The American Political Dictionary

The American Political Dictionary

Tenth Edition

Jack C. Plano
Western Michigan University

Milton Greenberg
American University

Harcourt Brace College Publishers
Fort Worth • Philadelphia • San Diego • New York • Orlando • Austin • San Antonio
Toronto • Montreal • London • Sydney • Tokyo

Publisher	Christopher P. Klein
Senior Acquisitions Editor	David C. Tatom
Developmental Editor	J. Claire Brantley
Production Manager	Serena Manning
Art Director	Lora Knox

Address for Editorial Correspondence:
Harcourt Brace College Publishers
301 Commerce Street, Suite 3700
Fort Worth, TX 76102.

Address for Orders:
Harcourt Brace & Company
6277 Sea Harbor Drive
Orlando, FL 32887-6777
1-800-782-4479, or 1-800-433-0001 (in Florida)

Library of Congress Catalog Card Number: 96–78286

Printed in the United States of America

ISBN: 0-03-017317-5

6 7 8 9 0 1 2 3 4 5 090 9 8 7 6 5 4 3 2 1

To Ellen and Sonia

Preface

The rise of the Information Age makes command of language more essential than ever for effective communication and for realistic analysis in the social sciences.

As teachers we find ourselves faced with the dilemma of how to present the realities and processes of American government while, at the same time, providing the student with the facts and language tools to probe into the excitement of government and politics in action. In an attempt to solve this problem, *The American Political Dictionary* emerged in 1962 as a guide both to the rich technical language of political science and to the actual operations of the American political system. In this, the tenth edition, *The American Political Dictionary* continues to fill a critical need in the study of American government. Comments from faculty and several generations of students, who used earlier editions of our book as a teaching/learning tool, support our belief in the utility of this approach to political lexicography. Media professionals—reporters, commentators, editors, and librarians—also find this reference work to be a useful resource.

This edition retains the unique format of the first nine editions: (1) an alphabetical arrangement of terms within subject-matter chapters so that each term is linked with similar concepts and placed in its proper frame of reference; (2) separate treatment of important agencies, court cases, and statutes; (3) a two-paragraph treatment of each term, one that provides a clear and precise definition, and another that indicates the significance of the term in its historical and contemporary applications; (4) an extensive cross-reference system that ties the item to related terms, subjects, and concepts; and (5) a comprehensive index of over 4,000 entries, including all important terms mentioned within major entries. Inclusion of the Constitution of the United States encourages learning about American government from the primary source.

This book features over 1,300 major terms, some new, most revised and updated, to reflect the dramatic political events of the 1990s. The format enables the teacher and student to reduce the time spent in the classroom defining terms and explaining their significance, freeing time for analysis and discussion. *The American Political Dictionary* can be used as a supplement to textbooks or books of readings and can serve effectively as a study guide for examinations (*see* A Note on How to Use This Book).

The authors are indebted in a general sense to all members of the political science discipline who have sought to achieve greater precision in the use of political vocabulary. We are also indebted to the faculty and students who have used earlier editions and have offered suggestions and criticism. These include George H. Cox, Jr., Linton R. Dunson, Timothy C. Evanson, James D. Gleason, James M. Graham, Michael Haag, John W. Smith, Aram Sogomonian, and William L. Swinehart.

For this tenth edition, special thanks go to Karl Irving and, for her special assistance in bringing this edition to completion, Ellen L. Plano.

It has become commonplace to speak of the need for an informed citizenry to maintain a free society. This truism is both real and urgent. The authors hope that this volume will contribute to the pursuit of that need.

A Note on How to Use This Book

The American Political Dictionary, tenth edition, serves as both a *dictionary* and a *study guide.* As a dictionary, terms are listed alphabetically by subject matter within each chapter; the reader can locate a term by consulting a particular chapter or, when in doubt as to the usage of a term, by consulting the index. As a study guide, a reading of a chapter will provide the student with basic information in a subject-matter area that will contribute to understanding lectures, preparing for class discussions, and studying for examinations.

The book is divided into fourteen subject-matter chapters that dovetail with the chapters or groups of chapters found in most American government textbooks. State and local government issues and procedures are integrated with national practice in most instances, since terms used to describe legislative, executive, and judicial functions are essentially the same at all levels of government. However, terms that have specific application to state and local governmental problems and practices are found in a separate chapter on state and local government.

Most chapters are divided into four sections. The first and longest in each case is an alphabetical listing of terms. Each concept is defined and then followed by a paragraph that explains its historical and current significance and relates it to the general field of American government. The listing of terms is followed by sections on important agencies, cases, and statutes. Each section contains an alphabetical listing of pertinent entries with a description and a statement of their significance. Many terms found in the first section of a chapter include references to agencies, cases, and statutes, but detailed treatment is given only to a select group. For most entries, cross-references are provided that send the reader to similar or closely related concepts that can add meaning and breadth to the term.

The index contains a complete listing of all major entries (with page numbers highlighted in **boldface** type) as well as all significant theories, agencies, cases, statutes, and events discussed within these entries. It includes more than 4,000 individual index entries, many of which have multiple page designations.

Contents

The American Political Dictionary

1

Political Ideas

Absolutism Unrestrained powers exercised by government. Absolutism is the opposite of constitutionalism, which provides for government limited by law. An autocracy is a form of absolutism that involves unlimited authority over others by a single individual. Constitutionalism or limited government may serve as a means for preventing the rise of absolute power, as in the American system. Once established, however, an absolutist regime typically defines and determines the scope of its own powers whether or not a constitution exists. *See also* DIVINE RIGHT, page 11; FASCISM, page 12; TOTALITARIANISM, page 27.

Significance Prior to the American and French revolutions, absolutism took the form of absolute monarchy based on the theory of the divine right of kings. In modern times, it has taken the form of dictatorships of the right (fascism) or of the left (Stalinist communism). The American Founding Fathers feared absolutism and established a system of separation of powers with checks and balances to safeguard against it. The historical struggle between absolutism and democratic constitutionalism continues today, both within and between nations. Although no government exercises completely unrestrained powers in all areas, the absolutist model provides a useful concept for political systems in which vast powers are exercised by governments free from *legal* and *political* restraints. Absolutist regimes typically remain in power unless overthrown by a popular uprising or revolution, by a coup d'état from within by a group that already exercises some share of power, or by intervention from a foreign state. In 1991 in the then still existing Soviet Union, a coup d'état was attempted but failed as a result of popular support for revolutionary political and economic changes carried on by Mikhail Gorbachev, president of the Soviet Union, and by Boris Yeltsin, president of the Russian Republic. With much of the world in a state of upheaval, absolutism remains a potential threat, especially in areas of Asia, Africa, and Latin America. In these regions ethnic, cultural, or tribal conflicts may produce leaders who aspire to absolute power.

Accountability The concept, underlying democratic representative government, that elected and appointed officials are responsible to the people for their actions. Accountability under law is one of the features distinguishing governments based on the concepts of constitutional democracy from those embracing the principles of absolutism. Elected officeholders ranging from

city commissioners to the President are both politically and legally accountable for their actions. Appointed officials are legally accountable through the
courts and can be held politically accountable through the elected officials
who appointed them or supervised their work. *See also* DEMOCRACY, page 9;
MASS MEDIA, page 87; REPRESENTATIVE GOVERNMENT, page 24.

Significance   Accountability implies that citizens in a democracy are
familiar with their elected officials and the decisions they make, and have an
opportunity to pass judgment on them. This in turn requires short ballots,
frequent elections, and an effective opposition. In the national government,
voters can hold the President accountable for decisions and actions undertaken in the executive branch because, under the Constitution, he alone is
accorded authority and responsibility for them. In Congress, accountability
is based on individual performance; frequent roll-call votes on important bills
and extensive press, television, and radio coverage of the activities of congressmen enable voters to judge members of the House every two years and
senators every six years. Cable-Satellite Public Affairs Network (C-SPAN) and
Cable News Network (CNN) are especially responsible for bringing congressional debates and other important public affairs to the attention of the
American people via their home television sets. When bills are killed through
minority blocking tactics, or when parliamentary maneuvers are used to
conceal political actions or to confuse voters, accountability is reduced.

Anarchism   The doctrine that government is an unnecessary evil and
should be replaced by voluntary cooperation among individuals and groups.
Anarchists regard the state as an instrument used by the propertied classes
to dominate and exploit the people. Anarchist thinking varies from individualism to collectivism, from pacifism to advocacy of violent revolution. All anarchists, however, hold the state's coercive system responsible for the evils
of society and the warping of the individual's personality, and look to the day
when every form of government will be abolished. *See also* LIBERTARIANISM,
page 17; NEW LEFT, page 91.

Significance   In Europe, anarchism has been represented primarily by
syndicalist parties that advocate a political and economic system in which
the workers own and manage industry; similarly, in the United States, anarchists have worked through the organization of Industrial Workers of the
World. Anarchism has never been a successful political ideology, but its advocates terrorized Europe's royal families and political leaders during the
nineteenth and early twentieth centuries by the widespread use of assassination as a political weapon. Anarchists have also had considerable influence
on other political theorists and movements. Marxian communism, for example, views government as an evil instrument of class exploitation and provides for a "final stage" in which government "withers away" and people in a
"stateless, classless society" spontaneously cooperate with one another. The
New Left movement during the 1960s produced a renaissance of anarchist
belief and action in many countries.

Aristocracy   The exercise of political power by a small ruling clique of a
state's "best" citizens. The selection of the aristocrats may be made on the
basis of birth, wealth, ability, or economic, social, or ecclesiastical position.

For Aristotle, aristocracy meant rule by the most virtuous, but in medieval Europe it came to mean rule by the upper classes, whom God had allegedly appointed to rule. *See also* ELITE, page 75; JEFFERSONIANISM, page 14.

Significance   Aristocracies are characterized by limited suffrage and great emphasis on property rights. Postrevolutionary America had characteristics of aristocracy, with most states having property and religious qualifications for voting and holding office. The "Jeffersonian Democracy" of that era emphasized rule by an aristocracy of ability. The democratic reforms ushered in during the age of Jackson provided a leveling influence. In modern America, an "establishment" of WASPs (White Anglo-Saxon Protestants) functioned for many years as an informal aristocracy in government, business, the professions, and the military. In Britain, an aristocracy based on inherited titles and wealth functions as a power elite, with a hereditary right to membership in the House of Lords.

Authoritarianism   Concentration of political authority in an individual or a small group. Authoritarian regimes emphasize obedience by the people to their rulers and the absolute power of rulers over their subjects. Individual freedoms and rights are subordinated to the power of the state. *See also* ABSOLUTISM, page 1; FASCISM, page 12.

Significance   Political history has been characterized by continuing struggles between the rival doctrines of authoritarianism and democracy. Although authoritarianism was set back by the defeat of the Axis powers in World War II, today it threatens again with many military takeovers in the developing countries. Changes of governments occur only rarely in Asia and Africa as a result of free elections. Modern authoritarian regimes often operate behind a façade of democratic and constitutional institutions. Fascism is a highly nationalistic form of authoritarianism of the extreme right that defends the established economic order; communism, conversely, is a doctrine of the extreme left that fosters revolutionary change. Both can be ruthless in pursuit of their objectives as, for example, in the struggle for power in many Latin American countries, carried on by right-wing "death squads" and by left-wing revolutionaries who seek to stamp out the defenders of the status quo.

Authority   Power and influence based on legitimacy. Authority involves acceptance of others' right to rule, to issue commands, to make rules, and to expect compliance with them. If an individual or a group recognizes and accepts another's control and direction, the latter functions in a legitimate or rightful capacity and exercises authority over the former. The relationship between them is based on psychological factors and moral imperatives, not necessarily on physical coercion or the threat of force. In a democratic political system, authority serves to keep the competition for power and influence restrained and peaceful. Those who voted for losing candidates and parties usually accept the verdict of the majority because the election provided legitimacy and bestowed authority upon the winners. Scholars who have studied the concept of authority have determined that, historically, its main sources are tradition and custom, law, and the charismatic personalities of leaders. *See also* LEGITIMACY, page 16; POWER, page 22.

Significance   Authority is the means by which political systems function effectively. It occurs because the ruled accept their rulers and recognize their right to rule. Some authoritarian leaders, such as Adolf Hitler, exercised dictatorial powers but at the same time sought to increase their authority so as to reduce the costs of gaining compliance through force and the threat of force. Typically, myths are used to convince the masses of the "rightful" nature of the power and influence exercised over them. Early legitimacy contests involved the myth of the divine right of kings that provided authority for the monarchs of Europe and the contract theory that involved a transfer of authority from the people to their constitutional rulers. Whenever the legitimacy and authority of rulers are widely questioned, the potential for revolution and civil war exists. During the colonial era, the authority of rulers was absolute, but once the colonial peoples rejected this authority by revolting, legitimacy and authority were shifted to the independence movements and new rulers. Many political groups use religious beliefs to support their cause and provide authority and legitimacy. In the American system of government, authority is the key to understanding the peaceful transitions of power that can occur with every election.

Capitalism   An economic system based on individual and corporate ownership of the means of production and a supply-demand market economy. Capitalism is often related to laissez-faire theory, which emphasizes the absence of governmental restraints on ownership, production, and trade. In classical economic theory, the natural balancing forces of the marketplace, guided by Adam Smith's "invisible hand," provided stability for the system. After World War II, the ideas of Keynesianism replaced laissez-faire theories, providing a central role for government in guiding and directing the economy. However, monetarism, a theoretical alternative to Keynesianism that is more compatible with laissez-faire, has received increasing support in capitalist countries. *See also* KEYNESIANISM, page 407; LAISSEZ-FAIRE, page 15; MONETARISM, page 409.

Significance   Capitalism is a working economic system developed in Europe and the United States in the late eighteenth and early nineteenth centuries, replacing the state-fostered mercantilist system. Historically, capitalism in its pure state has never been practiced for long, since each major economic group has soon looked to the government of its country to improve its own economic position. Each government in time has assumed a substantial promotional and regulatory role. Today, all capitalist states have mixed economies in which private ownership and market economies are matched with extensive governmental intervention. Free trade, a hallmark of capitalism, remains an ideal objective, but in many states economic activity is characterized by national and regional trade restrictions. In the global struggle between capitalism and communism, capitalism increasingly came to dominate the ideological, economic, political, and social competition between these two great shapers of human thinking. In the Eastern Bloc, a new era of capitalism began dawning in the late 1980s and early 1990s, replacing communism in both theory and practice in the Soviet Union and its former satellites. In the 1990s, democracy also replaced oligarchy as a working political system throughout Eastern Europe and Russia, following the dissolution of the Soviet Union.

Centrist   An individual or political group advocating a moderate approach to political decision making and to the solution of social problems. Centrists tend generally to uphold the status quo against demands by leftists or rightists for radical change. *See also* LEFTIST, page 15; RIGHTIST, page 25.

Significance   In the American political system, both major parties and most voters tend to view politics from a centrist perspective. Centrists are sometimes referred to as the "vital majority" that provides substantial support for "the establishment." European centrist parties, however, have been typically weak because of the tendency of voters to move toward political polarization and programmatic parties offering change to the voters. In the United States, centrists are often said to be engaging in "mainstream politics."

Collectivism   A generic term that describes various theories and social movements calling for the ownership and control of all land and means of production by the state or groups rather than by individuals. The term is often used synonymously with the more specific doctrines of socialism and communism. Collectivism rejects the economic freedoms and individual rights of capitalism in favor of group action and social welfare. *See also* COMMUNISM, page 5; SOCIALISM, page 26.

Significance   The major ideological conflicts of modern times have involved clashes between supporters of collectivist doctrines and defenders of individualism. The former have emphasized the advantages of cooperation and group effort, the latter the advantages of freedom, competition, incentive, and individual enterprise. In the early 1990s, many communist countries of Eastern Europe, along with Russia and the now-independent states of the former Soviet Union, concluded that collectivistic planning and control in their economies have failed, and all are now moving toward profit motivations and capitalist economies.

Communism   A political, economic, and social theory, also known as Marxism-Leninism, that is based on a collectivistic society in which all land and capital are socially owned and political power is exercised by the masses. Modern communism is based mainly on the theories and practices of Karl Marx, V. I. Lenin, and Josef Stalin, with variations provided by Mao Tse-tung and Josip Broz Tito. Communism, in theory, espouses the doctrines of historical inevitability, economic determinism, labor value, the "inner contradictions" of capitalism, class conflict, capitalist colonialism and imperialism, world wars resulting from competition for markets, the destruction of the bourgeoisie, the dictatorship of the proletariat, the socialist revolution, and the final "withering away" of the state. Plato and other political theorists have also advocated communism in the form of communal living, and various church and social groups have practiced it. *See also* CONVERGENCE THEORY, page 540; ECONOMIC DETERMINISM, page 11.

Significance   After World War II, communism as an ideology was used by communist states, especially the Soviet Union, in a worldwide ideological propaganda and political offensive against capitalism and democracy.

Communism, in theory, bases its main ideological attack on the evils and contradictions of capitalism, predicting its ultimate collapse. In practice, communism became increasingly pragmatic: Soviet leaders often supplemented their socialist approaches with capitalistic practices to provide incentives and to secure some degree of political stability and economic viability. During the alleged period of transition from socialism to communism—a period called "proletarian democracy" by Soviet ideologists—the "dictatorship of the proletariat" often proved to be a dictatorship by one man or rule by a ruthless oligarchy. Today, few ideological differences remain between East and West. In the 1980s, policies established under Soviet leader Mikhail Gorbachev were aimed at creating a new climate of internal liberalization and rapprochement with the West, with a new emphasis on disarmament. In the 1990s, communism is almost everywhere extinct or in retreat, replaced by democratic principles, institutions, and practices. Moreover, the Cold War has been replaced by expanded trade and cooperation on many levels between East and West. Communism remains a powerful ideological force in some Third World countries and in China, but it has failed completely in Eastern Europe and Russia as a practical political, economic, and social system.

Concurrent Majority   The political doctrine, expounded by John C. Calhoun of South Carolina prior to the Civil War, that democratic decisions should be made only with the concurrence of *all* major segments of society. Without such concurrence, Calhoun argued, a simple majority decision should not be binding on those groups whose interests it violates. *See also* CONSENSUS VERSUS CONFLICT, page 6.

Significance   The idea of concurrent majority was central to a systematic effort by Calhoun to justify the secession of southern states from the Union. He held that decisions made by Congress concerning tariffs and slavery were inimical to the interests of the South. Each southern state, therefore, had to decide whether it would accept these decisions or reject them and withdraw from the Union. Some contemporary democratic theorists reject majority rule and argue that only decisions reached by consensus are truly democratic.

Consensus versus Conflict   Alternative approaches to political action. Consensus involves agreement that approaches or achieves unanimity, usually without a vote. Consensus may range from the acceptance of a society's basic values to concurrence in a specific decision by members of a group. In a democracy, "government by consensus" sometimes replaces majority rule, which reduces the role of the opposition. A working bipartisan foreign policy, for example, might eliminate foreign policy issues from a subsequent election. Conflict, conversely, is an approach that involves the pursuit of political goals by force, the threat of force, or the application of pressure through the use of power. Civil war, a revolution, an international war, a coup d'état, an invasion, or an intervention are all examples of the use of conflict to achieve or attempt to achieve political objectives. *See also* CONCURRENT MAJORITY, page 6; MAJORITY RULE, page 18; POWER, page 22.

Significance   Consensus and conflict are opposing means that tend to dominate decision making. Typically, both are used by power wielders, but one or the other becomes the major approach used in pursuit of specific goals. Consensus provides the cementing force for a society. When consensual bonds are broken and conflict results, a new consensus must evolve if stability is to be restored. Strong leadership or compromise is needed to forge a consensus for a specific decision. Some observers believe that a highly pluralistic society may be more stable than one in which the leaders forge an artificially high level of consensus. The defeat suffered by the United States in the Vietnam War was partly the result of a breakdown in national consensus. The difficulty the United Nations had in achieving a peaceful solution to the conflict in the Balkans during the 1990s provided another example of controversy over whether the effort to restore peace should be by diplomatic consensus, military action, or both.

Conservatism   Defense of the status quo against major changes in the political, economic, or social institutions of a society. The classic statement of the philosophy of conservatism was expounded by the English statesman Edmund Burke. He held that political stability could be maintained only if the forces of change could be moderated by a slow and careful integration of new elements into time-tested institutions. *See also* LIBERALISM, page 16; REATIONARY, page 24.

Significance   Both major American political parties have conservative wings that frequently unite in opposing liberal legislation. Today, in American politics the term "conservative" has no precise meaning and is often used accusatorially against a rival party or candidate. The general conservative position on issues, however, has been fairly consistently opposed to governmental regulation of the economy, heavy government spending, and civil rights legislation. Conservatives tend to favor state over federal action, fiscal responsibility, decreased governmental spending, supply-side economics, the outlawing of abortion, more effective crime control, and lower taxes. Although conservatism received a setback in the 1964 defeat of Republican presidential candidate Barry Goldwater, conservative groups played a major role in Ronald Reagan's and George Bush's successful presidential election campaigns in the 1980s. In the 1994 off-year election, Republican conservative forces won control of the Congress for the first time in many years, and in 1995 numerous conservatives announced candidacy for the presidency in the 1996 election. Conservative strength in the United States is divided between the populist, radical, predominantly blue-collar wing, and the upper- and upper-middle-class liaison between the inheritors of wealth and the *nouveaux riches*. In the 1990 Middle East action against Iraq's Saddam Hussein, an action that followed the end of the threat of communism in Eastern Europe, some conservatives returned to their earlier isolationist base in criticizing President Bush's actions. These same conservatives also opposed President Bill Clinton's 1995 decision to send American troops as part of the NATO peacekeeping force in the Balkans.

Constitutionalism   The political principle of limited government under a written or unwritten contract (constitution). Constitutionalism assumes that the sovereign people draw up a constitution, by the terms of which a government is created and given powers. In the American system, the Supreme Court acts as the guardian of the Constitution through its powers to void governmental actions that exceed these limitations (judicial review). The Founding Fathers also incorporated various limitations that restrain the individuals who exercise power, including the separation of powers, checks and balances, federalism, subordination of the military to civilian control, and the Bill of Rights. *See also* CONTRACT THEORY, page 8; MADISONIANISM, page 18.

Significance The American system of constitutional government has been effective throughout most of its history in maintaining limitations upon government. In recent years, however, public sentiment has favored bigger government with more flexible approaches and expanded powers. The Industrial Revolution, depressions, wars, alien ideologies, and other domestic and foreign threats have overridden the fear of stronger government. Expanding democratic government is viewed by many as a means of achieving better protection for their personal rights, values, and welfare, rather than as a threat. Recent administrations have sought to reverse this trend through decentralization of programs and a revenue-sharing scheme to help state and local units finance them. The problem is essentially one of maintaining an equilibrium between liberty and order and of enabling government to meet new responsibilities while maintaining the restraints of constitutionalism. Some scholars subscribe to the "organic theory" of constitutional development, which holds that a constitution is not created but rather evolves out of the actual institutions and practices of a political community. Today, throughout Eastern Europe, new constitutions have been drafted to provide for changing to limited government and democracy from the authoritarian discipline of former communist regimes whose earlier constitutions were meaningless in protecting individual rights and freedoms.

Contract Theory A class of theories that seeks to explain the origin of society and government and to set out the respective authority and responsibility of government and individuals under their contractual obligations. Contract theorists regard the human race as having lived in a state of nature prior to the organization of civil society. Once a "body politic" has been created through a contract or compact among the people, a government is then founded and empowered through a second contract or constitution concluded between the people and the government. The nature of the relationship established by the governmental contract varies, in these theories, from the individualism of John Locke's popular sovereignty and limited government to the authoritarianism of Thomas Hobbes' *Leviathan*. *See also* CONSTITUTIONALISM, page 7; POPULAR SOVEREIGNTY, page 22.

Significance The contract theory was developed by various political philosophers during the Middle Ages as an intellectual challenge to the existing absolutism based on the theory of the divine right of kings. Progressively, the new doctrine gained adherents and the absolute power of some monarchs was mildly curtailed, but its full flowering and broad democratic implications emerged during the Age of Enlightenment. The advocacy of the doctrine by John Locke, Jean Jacques Rousseau, and James Harrington helped to gain the support of the intellectual classes and laid the foundations for the English, American, and French revolutions. The American Declaration of Independence, described by Thomas Jefferson as "pure Locke," based its justification of revolution on the violation of contract by the English government.

Although theories of a social contract are out of vogue today, the great ideas they fostered remain part of democratic theory and continue to support the ideas of individual rights and limited government.

Culture   A learned pattern of behavior that tends to govern individual lifestyle, beliefs, customs, and values. Political culture describes the forces that affect the individuals in pursuit of political goals. It can take the form of multiculturalism or cultural pluralism. Various cultures that seek to minimize their differences are using the Melting Pot or assimilation approach.

Significance   Most of the 200 states in the world are multicultural societies. As a result, competition and conflict among the groups often are inevitable as a result of cultural differences. In Canada, for example, the French-speaking minority has agitated for independence but seeks to achieve its political goals without armed conflict. In the Balkans, controversy among the various ethnic cultures led to war in the 1990s. Africa has proved to be a particularly difficult area to develop ethnocentric unity because of colonial-era boundaries that do not match long-existing tribal differences. Some progress is being made in developing a global culture through increased contacts among people throughout the world, producing a "global village" effect. In the United States, most cultural groups have been assimilated in the national culture. However, some groups, such as Afro-Americans and Hispanics, are torn between those who seek to live in the national culture and others who wish to remain a subculture but with their social, economic, and political rights fully recognized.

Democracy   A system of government in which ultimate political authority is vested in the people. The term is derived from the Greek words "demos" (the people) and "kratos" (authority). Democracy may be direct, as practiced in ancient Athens and in New England town meetings, or indirect and representative. In the modern pluralistic democratic state, power typically is exercised by groups or institutions in a complex system of interactions that involve compromises and bargaining in the decision process. The "democratic creed" includes the following concepts: (1) individualism, which holds that the primary task of government is to enable each individual to achieve the highest potential of development; (2) liberty, which allows each individual the greatest amount of freedom consistent with order; (3) equality, which maintains that all persons are created equal and have equal rights and opportunities; and (4) fraternity, which postulates that individuals will not misuse their freedom but will cooperate in creating a wholesome society. As a political system, democracy starts with the assumption of popular sovereignty, vesting ultimate power in the people. It presupposes that people can control their destiny and that they can make moral judgments and practical decisions in their daily lives. It implies a continuing search for truth in the sense of humanity's pursuit of improved ways of building social institutions and ordering human relations. Democracy requires a decision-making system based on majority rule, with minority rights protected. Effective guarantees of freedom of speech, press, religion, assembly, and petition and of equality before the law are indispensable to a democratic system of government. Politics, parties, and politicians are the catalytic agents that make democracy workable. *See also* CONSTITUTIONALISM, page 7; CONTRACT THEORY, page 8; RULE OF LAW, page 25.

Significance   Most Americans think of their political and social systems as best described by the term "democratic." Yet the term appears neither in the Declaration of Independence nor in the United States Constitution. For many centuries democracy was regarded as a dangerous and unworkable doctrine, but its ideas swept the Western world during the nineteenth and twentieth centuries as one of the forces unleashed by the American and French revolutions. In the twentieth century, democracy has clashed with new authoritarian ideologies, and the struggle continues, particularly in the nations of the Third World. Democracy is under attack not only from the ideologies of the extreme right and left, but from within as well—by those who oppose it as a mob rule that vulgarizes society and makes a virtue of incompetence and mediocrity, and by those who charge that it is a sham, impossible in practice because of an "iron law of oligarchy." Supporters of democracy reject such attacks, pointing to the evidence of the superiority of democracy as practiced in the United States, Britain, and Western Europe. Yet a façade of democracy exists in many countries where, despite forms and appearances, a small oligarchic group manipulates all power. Workable democracy seems to require a special environment, including an educated and responsible people, some degree of economic stability, and some social cohesion and consensus. Above all, it demands an acceptance of the democratic "rules of the game," namely, that there will be fair and frequent elections, that the losers will accept the verdict of the voters and allow the majority to govern, that the majority will respect the right of the minority to furnish opposition, and that if the minority wins a future election it will then be permitted to take over the reins of government. Democracy in practice will never achieve the perfection of the "democratic creed." Yet so long as such goals are held worthy and efforts are made to move in their direction, the system may be called democratic. American democracy, like its British counterpart, is an evolutionary and organic system that has pragmatically overcome obstacles and crises. In the 1980s and 1990s, democracy was imbued with new strength as many countries in Eastern Europe discarded communism in favor of democratic systems, and some Third World countries changed from authoritarian regimes to democratic systems embodying free elections and civil rights protection.

Democratic Socialism   An economic system established by a democratic nation in which the people, through industrial groups or government, take over ownership and direction of basic industry, banking, communication, transportation, and other segments of the economy. The extent of the government's role in the economy is determined by free elections rather than imposed by party oligarchies. Although a private sector of the economy may continue to exist, much effort is expended by government or groups in planning, directing, and regulating it and in providing welfare services for the needy. *See also* SOCIALISM, page 26; WELFARE STATE, page 27.

Significance   Democratic socialism has been partially instituted in several countries, particularly in Britain and Scandinavia. Some observers regard it as the best answer to the challenge of communism. Communists have been especially hostile toward democratic socialism because they felt its reformism would correct the evils and "inner contradictions" of capitalism upon which they placed their hopes for capitalism's economic collapse. American conservatives oppose it as a dangerous leftward step toward communism.

Direct Democracy   A system of government in which political decisions are made by the people directly rather than by their elected representatives. Under direct democracy, the citizens assemble periodically and function as a legislative body, or they vote on public issues to determine government policies. *See also* INITIATIVE, page 151; RECALL, page 107; REFERENDUM, page 163.

Significance   Direct democracy has been used in ancient Greece and Rome, in some Swiss cantons, in New England town meetings, and in some midwestern township meetings. A modern adaptation of direct democracy is found in about one-half of the American states—those that provide for initiative, referendum, and recall action by the people. Many local units of government also use binding and advisory referendums in reaching decisions on important issues. Direct democracy, however, is not provided for or recognized by the U.S. Constitution. The closest the Constitution comes to providing for a direct decision-making process is in the ratification of amendments by state conventions elected solely for that purpose. Ordinarily, direct democracy is practicable only in small communities and in resolving simple issues.

Divine Right   A theory supporting absolutism based on the divinity of a person or his or her office, or on a right to rule inherited from ancestors believed to have been appointed by a Supreme Being. *See also* ABSOLUTISM, page 1; THEOCRACY, page 27.

Significance   The political philosophy of the divine right of kings was accepted in theory and practiced throughout most of the Western world from the fifteenth through the eighteenth centuries. The system was perpetuated through family inheritance of the ruling power and the intermarriage of ruling families. Any challenge to or revolt against a king was regarded not only as a treasonable act but also as a sin. In time, the divine right of kings was first weakened and then overcome by the new contract theory, which held that a ruler's power was granted not by God but by the sovereign people.

Economic Determinism   The theory that the methods of production and exchange of goods control the form of a state's political and social organization and shape the intellectual and moral development of its people. Some economic determinists view history in terms of epochs in which the prevailing economic system pits the servile class against the dominant class, a struggle that eventually results in a new alignment. *See also* COMMUNISM, page 5; ECONOMIC INTERPRETATION OF THE CONSTITUTION, page 39.

Significance   Vague beliefs in some aspects of economic determinism are widespread and held by people of many persuasions. The most celebrated systematic theory was set forth by Marx and Engels, who used it to explain the movement of history in response to changing economic relationships.

Economic determinism is the core of such recently discredited or discarded communist theories as class struggle, the predicted collapse of capitalism, and the eventual victory of communism. Some historians view the American Revolution and the writing of the U.S. Constitution mainly as products of economic factors.

Fascism   The political system of the extreme right, which incorporates the principles of the leader (dictator), a one-party state, totalitarian regimentation of economic and social activity, and the arbitrary exercise of absolute power by the regime. After 1922, Benito Mussolini fashioned the fascist prototype in Italy and was emulated in the 1930s by Adolf Hitler in Germany, Francisco Franco in Spain, and Juan Perón in Argentina. Fascism's glorification of the leader makes the system unstable by posing serious problems of succession. Unlike communism, fascism retains private ownership of land and capital, but most economic activity is controlled and regimented by the state through a system of national socialism. *See also* ABSOLUTISM, page 1; TOTALITARIANISM, page 27.

Significance   Fascism is contemptuous of democratic parliamentarianism and personal liberty but is actively hostile toward communism. Fascists generally have come to power during a crisis in which the landed or industrial leaders of a state have feared the rise of communism. Although fascism was dealt a destructive blow by the defeat of the Axis powers in World War II, neofascism, in the form of such groups as "skinheads" and white supremacists, is on the rise.

Government   The formal institutional structure and processes of a society by which policies are developed and implemented in the form of law binding on all. Each government performs legislative (law-making), executive (law-enforcing), and judicial (law-interpreting) functions, with decision power exercised either by a majority (democracy), a small elite group (oligarchy), or a single, all-powerful individual (dictatorship). Government usually operates under the restrictive nature of a constitution, be it written or unwritten. The term "government" is also used to denote the individuals who have control of the decision-making machinery of a state, as in Britain, where the leaders of the majority party in Parliament are collectively referred to as "the Government." Both internal and external aspects of state sovereignty are always exercised by government. *See also* REPRESENTATIVE GOVERNMENT, page 24; SOVEREIGNTY, page 26; STATE, page 26.

Significance   No matter how it is organized, government is the most powerful instrument for social control ever devised. Without government, anarchy would prevail. Yet government has often been the main problem for people living in organized societies. It is government, for example, that declares war and makes peace, fosters both justice and injustice, makes fair as well as unfair laws, protects but also violates human rights, and levies burdensome, yet often necessary taxes. The role of government vis-à-vis the citizens it governs depends to a great extent on the degree of value consensus it has within the society. In the United States, the Great Depression of the 1930s resulted in a move away from laissez-faire to a great dependence on government to provide the leadership initiatives and regulatory activity needed to restore prosperity and meet the challenges facing individuals and groups in society.

Hamiltonianism   The philosophy of Alexander Hamilton, leader of the Federalist party, chief architect of the national monetary system, and promoter of a special government role in support of the nation's economic system. The Hamiltonian model incorporates the idea of a powerful national government with strong executive power providing unity for the nation and a base on which to build a viable national economy. *See also* JEFFERSONIANISM, page 14; MADISONIANISM, page 18; PATERNALISM, page 21.

Significance   Under Alexander Hamilton's energetic leadership, the new nation established a national banking system, a standard currency, business subsidies, a tax system, a national debt, a mint, and a protective tariff. The Federalist party generally espoused and supported the philosophy of Hamiltonianism. Many present-day Republicans regard Alexander Hamilton as the ideological godfather of the Republican party.

Ideology   The "way of life" of a people, reflected in their collectively held ideas and beliefs concerning the nature of the ideal political system, economic order, social goals, and moral values. Ideology is particularly concerned with the form and role of government and the nature of a state's economic system. Ideology is the means by which the basic values held by a party, class, group, or individual are articulated. *See also* IDEOLOGICAL WARFARE, page 553.

Significance   Ideology serves to justify an existing social system, or postulates a desirable future social order. Ideology provides the basic ammunition for psychological warfare. Each side seeks to "sell" its ideology to others through propaganda. Individuals tend to derive their attitudes and actions on political, economic, and social issues from the set of primary values that constitute their ideology. Historically, ideologies have often been color-coded for easy identification as, for example, red for revolution and white for counter-revolution, brown for fascism, black for anarchism, green for environmentalism, and blue for Zionism. American political parties are largely not ideological, as contrasted with European parties that range from the political extremes of radical socialism to fascism. Although communism suffered a major defeat in the Soviet Union and in Eastern Europe, it remains a powerful ideology in some Third World countries (especially Cuba, North Korea, and Vietnam) and in China.

Incrementalism   A doctrine holding that change in a political system occurs only by small steps, each of which should be carefully evaluated before proceeding to the next one. Incrementalism suggests a conservative, yet practical, approach for use by political leaders and administrators in decision making. *See also* CONSERVATISM, page 7.

Significance   Incrementalism recognizes that decision makers in a political system start with an existing store of knowledge, policies, programs, funding levels, and a particular mindset. Decision makers are regarded mainly as problem solvers and not initiators of broad new policies or searchers for alternatives. Incrementalism is particularly accepted in the field of American public administration as the logical approach to be used in bureaucratic operations, especially in budget making. Its support comes from a public that prefers modest, gradual change instead of dramatic, revolutionary departures from established policies and procedures.

Individualism   The political, economic, and social concept that places primary emphasis on the worth, freedom, and well-being of the individual rather than on the group, society, or nation. The concept of individualism may be contrasted with that of collectivism, which describes those systems in which primary emphasis is placed on the rights and welfare of the group. *See also* DEMOCRACY, page 9; LAISSEZ-FAIRE, page 15.

Significance   Individualism is the central idea in the political doctrine of constitutional democracy and in the economic theory of laissez-faire. The broad guarantees afforded to each person and to his or her property by the Constitution exemplify the American focus on individual rights. Although the term "individualism" was first used by Alexis de Tocqueville in 1840 in his classic *Democracy in America,* the concept is several centuries older.

Jacksonian Democracy   A political and social equalitarian movement in the United States that rejected political aristocracy and emphasized the "common man." The chief apostle of the new equality and democracy was Andrew Jackson, who brought to the presidency the leveling influences of the frontier. *See also* SPOILS SYSTEM, page 234.

Significance   The election of Jackson in 1828 ushered in an era of democratic changes on the national, state, and local governmental levels. Jacksonian Democracy emphasized and largely brought about universal manhood suffrage, popular election of officials, short terms of office, and the spoils system. The ideas of Jacksonian Democracy have continued to have an impact on government at all three levels—national, state, and local—especially in expanding the electorate.

Jeffersonianism   The philosophy of Thomas Jefferson, espousing a democratic, laissez-faire-styled agrarianism. Jeffersonianism rejected the Hamiltonian idea that a strong central government be created to spur the growth of urban industrialism and commercialism. The Jeffersonian model incorporates the ideal of an independent republic, democratically governed by an intellectual aristocracy under a strictly construed constitutional system, with a national government of limited powers and with major emphasis on individual freedom and responsibility and states' rights. Jefferson especially espoused the superiority of an agrarian economy and a rural society. *See also* ARISTOCRACY, page 2; HAMILTONIANISM, page 13; MADISONIANISM, page 18.

Significance   The ideal of Jeffersonianism has had an impact on the American political system for 200 years. Because it represents a relatively simple approach to meeting the needs of society and tends to be negative in relation to governmental powers, it has generally been placed on the defensive in a society that has demanded expanded economic growth and a larger and more powerful role by government. As the small farmer, laborer, businessperson, and artisan began to realize that they could cope with powerful business and industrial interest groups only by gaining political power, the two groups tended to exchange roles. Big business in the modern era espouses Jeffersonian laissez-faire freedoms, while the former Jeffersonians demand a more active central government.

Laissez-faire The economic theory basic to the principles of capitalism, propounded by the French physiocrats and popularized by Adam Smith (*The Wealth of Nations,* 1776), that calls for a "hands-off" policy by government toward the economy. Laissez-faire rejects state control and regulation and emphasizes economic individualism, a market economy, and natural economic laws to guide the production and consumption of goods. Tariffs and other trade restrictions are rejected in favor of a worldwide system of free trade. The economic system becomes self-regulatory in nature, and each individual's pursuit of self-interest contributes to the well-being of all. *See also* CAPITALISM, page 4; KEYNESIANISM, page 407; MONETARISM, page 409.

Significance The wide acceptance in practice of the theory of laissez-faire in the Western world during the eighteenth and nineteenth centuries ushered in the new economic era of capitalism. Laissez-faire was largely a reaction to the severe production and trade restrictions imposed by governments under the previous system of mercantilism. The American Revolution was a product of these economic forces of change, as well as of new political ideas based on individualism. Laissez-faire has been modified by the expanding role of government in economic affairs, so the United States now has a "mixed economy," combining capitalism with governmental promotion and regulation. Today, monetarist theories offer a return to the basic principles of laissez-faire economics by restricting government's role in the economy.

Leftist An individual or a political group advocating liberal, radical, or revolutionary political or economic programs, an expanded role by democratic government, or empowering the masses. Leftists include such categories as "welfare-statists," democratic socialists, Marxian socialists, communists, and anarchists. The use of the term stems from the practice in European parliaments of seating radical parties to the left of the presiding officer. *See also* NEW LEFT, page 91; RADICAL, page 23.

Significance The moderate leftist has played a significant role in advocating governmental action to correct injustices and shortcomings in existing societies. Leftists have been particularly active in calling for changes and modifications in capitalism and political democracy. American leftist movements have included the Progressive, the Socialist, the Socialist Labor, and the Socialist Workers parties. The New Left that functioned as a loose coalition of antiwar groups during the Vietnam War largely shunned political parties in favor of direct action through mass protests. Leftist views on social, economic, and political matters have often been in advance of popularly held beliefs. Extremes of the political left, like those of the right, tend to culminate in dictatorship. Leftist groups and parties have received little public support in American politics. The practice in European parliaments of seating radical and reactionary parties to the extreme left and right of the presiding officer, respectively, is an attempt to maintain order and prevent them from engaging in violent acts against each other.

Legitimacy Recognition and acceptance of the exercise of political power. Legitimacy is based on the conversion of the exercise of political power or the assumption of a political position into a situation of "rightful" authority. Within a nation, legitimacy means that the people accept the government and the role of the rulers in exercising power. Election victories thus assign power and create legitimacy. In foreign policy, legitimacy means that other countries recognize the existence of the state and accept the government in power as the sovereign authority of the nation. Although law functions as a legitimating device, social acceptance is needed if law is to reinforce the authority of the lawmakers and law enforcers. *See also* AUTHORITY, page 3; POWER, page 22.

Significance Legitimacy is the *sine qua non* (indispensable condition or essential thing) for effective government and the maintenance of political order. In the new American nation, acceptance of state governments as proper replacements for the English Crown provided a semblance of legitimacy following the Declaration of Independence. Victory in the War for Independence and international recognition by France increased the sense that the actions of the colonists were legitimate. Many observers emphasize the legitimacy and uniqueness in the world of the peaceful transfer of power in the United States. In foreign policy, the refusal of the United States for long periods of time to recognize the Soviet and Chinese communist regimes as legitimate encouraged a Cold War atmosphere. Efforts to bring down the Castro regime in Cuba by declaring it illegitimate also provoked a long period of hostility.

Liberalism A political view that seeks to change the political, economic, or social status quo to foster the development and well-being of the individual. Liberals regard the individual as a rational creature who can use his or her intelligence to overcome human and natural obstacles to a good life for all without resorting to violence against the established order. Liberalism is more concerned with process, with the method of solving problems, than with a specific program. *See also* CONSERVATISM, page 7; DEMOCRACY, page 9.

Significance Liberalism evolved in the eighteenth and nineteenth centuries as a doctrine emphasizing the full development of the individual, free from the restraints of government. The twentieth-century liberal, conversely, looks to government as a means of correcting the abuses and shortcomings of society through positive programs of action. In civil rights, for example, today's liberal views government as a positive force that can ameliorate wrongs and expand the freedom of the individual, rather than as, in the traditional sense, the major threat to individual freedom. Liberals have fought totalitarianism of the left and right by pursuing policies that seek to reduce economic and social inequalities. In the independent former republics of the Soviet Union and in Eastern Europe, "liberalism" describes a movement away from the rigidities of communism toward a system that is economically more flexible and politically more democratic.

Libertarianism   A political philosophy based on the freedom of the individual and the curtailment of state power. Libertarianism as an ideology resembles anarchism or Social Darwinism. Its American roots go back to the Revolution and eighteenth-century liberalism, and it is often referred to by its supporters as "the modern revival of classical liberalism." *See also* ANARCHISM, page 2; NEW LEFT, page 91.

Significance   Although libertarians preach opposition to the government and most of its programs, unlike the anarchists they do not call for a violent overthrow of the system. The Libertarian party has run candidates for many political offices in recent years. The Libertarian presidential candidate, for example, received about 1 percent of the national vote in the 1980 election, but since then the party has lost most of that support. Liberals oppose the libertarian call to eliminate all welfare programs, and conservatives reject libertarian demands that agencies like the CIA and FBI be eliminated and that military spending be greatly reduced. Like anarchists, libertarians believe that government and its programs are evil or ineffectual.

Litigious Society   A political or social community in which individuals and organizations resolve most controversies by legal action, such as adjudication, negotiation, mediation, and arbitration, with lawyers the predominant participants in resolving all forms of dispute. *See also* CIVIL LAW, page 253; CRIMINAL LAW, page 259; RULE OF LAW, page 25.

Significance   The United States is the leading example of a litigious society. It ranks first in the world in encouraging resolution of controversies through litigation. There are more than 800,000 lawyers in the United States or approximately 30 for every 10,000 people. This contrasts with Great Britain's 11, Germany's 8, and Japan's 1 for the same 10,000. It has been estimated that every minute, twenty new civil or criminal suits are filed in either a state or federal court. The growing roll of legal settlements of most disputes testifies to the importance of lawyers in American society and the importance of law schools, which each year produce thousands of additional lawyers. A major question raised in the world of government, business, and the media is, "Has this proposed course of action been lawyered?" Increasingly, however, citizens outside the legal community are becoming concerned at the extent of power wielded by lawyers. Much concern relates to the use of the "contingency fee" system, in which the lawyer is paid one-third to one-half of the award if the case is won and nothing if it is lost. No other country provides for such a system. Change will not come easily. The Trial Lawyers Association spends millions in lobbying and defending the status quo. Reforms are aimed at controlling product liability and malpractice suits and at encouraging "loser pays" laws. In 1995, medical malpractice cases produced the most frequent awards from lawsuits, followed by product liability cases.

Loyal Opposition   The role of a party out of power. In Britain, official recognition is given to the Leader of Her Majesty's Loyal Opposition, and a Shadow Cabinet is created that will become the government if the minority party wins a national election. The concept of loyal opposition permits the party out of power in a democratic system to criticize the majority and offer alternatives but not to sabotage its programs by devious means. In foreign policy, the loyal opposition approach often gives way to bipartisanship. *See also* BI-PARTISANSHIP, page 534; MANDATE, page 87.

Significance   In a democracy, the role of the loyal opposition is critical to the system's successful operation. Democracy thrives on criticism and the offering of alternative policies and programs. Yet the loyal opposition must be willing to accept the role of the majority to function as the legitimate government and to accept its electoral mandate to make policy decisions for the nation. In the United States, however, the system of separation of powers can result in confusion over which party should function as the loyal opposition when the presidency is held by one party and the other party controls one or both houses of Congress, as occurred in the Clinton Administration after the 1994 election. Also, political majority and opposition forces can be divided by liberal-conservative conflict both within and between the majority and minority parties.

Madisonianism   The philosophy of James Madison, espousing a political system based on checks and balances and the fostering of a harmony of interests. The Madisonian model begins with the assumption that the greatest dangers to republican government are those of the divisive power of faction and the threat of tyranny resulting from too great a concentration of political power. Madison's solution to these problems was to establish a powerful national government that could balance state and local units and maintain its own checks and balances to ensure moderation in the exercise of power. *See also* JEFFERSONIANISM, page 14.

Significance   Madisonianism as a philosophy of government has left a continuing imprint on the nature and functioning of the American system. The Constitution that finally emerged from the Philadelphia Convention of 1787 is often referred to as the "Madisonian system" because it incorporates Madison's basic idea that power must be checked and balanced to avoid tyranny. In his contributions to *The Federalist* papers (particularly No. 10 and No. 51) and during his presidential tenure, Madison did much to gain acceptance for a powerful central government limited by its internal system of power equilibrium. He is often regarded as the leading strategist of the American political system.

Majority Rule   A basic principle of democracy asserting that the greatest number of citizens in any political unit should select officials and determine policies. A majority is normally 50 percent plus one of the total vote cast or sometimes of the total number of potential voters. Special majorities are sometimes needed for decisions, as, for example, in the constitutional requirement that the Senate approve treaties by a two-thirds vote. In 1971, the Supreme Court held (*Gordon v. Lance*, 403 U.S. 1) that the requirement that a bond issue be adopted by a 60 percent extraordinary majority in a state election does not violate the equal protection clause of the Fourteenth Amendment. Majority rule is justified on the grounds that it rests on superior force, is commonly accepted in practice, and is a logical means for reaching decisions and that, pragmatically, no reasonable democratic alternative exists when there is no consensus. *See also* CONSENSUS VERSUS CONFLICT, page 6; PLURALITY, page 95.

Significance   Political philosophers have long debated whether it is more justifiable for the majority to impose its will on the minority than for the minority to rule. Some reject majority rule in favor of government by consensus or by a concurrent majority. In most cases, majoritarianism (rule by a majority) and egalitarianism (belief in the equality of all) stand in direct contrast to the principles and practices of elitism (rule by a small group that constitutes the "power structure" of a society). In the United States, majority rule is not rigidly adhered to; for example, in most cases only a plurality is needed to win an election. Other practices that depart from majority rule include the equal representation of states in the Senate, gerrymandering, the use of procedures and the committee system of Congress to thwart the majority, and the election of the president by the Electoral College. Also, when an extraordinary majority vote is required, such as a two-thirds vote, then one-third plus one of the minority can determine the outcome.

Majority Tyranny   Abuse of the minority by the majority through excessive use of power. Majority tyranny was a concern that helped to guide the Founding Fathers in shaping the American constitutional system. The tyranny of the majority, they believed, was just as much to be feared and avoided as the tyranny imposed on a people by an all-powerful ruler or a small ruling oligarchy. This fear led to the incorporation of certain basic principles in the new Constitution, such as those of separation of powers, checks and balances, federalism, and the rule of law. *See also* MADISONIANISM, page 18.

Significance   The fear of majority tyranny was part of the political culture of the American Revolution, developed and mythologized by the great political theorists of the Age of Enlightenment: John Locke, Thomas Hobbes, James Harrington, Thomas Paine, and Jean Jacques Rousseau. Others have feared the psychological oppression of the majority, who demand uniformity and intimidate those who would be different. The Frenchman Alexis de Tocqueville, for example, studied the American system during the early part of the nineteenth century and concluded that group pressures in American society tended to weaken the basic individualism that the American system expounds. Today, the struggle continues between those who place their main emphasis on individual freedom and the right to be different and those who strive to enforce conformity in thought and action.

Monarchy   Any form of government in which the supreme powers of the state are exercised, or ceremoniously held, by a king, queen, emperor, or other regal potentate. Monarchs may acquire their position through inheritance or election, although the latter is unusual. Absolute monarchs exercise full ruling powers, whereas constitutional monarchs either share governmental powers with elected parliaments or are mere figureheads. *See also* DIVINE RIGHT, page 11.

Significance   Absolute monarchs once ruled nearly all the states of Europe. Today, in the few countries that have retained their monarchs—Britain,

Sweden, Norway, the Netherlands, for example—the king or queen is assigned a ceremonial role as chief of state. In several semifeudal states of Asia, Africa, and the Middle East, however, monarchs continue to have absolute power.

Nation   Any sizable group of people united by common bonds of geography, religion, language, race, custom, and tradition, and through shared experiences and common aspirations. The term is often used interchangeably with "state," but not all national groups have achieved statehood, although they all aspire to it. Moreover, the nation and the state may be essentially the same, as in the case of a nation-state like Ireland or Israel, or a state may be multinational, as are Switzerland and Canada. Modern nations began to emerge from feudalism in the ninth century. The community of nation-states was given political and legal recognition by the Peace of Westphalia in 1648. *See also* NATIONALISM, page 566; STATE, page 26.

Significance   In the modern era, the nation has provided the unifying concept with which the individual can identify. The results have not always been good, for many national groups have built their unity on a real or imagined fear and a shared hatred of other groups or on a desire to bring others under their dominion. These conflicting national interests, which characterize the world's state system, have contributed to the instability of international relations and to the outbreak of wars. The breakup of Yugoslavia in the early 1990s into several independent political units and the military actions that followed demonstrates the powerful force of nationalism and the loyalty of individuals to their "nation."

Natural Law   The concept that human relations are governed by an immutable set of laws, similar to the physical laws of the universe and recognizable through human reason. Such laws are regarded as ethically binding in human society. The theory of *jus naturale* was expounded by the Stoics and was highly developed by the eighteenth-century natural-rights philosophers. *See also* NATURAL RIGHTS, page 327.

Significance   The concept of natural law has been influential in the development of legal and political theories and institutions, morals and ethics, and religion. Its main significance historically has been its use as a moral standard for judging individual and governmental conduct. Its ambiguities, however, subject it to conflicting interpretations and challenges. It constitutes the basis for the natural-rights philosophy that underlies democratic systems of government.

Oligarchy   Any system of government in which a small elite group holds the ruling power. Oligarchical systems are usually based on wealth, military power, or social position. *See also* ARISTOCRACY, page 2; ELITE, page 75.

Significance   Oligarchs traditionally rule with absolute power, unencumbered by democratic restraints. Even in democratic systems, however, oligarchic groups may temporarily hold a decisive influence over the government because of their economic position or social status. Two European philosophers, Robert Michels and Vilfredo Pareto, developed a theory of the "iron law of oligarchy," which propounds the impossibility of democracy in practice because of the tendency of elite groups to dominate and control the majority. Local communities are in some cases governed by the leaders of a political machine or by an elite "power structure" or "establishment."

Parliamentary System   A system of government, often based on the British prototype, in which governmental authority is vested in the legislative body (parliament) and in a cabinet headed by a prime minister or premier. The cabinet collectively exercises political leadership and directs the administration. Cabinet ministers are entirely or largely selected from the membership of parliament, and the cabinet continues in power so long as it commands the support of a majority of the parliament. Substantial disagreement between the parliament and the cabinet or within the cabinet results in either the appointment of a new cabinet or the election of a new legislature. *See also* PRESIDENTIAL GOVERNMENT, page 23.

Significance   The major advantage of the parliamentary system is that it avoids continuing controversy or deadlocks between the legislative and executive branches and provides for clear accountability to the people. These advantages, however, result in the loss of checks and balances; thus the American people have never seriously considered adopting this system. Most of the world's democracies are patterned after the British or continental European parliamentary systems, rather than after the American presidential system with its separation of powers.

Paternalism   A philosophy or governmental policy that holds that the state should act as a father-guardian of its citizen-children in looking out for their general welfare. Paternalism holds that the state has the responsibility to determine the best interests of its citizens for them and to inaugurate specific policies and programs aimed at achieving paternalistic goals. *See also* WELFARE STATE, page 27.

Significance   The ideas embodied in the philosophy of paternalism are more attuned to the welfare state than to the tenets of socialism. Examples of paternalism in the United States include Social Security, Medicare and Medicaid, unemployment insurance, fluoridation of water, and veterans' benefit programs. Paternalism is also used politically as a negative propaganda concept that connotes a lack of individual initiative and zeal that results from governmental handouts.

Political Science   An academic and research discipline that deals with the theory and practice of politics and the description and analysis of political systems and political behavior. Fields and subfields of the political science discipline include political theory and philosophy, national systems, cross-national political analysis, international relations, foreign policy, international law and organization, public administration, administrative behavior, public law, judicial behavior, and politics and public policy. Approaches to the discipline include classical political philosophy, structuralism, and behavioralism. Political science, as one of the social sciences, uses methods and techniques that relate to the kinds of data and the investigatory goals sought: historical documents, newspaper reports, scholarly journal articles, official records, personal observation, laboratory experiments, survey research, statistical analysis, model building, and simulation. *See also* INTERNET, page 81.

Significance   Political science in its broadest philosophical sense dates back even earlier than Plato and Aristotle. For many centuries, the study of politics was concerned mainly with normative determinations of what ought to be and with deducing the characteristics and functions of the ideal state. In time, usually regarded as starting with Machiavelli, modern political science, with its emphasis on direct empirical observation of the political institutions and actors, began to evolve. In the 1950s and 1960s, a behavioral revolution stressing the systematic and rigorously scientific study of individual and group political behavior swept the discipline. At the same time that political science moved toward greater depth of analysis and more specialization, it also moved toward a closer working relationship with other disciplines, especially economics, geography, sociology, anthropology, psychology, social psychology, biology, ecology, statistics, and communication sciences. Increasingly, students of political behavior have used the scientific method to create an intellectual discipline based on the postulating of hypotheses followed by empirical verification and the ascertainment of probable trends, and of generalizations that explain individual and group political actions. In the 1980s and 1990s, the discipline placed an increasing emphasis on "relevance," or the use of new approaches and methodologies to solve political and social problems. Statistical and mathematical analysis by computer has become the major analytical tool of the discipline. The main professional organizations of political scientists are the American Political Science Association (APSA), the International Political Science Association (IPSA), the International Studies Association (ISA), and various regional and state organizations.

Popular Sovereignty   The natural-rights concept that ultimate political authority rests with the people and can be exercised to create, alter, or abolish government. In practice, popular sovereignty is ordinarily exercised through representative institutions. *See also* SOVEREIGNTY, page 26.

Significance   Popular sovereignty was enunciated by the natural-rights philosophers in their attack on governmental absolutism based on the theory of divine right. The concept that the people possess supreme political power pervades the Declaration of Independence and the U.S. Constitution. Popular sovereignty is most directly practiced by the American people when engaged in writing, amending, and revising federal, state, and local constitutions or charters.

Power   The ability in politics to control or change the behavior of human beings in a way favored by the power wielder. Some political analysts link influence and force with power, whereas others regard them as distinct techniques employed in the pursuit of objectives. Power can be divided into political, economic, social, and military categories. Power can also be viewed as a means, an end, or both and as actual or potential. As a practical matter, A can be said to exercise power over B if A can get B to do something that B would otherwise not do or had refused to do. Although a number of means exist for exercising power—persuasion, friendship, propaganda, gifts, grants, ideology, moral suasion, and public opinion, for example—ultimately force may be required. A resort to violence may be viewed as resulting from the bankruptcy of political power. In international affairs, actions related to the national interest are almost always deeply involved in power politics. Thus, power politics is universally utilized in the foreign policy actions undertaken by states. The exercise of political power typically involves a psychological relationship between the elites who wield it and those who are influenced or controlled by it. *See also* AUTHORITY, page 3.

Significance   Power is one of the most widely used organizing concepts in the discipline of political science. Power can be utilized in the political arena in the allocation of values or to determine who gets what, when, and how. In the field of international relations, power is often used as a central organizing concept to gain an understanding of how and why decisions are made and actions undertaken. From a normative perspective, power is often regarded as a great evil when it is exercised by one's opponents and as the greatest good when utilized to achieve goals of national interest for one's own state. In government, decision making is rarely based on a rational process. Most decisions reflect the power and influence of those individuals and groups most directly affected. Some scholars and ideologues have regarded political and military power as subservient to the dictates of an economic class or elite. Although vague and elusive, the concept of power remains the key analytical tool for understanding the operations of government and the nature of society. In the sixteenth century, Niccolò Machiavelli, often regarded as the first political scientist because of his practical approach to politics, advised his prince to win and keep power by whatever means were needed and not to be limited by moral and ethical considerations.

Presidential Government   A system that features separation of powers between the legislative and executive branches and the independent election of an executive serving a fixed term. Presidential government is also used in the United States to describe the trend toward strong executive leadership, often at the expense of the legislative branch. *See also* GRIDLOCK, page 79; PARLIAMENTARY SYSTEM, page 21; PRESIDENT, page 196.

Significance   The main advantages claimed for the presidential system are the choice of the executive by the voters rather than by the legislature, the effective use of checks and balances, and the encouragement of strong executive leadership. Critics, however, claim that the system creates a gulf between the legislature and the executive, encourages disagreement and gridlock, and disperses responsibility. In presidential government, the executive tends to emerge as the central figure in the political system.

Radical   An advocate of substantial or fundamental political, social, and economic changes. Although no precise use of the term exists, a radical is generally regarded as a leftist or rightist who is extreme in demands for change. While the term usually refers to extremist individuals and parties of the political left, it can be used to describe anyone who favors drastic political, economic, or social change in the shortest possible time. The original Greek etymology of "radical" meant going to the root or origin of a matter; hence, a radical is one who asks basic questions or tries to answer them. *See* *also* DOMESTIC TERRORISM, page 73; LEFTIST, page 15; NEW LEFT, page 91; RIGHT-IST, page 25.

Significance   The American guarantees of freedom of speech, press, and association have encouraged the expression of radical views. Some radical parties have played a significant role in gaining popular support for some of their proposals, and these often have been incorporated into platforms of the major parties. Extreme radical parties of the Left are often Marxist-oriented. Ultraconservative groups in contemporary American politics are referred to, however, as the "radical right." The term "radical" is freely used in political campaigns in attempts to discredit opponents or their proposals.

Reactionary   A person who advocates substantial political, social, or economic changes, favoring a return to an earlier, more conservative system. Reactionaries believe that most social problems result from democratic excesses favoring the propertyless masses; they usually prefer government by oligarchy. Although the use of the term is not precise, reactionaries tend to be political rightists who are more extreme in their views than conservatives and more likely to adopt militant tactics to achieve their objectives. *See also* DOMESTIC TERRORISM, page 73; RIGHTIST, page 25.

Significance   Some of the new nations of Asia and Africa have come under the control of reactionary regimes after early failures of democracy following independence. In American politics, reactionaries have generally favored laissez-faire and have opposed social-welfare legislation. The term is freely used in political campaigns in attempts to discredit opponents or their proposals.

Representative Government   Any democratic system of government in which the people elect representatives to act as their agents in making and enforcing laws and decisions. Authoritarian regimes often have a façade of representative institutions, but they lack the vital element of accountability of democratic governments. *See also* DEMOCRACY, page 9; GOVERNMENT, page 12; REPUBLIC, page 24.

Significance   Any large and populous political unit must resort to some form of representative government, although small units may provide for direct decision making by the people. Representatives may act for a special class or group, as in medieval assemblies; for an occupational or social group, as in a system of functional representation; or for a geographical community, as in most contemporary legislatures. One theory, expounded by the English statesman Edmund Burke, holds that a representative should exercise his or her own intelligent discretion in reaching decisions; another theory views the representative to be an agent of the people who is expected to vote according to their wishes and interests.

Republic   A form of government in which sovereign power resides in the electorate and is exercised by elected representatives who are responsible to the people. Republican government stands in contradistinction to monarchical or oligarchical government, in which the rulers have a vested right to office. It is also to be distinguished from pure democracy, in which the people govern directly. *See also* REPRESENTATIVE GOVERNMENT, page 24; REPUBLICAN FORM OF GOVERNMENT, page 49.

Significance In the century following the American and French revolutions, republican government emerged in many countries to replace monarchical systems. The Founding Fathers wrote into the Constitution a guarantee by the national government of a republican form of government in every state. In American politics, the distinction between a republic and a democracy is frequently drawn by conservatives to emphasize the representative character of the American system in contrast to what they consider to be the "excesses" of direct democracy. The term "republic" is used to describe various kinds of political systems in the world. For example, in some communist states, such as the People's Republic of China, the ruling Communist party claims that it represents the interests of the public despite the lack of free democratic elections. Since 1991, the former republics that constituted the Union of Soviet Socialist Republics (USSR) have become independent states, and most are now voluntary members of the new Commonwealth of Independent States (CIS).

Rightist An individual or group advocating conservative or reactionary political or economic programs, a restriction on the power of the masses, and oligarchical rule. Rightists tend to favor laissez-faire and strong executive power; the extreme right wing supports fascist dictatorships. The term is derived from the common practice in European parliaments of seating conservative parties to the right of the presiding officer. *See also* REACTIONARY, page 24; RELIGIOUS RIGHT, page 108.

Significance Rightist parties exercise considerable influence in most democratic states. In the United States, both major parties have conservative members who hold positions of influence in Congress. Prominent American rightist movements active in recent years include the Ku Klux Klan, the Conservative party, the American Independent party, and the militias. Most rightists regard themselves as "moderates" or "middle of the road" in their approach to politics, whereas others in the American body politic may regard them as extremists. Extreme right-wing groups have never found much support in American politics.

Rule of Law An Anglo-American concept that emphasizes the supremacy of the law and restricts the discretionary power of public officials. The rule of law particularly stresses the protection of individual rights from the arbitrary interference of officials. *See also* DEMOCRACY, page 9; LITIGIOUS SOCIETY, page 17.

Significance The rule of law provides the foundation for democratic constitutionalism. In the United States, for example, the rule of law requires that each individual accused of a crime be treated equally under the law, receive a fair trial with established procedures, and be accorded due process in all official actions undertaken against him or her. Guarantees provided by the rule of law are in contrast with the operations of a police state. A vital maxim of democratic government is "government of law and not of men."

Socialism   A doctrine that advocates economic collectivism through governmental or industrial group ownership of the means of production and distribution of goods. Its basic aims are to replace competition for profit with cooperation and social responsbility and to secure a more equitable distribution of income and opportunity. Though these aims are common to all socialists, a wide variety of schools of thought have arisen, distinguished mainly by their approaches to the problem of how best to achieve socialism. These vary from the peaceful and democratic ideas of utopian and Christian socialists to the aggressive and sometimes violent approaches of anarchists and communists. *See also* DEMOCRATIC SOCIALISM, page 10.

Significance   Socialism has been a powerful social and political force, particularly in Europe, since the middle of the nineteenth century. In the United States, socialist parties have had little success at the ballot box, but their ideas have gained some measure of acceptance through liberal economic and social-welfare programs. The Democratic Socialist party of Eugene Debs and Norman Thomas had great influence on American politics but has waned in recent years. The more radical Trotskyite Socialist Labor party still runs a presidential candidate but has few adherents. The former communist states of Eastern Europe have in recent years changed to systems of democratic socialism, capitalism, or a combination of both.

Sovereignty   The supreme power of a state, exercised within its boundaries, free from external interference. The idea behind sovereignty is an ancient one, but it was first developed into an elaborate doctrine by philosophers of the sixteenth and seventeenth centuries. They sought to justify the absolutism of the kings of the new state system by cultivating the myth that the monarch had been accorded supreme power by divine action. *See also* POPULAR SOVEREIGNTY, page 22; SOVEREIGNTY, page 577.

Significance   The early absolutist implications of sovereignty developed by Jean Bodin and Thomas Hobbes gave way in time to the new concept of popular sovereignty developed by Jean Jacques Rousseau and John Locke. The idea of sovereignty remains a significant factor in international relations. The concept of absolute sovereignty, however, has been modified by state consent, as demonstrated in treaties, international law, and international organizations.

State   A political community occupying a definite territory, having an organized government, and possessing internal and external sovereignty. Recognition of a state's claim to independence by other states, enabling it to enter into international engagements, is important to the establishment of its sovereignty. The term is also used to describe territorial divisions within a federal system, such as the fifty American states. *See also* NATION, page 20.

Significance   More than 180 states comprise the community of nations. The state, the basic political unit of the world since the sixteenth century, is slowly giving way to evolutionary internationalism in the form of world and regional organizations. The basic challenge today is whether a stable system of international cooperation can be created before the state system destroys itself in a nuclear war.

Theocracy   Any political system in which political power is exercised directly or indirectly by clergy and in which church law is superior to or replaces civil law. The implication is that decisions are made by a Supreme Being and transmitted to human beings through agents who rule in a theocracy. *See also* OLIGARCHY, page 20.

Significance   Theocracies typically are nondemocratic systems in which political power is exercised by an oligarchic council of priests, ministers, monks, or other church officials, or by a single church leader. Examples of theocracies include Geneva under John Calvin, Tibet prior to the communist conquest, and Iran following the popular uprising that overthrew the Shah.

Totalitarianism   A modern form of authoritarianism in which the state controls nearly every aspect of the individual's life. Totalitarian governments do not tolerate activities by individuals or groups, such as labor unions and youth organizations, that are not directed toward the state's goals. Totalitarian dictators maintain themselves in power by means of a secret police, propaganda disseminated through the media of communication, the elimination of free discussion and criticism, and widespread use of terror tactics. Internal scapegoats and foreign military threats are created and used to foster unity through fear. *See also* ABSOLUTISM, page 1; FASCISM, page 12.

Significance   Totalitarianism has developed in the twentieth century through new techniques that mobilize entire populations in support of an authoritarian government and a political ideology. The main totalitarian governments have included Nazi Germany, Fascist Italy, the Soviet Union under Josef Stalin, and Communist China under Mao Tse-tung. Totalitarian systems, however, may not be as monolithic as they appear; they may hide a political process in which several groups—the army, political leaders, industrialists, and others—compete for power and influence.

Utopia   An imaginary human paradise created in the mind and writings of Sir Thomas More. More's ideal commonwealth was located on an island untouched by worldly vices and provided a nearly perfect society. The word "utopia" means literally "no place" and is taken from the title of More's book, published in 1516.

Significance   More's *Utopia* is part of the body of speculative political theory that has fostered the imaginative creation of ideal states and social systems, such as Plato's *Republic* and Tommaso Campanella's *City of the Sun.* The adjective "utopian" is also used to describe the idealistic nineteenth-century socialistic programs offered by Robert Owen, Claude Saint-Simon, and Francois Fourier. American democracy has been influenced by utopianism and the ideals embodied in the "democratic creed."

Welfare State   A concept that stresses the role of government as the provider and protector of individual security and social good through governmental economic and social programs. This role for government represents a shift from that of a minimal protector of persons and property to that of a positive promotor of human welfare. *See also* PATERNALISM, page 21.

Significance   The welfare state is a product of the Industrial Revolution, urbanization, and the social and economic consequences of depressions and wars. Opponents of government's welfare role charge that "cradle-to-grave" security destroys the individual's initiative and enterprise and promotes fiscal irresponsibility. Outspoken critics have sometimes been labeled "Social Darwinists" because they want to apply Charles Darwin's basic theory of "natural selection" to society. Supporters point out that programs involving social security, health, subsidized housing, and the like provide necessary minimum standards of life for all and that no civilized society can avoid this responsibility. Nearly all modern governments have engaged in some such practices, but the rich, industrialized nations have been able to afford the most extensive welfare programs. Some states having the most extensive welfare systems, such as Sweden and Norway, have also enjoyed the highest levels of economic growth. In the United States, massive debt and budget problems are making it difficult to maintain an effective "safety net" of welfare aid to the homeless, aged, sick, hungry, and others in desperate need. The Reagan and Bush administrations transferred much of the responsibility and cost of welfare programs to state and local units of government, which are severely limited in their ability to effectively administer many welfare programs because of massive debt and financial problems. In its 1994 Contract with America, the Republican party, utilizing its majority in Congress, sought to weaken some and eliminate other segments of the welfare state as it has developed since the Great Depression of the 1930s.

2

The United States Constitution and the Federal Union

Admission of New States   The constitutional power of Congress to admit new states to the Union (Art. IV, sec. 3). Limitations on this power are that no state may be created within an existing state and no state may be formed by the union of two or more states or parts of states without the consent of the states concerned and of Congress. The usual procedure for admission is: (1) The people of the territory petition Congress through their territorial assembly; (2) Congress passes an "enabling act" that, when signed by the President, authorizes the territory to frame a constitution; (3) Congress passes an act of admission approved by the President. Though Congress and the President may insist on certain conditions for admission to the Union, a state, once admitted, is equal with all other states. No state may constitutionally withdraw from the Union. *See also Coyle v. Smith,* page 55; DISTRICT OF COLUMBIA, page 38; TERRITORY, page 51.

Significance   The Founding Fathers recognized the desirability of expanding the federal Union by giving Congress power to admit new states. Political considerations, such as which political party the people of the area are likely to support, may influence the majority party in Congress. With the exception of the 13 original states, 30 were elevated from territorial status (including Alaska and Hawaii, the forty-ninth and fiftieth states, in 1959); 5 (Vermont, Kentucky, Tennessee, Maine, and West Virginia) were formed by separation from other states; and 2, Texas and California, were formed from an independent republic and by acquisition from Mexico, respectively. In 1980, the voters of Washington, D.C., approved a referendum to seek statehood for the District of Columbia. A convention drew up a constitution for a fifty-first state, "New Columbia," which, after approval by the voters and presentation to Congress, has remained dormant.

Amendment Process   The means by which changes in, or additions to, a constitution are made. In the United States Constitution, Article V spells out the methods. Amendments may be proposed by a two-thirds vote of both houses of Congress or by a convention called by Congress at the request of the legislatures of two-thirds of the states. Only the first method has been used. Such proposals must be ratified by either the legislatures of three-fourths of the states or by conventions called for that purpose in three-fourths of the states, as determined by Congress. Only the Twenty-first

Amendment (repealing Prohibition) was submitted to conventions. The President may not veto an amendment proposal. Congress may stipulate a time limit, usually seven years, within which a proposal must be ratified. A state that has rejected an amendment may change its mind, but once a proposal is ratified by a state legislature the validity of any subsequent rejection would be determined by Congress. Ratification by a state may not be accomplished by a referendum of the people, but only by the legislature or convention. Though thousands of proposals have been made in Congress to amend the Constitution, only 33 have received endorsement from both houses; of these, 27 have been adopted. Amendments are appended to the Constitution and not placed within the article or section that may have been changed, as is done in some state constitutions. *See also Coleman v. Miller,* page 54; CONSTITUTIONAL AMENDMENTS, STATE, page 612; CONSTITUTIONAL CONVENTION, page 96; EQUAL RIGHTS, page 309; TWENTY-SEVENTH AMENDMENT, page 173; USAGE, page 53. (See also other specific amendments.)

Significance A constitution, no matter how well designed, requires adjustment from time to time. A reasonable amendment procedure makes adjustment possible, without resort to force, in basic governmental arrangements. The Founding Fathers considered that proposal of amendments by the national government, with ratification controlled by the states, would safeguard the basic division of powers under the federal system. The executive and judicial branches are excluded from the proposal and ratification process. Several amendments adopted subsequent to the Bill of Rights relate to elections and have not involved fundamental changes in American government. Others, such as the Fourteenth and Sixteenth, have had profound effects. The present methods of amendment have been criticized largely on the ground that minorities may block the majority will because of the two-thirds- and three-fourths-vote requirements. However, less formal methods of change, such as judicial interpretation and custom and usage, have made frequent resort to the amendment process unnecessary.

Annapolis Convention A conference called by the Virginia legislature in 1786, whereby states were invited to send delegates to Annapolis, Maryland, to discuss trade regulations. Only five states were represented. Under the leadership of Alexander Hamilton and James Madison, the group urged Congress and the states to call another convention in Philadelphia in 1787 to consider revision of the Articles of Confederation. *See also* ARTICLES OF CONFEDERATION, page 31.

Significance The Annapolis Convention was an important prelude to the framing of the Constitution of the United States in Philadelphia the following year. Dissatisfaction with the Articles of Confederation, particularly in the area of trade and commerce, led to this movement for reform.

Antifederalists Persons who opposed adoption of the U.S. Constitution framed in Philadelphia in 1787. They opposed the centralist tendencies of the Constitution and attacked the failure of the framers to include a bill of rights. The group included many who had signed the Declaration of Independence or had strongly supported the Revolution. *See also* FEDERALIST PARTY, page 78.

Significance   A substantial number of people opposed ratification, but strong opposition to the Constitution rapidly dwindled after its adoption. The Antifederalist group, however, became the supporters of Thomas Jefferson, whose views on the nature of the Union, as distinguished from those of Alexander Hamilton and other Federalists, continue to be influential and controversial in American politics today. The Antifederalists were also known as "Democratic Republicans" and, in time, evolved into the Democratic party.

Articles of Confederation   The compact made among the thirteen original American states to form the basis of their government. Though prepared in 1776, the Articles were not officially adopted by all states until 1781 and were replaced in 1789 by the U.S. Constitution. The Confederation was a league of sovereign states. Each state had one vote in a one-house legislature. No provision was made in the Articles for a separate national executive or judiciary. The Congress was assigned a limited number of powers, but the approval of nine states was necessary for effective action. The central government lacked significant powers, including the powers to tax, to regulate commerce or the currency, or to make its laws directly applicable to the people without further state action. In short, the Congress could not force states or individuals to comply with its decisions and resembled, in many respects, an international organization. Any amendments to the Articles required the unanimous approval of the thirteen states. *See also* CONFEDERATION, page 34.

Significance   The Articles of Confederation, and the lessons learned under their operation, formed the backdrop against which the states could move toward "a more perfect union." The Confederation brought the Revolutionary War to a conclusion, accomplished much toward the development of the American continent through the Northwest Ordinance, and established the principle of interstate cooperation through such means as interstate rendition and full faith and credit. Many of the defects of the Articles were rectified in the U.S. Constitution.

Centralization   The tendency for political power and authority to gravitate from state governments to the national government. Though the functions performed by all governments in the United States have increased, the nationwide impact of political, social, and defense problems has led the national government to assume increased responsibility. *See also* COMMERCE POWER, page 33.

Significance   The proper division of powers between the national and state governments has been a cause for controversy throughout American history. It is argued that centralization permits more efficient handling of problems that are nationwide in scope. Opponents contend that decentralized activity prevents tyranny, permits experimentation, and encourages local solutions to problems. Various groups tend to support the management of a function by that level of government most responsive to their needs. The Reagan and Bush administrations and, with increasing intensity, the Republican-controlled Congress elected in 1994 sharpened the continuing debate over the centralization issue by emphasizing the return of functions to state and local governments and the dismantling of numerous national programs, especially public welfare programs.

Charter Colony   One of the three types of governments—charter, proprietary, royal—found in colonial America. Charter colonies, namely, Rhode Island and Connecticut, operated under charters agreed to by the colony and the king. The legislature was elected and allowed much autonomy by England. The governor was chosen by the legislature. *See also* PROPRIETARY COLONY, page 48; ROYAL COLONY, page 50.

Significance   Charter colonies enjoyed the greatest degree of independence from the Crown. The charters of Connecticut and Rhode Island proved so satisfactory for local self-government that they served as state constitutions until 1818 and 1842, respectively.

Checks and Balances   A major principle of the American governmental system whereby each department of the government exercises a check upon the actions of the others. The principle operates not only among the legislative, executive, and judicial branches but also between the two houses of the legislature and between the states and the national government. Each department has some authority to control the actions of one or more of the others by participation in their functions. Examples include the President's veto power and the congressional power to override the veto, judicial review of legislative and executive actions, presidential appointment of judges with senatorial approval, and the congressional power to impeach. *See also* DISTRIBUTION OF POWERS, page 38; SEPARATION OF POWERS, page 50.

Significance   Through the various devices of checks and balances, the framers of the Constitution sought to prevent the accumulation of all power in one branch, or in one or several persons, by giving each branch the authority to prevent the others' encroachment. The checks-and-balances system stresses the interdependence (rather than complete separation) of the various units of government and the need for compromise; it also prevents the usurpation of power. Major defects of this system are its tendencies to create gridlock and to prevent swift action during crises.

Commerce and Slave Trade Compromise   An agreement reached at the Constitutional Convention of 1787, giving the national government power to regulate foreign commerce, requiring the consent of two-thirds of the Senate to treaties, and prohibiting the national government from taxing exports or interfering with the slave trade until 1808.

Significance   One of the major purposes for the convention was to strengthen national control over commerce. Southern delegates, however, feared that northern majorities might cut off the slave trade and discriminate against the profitable cotton trade. They agreed to grant the national government control over foreign commerce provided that the South was given a check over treaties and that Congress would not tax exports. Southerners believed that a sufficient number of slaves would be available by 1808, although illegal slave traffic continued until the Civil War. The treaty and foreign commerce provisions continue to influence the making of American foreign policy.

Commerce Power   The authority delegated to Congress by the Constitution (Art. 1, sec. 8) to regulate commerce with foreign nations and among the states. The term "commerce" has been interpreted to include the production and buying and selling of goods as well as the transportation of persons or commodities. All of these functions are subject to national regulation and control if they affect more than one state or the free flow of commerce among states. *See also* COMMERCE, page 436; CONCURRENT POWERS, page 33; *Gibbons v. Ogden,* page 472; *United States v. Lopez,* page 56.

Significance   The commerce power is one of the major constitutional provisions used by Congress to expand national power. A broad interpretation of what constitutes interstate commerce has enabled Congress to regulate such matters as manufacturing, child labor, farm production, wages and hours, labor unions, civil rights, and criminal conduct. Any activity that in any way "affects" interstate commerce is subject to national rather than state control. So many functions are now interstate in character that the role of the states in the federal system has been considerably altered or diminished.

Commonwealth   A designation equivalent to the term "state," used in Pennsylvania, Massachusetts, Virginia, and Kentucky. The term "commonwealth" is generally used to indicate a federation of nations or states in which each unit has a large measure of self-government, such as those of the British Commonwealth of Nations. Puerto Rico and the Northern Marianas are each officially designated as a "free commonwealth" associated with the United States. *See also* CONFEDERATION, page 34; STATE, page 26; STATE SOVEREIGNTY, page 51; TERRITORY, page 51.

Significance   Significance "Commonwealth" refers to a body of equals united by a common interest. Although the term is used as the official name for several American states, it has no legal significance. However, its usage in connection with Puerto Rico does indicate special status for that area as an independent territory of the United States.

Concurrent Powers   Authority possessed by both the national and state governments. Examples include the powers to tax, maintain courts, and charter banks. The states exercise concurrently with the national government any power that is not exclusively conferred on the national government by the Constitution and that does not conflict with national law. *See also* DELEGATED POWERS, page 38; RESERVED POWERS, page 49; TENTH AMENDMENT, page 51.

Significance   Under the American federal system, it is essential that both national and state governments possess those powers necessary to enable them to function. The power to tax is a noteworthy example. The fact that this power is delegated to the national government does not mean that the states may not also tax. States frequently legislate in areas in which the national government has not, despite its power to do so. Should the national government determine to occupy a particular field of activity delegated to it under the Constitution, then the principle of national supremacy prevails. In the regulation of interstate commerce, the national government has frequently allowed state control over some elements of such commerce. The Supreme Court has disallowed state action when it has determined that national uniformity is desirable.

Confederation   A league of independent states. A central government or administrative organ handles those matters of common concern delegated to it by the member states. The central unit may not make laws directly applicable to individuals without further action by its member units. The governments under the Articles of Confederation and the Confederate States of America are two examples from American history. The United Nations is often referred to as a confederation. *See also* ARTICLES OF CONFEDERATION, page 31; FEDERALISM, page 40; UNITARY STATE, page 53.

   Significance   A confederation is generally distinguished from a federation, in which, as in the United States, the central unit is invested with supreme authority and may act directly upon individuals. American experience under the Articles of Confederation is credited with being an essential step toward the formation of a "more perfect union." A confederated structure enables sovereign states to cooperate in seeking solutions to mutual problems without giving up their autonomy.

Connecticut Compromise   The agreement reached in the Constitutional Convention of 1787 that resolved the question of representation in the national Congress. Each state is represented in the House of Representatives according to population, and in the Senate each state is represented equally. The compromise, also called the "Great Compromise," satisfied the small states in particular and enabled them to agree to the establishment of a strong central government. *See also* BICAMERALISM, page 130; NEW JERSEY PLAN, page 46; VIRGINIA PLAN, page 54.

   Significance   While the Connecticut Compromise was the "price of union" in 1787, it has had lasting significance. The equal representation of states in the Senate has resulted in a disproportionate influence of sparsely settled states and regions. Though the states are represented by population in the House, bills must pass both houses to become law. Thus the Compromise of 1787 is felt in the daily workings of Congress. The Connecticut Compromise was the crucial step in the formation of the Constitution.

Constitution   A fundamental or "organic" law that establishes the framework of government of a state, assigns the powers and duties of governmental agencies, and establishes the relationship between the people and their government. Constitutions may be written or unwritten. The British operate under an unwritten constitution, that is, one consisting largely of legislative acts, legal decisions, and customs that have never been comprehensively gathered in one document. American constitutions are written, but much fundamental law is unwritten and in the form of custom and usage. The U.S. Constitution went into effect on March 4, 1789, and has been formally amended 27 times. As the supreme law of the land, its basic principles include limited government, popular sovereignty, separation of powers, checks and balances, and federalism. *See also* CONSTITUTION (STATE), page 610; DISTRIBUTION OF POWERS, page 38.

Significance   The United States Constitution, the oldest and most successful written constitution in history, has served the nation with remarkably little formal alteration during periods of rapid social change. This is due to the wisdom of the framers, who wrote a brief and flexible instrument, and to the policy of liberal construction that has characterized many important Supreme Court decisions. The Constitution has not only served as an effective instrument of government and a guardian of human rights but also a revered symbol of how geographically dispersed people with diverse interests can live together in freedom.

Constitutional Construction   The method of interpreting the Constitution. Some favor a "loose" or "liberal" construction of constitutional phrases; others, a "strict" interpretation. The difference is largely expressed in terms of the interpreter's attitude toward broad grants of power to the national government (loose construction) as opposed to the retention of as much power as possible in the states (strict construction). *See also* ACTIVISM VERSUS SELF-RESTRAINT, page 247; JURISPRUDENCE, page 267; *McCulloch v. Maryland,* page 56; ORIGINAL INTENT, page 272.

Significance   The issue of loose versus strict construction arose early in American history and contributed to the emergence of political parties. The Federalist party favored a broad interpretation of national powers, while the Jeffersonian Antifederalists stood for a narrow construction of such powers. The legal issue arose in the famous case of *McCulloch v. Maryland,* 4 Wheaton 316 (1819), which involved the question of whether the national government was limited to those powers *expressly* delegated to it or whether it had *implied* powers. Chief Justice John Marshall resolved the issue in favor of the implied-powers doctrine and established the principle of, and necessity for, a loose construction of the Constitution. From time to time, the strict constructionists have had their way, depending largely on the party in power and the attitude of the Supreme Court. Loose construction, however, remains the basis for constitutional interpretation and has facilitated adaptation of the Constitution to the needs of the time.

Constitutional Convention   A body established by Congress on the application of the legislatures of two-thirds of the states to propose amendments to the Constitution. Article V of the Constitution provides for this method of proposing amendments as an alternative to proposals put forth by a two-thirds vote of both houses of Congress. In either case, ratification is accomplished by the approval of the legislatures or conventions of three-fourths of the states as provided by Congress. No national constitutional convention has been held in the United States since 1787, and no constitutional guidance exists as to the composition, procedures, or scope of authority of such a convention. *See also* AMENDMENT PROCESS, page 29; CONSTITUTIONAL CONVENTION (STATE), PAGE 612; CONSTITUTIONAL CONVENTION OF 1787, page 36.

Significance   A constitutional convention is viewed as the highest voice of the people. It is unclear under Article V whether a convention could be limited by Congress in its authority or procedures. Fear of a possible "runaway" convention, should one be called, is buttressed by the actions of the members of the Constitutional Convention of 1787 who wrote the United States Constitution. That convention was convened "for the sole and express purpose of revising the Articles of Confederation," a purpose that was essentially ignored, as was the ratification procedure required by the Articles. In the past, various states have called on Congress to call conventions to outlaw polygamy, limit federal taxing power, or to overturn specific Supreme Court decisions such as "one person, one vote" or prayer in schools. On occasion, a potential call for a convention has prompted Congress to propose an amendment, as was the case with the direct election of senators (Seventeenth). In recent years, nearly two-thirds of the states have petitioned Congress to call a convention to draft constitutional amendment proposals to require a balanced federal budget. This has prompted some action in Congress to consider procedures for the call of a convention, should that situation materialize.

Constitutional Convention of 1787   The convention held in Philadelphia from May 25 to September 18 that framed the Constitution of the United States. Called by the Confederation Congress to revise the Articles of Confederation, the delegates proceeded to draft an entirely new document. Rhode Island sent no delegates, and only 55 of the 74 men originally appointed as delegates attended. Presided over by George Washington, the deliberations were conducted in secret but have been made known through notes kept by James Madison. The delegates made compromises on various differences between large and small states, North and South, agrarian and commercial interests, and advocates of a strong or weak central government. They not only ignored their instructions merely to revise the Articles of Confederation but also ignored the provision of the Articles requiring unanimous consent of the state legislatures for revision by providing that the new constitution would go into effect when nine states ratified it in state conventions. *See also* COMMERCE AND SLAVE TRADE COMPROMISE, page 32; CONNECTICUT COMPROMISE, page 34; CONSTITUTIONAL CONVENTION, page 34; ECONOMIC INTERPRETATION OF THE CONSTITUTION, page 39; MADISON'S JOURNAL, page 45; NEW JERSEY PLAN, page 46; THREE-FIFTHS COMPROMISE, page 52; VIRGINIA PLAN, page 54.

Significance   The convention was a conservative reaction to the excesses of the Revolutionary period and to the commercial disorder under the Articles of Confederation. Its membership was young and well-informed on government and politics and representative of propertied and commercial interests. The convention has been the only national constitutional convention in American history, but, by law, another can be called by Congress on the request of two-thirds of the states.

Continental Congress   The body of delegates representing the colonies that first met to protest the British treatment of the colonies and eventually became the government of the United States. The First Continental Congress met in 1774 and drafted a Declaration of Rights. The Second Continental Congress, which began meeting the following year, adopted the Declaration of Independence, conducted the War of Independence, and served as the national government until the Articles of Confederation went into effect in 1781.

Significance   The First Continental Congress met in an atmosphere in which the colonists still considered themselves Englishmen who were being abused. The Second Continental Congress convened after open conflict with England had begun. Though the second Continental Congress rested on no legal base, it served as a de facto government. Delegates were selected by the state legislatures. While the states did not feel bound by decisions of the Continental Congress, it did bring the war to a successful conclusion. It also developed an American consciousness, which led to the adoption of the Articles of Confederation and, eventually, to the Constitution of the United States.

Cooperative Federalism   A concept that views the states and the national government as cooperating partners in the performance of governmental functions rather than as antagonistic competitors for power. The grant-in-aid programs typify this relationship between the national and state governments. *See also* BLOCK GRANT, page 388; FEDERAL AID HIGHWAY ACT, page 57; GRANT-IN-AID, page 404.

Significance   Many current problems cut across traditional divisions of authority between the national and state governments. Cooperation between these units to meet common problems has enabled American federalism to adjust to new problems and to find some middle ground between extreme centralization of power and unworkable decentralization. Some liken the relationship to a "marble cake," characterized by a mixing of functions at various levels. For example, a vast interstate highway system would be unlikely without national and state cooperation. Nevertheless, differences over the appropriate functions of national and state governments characterize American politics. Each president tends to promote a version of "new federalism," a term used by most recent presidents to call for greater assumption of responsibility by the state governments. President Reagan advocated and accomplished a transfer of responsibility from the national government to the state governments largely through budget cuts that put additional financial burdens on state and local governments. Increased use of block grants to the states to undertake formerly federally administered programs characterized the "new federalism" of the 1990s.

Declaration of Independence   The document adopted by the Second Continental Congress on July 4, 1776, declaring the independence of the American colonies from Great Britain and justifying the rebellion. It was drafted by a committee of five men: Thomas Jefferson, John Adams, Benjamin Franklin, Roger Sherman, and Robert Livingston. The draft was largely the work of Jefferson, who drew heavily from the natural-rights doctrine of the English philosopher John Locke. The Declaration enumerated the grievances against the Crown and eloquently defended human rights and the right of self-government.

Significance   The Declaration of Independence does not have any legal effect today. Nevertheless, it is recognized throughout the world as a basic statement of the American creed. Its famed opening passage declares as "self-evident" truths the equality of all men, the natural rights of man endowed by God, the principle of limited government, government by consent, and the right of people to rebel against tyrannical government.

Delegated Powers   Powers granted to the national government under the Constitution. Generally, the delegated powers are those enumerated in the first three articles of the Constitution, relative to the legislative, executive, and judicial branches of the national government. Article I, section 8 contains the main compilation of these powers. The terms "delegated," "enumerated," "granted," and "specific" may be used interchangeably *See also* IMPLIED POWERS, page 41; RESERVED POWERS, page 49; *United States v. Curtiss-Wright Export Corp.,* page 600.

Significance   Under American federalism, the national government is one of delegated powers. With the exception of foreign affairs, it must find justification for its actions in a specifically authorized power or in one that can be reasonably implied from those specifically authorized. The national government does not possess unlimited or general governmental power but only such power as is given to it in the Constitution.

Distribution of Powers   An underlying principle of the American constitutional system designed to prevent tyranny by assigning powers to different governments and agencies and by checking the exercise of power. The distribution takes the following forms: (1) dividing power between the national and state governments under a federal system; (2) separating power among the three major branches of the government—legislative, executive, and judicial—and giving each branch a check upon the operations of the others; (3) selecting the personnel of the three branches by different procedures and electorates, assigning them different terms of office, and making them responsible to different pressures; and (4) limiting all governments by specific constitutional restrictions. *See also* FEDERALISM, page 40; MADISONIANISM, page 18; SEPARATION OF POWERS, page 50.

Significance   Through a complex distribution of authority, the framers sought to prevent all governmental power from falling into the hands of any individual or group. They feared majority tyranny as much as minority or individual tyranny. Hence, they provided for a wide distribution of authority, limited in scope, and designed to effect a balancing of interests. The distribution of powers has been modified by the expanding role of the national government, the increasing influence of the President over legislation and foreign affairs, and the development of independent regulatory agencies that exercise some legislative and judicial power in their supervision of the economy.

District of Columbia   The seat of government of the United States of America, commonly called Washington, D.C. It consists of some 70 square miles of land carved out of the state of Maryland and is a densely urbanized area of about 600,000 inhabitants. Article I, section 8 of the Constitution grants Congress exclusive control over the nation's capital city. Until 1974, the District was managed by officials appointed by the President with the consent of the Senate, and Congress acted as the city council. In 1974, the voters of the

District approved a charter proposed by Congress providing for the election of a mayor and a thirteen-member city council. Congress, however, retains power to rescind council actions. Funds for the District are secured largely through local taxation. Under the Twenty-third Amendment to the Constitution adopted in 1961, residents of the District may vote in presidential elections and are alloted three electoral votes. Legislation enacted by Congress in 1968 authorized the District's first elected school board. In 1970, Congress granted the District a nonvoting delegate in the House of Representatives and established a local court system. A constitutional amendment proposal sent to the states by Congress in August 1978 would have treated the District as a state for representation in Congress and the Electoral College and repeal the Twenty-third Amendment, but it failed to receive ratification by three-fourths of the states. In 1980 the voters of the District adopted a referendum proposal to seek statehood and in 1982 adopted and sent to Congress a proposed Constitution (subsequently amended by the city council) for the fifty-first state, "New Columbia." Congressional inaction led to the election in 1990 of "shadow senators" under city council authorization.

Significance Congress has had to devote a great amount of time to affairs of the District, and even with home rule and possible statehood, some measure of congressional control is called for under the Constitution. The modified home rule acquired in 1974 was the culmination of many years of effort to secure self-government for the people of the District of Columbia. Major obstacles to statehood include the inability of Congress to agree on a scheme of government, racial issues (a major portion of the residents are black), and the city's record of mismanagement and corruption. Congress continues to monitor city council legislation very closely.

Economic Interpretation of the Constitution The theory that the framers of the Constitution represented the well-to-do classes and that the Constitution was designed to protect their interests. The theory was developed by the distinguished historian Charles A. Beard in his *An Economic Interpretation of the Constitution of the United States* (1913).

Significance Charles Beard's economic interpretation did not attribute any malice to the framers but demonstrated that they had much to gain from the creation of a strong and stable national government. He pointed out that the delegates were professional or propertied men with extensive holdings in public securities, land, manufacturing, shipping, and slaves. Although the framers were a conservative-minded group who were affected by their own backgrounds and interests, Beard and other historians have emphasized that economic interest was only *one* of the factors that motivated them.

Exclusive Powers Those powers that, under the Constitution, belong exclusively to, and may be exercised only by, either the national government or the governments of the various states. An example of an exclusive national power is that over foreign affairs; an exclusive state power is control over local government. *See also* CONCURRENT POWERS, page 33.

Significance The concept of exclusive power emphasizes the federal nature of the United States: two governments, existing side by side, each supreme within its own sphere of authority. Many problem areas, once considered within the exclusive realm of state power, have, however, under changing social conditions, fallen under national control. Civil rights and welfare programs illustrate how the national government has moved into fields previously under exclusive state control.

Federalism   A system of government in which a written constitution divides power between a central government and regional or subdivisional governments. Both governments act directly upon the people through their officials and laws. Both are supreme within their proper sphere of authority. Both must consent to constitutional change. By contrast, in a "unitary" system of government, the central government is supreme, and regional and local governments derive their authority from the central government. Federal systems are found in the United States, Canada, Switzerland, Mexico, Australia, India, and Germany, among others. In the United States, the term "federal government" is used as a synonym for the national government. American history has seen federalism defined and applied in various patterns, including (1) *cooperative* federalism, which assumes the two levels are essentially partners; (2) *dual* federalism, which holds that the two levels are functionally separate; (3) *creative* federalism, which involves common planning and decision making; (4) *horizontal* federalism, which involves interactions and common programs among the 50 states; (5) *marble-cake* federalism, which is characterized by an intermingling of all levels in policies and programming; (6) *picket-fence* federalism, which implies that bureaucrats and clientele groups help determine intergovernmental programs; and (7) *vertical* federalism, the traditional form of federalism, in which national government actions are supreme within their constitutional sphere. *See also* CONFEDERATION, page 34; UNITARY STATE, page 53.

Significance   Federalism is a compromise between an extreme concentration of power and a loose confederation of independent states for governing a variety of people, usually in a large expanse of territory. At the Constitutional Convention of 1787, this compromise was essential in order to convince the independent states to join together. Federalism has the virtue of retaining local pride, traditions, and power, while making possible a central government that can handle common problems. In the United States, federalism has facilitated growth through the admittance of new states to the Union. The basic principle of American federalism is fixed in the Tenth Amendment to the Constitution, which provides that the national government is to have those powers delegated in the Constitution with all other powers reserved to the states. In some countries using the federal system (for example, Canada), the pattern is reversed, with the regional governments possessing only delegated authority. The division of power under federalism is one of the major principles underlying the American Constitution and has a continuing impact on American life and politics.

Federalist Papers   A series of 85 essays written by Alexander Hamilton, James Madison, and John Jay (all using the name *Publius*), which were published in New York newspapers in 1787 to convince New Yorkers to adopt the newly proposed Constitution drafted in Philadelphia. These essays have been collected and published under the title *The Federalist*. *See also* MADISONIANISM, page 18.

Significance   *The Federalist,* although written in haste and for the specific purpose of winning support for the Constitution, is widely regarded as the best single commentary on the Constitution. Government officials, especially judges, often rely on *The Federalist* in interpreting the meaning of the Constitution. Moreover, it is considered the outstanding American contribution to political theory.

Full Faith and Credit   One of the obligations of each state in its relations with other states. Article IV, section 1 of the Constitution provides that "Full faith and credit shall be given in each state to the public acts, records, and judicial proceedings of every other state." The clause applies to civil but not criminal proceedings. It ensures that rights established under wills, contracts, and deeds and other property rights will be honored in all states. A judicial decision in one state will be honored and enforced in all states. *See also* HORIZONTAL FEDERALISM, page 41.

Significance   The full faith and credit clause was originally put into the Articles of Confederation to promote "mutual friendship and intercourse among the people of the different states in this Union." It was carried over to the Constitution and has contributed to the unity of the American people. It protects the legal rights of citizens as they move about the various states and prevents evasion of legal responsibilities. The increasing mobility of the American people and the expanse of business operations have increased the importance of the clause.

Horizontal Federalism   The relationships among the states of the Union either imposed by the Constitution or undertaken voluntarily. This term is used to distinguish state-state relations from national-state relations (denoted by the term "vertical federalism"). Requirements imposed by the Constitution are that each state afford full faith and credit to the public acts, records, and judicial proceedings of other states; grant the citizens of each state the privileges and immunities of citizens of their own state; and return fugitives from justice. Voluntary arrangements include interstate compacts, uniform laws, reciprocal agreements, and cooperation through consultation. *See also* FULL FAITH AND CREDIT, page 41; INTERSTATE COMPACT, page 44; INTERSTATE RENDITION, page 44; PRIVILEGES AND IMMUNITIES, page 47; UNIFORM STATE LAWS, page 629.

Significance   Under federalism, the relationships among the states may be of equal importance to the relationship between the national and state governments. Because each state retains a good deal of authority, certain requirements have been laid down to assure cooperation. The requirement of full faith and credit, for example, helps to guarantee legal rights of citizens throughout the country. The states have sought to forestall national intervention into problem areas that cross state lines by entering into voluntary agreements. States have not, however, shown sufficient initiative in meeting mutual problems, which results in increasing dependence by the people upon the national government.

Implied Powers   Authority possessed by the national government by inference from those powers delegated to it in the Constitution. For example, the power to draft men into the armed forces may be deduced from the power delegated to raise armies and navies. The implied-power concept derives from the "necessary and proper" clause in Article I, section 8, which empowers the national government to do all things necessary and proper to carry out its delegated powers. This principle was officially enunciated by the Supreme Court in *McCulloch v. Maryland,* 4 Wheaton 316 (1819). *See also* CONSTITUTIONAL CONSTRUCTION, page 35; *McCulloch v. Maryland,* page 56; NECESSARY AND PROPER CLAUSE, page 46.

Significance Through the use of implied powers, the national government has been able to strengthen and broaden the scope of its authority to meet many problems unforeseen by the framers. In the early days of the Union, conflicting opinions arose over whether the national government was limited to exercising only those powers expressly delegated to it in the Constitution. It is unlikely that the national government, or the United States as a nation, could have emerged as a powerful force had the more limited view prevailed.

Indian Tribes   Native American groups standing in a quasi-sovereign relationship to the United States. Slightly fewer than 2 million persons have been identified as American Indians and Alaskan Natives, about 20 percent of whom live on 314 reservations and Indian lands, covering about 3.6 million square miles. About 555 federally recognized tribes and Alaskan village communities are served by the Bureau of Indian Affairs in the Department of the Interior. The legal status of an Indian tribe is basically that of a "domestic dependent nation" exercising inherent sovereign authority over their members and territories (*Cherokee Nation v. Georgia,* 5 Pet. 1 [1831]). Most Indian lands are excluded from state jurisdiction, and only federal and tribal law applies. The Indian Reorganization Act of 1934 and the Indian Self-Determination and Education Assistance Act of 1975 strengthened tribal control over their own affairs, and the Indian Civil Rights Act of 1968 makes tribal government subject to limitations similar to those found in the Bill of Rights. The tribes do not have criminal jurisdiction over non-Indians but do over Indians from different tribes. Article I, section 8 of the Constitution authorizes Congress to regulate commerce with the Indian tribes. Since 1924, Indians born in the United States are citizens.

Significance Indian tribes stand primarily as remnants of conquered people. Tribal independence, acknowledged by nearly 400 treaties signed by the United States and various tribes between 1778 and 1868, has undergone severe strain. Contrary to popular belief, American Indians are not "wards" of the government; any payments made to tribes or individuals result from compensation for treaty violations or encroachments on Indian land. Broken treaties and unsuccessful efforts to assimilate American Indians into the mainstream of American life have left the Indians a seriously disadvantaged minority in terms of life span, education, employment, and housing. During the 1960s, American Indian groups adopted "Red Power" tactics, similar to those of the black civil rights movement, with emphasis on mass demonstrations, sit-ins, lobbying, and lawsuits to attract attention to their plight. The relatively small population and geographic isolation of American Indians have made progress difficult. The Native American Programs Act of 1974 authorizes grants to tribal organizations for educational, nutritional, and health assistance. Following a historic meeting between President Clinton and tribal leaders in 1994, steps were taken to encourage relationships between government departments and tribal governments in the provision of services, and Congress enacted the Tribal Self-Governance Act of 1994 to authorize tribes to contract with the federal government to manage entire Indian programs.

Inherent Powers   Authority vested in the national government, particularly in the area of foreign affairs, that does not depend upon any specific grant of power in the Constitution. Inherent powers, also known as "prerogative powers," derive from the fact that the United States is a sovereign power among nations. The Supreme Court has pointed out that even if the Constitution made no mention of it, the national government could still, for example, make international agreements or acquire territory. Whether or not the President has inherent powers to meet emergencies in internal affairs by virtue of his position as chief executive is a matter of dispute. *See also United States v. Curtiss-Wright Export Corp.,* page 600; WAR POWERS, page 591; *Youngstown Sheet and Tube Co. v. Sawyer,* page 217.

Significance   Since the national government has only delegated powers, justification for its actions must be found either directly or by implication from a specific grant of power. In the field of international affairs, however, the United States must be presumed to have the same power as any other nation in the world. Many presidents have taken unauthorized action to meet emergency situations, notably Abraham Lincoln during the Civil War. However, in 1952, during the Korean conflict, the Supreme Court ruled that the President could not seize private property (steel mills) without authorization from Congress (*Youngstown Sheet and Tube Co. v. Sawyer,* 343 U.S. 579).

Intergovernmental Tax Immunity   The exemption of state and national governmental agencies and property from taxation by each other. The doctrine of intergovernmental tax immunity had its origin in the case of *McCulloch v. Maryland,* 4 Wheaton 316 (1819), in which the Supreme Court declared that the states may not burden the national government by the taxation of its agents or functions. This doctrine was later extended to national taxation of state agents and functions. For a time, even the salaries of government employees and contractors were exempt from taxation; this is no longer the case. National governmental functions and properties are exempt from state taxation, but where hardship may result because of extensive federal holdings in a state, payments in lieu of taxes may be authorized by Congress. State or local activities may be taxed by the national government if the function is nongovernmental in character. An example of this is national taxation of state-owned liquor stores. *See also Graves v. New York,* page 55; *McCulloch v. Maryland,* page 56; PROPRIETARY FUNCTION, page 453; *South Carolina v. United States,* page 425.

Significance   Intergovernmental tax immunity prevents undue interference by one government with the proper exercise of power by another government. This rule is essential to the effective operation of a federal system of government. Without such a rule, one level of government might use its tax power to weaken or destroy the operations of the other. National taxation of state nongovernmental functions remains a matter of controversy, since it is questionable whether any state or local activity can be classified as non-governmental in character. The courts have been reluctant to interfere with congressional judgment on this matter.

Interposition   A concept that holds that a state may place itself between its citizens and the national government so as to prevent the enforcement of national law upon its citizens. According to this doctrine, each state may be the judge of the legality or constitutionality of national action and may "interpose" its sovereignty to nullify federal action. This theory was propounded by Thomas Jefferson and James Madison in the Kentucky and Virginia resolutions of 1799 protesting the Alien and Sedition Acts and by the South prior to the Civil War. Southern leaders reactivated the theory in the 1950s in opposition to the racial desegregation rulings of the Supreme Court. The federal courts, however, have rejected the interposition doctrine as contrary to the national supremacy clause of Article VI.

Significance   Interposition represents a challenge to national supremacy in an extreme form. Obviously, fifty different interpretations of the Constitution would dissolve the Union. From time to time, the right to interpose state sovereignty has been claimed by states in all sections of the country. This claim of state sovereignty has generally been made to cover up underlying social and economic interests of particular groups that feel themselves threatened by national policy. When interposition is invoked, it is a sign that the federal principle is under strain.

Interstate Compact   An agreement between two or more states. The Constitution (Art. I, sec. 10) requires such agreements or compacts to have the consent of Congress. Many agreements on minor matters, however, are made without such consent. Generally, any compact that tends to increase the power of the contracting states relative to other states or to the national government requires consent. One of the earliest and best-known compacts was concluded between New York and New Jersey in 1921 to establish the Port of New York Authority for purposes of regulating the New York harbor and other facilities. A great variety of other compacts cover a wide range of subjects from flood control to petroleum conservation. Congress has, at times, granted advance blanket approval to certain kinds of compacts, as in civil defense matters, nuclear waste storage, and water pollution. *See also* HORIZONTAL FEDERALISM, page 41; *Virginia v. Tennessee,* page 57.

Significance   One intent of the requirement that congressional consent be acquired for interstate compacts was to prevent the states from threatening the Union through alliances among themselves. Today, interstate compacts serve as means for the states to solve regional problems and counter the centralizing tendencies of recent years.

Interstate Rendition   The return of a fugitive from justice by a state upon the demand of the executive authority of the state in which the crime was committed. This is one of the obligations imposed upon the states by Article IV, section 2 of the Constitution. Though the language of the Constitution is positive on this obligation, until 1987 the federal courts would not order the governor of one state to deliver a fugitive wanted in another state; compliance by a governor was viewed as a moral duty (*Kentucky v. Dennison,* 24 Howard 66 [1861]). In 1987 the Supreme Court overruled the 126-year-old precedent, holding that the constitutional command of interstate rendition is mandatory and affords no discretion to the executive of an asylum state (*Puerto Rico v. Branstad,* 483 U.S. 219). Congress has supplemented the requirement by making it a federal crime to flee across state lines to avoid prosecution for certain felonies. When apprehended by federal agents, the fugitive is usually turned over to the state from which he or she fled. The term "extradition" is used to describe this practice among nations under international law. *See also* EXTRADITION, page 549; HORIZONTAL FEDERALISM, page 40.

Significance   Interstate rendition is designed to prevent an accused person from escaping prosecution by leaving a state. Rendition is routinely followed in most cases but, on occasion, a governor has refused to comply. Refusal was based on such grounds as the good behavior of the fugitive since the escape, the suspicion that a fair trial would not be granted, or for political or other reasons known only to the governor. The Supreme Court's decision in *Kentucky v. Dennison* was a political adaptation to the realities of the pre–Civil War period and the problem of fugitive slaves. In the 1987 *Branstad* case, the Court found no justification for distinguishing this particular constitutional duty imposed on states from others.

Madison's Journal   Notes kept by James Madison of the proceedings of the Constitutional Convention of 1787. Although an official journal of the convention was kept, it contained only formal motions and votes by states. Madison kept a record of the debates as well. These notes were not published until 1840, four years after Madison's death.

Significance   The proceedings of the convention were conducted in secrecy, and Madison's notes are the only reliable source of information. For more than 50 years, the Constitution was interpreted without the benefit of these materials, which cast important light upon the intentions of the framers.

Mayflower Compact   An agreement signed in 1620 by all adult men on board the ship *Mayflower,* prior to landing in Plymouth, to form a civil body politic governed by majority rule. *See also* CONTRACT THEORY, page 8.

Significance   The Mayflower Compact established the first government in New England based on the consent of the governed and remained the basis for government in the Plymouth Colony until it joined Massachusetts in 1691. The document also represents an underlying feature of American political theory that government results from a social contract among individuals for their mutual benefit.

National Supremacy   A basic constitutional principle of American government that asserts the superiority of national law. This principle is rooted in Article VI (the "supremacy" or "kingpin clause"), which provides that the Constitution, laws passed by the national government under its constitutional powers, and all treaties are the supreme laws of the land. The Article requires that all national and state officers and judges be bound by oath to support the Constitution regardless of any state constitutional or legislative provisions. Thus, any legitimate exercise of national power supersedes any conflicting state action; this is also known as "preemption." Determination of whether such a conflict exists rests in the hands of the judiciary, with the final decisions made by the Supreme Court. *See also Cohens v. Virginia,* page 286; *McCulloch v. Maryland,* page 56.

Significance   National supremacy is crucial to the successful operation of the federal system. The national government is the government of all the people; a state speaks for only some of the people. The application of the principle of national supremacy has been a source of constant conflict, with such extreme results as the Civil War. The major *legal* challenge to national supremacy was expounded by the Supreme Court in the concept of "dual federalism," which held that a grant of authority to the national government does not destroy local power reserved to the states. Since 1937, the Court has, with rare exception, rejected this concept and applied a broad construction of national authority.

Necessary and Proper Clause   The final paragraph (clause 18) of Article I, section 8 of the Constitution, which delegates legislative powers to Congress. It authorizes all laws "necessary and proper" to carry out the enumerated powers. This clause, sometimes called the "elastic" clause, was used by the Supreme Court in *McCulloch v. Maryland,* 4 Wheaton 316 (1819), to develop the concept of "implied powers." *See also* DELEGATED POWERS, page 38; IMPLIED POWERS, page 41; *McCulloch v. Maryland,* page 56.

Significance   Congressional authority is limited to its delegated powers. The necessary and proper clause, however, allows Congress to choose the *means* by which it will execute its authority. Broad construction of this phrase has enabled the national government to adapt its powers to the needs of the times. It has given elasticity to the constitutional system and has reduced the need for frequent constitutional amendments.

New Jersey Plan   A plan submitted by William Paterson of New Jersey to the Constitutional Convention of 1787 representing the views of the small states and states' rights advocates. It was expressly designed as a counterproposal to the strong nationalistic Virginia Plan. The essence of the New Jersey Plan was a single-house Congress, with each state having an equal vote. Moreover, the plan looked toward a moderate modification of the Articles of Confederation rather than the drafting of a new document. *See also* CONNECTICUT COMPROMISE, page 34; VIRGINIA PLAN, page 54.

Significance   The New Jersey Plan, along with the Virginia Plan, drew the major battle lines of the convention. Though the basic idea of the New Jersey Plan to retain the Articles of Confederation was defeated by the convention, the demand for equal representation resulted in the Connecticut Compromise. The assurance that the states would receive equal representation in one house of Congress made it possible for the convention to complete its deliberations.

Police Power   Authority to promote and safeguard the health, morals, safety, and welfare of the people. In the context of the American federal system, police power is reserved to the states. The national government, exercising only delegated powers, does not possess a general police power. Many national laws enacted under the commerce and postal powers, such as those that prohibit shipping impure drugs in interstate commerce or mailing obscene literature, are, however, examples of what may be termed "federal police power." State laws enacted under the police power may legally invade national jurisdiction if such laws are pertinent to the health, safety, or welfare of the people of the state, such as a state law regulating grade crossings for interstate trains. *See also* POLICE POWER (STATE), page 328; RESERVED POWERS, page 49; *United States v. Lopez,* page 56.

Significance   Police powers, in recognition of the responsibility of state government to safeguard individual well-being, are the most vital powers reserved to the states under the Constitution. The judiciary plays a large role in determining the proper scope for the exercise of police power. The police power enlarges the area of state and local control over the individual.

Preamble   The statement affixed at the beginning of the Constitution, stating the source of its authority and the purposes it is to serve: "We the people of the United States, in order to form a more perfect union, establish justice, insure domestic tranquility, provide for the common defense, promote the general welfare, and secure the blessings of liberty to ourselves and our posterity, do ordain and establish this Constitution for the United States of America." The Preamble to the U.S. Constitution has no legal effect but may serve as a guide to the intent of the framers.

Significance   Particular importance is attached to the fact that the Preamble begins with the words "We the People" rather than "The states of New York, …" The wording establishes the supremacy of the national Constitution as emanating from all the people rather than as a contract among sovereign states, which was of particular significance in the great debate over the nature of the Union prior to the Civil War. The Preamble is also noted as a concise statement of the enduring principles of a free people.

Privileges and Immunities   Special rights and exemptions provided by law. The Constitution contains two clauses that use the term "privileges and immunities." Article IV, section 2 provides that "The citizens of each state shall be entitled to all privileges and immunities of citizens in the several states." The Fourteenth Amendment provides that "No state shall make or enforce any law which shall abridge the privileges or immunities of citizens of the United States." The first provision is considered to be an instrument of federalism, one of the obligations of states in their relations with each other. Basically, it means that a citizen of one state is not to be treated as an alien when in another state and may not be discriminated against by denial of such privileges and immunities as legal protection, access to courts, travel rights, or property rights. Out-of-state residents, however, may be denied certain political rights, such as voting, or other privileges reserved to that state's residents, such as lower tuition at state universities. The full or precise meaning of the term has never been established by the courts. The Fourteenth

Amendment's privileges and immunities clause has, similarly, not received complete definition. It is basically an instrument of civil liberties, placing certain restrictions upon each state in its dealings with United States citizens. The clause has been interpreted to apply only to those privileges that apply to the individual by virtue of national citizenship (*Slaughterhouse Cases*, 16 Wallace 36 [1873]), including the rights to travel, to have access to national officials, and to engage in interstate and foreign commerce. As interpreted, the clause neither confers new rights on citizens nor affects the citizen in those privileges enjoyed by virtue of state citizenship.

Significance   Neither of the privileges and immunities clauses has proved to be of great importance in American history. The narrow interpretation given by the courts to the Fourteenth Amendment has disappointed those who saw in it a boon to the rights of blacks after the Civil War. Article IV has served, in part, to strengthen economic and social ties among the people of the various states, but its use has been limited, due to the vagueness of its language and uncertain judicial interpretation.

Proprietary Colony   One of the three types of governments—charter, proprietary, royal—found in colonial America. Proprietary colonies were governed by charters issued by the "proprietor," an individual to whom the king had made a land grant. Pennsylvania was established under such a charter bestowed by William Penn. Other proprietary colonies were Delaware and Maryland. Though the lower house of the legislature was elected, the upper house and the governor were chosen by the proprietor, subject to approval of the Crown. *See also* CHARTER COLONY, page 32; ROYAL COLONY, page 50.

Significance   The proprietor represented the Crown, and the colonies were largely ruled from England. Nevertheless, important lessons in self-government were learned. Increasing efforts by the Crown to control these colonies were contributing factors to the Revolution. The "frame of government" drawn up by William Penn for Pennsylvania was a relatively democratic document.

Regionalism   A method of decentralizing power on a geographical basis. In the United States, regionalism is often proposed as an alternative or supplement to the states. For example, the country could be divided into nine or ten regional subdivisions instead of into 50 states. The term is also applied to regional administration of federal projects, such as the Tennessee Valley Authority, and to regional interstate compacts and regional councils of government. Still another use of the term pertains to regionally shared political, economic, or cultural concerns (for example, "the South," "the Great Lakes States") that result in regional defense against other interests or sectional demands for favorable public policies. *See also* BLOC, page 132; COUNCILS OF GOVERNMENT, page 614; FIELD SERVICE, page 225.

Significance   Advocates of regionalism argue that since the states do not reflect realistic economic and social patterns, they should be united into regions having genuine unity, such as the Missouri Valley area and New England. People of the United States tend to take a regional or sectional rather than a state outlook on many problems. The strong tradition and constitutional power of the individual states make their elimination unlikely, but states are increasingly acting together to meet common problems.

Republican Form of Government   A government that operates through elected representatives of the people. It is generally distinguished from a pure democracy, in which the people govern directly. Article IV, section 4 of the Constitution, known as the "guarantee clause," provides that the national government shall guarantee to each state a republican form of government. The precise meaning of the guarantee clause has never been determined; the Supreme Court has held this to be a "political question" to be answered by Congress or the President. *See also Luther v. Borden,* page 55; *Pacific States Telephone and Telegraph Co. v. Oregon,* page 178.

Significance   The guarantee of a republican form of government is one of the obligations of the national government toward the states in maintaining the federal system. State citizens are thereby protected against arbitrary seizure of power by state government and abuse of state electoral systems. A state government is considered to be republican in form if the houses of Congress accept the elected representatives of the state. In addition, the President could conceivably use the armed forces to dispossess a state government considered by the President to be other than republican in form.

Reserved Powers   Powers of state governments under the American federal system. The concept that certain powers are "reserved" to the states is stated in the Tenth Amendment. The states retain all powers not delegated to the national government, or prohibited to them, by the Constitution. These powers are frequently referred to as "residuary." A definitive list of state powers is not possible because, in the very nature of the federal system, the states may exercise any power that is not delegated to the national government. These powers usually include authority over internal affairs of the state and general police power over the health, safety, morals, and welfare of the people. State constitutions may place specific restrictions upon state powers. *See also* DELEGATED POWERS, page 38; TENTH AMENDMENT, page 51.

Significance   The division of authority between national and state governments is a basic principle of American federalism. Exactly what constitutes a reserved power is often a matter of dispute. With problems continuously changing in scope, a power formerly exercised by a state may fall under national control, particularly in matters of commerce as these increasingly become interstate in character. The judiciary is frequently called on to determine the proper division of authority between the nation and the states.

Resulting Powers   Powers of the national government derived from a combination of delegated or implied powers, hence powers that "result" from a number of powers, rather than inferred from one of the delegated powers. *See also Legal Tender Cases,* page 425.

Significance   Resulting powers are an extension of the implied powers doctrine. They make possible an exercise of power that logically follows from a series of granted powers. For example, the United States Criminal Code provides that the violation of any national law is subject to punishment. The Constitution does not explicitly delegate this power, and it is not implied by any single grant of power. Rather, it "results" from the aggregate of power delegated to the national government.

Royal Colony   One of the three types of governments—charter, proprietary, royal—found in colonial America. Eight colonies were royal colonies. The lower house of the legislature was elected, but the upper house and the governor were appointed by the king. Royal governors exercised almost complete authority over the colony through instructions received from England. *See also* CHARTER COLONY, page 32; PROPRIETARY COLONY, page 48.

Significance   It was in the royal colonies that much of the resentment against the king grew, resulting in the Revolution. The royal governor, in particular, was the object of resentment and fear, and the first state constitutions reflected this problem by giving little authority to state governors. This tradition has lasted until recent times, though the tendency has been to strengthen executive power in the states.

Separation of Powers   A major principle of American government whereby power is distributed among three branches of government—the legislative, the executive, and the judicial. The officials of each branch are selected by different procedures, have different terms of office, and are independent of one another. The separation is not complete, in that each branch participates in the functions of the other through a system of checks and balances. The separation, however, serves to ensure that the same person or group will not make the law, enforce the law, and interpret and apply the law. *See also* CHECKS AND BALANCES, page 32; DISTRIBUTION OF POWERS, page 38; LEGISLATIVE VETO, page 155.

Significance   The separation of lawmaking, law enforcement, and law interpretation is designed to prevent tyranny. It also serves to make the three branches responsive to different pressures. At the same time, the system frequently results in lack of unity between the legislative and executive branches, particularly when they are controlled by different parties. This fragmentation of power is a major factor in the operation of the American governmental system. The judiciary plays the critical role in maintaining the branches within their assigned powers.

Shays' Rebellion   An armed revolt by farmers in western Massachusetts in 1786-1787, seeking relief from debts and possible foreclosures of mortgages. Led by Daniel Shays, a Revolutionary War officer, the group prevented judges from hearing mortgage foreclosure cases and attempted to capture an arsenal. They were repelled by the state militia.

Significance   While its seriousness may be questioned, Shays' Rebellion is credited with being a major factor in the demand for a revision of the Articles of Confederation. The event highlighted the economic difficulties facing the states at the time and caused alarm among the creditor and commercial interests.

State Sovereignty   Independence of a state from external control. The concept of state sovereignty was an integral part of government under the Articles of Confederation and was part of the great debate on the Union that took place prior to the Civil War. In effect, state sovereignty is a rejection of the principle of national supremacy under the United States Constitution. *See also* STATES' RIGHTS, page 51.

Significance   The states of the Union were sovereign under the Articles of Confederation. Prior to the Civil War, southern states claimed that the Constitution was a compact among states rather than among the people and that the states were free to secede. State sovereignty as a legal doctrine is rejected, although the states' rights political argument reappears from time to time, invoked by the opponents of expanding federal power.

States' Rights   A term used to connote opposition to increasing the national government's power at the expense of that of the states. States' rights adherents call for an interpretation of the Constitution that would place limits on the federal assumption of implied powers and give expanded interpretation to the reserved powers of the states. *See also* INTERPOSITION, page 44; STATE SOVEREIGNTY, page 51.

Significance   Strong support for states' rights usually comes from those groups who feel that their particular interest will be better served by state than by national action. Though the term is common in American political life, it has rarely been used with consistency. For example, state politicians who oppose national action in the field of civil rights actively seek federal grants-in-aid for state projects. The proper balance between national and state power is a continuing American problem under the federal system. The balance is usually determined by the strength of political forces rather than by the language of the Constitution.

Tenth Amendment   The final item of the Bill of Rights in the Constitution, which defines the principle of American federalism: "The powers not delegated to the United States by the Constitution, nor prohibited by it to the states, are reserved to the states respectively, or to the people." *See also* FEDERALISM, page 40.

Significance   The Tenth Amendment was added to the Constitution to make clear the position of the states in the Union. Although it was generally understood that the framers intended that the states would retain all powers not prohibited by the Constitution or delegated to the national government, the proponents of a bill of rights insisted upon an express provision to that effect. Exactly what is meant by the phrase "or to the people" has never been determined.

Territory   An area belonging to the United States that is not included within any state of the Union. Article IV, section 3 of the Constitution authorizes Congress to make rules respecting the territory of the United States. Authority to acquire territory also results from the national government's power to make treaties, admit new states, and make war that might result in conquest. The District of Columbia, though not a part of any state, is not considered a territory. Major territorial possessions of the United States now include Guam, Puerto Rico, the Panama Canal Zone, Samoa, the Virgin Islands, and parts of the Territory of the Pacific Islands. They enjoy varying degrees of self-governance or supervision by the Department of the Interior. The Panama Canal Zone, presently under a bilateral commission, is scheduled under a 1978 treaty to be turned over to Panama in the year 2000. *See also* ADMISSION OF NEW STATES, page 29; DEPARTMENT OF THE INTERIOR, page 492; NATIONAL, page 325; RESIDENT COMMISSIONER, page 165.

Significance Most of the territory acquired by the United States through purchase, conquest, or treaty has eventually become part of the United States. Current possessions are important mainly for strategic reasons. The United States has rarely used its territories as "colonies" to be exploited. Rather, inhabitants have been trained for self-government and given independence (the Philippines) or statehood (Hawaii). Residents of Guam, the Northern Marianas, Puerto Rico, and the Virgin Islands are citizens of the United States. Samoans are nationals of the United States. Puerto Rico and the Northern Marianas hold the status of free commonwealth associated with the United States. The Marshall Islands, the Federated States of Micronesia, and the Republic of Palau are in a "compact of free association" with the United States.

Three-fifths Compromise An agreement reached at the Constitutional Convention of 1787 to count only three-fifths of the slave population in determining representation in the House of Representatives and in apportioning direct taxes (Art. I, sec. 2). This provision of the Constitution is no longer pertinent.

Significance At the Constitutional Convention, the issue of whether to count slaves for representation and tax purposes sharply divided the northern and southern delegates. The issue was essentially that of representation of property interests, and the resultant compromise was one of many made at the convention.

Twenty-first Amendment An amendment to the Constitution, adopted in 1933, permitting the sale of intoxicating beverages in the United States. It repealed the Eighteenth Amendment, which had imposed Prohibition on the entire country. The Amendment protects states that retain Prohibition by barring the importation or transportation of liquor into such states and grants virtually complete control over distribution and consumption of alcohol to the states. *See also* FEDERAL AID HIGHWAY ACT, page 57.

Significance The Twenty-first is the only amendment that repeals a prior amendment. It is also the only one to have been ratified by conventions in the states rather than by state legislatures. By prohibiting the transportation of intoxicants into "dry" states, the Amendment lends national support to state laws. In a rare application of the Amendment, the Supreme Court held in 1972 that a state may ban obscene forms of entertainment in bars under the power given to states by the Twenty-first Amendment to regulate the importation and, therefore, the sale of liquor (*California v. LaRue,* 409 U.S. 109). A 1987 decision, however, held that it was not an unconstitutional intrusion into the powers reserved to the states by the Twenty-first Amendment for Congress to withhold highway aid funds from states refusing to raise the legal drinking age to 21 (*South Dakota v. Dole,* 483 U.S. 203). And, in ruling that a state may not prohibit advertising of liquor prices, the Court held that the Twenty-First Amendment does not override First Amendment free speech guarantees (*44 Liquormart v. Rhode Island,* 116 S. Ct. 1495 [1996]).

Unfunded Mandates Obligations imposed by Congress upon state and local governments or upon private-sector entities without providing the funds to pay for them. Examples include environmental controls, special facilities for the disabled, and workplace safety or family leave requirements. Legislation enacted in 1995 makes new unfunded mandates on state and local governments of more than $50 million subject to a point of order in either house which can be overcome only by a majority vote. Federal agencies must consult with state and local officials before imposing costly regulations and conduct a cost-benefit analysis of mandates. The Congressional Budget Office is to estimate the costs of all bills imposing mandates, including the costs of private-sector mandates in excess of $100 million.

Significance State and local officials have long complained about the enormous expenditures imposed upon them without their consent, without consideration of their ability to comply, or without concern for local priorities or local conditions. While the law's impact is yet to be tested, it represents a potentially important brake on national power. Critics of the law fear that it will become a vehicle to impede progress in environmental, health, and labor issues.

Unitary State A centralized government in which local or subdivisional governments exercise only those powers given to them by the central government. It differs from a federal system in which power is constitutionally divided between a central and a subdivisional government. The United Kingdom and France are examples of the unitary form. In the United States, local governments, such as cities and counties, stand in a unitary relationship to the state governments that assign specific rights and duties to them. An exception to this is found in those states in which cities or counties are given "home rule" by state constitutional provision. *See also* FEDERALISM, page 40.

Significance A unitary system provides a unified and consistent administration of policy while at the same time permitting variations to be made by the central authority. It allows more efficient handling of nationwide problems and is more sensitive to national majorities. Opponents of unitary government claim that federalism is superior because it permits more experimentation in local government and greater freedom in meeting local needs.

Usage A custom that, because it is well established, is regarded as a part of the American constitutional system. Though not precisely provided for in the words of the Constitution, such practices form an important element of the actual operations of government. Among these are such vital components as the role of political parties, the operations of the Electoral College, the presidential cabinet, and the inner organization of Congress.

Significance   Usage is one of the major methods by which the Constitution has been developed to meet practical problems. Little can be learned about how American government works solely by a reading of the Constitution. A full understanding of the American constitutional system requires a knowledge not only of the written document itself but also of the various usages. A well-established usage becomes part of the "unwritten constitution" and may have the same effect as, or a greater effect than, an actual constitutional provision.

Virginia Plan   A plan, submitted by Edmund Randolph of Virginia to the Constitutional Convention of 1787, that called for scrapping the Articles of Confederation and establishing a new and strong national government. It provided for a two-house legislature based on state population or wealth, a national executive, and a judiciary. Congress would have had power to disallow state legislation and was to be invested with broad power over matters of national concern. *See also* CONNECTICUT COMPROMISE, page 34; NEW JERSEY PLAN, page 46.

Significance   The Virginia Plan served as the major basis for discussion in the convention. Once a compromise over representation (equal representation in one house) that satisfied the small states was reached, the delegates proceeded to draft a constitution as envisaged by the Virginia Plan. A strong central government was established with power to act directly on individuals rather than through the states.

IMPORTANT AGENCIES

Advisory Commission on Intergovernmental Relations (ACIR)   An independent bipartisan body established by Congress in 1959 to study the operations of the federal system. It is composed of 26 members representing national, state, and local governments as well as the general public and concentrates on the impact of intergovernmental relations and the means by which they may be improved. *See also* FEDERALISM, page 40.

Significance   The ACIR has published numerous studies analyzing intergovernmental conflicts, particularly over the allocation of resources. It has issued recommendations for extensive legislative and judicial action on a wide variety of topics designed to increase efficiency within the context of the complex and overburdened federal system. The ACIR data collections and studies are widely noted by students of governmental relations.

IMPORTANT CASES

Coleman v. Miller,   307 U.S. 433 (1939): A case establishing the principle that the process of amending the Constitution is essentially political in nature and not subject to judicial interference. Specifically, the Supreme Court held that a state legislature may ratify the child labor amendment proposal after once rejecting it and that whether the pending proposal was still valid after many years is a political question for Congress to determine. *See also* AMENDMENT PROCESS, page 29.

Significance   The *Coleman* decision had the effect of removing the Court from involvement in the constitutional amending process, leaving procedures under Article V to Congress and the state legislatures. In 1982, however, the Court agreed to hear a set of cases challenging the right of Congress to extend the ratification period for the proposed Equal Rights Amendment and the authority of a state legislature to rescind prior approval of the proposal. When the extended ratification period expired and the proposal had failed, the Court dismissed the cases as moot (*National Organization for Women v. Idaho; Carmen v. Idaho,* 459 U.S. 809), thereby casting some doubt on the *Coleman* precedent

Coyle v. Smith,   221 U.S. 599 (1911): Established the principle that all states are admitted to the Union on an equal footing. Congress may not enforce conditions that would undermine the equality of the states. In this case, the Supreme Court upheld the right of Oklahoma to change its capital city contrary to a requirement in the congressional enabling act that preceded statehood. *See also* ADMISSION OF NEW STATES, page 29.

Significance   Congress may stipulate any conditions it chooses for the admission of a state. Once admitted to the Union, a state may not be compelled to abide by any condition that would interfere with its right to manage its internal affairs or that would create different classes of states.

Graves v. New York ex rel. O'Keefe,   306 U.S. 466 (1939): Held that a state may tax the income of a federal employee and that such a tax does not impose an unconstitutional burden upon the national government. *See also* INTERGOVERNMENTAL TAX IMMUNITY, page 43; *McCulloch v. Maryland,* page 56.

Significance   This was one of the last in a long line of cases that arose out of the decision, in *McCulloch v. Maryland,* that a state may not tax an instrumentality of the federal government, since the power to tax is the power to destroy. This doctrine was carried to the point that neither the state nor the national government could tax each other in any way, including the salaries of their respective employees. In the *Graves* case, the Court reversed its position and sustained congressional authorization of state taxation of federal employees' incomes. Federal taxation of state employees had been upheld the previous year in *Helvering v. Gerhardt,* 304 U.S. 405 (1938). In 1988, the Court held that there is no constitutional barrier to federal taxation of the interest on state and local bonds (*South Carolina v. Baker,* 485 U.S. 505). States do not tax income on federal bonds.

Luther v. Borden,   7 Howard 1 (1848): Held that the question of whether a state has a republican form of government is a political and not a judicial question. The Supreme Court refused to define a republican form of government, holding that Congress and the President must decide. The case arose out of Dorr's Rebellion in Rhode Island in 1841, when rival groups claimed to be the true government of the state. *See also* REPUBLICAN FORM OF GOVERNMENT, page 49.

Significance   The constitutional requirement that the national government guarantee each state a republican form of government will not be enforced by the courts. Congressional power to accept the state's representatives and the President's power to use force to quell a rebellion are the means by which the guarantee is honored.

Massachusetts v. Mellon,   262 U.S. 447 (1923): Rejected claims by a state that the federal grant-in-aid program to protect the health of mothers and infants was an unconstitutional invasion of the reserved powers of the states guaranteed by the Tenth Amendment. In a companion case (*Frothingham v. Mellon*), the Court rejected the claim of Mrs. Frothingham that the grant-in-aid program would take her property under the guise of taxation. *See also Frothingham v. Mellon,* page 260.

Significance   Three important rules were established by these two cases: (1) A state cannot validly seek to protect its citizens who are also citizens of the United States from the enforcement of federal laws; (2) a grant-in-aid system based on voluntary acceptance of programs by the states is a political and not a judicial question; and (3) an individual taxpayer who cannot show suffering and injury different from that of the general taxpaying public has no standing in court to challenge the constitutionality of tax laws (*Frothingham* rule). Today, under the *Frothingham* rule, it continues to be difficult for an individual to test the constitutionality of a tax law in the federal courts, unless it can be demonstrated that Congress may have exceeded a specific limitation on its taxing power, such as taxing and spending funds to violate the separation between church and state (*Flast v. Cohen,* 392 U.S. 83 [1968]).

McCulloch v. Maryland,   4 Wheaton 316 (1819): Upheld, in a landmark decision of the Supreme Court, the power of the national government to establish a bank and denied the state of Maryland the power to tax a branch of the bank. In the opinion by Chief Justice John Marshall, the Court held that it was not necessary for the Constitution expressly to authorize Congress to create a bank. Rather, the power to do so was implied from Congress' power over financial matters and from the "necessary and proper" clause of the Constitution. Maryland could not tax a legitimate instrumentality of the national government, said the Court, since this would be an invasion of national supremacy. "The power to tax involves the power to destroy...." From this was derived the principle of intergovernmental tax immunity. *See also* IMPLIED POWERS, page 41; INTERGOVERNMENTAL TAX IMMUNITY, page 43.

Significance   Two important principles of American government were firmly established by this decision: the doctrine of "implied powers," which has given the national government a vast source of power, and the principle of "national supremacy," which denies to the states any right to interfere in the constitutional operations of the national government. Had the decision favored Maryland, the national government would not have been able to meet the problems of an expanding nation and the Constitution would not have become a "living" document.

United States v. Lopez,   115 S. Ct. 1624 (1995): Struck down, as exceeding congressional authority under the commerce clause, a federal law that made it a crime to carry a gun within 1,000 feet of a school. The Court declared that the law had nothing to do with commerce and intruded upon the police power of the states. It held further that the federal commerce power extends only to regulation of an activity that "substantially affects" and not merely "affects" commerce. *See also* COMMERCE POWER, page 33; POLICE POWER, page 47.

Significance   The *Lopez* ruling was the first time in 60 years that the Supreme Court had denied Congressional action in utilizing the commerce power. The decision may well lead to numerous challenges to the exercise of the commerce power, particularly as it affects criminal behavior and education, two functions traditionally reserved to the states.

Virginia v. Tennessee,   148 U.S. 503 (1893): Denied a suit brought by Virginia to void the boundary line between it and Tennessee on the ground that the line had been established by agreement between the states without the consent of Congress. The Court held that the agreement did not constitute a compact between the states that required the positive approval of Congress. The only compacts or agreements requiring approval are those that tend to increase state power at the expense of the national government. In other instances, Congress may give its approval by implication. *See also* INTERSTATE COMPACT, page 44.

Significance   Although the Constitution prohibits states from entering into agreements or compacts without consent of Congress, this decision made it clear that the restriction did not apply to every agreement between states. This made it possible for states to solve mutual problems without involving Congress. Yet Congress is always free to intervene if it feels that the agreement threatens the national government in any way.

IMPORTANT STATUTES

Federal Aid Highway Act   A major example of national-state cooperation through federal grants-in-aid to the states; the first such grant was given in 1916 for the building of highways. From this time, grants have been given for trunk roads, secondary roads, urban extension of highways, and, since 1956, an extensive interstate highway system covering 42,500 miles. The states met national requirements regarding matching funds, maintenance of roads, location, engineering details, and speed limits. The national government financed 90 percent of the costs. The program is administered by the Federal Highway Administration in the Department of Transportation. *See also* CO-OPERATIVE FEDERALISM, page 37; GRANT-IN-AID, page 404; TWENTY-FIRST AMENDMENT, page 52.

Significance   The Federal Aid Highway Act is a leading example of both cooperative federalism and the use of grants to expand national power. Through it, the national government has shaped state and local road policy, although it does not actually build the highways. The grant-in-aid program has provided states with substantial revenue, but it has limited the discretion of the state and local authorities over a major function. A 1984 law withholds funds from states that do not enact a minimum drinking age of 21 and mandatory sentences for drunk driving convictions, which was upheld by the Supreme Court even though the Twenty-First Amendment gives states control over liquor laws (*South Dakota v. Dole,* 483 U.S. 203 [1987]). A 1987 law authorized states to increase the speed limit from 55 to 65 miles per hour on rural interstate highways, but all federal speed regulations (and motorcycle helmet laws) were dropped in 1995 and left to individual state regulation. The 1995 legislation also designated a new 160,000-mile National Highway System, which includes existing roads plus major expansion of roads in metropolitan areas and connectors to airports and other transport systems.

Northwest Ordinance   An enactment of the Congress under the Articles of Confederation in 1787 providing for the government of the territory north of the Ohio River and west of New York to the Mississippi River. The ordinance provided for the eventual statehood of areas of the territory when they acquired 60,000 inhabitants. Liberal provision was made for local self-government, civil and political rights, and education. Slavery was forbidden in the territory. A previous ordinance of 1785, establishing the township system of dividing land and providing for local schools, was reaffirmed in the Ordinance of 1787.

Significance   The Northwest Ordinance was the most significant measure passed by the Confederation Congress. It was readopted by Congress under the Constitution and served as the basis for later territorial acts. It established the important policy that territories were not to be kept in subjection but were to be developed for admission to statehood on an equal footing with other states.

3

Parties, Politics, Pressure Groups, and Elections

Absentee Voting   Provisions of state laws or constitutions that enable qualified voters to cast their ballots in an election without going to the polls on election day. A person who expects to be unable to vote on election day obtains a ballot within a specified period preceding the election, marks it, and returns the sealed ballot to the proper official. Fraudulent use continues to be a difficult problem in administering absentee voting. *See also* VOTING QUALIFICATIONS, page 119; VOTE-BY-MAIL, page 118.

Significance   All states have provisions for absentee voting. Congress initiated the process by providing for absentee voting by Federal troops during the Civil War. Several million potential voters, because of travel or illness, are unable to vote on election day, but few go to the trouble of securing an absentee ballot. Absentee voters can sometimes affect the outcome of an election, as in 1960, when a late count of absentee ballots in California swung that state's electoral votes from John F. Kennedy to Richard M. Nixon. In December 1995, the first congressional primary "vote-by-mail" election was held in Oregon to elect a replacement for Senator Bob Packwood, who resigned after the Senate Ethics Committee found him in violation of ethical standards. This primary was followed in January 1996 by a "vote-by-mail" general election in which Ron Wyden was elected to complete the term of Bob Packwood.

Absolute Majority   Any number over 50 percent of the total votes cast by *all* the voters participating in a given election. A *simple* majority, in contrast, is any number over 50 percent of the votes cast on any single issue in an election, even though many voters who go to the polls may not vote on that issue. A *plurality* consists of sufficient votes to win an election, but not necessarily a majority. In the United States Senate, cloture requires a three-fifths vote (60 of the 100 senators) and rule changes require a two-thirds vote (67 senators). *See also* MAJORITY RULE, page 18; PLURALITY, page 96.

Significance   No federal and only a few state and local elections require an absolute majority. Some states require an absolute majority of all voters participating in any phase of the election to vote "yes" to call a state constitutional convention or to ratify an amendment to a state constitution. Hence, failure to vote on that issue while otherwise participating in the election is the equivalent of a "no" vote.

Alienation   An individual's estrangement from society. Political alienation results when individuals believe they have lost their ability to participate effectively in the political process and to influence its outcome. Individuals tend to suffer political alienation when their government is unresponsive to their needs or hopes, or fails to quiet their fears. Alienation involves feelings of distrust, scorn, or fear toward a political system that may arise from anomie (a collapse of the social standards and values guiding society) and produce a rejection of the entire political system. *See also* NEW LEFT, page 91.

Significance   Various theories have sought to explain alienation and have offered, through political and economic ideologies, the means for overcoming it. Marxism, for example, posits that the destruction of capitalism will restore the individual's cooperative nature. Modern society has produced widespread feelings of anomie and rootlessness through the impersonalizing forces of machine technology and mass culture. Underlying mass movements and protest demonstrations by minorities, for example, is the alienation of such groups from the rest of society. Those alienated often fail to vote or participate in the regular arena for making political decisions. Increasing conservatism in the 1990s has led to demands for less governmental involvement in the economic life of the nation. In reacting to these changes, millions of Americans also feel alienated by the fear of the loss of support of the more liberal government of the past.

At Large   The election of members of a legislative body by the voters of an entire governmental unit rather than from subdivisions thereof. Congressmen at large, for example, may be elected by the whole electorate of the state when a state legislature fails to redistrict after a decennial census. United States senators and Electoral College electors are elected at large in each state. On the local level, members of city commissions are, in some cases, elected at large by the voters of the entire city rather than from wards, especially under the commission and city manager forms. *See also* SINGLE-MEMBER DISTRICT, page 112.

Significance   Election of representatives at large tends to foster a broader statewide or citywide approach to issues rather than the more restrictive "mirroring" of local interests by those chosen from districts or wards. The case against election at large is that representatives so chosen will not respond to the wishes or interests of the voters because of the size, population, and variety of views of the larger electorate. In contrast with the ward or district system, at-large elections also tend to limit or eliminate local government representation of minority groups who cannot usually muster enough citywide or countywide support to win. Proponents of election at large claim that it reduces parochialism in politics and makes fuller use of available political talent by allowing several good candidates living in the same area to be elected simultaneously, which is not possible under the single-member district system. Some advocates of change in the system of electing the President want to abolish the Electoral College and elect the President at large from the entire nation.

Australian Ballot   A secret ballot prepared, distributed, and tabulated by government officials at public expense. Voting machines are mechanical adaptations of the Australian ballot. *See also* BALLOT, page 62.

Significance   For over a century, many American voters were denied a secret ballot. Oral voting and differently colored ballots, prepared by the parties, were used. Extreme pressures could be exerted upon voters who were forced to cast their ballot publicly. Threats of retaliation frequently coerced voters into voting against their choice of candidates. Since 1888, all states have used the Australian ballot.

Availability   The evaluation of the qualifications of a potential candidate by a political party in making its selection of a nominee. A candidate who the party believes has the qualities and background to be a winner is "available." *See also* BALANCED TICKET, page 62; STALKING HORSE, page 113.

Significance   The question of availability is especially important in the selection of presidential nominees. Millions of members of each party meet the constitutional and legal requirements for the presidency, but few have the qualifications needed to win. Availability depends on whether the potential nominee has ever alienated a large economic, ethnic, or religious voting group; comes from a key state or strategic section; has demonstrated real vote-getting ability or is too closely identified with one wing or faction in the party; and on the public's perception of his or her family life—in short, whether the potential nominee's background and personal and political qualities all appear to add up to victory for the party in the presidential election. Increasingly, the availability qualifications of potential candidates are shaped by television and measured by public opinion polls. Candidates, however, may lose their availability by some act that alienates a large number of voters. Democratic presidential candidate Edmund Muskie, for example, dropped out of the 1972 campaign to win his party's nomination after reacting emotionally on the national media to a personal attack, and Gary Hart dropped out of the 1988 race as a result of media disclosures concerning his sex life. In the 1992 presidential election, however, Democratic candidate Bill Clinton was elected President despite allegations concerning sexual misbehavior and avoidance of military service in the Vietnam War.

Baby Boomers   The name used to describe the many millions of babies born in the period between 1946 and 1964. *See also* KEY ELECTION FACTORS: GENERATIONAL POLITICS, page 83; NEW LEFT, page 91.

Significance   The more than 75 million Baby Boomers born after World War II had a substantial impact from the start on the political, economic, social, and religious life of the nation. First they created huge markets for their childhood needs; then schools were built to accommodate their numbers. After high school, they filled the colleges and universities, and after graduation they sought and held jobs in the market that their very numbers had created. Unlike previous generations, the Baby Boomers cultivated a free, almost revolutionary lifestyle of "make love, not war." Thousands of young people demonstrated against the Vietnam War and sought ways to avoid the draft. They loved the Beatles, were more idealistic than materialistic, and set out to change the world. Now, as the first of the generation turn 50 years old, attitudes are changing from radical to conservative and from idealistic to materialistic, they are changing their political affiliations, and they are going back to religion. Liberal or conservative, they still desire to change the world. However, their overwhelming issue is financial security. While they remain hostile to government and its role in their lives, they have come to depend upon it for the economic security they seek. Some politicians fear that crisis may arise as the Baby Boomers reach retirement age.

Balanced Ticket   The influence of personal backgrounds and qualifications in the selection of candidates by a political party, with the objective of maximizing voter appeal. A balanced ticket may incorporate ideological, geographic, racial, ethnic, age, sex, or other diversities among the slate of party candidates. *See also* AVAILABILITY, page 61; PLURALISM, page 95.

Significance   A balanced ticket strategy typifies party activity in selecting slates of candidates. American pluralism dictates that successful party tickets recognize the extent of heterogeneity in the nation and in the states. The best-known historical example of ticket balancing has been in the selection of vice presidential candidates who have often provided the diversity necessary to supplement the broad-gauged appeal of presidential candidates.

Ballot   An instrument by which a voter indicates his or her preference in determining the outcome of an election. *See also* AUSTRALIAN BALLOT, page 60; LONG BALLOT, page 86; OFFICE-BLOCK BALLOT, page 93; PARTY-COLUMN BALLOT, page 94; SHORT BALLOT, page 111.

Significance   Various types of ballots have been developed in the United States to provide the means by which voting may be directly related to the democratic process. These range from the simplicity of marking an "X" on a paper ballot, to pulling a lever on a mechanical voting machine, and to punching a computer card to facilitate a quick vote count after the polls close.

Bandwagon Effect   A tendency in politics for some individuals to associate themselves with a cause, party, or candidate they believe will prevail. The bandwagon effect is identified with emotional behavior rather than with rational calculation that one's interests will be served by joining forces with the expected winner. In elections, for example, polls published prior to election day may change the outcome because some voters affected by the "herd instinct" seek to climb aboard the bandwagon of the candidate they expect to win. The *underdog effect* partly offsets the bandwagon effect when some voters feel sorry for a losing candidate or party and switch their votes. *See also* CAMPAIGN, page 63.

Significance   Studies have disclosed that voters in the United States are often influenced in their decisions by psychological factors, such as the bandwagon or underdog effects. Some states have tried to reduce the impact of such factors on election outcomes by, for example, prohibiting campaigning on election day. Congress recognized the impact that such factors might have on the outcome of federal elections and is considering a uniform poll-closing time for all states so that voters in states with different time zones would be less influenced by announcements of election results. Before many Californians went to the polls in past elections, for example, television commentators had already announced winners-to-be as the result of projections based on voting in the states in the eastern time zone. Voters on the West

Coast were substantially affected in the 1980 presidential election by television projections of a major sweep by Ronald Reagan, and by President Jimmy Carter's concession speech—all several hours before the polls closed on the West Coast. Congress, however, has not enacted uniform poll closing.

Boss   A political leader who dominates a highly disciplined state or local party organization that tends to monopolize power in its area. Political bosses retain power through patronage disposition, control over nominations, use of "honest" and dishonest graft, and manipulation of voting and elections. Sometimes the term "boss" is used to discredit the successful leader of an opposing party. *See also* DEMAGOGUE, page 71; POLITICAL MACHINE, page 98.

Significance   American politics has proved to be a fertile ground for the growth of political machines and party bosses. This growth stems largely from the decentralization of power in the party system and the apathy of large numbers of voters. Some of the leading party bosses in past years have been Richard Daley of Chicago, Edward J. Flynn of New York's The Bronx, Edward "Boss" Crump of Memphis, Ed Kelly of Chicago, Frank Hague of Jersey City, and Carmine DeSapio of the Tammany Hall machine in New York City. Political bosses have been equally successful in the countryside and in the big cities. The heyday of the political boss has waned, and few if any who remain are bosses in the old tradition. The direct primary, a better-educated electorate, electoral laws aimed at making elections fair and honest, and public welfare programs that have removed welfare aid from politics are among the chief reasons for the demise of "bossism."

Campaign   The competitive effort of rival candidates for public office to win support of the voters in the period preceding an election. Unlike the British system in which campaigning is limited to three weeks, some American candidates campaign actively for two years prior to the presidential election. Candidates use diverse means for reaching the voters—television, radio, telephone, the mails, door-to-door solicitation, speeches, coffee hours, and factory visits. Since the 1960s, political campaigns have increasingly depended on the impact of television. As a result, campaign costs have soared, and, with rare exceptions, only wealthy individuals or those with the financial support of major interest groups can compete effectively for national or state offices. In 1992, the Supreme Court limited campaign activity by upholding the provisions for a 100-foot campaign-free zone around polling places on election day (*Burson v. Freeman,* 504 U.S. 191). In 1995, the Court held that the First Amendment protects the right to distribute anonymous campaign literature (*McIntyre v. Ohio Elections Commission,* S. Ct. 1511). *See also* CORRUPT PRACTICES ACTS, page 69; FEDERAL ELECTION CAMPAIGN ACTS OF 1972 AND 1974, pages 122–123.

Significance   Campaigns and their financial support are the critical elements in seeking to win political office. This financial support is divided between "soft" and "hard" money. Soft monies can be contributed to the national parties in unlimited amounts under present laws. They come from such sources as corporations, labor unions, and wealthy individuals. Hard money, conversely, is contributed directly to the candidate and is limited by law to $1000 per candidate from any individual. Individuals can spend as much of their own money as they choose on their own campaign. There is, however, a legal limit of $37 million that a candidate's campaign can spend before the party's national convention. Soft money can help a presidential candidate by covering activities such as canvassing and advertising. Campaign stops can be planned around party fund-raising events or around "unity rallies" where the focus is on promoting other party candidates as opposed to a rally where the candidate speaks on his or her own behalf. The Supreme Court in 1996 seemed to create new loopholes when it ruled that as long as a political party spends money independently of any candidate's campaign, federal limits on contributions in congressional races do not apply (*Colorado Republican Federal Campaign Committee v. Federal Election Commission,* 116 S. Ct. 2309). An estimated $1.5 billion was spent on all federal elections in 1996, making it the most expensive election in history. Voters continue to demand greater control of the amount contributed by donors and spent by candidates.

Canvassing Board   An official body, usually bipartisan, that tabulates the election returns and certifies the election of the winners. When the polls close on election day, the returns from each precinct are forwarded to city and county canvassing boards. These boards consolidate the returns and forward them to the state canvassing authority, which, usually in a few days, certifies the election of the winners. The local group is the county board of supervisors or county board of election. The state canvassing board consists of several ex officio members of the state government, headed by the secretary of state. Each election winner receives a certificate of election from the county or state board. *See also* CHALLENGE, page 65.

Significance   Extensive coverage of election returns by newspapers, radio, and television makes the results of most elections known to the public before canvassing boards certify them. In exceptionally close elections, however, the final outcome may turn on the official tabulation and certification. Disputed elections are commonly settled in the courts or through an official recount. Poll watchers appointed by the major parties are often used to ensure the honesty of elections.

Caucus   A closed meeting of party leaders or rank-and-file members to select party candidates. In the early days of the Republic, party members in Congress and in the state legislatures selected their party's candidates for national and state office. Presidential candidates were chosen by party caucuses in Congress. Locally, leading members of each party met behind closed doors to select candidates for various local offices. Some local candidates are still nominated by caucus. The term "to caucus" is also commonly used to describe any private meeting of politicians seeking to reach agreement on a course of political action. *See also* CAUCUS, page 134; NOMINATION, page 92.

Significance   Most important decisions in American politics are officially ratified following agreements reached "in caucus" by political leaders. As a nominating device, "King Caucus" flourished for several decades of early American history. Because Andrew Jackson had been refused nomination for the presidency by the congressional Democratic caucus in 1824, he repudiated the system when he won office in 1828. By 1835, the legislative caucus as a means of making nominations for public office had almost disappeared. On both national and state levels, the nominating caucus was replaced by the convention method. Reasons for the demise of the caucus included: (1) its unrepresentative character, (2) its violation of the separation of powers theory, (3) use of secret deals and logrolling to manipulate the caucus, and (4) widespread use of the "snap caucus," by which small cliques control the nominating process by not notifying all eligible participants of a caucus meeting. Supporters of the nominating caucus, however, point out that it is less costly than primaries for all concerned, it tends to produce compromise among ideological wings and leaders within each party, and it tends to overcome the more divisive effects of the separation of powers system. Some states, such as Iowa, selected delegates to their party's national convention in 1992 by caucuses open for participation to anyone claiming to be a party member.

Challenge   An allegation by a poll watcher that a potential voter is unqualified or that a vote is invalid. Most states provide for a bipartisan group of election judges in each precinct to help decide disputes. An inspector usually takes charge of each precinct and makes the final decision. In some closed-primary states, a voter's party affiliation may be challenged. Voters who cannot prove their affiliation to the satisfaction of that party's poll watcher can be deprived of votes in the primary. *See also* CANVASSING BOARD, page 64.

Significance   Bipartisan selection of poll watchers and their right to challenge voters and votes are designed to prevent fraud in elections. This procedure is aimed at building confidence, not always warranted, in the incorruptibility of the ballot. In closed-primary states, the objective is to limit participation in the selection of candidates to bona fide party members.

Charisma   An attribute of leadership based on personal qualities of the individual. Charismatic leaders, typically, have magnetic personalities, a dedication to achieving their objectives, unusual powers of persuasion, and ability to excite and gain the loyalty of supporters. Although charismatic leaders are usually flamboyant, they may have mystical, withdrawn personalities. *See also* AVAILABILITY, page 61.

Significance   Every candidate for political office seeks to exude some degree of charisma that will set him or her apart as a leader. Charisma has, however, a potential for demagoguery, and excessive charismatic qualities characterize totalitarian leaders. Failure to achieve stated goals may weaken the position of charismatic leaders with their followers. Franklin Roosevelt's charisma enabled him to win four presidential elections in 1932, 1936, 1940, and 1944.

Closed Primary   The selection of a party's candidates in an election limited to avowed party members. Voters must declare their party affiliation, either when they register or at the primary election. In some states, party officials at the polls may challenge their right to vote in the closed primary. *See also* DIRECT PRIMARY, page 72; OPEN PRIMARY, page 93.

Significance   The closed-primary system seeks to prevent the "crossover" of registered voters of one party into the other party's primary for the purpose of trying to nominate its weakest candidate or to affect the ideological direction of the rival party. Party organizations tend to favor the closed primary because it promotes party unity, regularity, and responsibility. Many voters oppose it because it limits their freedom of action to select anew at each primary election the party in which they wish to choose nominees, as in the open primary. Independent voters are altogether excluded from participating in the nominating process in closed-primary states. Most states use the closed primary.

Coalition   The fusion of various political elements into a major American party. In multiparty countries, the coalition involves a fusion of a number of individual parties into a working parliamentary majority. In the United States, however, both major parties combine factions of liberals, moderates, and conservatives. Coalition is also used to describe any alliance among political groups, such as the congressional alliance between conservative Republicans and southern Democrats. *See also* MULTIPARTY SYSTEM, page 88; TWO-PARTY SYSTEM, page 117.

Significance   The coalition character of American major parties avoids black and white extremes of position that might split the American people into two hostile groups. Conversely, the American system has been criticized on the ground that the two parties are so similar in their makeup that satisfactory alternatives are not presented to the voters. Yet a number of active minor parties run candidates and thus permit voters to express their dissatisfactions.

Coattail Effect   The tendency for a candidate heading a party ticket to attract votes for other candidates of his or her party on the same ballot. Popular presidential, gubernatorial, and strong-mayor candidates typically offer the greatest pulling power for those running for lesser offices. Negative coattail impact may also exist, with an unpopular candidate for high office likely to prejudice voter sentiment against other candidates of the party on the same ballot. *See also* PARTY-COLUMN BALLOT, page 94; STRAIGHT TICKET, page 113.

Significance   The coattail effect is likely to be most pronounced in elections with party-column ballots that encourage straight-ticket voting. Examples of exceptional coattail pulling power include President Franklin D. Roosevelt in the 1936 election, and Mayor Richard Daley of Chicago in a number of local elections. Negative coattail effect was demonstrated in the Republican debacle of 1964, when Barry Goldwater headed the ticket; in 1972, when George McGovern headed the Democratic ticket; and in 1980, when Jimmy Carter failed to win reelection. An indirect coattail effect may occur in off-year elections as, for example, in 1974, when Independents and Republicans, angered by Watergate revelations of misconduct by the Nixon administration, helped to produce a major Democratic victory on national, state, and local levels.

Conflict of Interest   The situation that occurs when an official's public actions are affected by personal interests. A conflict-of-interest charge usually alleges that an elected or appointed official realized some direct or indirect financial gain from governmental actions he or she participated in, or that public decisions were motivated by efforts to protect personal financial interests or those of close friends or political supporters. The 1978 Ethics in Government Act tries to eliminate conflicts of interest by government employees, after as well as during their employment by the federal government, by imposing strict limits on their relationship with the agency that employed them. *See also* CORRUPT PRACTICES ACTS, page 69; ETHICS IN GOVERNMENT ACT OF 1978, page 242.

Significance The United States has been plagued with conflict-of-interest problems throughout its history, dating back to the Yazoo Land Fraud of 1795, which involved almost every member of the Georgia legislature. The extent of American involvement in conflict-of-interest problems may relate to the extremely large number of part-time politicians with predominantly private interests, to the American value system (which tends to tolerate similar practices in the private world of business and finance), or to the historical role of party bosses and machines steeped in the pursuit of "honest" graft. In the national government, both the executive and legislative branches have undertaken policies to control conflicts of interest by developing codes of ethics and requiring disclosures of private financial interests. In the House and Senate, members are required to make reports to ethics committees. In the 1970s, grand jury and congressional investigations divulged numerous cases of conflict-of-interest behavior among high officials of the Nixon administration, leading to new efforts to control the problem, especially by financial disclosure and regulatory laws. These, however, failed to deter officials in the Reagan and Bush administrations, which during the 1980s were charged with a record number of conflict-of-interest activities.

Congressional and Senatorial Campaign Committees House and Senate groups consisting of Republican and Democratic members selected by fellow party members in their respective chambers to organize and to help finance election campaigns. The House Republican Campaign Committee consists of one congressman from each state having Republican representation in the House. House Democrats use this formula also, but supplement it with women members from some states as selected by the committee chairman. Senate committees consist of six or seven members selected from the Senate by each party's caucus chairman. *See also* CAMPAIGN, page 63.

Significance In a presidential election year, each committee may integrate its efforts with those of its national committee, depending upon the "coattail" vote-pulling potential of the party's presidential candidate. In off-year contests, the committees operate more independently. Maintaining permanent staffs, the committees raise funds, furnish speakers, distribute literature, and generally take charge of congressional campaigns. Their efforts may also be integrated with those of state and local committees of their parties.

Contract with America A comprehensive action plan primarily associated with Newt Gingrich, who after the 1994 election became Speaker of the House of Representatives. As a campaign strategy, the Contract with

America provided the voters with a time table for achieving a list of specific issues to be addressed during the first 100 days of the new Congress. The action agenda embodied in the Contract included the following components: (1) fiscal responsibility (e.g., a balanced budget amendment, line item veto, and a tax policy change); (2) an anticrime package (e.g., victim restitution, truth in sentencing, and crime prevention block grants); (3) personal responsibility (welfare reform); (4) family reinforcement (e.g., child support enforcement, strong child pornography laws, and elderly care tax credit); (5) American dream restoration (e.g., $500-per-child tax credit and repeal of marriage tax penalty); (6) national security restoration (e.g., no U.S. troops under United Nations command and strengthened national defense); (7) senior citizen fairness (social security reform); (8) job creation and wage enhancement (e.g., reduce capital gains tax, no unfunded mandates, and regulatory overhaul); (9) commonsense legal reform (e.g., loser-pay laws and frivolous suit restrictions); and (10) citizen legislature (term limits). *See also* REPUBLICAN REVOLUTION, page 109; RESPONSIBLE PARTY SYSTEM, page 110.

Significance   With the Contract with America, the Republican party for the first time in more than a century presented the voters with a comprehensive action plan—the "Republican Revolution." The voters, in an angry mood, threw out the Democrats, and for the first time in 40 years the Republicans were in control of both the House and the Senate. The House as promised, passed the Contract with America within the first 100 days. The Senate, however, rejected, rewrote, or delayed action on most of the Contract's provisions. As a preface to the Contract, the Congressional Accountability Act was passed in 1995. For the first time, the Congress will be governed by nine workplace laws that have covered the rest of the nation for years. Adhering to the Fair Labor Standard Act will be the most difficult, as members and committees decide which employees are exempt as "executives," "administrators," or "professionals" and pay overtime rates for every hour over 40 hours per week to those who are not. The proclamation and passage of a "platform" is a rarity in American politics. The ultimate role of the Contract with America will be decided by the Senate and the voters in future elections.

Convention   A meeting of party delegates at the national, state, or local levels to decide upon party policy and strategy and to nominate candidates for elective office. Each major party holds a national convention every four years to nominate its presidential candidate and adopt a platform. In most states, both parties hold county and state conventions annually. Typically, delegates to the county conventions are selected by party voters in precinct elections, delegates to state conventions are selected by county conventions, and delegates to national conventions are selected by state or district conventions or, in more than half of the states, by voters in presidential primaries. *See also* NATIONAL CONVENTION, page 89; NOMINATION, page 92.

Significance   Although state and local conventions have lost most of their nominating power, they continue to serve as the basic policymakers of the American political parties. Decisions made at national, state, and local conventions give direction to party committees and chairmen in the periods between conventions. On state and local levels, nomination for most elective offices has been taken from conventions and placed under direct primary systems. This has been the result, partly, of increasing democratization of elections and, partly, of convention malpractices that allowed small cliques to dominate them through manipulation. An advantage of the convention system in making policy and deciding nominations is that it tends to force conflicting wings of the party to work out compromises that help hold tenuous intraparty coalitions together.

Corrupt Practices Acts   Laws that seek to limit and regulate the size and sources of contributions and expenditures in political campaigns. Since 1925, a variety of federal corrupt practices acts were enacted to regulate campaign finance, but they proved unrealistic and unenforceable. For example, the Political Activities Act of 1939 (Hatch Act) outlawed political activity by federal employees, forbade a political committee to spend more than $3 million in any campaign, and limited individual contributions to a committee to $5,000, both of which committee restrictions could be circumvented by the creation of additional committees. The Federal Election Campaign Acts of 1972 and 1974 swept aside many past laws and instituted major reforms that tried to take into account the problems of reaching a large electorate. In a related action, designed to broaden the base of campaign financing, Congress authorized, in the Revenue Act of 1971, a system of individual voluntary one-dollar checkoffs (raised to three dollars in 1994) on federal income tax returns for a general campaign fund to be made available to major-party presidential candidates. Mass support for candidates was also encouraged by provisions of the law that permitted small contributions to be used to reduce one's federal income tax. State and local political campaign finances are regulated by state laws, which vary considerably. *See also* FEDERAL ELECTION CAMPAIGN ACTS OF 1972 AND 1974, pages 122–123.

Significance   The underlying purposes of corrupt practices legislation are to free public officials from being beholden to heavy contributors and to restrain the increasing tendency to limit office seeking to people of means. The Federal Election Campaign Acts of 1972 and 1974 modernized rules governing campaign finance by taking cognizance of the vast costs of mass media advertising, but they left uncovered many areas of financial strain for candidates, such as direct mail advertising, staff salaries, and travel costs. The new law, like its past counterparts and similar state and local restrictions, will be difficult to monitor without a considerable amount of bureaucratic oversight. In the wake of Watergate campaign scandals and other disclosures of irregularities, most of the states followed the national government's lead and enacted new laws requiring open meetings, lobby controls, campaign reforms, and financial disclosures. In a key decision rendered in 1972, the Supreme Court ruled that the Corrupt Practices Act that bars contributions by labor organizations to any federal election campaign does not prohibit union contributions from funds obtained from voluntary contributions made without deception or threat of reprisal (*Pipefitter Local Union v. United States,* 407 U.S. 385 [1972]). In 1978, the Court struck down a state law that forbade corporations to spend money to influence voters on a referendum issue because it violated First and Fourteenth Amendment guarantees of free speech (*First National Bank of Boston v. Bellotti,* 435 U.S. 765 [1978]). The Tax Reform Act of 1986 eliminated political-contribution deductions from federal income tax. In 1976, the Supreme Court found that no limits can be placed on an individual's right to spend his own money on a political campaign, with the result that some recent candidates have spent millions of dollars on their own campaigns (*Buckley v. Valeo,* 424 U.S. 1).

Countervailing Theory of Pressure Politics   The theory that in American politics the competition among business, labor, farm, racial, and other interest groups tends to balance their respective power and influence. *See also* PRESSURE GROUP, page 104; PUBLIC POLICY MODELS, page 107.

Significance   The countervailing theory of pressure politics seeks to explain why democratic pluralism can continue to exist in the United States and why no single dominant social group controls the direction of American politics and policies. The theory postulates that from this competition of diverse interests, the public interest tends to emerge. Some investigators challenge the theory and hold that empirical evidence refutes the ideas of "balance" and the emergence of the public interest from group conflict. Many American liberals believe the power scales are overloaded in favor of business and industry, whereas many conservatives believe that labor unions and the media have upset the balance. In some cases, one interest group is able to transform a competitor into an ally through a process known as co-optation.

Credentials Committee   A committee used by political parties to determine which delegates may participate in their conventions. The credentials committee prepares a roll of all delegates entitled to be seated at the convention. Controversy over contested seats arises when rival groups claim to be the official party organization for a county, district, or state. In such cases, a credentials committee makes recommendations to the convention. *See also* NATIONAL CONVENTION, page 89.

Significance   Recommendations made by the credentials committee to the convention are usually approved without debate or roll call. Conventions have, however, on occasion rejected these recommendations in whole or in part. In national conventions, decisions on seating of delegates from certain states, when two or more rival delegations appear at the convention, may be a decisive factor in the selection of the presidential nominee. As an example, in 1952 at the Republican Convention, rival delegations supporting General Dwight D. Eisenhower and Senator Robert A. Taft arrived from five southern states. The success of the Eisenhower supporters in getting their delegates seated was instrumental in securing the General's nomination. In the 1972 Democratic National Convention, a new delegate-selection process gave greater representation to women, the poor, and minority groups. In a controversy over seating Illinois delegates to that convention, the Supreme Court held that national political parties have a right to political association, and state courts cannot interfere with their right to determine which delegates should be seated (*Cousins v. Wigoda,* 419 U.S. 477 [1975]). In 1981, the Court strengthened this position, holding that a state may not compel a national political party to seat a state delegation chosen in a way that violates party rules (*Democratic Party of the United States v. LaFollette,* 450 U.S. 107).

Cumulative Voting   A method of voting in which the individual casts more than one vote in the simultaneous election of several officials, as a means of securing greater representation for minor parties. Each voter is allowed two or more votes, which can be cast for a single candidate or distributed among several. Candidates of minor parties can usually win seats because their supporters concentrate their additional votes for them, whereas major party supporters tend to distribute their votes among several candidates. Cumulative voting is used in electing members of the lower house of the Illinois legislature, with three representatives elected from each district and with each voter casting three votes. *See also* PROPORTIONAL REPRESENTATION, page 106.

Significance   Cumulative voting is an attempt to provide some direct representation for minority groups. Proponents support it as more accurately representative (and, hence, more democratic) than the two-party, single-vote, winner-take-all system. Opponents point out that it may foster a host of splinter parties with the result that, frequently, none is able to gain a majority and unstable coalition government results. Most political battles over whether a cumulative voting system should be established occur on the local level.

Dark Horse   A marginal candidate or noncandidate for public office who has little support and almost no chance to win nomination or election. When a consensus cannot be achieved in support of one of the leading candidates, however, the party or voters may suddenly and dramatically shift their support to a dark horse. The role of the dark horse in American politics relates particularly to the presidential nominating conventions of the two major political parties. *See also* AVAILABILITY, page 61; PRESIDENTIAL ELECTION PROCESS, page 102.

Significance   Because the two major American political parties are coalitions of diverse and often antagonistic ideological and sectional wings, convention deadlocks over the selection of presidential candidates have not been uncommon. Historically, a dark horse candidate remained a definite possibility at almost every major party convention, except for those renominating an incumbent president. More recently, increased party discipline and the expenditure of millions of dollars on mass media have almost eliminated the opportunity for a dark horse or surprise candidate to be nominated. However, a candidate choosing to run as an independent for an office may assume the role of a dark horse candidate.

Demagogue   An unscrupulous politician who seeks to win and hold office through emotional appeals to mass prejudices and passions. Half-truths, outright lies, and various means of cardstacking may be used in attempts to dupe the voters. Typically, a demagogue may try to win support from one group by blaming another for its misfortunes. *See also* BOSS, page 63; MCCARTHYISM, page 325.

Significance   Demagogues may thrive in either a dictatorship or a democracy. In the latter, however, because of free speech and press guarantees and frequent elections, the chances of unseating a demagogue are infinitely greater. Generally, the success of American demagogues has been short-lived, with the exception of a few powerful political bosses.

Democratic Party   A major American party that evolved from the Democratic-Republican group supporting Thomas Jefferson. Andrew Jackson, regarded by Democrats as cofounder with Jefferson, changed the name to Democratic party in keeping with his ultrademocratic philosophy. Further development of party principles occurred under the more recent leadership of Woodrow Wilson and Franklin D. Roosevelt. From 1932 to 1952, the Democratic party dominated the American political scene, holding the presidency for those 20 years. In the next 44 years, 1953 to 1997, however, the Republicans held control of the presidency for 28 years (the 8 Eisenhower years, 1953–1961; the 8 Nixon-Ford years, 1969–1977; the 8 Reagan years, 1981–1989; and the 4 Bush years, 1989–1993). The Democratic presidents during these years were: John F. Kennedy, 1961–1963; Lyndon Johnson, 1963–1969; Jimmy Carter, 1977–1981; and Bill Clinton, 1993–1997. The Democrats, however, held a majority of the seats in the House of Representatives from 1932 to 1994, with the exception of the periods 1946 to 1948 and 1952 to 1954, and in the Senate except for the years 1980 to 1986. *See also* JACKSONIAN DEMOCRACY, page 14; JEFFERSONIANISM, page 14; POLITICAL PARTY, page 98; REPUBLICAN PARTY, page 109.

Significance   Many studies show strong Democratic party preference by low-income groups, organized labor, and religious and racial minority groups. In recent years, the Democratic party has generally stood for freer trade, more extensive international commitments, and expanded civil rights guarantees. On the issue of states' rights, the party has reversed its early position and, in modern times, has consistently favored expanded national responsibilities. Its policies have generally been more liberal than Republican party policies, although both parties include a coalition of liberals, moderates, and conservatives. Polls indicate that there are considerably more Democrats than Republicans registered to vote in the United States. Ideologically based groups that have functioned in Congress within the Democratic party include the liberal Democratic Study Group and the conservative Democratic Forum, often called the Boll Weevils.

Direct Primary   An intraparty election in which the voters select the candidates who will run on a party's ticket in the subsequent general election. Primaries are also used to choose convention delegates and party leaders. In a *closed* primary, used in most states, the selection process is limited to avowed party adherents; in an *open* primary, voters participate regardless of party affiliation or the absence of any affiliation. In the states of Alaska and Washington, a "blanket primary" permits the voter to split his or her ticket by voting for candidates of more than one party. Other than these exceptions, voters are limited in both open and closed primaries to selecting candidates of a single party. Some state and local governments use primaries to reduce the number of candidates for nonpartisan elections. Candidates get their names on a primary ballot, typically, through petitions signed by a required number of registered voters. Other means include caucus, preprimary convention, and self-announcement. *See also* CLOSED PRIMARY, page 65; OPEN PRI-

MARY, page 93; PRESIDENTIAL PRIMARIES, page 103; RUNOFF PRIMARY, page 111; *Smith v. Allwright,* page 121.

Significance Since 1900, the direct primary has gradually superseded the convention as a nominating device. All states today use the direct primary system, in one form or another, for some offices. The primary system gives rank-and-file voters a larger voice in party affairs and enables the voters to get rid of an unpopular, but strongly entrenched, elected official or party leader. Disadvantages include greater expense for the candidate and taxpayer and, generally, a weakening of party organization and responsibility. Presidential nominations involve both the election of delegates in presidential primaries in more than 30 states and the holding of national conventions to nominate each party's presidential and vice presidential candidates. The United States is unique in the world in its use of the direct primary as a nominating election.

Disfranchise Taking away the right to vote. Persons may be deprived of their franchise or vote if they lose their citizenship, if they fail to register when required, or if they are convicted of certain crimes. Many people are disfranchised temporarily when they move, either within the state or from state to state, until they establish new residence. Voters may also be wholly or partially disfranchised indirectly as a result of dishonesty in ballot counts or through political manipulation, such as gerrymandering. *See also* VOTING QUALIFICATIONS, page 119.

Significance Each election finds many Americans denied the privilege of voting despite their previous participation. Disfranchisement for loss of citizenship and conviction for crime is infrequent. Failure to register or reregister is the main cause for disfranchisement in the United States. Much voter disfranchisement would be removed by reducing residence requirements for most elections and eliminating them for presidential contests. Judicial oversight of state redistricting to ensure substantial equality in voting power and increased federal action to prevent disfranchisement because of color or race through the Civil Rights Acts have reduced both indirect and direct disfranchisement. "Grandfather clauses" used by southern states to bestow the vote on whites who were otherwise disfranchised by tax and literacy requirements intended to keep blacks from voting were found unconstitutional by the Supreme Court (*Guinn v. United States,* 238 U.S. 347 [1915]). The Court also has held that states do not violate the equal protection guarantee by disfranchising convicted felons (*Richardson v. Ramirez,* 418 U.S. 24 [1974]).

Domestic Terrorism A relatively new and growing problem facing American Society in the 1990s. Domestic terrorism has increasingly been linked with political movements that seek to utilize fear, oppression, and violence to achieve their goals. *See also* ANTITERRORISM AND EFFECTIVE DEATH PENALTY ACT OF 1996, page 375; INTERNATIONAL TERRORISM, page 558.

Significance American society has become a target for not only terrorism from abroad, such as the 1993 bombing of the World Trade Center in New York City by Muslim fundamentalists, in which 6 people were killed and more than 1,000 were injured, but also terrorist action perpetrated by Americans, born and raised in the United States. Recent happenings include the bombing of the Federal Building in Oklahoma City in 1995, the Amtrak derailment in Arizona in 1995, and the actions of the Unabomber, who has killed 3 and maimed 23 in 16 bombings directed at airlines and techno-industries over a 17-year period. New weapons, such as bombs made from fertilizer and fuel oil, have given domestic terrorists a new and potent way to present their demands for change. Terrorist actions are often aimed at changing the status quo but have also been used to seek revenge for governmental or societal actions against them or their groups that they believed were wrongfully committed. Some terrorists have been motivated by religious doctrines to murder doctors and receptionists and bomb abortion clinics; by racial concerns, for example, white supremacist groups like the Klu Klux Klan, White Aryan Resistance, and neo-Nazis; and by far-right antigovernment attitudes, such as those held by the Freemen in Montana and the militiamen. Members of the militias believe that only an armed citizenry can keep the federal government in check. They see the government as an enemy and have a list of conspiracy theories involving the United Nations and foreign troops training in the United States for eventual invasion. They see the Brady Bill and assault weapon ban as part of a large conspiracy to take over the government. This outlook all came to public attention following the Oklahoma City bombing, in which 168 people were killed, and many men, women, and children were injured. This bombing occurred exactly two years to the day following the Waco, Texas, disaster, in which agents of the Bureau of Alcohol, Tobacco, and Firearms and later the FBI, besieged the Branch Davidians' compound. The standoff ended with the compound erupting into flames and the deaths of 82 men, women, and children. Letters mentioning the WACO incident and the botched federal raid by ATF agents at Ruby Ridge on the white separatist, Randy Weaver and his family, were found at the Amtrak derailment. These happenings have convinced Americans that terrorism has become a feature of life in the United States. In 1996, President Bill Clinton signed the Terrorism Bill, which limits federal appeals by inmates on death row, makes it easier to deport or exclude foreign terrorists, prohibits Americans from raising money for terrorist organizations, and allows law enforcement agencies to spend $1 billion for fighting terrorism.

Electoral College   The presidential electors from each state who meet in their respective state capitals, following their popular election, and cast ballots for president and vice president. The Electoral College never meets as a national body. The process starts with the nomination of partisan slates of electors by party conventions, primaries, or committees in each state. The number of electors in each state is equal to its number of representatives and senators; the Twenty-third Amendment allots three electors for the District of Columbia, making a total electoral vote of 538. In the November presidential election, the slate of electors receiving a plurality of popular votes in each of 48 states is elected. In two states—Maine and Nebraska—the electoral votes are divided proportionally to the popular vote. The electors pledge themselves to vote for their party's candidates for president and vice president, although the Constitution permits them to use discretion. After casting electoral ballots in their respective state capitals in December, the ballots are counted and certified before a joint session of

Congress early in January. The candidates who receive a majority of the electoral votes (270) are certified as president-elect and vice president–elect. If none receives a majority of the electoral vote, the election of the president is decided by the House of Representatives from among the three highest candidates, with each state having one vote; that of the vice president is decided by the Senate from between the two highest candidates, with each senator having one vote. Normally, the people of the United States know who has been elected following the popular election in November, and the rest of the process is largely a formality. The rise of political parties that nominate pledged electors has distorted the original intention of the Founding Fathers. *See also* ELECTORAL COUNT ACT, page 122; MINORITY PRESIDENT, page 195 PRESIDENTIAL ELECTION PROCESS, page 102; TWELFTH AMENDMENT, page 115.

Significance   The Electoral College system has on three occasions— 1800, 1824, and 1876—failed to elect a president and vice president, thus throwing the election into Congress. The system has come under severe criticism at times in American history. Several recurring grounds for criticism have been: (1) Sometimes candidates with a minority of the popular vote have won election, (2) the machinery has become an anachronism because the electors no longer actually perform the selecting function envisioned by the Founding Fathers, (3) the unit system under which all of a state's electoral votes go to the party that polls a statewide plurality is unfair to other candidates and their supporters, and (4) the complicated nature of the entire system tends to confuse voters and complicate the selection process. Proposals for reform include: (1) discarding the Electoral College machinery and placing the election on a direct popular vote on the basis of a nationwide constituency, (2) eliminating the electors but retaining a state basis for voting, with a plurality needed in a majority of states to win, (3) eliminating the electors but retaining an electoral vote divided in each state at approximately the same ratio as the popular vote, (4) selecting electors in each state in the same manner as members of the House and Senate are chosen, and (5) continuing to use the Electoral College system but adding a "national bonus plan" that would award 102 bonus electoral votes to whichever candidate won the nationwide popular vote. The Congress has rejected several constitutional amendment proposals that would have provided for the elimination or substantial alteration of the Electoral College. Opposition to direct election of the president, for example, reflects the fears of small states of being overwhelmed by the large urban vote of big states, and the concern of the major parties that the change would give minor parties a more influential role. Political leaders as well as the general public tend to be wary of changing the basic system for electing the president because they fear how change would affect the outcome of future elections.

Elite   Persons who exercise a major influence on, or control the making of, political, economic, and social decisions. Elites achieve their power position through wealth, family status, caste systems, or intellectual superiority. Elites constitute the "power structure" or "establishment" of local and national communities. *See also* OLIGARCHY, page 20; PUBLIC POLICY MODELS, page 107.

Significance   An elite group may hold power openly and officially or may exercise control over those in authority. On the national level in the

United States, no elite group is dominant; on specific issues, however, business, labor, military, and other elites may exercise a decisive influence. In many cities, a business elite constitutes "the establishment" or power structure. Elitism contravenes democratic theory but in practice pervades most institutions. Much political science literature is concerned with description and analysis of the role of elites in decision making.

Equal Time Rule   A policy established by the Federal Communications Commission (FCC) that stipulates that all candidates for a public office be given equal access to the free or paid use of television and radio. The equal time rule is enforced through the authority of the FCC to renew broadcast licenses periodically. A related policy, the "fairness doctrine," was established by the FCC in the late 1940s to require radio and television stations to present all sides of important public issues. The fairness doctrine was repealed by the FCC in 1987 on the grounds that it unduly restricted broadcasting, that the number of radio and television stations had expanded greatly, and that broadcast freedom would result in a fair hearing for public issues. In 1989, however, Congress tried to reimpose the fairness doctrine and authorize the FCC to fine broadcasters who violated it, but the measure was killed by a presidential veto. In 1990, the Supreme Court refused to reinstate it as a constitutional requirement. A third rule, the "right of rebuttal," gives individuals a chance to respond to personal attacks made on radio or television. This rule was supported by a 1969 decision of the United States Supreme Court (*Red Lion Broadcasting Co. v. Federal Communications Commission,* 395 U.S. 367). Another related FCC rule requires all stations to devote some of their broadcast time to public service activities. *See also* CAMPAIGN, page 63; FEDERAL COMMUNICATIONS COMMISSION, page 464.

Significance   The equal time and related rules were based on the assumption that democracy requires that people have the opportunity to hear the candidates and opposing views on political issues before making up their minds. Unlike newspapers and other published materials, which are not governed by "equal space" or "right to rebuttal" provisions, radio and television use public property in beaming their broadcasts over the airwaves, and are therefore subject to control by Congress through regulation by the FCC. Congress exempted the Kennedy-Nixon, The Ford-Carter, the Carter-Reagan, and the Bush-Dukakis television debates from the equal time provision so that a number of minor parties could not demand equal time. During the 1992 campaign for presidency, Bush and Clinton were joined by the independent Ross Perot in a three-way debate. Most candidate and party radio and television presentations are limited to paid advertising because the station would have to provide free time to as many as a dozen or more minor parties if they offered it to the two major parties. The public educational media, however, provide some free time for candidates of all parties. These media include many local stations and the Public Broadcasting Service (PBS) in television and National Public Radio (NPR), which produce and distribute programs over national networks. They receive support from the Corporation for Public Broadcasting (CPB), a private, nonprofit corporation that administers funds provided partly by Congress. In 1987, Congress tried to make the fairness doctrine a permanent statutory limitation on the American media, but President Ronald Reagan vetoed this effort. He held that the rule is unconstitutional, that bureaucratic regulation of the media is self-defeating, and that complete freedom and competition should prevail. The equal time and related rules currently apply to approximately 10,000 radio and 1,300 television stations. President Clinton suggested in his 1995 State of the Union message that broadcasters give politicians free air time since broadcasters have free use of the public airwaves. The broadcasters replied that this would be "welfare for politicians" and that they would challenge any such proposal in the courts.

Faction   A political group or clique that functions within a larger group, such as a government, party, or organization. Factions are often linked with strife, instability, and intrigue. Factions usually identify themselves by their perceptions of common belief or purpose rather than by simple membership. A fear of factions motivated much of the support for sixteenth- and seventeenth-century monarchy, and in the eighteenth century Age of Enlightenment check and balance features were considered essential in democratic institutions to control the power of factions. *See also* MADISONIANISM, page 18.

Significance   James Madison, in *Federalist Paper* No. 10, warned that special interests (factions) always exist in a free society. In effect, Madison was warning that political parties could misuse freedom and create conflict by pitting the interest of one against another. To Madison, the most common and durable source of factional conflict was the uneven distribution of property. Madison's defense against the threat of factionalism in the new Constitution was to build in safeguards that could control the encroachments of government and its officials, whereby the system "must first enable the government to control the governed; and in the next place oblige it to control itself." Despite Madison's warnings, political parties soon emerged in the new system of government and, over a period of two centuries, have contributed much to the democratization of the American system. In the contemporary world, faction is used to describe subgroups that are part of the main political parties, such as the conservative wings of the Republican and Democratic parties.

Favorite Son   A state political leader—often the governor—whose name is placed in nomination for the presidency at a national nominating convention by members of his state's delegation. Usually a favorite son is not a serious candidate, and his nomination is merely a means of honoring him or of delaying commitment of the state delegation's votes. *See also* DARK HORSE, page 71; STALKING HORSE, page 113.

Significance   A "favorite son" nominee is seldom given serious consideration by the convention. Delegation members generally vote for their favorite son on the first ballot, especially if a real contest between leading candidates is shaping up. In this way, the delegation can remain noncommittal until the first ballot gives some indication of the relative strength of leading candidates. At this point, the favorite son will probably withdraw his own nomination and throw his delegation's votes to one of the front-runners. If the recipient of these votes should go on to win the presidency, the favorite son will be in a good bargaining position to obtain a high-level political appointment or other favors. In order to broaden grass-roots participation and reduce backroom manipulation, the Democratic party, in 1970, required that to be placed in nomination, a candidate must have the support of at least 50 delegates, including no more than 20 from one state.

Federalist Party   The first American political party, which evolved during the later phases of George Washington's presidency. Its leaders, Alexander Hamilton and John Adams, gained the support of the financial, industrial, and commercial interests for the new party. Many of its members had strongly supported the adoption of the new Constitution and the creation of the federal Union. *See also* HAMILTONIANISM, page 13; MADISONIANISM, page 18; REPUBLICAN PARTY, page 109.

Significance   The Federalist party developed national financial and economic programs, which included a protective tariff, an excise tax, the creation of a national bank, and the assumption of state debts by the national government. To justify the expansion of national powers, the Federalists insisted on a loose interpretation of the Constitution. As a reaction to these policies, Thomas Jefferson and James Madison rallied the small farmers and artisans and the planters of the South into a coalition of Anti-Federalists. In this manner the two-party political system was born in the United States. After Jefferson's defeat of the Federalists in the election of 1800, the party began to decline in popularity. In 1816, it disappeared completely from the American scene. Its demise resulted from quarrels among its leaders and from its discredit for both its attempt to silence the opposition through the Alien and Sedition Acts and its failure to support the War of 1812. In 1832, the Whig party evolved as a successor to the Federalists, and in 1860 the Republican party replaced the Whigs.

Fifteenth Amendment   An amendment to the Constitution, adopted in 1870, that forbids a state to deny a person the right to vote because of race, color, or previous condition of servitude. *See also* CIVIL RIGHTS ACTS, pages 376–379; *Smith v. Allwright,* page 121.

Significance   Although the Fifteenth Amendment does not give anyone an absolute right to vote, it does prohibit any discrimination because of race or color. Not until recent years have blacks made significant advances in realizing the goals established by the Amendment. In 1960, for example, the Supreme Court ruled that the racial gerrymandering of Tuskegee, Alabama, so as to exclude all black voters from city elections violated the Fifteenth Amendment (*Gomillion v. Lightfoot,* 364 U.S. 339). The Civil Rights Acts of 1957, 1960, and 1964 and the Voting Rights Acts of 1965, 1970, 1975, and 1982 were passed by Congress, and the Twenty-fourth Amendment prohibiting poll taxes was adopted to aid blacks in overcoming the various devices used by some southern states to frustrate the purposes of the Fifteenth Amendment.

Filing   The legal act of declaring candidacy for a public elective office. Most states provide that aspirants first circulate candidacy petitions to be signed by a stipulated number of registered voters. The aspirant presents the petitions and files for candidacy with the appropriate official (secretary of state, county clerk, or city clerk). The candidate may then run against other candidates of the party for the office in a direct primary election to determine which of them will become the party's standard-bearer in the general election. In some states, persons seeking candidacy for local office may file simply by declaring their intentions before an official. In other states, a candidate may file by depositing a sum of money in lieu of petitions, which may be refunded if the candidate polls enough votes. *See also* NOMINATION, page 92; PETITION, page 94.

Significance   Filing is a means by which running for office can be limited to "serious" candidates. A balance must be struck: If the requirements are too difficult, then competent, public-spirited citizens may be discouraged from seeking candidacy; if too lenient, a horde of candidates may confuse the voters. In Britain, this problem is met by requiring all candidates to deposit a modest filing fee, which is forfeited if the candidate fails to secure a minimum percentage of the vote. In 1972, the U.S. Supreme Court declared that filing fees must be kept at a reasonable level (*Bullock v. Carter,* 405 U.S. 134).

General Election   A statewide election, usually held shortly after a primary election, to fill state and national offices. States hold national presidential elections every four years and national congressional elections in the even-numbered years. Typically, states hold state and county general elections every November in the even-numbered years, although some states elect some important state officials and judges in general elections held in odd-numbered years, frequently in the spring. *See also* DIRECT PRIMARY, page 72; PRESIDENTIAL ELECTION PROCESS, page 102.

Significance   Voters make their final choice in selecting their public officials in the general election. Such an election is to be distinguished from a primary election, which is a nominating process, and from special elections, which are called at irregular intervals. General elections are conducted by states and are governed largely by state constitutional and statutory provisions, although the national government has become increasingly involved in expanding and protecting voting rights. In 1986, the Supreme Court held in *Munro v. Socialist Workers' Party* (479 U.S. 189) that freedom of association was not violated by requiring a minimum primary vote to qualify a party to be placed on a general election ballot.

Gridlock   The freezing of action on an issue as a result of the sometimes overly effective operation of the separation of powers and the checks and balances system provided by the U.S. Constitution and by the natural functioning of the two-party system. The ultimate test for a gridlock situation occurs when government seeks to deal with a budget crisis. *See also* BUDGET, page 390.

Significance   Gridlock is often the product of a president of one party and Congress of another. It can also result from a conservative-liberal division within the majority party; in foreign policy, it often takes the form of a political battle between isolationists and interventionists or hawks versus doves. Gridlock has often killed or postponed positive action, especially by the national government. For the government to function, each year the Congress must pass appropriation bills and the President must sign them. When there is wide disagreement between the two branches, the process breaks down and there is fiscal budgetary gridlock, also referred to as a "train wreck." Nine times since 1981 there have been temporary shut-downs of the government, but they were short term with minor inconvenience. In 1995 and early 1996, however, the government was shut down for nearly a week on one occasion and later for three weeks, except for functions labeled "essential." Some political experts view these actions as political ploys. With a Democratic executive and a Republican legislature, the divisive nature of dealing with critical financial questions became acute, with each party determined to show the voter that its approach to balancing the budget in a specific number of years was the best way to achieve the budgetary goal.

Incumbent   A person who holds an office or an official position. Many states make voters aware that some candidates are incumbents by printing their official titles or offices on the ballot beside their names. *See also* TERM LIMITATION, page 114.

Significance   An incumbent usually has an advantage in seeking reelection, since he or she has an established following, is known to the voters, and has campaign experience. Printing offices or titles on the ballot gives an advantage to incumbents because the voter is thus given a choice between a candidate who obviously has had experience in the office and other untried and often unknown persons. Studies have disclosed that incumbents usually win elections whether or not they are identified on the ballot. Disagreement exists as to whether a person appointed to fill an elective office is an incumbent. Incumbency may also produce negative results for candidates when voters become exasperated with governmental actions or inactions or with the performance of individuals. This contributed to the Republican victory in 1994. The major share of political contributions goes to incumbents, regardless of their party affiliation. Incumbency has played a major role in congressional races for the House and Senate. In the eight elections for the House of Representatives prior to the 1986 election, for example, 93 percent of incumbents of both major parties won reelection. In the 1990, 1992, and 1994 elections, however, some voters in both primaries and general elections turned against incumbents because of a disenchantment with politics and politicians who, they believe, often do not translate their campaign pledges into meaningful policy. This attitude led to efforts to provide term limitations for members of Congress and the state legislatures.

Independent   A voter who disregards party affiliation of candidates running for elective office and casts the ballot for the "best person" or on the basis of issues. Empirical studies of voting behavior tend to show that most independents are politically apathetic. In 1992, however, Ross Perot, an independent candidate for the presidency, awakened the American electorate with a campaign aimed at gaining maximum support and participation. *See also* CLOSED PRIMARY, page 65; POLITICAL ACTIVIST, page 97.

Significance   Although independents are often criticized for not contributing actively to the democratic process through political parties, they are wooed by both major parties. Independent voters may be decisive in determining the outcome of elections, including presidential contests. A large number of independent voters encourages political parties to focus on crucial issues in the campaign. Some political analysts question whether there is such a thing as an independent, holding the view that all voters have a predisposition toward one party or the other. In 1983, the Supreme Court voided Ohio's early filing requirement for presidential candidates—they must file by March to be on the November election ballot—on the grounds that it discriminated against independent candidates and their supporters (*Anderson v. Celebrezze,* 460 U.S. 780).

Indicator (or Bellwether) Precincts Voting units that tend to serve as election barometers. An indicator precinct typically constitutes a micro-cross-section of the electoral system because the factors that affect general voting behavior are present. Such precincts may also be used to predict how ethnic, racial, or social groups will react to candidates or issues. *See also* PRECINCT, page 102.

Significance Political parties, candidates, campaign managers, political scientists, the news media, and others have devoted much time and effort to discovering indicator precincts. The ability to predict election outcomes is often closely related to the judicious selection of indicator precincts as well as to interviewing and polling techniques. Some indicator precincts, for example, have voted for the winning candidates in every presidential election in the twentieth century. As a result, their role in the selection of presidential nominees for both major parties is substantial. Two counties, one in Oregon and the other in Iowa, rate high in their ability to predict outcomes since both have voted for the winner in all 23 presidential elections since William McKinley beat William Jennings Bryan in 1896.

Internet A computer network that links most colleges and universities as well as many businesses, governmental offices, and individuals. Internet is the heart of the growing information superhighway. In 1995, it was estimated that more than 30 million individuals were using modems (devices that connect computers to telephone lines) to tap into global networks. Via telephone lines, computer users can gain access to government archives and university libraries and can send private messages (E-mail). *See also* POLITICAL SCIENCE, page 21; TELECOMMUNICATION ACT OF 1996, page 479.

Significance Internet was first established in 1969 as a military communication system. The fastest-growing segment of the Internet is the World Wide Web with its multimedia sites and integration of audio, video, graphics, and text. Online services are available through commercial providers such as America Online, CompuServe, Prodigy, and the most recent, Microsoft Network. The U.S. government is also online through "Thomas," the Library of Congress's legislative informational system on the Internet, which is nonpartisan and available for research and communication. All Congressional members will be online and able to reach constituents with their records and stands on issues. It will redefine democracy, making possible electronic town meetings and instant voter-legislator communication. A negative aspect is that organizations can flood the Internet with messages from only one side of an issue. Other negative factors are concerns about access to pornography by children and the issue of privacy versus the right to know.

The computer is evolving into an information appliance but is not yet as easy to use as the telephone or available to all.

Iron Triangle   A phrase used to describe a strong, resilient relationship among three distinct political entities. Used in political subfields as diverse as geopolitical strategy and domestic policy analysis, the concept of "iron triangle" implies an association with a peculiar degree of autonomy or self-sufficiency. In the context of domestic policy making, the iron triangle (sometimes called a "cozy triangle") consists of special interests, congressional committees, and bureaucratic units associated in such a way as to routinize policy making to the benefit of the involved parties. *See also* DEFENSE CONTRACT, page 544; PRESSURE GROUP, page 104.

Significance   Iron triangles that exist within the policy arena are sometimes referred to as "subgovernments." They are generally considered to have a negative impact on the policy process. An often cited example of an iron triangle is the relationship that exists among the Pentagon, the defense industry, and the congressional committees responsible for defense appropriations. Each of the parties in the triangle benefits from the defense budget, and the self-interest of each in such a relationship leads to a policy bias that favors an unnecessarily large national defense budget.

Key Election Factors: Class   The classification of people into various socioeconomic and political groups for the purpose of analysis and evaluation.

Significance   Political scientists have increasingly used class as a factor in voting behavior studies. Class is often linked in studies with other relevant factors such as race, economic position, population makeup, and gender so that interviewing techniques can provide a more realistic base of factors. Although the United States is generally regarded as a classless society, some analysts have described the situation as one of a perpetual and increasingly divisive class war between the rich and the poor or the haves and have-nots. Nevertheless, 90 percent of Americans consider themselves to be middle class. Those living below the poverty line are usually called the "underclass." The overclass constitutes the new American elite, the estimated upper 5 percent of American society. Most members of the overclass are economic conservatives who generally support the Republican candidates with money but tend to favor many of the causes set forth in the Democratic agenda. They do not regard themselves as part of the ruling class.

Key Election Factors: Ethnic Politics   Political activity carried on by people who belong to the same cultural, racial, religious, national origin, or linguistic group. Along with gender and sexual politics, which are based on sexual orientation as it relates to political activity, and generational politics as it relates to age groups, ethnic politics has a substantial impact on political outcomes. The term "ethnic" comes from the Greek "ethnos," a tribe; ethnic politics relates to what can be called tribal groups that often compete with each other in the struggle for political power. *See also* KEY ELECTION ISSUES, page 85; POLITICS, page 100; VOTING BEHAVIOR, page 119.

Significance   The world is filled with ethnic or tribal groups, with each group peacefully or violently seeking to win political power. In many countries, such as Russia, the former Yugoslavia, Canada, and India, ethnic politics threatens to destroy or greatly weaken the existing political system. In the United States, the trend has been toward integration and assimilation, although black and Hispanic ghettos still exist. Likewise, other groups, such as Palestinian Arabs, Vietnamese, and Orthodox Jews, tend to live together and vote together in sections of large American cities. Polls have demonstrated a high level of consistency in voting behavior among the members of many ethnic groups, but the greater the assimilation, the less consistency can be demonstrated.

Key Election Factors: Gender Politics   The role of men and women, especially women, in developing positions as a group on political issues, candidates, and other forms of political activity. Polls tend to demonstrate the differences between men and women in things political. Women have been an active political force since they successfully agitated for the right to vote and achieved the adoption of the Nineteenth Amendment in 1920. As a result, men also became an identifiable political force, with some radical individuals agitating against women's rights. *See also* EQUAL RIGHTS, page 309; KEY ELECTION ISSUES, page 85.

Significance   Polls and voting studies of various kinds have tended to demonstrate that gender politics is a reality, although not a decisive force in electoral politics in the American system. Several million more women than men voted for Jimmy Carter in 1980, for Walter Mondale in 1984, and for Michael Dukakis in 1988 than voted for Ronald Reagan and George Bush. Roughly 61 percent of the male voters and 57 percent of the female voters supported the two Republican candidates. Studies have also shown that women differ from men in that women are more likely to be registered voters, are more likely to be registered as Democrats and vote for Democratic candidates, and are more likely to take liberal positions on leading issues, such as abortion rights, health care, education, family values, and care of the elderly. In 1991, sexual harassment became a national topic for gender politics discussion and debate as a result of charges and countercharges made over the national media during the Senate Judiciary Committee's consideration of Judge Clarence Thomas's appointment to the United States Supreme Court. The impact of gender—especially charges of alleged sexual harassment—on election outcomes may be substantial as a result of the feminist movement.

Key Election Factors: Generational Politics   The determination of an individual's political orientation because of his or her age. Generational politics involves similar attitudes and actions in the political milieu by cohort groups of youths, middle agers, and the elderly. *See also* BABY BOOMERS, page 61; KEY ELECTION ISSUES, page 85; OLDER AMERICANS ACT OF 1965, page 526.

Significance   The role of generational politics in the determination of election outcomes has been increasing in recent years. The group that lived through the Great Depression and World War II has a different outlook than other age groups on, for example, matters dealing with the economy, social security, health care, and American involvement in military actions abroad. The youth of America became highly politicized during the Vietnam War period of the 1960s and early 1970s, with some holding extremely radical positions on issues relating to the war and American society. Although generational influences always exist in the political arena, their intensity will depend on the issues that challenge the electorate and how these issues relate to different age groups and to historical events. In 1996, an estimated 30 million of a total U.S. population of 260 million were older than 65. Baby boomers, those born between 1946 and 1964, number approximately 75 million. Those belonging to Generation X, born between 1965 and 1977, number approximately 41 million; 72 million were born between the years 1978 and 1995. Economic policymakers fear future crises when the baby boomers reach retirement age and are eligible for social security benefits. Baby boomers and Generation Xers feel that they are putting more into Social Security than they will ever receive. Generation Xers are the least involved but face the worst scenario from earlier and later generations. One continuing issue, the national public debt, will likely provoke a more open struggle between the elderly and the young as huge deficit spending leaves mountainous debt for the younger and future generations to grapple with. Polls and voting studies show that since the Vietnam War era, young people have become increasingly less interested in issues, elections, and the political process.

Key Election Factors: Population/Power Shifts   The profound changes in political power that have occurred as substantial segments of the population have shifted from the North and the East to the coastal and southwestern states. Three states—California, Texas, and Florida—have benefited most politically from these population movements. States like New York have had to pay the price of eight congressional seats for the shifts in population between 1980 and 1990. California today has a population of more than 31 million, 60 percent greater than the next most populous state, Texas. In 1950, Texas had a population of only 1.5 million; by 1995 it had increased eightfold to a population of more than 18 million and had replaced New York as the second most populous state. Florida, which contained fewer than 3 million people in 1950, currently has a population of more than 14 million, which ranks it fourth in the nation. Other states that have gained congressional seats after the most recent census include Arizona, Colorado, Georgia, Nevada, New Mexico, North Carolina, Oregon, Tennessee, Utah, Virginia, and Washington. *See also* APPORTIONMENT, page 128; KEY ELECTION ISSUES, page 85; PIVOTAL STATES, page 95; REDISTRICTING, page 162.

Significance   Population and political power have shifted dramatically since World War II. Population movements have related mainly to economic factors, such as availability of jobs and lower energy costs. Because a large portion of the federal budget relates to purchases of military and civilian manufactured products, contract awards to companies located in the coastal and southwestern states have produced jobs, which have encouraged population flows, which in turn have increased political power and the ability to get contract awards. The process is circular and feeds on itself. Examples of factors that produce change are the end of the Cold War, downsizing of governmental operations, efforts to secure a balanced budget, and the impact of foreign trade on the nation's economy. Population growth in coastal states also can be explained by the influx of millions of aliens, both legally and illegally. In addition, weather and cultural factors have attracted millions of others to the "sunbelt" and "new lifestyle" states.

Key Election Factors: Race   The impact of race in making voting decisions and in determining the outcome of elections. For blacks, Hispanics, Asians, and other minority racial groups, voting is largely a group experience. Although blacks are the largest minority group, Hispanics, or Chicanos, are increasing at a faster rate and, early in the twenty-first century, will likely pass blacks in potential voting strength. The rapid rate of increase is the result of a high birth rate and a continuing immigration, both legal and illegal. *See also* KEY ELECTION ISSUES, page 85; VOTING RIGHTS ACT, page 124.

Significance   Contemporary minority participation in voting and helping to determine election outcomes is the product of a long historical process by which, incrementally, minorities slowly but surely won the right to participate. Legal steps include the Thirteenth, Fourteenth, and Fifteenth Amendments, numerous Supreme Court decisions that expanded the political participatory rights of minority groups, a number of civil rights laws enacted by Congress and state legislatures, and the Voting Rights Act. The last of these effectively solved the legal problems that had for many years placed obstacles in the way of potential minority voters, especially blacks in the southern states. Studies show that minority groups exercise a high level of solidarity in casting their ballots, with typically 85 to 90 percent of blacks voting the straight Democratic party ticket (a considerably lower level of unity is demonstrated within Hispanic and Asian groups). Whites are predicted to constitute less than half the population of the United States sometime during the next century, and, even though participatory levels are currently lower, minorities may one day outnumber whites at the polls as well.

Key Election Issues   Controversial solutions to public policy problems offered by rival candidates in election campaigns. Social problems tend to become issues after they have crossed the political threshold. They are matters over which reasonable—and sometimes unreasonable—people in the body politic can and do disagree. Issue orientation involves voter perceptions of policy positions taken by candidates and how these positions relate to the voter's own policy preferences. *See also* KEY ELECTION FACTORS, pages 82–85.

Significance   While many people who vote in American elections are influenced decisively by such factors as ethnicity, gender, sexual preference, age group identification, geographical location, and economic position, many make their decision after studying the issues and candidate positions on them. Key issues in recent national and state elections have included abortion politics, a balanced-budget amendment, capital punishment, environmental protection, the foreign-trade gap, health care, tax equity, and state and local problems. Because many voters feel so strongly about these and related issues, other more institutionalized factors have lost some of their traditional ability to determine election outcomes. Some voters are completely "captured" by a single issue and make all of their voting decisions based on that issue as, for example, in the case of many members of the National Rifle

Association (NRA) whose voting decisions are governed by the position taken by political candidates on the issue of gun control.

Literacy Test A suffrage qualification used to determine fitness for voting by means of a reading or "understanding" test. Because literacy tests were used to discriminate against prospective voters in several states, Congress suspended their use in the Voting Rights Act. *See also* VOTING QUALIFICATIONS, page 119; VOTING RIGHTS ACT, page 124.

Significance Literacy tests offered an effective means of discriminating against voters because examining officials had great discretion, especially when the tests were administered orally. In some southern states, for example, black college graduates were once disqualified because they failed to interpret constitutional passages to the satisfaction of a white board of examiners. Evidence of discriminatory use of literacy and related tests in six southern states led to passage of the Voting Rights Act of 1965. This Act, continued and expanded in 1970, 1975, and 1982, suspended the use of such tests and authorized appointment of federal voting examiners to order registration of blacks in states and voting districts where fewer than 50 percent of eligible voters were registered. The suspension of all literacy tests by the Voting Rights Act of 1970 was upheld by the Supreme Court in *Oregon v. Mitchell*, 400 U.S. 112 (1970).

Lobbyist A person, usually acting as an agent for a pressure group, who seeks to bring about the passage or defeat of legislative bills or to influence their contents. Lobbyists, often called the "Third House" of the legislature, are experts who testify before committees and present important facts on legislative proposals to support their clients' interests. They also often use large sums of money in a variety of ways to influence legislative outcomes. Many states and the national government require the registration of lobbyists and disclosure of information concerning their employers, their salaries, and the amounts spent to influence legislation. Lobbyists are also active in trying to influence decisions made by executive officials, administrators, and the courts. See also POLITICAL ACTION COMMITTEES (PACS), page 96; PRESSURE GROUP, page 104; REGULATION OF LOBBYING ACT, page 181; *United States v. Harriss*, page 179.

Significance Lobbyists furnish important factual data to legislators and provide effective representation for organized groups. They are criticized because they use selected facts, often distorted for propaganda purposes, and are more concerned with particular interests than with general interests. Except for laws prohibiting bribery and related criminal offenses, governmental action toward lobbyists has not sought to restrict their activities but to publicize them. Attempts by government to restrict lobbyists and lobbying unduly might be regarded by the courts as an infringement of the First Amendment freedom to petition the government. In 1989, Congress passed the Lobbying Reform Act, which for the first time required those receiving federal grants, contracts, and loans to publicly account for payments made to lobbyists to influence Congress and government agencies.

Long Ballot The typical state and local ballot, sometimes called the "bedsheet ballot" or "jungle ballot," which has a large number of offices to be filled, candidates to be selected, and issues to be decided. *See also* BALLOT, page 62; PARTY-COLUMN BALLOT, page 94; SHORT BALLOT, page 111.

Significance The long ballot emerged during the era of Jacksonian Democracy in the 1830s on the theory that the way to expand democracy is to increase the number of elective officials. Today, political observers question this assumption. They argue that with a smaller number of elective officials, the voter can know the candidates, their qualifications, and the issues of the campaign. The long ballot may enable political machines to retain power because of voter apathy or confusion. The short ballot movement, which started in the early 1900s, has had some success in reducing the length of the ballot in a few states, but the basic problem remains. The party-column ballot also provides a means for meeting the long-ballot problem by permitting voting for all of a party's candidates for local, state, and national office by marking a single "X" or pulling a single lever on a voting machine.

Mandate Popular support for a political program. A mandate is assumed to emerge from an election as a result of popular support given to a political party or to elected officials who ran on a set of pledges to the voters. A mandate may be vague or specific, depending upon the clarity with which alternatives are presented to the voters. *See also* CONTRACT WITH AMERICA, page 67; REPUBLICAN REVOLUTION, page 109; RESPONSIBLE PARTY SYSTEM, page 110.

Significance The mandate concept is best implemented where a responsible, well-disciplined party, ready and able to carry out its promised program, exists. The American party system, unlike the British, lacks these qualities, and the mandate concept is consequently weakened. Other factors in the American political milieu that weaken the applicability of the mandate concept include the separation of powers, bicameralism, and gerrymandering. The trend, however, is toward evolving a political system in which voter action produces political change. One such movement has been carried on by Ross Perot, whose demand for changes in the governmental system is aimed at gaining a mandate from the American people for his independent program. Another effort to secure a mandate occurred in the 1994 election, when the Republicans offered a program to the voters in the form of the "Contract with America." The Republican party won control of both the House of Representatives and the Senate for the first time in several decades. They believed they had won a mandate from the people for major changes in the basic policies of the national, state, and local governments.

Mass Media The technical means of communication with millions of people, exemplified by television, radio, newspapers, motion pictures, magazines, and periodicals. Television, in particular, is used with increasing impact to build an "image campaign" in which special techniques (contrived situations, spot announcements, editing of videotapes, and the like) are used to achieve short-term shifts in voter behavior. *See also* CAMPAIGN, page 63; EQUAL TIME RULE, page 76; INTERNET, page 81; PROPAGANDA, page 105; TELECOMMUNICATION ACT OF 1996, page 479.

Significance The mass media of communication have become extremely important to government and politics as a means of informing and influencing millions of citizens. Objectives include winning elections, marshaling support for or opposition to programs, and educating the public on major issues. Political scientists, aware of the increasing significance of the mass media in decision making and of their abuse in totalitarian states, have expressed concern for their effect on the democratic process. The trend in the United States is toward concentration of the ownership of the mass media in fewer hands. The problem of seeking corrections for this situation raises many serious issues, including those concerning the constitutional rights of free expression and property. The Corporation for Public Broadcasting, however, offers a different media perspective over its Public Broadcasting Service (PBS) television with programs such as "News Hour with Jim Lehrer" and on its National Public Radio (NPR) FM radio programs such as "All Things Considered." The Cable-Satellite Public Affairs Network (C-SPAN and C-SPAN 2), created by Brian Lamb in 1979, provides live broadcasts of the House and Senate proceedings and various other political events such as press conferences and special committee hearings. Cable News Network (CNN) also covers presidential, congressional, and other public affair events.

Minor Party   A party movement, often based on a single idea or principle, that usually has little influence on elections because its support is either localized or widely scattered. Some American political observers distinguish a minor party from a third party, a new party based on a protest movement that may influence the outcome of a major election. Minor parties are often called "doctrinaire parties" because of their commitment to an ideology or cause. *See also* LIBERTARIANISM, page 17; SOCIALISM, page 26; THIRD PARTY, page 114; UNITED WE STAND AMERICA, page 118.

Significance   Minor parties have played a significant role in American political life in initiating and successfully publicizing political, economic, and social reforms over a period of years. When a minor party gains a substantial number of adherents to its basic principles, a major party often incorporates these principles into its own platform to gain voter support. The Prohibition party, for example, convinced large numbers of people of the wisdom of prohibition; the Republican party thereupon included a prohibition plank in its platform and, after winning at the polls, instituted prohibition. Minor parties found on the ballot in many states today include the American Independent, Libertarian, Socialist Labor, Socialist Workers, and the Green party.

Multiparty System   An electoral system, usually based on proportional representation, that often requires a coalition of several parties to form a majority to run the government. Multiparty systems are typical of continental European democracies. The system can be distinguished from the Anglo-American "winner-take-all" two-party system, not by the existence of numerous parties but rather in that many parties seriously compete for, and actually win, seats in the legislature. *See also* PROPORTIONAL REPRESENTATION, page 106; TWO-PARTY SYSTEM, page 117.

Significance   Multiparty systems tend to provide a broader, more diverse representation of the electorate. This strength is, at the same time, a major weakness. Coalition governments, by their very nature, are unstable governments that tend to disintegrate when the parties comprising the coalition have a falling out over a major issue. France, for example, had twenty coalition governments during the period of the Fourth Republic, from 1946 to 1958. In Italy, since World War II, governments have changed with even greater frequency. The American people have shunned a multiparty approach to politics by refusing to give substantial support to any but the two major parties. Moreover, the single-member district system, as distinguished from multidistrict proportional representation, tends to perpetuate the two-party system because typically only two parties have the voting strength to compete effectively for political power.

National Chairman   The chairman of a political party's national committee. The national chairman is generally chosen by the party's presidential candidate, with the national committee ratifying the choice. *See also* NATIONAL COMMITTEE, page 89.

Significance   The major responsibility of a national chairman is the management of the national election campaign. Working through the national committee, the chairman may exercise a considerable influence over state and local party organizations, although no formal control mechanism exists. Specific responsibilities include establishing national party headquarters, directing party affairs during and between campaigns, and raising and distributing campaign funds.

National Committee   A standing committee of a national political party established to direct and coordinate party activities during the four-year periods between national party conventions. The Democratic National Committee includes two members, a man and a woman, from each state, from the District of Columbia, and from several territories; the Republican National Committee uses the same formula but adds state chairmen from all states carried by the Republican party in the preceding presidential, gubernatorial, or congressional election. National committeemen and committeewomen are chosen every four years by the various delegations to the national convention. Each committee ratifies the presidential nominee's selection of a national chairman, who acts as spokesman for his or her party. *See also* NATIONAL CHAIRMAN, page 89.

Significance   Although the national committee appears to top the hierarchical permanent structure of each party, its power and influence are not great. The real focus of power in both party organizations remains at the local and state levels. Each national committee is concerned mainly with planning the next presidential campaign. Other important functions include planning the national convention, securing financial contributions, and publicizing the party.

National Convention   A quadrennial meeting held by each major party to select presidential and vice presidential candidates, write a platform, choose a national committee, and conduct party business. Party presidential candidates have been nominated by the convention method in every election since 1832. Delegates are apportioned on the basis of state representation with bonuses for states showing voting majorities for the party in preceding elections. Delegates are selected by party conventions or committees in some and by presidential primaries in most states. Both parties also accredit delegates from the District of Columbia, Puerto Rico, and the Virgin Islands. The nomination of, and voting on, candidates is conducted by a call of the states in alphabetical order. Since 1972, both parties have restricted the use of the unit rule, by which state delegations cast their total votes in a block for a single candidate. Both conventions nominate their candidates by an absolute majority vote. In 1980, President Jimmy Carter called for adoption of the "faithful delegate rule," which requires all delegates to vote on the first ballot for the candidate to whom they have pledged their vote. This rule helped him capture the Democratic party nomination at a time when his support was waning. *See also* CREDENTIALS COMMITTEE, page 70; PLATFORM, page 95.

Significance   Although national party conventions are typified by excitement, both artificial and natural, their responsibilities are extremely important. Most convention efforts and oratory are pointed toward the imminent fall campaign. Despite extensive television coverage in recent years, the national convention remains a puzzling phenomenon for most Americans. Much criticism has been directed at it for its clownish atmosphere, the use of pressure tactics and secret bargains, and the lack of popular participation in the candidate-selection process. Yet conventions seldom ignore public opinion and have chosen many distinguished candidates. Conventions generally are free from state and federal regulation. The main difference between the Democratic and Republican national conventions is in the number of participants, with the Democrats involving almost twice as many delegates in the process.

National Elections   The schedule of on-year, off-year presidential and congressional elections. On-year elections occur every other even-numbered year and provide for the election of a president, vice president, one-third of the Senate, and the entire House of Representatives. Off-year elections occur in every other even-numbered nonpresidential election year and provide for the election of one-third of the Senate and the entire House of Representatives. *See also* VOTER TURNOUT, page 118.

Significance   In on-year and off-year elections, presidents are often confronted by a House and Senate controlled by the other major party. Typically, in off-year elections the President's party tends to lose seats in the House of Representatives and, often, in the Senate as well. The "out" party in the House of Representatives has gained seats in every off-year election in the twentieth century except in 1934, which was part of a realigning election. Some political scientists have recommended that the national elections schedule be changed to elect a president and vice president along with the entire Senate and House of Representatives every six years. Supporters of this change claim that it would make the system more democratic and more responsive. Opponents regard the existing system as compatible with the constitutional system of checks and balances and capable of reflecting changes in public opinion every two years.

Nepotism   Granting political favors to relatives, often in the form of appointments to office. Civil service merit systems have helped to reduce the incidence of nepotism.

Significance Nepotism has been carried on by various kinds of public officials on all levels of government throughout American history. Although nepotism occasionally may result in the appointment of capable, highly qualified individuals to public office, it is more likely to result in the appointment of less capable persons and therefore is generally frowned upon by the voting public.

New Left A radical-liberal mass movement, particularly of college youth, that emerged during the 1960s. The New Left subscribed to a multifaceted radical ideology, with many uncoordinated campaigns and organizations challenging the established political, social, and economic order. The main unifying themes of the New Left were common opposition to the Vietnam War, the draft, the military-industrial complex, racial discrimination, the machinations of the establishment or power structure, the plundering and pollution of the planet, and economic deprivation of poor people. The New Left also provided the vanguard of the cultural revolution of the 1960s and 1970s, which changed the attitudes and social practices of millions concerning hair styles, drugs, sex, rock music, religion, education, and pornography. "Participatory democracy," or direct decision making by interested, active local mass groups, became the basic political objective, a means by which the New Left sought to reform what it regarded as the perversion of the democratic process by the rich and powerful. These changes have left an impact on American society that is still cogent in the world approaching the twenty-first century. *See also* ALIENATION, page 60; BABY BOOMERS, page 61; POLITICAL ACTIVIST, page 97; WOMEN'S LIBERATION MOVEMENT, page 120.

Significance The origins of the New Left movement can be traced to the Free Speech campaign at the University of California at Berkeley in the late 1950s. During the 1960s and 1970s, the New Left proved to be one of the most powerful protest movements in American history, radically changing many aspects of individual and social life. Its impact spilled over American borders, and it became an almost worldwide phenomenon, although most pronounced in its impact on rich, industrialized countries. The New Left differed from the "Old Left" of Communist and Socialist party members mainly in its broad heterogeneity, its lack of discipline, its shifting leadership, its lack of clear ideological goals for establishing the "best" society, its emphasis on protest, reform, and change rather than revolution, and its libertarian emphasis on individualism and freedom. Although the New Left began as a pacifist, antiauthoritarian force, repression from the police and the military led to a growing militancy within the movement. The New Left, like other radical movements in American history, was relatively short-lived in generating mass support, but some of its ideas have had a lasting impact on the American political and social system.

Nineteenth Amendment An amendment to the Constitution, adopted in 1920, that prohibits any state from denying the right to vote to any citizen because of their sex. Wyoming took the initiative, in 1869, in granting suffrage to women, but only a few states followed this lead. Suffragette agitation during the early part of the twentieth century culminated in the Nineteenth Amendment, which was adopted in time for women to vote in the presidential election of 1920. *See also* EQUAL RIGHTS, page 309; WOMEN'S LIBERATION MOVEMENT, page 120.

Significance   Like the Fifteenth Amendment, the Nineteenth does not grant an absolute right to vote to anyone, but it does restrict the states from discriminating on the basis of gender. The Amendment resulted in the largest increase in the electorate in American history. Since 1920, there have been no attempts to interfere with the voting rights of women. Because women voters outnumber eligible male voters today, campaigns have acquired more of a feminine touch. Most political campaigners publicly recognize "equal rights" for women, and the Nineteenth Amendment is often described as the forerunner to the Equal Rights Amendment campaign. Polls have shown that women tend to offer greater support for the Democratic party, whereas men tend to favor the Republicans.

Nomination   The official designation of an individual as a candidate for public office. Methods for selecting candidates in the United States have included the rank-and-file party caucus, legislative and congressional caucuses, the mixed caucus (legislators and party representatives), the party convention, the primary, and petition. *See also* CAUCUS, page 64; CONVENTION, page 68; DIRECT PRIMARY, page 72; FILING, page 78; NATIONAL CONVENTION, page 89; PETITION, page 94.

Significance   The direct primary is the most widely used nominating device, being mandatory or optional in all 50 states. The convention system, discredited and largely replaced by the direct primary by 1910, is once again gaining acceptance on state and local levels. Some disillusionment with the primary system exists, and the convention method is credited with giving greater emphasis to party responsibility and selection of able candidates. The selection of the candidates for the presidency remains in the hands of each party's quadrennial convention. Nomination also refers to appointment of executive and judicial officials if executive nomination must be followed by confirmation of the nominee by the legislative branch.

Nonpartisan Election   An election in which candidates have no party designations and political parties are prohibited from running candidates. Nonpartisan elections are typically used to elect state and local judges and municipal officials. They are often preceded by nonpartisan primaries in which the number of candidates for each office is reduced to two. *See also* PLURALITY, page 96.

Significance   A progressive movement active early in the twentieth century proposed to get rid of corruption by eliminating political parties and partisan elections. Many nonpartisan electoral reforms were introduced, especially on the local level. Most nonpartisan systems, however, have not produced the anticipated results because candidates often remain identified with parties and parties may seek to influence the election. On the other hand, nonpartisan elections that succeed in divorcing the party from the election tend to rob the voter of his most effective cue-giving source—the party. Political parties have also been weakened by severance from their grass roots.

Nonpartisan elections, however, have the major advantage of reducing the impact of state and national partisan issues on local elections.

Office-block Ballot   A form of general election ballot in which candidates for elective office are grouped together under the title of each office. The "office block" or "Massachusetts ballot" is in contradistinction to the other common type of ballot, the "party-column" or "Indiana ballot," in which all candidates of a particular party are arranged in one column. *See also* BALLOT, page 62; PARTY-COLUMN BALLOT, page 94.

Significance   The office-block ballot is now used, in some form, in about twenty states. Politicians dislike it because it places more emphasis on the office than on the party and tends to discourage "straight-ticket" voting. Studies have shown that it definitely encourages voters to "split their ticket" in general elections, compared with a tendency for straight-ticket voting on party-column ballots.

Open Primary   A voting system—also known as the crossover primary—that permits voters to choose the party primary of their choice without disclosing party affiliation or allegiance, if any. In an open primary, voters make their choice in the privacy of the voting booth. Each is limited, however, to casting votes for candidates of only one party. *See also* CLOSED PRIMARY, page 65; DIRECT PRIMARY, page 72.

Significance   Few states use the open-primary system. Unlike the closed primary, it permits independents to vote in primaries and does not require public disclosure of party affiliation, regarded as distasteful by many voters. The open primary is criticized because it reduces party responsibility and permits "raiding" by voters of one party who cross over and try to nominate weak candidates for the opposing party. The open primary is used in some states to select delegates for presidential conventions and candidates for congressional and state offices. In 1986, the Supreme Court held that a state could not bar a political party from holding an open primary in which nonmember independent voters could take part without offending freedom of association (*Tashjian v. Republican Party of Connecticut,* 479 U.S. 208).

Participatory Democracy   Maximum direct participation in political, economic, and social decision making by interested, active, and knowledgeable local groups. Participatory democracy became a basic objective of the New Left movement during the 1960s. The League of Women Voters has been active for many years in encouraging participation in politics. *See also* DIRECT DEMOCRACY, page 11; NEW LEFT, page 91; PUBLIC POLICY MODELS, page 107.

Significance   Participatory democracy establishes the ideal of maximum feasible mass action in public decision making. Historically, the idea of mass participation in the political process was applied in the Greek city-states, the Swiss cantons, and the New England town meeting. More recently, it has been tested in the neighborhood block movement in the inner cities. Critics of participatory democracy cite the masses' lack of interest in politics, their lack of knowledge, and the "iron law of oligarchy," which postulates the impossibility of mass democratic decision making.

Party-column Ballot   A form of general election ballot in which candidates for various offices are arranged in one column under their respective party names and symbols. The "party-column" or "Indiana ballot" can be contrasted with the other common type of ballot, the "office-block" or "Massachusetts ballot," in which candidates are grouped under each elective office. *See also* BALLOT, page 62; COATTAIL EFFECT, page 66; OFFICE-BLOCK BALLOT, page 93; STRAIGHT TICKET, page 113.

Significance   The party-column ballot permits voting for all of a party's candidates for local, state, and national offices by marking a single "X" or by pulling a single lever. Some variation of this kind of ballot is used today in about 30 states. Politicians generally prefer the party-column ballot because it simplifies and encourages "straight-ticket" voting, particularly when a party has an exceptionally strong presidential or gubernatorial candidate to head the party ticket, producing a coattail effect.

Patronage   The power to make partisan appointments to office or to confer contracts, franchises, licenses, honors, or other special favors. Patronage powers are vested primarily in the President, in governors and other state elective officials, in mayors, and in various county officers. Through senatorial courtesy and similar practices, legislators on all levels of government also share in patronage disposition. *See also* CIVIL SERVICE REFORM ACT OF 1978, page 241; *Rutan v. Republican Party of Illinois,* page 239; SENATORIAL COURTESY, page 167; SPOILS SYSTEM, page 234.

Significance   An era of unrestricted patronage was ushered in on the national level by the Jackson administration's spoils system in 1829. Presidential patronage reached a high-water mark during Abraham Lincoln's first term (1861–1864) but began to lose ground progressively after the enactment of the Civil Service Act of 1883 (Pendleton Act). Patronage is often defended as an essential feature of the party system to provide inducements and rewards for party workers. It also enables a chief executive to surround himself with loyal subordinates who support his views and help him redeem his campaign pledges. Antipatronage forces counter these arguments by pointing to the long, disreputable history of the spoils system. Intelligent and well-trained personnel, it is argued, can work effectively with administrations of either party. The county is the major remaining stronghold of the patronage system in the United States, although executives on all levels continue to make some patronage appointments. The Supreme Court has seriously weakened the patronage system at the local level by holding that non-policy-making jobs may not be conditioned on political beliefs or political affiliations (*Rutan v. Republican Party of Illinois,* 497 U.S. 62 [1990]).

Petition   A method of placing a candidate's name on a primary or general election ballot by submitting a specified number, or percentage, of signatures of registered voters to an appropriate state or local official for certification. Petitions may also be used to commence the initiative, referendum, and recall procedures in several states. *See also* DIRECT LEGISLATION, page 143; FILING, page 78.

Significance   The petition requirement to get an aspirant's name placed on a primary ballot is intended to help restrict the election to serious candidates. In general elections, the petition method provides a means for political independents to get their names on the ballot. Petitions frequently become matters of political controversy, involving charges of invalid signatures.

Pivotal States   Those states with large electoral votes that are crucial in winning a presidential election and in which the outcome is doubtful. The term "pivotal states" is also used to describe the twelve most populous states that have a majority of electoral college votes and potentially could elect a president and vice president over the opposition of the other 38 states and the District of Columbia. *See also* APPORTIONMENT, page 128; ELECTORAL COLLEGE, page 74.

Significance   When reapportionment occurred following the 1990 census, some of the pivotal states—California, Florida, and Texas—gained congressional seats and electoral votes, whereas other members of the "pivotal club"—New York, Michigan, and Illinois, for example—lost seats and electoral votes. Each major party usually concentrates much of its organization, campaign funds, and candidate appearances on the eight most populous states that together comprise 228 of the 270 electoral votes needed to elect a president: California (54), New York (33), Texas (32), Florida (25), Pennsylvania (23), Illinois (22), Ohio (21), and Michigan (18). In most elections, these states have also been given "doubtful" status, adding to the attention given them during campaigns by both parties and their candidates. Popular leaders from pivotal states are also likely to be nominated as presidential and vice presidential candidates.

Platform   A statement of principles and objectives espoused by a party or a candidate that is used during a campaign to win support from voters. Platforms are typically written by platform committees and adopted by national, state, or county party conventions. *See also* MANDATE, page 87; NATIONAL CONVENTION, page 89.

Significance   American party platforms consist of specific promises plus many generalities and platitudes. They extol the vast accomplishments of their party while indicting the opposition party for its failures. The language used to elaborate positions on those issues on which the party is united, however, is precise and the commitment clear. Party platforms are supplemented and modified by candidates, but few consider themselves bound by platform commitments when elected. In the British system of responsible parties, conversely, the platform of the winning party is an excellent guide to future governmental actions.

Pluralism   The concept that modern society is made up of heterogeneous institutions and organizations that have diversified religious, economic, ethnic, and cultural interests and share in the exercise of power. Democratic pluralism is based on the assumption that democracy can exist in a society where a variety of elites compete actively in the decision process for the allocation of values and that new elites can gain access to power through the same political processes. The countervailing theory of pressure politics posits that competition among major interest groups tends to balance power against power, with the result that none is able to dominate the American political system. Some analysts reject the theory and have described the American political system as one dominated by a power elite of military, business, and governmental groups and organizations. *See also* COUNTERVAILING THEORY OF PRESSURE POLITICS, page 70; PUBLIC POLICY MODELS, page 107; SECTIONALISM, page 111.

Significance   The greater the variety in a population, the greater the degree of pluralism. Some react with fear in the presence of differences, whereas others derive satisfaction. While diversity is a potential threat to unity, uniformity is a threat to freedom. In countries like the United States, pluralism has given rise to a tremendous proliferation of organized groups, many with some impact on public policy, representing all manner of interests. It has also resulted in a greater variety of approaches to issues than will be found in homogeneous societies. The countervailing theory of pressure politics has been weakened in recent years by the growth in the number of single-interest groups that are ideologically committed to their goal. The power of the National Rifle Association to block gun control legislation, for example, is not balanced by pro-gun control lobby groups.

Plurality   The winning of an election by a candidate who receives more votes than any other candidate but not necessarily a majority of the total vote. Winning by plurality means that it is possible to win an election with only 30 or 40 percent of the vote. In 1992, Bill Clinton won the presidency with 43 percent of the popular vote. Plurality is often used to describe the margin of votes received by the winner over the losers. *See also* MAJORITY RULE, page 18.

Significance   Most American electoral laws for national, state, and local elections provide for winning by a plurality vote. Whenever there are more than two strong candidates running for an office, the winner usually secures a plurality rather than a majority vote. An exception is found in the runoff primary system used in several southern states whereby, if no candidate receives a majority vote, a second, runoff election is held between the two highest vote-getters. Nonpartisan primaries may also be used to reduce the number of candidates for each office to two, thereby ensuring that the winner will receive a majority vote.

Political Action Committees (PACs)   Interest groups that collect money from their members and contribute these funds to candidates and parties. Political action committees were authorized by the Federal Election Campaign Act of 1974, and corporations, labor unions, and other special-interest groups were permitted to raise and disburse funds by seeking contributions from members of their organizations. Under the 1974 law, contributions of up to $5,000 may be given to up to five candidates in a federal election, provided the money was received as contributions freely given from a minimum of 50 donors. Congress provided that each corporation or union is limited to having only one PAC, and it must operate under strict accounting rules and obey federal regulations. There are two types of PACs: the segregated fund type (not permitted to solicit funds from the public and fully accountable to the organization that created it) and the "nonconnected" political committee (raises money from the voting public and expends it in support of political candidates). *See also* CAMPAIGN, page 63; FEDERAL ELECTION CAMPAIGN ACT OF 1974, page 123.

Significance Beginning with the Committee on Political Education (COPE) in the 1940s, political action committees have developed to the point where they have revolutionized fund raising and political campaigns. Some observers fear that PACs may substantially reduce the role of political parties in campaigns because of their financial power: PAC congressional campaign spending rose from about $34 million in 1977–1978 to more than $132 million in 1985–1986, and for all political campaigns combined it was more than double these amounts. In the 1986 congressional elections, candidates spent a total of about $450 million, with nearly one-third provided by PACs. In electing a new Congress, most PAC money goes to support incumbents who have lent support to the group that has supplied them with campaign funds and, it is believed, will continue to give support. Thus far, Democratic and Republican candidates have received about equal financial support from PACs. Decisions by PACs to support candidates are generally made not on the basis of partisanship but usually in support of incumbents, with the self-interest of the donor group paramount in its decision making. In 1995, due to pressures from the citizenry, Republicans and Democrats joined in passing a lobby reform act and a ban on gifts, the first successful effort to regulate lobbying in 49 years. The act requires lobbyists to register and report who pays them, how much they are paid, and with which issues they are involved. Clients who spend less than $5,000 on lobbying in six months or organizations that spend less than $20,000 in six months are exempted from registering.

Political Activist An individual who is extensively and vigorously involved in political activity, either within or outside the party system. Political activists within the party system participate in decision making at various levels, verbalize their ideas, attend party functions, campaign, work at the polls, help collect funds, support party candidates, and carry on other forms of activity within the party framework. Political activists outside the party typically are protestors who build their interest and activity around a major issue, idea, or ideological point of view. Studies of political participation have produced operational definitions and varied categories of activist behavior. *See also* ALIENATION, page 60; NEW LEFT, page 91.

Significance New social movements are born when major issues or ideas tend to create large numbers of political activists with similar views on controversial issues and common demands for change in "the system." The decade of the 1960s saw the emergence in the United States of a vast number of protest movements comprised of individuals who had lost confidence in the party system and other institutions of peaceful change. They became politically active as a result of their search for fundamental change in the political system. Political activism is a useful component of a democratic system of government so long as it is directed toward nonviolent change. In the 1980s, increasing numbers of women and minority group members became active in politics. In the 1992 election, women, blacks, and Hispanics increased their membership in the House of Representatives, and four of the twelve newly elected members of the Senate were women. Carol Mosely Braun (D-IL) was the first black woman elected to the Senate.

Political Correctness   A term used, especially by conservatives, to attack the application of affirmative action and various forms of censorship carried on at many American colleges and universities. Liberals, conservatives charge, engage in political correctness in demanding campus rules that prohibit students from making comments considered offensive to groups such as homosexuals, African Americans, and women. Some educational institutions carry on "sensitivity training" to instill "correct" thoughts and attitudes concerning race, gender, and sexual preference.

Significance   Political correctness involves a measure of social engineering that has tended to corrupt the civil rights cause. In its most flagrant forms, it has weakened academic standards, distorted admissions policies, provided a measure of censorship, and fostered a campaign to "break the white, male, Eurocentric racist grip" on the teaching of American history. Supporters of affirmative action programs and limits on speech and teaching argue that offensive speech and written materials should be censored because they disrupt the open learning environment. Both sides—the political left and the political right—appear to many observers to be more interested in pushing their own political agenda than in improving education and protecting student rights. Future elections may be dramatically influenced by whichever group succeeds in winning the battle over political correctness on the nation's campuses.

Political Machine   A well-entrenched party organization headed by a boss or small group of autocratic leaders. Political machines usually operate at the city or county level and occasionally on a statewide basis. They may use ruthlessly efficient methods in maintaining themselves in power through such techniques as bribery, patronage, "honest" and dishonest graft, control over nominations, and the rigging of elections. Any successful political organization may, however, be dubbed a "machine" by its opponents. *See also* BOSS, page 63; WATERGATE, page 211.

Significance   Political machines have flourished throughout American history, although their number and effectiveness have been reduced in recent years. The direct primary was instituted in the early twentieth century largely as a reform to clean up politics by wresting power from political machines, but new techniques were developed by the bosses to control primaries. A high level of interest, participation, and civic spirit in an aroused community is the best answer to machine politics, but reform movements that incorporate these attributes are often short-lived in their vigor and interest, resulting in a return to power of the machine. Historically, political machines performed certain useful functions that are sometimes overlooked. These included helping to assimilate new immigrants, improving their social condition, and providing a channel through which many aggrieved groups could express their discontent and seek remedies for it.

Political Party   A group of individuals, often having some measure of ideological agreement, who organize to win elections, operate government, and determine public policy. A party differs from a pressure group mainly in its basic objective of winning control of the machinery of government, whereas a pressure group seeks to influence the actions of government. In the United States, political parties are organized on precinct, county, congressional district, state, and national levels, with most decisions made by conventions, chairmen, and committees at the county, state, and national levels. Unlike parties in most countries, power in American political parties is highly decentralized except during times of national crisis. *See also* DEMOCRATIC PARTY, page 72; MINOR PARTY, page 88; MULTIPARTY SYSTEM, page 88; REPUBLICAN PARTY, page 109; TWO-PARTY SYSTEM, page 117.

Significance   Neither of the two major American parties requires either formal membership or ideological conformity as a requirement for participation. In an authoritarian state, a single party, typically requiring rigid adherence to its ideological dogma, is used to develop policies and run the government through dual party and governmental leadership positions. In multiparty democratic states, in which each party can compete for a share of political power, individuals join the party that best promotes their economic and social interests. Political parties in the United States: (1) stimulate interest in the political process; (2) publicize political issues; (3) recruit candidates and carry on national, state, and local campaigns; (4) raise finances for political activity; (5) help maintain the honesty of elections; (6) take responsibility for operating the machinery of government or providing an organized opposition; (7) mobilize mass political power to control elite groups; (8) help to manage conflict; and (9) contribute to the building of intersectional and interclass consensuses.

Political Socialization   The process by which young people acquire views and orientations about politics and political life. Through political socialization, individuals adopt general as well as specific beliefs, feelings, attitudes, and values concerning the political system and their role in it. Socializing agents in the American political system include the family, the educational system, the mass media, religion, clubs, organizations, friends, and other elements in society to which the individual is exposed in some politically relevant way. The range of orientations that shape political views in the socialization process can be extremely broad. Then again, a single source of orientation, such as the family, may be decisive for some individuals. *See also* KEY ELECTION ISSUES, page 85; POLITICAL CORRECTNESS, page 98; VOTING BEHAVIOR, page 119.

Significance   Political scientists have devoted much time and effort in researching the political socialization process, especially as it affects voting behavior in the United States. Voting, party, and candidate support are rarely the product of careful analysis and evaluation by the individual. Generally, individuals believe and act politically in their adult lives in the same manner their social environment led them to accept during their youth. Dramatic change in political beliefs is rare but does occur. President Ronald Reagan, for example, changed from an avid Democratic liberal supporter of New Deal policies to a staunch Republican conservative. The general liberal-conservative dichotomy is believed to be largely a product of different social exposures during early years of life. Although many studies have been made of the impact of political socialization on the American political system, much remains to be done in exploring the linkages between socialization and the functioning of the political system.

Politics   The means or processes by which decision making and decision implementation are carried on within and between societies. Every social group through the activity of "politics" decides who shall receive benefits and who shall pay the costs. It is closely associated with the exercise of influence and the struggle for power that characterize every political system. Politics is usually carried on through instruments of government that provide for the authoritative or legitimate exercise of power. Political scientists have defined politics in a variety of ways, including "the art of the possible," "who gets what, when, and how," and "the competition among individuals and groups over the allocation of values or rewards." *See also* AUTHORITY, page 3; DEMOCRACY, page 9; LEGITIMACY, page 16; POWER, page 22.

Significance   In its broadest scope, politics is the means by which decisions are made and implemented in all human social units and institutions, including the family, religious groups, educational institutions, the national and local economies, and nongovernmental organizations of every kind. However defined, politics has come to be accepted as a universal phenomenon that is particularly important in making and carrying out governmental decisions and policies. Politics is an inescapable human activity if universal anarchy and chaos are to be avoided. Because of the great number and variety of demands that human beings make on each other, some means must be available to resolve conflicts. This need takes the form of politics. In the American political system, politics is shaped and influenced predominantly by the United States Constitution, especially provisions that have instituted federalism, the separation of powers, and checks and balances. In the world community, politics among nations best describes the nature of international relations.

Poll   An attempt to determine public opinion concerning issues or to forecast an election. Public opinion polling has developed from the early newspaper straw-vote poll of its subscribers to the personal interview technique, based on scientifically determined quota sampling of the voting population. Polling methods in use today involve random or probability sampling, in which representative precincts are used as barometers to indicate prevailing opinions. Poll results are checked against the actual voting records of the precincts. *See also* INDICATOR PRECINCTS, page 81; POLL SAMPLE, page 101; PUBLIC OPINION, page 106; VOTING BEHAVIOR, page 119.

Significance   The best-known polls include those conducted by George Gallup, Elmo Roper, Lou Harris, A. M. Crossley, the Survey Research Center of the University of Michigan, and the Princeton Research Service. Most polling interest is directed toward presidential elections, in which pollsters have often accurately predicted voting behavior. In the 1948 presidential election, however, polling groups failed to predict the Truman victory, resulting in considerable public skepticism of polling techniques and suspicion of pollsters' objectives. New techniques developed since 1948, including the use of electronic computers, have increased predictive accuracy. Major prediction problems still occur, however, especially if large numbers of voters remain "undecided" up to election day. The 1980 presidential election provided an example of this, with a surprising last-minute swing of millions of undecided voters to Ronald Reagan. Polls have also become increasingly useful as a means of keeping elective officials aware of public opinion on important issues and in the selection of presidential nominees by the major parties. Supporters of polling regard it as a major democratic advance, whereas opponents fear the rigging of polls to influence elections and the restrictions polls may place on policymakers.

Poll Sample   A selected representative portion of a larger population for the purpose of determining through extrapolation the views, actions, or intentions of that population. Random samples, in which each person who is a member of the population being surveyed has an equal chance of being selected for the samples, are regarded as the best scientific approach. Random sampling is used in most public-opinion polling. *See also* POLL, page 100.

Significance   Sampling errors can destroy the utility of polling results. The sample must be truly representative of the total population if it is to yield valid results. The most famous example of a biased sample ruining a poll's results occurred in 1936 when the *Literary Digest* magazine sought to discover and predict the winner of the presidential election contest between Franklin Roosevelt and Alfred Landon. A sampling of 10 million potential voters was sent opinion cards requesting that the recipient indicate whether he or she intended to vote and what was his or her preference. Only 2 million of the cards were returned, which alone made the sample suspect. Moreover, the mailing lists compiled included mainly middle- and upper-middle-class individuals, whose names were selected from automobile registrations, clubs and organizations, telephone books, and the like. Workers, lower-middle class families, and the millions of unemployed were not included in the sample for the most part. Whereas the poll indicated that Landon would win by a wide margin, in the actual election President Roosevelt was overwhelmingly reelected, winning all states but two. As a result of this polling fiasco, the *Literary Digest* disappeared from the American scene.

Populist Movement   A radical social and political philosophy and grassroots action program developed by farmers in the South, West, and Midwest. The movement resulted in the emergence in the late nineteenth century of the Populist party, which favored government ownership of the railroad, free coinage of silver, a vastly expanded supply of paper money, elimination of monopolies, and a graduated income tax. Populism as a continuing American political philosophy characterizes the role of large numbers of rural and urban poor, who seek by democratic means to use the power of government to cope with the financial giants of business, industry, and commerce. *See also* FARM BLOC, page 146; PARTICIPATORY DEMOCRACY, page 93.

Significance   The agrarian populist movement has had a radical impact over the years on political, social, and economic policies on both the state and national levels. Although the Populist party failed to displace one of the major parties in the American two-party system, its action program was largely incorporated into the Democratic party's platform in 1896, when

William Jennings Bryan won control of that party. The populist movement contributed much to the development of federal regulatory controls over the railroads, to support by the national and state governments for economic and social programs to aid farmers, and to enactment by Congress of the Sherman Act and other antitrust legislation.

Precinct   The basic unit in the United States in the election process and for party organization. Cities and counties are divided into precinct polling districts, each containing from 200 to more than 1,000 voters and a polling place. In political organizations, each party usually elects or appoints a precinct captain or committeeman who functions as a party leader within the precinct. Precinct leaders in the cities may represent their precincts in party ward committees. The precinct also serves for the election or appointment of delegates to city or county party conventions. *See also* INDICATOR PRECINCTS, page 81.

Significance   The precinct, as a small voting district, provides easy access to the polls. The precinct organization of the parties is the key to election success, especially in the metropolitan areas. An effective precinct leader is expected to work tirelessly the year round gaining party converts, getting voters registered, carrying on routine party business, and, most significant for his or her political future, turning out large majorities for the party on election days.

Presidential Election Process   The procedures by which the American people select their president. The presidential election process involves two races: the first, in which the aspirants seek to obtain their party's nomination, and the second, in which the nominees of the two major and several minor parties contest. The climax of the aspirant's race for nomination takes place in the summer of the presidential election year at his party's national nominating convention. This convention is composed of delegates chosen in some states by conventions or committees and in most by the voters in presidential primaries. Following the conventions, the autumn campaign between the major party candidates begins in earnest. In the national election, held on the first Tuesday after the first Monday in November, the voters in the 50 states and the District of Columbia cast ballots for their choice for president, although in fact they are legally electing only members of the Electoral College. The electors meet in their respective state capitals in December and cast their ballots for president. In early January, a joint session of Congress opens the Electoral College ballots and certifies the winners, who are subsequently sworn into office on January 20. In brief, here is a major party candidate's typical schedule in a presidential election year: *late winter or earlier,* announce candidacy; *spring,* campaign vigorously in key contests, particularly in Iowa (the first caucus) and in New Hampshire (the first primary) and in several pivotal states; *early summer,* continue primary races while striving to win delegates at party caucuses in nonprimary states; *late summer,* marshal all possible party strength for final drive to obtain nomination at party's national nominating convention; *early autumn,* resume campaigning with increasing tempo and a broader focus to attract votes from independents and rival party members as well as from members of candidate's own party; *late fall,* build campaign to a climax, with major speeches and saturation of television and radio with partisan propaganda; *postelection period,* congratulate opponent and go into seclusion or, if victorious, prepare to take over the reins of power in January. *See also* ELECTORAL COLLEGE, page 74; PIVOTAL STATES, page 95, PRESIDENTIAL PRIMARIES, page 103.

Significance The presidential election process is basically a peaceful struggle for political power waged by the "outs" in their effort to defeat the "ins" and take over operation of the government. The process, described by some pundits as "that quadrennial madness," is often replete with ballyhoo, appeals to the voters' emotions, and a carnival-like atmosphere. Millions of dollars have been spent by each major presidential candidate on television programming alone. Over the years, the presidential election process has produced several great presidents, but it also has resulted in the election of some inferior presidents. Some critics point out that the process has often resulted in a "Hobson's choice" for the voter—that is, no real choice because both major candidates are undesirable. While most presidential elections merely continue the prevailing partisan political situation (*maintaining* elections), they may, as the result of some unusual event or candidate, lead to the defeat of the majority party (*deviating* elections), as in the case of Dwight D. Eisenhower's, Richard M. Nixon's, and Ronald Reagan's elections. Such an upset often leads to a recapturing of the presidency by the dominant party after the event or personality that led to the disruption leaves the scene (*reinstating* elections). By contrast, an event may be so dramatic or catastrophic that large numbers of voters change their party identifications (*realigning* elections), as in the struggle over slavery and in the Great Depression, with the result that a new dominant party emerges.

Presidential Primaries The process of electing delegates to a party's national presidential nominating convention. Most of the states and the District of Columbia hold some form of presidential primary in the weeks or months preceding the conventions; delegates are selected in the other states by political party caucuses, conventions, or committees with Iowa being the traditional leader by virtue of its early February caucus. Republican party primaries differ from Democratic ones in that the former are generally based on the winner-take-all principle, whereas the Democrats split the delegates largely on the basis of votes received by each presidential candidate. Delegates selected in the primaries may or may not be "pledged" to vote for a presidential aspirant. In a few states, delegates are selected by the party organization and are bound to support the candidate designated by the voters in a so-called popularity contest. Although each state can determine when and how delegates are chosen, during the past three presidential elections a block of predominantly Southern states — including two major delegate-selection states, Texas and Florida — have participated in a "Super Tuesday" in March. During this multiple-state primary, a large portion of the delegates to each party's presidential nominating convention are selected on the same day. Twenty states participated in 1988, eleven in 1992, and only seven in 1996. In 1996, 30 states had their primaries or caucuses by the end of March and selected 70 percent of the national convention delegates. In addition to those delegates elected in primaries or selected by caucuses or conferences, so-called "Super Delegates" are entitled to become delegates to their party's nominating convention by virtue of their position in government or in the party hierarchy. *See also* DIRECT PRIMARY, page 72; NATIONAL CONVENTION, page 89.

Significance   The presidential primary was pioneered by Wisconsin in 1905. By 1916, both parties selected a majority of their national convention delegates by this method. Then it lost considerable ground, but more recently it has regained much of it. Today, about 40 states hold presidential primaries, with over half of the national convention delegates elected in these primaries. The main controversy surrounding the presidential primary concerns the "preferential" problem—that is, should pledged or unpledged delegates be elected. Popular influence is reduced because pledged delegates are under no legal—and little moral—obligation to honor such pledges beyond the first ballot and because many are elected as unpledged delegates. As a result, the presidential primary has not always been of great significance in choosing presidential nominees. In 1952, for example, Estes Kefauver won most of the delegates in the preferential primary states but was not selected for the presidential nomination by the Democratic convention; Adlai Stevenson, conversely, did not enter any presidential primaries and yet won the Democratic nomination. Presidential primaries, however, are gaining in significance by eliminating those who lack vote-getting ability, building the stature of those who demonstrate widespread popular support, and discouraging incumbent presidents from running for reelection. Presidents Harry S. Truman and Lyndon B. Johnson, for example, announced their decisions not to seek reelection in 1952 and 1968, respectively, shortly after the New Hampshire primary demonstrated lack of party support. Conversely, when John F. Kennedy won the Democratic primary in heavily Protestant West Virginia, he overcame the long-held belief that Catholicism was an insurmountable barrier to the presidency. The "power of the primaries" was most forcefully demonstrated in 1976, when Jimmy Carter gained the Democratic party's nomination despite opposition from many party regulars. Supporters of preferential primaries argue that they prevent bosses from dominating conventions, build interest for the presidential election, and expand democratic influence. Those who oppose them point out that they are not decisive because voter opinion often is split in many directions, that they prolong the presidential election spectacle until voters get weary, and that only a convention free from voter pledges can reconcile party differences and unite the party behind a candidate. Although popular demands have increased in recent years for a nationwide preferential primary system, most professional politicians believe such a system would be too costly in money, energy, and confusion.

Pressure Group   An organized interest group in which members share common views and objectives and actively carry on programs to influence government officials and policies. Unlike political parties, which seek to win control of and operate the government, pressure groups are mainly interested in influencing the determination of public policies that directly or indirectly affect their members. Such groups vary considerably in size, wealth, power, and objectives. Their methods, however, are quite similar and include lobbying, electioneering, and propagandizing to influence public opinion. Pressure groups seek to influence decisions in the legislative, executive, and judicial branches. *See also* BUSINESS AND PROFESSIONAL ORGANIZATIONS, page 433; CIVIL RIGHTS ORGANIZATIONS, page 300; COUNTERVAILING THEORY OF PRESSURE POLITICS, page 70, FARM ORGANIZATIONS, page 484; LABOR UNIONS, page 445; LOBBYIST, page 86; VETERANS ORGANIZATIONS, page 514.

Significance In America's pluralistic society, groups rather than individuals exercise most political influence. The most powerful interest groups are those that have emerged out of the three basic economic areas: agriculture, business, and labor. Other significant groupings that carry on pressure activities include professional societies, women's groups, patriotic and veterans' organizations, and religious and racial groups. Pressure-group efforts are directed toward an identification of their particular interests with the general interest. The countervailing theory of pressure politics holds that the major interest groups, powerful as they may be, tend to counteract and balance each other's power, which keeps any one from exercising a dominant influence. Many critics have disputed this theory, with conservatives typically charging labor dominance, and liberals attributing a decisive role to business and industry. Congress in 1946 sought to regulate the lobbying activities of pressure groups through the Federal Regulation of Lobbying Act. The Act is largely concerned with publicizing lobbying groups and their activities, but its vague and confusing language and the absence of an enforcement agency have encouraged much noncompliance. The enactment of stiffer laws involving extensive regulation of pressure groups and their activities would likely involve serious questions of constitutionality concerning basic rights of assembly and petition. Some of the more effective pressure groups involved in direct political action have included the Moral Majority, a large organization of conservative evangelical Christians, and the National Conservative Political Action Committee (NCPAC), both of which played a role in Ronald Reagan's election. Perhaps the most successful pressure group over the years has been the National Rifle Association (NRA), which had until 1994 prevented any meaningful federal gun control laws from being passed, despite strong public support for such legislation. In that year Congress passed the long-debated Brady gun control bill, which imposed a five-day waiting period for handgun purchases so that officials can check on the buyers' credentials.

Propaganda Communication aimed at influencing the thinking, emotions, or actions of a group or public. The use of propaganda assumes that changes in people's thinking will prompt changes in their actions. Propaganda is not necessarily true or false; it is based on a careful selection and manipulation of data. *See also* MASS MEDIA, page 87; PUBLIC OPINION, page 106; UNITED STATES INFORMATION AGENCY, page 598.

Significance The development of mass media has encouraged the use of propaganda to influence governmental decisions indirectly through public opinion. Government also uses propaganda to cultivate support for its programs and policies and to answer criticisms. Propaganda techniques include the use of simple slogans, the identification of propaganda with local situations, the "straight news" approach, the distortion of facts, appeals to idealism, and the "big lie" technique of Adolf Hitler. As a rule, successful mass propaganda must be simple, interesting, credible, consistent, and supported by actual events or experiences. Democracies are characterized by a variety of competing propagandists and their propaganda; dictatorships are maintained by government monopoly of propaganda. Typically, propaganda differs from education in that the latter involves critical judgments and the making of choices, whereas propaganda is aimed at persuasion through propagation. Major American propaganda efforts have been carried on in the world by the Voice of America (VOA), by Radio Marti directed at Cuba, by Radio Free Europe aimed at the peoples of Eastern Europe, and by Radio Liberty, which broadcast to the Soviet Union. With the collapse of the Soviet Union and the end of the Cold War, Radio Liberty operations have been curtailed. With the apparent ending of the Cold War, the future role of these propaganda organizations remains problematical, as do their financing and operational objectives.

Proportional Representation (PR)   An electoral system that allocates seats in the legislative body to each party or group approximately equal to its popular voting strength. Under a system of proportional representation, for example, a number of legislators may be elected from the same district by the same voters. A minority party that receives 5 percent of the total vote in that election will win about 5 percent of the legislative seats. The most commonly used systems of PR are the list system, based on voting by party, and the Hare system, based on voting for individuals using the single transferable vote. *See also* CUMULATIVE VOTING, page 71; MULTIPARTY SYSTEM, page 88.

Significance   Several American cities, including New York, have experimented with the Hare system to provide some measure of minority representation. Most democratic countries use the continental European PR multimember district list system in preference to the Anglo-American, single-member district system. Proponents of PR point out that it provides representation for minority parties, reduces or eliminates machine politics, and is more democratic. Opponents argue that PR tends to proliferate parties, is too complicated for the average voter, and inevitably results in unstable coalition governments. In recent years, the Democratic party has used a system of proportional representation to increase the participation of women and minority groups as delegates to the party's national convention.

Public Opinion   An aggregate of individual views, attitudes, or beliefs shared by a portion of a community. No single public opinion in the sense of a general will exists; rather, a number of publics hold various opinions on a host of issues. Public opinion can be made known in a democracy through elections, referendums, lobbying and pressure group activities, polls, and by elected representatives who "sound out" grass-roots sentiment. Essentially, public opinion consists of those opinions held by private persons and groups that government finds it prudent to heed. *See also* MASS MEDIA, page 87; POLL, page 100; POLL SAMPLE, page 101.

Significance   A common problem of democracies involves the question of how responsive to public opinion elected representatives should be. Should they, for example, exercise their own best judgment in voting on issues, or should they follow the public opinion positions of their constituents? If the latter, there remain the difficult problems of how to determine the existence of public opinion and how to measure it. Opinion research reveals the existence of a small "attentive public," with the mass public unaware of most issues. Although public opinion is a vague concept, political leaders recognize its significance in the political process and seek to shape it in support of their major policies. Public opinion functions as a *supportive* factor when the general public tends to bolster governmental policies and programs, in a *directive* capacity when it offers cues to political leaders, and as a *permissive* factor when it establishes toleration limits for policy alternatives.

Public Policy Models   Theoretical efforts to explain how public policy is made—or should be made—in the American system of government. Public policy models include: (1) the power elite model, which posits that all important decisions in the American system are made by a small group of upper-class or establishment persons who, along with their lackeys, run the private and public sectors; (2) the pluralist model, which holds that policy is the product of group conflict and that the public interest tends to emerge out of the welter of competing individual and group claims; (3) the participatory democracy (or mass mobilization) model, which prescribes a changeover to a system wherein the entire citizenry participates directly in the policy process; (4) the Marxist model, which claims that every political system is controlled by the dominant economic class that uses the system to maximize its own interest; (5) the Weberian or bureaucratic model, which holds that all of society's institutions are under the control of large bureaucracies whose expertise is essential in problem solving; and (6) the traditional or liberal democratic model, which accepts the basic principles of democracy, such as representation, majority rule, and the rule of law, as the means by which the system functions. *See also* ELITE, page 75; PARTICIPATORY DEMOCRACY, page 93; PLURALISM, page 95.

Significance   Political scientists have disagreed over which of the public policy models most accurately describes the decision processes of the American political system and which is to be prescribed as the most cogent. Many observers have concluded that no one model describes the many-faceted system and that all contribute to an understanding of its functioning. Public policy models are aimed at answering basic political questions, such as who governs, who gets what, when, why, and how, and who pays the bill.

Recall   A procedure enabling voters to remove an elected official from office before his or her term has expired. The required number of valid signatures on petitions (typically 25 percent of voters in the last election) results in the calling of a special election. If the majority of voters favors recall, the official is replaced by a successor who is either chosen on the recall ballot or in a subsequent election. Several states and numerous local units of government provide for the recall of elected officials. Fourteen state constitutions provide for the recall of state officials, and many others apply the procedure to local officials. *See also* ACCOUNTABILITY, page 1; DIRECT DEMOCRACY, page 11.

Significance   The recall enables the voters to hold their public officials continuously responsible. It is used infrequently, but the threat of recall is ever-present and does not go unnoticed by elected officials. No provision is made for the recall of federal officials, but each house of Congress has the power to remove any member who fails to meet the qualifications it requires of its members, and the president and vice president are subject to impeachment action. The recall, along with the initiative and referendum, constitute the basic instruments of direct democracy. Use of the recall does not require charges of illegal actions; voters may merely be dissatisfied with the elected official's performance in office. In 1984, the effectiveness of recall was demonstrated in Michigan, where voters, stung by a large tax increase, successfully recalled several legislators and changed party control of the state senate as a result. Ordinarily, voter turnout in a recall election is small.

Registration　Enrolling prospective voters prior to their participation in elections. Under a system of *permanent* registration, the voter, once qualified, remains on the eligible list until he or she dies, moves, or fails to vote in several consecutive elections. *Periodic* registration requires that the voter enroll at the appropriate local office annually or at fixed intervals. Almost all states now use some form of permanent registration. *See also* VOTING QUALIFICATIONS, page 119.

Significance　Registration permits the orderly enforcement of voting qualifications and helps to maintain the honesty of elections. Permanent registration is more economical and less bothersome to voters than periodic, but it involves the problem of keeping voting lists up-to-date by enrolling new voters and deleting those who die, move, or are otherwise disqualified. Partisan or apathetic administration of these functions can result in fraudulent voting. Under periodic registration, lists are kept relatively up-to-date, and vote frauds are discouraged. Periodic registration is most useful in large cities where the mobility of population is high. Under the Voting Rights Act, federal registrars have enrolled blacks in southern communities where racial discrimination had foreclosed their registration for many years. Registration has been facilitated by the 1993 National Voter Registration Act, known as the Motor Voter bill, which permits people to register to vote when obtaining a driving permit or license. It also allows registration at welfare and disability agencies, at military recruitment offices, and by mail. The first year resulted in a record 11.2 million people registering to vote or updating their registration, including 5.7 million at drivers' license bureaus, 1.3 million at public assistance agencies, and 2 million by mail. For the 1996 presidential election, there will be an estimated 154 million registered voters.

Religious Right　Ultraconservative religious groups that seek to bring about major changes in the American political system. The religious right has greatly expanded its political role by creating the Christian Coalition, consisting of many diverse groups, thereby producing a major impact on the political process at all levels from electing a president to the local school board. The religious right has also expanded into the world of business. These Christian capitalists who blend commerce, religion, and politics are mostly managers, professionals, and small-business owners. *See also* REPUBLICAN REVOLUTION, page 109.

Significance　The religious right has created a coalition to expand its power and influence on American elections. It was organized by Pat Robertson, with Ralph Reed as director and spokesperson. It began in 1989 with 1,000 members and has since expanded to an estimated 2 million. It has been a major player in the elections of the 1990s, providing the Republican party with money, votes, and workers in the political vineyard. Its membership consists mainly of Protestant evangelicals, with efforts being made to bring in other Christians, including Roman Catholics. The Christian Coalition has strongly supported the Republican party's Contract with America. It has supplemented it with its own campaign position, known as the "Contract with the American Family," which stresses parental rights, prayer in schools, and opposition to abortion. Some moderate Republicans are concerned about this program and its divisive nature. They fear that core issues, such as balancing the budget and reducing unemployment, may be relegated to a secondary position in the political battles that lie ahead. This situation may have the effect of encouraging a third party independent movement.

Republican Party   A major American party, often called the GOP or Grand Old Party, that emerged in the 1850s as an antislavery party. The Republican party is the successor to two earlier major parties—the Federalists and the Whigs. It became firmly established in American politics when its candidate, Abraham Lincoln, won the presidency in 1860 and successfully prosecuted the Civil War. The period from 1860 to 1932 was characterized largely by Republican dominance of the American political scene. Then, starting with Franklin Roosevelt's election in 1932, the Democrats dominated the presidency for twenty years, followed by another Republican era which included the elections of Dwight Eisenhower, Richard Nixon, Ronald Reagan, and George Bush. *See also* DEMOCRATIC PARTY, page 72; HAMILTONIANISM, PAGE 13; MADISONIANISM, page 18.

Significance   Studies have shown that Republican support among voters tends to increase as their income, property-owning, and educational levels rise. Traditionally, manufacturing, business, financial, and farming interests have been influential in the party. The Republican party has historically advocated individual initiative, free enterprise, fiscal responsibility in the form of a balanced federal budget, and sound-money policies. Its policies have generally been more conservative than Democratic party policies, although both include a coalition of conservatives, moderates, and liberals. Ideologically based groups that have recently functioned in Congress with the Republican party include the relatively conservative Wednesday Club and the relatively liberal Gypsy Moths. Historically, Republicans have favored a high protective tariff and isolationism, although in recent years the party has supported lower tariffs and various American international commitments. It has generally opposed the ideas of the welfare state and big government. Republicans generally have favored military interventions to cope with the threat of communism in the Third World, as, for example, in the 1983 invasion of the island of Grenada, and when a threat to our national interest becomes apparent, as in the 1991 Persian Gulf War. In 1995, the Republican-controlled Congress lent some support to President Bill Clinton's sending of troops as part of the NATO implementation force (IFOR) in Bosnia.

Republican Revolution   A major electoral victory in the Congressional election of 1994 that placed legislative power in the hands of the Republicans in both houses of Congress. The vast changes anticipated by the leadership in the House will, if successful, dramatically change the relationship between the government and the American people. It has followed a three-step process: (1) the formation of a comprehensive legislative program (Contract with America), (2) a successful 1994 election campaign that resulted in the Republican party gaining control of both the House and the Senate, and (3) the formal process of bringing the contract to fruition through adoption of a series of legislative bills. *See also* CONTRACT WITH AMERICA, page 67.

Significance   The Republican Revolution was largely a product of widespread disillusionment with both major parties. The new speaker of the House of Representatives, Newt Gingrich, orchestrated the 1994 GOP sweep and wrote the scenario for 1995. With the leadership of the Speaker and the dedication and zeal of the 73 members of the Republican freshman class, the "Revolution" achieved the prescribed goals during the first 100 days of the 104th Congress. The Revolution has slowed because a cautious Senate has been pitted against a zealous House, because an energetic Democratic president has cultivated his own program and threatened extensive use of his veto power, and because of some measure of disarray within the Republican party, itself. The dynamism of the 1995 Revolution, however, gave way to the realism of 1996 and the gridlock it produced in trying to secure agreement on balancing the budget. The future of the Republican Revolution will depend on the voters' decisions in the 1996 elections.

Residence   A qualification for voting based on domicile. Such laws require that a person live in the state for a specified period of time, commonly one year, and within a county and a voting precinct, typically 90 days for the former and 30 days for the latter. In 1972, the Supreme Court declared invalid lengthy state (one year) and local (90 days) residence requirements and suggested 30 days as sufficient (*Dunn v. Blumstein,* 405 U.S. 330). In the Voting Rights Act of 1970, Congress provided that 30 days' residence in any state would qualify citizens to vote in presidential elections. *See also* DISFRANCHISE, page 73; RESIDENT, page 623; VOTING QUALIFICATIONS, page 119.

Significance   Residence requirements are intended to prevent the importing of "floaters" to win elections and to ensure that the individual is acquainted with state and local problems and candidates before becoming eligible. The qualification, however, disfranchises temporarily several million voters in each major election as a result of the increasing mobility of the American people. This mobility led the Supreme Court in 1972 to find lengthy residence requirements for voting an interference with the right to travel and change domicile. Congress has also considered legislation that would eliminate residence requirements in all national elections. Residence also refers to the fact that American candidates are residents of the districts or states in which they run for election, unlike many other countries, such as Britain, where no residence requirement exists either in law or practice.

Responsible Party System   A democratic political system in which parties accept full accountability to the voters in developing policy and operating the government. A responsible party requires internal discipline, so that its members give support to its objectives and platform promises. Following an election, the real test of responsibility is whether the majority party can redeem its pledges to the voters. *See also* CONTRACT WITH AMERICA, page 67; MANDATE, page 87.

Significance   American political parties are fundamentally irresponsible in that they are highly decentralized and lack ideological cohesion. Moreover, separation of powers, federalism, and sectionalism provide a political milieu not conducive to the growth of responsibility. In contrast, British parties are hierarchically structured, are disciplined through the party-whip system, and therefore can turn party promises into government policies. Critics of American parties have suggested a realignment of party wings into a new conservative-liberal two-party system so that both could function more responsibly. Reapportionment of American legislative bodies has helped to overcome the divisive impact of the separation of powers on party responsibility. Recent studies indicate that both major parties have increasingly acted more responsibly in implementing their platform pledges after winning elections except in budget-balancing and debt reduction matters. In 1992, disclosures of great irresponsibility of both Democratic and Republican members of the House in personal banking matters involving thousands of no-fund checks led to public castigation and, for some, defeat in subsequent elections.

Runoff Primary   A nominating system used in a number of southern states (ten in 1991), in which a second primary election is held between the top candidates if no candidate in the first primary polls a majority vote. *See also* DIRECT PRIMARY, page 72; PLURALITY, page 96.

Significance   The runoff primary is particularly advantageous in one-party states, where winning the primary is tantamount to election. It guarantees that the nominee will have the majority support of the voters rather than a mere plurality when three or more candidates are in the running. It also gives supporters of losing candidates in the first primary a chance to coalesce their support in the runoff or second primary. Some critics of the runoff primary claim that it is used to weaken the chances of black candidates who might win a plurality in the first primary and then lose in the runoff.

Sectionalism   The influence of local or regional loyalties on state or national elections, issues, or party unity. Sectionalism contributes to the heterogeneity that typifies democratic pluralism. *See also* PLURALISM, page 95.

Significance   Traditionally, national unity has been seriously challenged by sectional cleavage on such vital issues as slavery, civil rights, "free silver," and the tariff. Most deep-rooted sectional loyalties of the early American period have given way, in the course of a century and a half, to nationalizing and unifying forces. The position of the South on civil rights issues, for example, is today not substantially different from that of other sections of the country.

Short Ballot   A ballot containing relatively few offices to be filled by election. It is differentiated from the long ballot, which contains numerous elective offices, especially in the executive and judicial branches. Several states, such as New Jersey and Alaska, have reduced the number of statewide elected executive officials to governor and lieutenant governor and have considerably cut down the number of judicial elections. The national election ballot is already a "short" one, providing for the casting of a single vote for president and vice president, the election of a single representative, and in two of three elections, of a senator. The longest ballots, typically, are found on the local government level, especially in the county. *See also* BALLOT, 62; LONG BALLOT, page 86.

Significance   During the era of Jacksonian Democracy, the view that "the more numerous the elective offices, the more democratic the system" gained widespread acceptance. In the twentieth century, the short-ballot movement was established to try to reverse this situation. Advocates of the short ballot have called for patterning the state, county, and municipal ballots after the national, by providing for the election of legislators and one or two executive officials, with other executives and judges to be appointed. Underscoring the short-ballot movement is a belief that not only do shorter ballots simplify elections but also they make them more democratic by securing larger and more intelligent voter participation. Opponents adhere to the older doctrines that democracy thrives on numerous elections and that responsibility of officeholders can be secured only with a long ballot.

Single-member District   An electoral district from which a single legislator is chosen, usually by a plurality vote. The single-member district voting system is used in the United States, Britain, and many former British colonies. It differs from the multimember districts typical of most continental European electoral systems based on proportional representation and from at-large districts in the United States. France also uses a single-member district system, but a candidate can win only with a *majority* vote either in the initial election or in a subsequent runoff between the two highest vote-getters. *See also* TWO-PARTY SYSTEM, page 117.

Significance   The single-member district system with a single plurality ballot is one of the factors that contributes to maintaining a two-party system because elections are based on the principle of "winner take all." Minor parties as a result are usually unable to win any share of political power and become parties of principle. Some American states depart from the single-member district system in holding elections for one house of the legislature, and many cities have instituted multimember systems with at-large elections. Other than these exceptions, American elections are based on single-member districts. Supporters of the single-member district principle argue that it avoids confusion, helps guarantee a majority party, and avoids the pitfalls of government by coalition. Those who oppose it point out that the votes of defeated parties and candidates are wasted, that the principle distorts the final election results, and that it fosters a false majority that does not democratically reflect voter sentiment.

Split Ticket   Voting for candidates of two or more parties for different offices. Split-ticket voting is not permitted in primaries. *See also* OFFICE-BLOCK BALLOT, page 93; STRAIGHT TICKET, page 113.

Significance   Split-ticket voting is encouraged by the "office-block" ballot, which emphasizes individual choice for each office rather than straight-ticket party voting. Some observers regard split-ticket "voting for the best candidate, not the party" as the most desirable approach to politics. Others oppose it on the grounds that the voter can too easily be fooled by personality and glibness, that issues rather than individuals are most important, and that it tends to weaken party and government responsibility. A frequent result of split-ticket voting is a government in which different parties control the executive and the legislature and in which deadlocks and stalemates are common, with the voters unable to fix responsibility for action or inaction. Studies show that America voters tend to engage in split-ticket voting more often than straight-ticket voting.

Stalking Horse   A candidate for public office, especially for the presidency, whose only role is to function as a cover or decoy on behalf of a stronger but unannounced candidate. The term "stalking horse" comes from the Great Plains states where hunters once used their horses as cover, due to lack of foliage and other natural cover, to move in for a close-range shot at bison or other game. Unlike a favorite son candidate, a stalking horse tries to convey the appearance of being a serious candidate so that his or her impact on the voters can be accurately assessed, and the base prepared for the subsequent candidacy of the party leader for whom the stalking horse has fronted. Nevertheless, favorite son candidates may also function in the capacity of stalking horses. *See also* PRESIDENTIAL ELECTION PROCESS, page 102.

Significance   The stalking horse technique relates especially to the hectic preconvention period of intraparty rivalry among prospective candidates for the presidential nomination. Candidates often accuse each other of being a stalking horse for another as a means of challenging each other's credibility as a serious contender. The main objectives of a stalking horse are to test voter support or to try to divide the opposition. A stalking horse might, for example, want to test voter reaction to a candidacy from a particular wing of the party or the extent of grass-roots support for a candidate who takes a stand on a major controversial issue. Widespread public opinion polling has substantially reduced the role of stalking horses in presidential nomination contests.

State Central Committee   The principal committee of a political party within a state. State central committees are composed of members representing congressional districts, state legislative districts, or counties. *See also* POLITICAL PARTY, page 98.

Significance   The state central committee has responsibility for carrying out policy decisions of the party's state convention. During political campaigns the committee makes decisions concerning strategy and the use of party campaign funds. It also may give direction to the party's state chairman but, typically, has little influence with the party's state legislators or executive officials after they are elected.

Straight Ticket   Voting for all candidates of a single party for all offices. *See also* COATTAIL EFFECT, page 66; PARTY-COLUMN BALLOT, page 94; SPLIT TICKET, page 112.

Significance   Straight-ticket party voting is encouraged by the use of "party-column" ballots, which require the marking of a single "X" or the pulling of a single lever to vote for all party candidates for all offices. Straight-ticket voting is also encouraged by the "coattail effect," when a popular presidential or gubernatorial candidate heads the party's ticket. Some observers prefer straight-ticket voting because it reduces the impact of personality, places major emphasis on issues, and promotes party and government responsibility. The case against straight-ticket voting is based on the assumption that intelligent voters should "vote for the person, not the party," that a split ticket encourages the exercise of judgment by the voter, and that an individual can more directly influence policy by voting for a liberal or a conservative, regardless of party affiliation.

Term Limitation   An approach aimed at decreasing the number of career, professional politicians in office by limiting the number of terms of reelection. The current campaign of the 1990s has sought to limit the terms of elective offices in the state and federal elections. By 1995, 23 states had established term limits for their congressional representatives. *See also* CONTRACT WITH AMERICA, page 67; TWENTY-SECOND AMENDMENT, page 209.

Significance   The first elective office affected by term limitation was that of the president, who was limited to two elective terms in 1951 by the adoption of the Twenty-second Amendment to the Constitution of the United States. Term limitation to establish a citizen legislature was part of the Republican Contract with America but became the only feature of the contract rejected by the members of the House. Supporters say term limits will oust career politicians who have lost touch with their constituents. Opponents say it denigrates the value of experience by eliminating the small corps of experienced legislators who provide the institutional memory; it would increase the power of bureaucrats, staffers, and lobbyists; and it would deprive voters of their democratic right to choose the person they want to represent them. In a decision rendered in 1995, the Supreme Court rejected term limitation for Congress and held that the decision involved a critical question concerning the workings of our federal system of government and was inconsistent with the framers' vision. A consitutional amendment is the only way this can be accomplished (*U.S. Term Limits v. Thorton,* 115 S. Ct. 1842). It forecloses any attempt in Congress to impose limits by enacting a statute. Term limitation seems to have secured voter support. Since 1990, 21 states have limited the terms of their state legislators, 40 states have gubernatorial term limits (19 since 1990), and approximately 3,000 cities have enacted term limits on municipal offices. However, voting remains the most effective method of limiting terms by voting the incumbent out of office.

Third Party   A new party, usually comprised of independents and dissidents from the major parties in a two-party system, that typically is based on a protest movement and that may rally sufficient voter support to affect the outcome of a state or national election. A third party may be distinguished from a *minor* party, an ideological or doctrinaire party that seldom affects a specific election outcome. The objective of American third parties may be to encourage a large protest vote or to seek to prevent either major party candidate from winning a majority of electoral votes, so that the election of the President would be thrown into the House of Representatives. Third parties are also known as *splinter* or *secessionist* parties because they are composed largely of adherents who have broken away from one or both major parties. *See also* MINOR PARTY, page 88.

Significance   Third parties have played an important role in American politics by influencing the adoption of reforms and by keeping the major parties from becoming too similar in their approach to issues, or too indifferent. When a political, economic, or social consensus breaks down, third-party movements have their best opportunity to affect the outcome of an election. For example, in 1856 the Republican party was a third party that took the initiative away from the Whig party with a forthright antislavery program and replaced it as a major party. Another significant third-party movement was Theodore Roosevelt's "Bull Moose" party, which split the Republican vote and enabled Woodrow Wilson to win in 1912. The Dixiecrat party in 1948 was a sectional third party that failed to change the election outcome because of a lack of sympathy outside the Deep South for its protest position. It did, however, win 38 electoral college votes from four states. Recent third-party movements include that headed by John Anderson, who broke away from the Republican party to run as an independent third-party candidate in 1980, and received 7 percent of the votes cast. Ross Perot, who ran as an independent in 1992, received 19 percent of the popular vote, the highest proportion for an independent third party candidate since 1912. In September of 1995, Ross Perot announced that he would form a Reform party to back any presidential candidate willing to address the concerns of the Reform party, which were set forth in the United We Stand America movement. Speculation remains that Perot himself may be the presidential candidate of the party.

Trade-off   The price an individual or a group must pay to gain political support for a desired policy or program. Trade-offs in domestic politics resemble international bargaining tactics based on quid pro quo (something for something). In each case, domestic and foreign, the compromises engendered by trade-offs are essential to reaching agreement. The general public, however, often tends to equate trade-off with "sell-out" or appeasement. *See also* LOGROLLING, page 156; QUID PRO QUO, page 574.

Significance   Almost all political decisions involve trade-offs because all efforts to solve social, economic, and political problems tend to produce political issues. An issue can be defined as a problem over which reasonable people (and sometimes unreasonable ones) can disagree. Party leaders, government officials, and ordinary citizens may play the role of "political broker" in working out solutions to political issues through trade-off bargaining. This role is a critical one, for example, when a president tries to bring inflation under control by negotiating an agreement on budget cuts among various groups that will be adversely affected. In the American system, most decisions involve trade-off bargaining, such as that carried on in congressional conference committees.

Twelfth Amendment   An amendment to the Constitution, adopted in 1804, that provides for separate ballots to be used by the electors in voting for president and vice president. Previously, the vice presidency went to the runner-up in the Electoral College vote. The Amendment also reduces the range of choice of the House of Representatives from the five highest to the three highest candidates when none has received an electoral vote majority. The Senate's choice of vice president under these circumstances is limited to the two highest candidates. *See also* ELECTORAL COLLEGE, page 74.

Significance   The Twelfth Amendment developed out of the confusion in the election of 1800, in which party-pledged electors were chosen for the first time. Since each elector voted for two candidates, the result found Thomas Jefferson, the presidential candidate, tied with his own vice presidential candidate, Aaron Burr. The election was thrown into the House, where the lame-duck Federalist party majority finally elected Jefferson president after toying with the idea of electing Burr to embarrass the Jeffersonian Republican party. To avoid such confusion in subsequent elections, the Twelfth Amendment specified that electors "name in their ballots the person voted for as President, and in distinct ballots the person voted for as Vice President." The Amendment adapted the Electoral College to the new political party system, which had not been anticipated by the Founding Fathers.

Twenty-fourth Amendment   An amendment to the Constitution, adopted in 1964, that forbids the levying of a poll tax in primary and general elections for national officials, including the president, vice president, and members of Congress. Although the Amendment does not apply to elections for state or local officials, the Supreme Court in 1966 declared that the levying of a poll tax for *any* election is unconstitutional (*Harper v. Virginia State Board of Elections,* 383 U.S. 663). *See also* VOTING QUALIFICATIONS, page 119.

Significance   At the time of the ratification of the Twenty-fourth Amendment, only five states levied poll taxes, and the Amendment was generally viewed as an attempt to placate growing black demands for voting rights. Failure to outlaw poll taxes in state and local elections made the Amendment largely ineffective, with the result that Congress, in the 1965 Voting Rights Act, authorized a legal test of all poll taxes, which led to the *Harper* decision.

Twenty-sixth Amendment   An amendment to the Constitution, adopted in 1971, that lowers the legal voting age to eighteen in the United States. Although eighteen-year-olds had already been accorded the vote in national elections by the Voting Rights Act of 1970, the Twenty-sixth Amendment assured them the vote in *all*—national, state, and local—elections. The amendment proposal was ratified by the necessary 38 state legislatures in record time during 1971 so that the measure could take effect for the 1972 presidential election. Voting opportunities were increased by the Amendment at the time of its adoption for an estimated 11 million young people. *See also* VOTING QUALIFICATIONS, page 119; VOTING RIGHTS ACT, page 124.

Significance   The Twenty-sixth Amendment accomplished what Congress had unsuccessfully attempted to do by statute. In the Voting Rights Act of 1970, Congress lowered the legal voting age to eighteen in all elections, but the Supreme Court ruled subsequently in *Oregon v. Mitchell,* 400 U.S. 112 (1970), that Congress had the constitutional power to lower the voting age requirements for national but not for state and local elections. The Twenty-sixth Amendment resulted from that decision. Two factors that encouraged early ratification of the Amendment were the prospective increases in state expenses for maintaining separate registration systems and ballots for national and state elections, and the political backing given to the measure by the Democratic party, whose members anticipated substantial support from the younger voters. Opponents of the Amendment pointed out that the voters in many states had earlier rejected referendums aimed at extending the vote to eighteen-year-olds. The impact of the Twenty-sixth Amendment has been moderate because only a small percentage of young people turn out to vote.

Twenty-third Amendment   An amendment to the Constitution, adopted in 1961, that enables the people of the District of Columbia to participate in the election of the President. The Twenty-third Amendment allots the District of Columbia three electoral votes. *See also* DISTRICT OF COLUMBIA, page 38.

Significance   The Twenty-third Amendment increased the size of the Electoral College from 535 to 538 electors. Although President Kennedy proposed that voting eligibility in the District be established by 90 days' residence and the age of eighteen, the Congress, in 1961, prescribed a residence of one year and a minimum voting age of twenty-one. Various groups in the District are continuing their agitation for congressional representation. In 1978, Congress approved a constitutional amendment proposal that would have repealed the Twenty-third Amendment and authorized full representation for the District in Congress and in the Electoral College, but it failed to be ratified by the state legislatures. Various groups in the District are continuing to agitate for congressional representation and full statehood.

Two-party System   Division of voter loyalties between two major political parties, resulting in the virtual exclusion of minor parties from seriously competing with the major parties or sharing in political power. A state in which the two major parties compete on fairly equal terms may nevertheless contain many electoral districts that are basically one-party in voter support, and some may be dominated by a third party. The two-party system is the traditional British system, which has been adopted in many Commonwealth countries and by the United States. *See also* MULTIPARTY SYSTEM, page 88; SINGLE-MEMBER DISTRICT, PAGE 112.

Significance   The two-party system stems from tradition, the tendency to view problems in terms of black-or-white alternatives, and the use of the single-member district system. The two-party monopoly on governmental power has, on several occasions in American history, been seriously challenged by the rise of a third party. Under a single-member district electoral system, however, the third party cannot compete effectively for political power unless it displaces one of the major parties, as when the Republicans took over the major party status of the Whigs in 1860. Americans who support the two-party system point out that it assures the election of legislative majorities, provides an effective and cohesive opposition, simplifies the role of the voter, and generrally provides stability in government. Opponents of the two-party system, however, charge that it creates artificial legislative majorities, narrows the voter's choice to two alternatives when there may be many, and makes a fetish of stability while denying minority parties and groups representation in the government.

United We Stand America   The movement created by Ross Perot in 1992 composed largely of frustrated members of the two major parties who had become disenchanted with the current political milieu. Examples from the agenda established by Ross Perot included: Congressional term limits, passage of a balanced budget amendment, restructuring the tax system, a reduced role by government, reform and stabilization of Medicare and Medicaid programs, and extensive reforms of lobbyists and lobbying. *See also* THIRD PARTY, page 114.

Significance   The United We Stand America movement is not a unique phenomenon in American politics. Historically, independent candidates for the presidency have faced the problem of overcoming the attachment of voters to one of the two major parties. The main source of strength for this movement is the large-scale disaffection of millions of voters from candidates who failed to produce once elected. For example, most presidential candidates for many years have promised the voters a balanced budget, but once elected the promise has become meaningless. The impact of Ross Perot and his organization on future elections will likely be determined by whether he runs himself as an independent third-party candidate for the presidency or throws his support to one of the major party candidates who may incorporate his agenda.

Vote-by-Mail   An alternative method of voting. Voting by mail is not a new phenomenon. Voters have used absentee ballots for many years, and some states have used mail balloting for local issues. *See also* ABSENTEE VOTING, page 59.

Significance   Vote-by-mail is one of the alternative methods used by states as they seek to increase voter participation. Oregon was the first state to use a mail-in ballot for an election to fill a vacancy in the U.S. Senate. In 1996, North Dakota became the first state to use a mail-in ballot for a presidential primary. One polling place in each county was open for conventional voting on the regular election day. Election officials stated that vote-by-mail is the most cost-efficient way to conduct a statewide election. It is much less expensive than staffing and equipping polling places. There is the added benefit of a 10 to 20 percent higher turnout of voters, and it makes voting more accessible for the handicapped and senior citizens. Opponents say, if mail-in-voting increases participation, it also increases the possibility for ballot-tampering. The custom of gathering at the neighborhood polling place offers more than security; it also is a reminder that the responsibility of citizenship requires a little effort.

Voter Turnout   The number of voters who actually participate in an election compared to the total number who are eligible to vote in that election. Voter turnout tends to be higher in presidential elections than in off-year elections, in national elections more than in state and local contests, and in general over primary or special elections. Other factors that may influence the size of voter turnout include geography (higher in the North than in the South and in small towns than in big cities), the type of election (in one-party states, the primary draws better than the general election), and electoral factors (spirited campaigns and glamorous candidates attract voters, whereas elections without them suffer from reduced participation). *See also* VOTING QUALIFICATIONS, page 119.

Significance   Political scientists have discovered that the size of voter turnouts often affects election outcomes. A low turnout, for example, tends to favor Republican candidates. If critical economic issues are at stake in an election, Democratic voters tend to turn out in larger numbers. As a general rule, independents tend to have a poorer turnout record than those who have a party preference. Uncontrollable factors, such as the weather on election day, may also help to determine the size of the turnout and the election outcome. Some nations have tried to increase voter turnout by systems of compulsory voting in which the eligible voter who fails to go to the polls may be fined or lose certain citizenship privileges. Historically, in presidential elections Lyndon B. Johnson received the highest percentage of votes from those eligible to vote (37.8 percent), whereas Martin Van Buren received the lowest (11.4 percent) of all winning candidates. Presidential elections usually encourage large turnouts. The two lowest voter turnouts in the twentieth century occurred in the off-year (nonpresidential) elections of 1942 and 1986.

Voting Behavior   The ways people vote in public elections and the factors that influence them in their voting decisions. Voting behavior studies are carried on by political scientists in their efforts to understand how and why individuals and groups tend to vote the way they do. Factors identified as having a critical influence on voting behavior include party affiliation, family and friends, the role of the mass media, the impact of the educational system, age, religion, one's business and personal environment, occupation, nationality, location of residence, income, economic and social status, personality type, ideological convictions, and susceptibility to campaign propaganda. *See also* POLITICAL SOCIALIZATION, page 99; VOTER TURNOUT, page 118.

Significance   Political scientists have increasingly examined voting behavior through the device of survey research. By studying representative samples of major voting populations, elections can be predicted or explained with a high level of accuracy. Tendency statements have been developed as theories that seek to explain causal factors in voting behavior. Prediction becomes difficult, however, when large numbers of voters remain "undecided" up to election day and, in some cases, until they walk into the polling booth. In the 1980 presidential election, for example, pollsters and political scientists predicted a very close race between incumbent President Jimmy Carter and challenger Ronald Reagan, but the latter won an electoral vote sweep. In addition, none of the pollsters had predicted that Republicans would win control of the Senate. Numerous polling organizations collect data and refine their techniques in efforts to gain precision in understanding the democratic process at work in elections. Recent studies have tended to reaffirm that party affiliation is the most important factor influencing voting behavior in a particular election, and that family influence is among the most powerful socializing factors influencing general political behavior, including party affiliation.

Voting Qualifications   Legal requirements that prospective voters must fulfill to exercise their franchise or right to vote. Qualifications imposed in all of the states include citizenship, age (eighteen for all elections since the adoption of the Twenty-sixth Amendment in 1971), and residence (although Congress in the Voting Rights Act of 1970 provided that 30 days' residence would qualify citizens to vote in presidential elections). Special qualifications involving lengthy residence, tax payments, property ownership, and literacy may no longer be imposed under Supreme Court rulings. Most states, however, disqualify mental incompetents, prison inmates, election-law violators, and vagrants. According to the Fifteenth and Nineteenth amendments to the Constitution, no person may be disqualified by a state from voting because of race or sex. *See also* DISFRANCHISE, page 73; LITERACY TEST, page 86; REGISTRATION, page 108; RESIDENCE, page 110; TWENTY-FOURTH AMENDMENT, page 116.

Significance   Fewer than 50 percent of the potential voters actually participate in most elections, and the best turnouts in presidential contests have only slightly exceeded 60 percent. Many potential voters are denied the ballot because of failure to qualify. Suggestions for improving voter participation include: (1) reducing residence requirements for most elections and eliminating them for presidential contests and (2) vigorously enforcing federal Civil Rights Acts and the Voting Rights Acts to prevent disfranchisement because of color or race. Although much can be accomplished by such actions, many observers believe that alienation, inertia, and lack of interest by millions of people remain the major difficulties.

Women's Liberation Movement   A contemporary militant feminist movement aimed at achieving status and rights for women in society equal to those of men. Commonly referred to as "Women's Lib," it consists of several national and numerous local organizations and informal groups. The main goal of the movement is to change society and its culture so that the "dominant-inferior relationship of men to women" can be changed. Particular objectives for the more radical elements of the movement include ending the "power-structured system of patriarchy," by which the father dominates family life, and wiping out "sexism," the conscious or unconscious male chauvinist attitudes that treat women as sex objects. Most liberationists, however, are concerned with less philosophical and more immediate problems, such as ending job and pay discrimination, securing abortion reform, setting up tax-supported child-care centers, and securing equal treatment under national, state, and municipal laws. *See also* EQUAL RIGHTS, page 309; KEY ELECTION FACTORS: GENDER POLITICS, page 83; NINETEENTH AMENDMENT, page 91.

Significance   The origins of the Women's Liberation Movement in the United States can be traced back to the nineteenth-century feminist campaigns to secure the ballot. The assumption of the feminists in those days was that the achievement of other basic rights and a dignified position in society would follow suffrage. The contemporary movement, which began in the early 1960s and gained momentum over the next decade, recognizes that this assumption has proved false and that political, economic, and social discrimination against women still permeates American society. Women's Lib has occasionally taken on some of the characteristics of a radical mass movement, with protests, marches, invasions of male sanctuaries, condemnation of female sex symbols, and direct and indirect political involvement. Some scholars relate Women's Lib to the general problems of anomie and alienation growing out of the increasing urbanization and depersonalization of modern life. Since women constitute a majority of Americans of voting age, major political consequences could result from the movement's growing base of support. During the 1970s and 1980s, most Women's Lib activities were aimed at securing ratification of the proposed Equal Rights Amendment (ERA), led by the National Organization for Women (NOW), but the campaign failed. In 1984 Women's Lib hailed Walter Mondale's choice of Geraldine Ferraro as vice-presidential candidate. In the 1980s and 1990s, increasing numbers of women and minority group members became active in politics. Women, for example, in 1988 comprised 15.5 percent of the nation's elected state legislators, up from only 4 percent in 1969. Moreover, voting studies show that women were more liberal, men more conservative, in voting in presidential elections in the 1980s. In 1980, for example, men voted 54 percent for Ronald Reagan whereas women gave him only 47 percent, a 7-point gap. In 1984, the gap increased to 8 points. In 1988, George Bush received 57 percent of male votes but only 50 percent of women's, another 7-point gap, and in 1992 Bill Clinton received 46 percent of votes cast by women to 37 percent for George Bush, a 9-point gap.

IMPORTANT CASES

Hadley v. Junior College District of Kansas City,   397 U.S. 50 (1970): Ruled that the "one person, one vote" principle applies generally to *all*—national, state, and local—elections of government officials. The *Hadley* case declared that the "dilution" of the votes of people living in one of the districts comprising the Junior College District of Metropolitan Kansas City violates the equal protection clause of the Fourteenth Amendment. The unconstitutional dilution involved a state apportionment formula whereby 60 percent of the total electorate of the district could elect only 50 percent of the junior college trustees. *See also* APPORTIONMENT, page 128; *Baker v. Carr,* page 176; REDISTRICTING, page 162.

Significance   The *Hadley* decision climaxed a series of apportionment cases that began with *Baker v. Carr* in 1962 by declaring conclusively that equal voting power in all popular elections is a fundamental right enjoyed by every American. This right, according to the Court, is "protected by the United States Constitution against dilution or debasement." The *Hadley* decision expanded upon the 1963 ruling of the Court in *Gray v. Sanders,* 372 U.S. 368, in which it held that each person's vote must count equally in all statewide elections.

Smith v. Allwright,   321 U.S. 649 (1944): Established, finally and conclusively, that the "white primary" was a violation of the Fifteenth Amendment. The case arose over the denial of a ballot to Smith, a black resident of Houston, Texas, in the Democratic primary of 1940 for nominating candidates for congressional and state offices. The Court recognized that its earlier decision, allowing the exclusion of blacks from "private" party primaries, in the case *Grovey v. Townsend,* 295 U.S. 45 (1935), had been "in error." The Court reasoned that the party was actually performing a state function in holding a primary election and was not acting as a private group. Moreover, the Court pointed out that a primary is an integral part of the election process. *See also* DIRECT PRIMARY, page 72.

Significance   In southern states, nomination in the Democratic primary was for many years almost tantamount to winning the election. By being denied a vote in the primary, blacks were prevented from effectively participating in the selection of public officials. By invoking the Fifteenth Amendment against a private group (political party), the Court closed a loophole it had opened with its earlier interpretation. This case stands as an important landmark in the continuing legal battles to ensure voting rights for all. The *Smith* decision also augmented the Court's earlier ruling in *United States v. Classic* (313 U.S. 299 [1941]), which upheld the power of Congress to supervise the holding of state primary congressional elections to ensure the right of the people to vote and have their ballots counted regardless of their race or color.

IMPORTANT STATUTES

Electoral Count Act   An 1887 act of Congress that provides for settlement of disputes over the election of presidential electors. When two or more sets of electors are certified by different authorities of a single state, Congress, voting as two separate houses, decides which to accept. If Congress fails to agree, the electors certified by the governor are accepted. *See also* ELECTORAL COLLEGE, page 74.

Significance   The Electoral Count Act resulted from the great confusion in the election of 1876. Hayes finally won the presidency over Tilden, 185 electoral votes to 184, after 20 contested electoral votes were awarded to Hayes on a strictly partisan basis by an Electoral Commission hastily created by Congress. The establishment of regular procedures is important because the outcome of such disputes may affect the outcome of a close presidential election. The democratic process depends upon popular confidence in the honesty of elections.

Federal Election Campaign Act of 1972   An act to control the raising and expenditure of funds for political campaigns. Its major provisions include (1) a limitation on the amount that can be spent for political advertising to 10 cents for every eligible voter—in a congressional district for House contests, statewide for Senate contests, and nationwide for presidential races—with a limit of 60 percent of that sum usable for broadcast advertising and (2) a requirement of complete disclosure of contributions in excess of $10 and expenditures in excess of $100. Other provisions regulate the activities of political campaign committees, labor unions, and corporations, and establish reporting procedures. *See also* CORRUPT PRACTICES ACTS, page 69; FEDERAL ELECTION CAMPAIGN ACT OF 1974, page 123.

Significance   The Federal Election Campaign Act of 1972 replaced various federal corrupt practices legislation enacted since 1908 and is designed to reduce the influence of heavy campaign funds and personal wealth on elections. The limits on broadcast advertising reflect both the huge costs involved in television exposure for candidates and recognition of the impact of television saturation of the electorate. While not all campaign expenditure pressures on candidates are covered by the Act, such as travel and other non-mass-media advertising costs, the extensive reporting and disclosure requirements may temper both the giving and spending of funds. Disclosures of widespread illegal and corrupt actions during the 1972 presidential election led Congress to enact the Campaign Act of 1974.

Federal Election Campaign Act of 1974   A major law that alters and supplements the Federal Election Campaign Act of 1972 in regulating campaign financing in national elections. The Federal Election Campaign Act provides for mainly public financing for presidential general elections, with $46 million provided in 1988 for each major party candidate, and with minor party candidates receiving a proportion of that amount based on votes received. In the drive to win their party's nomination, qualified aspirants can use a mixture of private and public funds. To qualify for public financing in the party's nomination campaign, a candidate must first raise $5,000 in each of 20 states in contributions no larger than $250 each. Funds for all public financing will be derived from a $1 ($3 after 1994) voluntary checkoff on personal income tax returns. Other provisions of the law limit individual contributions to a maximum of $1,000 for a candidate in a national primary or general election, with a $25,000 limit set on any person's total contributions during an election year. Special interest groups and political committees may contribute no more than $5,000 to any candidate in a national primary or general election. Spending limits start with a base figure of $70,000 for each primary and for each general election for House candidates, plus a variable system that could raise the total ceiling for some House candidates to over $100,000. Senate candidates are limited in spending for each primary to a base figure of $100,000 or 8¢ per eligible voter, whichever is greater, and to $150,000 or 12¢ per eligible voter for each general election. Spending by each national party organization is limited to $10,000 per candidate in House general elections, to $20,000 or 2¢ per voter for Senate general elections, and to 2¢ per voter in presidential general elections. Enforcement of the campaign finance laws is placed in the hands of a bipartisan six-member Federal Elections Commission, appointed by the President with Senate consent. The Commission is assigned extensive civil enforcement powers, but criminal actions are handled by the Department of Justice. Finally, the Act repealed provisions of the Hatch Act of 1940, which for 35 years barred state and local employees paid in whole or part with federal funds from engaging in partisan political activity. Currently, federal employees are permitted to engage in off-duty political activity—campaigns and fund raising. However, it excludes members of the Senior Executive Service and all workers in certain security-sensitive agencies such as the CIA. *See also* CORRUPT PRACTICES ACTS, page 69, FEDERAL ELECTION CAMPAIGN ACT OF 1972, page 122; POLITICAL ACTION COMMITTEES (PACS), page 96; WATERGATE, page 211.

Significance   The Federal Election Campaign Act of 1974 was largely the product of public pressures generated by revelations of big-money financing scandals during the 1972 presidential election involving President Richard M. Nixon's reelection committee and various special interests. It was also partly a result of the effective tactics employed by Common Cause, a powerful citizen's public interest lobby group. Not all provisions of the 1974 Act, however, were aimed at strengthening the 1972 Act; for example, the 1974 law included an amendment shortening the statute of limitations from five to three years for exempting corporations and their officers from prosecution. The main changes in the 1974 amendments to the 1972 law involve public financing of presidential election campaigns, and the creation of a special regulatory commission to enforce the provisions of both congressional enactments. Although Congress agreed on public financing for presidential elections, the House refused to support the idea of public financing of congressional campaigns on the ground that it would be mainly advantageous to candidates opposing House members. It now costs over $500,000 on average to win a seat in the House, and more than $4 million to get elected to the Senate. Many presidential candidates have been helped by the federal financing provisions of the 1974 Act. Ronald Reagan, for example, received more than $90 million in federal funds in his three campaigns for the presidency, two of them successful. The 1972 and 1974 Acts were the first major election campaign reform acts passed in a half century. Although the 1940 Hatch Act was repealed, some provisions of the Hatch Act of 1939 limiting the political activities of *federal* employees remain in force. The Supreme Court upheld them in the 1973 case, *United States Civil Service Commission v. National Association of Letter Carriers,* 413 U.S. 548. In 1976, the Court struck down provisions of the 1974 Act that placed limits on the amount of money candidates could spend and the law's limits on amounts an individual candidate could spend of his own money (*Buckley v. Valeo,* 424 U.S. 1). As a result, amendments were adopted to the Act in 1976 and in 1979 that, *inter alia,* simplified reporting requirements and changed the role that state and local party organizations could play in presidential elections. In 1986, the Supreme Court declared unconstitutional a section of the Federal Election Campaign Act in violation of the First Amendment, as applied to a small nonprofit prolife corporation (*Federal Election Commission v. Massachusetts Citizens for Life,* 479 U.S. 238). In *Federal Election Commission v. National Conservative Political Action Committee,* 470 U.S. 480 (1985), the Court struck down a section of the Presidential Election Campaign Fund Act limiting spending by a political action committee to $1,000 for a presidential candidate as a violation of free speech.

Voting Rights Act   Major law enacted by Congress in 1965 and renewed and expanded in 1970, 1975, and 1982 that has sought to eliminate restrictions on voting that have been used to discriminate against blacks and other minority groups. A major provision of the 1965 Act suspended the use of literacy and other tests used to discriminate. The Act also authorized registration by federal registrars in any state or county where such tests had been used and where less than 50 percent of eligible voters were registered. Seven southern states were mainly affected by these provisions. The Act also authorized a legal test of poll taxes in state elections, and the Supreme Court in 1966 declared payment of poll taxes as a condition of voting to be unconstitutional (*Harper v. Virginia State Board of Elections,* 383 U.S. 663). Major provisions of the 1965 Act were upheld by the Court as a valid exercise of power under the Fifteenth Amendment (*South Carolina v. Katzenbach,* 383 U.S. 301 [1966]). The Voting Rights Act of 1970: (1) extended the 1965 Act for five years; (2) lowered the minimum voting age for all elections from twenty-one to eighteen; (3) prohibited the states from disqualifying voters in presidential elections because of their failure to meet state residence requirements beyond 30 days; and (4) provided for uniform national rules for absentee registration and voting in presidential elections. In 1970, the Court upheld the eighteen-year-old vote for national elections (*Oregon v. Mitchell*, 400 U.S. 112) but found its application to state and local elections unconstitutional. In 1975, the Act was continued for seven years. Federal voting protection was extended to all or parts of ten additional states, bilingual ballots were required, election law changes in states covered by the Act were required to be approved by either a United States Attorney or a federal court, and legal protection of voting rights was extended to Spanish-Americans, Alaskan natives, American Indians, and Asian-Americans. The 1982 Act extends the law for 25 years, authorizes a "bail-out" for covered states showing a clear record for 10 years, and provides that intent to discriminate need not be proven if the results demonstrate otherwise. Although the 1982 extension does not require racial quotas for city councils, school boards, or state legislatures, a judge could under the law redraw voting districts to give minorities minimum representation. *See also* CIVIL RIGHTS ACTS, page 376; TWENTY-SIXTH AMENDMENT, page 116; VOTING QUALIFICATIONS, page 119.

Significance The Voting Rights Acts were passed in response to demonstrations by black Americans protesting voting discrimination. Existing legislation that relied on slow-moving judicial procedures to control discriminatory practices had proved ineffective. Under the Acts' federal registration procedures, thousands of minority voters were added to the voting rolls. The Acts have had a major impact upon southern and national elections, and numerous black officeholders have been elected. Federal intervention to expand the electorate was sustained by the Supreme Court through a broad interpretation of the Fifteenth Amendment. The Twenty-sixth Amendment, which provides for a minimum voting age of eighteen in *all*—national, state, and local—elections, was proposed by Congress and ratified by the states following the *Oregon* decision, which had limited the eighteen-year-old vote to national elections. In 1980, the Supreme Court upheld provisions of the Voting Rights Act that prohibit changes in voting practices that have a discriminatory effect, even if not so intended (*City of Rome v. United States*, 446 U.S. 156). In another 1980 case, the Court refused to declare an at-large election system discriminatory because no black had ever been elected to a city commission even though blacks comprise about 35 percent of the city's population (*City of Mobile v. Bolden*, 446 U.S. 55). The success of the Voting Rights Act results from the application of federal power to correct abuses at the state and local levels. Several million blacks and other minority voters have been registered since the law went into effect. In an important case in 1983, the Supreme Court upheld changes in city government that continued but did not worsen the racially discriminatory effect of the election system, against the position that the Voting Rights Act was intended to prevent perpetuation of past discrimination (*City of Lockhart v. United States*, 406 U.S. 125 [1983]). In 1986, in *Thornburg v. Gingles*, 478 U.S. 30, the Supreme Court ruled for the first time on the 1982 amendments to the Voting Rights Act of 1965 that require courts to look at the *results* of electoral practices and not merely the *intent* as expressed in regulations. In that case, which involved a redistricting plan using multimember districts, the

Court ruled that the fact that some minority candidates were successful does not foreclose investigation into the extent to which minority voting is diluted. In 1991, the Court ruled that the Voting Rights Act is applicable to the election of state (*Chisom v. Roemer,* 501 U.S. 380) and local (*Houston Lawyers' Association v. Attorney General of Texas,* 501 U.S. 419) trial judges. In 1992, the Court held that the Act did not apply to an internal governmental reorganization that resulted in reduction of the authority of a government commission after some blacks were elected to the formerly all-white agency (*Presley v. Etowah County Commission,* 502 U.S. 491). In *Holder v. Hall,* 114 S. Ct. 2581 (1994), the Court held that the Act cannot be used to challenge the size of a governmental body—that is, a one-person "commission"— to which no black had been elected. Again in 1994, the Court held that the Act does not require that the maximum number of minority legislative districts be established. A "rough proportion" satisfies the Act (*Johnson v. De Grandy,* 114 S. Ct. 2647).

4

The Legislative Process: Congress and the State Legislatures

Adjournment   Termination of a session of a legislative body. Adjournment *sine die* means to end the session without definitely fixing a day for reconvening. It is used to end a congressional session officially. "Adjournment to a day certain" means adopting a motion or resolution that specifies the date and time of the next meeting. Neither house of Congress can adjourn for more than three days without the concurrence of the other. *See also* LEGISLATIVE DAY, page 154; SESSION, page 168.

Significance   Under the Legislative Reorganization Act of 1946, Congress adjourns no later than the last day of July, unless Congress specifically provides otherwise. Under the Constitution, if the two houses of Congress cannot agree on an adjournment day, the President can determine it. This has never occurred.

Advice and Consent   The power vested in the U.S. Senate by the Constitution (Art. II, sec. 2) to give its advice and consent to the President in treaty making and appointments. A two-thirds vote of the senators present is required for treaties. Appointments are confirmed by a simple majority vote. The Senate may give its advice through consultations between Senate leaders and the President, by resolutions setting out its position, or by delegating some of its members actually to sit in on treaty negotiations. *See also* CONFIRMATION, page 138; RATIFICATION, page 161.

Significance   Although the Constitution's phraseology seems to associate the Senate with the President throughout the treaty-making process, President Washington, after several attempts to consult with the entire Senate, found it impractical, and initiated the tradition of consulting with the Senate only after a treaty has been negotiated and signed or an appointee has been nominated. Since World War II, however, presidents have increasingly expanded the "advice" role of the Senate by inviting influential senators to participate in the negotiation of the treaty that created the United Nations, several treaties that established military alliances, and other significant treaties. The Senate generally accepts the nominees of the President for high-level positions, but in the case of many presidential appointments to federal positions located within states, the rule of "senatorial courtesy" applies. Politics has played an important role in the advice and consent function throughout American history. In making nominations to the Supreme Court, for example, of 139 individuals nominated in the Court's 200-year history, 26 failed to be confirmed by the Senate. In a 1987 case, Robert H. Bork was rejected in a full Senate vote despite unprecedented efforts by President Ronald Reagan to win majority support. A factor in many of the Senate rejections of nominees has been the "lame duck" status of the nominating President, with the Senate opposition aimed at saving the appointment for the President's successor.

Amendment   An action of a legislative body to delete, alter, or revise the language of a bill or an act. Bills in Congress may be amended by either house at any one of a number of stages in the legislative process. Generally, amendments are printed, debated, and voted upon in the same way as a bill. Most laws enacted by Congress are, in fact, amendments to existing laws. *See also* AMENDMENT PROCESS, page 29.

Significance   Through the amending process, a bill may undergo such extreme revision or modification that it loses much of its original character. Often, instead of attempting to kill bills outright, legislators add amendments to make them innocuous. Legislators may also try to kill bills by attaching amendments that are unacceptable to the majority of their house or the other chamber. Once a bill is enacted into law, it can be amended only through passage of new legislation. The Rules Committee in the House usually limits the amending process severely, but in the Senate numerous amendments may be proposed and considered. Congress also can propose amendments to the United States Constitution by a two-thirds vote in each chamber, or may call a national constitutional convention on petition of two-thirds of the state legislatures. Thus, an instrumentality of the national government controls the proposal stage for constitutional amendments, with the ratification or final approval stage controlled by the states either through legislative actions by three-fourths of the state legislatures or by favorable action of three-fourths of state conventions elected solely for the purpose of considering ratification. Only once, in the adoption of the Twenty-first Amendment, has the convention method been used. In 1933, a convention provided for the repeal of Prohibition, which had been adopted by the Eighteenth Amendment in 1919. By providing that constitutional changes must be approved by both levels of government, the constitutional framers sought to protect the federal system.

Apportionment   The allocation of legislative seats. The Constitution (Art. I, sec. 2) and the Fourteenth Amendment (sec. 2) provide that representatives shall be apportioned among the several states according to their respective numbers. Under the Apportionment Act of 1929, Congress fixed the number of House seats at 435 and provided that the Census Bureau after each decennial census redistribute the seats among the 50 states, subject to congressional control. Each state is assigned one representative before a population formula is applied. Following the reapportionment decisions, each state that gains or loses seats in the House must be redistricted by its legislature. Politics typically plays a major role in this process. Under the 1970 reapportionment, nine states lost seats in the House and five states gained. California led with an increase of five seats. Under the 1980 reapportionment, ten states lost seats (five in New York, two each in Illinois, Ohio, and Pennsylvania, and one each in Indiana, Massachusetts, Michigan, Missouri, New Jersey, and South Dakota), while eleven states gained seats (four in Florida, three in Texas, two in California, and one each in Arizona, Colorado, Nevada, New Mexico, Oregon, Tennessee, Utah, and Washington). Following the 1990 census, gainers of House seats included California (seven), Florida (four), Texas (three), and Arizona, Georgia, North Carolina, Virginia, and Washington, (one each). As a result of reapportionment, California has an unprecedented 52 seats, about 12 percent of the entire House of Representatives. States that lost seats included New York (three), Illinois, Michigan, Ohio, and Pennsylvania (two each), and Iowa, Kansas, Kentucky, Louisiana, Massachusetts, Montana, New Jersey, and West Virginia (one each). In 1995, the Supreme Court held that redistricting decisions based solely on racial considerations violate the Constitution of the United States (*Miller v. Johnson,* 115 S. Ct. 2475). *See also* GERRYMANDERING, page 148; KEY ELECTION FACTORS: POPULATION/POWER SHIFTS, page 84; PIVOTAL STATES, page 95; REDISTRICTING, page 162.

Significance   With the mobility of the American people, gross under- or overrepresentation of states in the House is avoided through the "automatic" reapportionment by the Bureau of the Census that follows each ten-year census. Within the states, however, the responsibility for redistricting congressional seats is placed upon the majority party in each state legislature, leading to gerrymandering and other actions aimed at gaining political advantage. Population, and thus power in the House of Representatives and the Electoral College, has continued to shift from the "snowbelt" states of the East and North to the "sunbelt" states of the South and West. In a 1992 case, the Supreme Court rejected the claim of the state of Montana (*U.S. Department of Commerce v. Montana,* 503 U.S. 442) that the mathematical formula for allocating representatives—known as "equal proportions"—was unconstitutional because it left the state with a single congressional district of 803,655 people, far larger than the national average of 572,466. This, Montana held, violated the constitutional requirement that representatives be apportioned among the states "according to their respective numbers."

Appropriation   A legislative grant of money for a specific purpose. The executive branch pulls together thousands of individual items for the next fiscal-year period and submits them as an omnibus budget for consideration by the legislative branch. In the national government, authorization bills establishing specific programs are first enacted by Congress. Then, an appropriation bill must be passed to provide the money to carry out the program. *Appropriation* bills originate in the House of Representatives *by custom; revenue* bills to provide the income to cover appropriations must originate in the House under the Constitution. A *supplemental* appropriation is a legislative authorization of additional money for specific purposes after the regular appropriation bills have been enacted. A *deficiency* appropriation is a special bill providing funds to make up the difference between an agency's appropriation for the fiscal year and the amount needed to continue its operations for the full fiscal year. Unlike regular appropriations, which are made for the next fiscal year, deficiency appropriations are used to make up shortages in the same fiscal year in which they are passed. *Continuing* resolutions relate to the start of a new fiscal year when the legislative body has failed to adopt the budget and authorizes the continuing of appropriations to government agencies at the level of the previous fiscal year. *See also* AUTHORIZATION, page 130; BUDGET, page 390; BUDGET COMMITTEES, page 133; POWER OF THE PURSE, page 159.

Significance In the American system of government—including national, state, and local levels—no expenditure of public money can be made unless authorized by law. Thus, Congress, the state legislatures, and local councils, commissions, and boards exercise "control over the purse strings"—one of the most important powers of legislative bodies. Because money is needed to implement most new laws, the appropriations committees wield great power in the House and Senate of the Congress and in the state legislatures. Supplemental appropriations are useful in correcting miscalculations in the budget process, in meeting new problems, and in reacting to changes in public opinion. Deficiency bills typically are enacted later in the budget year to provide funds for ongoing projects that are threatened by the lack of financial resources to keep them going. Because federal budgets have become major instruments of fiscal policy for maintaining a healthy economy, supplementary and deficiency appropriations may also be called for when the economy needs some stimulative action. Continuing appropriations resolutions, by contrast, must be adopted when the legislative process is stalemated to forestall, for lack of money, an imminent breakdown in governmental operations, referred to as a "train wreck." Spending money has proved to be far more popular in Congress than raising it through taxation, with the result that by 1996 the national public debt had soared above $5 trillion.

Authorization A legislative action that establishes or continues a substantive program, specifies its general purpose and the means for achieving it, and indicates the approximate amount of money needed to implement the program. An authorization bill is ordinarily enacted before the appropriation bill providing financing for the program is considered by Congress. State legislatures also require authorizations prior to the enactment of appropriation measures. *See also* APPROPRIATION, page 129; IMPOUNDMENT, page 193.

Significance Because programs must be authorized before public money can be appropriated to support them, legislative bodies typically have two opportunities to consider them. Four different committees of Congress— the House and Senate appropriations committees and a substantive committee in each house—thus have an opportunity to kill, modify, add to, or otherwise change major programs. Although authorization laws specify ceilings on the amounts that can be spent to support programs, appropriation bills seldom provide the full amount permitted.

Bicameralism The principle of a two-house legislature, in contrast to unicameralism, or a legislature based on one house. At the Philadelphia Convention of 1787, the Founding Fathers adopted a compromise solution for representation in Congress. This "Connecticut Compromise" established a balanced bicameral legislature with one house (House of Representatives) based on population and the second (Senate) based on equality of states. In the states, Nebraska has the only unicameral legislature, but all local units of government in the United States have unicameral systems. In a bicameral legislature, all bills must pass both houses before becoming law. *See also* CONNECTICUT COMPROMISE, page 34; *Reynolds v. Sims,* page 178; UNICAMERALISM, page 173.

Significance   A two-house legislature provides opportunity for different types of representation and responses to varying interests, such as population, area, and existing political units. Also, the second house can function in a capacity of revising and correcting mistakes made by the first chamber. Bicameralism is consistent with the principle of checks and balances. Opponents of bicameralism regard a single-house legislature as more economical and efficient. Although the Supreme Court has declared that the electoral districts for both houses of state legislatures must be based on population (*Reynolds v. Sims,* 377 U.S. 533 [1964]), the American people continue to support bicameralism. The Supreme Court in the *Reynolds* case rejected the "federal analogy" argument, holding that the upper houses of state legislatures have no constitutional base and, unlike the U.S. Senate, must be redistricted on the basis of equal voting power.

Biennial Session   A regular meeting of a legislature held every two years. A majority of state legislatures convene in regular session once every two years, while the rest meet annually. In biennial session states, typically, legislatures hold their sessions in the odd-numbered years. *See also* SESSION, page 168.

Significance   The biennial session was established for the state legislatures by state constitution framers early in our nation's history, partly from a desire to save money and partly because of suspicions that if the legislature convened too frequently it might engage in mischievous doings. Biennial sessions have proved inadequate to meet the vast number of complex problems facing state governments today, and frequent special sessions are necessary. Legislators often refer to "the biennium," meaning the two-year session of the state legislature.

Bill   A proposed law. Most legislative proposals before Congress are in the form of bills. Members of the House officially "introduce" bills by dropping them into a "hopper"; in the Senate, bills are introduced by verbal announcement. All bills introduced during a two-year congressional term are designated "HR" in the House and "S" in the Senate, with consecutive numbers assigned in the order in which they are introduced in each chamber. After introduction, bills are sent to a standing committee, where, typically, they receive their most thorough airing and consideration. Committees and subcommittees often revise bills in a process called a "markup session" in which the bill is approved or revised on a section-by-section basis. On occasion, the committee will completely rewrite a bill during a markup session, with the new version called a "clean bill." Each bill must have three readings in each house, be approved by a majority vote in each house, and, normally, be signed by the President to become law. A bill passed in one house is called an "engrossed bill," and the final authoritative copy of a bill passed by both houses and signed by their presiding officers is called an "enrolled bill."

Public bills deal with matters of general concern and may become public laws. Private bills are concerned with individual matters and become private laws if approved. *See also* BILL DRAFTING, page 132; PRIVATE BILL, page 160; READINGS, page 162.

Significance   Thousands of bills are introduced into every Congress. They are drawn up by pressure groups, interested citizens, congressional committees, individual congressmen, and members of the executive branch. Only members of Congress, however, can introduce bills in their respective chambers. The great majority of these bills are killed because committees in either or both houses do not act upon them. Some bills are concerned with new issues, but many public bills enacted into law are amendments to existing laws. Technically, a bill passed by one house is referred to in Congress as an "act," but the term "act" is generally used to denote a bill passed by both houses that becomes a new law. A bill may be delayed or killed by a motion to "lay on the table" or by returning it to committee. Most bills that become law are written by bureaucrats in the executive branch and are amendments to existing statutes.

Bill Drafting   The process of formulating legislative proposals. Congress and many state legislatures have staff agencies to aid members in this process. In Congress, members seeking assistance in study and research have access to the Congressional Research Service in the Library of Congress. Aid in drawing up bills is supplied by legislative counsel. Some of the most important bills are often drafted by House and Senate standing committees. Many bills are also drawn up by lawyers representing interest groups that will benefit from the legislation. *See also* BILL, page 131; LIBRARY OF CONGRESS, page 175.

Significance   Bills must be drafted with precision. If enacted, the courts may refuse to sanction their enforcement if they are drawn in vague language that allows enforcement officers to exercise too much discretion. As a result of pressures from Common Cause, a citizen lobby group, most committee bill-drafting sessions, formerly secret, are now open to public scrutiny. Although most public bill drafting occurs in the executive branch, Congress has attempted to check this drift of power by strengthening its staff aides. Bills drafted in executive agencies are officially introduced in the Congress by "friendly" members of the House and Senate, who work closely with executive officials.

Bloc   Members of a legislative body, not necessarily of the same party, who have common aims and goals. Some historical examples include the farm bloc, civil rights bloc, and the international trade bloc. *See also* FARM BLOC, page 146.

Significance   Bloc voting in Congress and in state legislatures is a means by which the interests of a segment of the population can be effectively represented. It is basically a bipartisan approach. The danger inherent in voting blocs results from their narrow positions on specific issues, for thus rivalry is intensified and the legislative body may be split into warring factions. Bloc voting tends to reduce party responsibility because blocs typically represent interests that cross party lines.

Budget Committees   House and Senate committees that recommend policy guidelines each fiscal year to aid Congress in considering the annual federal budget. Recommended in 1973 by a joint budget-reform study committee, Congress created the two committees in the Congressional Budget and Impoundment Control Act of 1974 to function as the main instruments for implementing legislative budget reform. *See also* APPROPRIATION, page 129; BUDGET POWER, page 184; CONGRESSIONAL BUDGET AND IMPOUNDMENT CONTROL ACT OF 1974, page 180; LINE ITEM VETO, page 194.

Significance   Budget-reform legislation and the creation of the powerful House and Senate Budget Committees to function as super fiscal agents of Congress were aimed at restoring a greater measure of control over the budget process. For years, the President's budgetary powers had steadily increased, and these new committees were intended to restore the "power of the purse" to its constitutional source—the legislative branch. Under the enacting legislation, five members of the House Budget Committee must also serve on the House Appropriations Committee, and five on the tax-writing Ways and Means Committee, to coordinate fiscal policies developed by Congress. In the Senate, Budget Committee membership was similarly linked with the Appropriations and Finance Committees. Whether congressional budget committees can restore weakened budgetary powers to the legislative branch remains problematic. Since 1974, the Senate and House Budget Committees have routinely operated under different economic assumptions, widely varying estimates have been produced, and timetables have often been ignored. The result has been huge deficits aggregating to over $5 trillion by 1996. As a means of seeking greater control over the budget process, Congress in 1996 gave the President line item veto authority, which took effect in January 1997.

Calendar   An agenda or list that contains the names of bills or resolutions to be considered before committees or in either chamber of a legislature. When a standing committee of the House of Representatives reports out a bill, it is placed on one of the five possible calendars: *Consent* (noncontroversial bills), *Discharge* (discharge petitions), *House* (nonfiscal public bills), *Private* (private bills), and *Union* (appropriation and revenue bills). In the Senate, all bills reported out go on a single Calendar of General Order, although nonlegislative matters (treaties and confirmations of appointments) are placed on the *Executive* calendar. *See also* DISCHARGE RULE, page 144.

Significance   The placement of a bill on a calendar is no guarantee that the bill will be considered by that chamber or that it will be taken up in the listed order. Decisions as to which bills will be debated and voted on are made in the House by the Rules Committee and by the House party leaders, and in the Senate by the Majority Leader. In the Senate, the Minority Leader is consulted frequently in order to ensure unanimous consent agreement to consider bills. Many bills are killed by failing to have them put on a specific calendar or because they are still on a calendar at the end of a two-year Congress. In addition to the formal calendars, the legislative process is influenced by informal partisan, executive, and hidden calendars.

Calendar Wednesday   A procedure of the House of Representatives whereby Wednesdays may be used to call the roll of the standing committees for the purpose of bringing up bills for consideration from the House or the Union Calendars. General debate on each bill called up in this way is limited to two hours. Calendar Wednesday is not observed during the last two weeks of a session and, by a two-thirds vote, may be suspended any Wednesday, which usually is the case. *See also* CALENDAR, page 133; DISCHARGE RULE, page 144.

Significance Calendar Wednesday is a device by which the committee chairs in the House of Representatives can, when the rule is operative, bypass the Rules Committee and place a controversial bill before the House for debate and a vote. The frequent suspension of Calendar Wednesday testifies to the power of the House leadership to control the legislative process. A new device called "Corrections Day" was introduced in the House in 1995 by Speaker Newt Gingrich. This process devotes one day each month to correcting federal regulations.

Caucus A meeting of party members in one of the houses of a legislative body for the purpose of making decisions on selections of party leaders and on legislative business. Republicans in both houses of Congress and the Democrats in the Senate prefer to call their party meeting a "conference." The term "to caucus" is also commonly used to describe any informal meeting seeking to reach agreement on a course of legislative action. Caucuses of party members are also used in many states to select delegates to the party's national presidential nominating convention. *See also* CAUCUS, page 64; POLICY COMMITTEE, page 158.

Significance The majority caucus or conference in each house makes important decisions regarding the organization of its chamber; these decisions then become official when they are ratified by that house in regular session. In Congress, the Democrats until 1975 provided for "binding" caucus decisions regarding party stands on bills, with a two-thirds vote of the caucus required. No member was bound, however, if the party position involved a question of constitutional construction or a measure contrary to a pledge given by the member to his or her constituents. The "binding rule" was repealed in 1975. Republicans operate their conference on a majority-vote basis and, like the Democrats, do not seek to bind their members on voting positions. Some observers have recommended that the role of party caucuses in Congress be strengthened by providing for *binding* decisions on all important legislative proposals. This, they suggest, would strengthen the democratic process by making the parties more responsible.

Censure A power vested in a legislative body by which each chamber can discipline its own members. Under the Constitution, "Each house may...punish its members for disorderly behavior, and, with the concurrence of two-thirds, expel a member" (Art. I, sec. 5). *See also* EXPULSION, page 146; MCCARTHYISM, page 325.

Significance Cases of either house of Congress censuring a member are rare. They include the Senate's motion to "condemn" Senator Joseph McCarthy of Wisconsin in 1954 and the House's vote in 1967 to exclude New York Congressman Adam Clayton Powell Jr., remove his seniority, and fine him $25,000 for misconduct. Disciplinary measures can range in severity from adoption of a simple motion of censure to withdrawal of privilieges and, in extreme cases, expulsion of a member. A censured legislator suffers the ostracism of colleagues and loses much effectiveness as a legislator. Several congressmen were censured in the early 1980s as a result of "Abscam"—accepting bribes from FBI agents who posed as Middle Eastern sheiks—but most punishment occurred outside Congress, with a dozen congressmen convicted in court, and those who sought reelection were defeated. In 1995, the threat of expulsion from the Senate for sexual misconduct by Senator Bob Packwood of Oregon led to his resignation. This was the first time since the Civil War that such actions were undertaken or threatened by the Senate.

Census   A decennial enumeration of the total population of the United States, conducted by the Bureau of the Census. The Constitution provides that the population count be used for purposes of apportioning direct taxes and representatives among the several states (Art. I, sec. 3). Since the first census in 1790, new ones have been taken every ten years. Approximately half of the states conduct a mid-decade census along the same lines. The Census Bureau also collects data on a wide variety of subjects useful to Congress and the general public on such matters as business, housing, and units of government. *See also* APPORTIONMENT, page 128; BUREAU OF THE CENSUS, page 461; KEY ELECTION FACTORS: POPULATION/POWER SHIFTS, page 84; REDISTRICTING, page 162.

Significance   The American people have become extremely mobile, with considerable shifts in population occurring within the ten-year periods. The flow of population today is toward the West and the South, resulting in a shift of political power in the same directions. After each census, the Bureau reapportions the seats in the House of Representatives on the basis of the new population statistics. No direct taxes are now levied by the federal government. States use census figures in apportioning grants and allowances for local governments. Census data have also proved useful for scholarly researchers, especially social scientists. In 1982, the Supreme Court ruled that raw, individual census data are confidential and may not be disclosed under the Freedom of Information Act or federal court discovery rules (*McNichols v. Baldrige; Baldrige v. Shapiro,* 455 U.S. 345). These cases dealt with questions of accuracy of the census count for apportionment of federal funds and redistricting of legislative seats. Criticisms of the 1990 census and the count for apportionment and related purposes were widespread. These included charges that many households remained unlisted on the Census Bureau's address list and that many people did not complete a census form, whether through fear, ignorance, or misunderstanding of the Census Bureau's complicated instructions. It has been estimated that there was a 9 million undercount in 1980—a figure greater than the population of eleven states—and that in 1990 it was even larger. In *Wisconsin v. The City of New York,* 116 S. Ct. 1091 (1996), the Court upheld the Secretary of Commerce's refusal to adjust the 1990 census to rectify an alleged undercount of minorities. Accuracy is important because political power tends to shift with the population count.

Cloture (or Closure)   A parliamentary technique used by a legislative body to end debate and bring the matter under consideration to a vote. Cloture can be invoked under an amendment to Rule 22 in the Senate, which provides the method by which debate can be limited and a filibuster broken. One-sixth of the Senate membership can initiate action under cloture by petitioning the Senate to close debate on a pending measure. If such a petition is approved by three-fifths of the Senate (60 senators), thereafter no senator may speak for more than one hour on the bill or resolution being considered. Hence, in a short time, the measure will come up for a vote and the attempt of the minority to "talk the bill to death" by filibuster will have been defeated. *See also* FILIBUSTER, page 146; FREEDOM OF DEBATE, page 147.

Significance   Cloture safeguards majority rule by limiting the power of the Senate minority to kill bills by parliamentary maneuvers. Since Rule 22 was amended in 1917, there have been more than 100 cloture votes, of which only 20 percent have succeeded, including the following notable votes: Versailles Treaty, 1919; World Court, 1926; Branch Banking, 1927; Prohibition Reorganization, 1927; Communications Satellite, 1962; Civil Rights, 1964; Voting Rights, 1965; Open Housing, 1968; Draft Extension, [twice] 1971; Equal Job Opportunity, 1972; and Public Campaign Financing, 1974. The reluctance of senators to vote cloture stems from pride in the Senate's tradition of freedom of debate, as well as from the practical fear of jeopardizing the minority weapon of filibuster, which each senator may someday want to use. Attempts to invoke cloture have occurred with increased frequency since 1960. In 1975, after many unsuccessful attempts since 1917 to make it easier to limit debate, the Senate changed Rule 22 to make it possible to invoke cloture of debate by three-fifths of the entire Senate rather than by the traditional two-thirds of senators present and voting. The two-thirds rule, however, still applies to debate on Senate rule changes.

Committee Chair   The member of the majority party who heads a standing or select legislative committee. In Congress, the chairs of the nineteen House and sixteen Senate standing committees have been selected mainly under the rule of seniority, although since 1971 the party caucuses must give approval in the House. In most state legislatures, the committee chairs are appointed by the Speaker in the lower house and are usually selected by a committee on committees in the upper chamber. *See also* REFER TO COMMITTEE, page 164; STANDING COMMITTEE, page 171.

Significance   A committee chair can exercise an almost decisive control over bills assigned to that committee. The chair normally determines when and if the committee will meet, which bills it will consider and the order of their consideration, whether public hearings will be held, and the appointment of subcommittees. The Legislative Reorganization Act of 1970, however, permits a committee majority to call a meeting of the committee over the opposition of its chair. But the chair may, given enough political acumen and personal relationships, push bills through the committee, guide them through floor debate, and serve as a member of a conference committee. Next to the Speaker of the House and the Majority Leader in the Senate, committee chairs exercise the greatest influence over the legislative process. A committee majority seldom overrules its chair because of a reluctance to challenge "the establishment." In 1975, several powerful committee chairs of long seniority in the House were replaced by action of the Democratic Steering Committee and/or by decision of the Democratic Caucus.

Committee of the Whole   An informal procedure used by a legislative body to expedite business by resolving the official body into a committee for the consideration of bills and other matters. In Congress, this procedure is used only by the lower house, which becomes "The Committee of the Whole House (of Representatives) on the State of the Union." A temporary chair is appointed by the Speaker, and the formal rules are suspended; any members of the House may participate, with a minimum of 100 needed instead of the official quorum of 218 required by the House to conduct business.

Significance   Most House business is transacted in the Committee of the Whole. Advantages of this procedure include: (1) only 100 members need be present to constitute a quorum; (2) business is expedited through relaxed procedures; and (3) the full House retains control, in that it must act upon all decisions made by the Committee of the Whole to make them official. Since 1970, members' votes in Committee of the Whole may be required to be individually recorded. State legislatures also make use of Committee-of-the-Whole procedures to expedite their business.

Committee on Committees   Party committees that determine the assignments of party members to standing committees in the House of Representatives. The Republican Committee on Committees consists of one representative from each state having Republican members in the House. In voting within the Committee on Committees, each member casts the number of votes equal to the number of Republican members that state has in the House. The Democrats have given the power to the House Democratic Steering and Policy Committee, subject to oversight by the Speaker and the Caucus. In the Senate, where only one-third of the seats are filled in each biennial election, a majority party Steering Committee makes the necessary adjustments for each standing committee. In the state legislatures, committees in the lower house are appointed by the Speaker of the House. In the upper house, the procedure varies: Selections may be made by the presiding officer, by the chamber as a whole, or by a committee on committees. *See also* STANDING COMMITTEE, page 171.

Significance   Selections of standing committee personnel made unofficially by committees on committees are, typically, approved by the respective party caucuses and thence by their respective chambers. The power to assign committee members is significant because it largely determines the role that an individual legislator will play in that chamber and may affect the consideration of bills by standing committees for many years. In effect, a committee on committees can determine the power structure in a legislative body. In 1975, a dramatic change in the seniority system occurred when the Democratic Steering and Policy Committee and the House Democratic Caucus removed several powerful chairmen of long seniority from their chairmanships by secret ballot.

Concurrent Resolution   A special measure passed by one house of Congress with the other concurring, but not requiring the President's signature. Concurrent resolutions are used to make or amend joint rules or to express the sentiment of Congress on some issue or event. Concurrent resolutions are also used in the congressional budgetary process. *See also* JOINT RESOLUTION, page 153; SIMPLE RESOLUTION, page 169.

Significance   The most important use of concurrent resolutions since 1932 has been as a legislative veto over the President's exercise of powers delegated to him by Congress. Examples have included congressional disapproval of presidential reorganization plans or congressional action fixing the date for adjournment, creating joint committees, and welcoming official foreign visitors. In 1983, however, the use of the legislative veto was proscribed by the Supreme Court as a violation of the separation of powers (*Immigration and Naturalization Service v. Chadha*, 462 U.S. 919 [1983]). Under the War Powers Act of 1973, Congress may use a concurrent resolution not subject to a presidential veto to require the President to disengage American troops involved in hostilities abroad. However, all presidents since 1973, Republican and Democrat alike, have charged that the Act is unconstitutional and violates the President's power to make and carry out foreign policy.

Conference Committee   An ad hoc or special joint committee appointed to reconcile differences when a bill passes the two houses of Congress in different forms. A joint conference committee usually consists of three to nine "managers" appointed by the Speaker of the House and the President of the Senate. Efforts are directed toward a compromise version of the bill, which must be approved by a majority of the managers for each house voting separately. This compromise version, in the form of a "conference report," then goes for approval to each house, where it cannot be amended; if rejected by either house, it goes back to conference for further negotiation. *See also* BI-CAMERALISM, page 130; QUID PRO QUO, page 574.

Significance   Important bills frequently end up in conference committees; differences over bills of lesser importance are usually ironed out by securing the agreement of each chamber to the other's amendments. Frequently, great power is wielded by conference committees. Many important bills are substantially rewritten in conference or are killed through failure to achieve a compromise agreement. Meetings of the committees are always secret. Their power is reflected in the large number of times that the two houses accept conference reports and enact them into law. A number of conference committees may be operational simultaneously, and several may consider different aspects of the same major bill. Senator George Norris, Nebraska Republican, was responsible for creating the unique Nebraska unicameral state legislature to eliminate the need for conference committees.

Confirmation   The power of a legislative body to approve nominations made to fill executive and judicial positions. Nominations for such offices made by the President must be confirmed by the Senate with a majority vote. In addition, the Twenty-fifth Amendment gives the President the power to fill a vacancy in the office of Vice President with the approval of a majority of both houses of Congress. Many of the appointments made by the governors in the various states must also be approved by the upper houses of the legislatures. *See also* APPOINTMENT POWER, page 183; SENATORIAL COURTESY, page 167.

Significance   All federal judges are appointed subject to senatorial confirmation. Most important diplomatic and administrative positions not under civil service or other merit systems also come under senatorial scrutiny. Often the President confers with Senate leaders before nominating an individual for a cabinet position to determine in advance that he or she is *persona grata* (acceptable). In the case of appointments to federal positions located in the several states, the senior senator of the President's party from the state in which the appointment is to be made actually selects the appointee and gives the name to the President, thus in effect reversing the constitutional procedure. This is known as "senatorial courtesy."

Congressional Budget Office (CBO)   An agency of Congress established by the Congressional Budget Act of 1974, which also created a procedure by which Congress considers and acts upon the annual budget presented by the President. The CBO provides Congress with an assessment of the economic impact of the federal budget and offers alternative fiscal budgetary and programatic policy issues. *See also* CONGRESSIONAL BUDGET AND IMPOUNDMENT CONTROL ACT OF 1974, page 180; OFFICE OF MANAGEMENT AND BUDGET (OMB), page 423.

Significance   The Congressional Budget Office performs tasks for Congress similar to those the Office of Management and Budget (OMB) does for the executive branch. Frequently, figures issued by the CBO conflict with those of the OMB and become part of the negotiating battles between the executive and legislative branches on how to balance the budget. This occurred in 1995 and 1996, when President Bill Clinton personally entered the budget-balancing effort, along with Newt Gingrich, Speaker of the House, and Bob Dole, Senate Majority Leader. Agreement was finally reached to try to balance the budget in seven years with figures provided by the CBO.

Congressional Directory   A handbook published annually that contains information regarding the organization of Congress and its committees and brief biographical sketches of the senators and representatives. *See also* UNITED STATES GOVERNMENT MANUAL, page 235.

Significance   The *Congressional Directory,* which can be found in most libraries, is a useful reference guide for citizens and students of government. It supplements the *United States Government Manual,* which gives pertinent information about the three branches of American government.

Congressional District   A political-geographical division of a state from which one member of the House of Representatives is elected. A congressional district is usually a portion of a state, but if a state's population entitles it to only one representative, as in the case of seven states (Alaska, Delaware, Montana, North Dakota, South Dakota, Vermont, and Wyoming), the entire state is the congressional district. *See also* GERRYMANDERING, page 148; REDISTRICTING, page 162; *Wesberry v. Sanders,* page 179.

Significance   Districts generally are drawn up by partisan majorities in state legislatures to favor their party's candidates in congressional elections (gerrymandering). For many years, Congress provided that state legislatures draw up congressional districts as "compact and contiguous" areas, substantially equal in population, but since 1929, Congress has not specified criteria for redistricting. The Supreme Court's 1964 decision in *Wesberry v. Sanders,* 376 U.S. 1, holds that congressional districts must be based on substantial equality of population, but this decision does not eliminate gerrymandering.

In 1995, the U.S. Supreme Court held that race alone cannot be used as a determining factor in drawing up legislative districts (*Miller v. Johnson,* 115 S. Ct. 2475).

Congressional "Perks"   Benefits that Congress has voted for its members. Perquisites for members have included the authority to set their own salaries, liberal expense accounts, the franking privilege, free medical care, low-cost lunches, sports and exercise facilities, special banking arrangements, low-cost consumer goods, and congressional pensions. *See also* FRANKING PRIVILEGE, page 147; TWENTY-SEVENTH AMENDMENT, page 173.

Significance   A recent study of congressional "perks" indicates that the typical House member will collect more than $1.5 million in lifetime pension benefits alone. The voting public, however, has increasingly voiced strong disapproval of many of the congressional benefits, often placing members of Congress on the defensive. Voter disgust with congressional perquisites has led to a growing support for a "term limitation" constitutional amendment. In 1991, observers concluded that Congress as an institution needs structural overhaul. As a result, some members of both houses undertook the creation of a Joint Committee on the Reform of Congress. Such a committee would, inter alia, recommend that Congress either end or limit most "perks." In 1992, a special banking arrangement for members of the House of Representatives was exposed by the national media. Many members wrote no-fund checks and in this way received, in effect, interest-free loans, some for thousands of dollars. The American public was shocked at this revelation and punished some members of Congress at the polls. In 1995, pressure from voters led the Senate to ban free vacations, gifts of over $100 from an individual per year, and lobbyists' contributions to their legal defense funds and to so-called policy-making retreats. The process over the years of adding new perks has now been replaced by actions curtailing or eliminating existing perks. The House has passed a similar bill.

Congressional Record   A record of the proceedings (debates, speeches, and votes) in both the House and the Senate, printed daily. Members may edit their remarks and speeches before they are printed, and they may also insert material, called "extension of remarks," that was not actually delivered on the floor of their chamber. In a process known as "correcting the record," members of Congress may change recorded votes after a vote has been recorded in the Senate, and in the House if the vote was not electronically recorded but was recorded on a roll call. *See also* WEEKLY COMPILATION OF PRESIDENTIAL DOCUMENTS, page 212.

Significance   The *Congressional Record* is a valuable source of data. The inclusion of committee reports enhances its utility. The increasing length, the propagandistic nature of much of the material (excerpts are often used for campaign purposes), and rising costs of the *Record,* however, are matters of concern often voiced by congressional critics. Because many congressmen substantially alter their floor comments by "revising and extending" their remarks, the *Congressional Record* is not a verbatim record of the House and Senate proceedings. Nevertheless, judges often turn to the

Congressional Record and to committee reports in efforts to determine legislative intent.

Congressman at Large   A member of the House of Representatives who is elected by the voters of an entire state rather than by those of a specific district. If a state gains seats following a decennial reapportionment and fails to redistrict, the new seats will be filled by election at large. If a state loses seats and fails to redistrict, then all of the state's congressional members will be elected at large. States with only one member of the House will, of course, always elect that one at large. Decisions concerning redistricting are made by the majority party in each state legislature, but these decisions are subject to judicial oversight. *See also* CONGRESSIONAL DISTRICT, page 139; AT LARGE, page 60.

Significance   Election of representatives at large in states with more than one member of Congress usually results from a partisan legislative deadlock or the refusal of a court to accept a redistricting plan. Increasing pressures from the courts to redistrict on a population basis after each decennial census, however, have reduced the likelihood of electing members of Congress at large. When all of a state's representatives are elected at large, the possibility that one party will win all the seats is substantially increased.

Constituent   A resident of a legislator's district. The district itself is sometimes referred to as the member's constituency. *See also* CONGRESSIONAL DISTRICT, page 139.

Significance   Legislators must act in the capacity of a go-between in the relationship of the average citizen with the national and state governments. Much of a legislator's day must be spent in answering letters, showing the sights to visitors, and similar activities on behalf of constituents. Although this keeps a representative in close contact with the voters, the legislator may be overburdened and unable to devote sufficient time to the lawmaking function. However, helping constituents is often critical for reelection.

Constituent Power   Participation in the process of making, amending, or revising a constitution. The constituent power of Congress consists of its authority to propose amendments to the U.S. Constitution by a two-thirds vote of both houses or to call a national convention for this purpose on petition of two-thirds of the state legislatures. Amendment proposals must be ratified by three-fourths of the state legislatures or by specially elected conventions in three-fourths of the states. In the states, the legislatures are usually empowered to propose specific amendments to their state constitutions. Extensive revisions of state constitutions are generally done by constitutional conventions established solely for that purpose. Ratification or final approval of state constitutional changes is vested in the voters of that state. *See also* AMENDMENT, page 128; CONSTITUTIONAL CONVENTION, page 35; RATIFICATION, page 161.

Significance   Under a system of limited government, the fundamental law found in the constitution provides for the regulated exercise of power by the three branches of government. To the extent that the legislature exercises powers of a constituent nature, it can affect the nature of the limitations placed upon itself as well as those placed upon the other two branches of government. This can be accomplished not only by participating in the formal amendment process but also by constitutional interpretation through statutory enactments.

Contempt of Congress   Willful obstruction of the legislative process. Authority is vested in both houses of Congress and in their investigating committees to cite for contempt of Congress any subpoenaed witness who refuses to appear or to give testimony under oath. The Supreme Court has upheld this power by asserting: "It is unquestionably the duty of all citizens to cooperate with the Congress ... to respond to subpoenas ... and to testify fully with respect to matters within the province of proper investigation" (*Watkins v. United States*, 354 U.S. 178 [1957]). Contempt citations are referred by the presiding officer of the offended chamber to the Department of Justice for criminal prosecution through the federal courts. *See also* INVESTIGATING COMMITTEE, page 152; *McGrain v. Daugherty*, page 177; *Watkins v. United States*, page 179.

Significance   The contempt power of Congress, though it might occasionally be misused, is essential if Congress is to have the authority to conduct meaningful investigations to learn facts on which to base legislative decisions. As currently interpreted by the courts, valid contempt citations may not be issued for refusal of a witness to testify when: (1) the subject under examination is beyond the proper scope of authority of the committee; (2) questions directed to a witness are not pertinent to the subject being investigated; or (3) answers of the witness might provide evidence that could be used against him or her in a criminal case. Most contempt citations of the Congress have been issued by its committees investigating "un-American activities" and organized crime.

Contested Election   Controversy over seating competing claimants to a legislative seat or the qualifications of an elected member. Article I, section 5 of the Constitution states: "Each house shall be the judge of the elections, returns, and qualifications of its own members..." State constitutions have similar provisions. When the election of a member is contested, the chamber concerned sets up a committee to conduct an investigation. Similarly, if controversy arises over rival claims of election to the Electoral College, Congress may determine which electors shall be accredited and have their votes counted in the election of the President. *See also* ELECTORAL COUNT ACT, page 122; EXPULSION, page 146.

Significance   The Constitution makes Congress the exclusive judge of the qualifications of its members, but the Supreme Court has changed the application of this provision by limiting the role of Congress to making judgments on specific constitutional requirements, such as whether the elected member met the minimum age requirement (25 years old) for all members. Historically, however, the House and the Senate on occasion have refused to seat elected members for reasons other than those related to constitutional qualifications. Examples include the barring of a polygamist in 1900, of a socialist in 1919, of two senators in 1926 because they had exceeded lawful campaign expenditures, and of Adam Clayton Powell Jr. in 1967 because of misuse of public funds. Similar cases have occurred in several state legislatures. The main Electoral College issue arose in 1877, when Hayes won over Tilden after twenty contested electoral votes were awarded to Hayes on a partisan basis.

Delegation of Power   The transfer of authority from one government or branch of government that has been constitutionally assigned the power to another branch or specific agency. Generally, delegations of power have involved the transfer of legislative power by Congress to the President, to an executive department or office, or to independent agencies or regulatory commissions. *See also Opp Cotton Mills v. Administrator of Wage and Hour Division,* page 239; QUASI-LEGISLATIVE, page 232.

Significance   The tendency of Congress and state legislatures to delegate legislative powers has increased as legislative workloads have become burdensome and highly technical. Involved in all such delegations, however, is the constitutional question of the legality of the transfer. The Supreme Court, for example, struck down the National Industrial Recovery Act of 1933 in two significant cases in 1935, holding that Congress could not constitutionally transfer its legislative power to the President or to an executive agency (*Panama Refining Co. v. Ryan,* 293 U.S. 388 [1935]; *Schecter Poultry Corp. v. U.S.,* 295 U.S. 495 [1935]). In another case, the Supreme Court held that Congress may not delegate its constitutional powers to the states (*Knickerbocker Ice Co. v. Stewart,* 253 U.S. 149 [1920]). In the field of foreign affairs, however, the Supreme Court upheld a sizable delegation of power to the President by Congress on the ground that the President has a special responsibility in foreign affairs (*United States v. Curtiss-Wright,* 299 U.S. 304 [1936]). The Supreme Court has also laid down the general rule that, if delegations of legislative power are to be considered valid, Congress must determine the general policies and establish clear standards to guide the President or agency in making detailed applications of the general law.

Dilatory Motion   An irrelevant or nongermane motion in a legislative body to delay action on a bill. Dilatory motions are not allowed under the rules of either house of Congress, but considerable discretion is left to the presiding officers in enforcement of these rules. *See also* FILIBUSTER, page 146.

Significance   Dilatory motions are often used by the minority to force concessions by disrupting the time schedule of the majority. In the Senate, their most effective use is by a minority that is trying to kill an important bill by use of the filibuster. Disagreement often exists as to whether a particular action is a dilatory motion or whether it is a relevant and germane motion that should be given careful consideration.

Direct Legislation   Electoral devices that enable voters to participate directly in deciding governmental policies. Direct methods include the initiative and the referendum. The recall, a technique by which the people can remove elected officials before their term of office ends, can also indirectly affect government policies. *See also* DIRECT DEMOCRACY, page 11; INITIATIVE, page 151; RECALL, page 107; REFERENDUM, page 163.

Significance   About half of the states authorize the initiative and/or the referendum. The initiative enables the people of a state to circumvent the inaction of their state legislature. The referendum is a means by which the people can "veto" laws passed by their state legislature before they become effective. In both the initiative and the referendum, the legislature cannot repeal the action of the people. There are no provisions for direct legislation in the national government. New England town meetings and Midwestern township meetings involve direct participation by citizens in deciding policies and budgets.

Discharge Rule   A procedure by which a bill in the House of Representatives may be forced out of a committee (discharged) that has refused to report it out for consideration by the House. Bills not reported out within 30 days after referral to a committee may be subject to discharge, although the Rules Committee may be discharged of a bill after it has held it for only seven legislative days. The discharge petition must be signed by an absolute majority (218) of the House membership. After a week's delay, any member who has signed the petition may move that the bill be discharged from committee. If the motion is carried by a simple majority vote, consideration of the bill then becomes a matter of high privilege. Similar to the House discharge rule is the discharge resolution in the Senate, which may be initiated by an ordinary motion. Many state legislatures also vest discharge powers in the majority of each house. *See also* CALENDAR WEDNESDAY, page 133; PIGEONHOLE, page 158; STANDING COMMITTEE, page 171.

Significance   The discharge rule is one means by which the majority of the House can overcome the "minority" power of legislative committees, which can kill bills by refusing to report them out for consideration. It is used only on rare occasions, since it is a complex procedure and because members are reluctant to challenge the prerogatives of committees and their chairs. Senate discharge has been used only fourteen times in the history of that body, most recently in 1964.

Ethics Codes   Codes of conduct intended to govern the activities of House and Senate members. Each of the two houses of Congress has its own ethics code, and each has its own special Ethics Committee, although the two systems are quite similar. Both House and Senate codes: (1) require full financial disclosure by each member; (2) limit the amount of income each member may earn outside Congress; (3) impose a maximum of a $1,000 fee members can accept for an activity such as giving a speech or writing an article; (4) limit gifts from lobbyists to no more than $100 in value; (5) abolish all unofficial funds used to pay for activities not covered by official allowances; (6) limit the free mailing privileges of members of Congress; and (7) restrict the travel of members who have been defeated for reelection. *See also* ETHICS IN GOVERNMENT ACT OF 1978, page 242; EXPULSION, page 146.

Significance   For many Americans who are growing increasingly cynical about the behavior of elected officials, the phrase "congressional ethics" has become an oxymoron. Congressional investigating committees have uncovered countless cases of abuses and unethical conduct by members of Congress. The problem particularly relates to contributions that individual representatives have accepted from domestic and foreign lobbyists, especially from political action committees (PACs), which captured the headlines in the nation's press over a period of several years. The ethics codes and the oversight committees in each chamber are aimed at avoiding a "congressional Watergate" set of scandals. They represent the pressure of public opinion, the work of public interest lobbies like Common Cause, and fear of voter wrath on the part of incumbent members of Congress. Congress has also undertaken to develop major ethics and disclosure codes and enforcement procedures for the executive and judicial branches of government. Despite efforts to influence ethical congressional conduct, a dozen members were convicted in 1980. Their trials were based on evidence secured by FBI agents masquerading as Middle Eastern sheiks who offered bribes to the congressmen in exchange for their votes, a situation called "Abscam." Issues concerning ethics in government beyond the role played by Congress in its oversight of the conduct of its members developed in 1987. At that time, Congress investigated covert actions carried on by personnel in the Executive Office of the President involving secret sales of arms to Iran and diversion of the funds to aid the Nicaraguan contras. This "Iran-contra affair" involved a double ethics violation in that, under existing law, it was illegal to sell arms to Iran, and it was illegal to fund the contra rebels in Nicaragua beyond the limits established by Congress in the Boland Amendments. To attempt to deal with other ethical problems, Congress enacted the Post-Employment Restrictions Act of 1988, which expanded the Ethics in Government Act of 1978 by tightening restrictions on lobbying, and would have applied them for the first time to members of Congress and their staffs. President Ronald Reagan vetoed it, however. In 1995, Senator Bob Packwood of Oregon resigned under threat of expulsion by the Senate Ethics Committee for unethical conduct—especially in his role as chair of the powerful Senate Finance Committee—including such actions as receiving and granting favors to lobbyists on a large scale. The Packwood case came to public attention when many of his female employees accused him of improper sexual conduct. Thus Senate actions can take the form of investigation and condemnation of ethical code violators, followed by the full Senate dealing with questions of expulsion. Voters constitute the final control, as in the senatorial election of 1994, when the voters defeated Oliver North, even though his conviction for lying to Congress about the Iran-contra affair had been reversed on appeal.

Executive Session A meeting of a legislative body, board, commission, or committee that is closed to the public. Executive sessions are used mainly by committees to consider classified material, interrogate witnesses, and discuss controversial bills. Under the Legislative Reorganization Act of 1970, all votes taken in secret committee sessions must be made part of the public record. *See also* LEGISLATIVE REORGANIZATION ACT OF 1970, page 180.

Significance Executive sessions permit greater freedom for members to express themselves, knowing they will not be put on record. The main disadvantage is that they may tend to encourage irresponsible action, which can be hidden from public view. Although most committee decisions are made in closed sessions in Congress and in state legislatures, the vote of individual members of Congress must be made available to the public. City commissions and councils and other local policy-determining bodies often make important decisions in executive session prior to the public meeting. Thus, in the formal meeting the group may give the impression of consensus and agreement, when, in reality, major battles have already been fought out at the earlier secret session. All levels of government are moving in the direction of reducing or abolishing the use of executive sessions of public bodies as a result of new "sunshine" statutes and court decisions.

Expulsion   The power of a legislative body, usually exercised by each chamber separately, to expel a member as an extreme disciplinary measure. Typical grounds for expulsion include conduct unbecoming a member, disloyalty, and moral turpitude. By Article I, section 5 of the Constitution, each house is empowered to expel a member with the concurrence of two-thirds of the members of that chamber. State constitutions generally vest similar powers in state legislatures. *See also* CENSURE, page 134; ETHICS CODES, page 146.

Significance   Expulsion is a rarely used power of legislative bodies. Only four persons have been expelled from the House, three during the Civil War for supporting rebellion and one in 1980 for corruption. Fifteen senators have been expelled, one in 1797 and fourteen during the Civil War. Members usually try to reconcile differences and, if absolutely necessary, to mete out punishment only in the form of censure or denial of privileges. In addition to expulsion, each chamber of Congress has the power, subject to judicial review, to refuse to seat an elected member. This power was limited by the Supreme Court in 1969, when it held that a member-elect could be barred only if he or she failed to meet constitutional qualifications (*Powell v. McCormack,* 395 U.S. 486).

Farm Bloc   A group made up of both Democratic and Republican representatives and senators from the farm states, who put aside party differences to pass legislation favorable to the farmers. The creation of this voting bloc in the early part of the twentieth century followed the attempts of the farmers to achieve their aims through the creation of various farmers' parties that were unsuccessful in challenging the two major parties. *See also* BLOC, page 132; FARM ORGANIZATIONS, page 484.

Significance   The farm bloc was for many years one of the most consistently successful voting alignments in Congress and in most state legislatures, largely because of overrepresentation of rural areas. Increasing urban and suburban representation is modifying the power of the farm bloc. Moreover, the farm bloc has lost some of its effectiveness because of the failure of farmers and farm organizations to agree on solutions to farm problems. The annual subsidies secured by the farm bloc since President Roosevelt's New Deal days of the 1930s came under increased scrutiny in the 1990s, as efforts were made to balance the federal budget. This involved a planned phase out of general subsidies to farmers over a seven-year period.

Filibuster   A parliamentary device used in the U.S. Senate by which a minority of senators seeks to frustrate the will of the majority by literally "talking a bill to death." Senators are proud of their chamber's reputation for being the world's greatest forum for free discussion. Custom and Senate Rule 22 provide for unlimited debate on a motion before it can be brought to a vote. A filibuster is a misuse of this freedom of debate, since full exploration of the merits and demerits of the pending measure is not its objective. Rather, the minority of senators seeks to gain concessions or the withdrawal of the bill by delaying tactics. These include prolonged debate and speeches on relevant and irrelevant topics, parliamentary maneuvers, dilatory motions, and other tricks of the legislative game. The objective of the minority is to delay action on the measure interminably, until the majority is forced by the press of other business to withdraw it from consideration. *See also* CLOTURE, page 135; FREEDOM OF DEBATE, page 147; LEGISLATIVE DAY, page 154.

Significance   Over the years, many important bills have been filibustered to death. Many more have been killed by using the threat of a filibuster to force withdrawal of a bill. Until the enactment of the Civil Rights Act of 1957, for example, the filibuster or threat of it had been used successfully for many years by southern senators to forestall civil rights legislation. Senator Strom Thurmond of South Carolina holds the record for the longest individual filibuster, speaking for more than 24 hours against enactment of civil rights legislation in 1957. In 1975, the use of the filibuster to kill legislation was weakened in the Senate by making it easier to invoke cloture on debate under Rule 22. Since 1975, three-fifths (60) of the Senate membership of 100 can invoke cloture, thereby breaking a filibuster. Amending the rules of the Senate requires a two-thirds vote of senators present and voting. Filibusters may also be defeated by extending the legislative day and holding round-the-clock sessions of the Senate. The use of the filibuster has increased in recent years. There were only 16 filibusters in the entire nineteenth century, contrasted with 34 in the 103d Congressional session ending in 1994.

Franking Privilege   A policy that enables members of Congress to send material through the mail free by substituting their facsimile signature (frank) for postage. Free mail privileges have also been accorded by Congress to other officials and agencies of the national government. *See also* CONGRESSIONAL "PERKS," page 140.

Significance   The franking privilege provides a means by which members of Congress can keep their constituents informed on issues, voting records, and other business. It is a recognition that the "representative" function of Congress requires that means be provided by which the individual representative can keep in contact with constituents. Controversies often arise during election years over the alleged misuse of the franking privilege to distribute campaign propaganda. The Federal Election Campaign Act of 1974 prohibits members of Congress from using their franked mail to solicit campaign funds. In 1989, Congress reduced by 50 percent the amount of postal patron mass mailings a senator or House member could make in the 1990 fiscal year. The citizens' lobby Common Cause has estimated that in an election year, over 40 million pieces of franked mail are sent out each month by members of the House of Representatives.

Freedom of Debate   The right of members of a legislative body in a democratic system of government to freely discuss, deliberate, and act upon matters of policy without fear of legal action. The Constitution (Art. I, sec. 6) provides that "for any speech or debate in either House, they [senators and representatives] shall not be questioned in any other place." Utterances that might otherwise be unlawful are privileged, therefore, when made in Congress (*United States v. Johnson*, 383 U.S. 169 [1966]). Immunity to suit does not ordinarily apply to statements made outside of Congress, as in press releases, newsletters, television programs, and phone calls (*Hutchinson v. Proxmire*, 443 U.S. 111 [1979]). In all cases, however, whether such statements are made in or out of Congress, members can be held to account through the disciplinary powers of their own house. State constitutions also provide immunity for legislators. Freedom of debate is sometimes used to describe the right under Senate Rule 22 to speak indefinitely on a pending measure in the U.S. Senate unless limited by the invoking of cloture or by unanimous consent. *See also* CLOTURE, page 135; FILIBUSTER, page 146; GAG RULE, page 148.

Significance   The purpose of ensuring maximum freedom of debate is to guarantee that decisions will be freely made after thorough debate. Without such a guarantee, members might become too restricted in their deliberations to do a good job of legislating. A member can abuse this right by unjustly slurring the reputation of a citizen, who has no recourse in the courts. In the Senate, a small group can delay action and frustrate the majority will by the use of the filibuster, which constitutes an abuse of freedom of debate. In the House, but not the Senate, debate must be germane (relevant).

Gag Rule   A legislative rule that arbitrarily limits the time available for consideration of a measure. The term "gag rule" refers generally to any special rule that limits debate on a pending bill or resolution beyond that provided by the chamber's regular legislative rules. *See also* CLOTURE, page 135; RULES COMMITTEE, page 166.

Significance   The use of gag rules by a legislative body tends to expedite the legislative process but may give excessive influence to minority elements that have the power to impose special rules. By prohibiting or limiting the proposal of amendments or other parliamentary tactics, a gag rule may have a profound effect on the outcome of the voting on a measure and on the substantive product as well. A special rule is provided by the Rules Committee of the House of Representatives for the consideration of each legislative matter, but in the Senate, freedom of debate may be limited only by invoking cloture, or by unanimous consent.

Gerrymandering   The drawing of legislative district boundary lines to obtain partisan or factional advantage. Gerrymandering is engaged in by partisan majorities in state legislatures when they are drawing up congressional and state legislative districts. The objective is to gain partisan electoral advantage by spreading support for one's own party over many districts and concentrating the support for the other party in few districts. Gerrymandering is possible because of the pattern of consistency in voting behavior of most Americans. The term emerged in Massachusetts in 1811 when Governor Elbridge Gerry signed a redistricting bill that created a district resembling a salamander in its shape; it was referred to by pundits of the day as a "gerrymander." *See also* REDISTRICTING, page 162; *Reynolds v. Sims,* page 178; *Wesberry v. Sanders,* page 179.

Significance The shape and composition of each legislative district can dictate a candidate's strategy and tactics and help determine an election outcome. Most redistricting laws enacted by state legislatures show evidence of varying degrees of boundary manipulation for partisan advantage. After the 1990 census, for example, a 160-mile-long ribbon-shaped district was created to increase black representation. In *Shaw v. Reno* (509 U.S. 630 [1993]), the Court held that this racial gerrymandering was in violation of the equal rights of white voters. It concluded that a state must show a compelling interest to disregard the tradition of "compact and contiguous" districts. Historically, gerrymandering resulted in gross overrepresentation of rural areas in the House of Representatives and in most state legislatures. In 1964, the Supreme Court ruled on this issue (*Wesberry v. Sanders,* 376 U.S. 1), holding that state and congressional districts should be drawn on a basis of substantial equality of population. Nevertheless, the boundaries of districts that are substantially equal in population may still be drawn to secure partisan advantage, and gerrymandering persists. Thus, a minority of a state's voters may elect a majority of that state's congressional delegation and a majority in both houses of the state legislature. A legislative majority can often maintain its power position by influencing elections through its control over district boundaries. Critics of gerrymandering claim that it violates the "one person, one vote" rule laid down by the Supreme Court in a number of apportionment decisions because gerrymandering can add to or subtract from the electoral power of voters. In 1986, the Supreme Court ruled on this issue (*Davis v. Bandemer,* 478 U.S. 109) when it held that partisan political gerrymandering is subject to constitutional challenge even if the "one person, one vote" rule is met. Such a challenge may stand, said the Court, if the drawing of lines results in continual frustration of the majority will or the effective denial of influence to a majority. The Court, however, failed to clarify what standards would prove that the state legislature had engaged in a "legally unacceptable partisan gerrymander." Gerrymandering problems have been further complicated by questions regarding the accuracy of federal censuses, including that of 1990.

Hearing A public session of a committee of a legislative body to obtain information on a proposed law or resolution. In Congress, public hearings are commonly functions of subcommittees, which report their findings to the full committees. The theory behind hearings is that out of the "combat" between contestants using every ethical means to convince committee members of the wisdom of their positions will emerge the "true facts." The members can then make their decision, much like a judge and jury in a judicial proceeding. The hearings thus serve as a means by which American citizens can "petition" their elected representatives and seek to influence their decision making. *See also* INVESTIGATING COMMITTEE, page 152.

Significance Most hearings involve only professional lobbyists. Administration officials are often pitted against private lobbyists. In recent years, there has been an increasing tendency in Congress for committees to use hearings to try to influence public opinion or executive action, as in the areas of communism, foreign policy, and crime. Public hearings are used extensively and are a valuable legislative aid. State legislatures also provide for public hearings on important measures.

High Crimes and Misdemeanors   The Constitution provides in Article II, section 4 that the President, Vice President, and all civil officers of the United States are subject to impeachment and removal from office upon conviction for "treason, bribery, or other high crimes and misdemeanors." No precise definition of what acts might constitute high crimes and misdemeanors has been developed. Discretion is vested completely in Congress. *See also* IMPEACHMENT, page 150.

Significance   In practice, probably based on English historical precedent, the grounds on which impeachment action is taken are usually restricted to unethical conduct and criminal offenses. Congress has not regarded incompetence or political disagreement as grounds for invoking its impeachment powers. Yet, because so much discretion is vested in Congress by the Constitution, the threat of its use may sometimes constitute a potent weapon. In 1974, the House wrestled with the problem of defining and applying "high crimes and misdemeanors" to the conduct of President Richard M. Nixon to determine if he should be impeached. The President's resignation occurred, however, before the House acted.

House of Representatives   The lower house of the bicameral Congress, in which representation is based on population. The upper house, the Senate of the United States, is based on the principle of state equality. The House was intended by the Founding Fathers to be the popular chamber of Congress, and it was made larger and more responsive to the public will than the Senate, which was intended to represent the states and to function as the more deliberative body. Each state is guaranteed at least one representative. Since 1910, the House has had a permanent membership of 435. The ratio of population to representatives has been steadily increasing until now it is more than 500,000 per representative. The Constitution vests certain powers exclusively in the House, including (1) the impeachment power, (2) the initiation of revenue bills, (3) the election of a President if no candidate obtains a majority in the Electoral College, (4) the determination of its own rules of procedure, and (5) the discipline of its members. *See also* SENATE, page 167.

Significance   Some critics reject the assertion that the House is the more representative of the two houses of Congress. They point out that because many representatives tend to stress local interests, the House may be less responsive to national problems than the Senate. Its unwieldy size and the power vested in its Rules Committee often make it less able than the Senate to cope with contemporary problems. Nevertheless, American voters tend to regard their representatives as their most direct contact with the national government. In 1979, the House decided to permit live coverage of routine sessions by public and commercial television, such as C-SPAN.

Impeachment   A formal accusation, rendered by the lower house of a legislative body, that commits an accused civil official for trial in the upper house. Impeachment is, therefore, merely the first step in a two-stage process. In the national government, constitutional authority to *impeach* is vested in the House and the power to *try* impeachment cases rests with the Senate (Art. I, sec. 2 and 3; Art. II, sec. 4; and Art. III, sec. 2). All civil officers of the United States are subject to impeachment, excluding military officers and members of Congress. The impeachment process begins with the preferring of charges by a representative, followed by referral to either the Judiciary Committee or to a special investigating committee. A simple majority vote of the House is sufficient to impeach. "Articles of Impeachment" are drawn up, setting forth the basis for removal. The House appoints managers who prosecute the case in a trial before the Senate. If the President is on trial, the Chief Justice of the United States presides. The procedure during the trial closely resembles that of a court of law. A two-thirds vote of the Senators present is necessary for conviction. The only punishments that may be meted out are removal from office and disqualification from holding any office in the future. Once removed, however, the individual may be tried in a regular court of law if he or she has committed a criminal act. The President's pardoning power does not apply to impeachment convictions. *See also* GOOD BEHAVIOR, page 263; HIGH CRIMES AND MISDEMEANORS, page 150.

Significance   In the course of American history, the House has instituted impeachment proceedings against 50 individuals, but only 14 have been impeached, the most recent in 1986. Twelve have come to trial before the Senate, and only 5—all judges—have been convicted. Charges have included bribery, incompetence, immorality, treason, sedition, insanity, tyranny, and advocacy of secession. In one notable case, President Andrew Johnson was acquitted by the margin of a single vote in 1868 of the charge of violating the Tenure of Office Act by removing an appointed official without congressional consent (the Act was later declared unconstitutional by the Supreme Court); in another case, Justice Samuel Chase was acquitted in 1805 of alleged political conduct on the Supreme Court. Few state officials have been convicted and removed by state legislatures. Occasionally, partisan politics may influence the exercise of the power, as was true in the Johnson case, and in the removal of several state officials by their legislatures. The process is always political in nature, but open partisanship can weaken public support. In 1974, President Richard M. Nixon resigned in the face of House preparations to begin impeachment proceedings. The *threat* of impeachment is often effective in securing the resignation of the official. However, in 1986 the Senate convicted and removed federal judge Harry E. Claiborne of Nevada when he refused to vacate the judgeship even though serving a two-year prison sentence for tax evasion. In 1991, the federal Court of Appeals ruled that the United States Senate may use a special committee rather than the full Senate to hear evidence in an impeachment case. The case involved the 1989 impeachment conviction of U.S. District Judge Walter L. Nixon Jr. of Mississippi, and the Court reaffirmed that impeachment is not a matter for the courts.

Initiative   An electoral device by which interested citizens can propose legislation or constitutional amendments through initiatory petitions signed by the required number of registered voters. The number of signatures varies from 5 to 15 percent of the voters in the different states. The proposition is then voted on by the people. Constitutional amendment proposals usually require a greater number of signatures on the petitions. The "direct" initiative involves a vote of the people following the filing of petitions. The "indirect" provides that the proposal, after being filed, be sent to the legislature; if not approved, it then goes before the voters. *See also* DIRECT DEMOCRACY, page 11; DIRECT LEGISLATION, page 143; REFERENDUM, page 163.

Significance   Approximately half of the states provide for the initiative in either form. About twenty states permit its use for ordinary laws, and seventeen for constitutional amendments. Only one state, Alaska, has adopted the initiative since 1918. The U.S. Constitution does not provide for a national initiative, but groups have, from time to time, advocated its adoption. In some states, especially California, the ease with which initiatory proposals can be placed on the ballot has contributed to the "long ballot" problem. In recent years, tax reduction or limitation amendment proposals have been placed on the ballot in many states through the initiative. In *Meyer v. Grant*, 486 U.S. 414 (1988), the Supreme Court nullified a state law prohibiting payment to circulators of petitions to amend the state constitution as a violation of freedom of speech.

Investigating Committee   A legislative committee that exercises a fact-finding role as an aid to the lawmaking process. Investigating committees may compel witnesses to attend and to produce relevant materials. Investigations are conducted by both the regular standing committees and by special committees created for that purpose. The purposes behind investigations include (1) finding of facts on which to base legislation, (2) discovering or developing of public opinion, (3) overseeing of administrative agencies, (4) uncovering the questionable activities of public officials and private individuals, and (5) sometimes securing personal or partisan political gain. In terms of time, effort, and publicity, the investigatory activities of Congress and of some state legislatures have in recent years rivaled their legislative functions. A legislative body may investigate any subject that is properly within the scope of its legislative powers. *See also* McGrain *v. Daugherty,* page 177; WATCHDOG COMMITTEE, page 175; *Watkins v. United States,* page 179.

Significance   Many important topics have been investigated in the more than 800 congressional investigations in the nation's history. Some have been mere "fishing expeditions," and others were politically motivated by attempts to embarrass the rival party. Increasingly, Congress has relied on investigations as a means of seeking to regain its position of power vis-à-vis the executive branch, which has steadily gained in relative power during this century. Serious questions have been raised concerning the scope of congressional inquiries, the rights of witnesses who appear before committees, the fairness of procedures, and the extraction of testimony from unwilling witnesses. Congress has sought to deal with some of these problems through the study and correction of procedures and the setting up of a "fair play" guarantee for witnesses. Several presidents have invoked executive privilege in refusing to permit executive officials to appear before investigating committees on matters pertaining to national security or executive prerogatives. Some of the more recent and important investigations have been on Watergate, the Iran-contra affair, the Waco siege, and the Whitewater hearings. In the last case, a special Congressional committee has searched for evidence of wrongdoing by Bill and Hillary Clinton while he was governor of Arkansas and she worked for the Rose Law Firm, which represented the interests of a bankrupt savings and loan, Madison Guaranty, that had investments in the Whitewater resort development project.

Joint Committee   A legislative committee composed of members of both houses. The number appointed to a joint committee is usually divided equally between the two houses, with each member having one vote. On some, such as conference committees, each chamber may determine the size of its membership on the committee, and the two groups vote separately on measures. Joint committees are usually select (special) committees appointed for a specified purpose: typically, to conduct investigations. Congress has created a few standing (permanent) joint committees, such as the Joint Committee on the Economic Report and the Joint Committee on Atomic Energy. *See also* CONFERENCE COMMITTEE, page 138.

Significance   Joint committees make it possible for the two houses of a legislative body to work out compromises on bills or resolutions. They tend to encourage greater cooperation between the two chambers. Some observers have recommended that all standing committees of Congress be joint committees, so that time-consuming duplication of the existing dual-committee system could be eliminated. Supporters of this proposal believe that it would result in quicker and more effective action on most bills and would eliminate the need for two appearances before separate House and Senate committees by persons wishing to testify for or against a bill. Opponents point out that such a change would eliminate much of the effectiveness of the checks and balances system inherent in a bicameral legislative body, and it would be likely to result in less careful scrutiny of pending legislation.

Joint Resolution   A measure, similar to a bill, that must be approved in both chambers and by the executive. In Congress, joint resolutions are designated "H J Res" and "S J Res" and, if passed by a simple majority in both houses, must be signed by the President to become law. The procedure is identical to that used in passing a bill into law except when the joint resolution is used to propose an amendment to the Constitution. Then the President's signature is unnecessary. About half of the state legislatures also employ the joint resolution in enacting laws and proposing constitutional amendments. *See also* CONCURRENT RESOLUTION, page 137; SIMPLE RESOLUTION, page 169.

Significance   Joint resolutions are employed by Congress to approve of executive actions in foreign affairs or to take the initiative in foreign policy. They have occasionally proved useful in circumventing the two-thirds vote requirement in the Senate on treaty matters, as in the annexations of Texas and of Hawaii. Joint resolutions are also used for such limited matters as the passing of a single appropriation bill for a designated purpose. The Tonkin Gulf Resolution, which was adopted by Congress in 1964 to authorize the President to take whatever military action he deemed necessary to protect American forces in Asia, became one of the most controversial joint resolutions. In 1970, because of congressional disenchantment with the Vietnam

War and disclosures of alleged perfidy in reporting the incidents to Congress that led to its adoption, the Resolution was repealed.

Joint Session   A meeting of the members of both chambers of a legislative body. Congress meets in joint session to count the electoral votes and certify the election of the President, and when addressed by the President or a foreign dignitary. A joint session is never used to consider specific bills. Most state legislatures meet in joint session to receive the governor's annual message. *See also* SESSION, page 168.

Significance   Legislative bodies typically use joint sessions to consider noncontroversial matters and to be informed on current issues. Such sessions of the Congress are often televised since they are auspicious occasions. Most joint sessions are called to receive messages or reports from the chief executive officer, or to welcome foreign officials.

Legislative Council   An interim committee employed by some legislatures between sessions to study state problems and to plan a legislative program. In some states, legislative councils have pursued extensive fact-finding research programs. The councils range in size from five members to the entire legislature. Usually, membership is selected from the two houses of the legislature, but, in several states, the governor is authorized to include representation from the executive branch.

Significance   Legislative councils are a means by which the legislatures of three-fourths of the states have sought to develop leadership and planning facilities staffed by their own members. In this way, dependence on the executive to formulate a comprehensive program for consideration by the legislature is reduced. Moreover, as the work load becomes heavier and more complex, legislatures are becoming more dependent upon well-prepared programs worked out carefully in advance. The fear that power might become too concentrated in the hands of those legislators making up the councils has not been justified in the experience of the states that have adopted the plan.

Legislative Day   The official meeting of a legislative chamber that begins with a formal call to order and opening of business and ends with adjournment. A legislative day may cover a period of several calendar days, with the chamber merely recessing at the end of each calendar day rather than adjourning. *See also* FILIBUSTER, page 146; MORNING HOUR, page 156.

Significance   The objective of continuing a legislative day over a period of several calendar days may be to expedite business, to avoid the introduction of new, controversial issues before current business has been disposed of, or to facilitate bringing a major bill to a vote. In any case, it is a technique used by the leadership to help in the achievement of some goal. In the Senate, for example, one approach to defeat a filibuster is to use the rule that permits each member to speak no more than twice during a legislative day. By recessing instead of adjourning, the legislative day is continued indefinitely without adjournment until each senator has had an opportunity to speak. In this way, debate ultimately ends and a vote is taken. By using this procedure and holding night and day sessions, the Senate leadership has been able to defeat a filibuster on several occasions.

Legislative Service Organizations   Groups whose members—either Republican, Democratic, or bipartisan—join together to debate and take policy stands on issues of mutual concern. The first such informal legislative caucusing group was the Democratic Study Group. Its success in providing members with useful information on pending legislation led others to form similar groups on various issues. Congressional funding was available from 1979 to 1995. At that time, budget considerations and a promise to voters for change toward less government led the Republican-controlled Congress to end all financial support. *See also* CAUCUS, page 134.

Significance   The success of these legislative service organizations that function as informal caucusing groups was demonstrated by their rapid increase to more than 100, by the acceptance of their role by the leadership of the House and Senate, and by the decision-making power that they have possessed. Some of the most effective groups have been the Democratic Study Group, Conservative Democratic Forum ("boll weevils"), Republican Study Group, Northeast-Midwest Republicans Coalition ("gypsy moths"), the Republican Freshman Class (especially of the 104th Congress, who, because of their numbers and belief in the mandate that brought them to Washington, exerted great power and influence on issues before the House, most notably in obtaining agreement on a balanced budget in seven years), the Congressional Black Caucus, Congressional Human Rights Caucus, the bicameral Caucus for Women's Issues, and the Senior Citizens Caucus. The influence of specific caucus groups changes with the party in power, especially for the Black Caucus under the Republican-controlled Congress. However, all legislative service organizations, having been deprived of financial support, a working staff, and office space have lost much of their ability to affect policy.

Legislative Veto   Rejection of an action of the executive or of an administrative agency by the legislature without the consent of the chief executive. Legislative veto authority was made part of about 200 acts of Congress to enable one or both houses of Congress or, in some cases, a committee of Congress, to veto an executive or administrative action. While some explicitly applied to the President (for example, the War Powers Act of 1973 and the Congressional Budget and Impoundment Control Act of 1974), most were enacted to restrain regulatory commissions and the vast number of administrators engaged in rule making. Under such authority, one or both houses of Congress could veto a specific administrative rule or regulation prior to its taking effect, without subsequent acceptance or veto by the President, as in the case of ordinary legislation. In 1983, the Supreme Court stunned Congress by holding in *Immigration and Naturalization Service v. Chadha* (462 U.S. 919) that the legislative veto is an unconstitutional violation of the separation of powers. *See also* ADMINISTRATIVE ORDER, page 219; *Immigration and Naturalization Service v. Chadha,* page 177; QUASI-LEGISLATIVE, page 232; SEPARATION OF POWERS, page 50.

Significance   The legislative veto controversy offered a classic test of the separation of powers doctrine underlying the U.S. Constitution. Supporters of the legislative veto argued that lawmaking is the responsibility of elected legislative bodies but that most of the rules governing behavior are actually promulgated by either the executive or unelected bureaucrats. Much legislation would not have been enacted, it is argued, without the safeguard of the legislative veto; otherwise, Congress would have to be much more specific in legislating than is often possible or desirable. Opponents contended (and the Supreme Court agreed) that the legislative veto violated the separation of powers by invading the administrative prerogatives of the executive branch and by bypassing the President's responsibility to sign or veto legislation. Though the legislative veto was not used to a great extent, its existence affected Congress's willingness to enact legislation and served to restrain administrative action.

Logrolling   An arrangement by which two or more members of a legislative body agree in advance to support each other's bills. The term "logrolling" refers to a lumberjack's game in which two men must cooperate to maintain their balance on a floating, spinning log. The technique pertains especially to the trading of votes among legislators in order to gain support for appropriations beneficial to each legislator's home district. *See also* PORK BARREL LEGISLATION, page 158; TRADE-OFF, page 115.

Significance   To the extent that logrolling exists, it probably results from the American belief that a representative should seek to "deliver the goods" for the home district. Also called "horse trading" or "mutual back scratching," logrolling is inevitable in legislative bodies in which strong party discipline does not prevail. No control over logrolling exists except for the adverse publicity that may result and the ultimate action of the voters on election day.

Majority Floor Leader   The chief spokesman and strategist of the majority party, who directs the party's forces in legislative battles. In the House, only the Speaker is considered to be more influential. In the Senate, the majority leader is the undisputed leader of his or her party. Floor leaders seek to carry out decisions of their party's caucus or conference and are aided by party whips. Their counterparts in the other party are the minority floor leaders. Floor leaders are selected by their respective party caucuses. Similar party leadership positions exist in most state legislatures. *See also* CAUCUS, page 134; POLICY COMMITTEE, page 158; WHIP, page 175.

Significance   Much of the success of a majority floor leader depends on ability. A floor leader who is an able organizer and possesses personal leadership characteristics can exercise considerable influence on legislation. In the Senate, the majority leader must work closely with the minority leader, since much business is transacted through unanimous consent. Because floor leaders hold critical positions in Congress, they are summoned often to the White House for conferences concerning the President's legislative program.

Morning Hour   A period, not limited to mornings, reserved in Congress at the start of a legislative day to consider routine business. The Senate sets aside the first two hours of each new legislative day for such matters as committee reports, the introduction of bills and resolutions, and the receipt of presidential messages. During the first hour, a bill can be considered only through unanimous consent. In the House, the morning hour is seldom used, since most routine business is transacted in the Committee of the Whole, and bills are introduced by simply dropping them into the "hopper." *See also* COMMITTEE OF THE WHOLE, page 137; LEGISLATIVE DAY, page 154.

Significance   The morning hour frees the remainder of the Senate's legislative day for consideration of pending legislation. During the morning hour, senators may speak on a variety of topics not necessarily related to current business. Senate committees often meet during that chamber's morning hour.

Ombudsman   A special official or commissioner appointed by a legislative body or governing board to hear and investigate complaints by private individuals against public officials or agencies. The office of ombudsman, which originated in Scandinavia, is utilized currently in many countries by national, state, and local units of government and other public bodies, including some local agencies in the United States. Typically, the ombudsman has no decision-making authority but is empowered to carry on inquiry and mediation functions. The title of the office has increasingly been changed to "ombudsperson" because of the growing number of women appointed. *See also* CONSTITUENT, page 141; PRIVATE BILL, page 160.

Significance   Several American congressmen have recommended the creation of the office of ombudsman to function as an agent of Congress. The objective would be to free members of Congress for legislative business by turning citizen complaints over to a professional who would focus full attention on handling problems on a nonpartisan, nonpolitical basis. Most members of Congress, however, have been reluctant to turn their constituents over to an ombudsman or administrative agency for relief, since solving citizen problems is regarded as a lucrative source of votes for reelection. Some ombudsmen are given general jurisdiction whereas others have specialized jurisdiction or serve as quasi-ombudsmen. Many colleges and universities and some private companies have created ombudsmen offices. The United States Association of Ombudsmen (USAO) seeks to establish and improve governmental ombudsmen offices at all levels, and the International Ombudsmen Institute in Canada promotes the idea internationally.

Pair   An understanding reached in advance between two legislators, holding opposing views on a bill, to withhold their votes on a "yea and nay" roll call. In this way, each is assured that his or her absence from the chamber during the vote will not affect the outcome. In effect, each member of the pair cancels out the other's vote, with one "paired for" the measure and the other "paired against" it. A "special" pair applies to one or several votes taken on the same subject. A "general" pair, used in the House and occasionally in the Senate, applies to all votes taken over a specified period of time. A "live" pair indicates how each member would have voted. On a question requiring a two-thirds vote, two members must be "paired for" the measure to balance off one "paired against" it. *See also* VOTING (LEGISLATIVE), page 174.

Significance   The advantage of pairing lies in the nature of the "gentlemen's agreement" between the two lawmakers. Neither can show up unexpectedly and vote in the roll call without breaking the agreement. Each, in effect, casts a vote by canceling out the other's vote, although they are not counted in "yea" and "nay" vote totals. Members of Congress frequently find it necessary to be absent from their chamber, and pairing enables them to put their position on bills on record.

Pigeonhole   To kill a bill in committee by putting it aside and not reporting it out for consideration by the chamber. The term relates to the old-time desks in committee rooms of Congress, which had open "pigeonholes" or cubicles for filing papers. To pigeonhole a bill means to file the bill away and forget it. This usually kills the bill. Killing a bill by pigeonholing is typically accomplished by a committee chair when a majority of the committee members do not object. *See also* COMMITTEE CHAIR, page 136; DISCHARGE RULE, page 144.

Significance   More bills die in committee through pigeonholing each congressional session than are rejected outright by the two houses. The same is true in the state legislatures. Chances for a pigeonholed bill to be enacted into law are slight because members of the committee and chamber are reluctant to challenge the authority of the chair or to use the extraordinary procedures required to discharge bills from committee.

Policy Committee   A party committee in Congress that functions as an agent of the caucus or conference in formulating legislative plans and strategy. Although the reorganization of Congress in 1946 provided for policy committees to replace the old steering committees, only the Senate at that time formally created such bodies. House Republicans converted their steering committee into a policy committee in 1949, and more recently House Democrats established a combined Steering and Policy Committee. In the Senate, the Democrats retained their steering committee to function solely as a committee on committees to fill vacancies on Senate committees. *See also* CAUCUS, page 134; COMMITTEE ON COMMITTEES, page 137.

Significance   In both the Senate and House, the policy committees have superseded the steering committees as the basic party strategy organs and agents of the caucus or conference. In the Senate, the majority policy committee, along with the floor leader, often determines the order in which measures will be considered. Representation on the policy committees is given to all major regions of the nation and to important factions within the party. Their importance in the legislative process varies, depending upon the degree of party unity and the personalities and drive of the individuals on the committees.

Pork Barrel Legislation   Appropriations made by a legislative body providing for expenditures of sums of public money on local projects not critically needed. The term is closely related to logrolling, in that members of the legislative body usually do not question each other's pet projects for fear that their own may be voted down. It is frequently a simple matter of *quid pro quo*—that is, "You scratch my back and I'll scratch yours." *See also* LOGROLLING, page 156.

Significance   Pork barrel legislation has resulted in the expenditure of large sums of money each year. Basically, the problem relates to the theory of representation. The American representative goes to the legislature or to Congress as the representative of the people of his or her district rather than of the state or nation. This means that constituents expect their representative to perform creditably on their behalf. By obtaining "pork" (appropriations for local highways, river and harbor construction projects, and so forth) by raiding the pork barrel (the state or national treasury), the representative is likely to improve his or her chances for reelection. Recent studies show that, whereas the "snowbelt" states of the North and East contribute billions of dollars more in taxes than they receive in federal benefits, the "sunbelt" states receive far more from federal spending programs than they contribute in taxes, largely because of the concentration of military bases, defense industries, and retired people in states such as Florida, Arizona, Nevada, Texas, and California. This is a form of pork-barreling that has seriously unbalanced the nation's economy.

Power of the Purse   The historic power of democratic legislative bodies to control the finances of government. The power of the purse extends to both revenue and appropriation functions. In the national government, the Constitution specifies that "No money shall be drawn from the Treasury, but in consequence of appropriations made by law" (Art. I, sec. 9). New programs must be twice approved: first, through authorization and, second, through appropriation to finance them. Expenditures by the executive must be validated by the General Accounting Office to ensure that such outlays fall within the limits of appropriations made by Congress. Additional checks are carried on through the "watchdog" oversight committees of Congress. *See also* APPROPRIATION, page 129; AUTHORIZATION, page 130; IMPOUNDMENT, page 193.

Significance   The power of the purse remains a major power of all legislative bodies. The power can be used in an affirmative manner to force positive action by government as well as in a negative way to stop action. The threat of budget cutting is usually enough to elicit cooperation from executive officials. Historically, legislative bodies first succeeded in limiting executive absolutism through control of the purse. One of the major grievances leading to the American Revolution was the taxation of the colonists without their consent. Some measure of the impact of the power of the purse may be assessed from the fact that Congress appropriates hundreds of billions of dollars each fiscal year.

President Pro Tempore   The temporary presiding officer of the Senate in the absence of the Vice President. The President pro tempore is elected by the Senate, following nomination by the majority party caucus, and is eligible for the presidency of the United States following the death or disability of the President, Vice President, and Speaker of the House. State senates also select presidents pro tempore. *See also* PRESIDENTIAL SUCCESSION, page 204; VICE PRESIDENT, page 174, 210.

Significance   Like the Speaker of the House, the President pro tempore is a partisan officer who may use the position to aid the program of the majority party. In presiding over the Senate, however, the President pro tempore usually functions in an objective, nonpartisan manner. Although the office is usually overshadowed by that of the majority floor leader, it is one of considerable prestige and is usually awarded to the senior member of the majority party in the Senate.

Previous Question   A motion in a legislative body to cease debate and force a vote on a pending measure. In Congress, the rules permit previous question motions in the House but not in the Senate. The motion itself cannot be debated or laid on the table. If the motion carries before any debate on the bill has occurred, each side is allowed twenty minutes to present its case. State legislatures use similar rules to limit debate. *See also* SUSPENSION OF RULES, page 172; UNANIMOUS CONSENT, page 173.

Significance   The previous question rule in the House makes it possible to avoid unlimited discussion, such as occurs during a filibuster in the Senate. With 435 members in the House, such a rule is necessary to prevent the chamber from bogging down in endless debate. It is also used as a parliamentary device to prevent amendments that might cripple a bill, or it may be employed by supporters or by opponents of a bill who may regard an extensive debate of its merits as detrimental to their position. Previous question is augmented by other parliamentary devices to speed up the legislative process, such as suspension of rules and unanimous consent.

Private Bill   A bill introduced into a legislative body that deals with specific matters and individuals rather than with general legislative affairs. In Congress, although the number of private bills was considerably reduced by the Reorganization Act of 1946, several thousand—about one-tenth of the total bills introduced—are still introduced at each session. The main categories include: (1) immigration and naturalization bills applying to specific individuals, (2) claim bills not subject to administrative resolution, and (3) land bills assigning title to individuals. Private bills are introduced by members of Congress who are petitioned by their constituents to right a government-inflicted wrong or to deal with a matter not covered by general statute. If enacted, they become private law and apply only to specific individuals named in the act. All state legislatures allow introduction of private bills. *See also* BILL, page 131; OMBUDSMAN, page 157.

Significance   Many observers believe that it would add considerably to the efficiency of Congress to reduce further the categories of private bills. Approximately one-third of the laws passed by Congress are private laws, despite efforts to reduce or eliminate the need for such actions. Private bills tend to force the legislative body into performing a judicial function in determining the merits of particular claims made by individuals. They are time-consuming and detract from the general lawmaking function of Congress, as well as of the legislatures in the states. Further use of administrative agencies to handle these matters could lighten the burden of the legislative body. Nevertheless, many believe that it is part of the democratic system of government that the legislative body have the power to right governmental wrongs against individuals. In Congress, a private bill is unlikely to become law unless the representative who introduces it gives it personal attention and strong support.

Quorum   The minimum number of members of a legislative chamber who must be present in order to transact business. The Constitution specifies that "a majority of each [house] shall constitute a quorum to do business" (Art. I, sec. 5). This means 218 in the House and 51 in the Senate. In the House, the quorum for the Committee of the Whole is 100. Typically, state legislatures also require a majority of members to be present for the transaction of business. *See also* COMMITTEE OF THE WHOLE, page 137.

Significance The House frequently escapes the quorum requirement of 218 by dissolving into the Committee of the Whole. Decisions reached, however, must be ratified by the duly constituted House. Both chambers often proceed with fewer than a quorum present unless challenged by a point of order. When this occurs, either the chamber must adjourn or the Sergeant at Arms is instructed to round up the absent members. Frequent "quorum calls" or demands that the members present be counted to determine if a quorum is in fact present may be used as a delaying tactic.

Ranking Member That member of the majority party on a legislative committee who ranks first after the chair in years of continuous service (seniority) on the committee. The ranking minority member is the minority party member with the longest continuous service on the committee. *See also* COMMITTEE CHAIR, page 136; SENIORITY RULE, page 168.

Significance In Congress, the ranking member is the one who is likely to succeed to the chair of a committee if that post is vacated while his or her party has majority control of that house. The ranking member is often accorded the chair of one of the committee's important subcommittees. Many state legislatures follow the same procedures, although factors other than seniority—for example, the political influence of nonsenior members and pressures exerted by powerful interest groups—may be more decisive in making such selections. In Congress, the ranking minority member is likely to succeed to the chairmanship of the committee when his or her party wins control of that house. Meanwhile, the ranking minority member provides some leadership for the minority members on the committee.

Ratification (Legislative) A power vested in a legislative body to approve (or reject) agreements entered into with other states, as well as constitutional amendment proposals. In the states, interstate compacts negotiated by the governors of several states must be ratified or approved by the state legislature of each and approved by Congress before becoming effective. Amendments proposed to state constitutions, however, must be ratified by a vote of the people of that state. The term "ratification" is also popularly used to describe the "consent" function of the United States Senate regarding treaties negotiated by the United States with foreign nations, although here the term more properly applies to the role of the President in accepting or rejecting the Senate-approved version of a treaty. *See also* AMENDMENT, page 128; RATIFICATION (EXECUTIVE), page 205.

Significance Ratification gives the legislative body an effective check over agreements entered into with other states and over changes made in the fundamental law. Often, important agreements and amendment proposals are killed by the failure of legislatures to bring them to a vote or by the failure of proponents to secure the necessary extraordinary majority vote. All amendments to the U.S. Constitution have been ratified by state legislatures except the Twenty-first, ending Prohibition, which was ratified by specially elected conventions in the states.

Readings   The three readings of a bill required at different stages of the legislative process. In Congress, the first reading occurs when the bill is introduced and printed by title in the *Congressional Record*. The second, often a reading in full, takes place when the bill is brought out of committee for consideration before the chamber. The third reading, usually by title only, comes after amendments have been voted on and the bill is up for a final vote. State legislative procedure is similar. *See also* BILL, page 131.

Significance   The required three readings of a bill, based on traditional parliamentary procedure, are expected to ensure careful consideration of all bills and to prevent any from sneaking through almost unnoticed. The procedure is of little utility today in the legislative process of Congress and the state legislatures. On occasion, full reading of a bill may be demanded and used as a delaying tactic. Cases abound wherein legislators have voted for bills without realizing their contents or consequences despite their three readings. Because of the huge volume of legislative business, readings have often been made through the process of unanimous consent, whereby if no member objects it is assumed the reading has occurred.

Recommittal   The action of a legislative body of sending a bill back to the committee that had reported it out for consideration. A motion to recommit may instruct the committee to report the bill out again with certain amendments or at a later date. Most motions for recommittal, however, simply call for further study by the committee. *See also* BILL, page 131.

Significance   In most cases, the adoption of a motion to recommit to committee is considered a death blow for a bill. Often legislators prefer not to alienate constituents who support a bill by directly voting it down. Recommittal can accomplish the same purpose without giving the appearance of killing the bill.

Reconsideration   A motion in a legislative body to renew debate and undertake a new vote on a measure that it had already acted on. The motion has the effect of suspending action on the bill until it can be reconsidered. In Congress, both the Senate and the House permit motions for reconsideration from members who have voted with the majority, and the Senate additionally permits them from members who have not voted on the bill. Most state legislatures use similar procedures. *See also* BILL, page 131.

Significance   Motions to reconsider votes taken on controversial pieces of legislation are quite common in the Senate. Typically, they are defeated by a subsequent motion to table the reconsideration motion, an action that is usually supported by the majority that passed the bill when it was first considered. In the House, motions to reconsider are routinely made after each important bill has been passed. Subsequent tabling removes the passed bill from future reconsideration except by unanimous consent. Reconsideration is, in effect, a last-ditch effort to prevent or delay passage of an important piece of legislation.

Redistricting   The action of a state legislature or other body in redrawing legislative electoral district lines following a new population census. Redistricting occurs in those states that gain or lose seats in the reapportionment that occurs after each decennial federal census. After the 1990 census, for example, 13 states lost seats in the House, and 8 states gained, requiring all 21 state legislatures to act on congressional redistricting plans. State legislatures are also required by most state constitutions to redraw district boundary lines for electing state representatives and senators to the state legislatures following each federal census. *See also* APPORTIONMENT, page 128; *Baker v. Carr,* page 176; GERRYMANDERING, page 148; *Hadley v. Junior College,* page 121; *Reynolds v. Sims,* page 178; *Wesberry v. Sanders,* page 179.

Significance   Redistricting decisions typically are made by partisan majorities in the legislatures, and the partisan nature of the undertaking is often reflected in the final results, called "gerrymandering." In the past, large cities were underrepresented, and rural areas tended to be grossly overrepresented because of state legislative refusals to redistrict on a population basis. Since 1962, federal and state court rulings have required that districts be drawn on a basis of substantial equality of population. This new pattern of redistricting has radically altered the distribution of political power in American legislative bodies in favor of urban and suburban interests. In 1983, the Supreme Court struck down a New Jersey congressional redistricting on the ground that even slight variations from the "one person, one vote" rule must be justified as being in pursuit of a reasonable legislative goal (*Karcher v. Daggett,* 462 U.S. 725 [1983]). This decision casts doubt on the validity of several state congressional districts. In another case (*Brown v. Thompson,* 462 U.S. 835 [1983]), the Wyoming state legislature redistricting map was upheld even though wide variations existed. The Court accepted the reasoning that each county should have a legislative seat, regarding it as a nondiscriminating departure from "one person, one vote." Under the Voting Rights Act, redistricting plans must be approved for each state with changes by Department of Justice officials in Washington, D.C., to ensure the new districts are nondiscriminatory. When a state's legislature and governor are unable to agree on fair redistricting, the issue may be resolved in federal court. In 1995, the Supreme Court held that districts gerrymandered to ensure that racial minorities had representation are unconstitutional when they are based solely on race (*Miller v. Johnson,* 115 S. Ct. 2475). This decision was reinforced by 1996 Supreme Court rulings, which held that racial gerrymandering is unconstitutional. Race can be intentionally used in redistricting but cannot be the overriding factor. (*Bush v. Vera,* 116 S. Ct. 1941) and (*Shore v. Hunt,* 116 S. Ct. 1894).

Referendum   An electoral device, available in many states, by which voters can "veto" a bill passed by their legislature. Emergency and financial bills are commonly excluded from referendum action. In states providing for the referendum, bills passed by the legislature do not take effect for a specified period (usually 90 days), during which the bill may be suspended by obtaining the required number of voters' signatures on petitions (usually 5 percent of the total votes cast in a preceding election). A suspended bill is voted on by the electorate and, if disapproved by a majority, it is killed. The *constitutional referendum* gives voters an opportunity to approve or reject amendments or revisions of state constitutions. Many state and local governments may also use the *optional* or *advisory referendum,* by which a legislative body may voluntarily refer a measure to the voters for an expression of popular sentiment. *See also* DIRECT DEMOCRACY, page 11; DIRECT LEGISLATION, page 143.

Significance   The referendum was adopted by many states in the early part of the twentieth century as an ultrademocratic weapon to check the objectionable enactments of the legislatures. It is not intended for regular use, but rather remains a "gun behind the door," by means of which the people hold a continuing veto power. The referendum has been used infrequently. Supporters of the referendum regard it as a useful check on ill-considered or dangerous actions by the legislature and as an expansion of democracy. Those who oppose it regard it as an unnecessary check on representative government that weakens legislative responsibility, gives great power to organized groups, and provides for the making of decisions on complex or technical issues by the average citizen, who may be incapable of voting knowledgeably on them. Along with the initiative and the recall, the referendum serves as an instrument of direct democracy.

Refer to Committee   Send a bill that has been introduced into one of the houses of a legislative body to a standing committee. In Congress, public bills are assigned to committees by the parliamentarian under the scrutiny of the presiding officer in each house. Private bills are usually referred to the committee requested by the senator or representative who introduces the bill. *See also* COMMITTEE CHAIR, page 136; STANDING COMMITTEE, page 171.

Significance   Referral of bills to the proper committee is generally a routine matter. Some bills may include subject matter pertinent to several committees. In such cases, the presiding officer in each house may exercise some discretion in assigning bills, which may have a significant effect on whether those bills are killed in committee or reported out. For example, the Speaker of the House would be likely to refer a bill to a committee favoring such legislation if he personally supported it. In each house, in a rarely used procedure, the majority of members can overrule the decision of the presiding officer by removing a bill from one committee's jurisdiction and assigning it to another. Initial consideration of bills is usually carried on by subcommittees, which report to the full committee.

Report   The action of a legislative committee in sending out its findings and recommendations to its chamber following consideration of a bill or investigation of some matter. The report explains the reasons for the committee's actions. Most committee reports are favorable, but on rare occasions a committee reports out a bill with a recommendation that its parent chamber kill the bill. In any case, many reports are not unanimous, and those members of the committee who dissent may file a minority report. If a bill has been amended in committee, the majority report provides an explanation for this action. *See also* DISCHARGE RULE, page 144; RULES COMMITTEE, page 166; STANDING COMMITTEE, page 171.

Significance   Typically, the great majority of bills introduced each session in most legislative bodies fail to become law because they are not reported out by the various committees to which they have been assigned. Some state legislatures require committees to report out all bills. In the House of Representatives, a committee's refusal to report out a bill for consideration can be overridden only by the rarely used discharge rule, and in the Senate the discharge resolution can be used. Most bills and resolutions reported out with recommendations to the chamber that they be passed are acted on favorably. Recommendations on bills of a controversial political nature are of lesser importance in influencing action in the chamber. In the House, bills reported out by committees are sent first to the Rules Committee, which exercises the power to determine when and how bills will be considered on the floor of the chamber.

Representative   A member of the House of Representatives in Congress or of the lower house of a state legislature. Representatives are elected for two-year terms and, in keeping with the idea that the lower house is to be the more representative of the two chambers, all members' terms end together. The Constitution provides that a representative must be at least 25 years of age, a citizen for 7 years, and a resident of the state from which he or she is elected. Vacancies are filled by special election called by the governor. *See also* HOUSE OF REPRESENTATIVES, page 150; REPRESENTATIVE GOVERNMENT, page 24.

Significance   In Congress, representatives, also called "congressmen and "congresswomen," serve as the most direct contact between the citizen and the government. The two-year term makes it necessary for the representative to keep in touch with constituents if he or she wishes to be re-elected. Several presidents have proposed a four-year term coterminous with that of the President to alleviate the pressures of constant campaigning and to provide greater continuity. While neither national nor state representatives enjoy the same prestige accorded members of upper chambers, many who have acquired seniority through long service exercise considerable political power.

Resident Commissioner   Delegate elected by the people of Puerto Rico to represent them in the House of Representatives. A resident commissioner may speak in the House and serve on committees but cannot vote. The resident commissioner's salary is the same as that of all congressmen. American Samoa, the District of Columbia, Guam, and the Virgin Islands elect nonvoting delegates to the House. The Northern Marianas have commonwealth status similar to Puerto Rico and have a nonvoting "resident representative." The people of the Northern Marianas refer to this person as their "Washington representative." *See also* TERRITORY, page 51.

Significance   Permitting a territory to elect a resident commissioner or a nonvoting delegate to Congress demonstrates willingness to prepare the territory for self-governance and possible statehood or independence. Since the people of territories are subject to many federal laws, they are entitled to have their interests represented. Nationalistic groups in several of these areas point out that the nonvoting role of their commissioner, delegate, or representative is proof of the continuing colonial status of their people.

Rider   A provision, unlikely to pass on its own merits, added to an important bill so that it will "ride" through the legislative process. Riders become law if the bills to which they are attached are passed. What may be considered a rider by one legislator may be regarded by another as an important and germane amendment to the bill. *See also* LINE ITEM VETO, page 194.

Significance   In Congress many riders are attached to appropriations bills, although this procedure is technically banned under the rules of the House and Senate. Before the line item veto was adopted, opponents of the rider and the President were forced to accept the provision if they wanted the appropriation or other major bill to become law. In many states, the governors have the line item veto power; it permits them to veto only those sections of an appropriation bill with which they disagree, allowing the remainder to become law. In 1995, a major effort was made to secure a line item veto for the President as part of the Republican Contract with America. This effort was successful in 1996, when it passed both houses and was signed by the President and became effective January 1997.

Rules Committee   A standing committee of the House of Representatives that can provide special rules under which specific bills will be debated, amended, and considered by the House. The Rules Committee functions as a valve or sifting device to control the flow of bills from House standing committees to the floor for consideration, a power that can be abused by its selective use. *See also* CALENDAR, page 133; DISCHARGE RULE, page 144; GAG RULE, page 148.

Significance   Because more bills are reported out of committees than the House has time to consider, the Rules Committee functions as a legislative traffic-control officer. In this role it can exercise a virtual veto power over bills reported out by other committees. It can, conversely, send out bills to be considered under favorable procedures. If a majority of the committee favors a bill, their approval will most likely be reflected in the rule specified for consideration of that bill. The committee may also provide a "gag" rule by which amendments to the bill may be forbidden or limited to specified areas. Because of these powers, the Rules Committee can exercise great influence over legislation in the House. Under the House procedure, a bill can be pulled out of the Rules Committee after seven days by means of a discharge petition signed by a majority of House members. This method has not proved satisfactory because of representatives' reluctance to challenge committee leadership and prerogatives. In 1961, the membership of the Rules Committee was enlarged by three to a total of fifteen in an attempt to offset the traditional conservative control of the committee by the addition of liberals. A change in the majority-minority party ratio of the committee from 8 to 4 to 10 to 5 was also effected.

Select Committee   An ad hoc legislative committee established for a limited time period and for a special purpose. Select committees may be created by either house or may include members from both houses (joint committee). *See also* INVESTIGATING COMMITTEE, page 152; WATCHDOG COMMITTEE, page 175.

Significance   Select committees are given assignments that do not fall within the jurisdiction of any standing committee or that the latter may prefer not to carry on. Most special committees have been given investigative duties, although others have been assigned supervisory, housekeeping, and coordination responsibilities. The Legislative Reorganization Act of 1946 reduced the need for select committees by placing primary responsibility for investigations in the standing committees. Currently, House select committees include those on Aging, Intelligence, Narcotics Abuse and Control, and the Outer Continental Shelf. Senate select committees include Ethics, Indian Affairs, Intelligence, Small Business, and Aging.

Senate The upper house of the United States Congress and of 49 state legislatures (one state, Nebraska, has a unicameral legislature). Representation in the United States Senate is based on the principle of state equality, and the Constitution specifies that no state may be deprived of its equal representation in the Senate without its consent. The Senate is comprised of 100 senators from 50 states. Most state senates have fewer than 50 members. The Vice President is the presiding officer of the Senate; in the state legislatures, the lieutenant governor normally presides. In the absence of a presiding officer, a president pro tempore elected from the membership assumes that role. *See also* HOUSE OF REPRESENTATIVES, page 150; SENATOR, page 167.

Significance Many observers regard the Senate as more responsive to national interests than the House because it tends to respond more to the needs of the nation than to local interests. Aside from lawmaking and representational functions, the Senate is also vested with special powers, including the power to try impeachments and to give advice and consent to treaties and appointments. If no candidate for the vice presidency receives a majority of the electoral vote, the Senate then elects the Vice President from the two candidates with the highest electoral votes. State senates, too, exercise special powers, such as confirmation of appointments and trial of impeached officials.

Senator A member of the U.S. Senate or of the upper house in state legislatures. United States senators have been directly elected by the people of their respective states since the adoption of the Seventeenth Amendment in 1913. The term of office is 6 years, with one-third of the Senate seats up for election every 2 years. Vacancies are usually filled by appointment by the state's governor, although the legislature may provide for a special election. The Constitution provides that a senator must be at least 30 years of age, a citizen for 9 years, and a resident of the state from which elected. In state legislatures, senators are elected in districts by the people, usually for 4 years. *See also* REPRESENTATIVE, page 165; SENATE, page 167; SEVENTEENTH AMENDMENT, page 169.

Significance In Congress, because there are fewer than one-fourth as many senators as representatives and because of their longer terms and special powers, senators generally are accorded greater prestige than their colleagues in the lower house. Many representatives aspire to achieve election to the Senate, and many senators seek the presidency. Most senators represent more constituents than do House members, and the smaller size of the chamber encourages more thorough deliberation on measures. In state legislatures, the average senator also represents more constituents than does a member of the lower house and usually exercises greater influence in state matters.

Senatorial Courtesy An unwritten agreement among senators that requires the President to confer with the senator or senators of his party from a state before he makes a nomination to fill a federal office located in that state. The Senate almost invariably shows "courtesy" to one of its members by rejecting a presidential nominee when the senator involved raises a personal objection. When neither senator of a state is of the President's party, the President is apt to consult state party leaders. *See also* APPOINTMENT POWER, page 183; CONFIRMATION, page 138.

Significance   Senatorial courtesy transfers federal patronage within a state from the President to the senators of his party. This means that such senators normally choose the appointees and give their names to the President for formal appointments. Federal positions affected by senatorial courtesy include judges, district attorneys, customs officials, and field service officials of most important agencies. Presidents may reject senatorial recommendations, but this rarely occurs.

Seniority Rule   A custom, nearly always followed in both houses of Congress, of awarding the position of chair for each committee to the majority party member who has the longest number of years of continuous service on the committee. Each party, majority and minority alike, strictly lists its members on the various committees according to the seniority rule. When a high-ranking member leaves the committee, all members of that party move up one notch on the seniority list. Many state legislatures follow the seniority rule, although other political and personal factors may modify or override seniority. Under public pressure to change the seniority system, both parties in the House agreed in 1973 to permit election of committee chairs by their respective party caucuses or their agents, but seniority generally continues to be honored in the selection process. *See also* COMMITTEE CHAIR, page 136; RANKING MEMBER, page 161.

Significance   The seniority rule, which emerged in Congress during the latter part of the nineteenth century, has been a source of much controversy. Supporters of seniority argue that it (1) guarantees chairs will have had long experience in committee matters; (2) avoids intrigues, conflicts, and deadlocks within the party organizations that would inevitably occur whenever a new chair is chosen; (3) makes it possible for members of congress from small states to rise in positions of importance; and (4) has produced leaders of ability and stature in the important committees. Opponents of seniority argue that it (1) tends to hold back individuals of ability while it often moves mediocre persons steadily ahead; (2) requires nothing more than that a member continue living and getting reelected; (3) tends to favor stagnant, one-party voting areas of the nation over two-party competitive areas that reflect changes in public opinion; and (4) reduces party responsibility by filling many key power positions in both houses with members from the conservative wings of either party. The likelihood of eliminating seniority is remote. Denial of an incumbent's seniority rights may occur, however, in selection of committee chairs. In 1975, for example, the House Democratic Caucus denied seniority rights in removing several powerful chairmen from key committees. In 1995, the Republicans denied chairs to some who, because of seniority, would automatically have received them in the past.

Session   The period during which a legislative body assembles and carries on its regular business. Each Congress has two regular sessions, based on the requirement in the Constitution that Congress assemble at least once each year. In addition, Congress may be summoned into special session by the President. The first session of a Congress usually begins during the first week of January of odd-numbered years, with the start of the terms of all representatives and one-third of the senators. The second session begins in January of even-numbered years. The Congress that assembled in January 1995, for example, was the 104th Congress, first session. Adjournment is left up to Congress, although the Constitution provides that if the two houses cannot agree on a date, the President may adjourn them at his discretion. No President has exercised this authority. In the states, most legislatures convene in regular session every two years, although many have regular annual sessions. Most state constitutions limit the length of legislative sessions either by specifying the number of days or by cutting off pay and allowances for legislators after a certain date. *See also* SPECIAL SESSION, page 170; TWENTIETH AMENDMENT, page 172.

Significance   To cope with the many complex problems of modern society, a legislative body must be in session regularly and not only at widely separated intervals. Because the Constitution leaves sessions pretty much up to the discretion of Congress, this problem does not exist in the national government. In some of the states, however, sessions continue to be held infrequently and are generally short. Constitutional revision is needed in many states to free the legislatures from restrictions that date back more than a century. Some states have met this problem by calling special sessions of the legislature annually or every other year.

Seventeenth Amendment   An amendment to the Constitution, adopted in 1913, that provides for the direct election of United States senators by the voters of each state. The Amendment changes those sections of Article I that authorized senators to be chosen by the legislatures of the states. It also provides that, when a vacancy occurs, the legislature may authorize the governor to make a temporary appointment until an election can be held. Most legislatures have so authorized their governors. *See also* SENATOR, page 167.

Significance   Prior to the adoption of the Seventeenth Amendment, selection of senators frequently resulted in lengthy distractions from normal state legislative business. Deadlocks in the selection process often kept states unrepresented in the Senate for many months. Although popular election is no guarantee of fitness, most observers believe that senatorial abilities, stature, and responsiveness to the will of the public have all tended to increase since 1913. The Seventeenth Amendment signified a shift for senators from representing "sovereign" states to representing the people of their states.

Simple Resolution   A measure adopted by one chamber of a legislative body. It does not require approval either by the other house or by the President. Simple resolutions are designated either "H Res" or "S Res." *See also* CONCURRENT RESOLUTION, page 137; JOINT RESOLUTION, page 153.

Significance   Simple resolutions do not have the force of law. They are usually adopted for the purpose of making or amending rules of procedure. In Congress, one chamber may adopt a resolution to express its sentiment on a current issue or to give advice to the President on foreign policy or other areas of executive responsibility.

Speaker of the House The presiding officer in the House of Representatives and in the lower chamber of state legislatures. The Speaker's election by the House is a formality that follows selection by the majority party caucus. As a member of the House, the Speaker may engage in debate and vote on measures. The Speaker follows the Vice President in the line of succession to the presidency under the Presidential Succession Act of 1947. *See also* PRESIDENTIAL SUCCESSION, page 204; REFER TO COMMITTEE, page 164.

Significance The Speaker is the most powerful and influential member of the House. As presiding officer, he recognizes members wishing to speak, interprets and applies the rules, and decides questions of order. Although the Speaker can be overruled by the House, this rarely occurs. The Speaker also appoints select and conference committees and refers bills to committee. The real influence of the office lies in the fact that, in exercising the foregoing powers, the Speaker may use discretion and political acumen and is thus placed in a strategic position to influence the passage or rejection of bills at almost every stage in the legislative process in the House. As the leader of the majority party in the House, the Speaker also exercises considerable power in shaping and implementing party decisions on pending legislation. Most Speakers have been persons of ability, stature, and tact, able to provide the kind of leadership needed by the majority party. In 1995, Newt Gingrich demonstrated the powerful role the Speaker can play by providing program development in the form of the Contract with America and by showing dynamic leadership in guiding the passage of the program through the legislative process in the House. The role and powers of speakers in the various state legislatures are analogous to those of the Speaker of the House of Representatives, and they often have the additional power to appoint members of standing committees.

Special Session An extraordinary session of a legislative body, convoked usually on the initiative of a chief executive. The Constitution grants power to the President to summon Congress or either house into session "on extraordinary occasions" (Art. II, sec. 3). Although the House has never been called into special session, the Senate has been convoked to act upon executive appointments or treaties. In all 50 states, the governors are empowered to call special sessions of the legislatures. In several states, a stipulated number of legislators may petition the governor to call the legislature into session. In a few others, the legislature can call itself into special session. *See also* JOINT SESSION, page 154; SESSION, page 168.

Significance Congress, when called into special session, possesses full constitutional power to legislate. In about half of the states, legislatures convened in special sessions are similarly free to act, whereas in the other half they are limited to acting upon what the governor specifies in the call. Special sessions may be useful in meeting a sudden crisis or new problem. A chief executive can use the call of a special session as a political weapon to focus public attention on an issue and pressure the legislative body to consider it. Although executive officials may summon legislative bodies into special sessions, they cannot exercise appreciable control over legislative action or inaction once the body convenes.

Standing Committee   A regular committee of a legislative body that considers bills within a subject area. In Congress, there are 19 House and 16 Senate standing committees. In addition, there are about 140 subcommittees in the House and about 90 in the Senate, each with its own chair. House committees range in size from 9 to 51 members and Senate committees from 12 to 29 members. Representatives are normally assigned to only one or two standing committees, senators to two or three. In the House, the leading standing committees include Rules, Ways and Means, Appropriations, Armed Services, Judiciary, Foreign Affairs, Commerce, and Agriculture. In the Senate, influential committees include Foreign Relations, Appropriations, Finance, Judiciary, Armed Services, and Banking and Currency. The majority party in each chamber holds a majority vote and the chair on each committee. Positions of importance on the committees are usually determined by seniority. Under the Legislative Reorganization Act of 1970, committee votes in executive (secret) sessions must be made public, and committee hearings may for the first time be opened to radio and television coverage if witnesses and a majority of the committee do not object. *See also* COMMITTEE CHAIR, page 136; COMMITTEE ON COMMITTEES, page 137; REFER TO COMMITTEE, page 164; SENIORITY RULE, page 168.

Significance   The standing committee system operates on the principle of specialization secured through a division of labor. Most bills receive their most thorough consideration at the committee stage. Members of Congress usually respect the decisions and recommendations made by the standing committees on pending litigation. Thus, the fate of most bills is decided in committee rather than on the floors of the two chambers. This great power led Woodrow Wilson to describe the American political system as "government by the standing committees of Congress." Individual committee members of long seniority who have developed expertise in some area of the committee's operations can also become highly influential in the congressional decision process and are often consulted by the leadership.

Statute (Act)   A law enacted by Congress or by a state legislature. Simple, concurrent, and joint resolutions adopted by Congress are not considered statutes. Statutes take the form of public and private laws and are numbered consecutively in each session of Congress. In Congress, a bill passed by one house is called an "act," but the term is generally used to describe a bill passed by both houses that becomes a new law. *See also* BILL, page 131; CODE, page 254.

Significance   All acts of Congress are published first in the form of "slip laws" and are bound after each session in the *Statutes at Large of the United States.* Those public acts applicable today can be found in the *United States Code,* which is revised every six years and supplemented annually. The *Code* is organized on a subject-matter basis. State laws are published but not codified regularly. Some statutes have a delayed implementation date because of the need to set up administrative machinery to carry out the new program.

Sunset Law   Statutes that include provisions for automatic expiration at the end of a specified time period. Sunset laws typically require a reauthorization of programs by the legislative body at stipulated intervals, such as five years. Without such reauthorization, the program lapses, or the conditions set forth under the sunset provisions take effect. *See also* BUDGET, page 390; INDEXING, page 406.

Significance   Sunset provisions are regarded as one approach that can be used to bring the federal budget under a measure of control, with reduction or elimination of the program as possible courses of legislative action. Because three-fourths of the nation's budget expenditures are for entitlement programs—a form of almost uncontrollable spending based on the rights of client groups to receive federal funds—sunset legislation is essential if the lawmakers want to maintain a continuing control. Numerous efforts to enact sunset legislation for all congressional enactments have failed because of the pressures of interest groups and the general belief in Congress that it is not practicable. The problem is particularly urgent if a program has been "indexed" to the Consumer Price Index (CPI) so as to adjust payments for inflation.

Suspension of Rules   A time-saving procedure used by a legislative body to bring a measure to a vote. In the House of Representatives, a motion to "suspend the rules and pass the bill" requires a two-thirds vote of members present for passage. Debate on the bill is limited to 40 minutes, and no amendments are permitted. *See also* PREVIOUS QUESTION, page 160; UNANIMOUS CONSENT, page 173.

Significance   The suspension of rules procedure keeps the House from getting bogged down with its complex rules system. Because of the size of the House, a means by which debate can be closed and a measure brought to a vote quickly is necessary to maintain the flow of business. The Senate, with its rules for unlimited debate, can obtain these results only through unanimous consent. Suspension of rules is augmented by other parliamentary devices to speed up the legislative process, such as previous question and unanimous consent, but the former is not used in the Senate.

Twentieth Amendment   An amendment to the Constitution, adopted in 1933, that provides that a new Congress elected in November of even-numbered years will convene on January 3 of the following year unless Congress sets a different date. Prior to its adoption, a newly elected Congress did not convene in regular session until December of the following year—a lapse of thirteen months. The old Congress, meanwhile, with many members who had failed to win reelection ("lame ducks"), met in perfunctory session for four months following the election. The Amendment also changed the presidential term to start a month and a half earlier, on January 20 instead of on March 4. *See also* TWENTIETH AMENDMENT, page 208.

Significance   The Twentieth Amendment provides for more democracy and greater efficiency. By reducing the interim period between an election and the assumption of office by newly elected members of Congress, the people's mandate may be more quickly and accurately realized. By changing the

President's term to start at an earlier date, a new President has the opportunity to present his legislative and budgetary programs to a new Congress. Some observers, including former presidents, have suggested that the interim period be reduced still further to enable a new Congress and President to come to grips with pressing problems of government at an even earlier date.

Twenty-seventh Amendment   An Amendment to the Constitution of the United States, adopted in 1992, that prohibits members of Congress—the House of Representatives and the Senate—from voting themselves a midterm pay raise. The Twenty-seventh Amendment contains only one sentence: "No law, varying compensation for the services of the senators and representatives, shall take effect until an election of representatives shall have intervened." *See also Coleman v. Miller,* page 54.

Significance   The Twenty-seventh Amendment to the Constitution of the United States was officially proposed by James Madison in 1789 as part of a package of twelve initially proposed amendments. Ten were ratified by 1791 and became the Bill of Rights. The pay-raise limitation amendment proposal lacked support from the state legislatures, as did a proposal on legislative apportionment. In the 1980s, deep resentment by the voters to Congress's action in voting itself several pay raises during the decade led to surprise ratification of the amendment proposal in 1992. The legal question of whether the proposal was still valid after more than 200 years was resolved by the Archivist of the United States, who officially proclaimed it to be the Twenty-seventh Amendment, which Congress then confirmed.

Unanimous Consent   A time-saving procedure, also known as "without objection," used by a legislative body to adopt noncontroversial motions, amendments, and bills without submitting them to a vote. Both houses of Congress use the procedure to expedite business. In the House, an objection from a single member results in the tabling of the bill or motion for two weeks. *See also* PREVIOUS QUESTION, page 160; SUSPENSION OF RULES, page 172.

Significance   Unanimous consent can be a useful parliamentary procedure for rapidly disposing of a host of minor matters cluttering up a legislative chamber's agenda. By expediting noncontroversial measures, additional time may be made available for dealing with more critical and controversial issues. Unanimous consent is augmented by other parliamentary devices to speed up the legislative process, such as previous question and suspension of rules.

Unicameralism   The principle of a one-house legislature, as contrasted with bicameralism, a legislature based on two houses. One state legislature— Nebraska's—is unicameral, as are local governmental policy-determining bodies, such as county boards, city councils, township boards, and school boards. *See also* BICAMERALISM, page 130.

Significance   The merits claimed for unicameralism include (1) greater economy and efficiency of operation; (2) greater prestige, which attracts outstanding citizens; (3) elimination of deadlocks resulting from rivalry and friction between two houses; (4) elimination of the need for conference committees to iron out differing versions of a bill passed by the two chambers; and (5) more accurate fixing of responsibility of elected representatives by the public. Arguments against unicameralism include the following: (1) Hasty, careless, ill-considered legislation may result; (2) special interest lobbies can concentrate their influence more effectively against one house; (3) one house may be more susceptible to aroused popular passions and other democratic excesses; and (4) control over a one-house legislature may be focused in a single major interest group or in a small geographical area.

Vice President   The second highest executive officer of the United States, who is designated the presiding officer of the Senate by the Constitution. Although the Vice President's constitutional duties are primarily legislative, in modern times presidents have tended to assign them executive responsibilities. *See also* TWENTY-FIFTH AMENDMENT, page 208; VICE PRESIDENT, page 210.

Significance   Unlike the Speaker of the House, the Vice President as President of the Senate is not the chosen leader of the majority party in the Senate or a member of the Senate. The Vice President cannot speak from the floor on issues and, as presiding officer, must not show partisanship. He or she can cast a vote only in case of a tie. Although the Vice President's powers are negligible, some have exercised considerable influence in the Senate's decision making by ability and personal powers of persuasion. If the Vice President is a leader in the majority party of the Senate, his or her potential influence is increased. In recent years, a succession of vice presidents selected from Congress—John N. Garner, Harry S Truman, Alben W. Barkley, Richard M. Nixon, Lyndon B. Johnson, Hubert H. Humphrey, Gerald R. Ford, Walter F. Mondale, George Bush, and Albert Gore—have proved to be valuable liaison agents between the President and the Congress. Spiro T. Agnew and Nelson A. Rockefeller suffered in the role of legislative liaison agent because of their lack of congressional experience and because Congress was controlled by the opposing major party.

Voting (Legislative)   Various methods that legislative bodies use to make decisions. Voting procedures typically include (1) a "record" or "yea or nay" roll-call vote, registered instantly on an electric scoreboard, in which each member's vote is required to be recorded individually; (2) a "division" or standing vote in which members voting for and against a motion alternately rise and are counted by the presiding officer; (3) a "teller" vote in which members are counted as they file past either a "yea" or a "nay" teller; and (4) a "viva voce" or voice vote in which a presiding officer determines the outcome from the volume of response from those for and those against the measure. In Congress, the Constitution requires a record roll-call vote for overriding a presidential veto, and whenever one-fifth of the members demand it. Members not voting for or against a measure will either be "paired" or "present." Since 1973, the House of Representatives has used an electronic voting system to speed up the roll-call process. *See also* LEGISLATIVE REORGANIZATION ACT OF 1970, page 180; UNANIMOUS CONSENT, page 173.

Significance   Although all four voting procedures are used in the Congress and in most state legislatures, important decisions are almost always made by a record vote. For many years the teller vote was used in the House to achieve an accurate vote count while not putting its members on record for or against a measure. The Legislative Reorganization Act of 1970 sought to achieve greater accountability of members by providing that one-fifth of a House or Committee of the Whole quorum may require that members' teller votes be put on record. In a representative system of government, it is essential that the voters have an opportunity to examine their legislators' voting records.

Watchdog or Oversight Committee   A committee established by a legislative body or assigned the duty of overseeing the administration of the laws. In Congress, prior to 1946, each house created a number of select committees to perform this oversight function. In the Legislative Reorganization Act of 1946, Congress vested the "watchdog" responsibility in the standing committees, each responsible for overseeing the execution of laws within its jurisdiction. *See also* INVESTIGATING COMMITTEE, page 152; STANDING COMMITTEE, page 171.

Significance   In its report in 1946 that led to the Reorganization Act, the Joint Committee commented on the watchdog committee function: "Without effective legislative oversight of the activities of the vast executive branch, the line of democracy wears thin." The committee recommended "a continuous review of the agencies administering laws originally reported by the committees." The Government Operations Committees of the House and the Senate have been given the special responsibility of "studying the operation of government activities at all levels with a view to determining its economy and efficiency." Congressional "watchdog" oversight can be distinguished from congressional investigations in that the former is a continuing scrutiny of executive operations, whereas the latter involves a more intense digging for facts within a limited problem area.

Whip   An assistant floor leader who aids the majority or minority floor leader of each party in each house of Congress. Whips are selected in party caucuses, usually on the recommendation of the floor leaders. Each whip in the House appoints several assistants, whereas the Senate whips are aided by the secretaries of their respective party policy committees. *See also* CAUCUS, page 134; MAJORITY FLOOR LEADER, page 156.

Significance   The duties of the whips include (1) canvassing fellow party members on key issues to inform party leaders of the votes that can be counted on, (2) bringing the full voting power of their party to bear on key issues, and (3) acting for the floor leaders when they are absent from the chamber. On crucial issues, when close votes are anticipated, much depends on the effectiveness of the whips' operations. Unlike party whips in the British Parliament, congressional whips operate in a system with little party discipline.

IMPORTANT AGENCIES

Library of Congress   The national library of the United States, which serves the entire national government and state and local governments as well as the public. The Library of Congress was created in 1800 by Congress and is headed by the Librarian of Congress, who is appointed by the President with Senate approval. Two important divisions of the Library are the Copyright Office and the Congressional Research Service (CRS). The latter functions exclusively to serve the needs of Congress "in the analysis, appraisal and evaluation of legislative proposals. ..." *See also* INTERNET, page 81.

Significance   The Library of Congress is particularly useful to Congress and the executive branch because it is a vast storehouse of official records and documents. With its access for the general public of the United States and for scholars from every country, it has become the world's research library. Much legislation involves extensive studies and research, and the role of the Library has grown as governmental activities have increased and grown more complex. Copyrighted publications are given a Library of Congress catalog card number. Today, the Library has more than 20 million books, more than 30 million manuscripts, and vast numbers of maps, records, films, and photographs in its collection. The CRS receives several thousand inquiries from members of Congress daily. Its staff of nearly 500 specialists provide answers about past, present, and future legislation concerning both domestic and foreign policy. In recent years the development of a vast information superhighway system (Internet) has opened up a new means of communication for legislators, scholars, and other frequent users.

IMPORTANT CASES

Baker v. Carr   369 U.S. 186 (1962): Ruled in an epic Supreme Court decision that federal courts have jurisdiction over lawsuits challenging the apportionment of legislative districts, on the ground that malapportioned districts may violate the equal protection clause of the Fourteenth Amendment. The case had the effect of overturning *Colegrove v. Green,* 328 U.S. 549 (1946), in which the Court held that the issue of malapportioned legislative districts was a political question and relief should be sought through the political process. The *Baker* case involved a suit to compel the Tennessee legislature to redistrict state legislative districts on a population basis, a provision of the Tennessee Constitution that the legislature had ignored for over 60 years. *See also* GERRYMANDERING, page 148; REDISTRICTING, page 162.

Significance   Before the *Baker* case, many state legislatures had long refused to provide for equitable apportionment for state legislative and congressional election districts. The *Baker* decision reflected the new view of the Court's majority that it is unrealistic to seek to achieve a fair system of representation through the ballot box, since state legislators often maintain themselves in power through gerrymandering and refusals to redistrict. The *Baker* case led to a number of challenges to districting patterns in other states. Subsequently, the Supreme Court ruled that in statewide primary elections for United States senators and state executive officers, each person's vote must count equally (*Gray v. Sanders,* 372 U.S. 368 [1963]), that congressional districts must be substantially equal in population (*Wesberry v. Sanders,* 376 U.S. 1 [1964]), and that both houses of a bicameral state legislature must be apportioned on a population basis (*Reynolds v. Sims,* 377 U.S.

533 [1964]). These and later decisions have affirmed that the basic constitutional principle of voting equality can mean only one thing—"one person, one vote." Many observers regard the *Baker* and subsequent apportionment decisions as the most important precedents established by the Warren Court because of their impact on legislative decision making. A further refinement occurred in 1995, when the Court held that race cannot be the sole factor for districting congressional seats.

Immigration and Naturalization Service v. Chadha   462 U.S. 919 (1983): Held that a legislative veto to invalidate an act of the executive branch is unconstitutional as a violation of the separation of powers. In the *Chadha* case, the Court struck down a law authorizing one house of Congress to veto a decision of the Immigration and Naturalization Service to allow a deportable alien to remain in the United States. Such action, said the Court, requires passage of a bill by a majority of both houses and its presentation to the President for his approval or veto. *See also* LEGISLATIVE VETO, page 155.

Significance   The *Chadha* decision called into question the validity of about 200 acts of Congress with legislative veto provisions. While the decision appeared to strengthen the executive branch, many observers believe that Congress may become reluctant in the future to grant the executive the administrative discretion necessary to carry out complex policies. The judiciary, in turn, would be affected by the degree of specificity of legislation in exercising its own decision making. The *Chadha* decision gave renewed vitality to the constitutional provisions that the application and interpretation of laws not be done by the same unit that makes the law. The Court pointed out that Congress could not, without the veto authorization, require the deportation of an alien and that Congress must abide by its delegation of authority until it is revoked by other legislation. Finally, the Court noted that any specific provisions for action by one house of Congress (for example, in Senate ratification of treaties) is clearly spelled out in the Constitution. The *Chadha* case illustrates the independence of each of the branches of government when acting within its sphere of constitutional authority.

McGrain v. Daugherty   273 U.S. 135 (1927): Decided that Congress has the right to compel testimony from private individuals as an aid to its power to pass laws. The *McGrain* case concerned congressional investigation of the Teapot Dome scandal involving bribery and other illegal acts by public officials. The Court held that Congress could subpoena a private individual as well as a public official when this action is pertinent to a proper legislative function. *See also* INVESTIGATING COMMITTEE, page 152.

Significance   The *McGrain* case established the constitutional basis for legislative investigations, along with the power to compel testimony and production of papers and other materials. So long as an investigation has a legislative purpose, the courts will not inquire further into the motives of Congress. This includes investigations aimed at gathering information that relates to possible impeachment actions by Congress against executive and judicial officials. The Watergate investigation that led to the resignation of Richard M. Nixon was strengthened by the precedents established in the

McGrain case. More recent congressional investigations of executive branch actions include (1) the War Powers Act, used to justify intervention in Vietnam; (2) the Iran-contra affair, in which weapons were illegally sold to Iran and the money secretly diverted to continue the guerrilla war in Nicaragua; (3) the Waco hearings, which sought to determine if the action of the Alcohol, Tobacco, and Firearms agents against the Branch Davidians was justified; and (4) the Whitewater affair, which sought to involve the President and First Lady in past questionable financial dealings in Arkansas.

Pacific States Telephone and Telegraph Co. v. Oregon   223 U.S. 118 (1912): Involved the question of whether the initiative and referendum provisions of the Oregon Constitution destroy the republican form of government guaranteed to all states by the U.S. Constitution in Article IV, section 4. The Court held it to be a political question not open to judicial inquiry. *See also* INITIATIVE, page 151; POLITICAL QUESTION, page 274; REFERENDUM, page 163; REPUBLICAN FORM OF GOVERNMENT, page 49.

Significance   Although no provision is made by the Constitution for direct action by the people in the lawmaking process, the Court, in effect, recognized in the *Oregon* case that the states may validly adopt such measures. About half of the states and numerous cities have adopted the initiative and referendum, most of them during the first two decades of the twentieth century.

Reynolds v. Sims   377 U.S. 533 (1964): A landmark decision that provides that under the equal protection clause of the Fourteenth Amendment both houses of a bicameral state legislature must be apportioned on the basis of population. The Court rejected the "federal analogy" that, like Congress, a state legislature could have one house based on a factor other than population. It held that political subdivisions in states are not "sovereign entities" (on which equal representation of states in the Senate was predicated). Since both houses of a legislature must agree to enact legislation, representation on factors other than population dilutes the votes of citizens living in heavily populated areas. "Legislators represent people, not trees or acres," said the Court, and an apportionment scheme cannot discriminate on the basis of residence any more than it can on the basis of race or economic status. *See also* BICAMERALISM, page 130; REDISTRICTING, page 162.

Significance   The *Reynolds v. Sims* case is among the most important decisions in American history, overcoming years of inaction by legislative bodies on the representation problem. It transformed the American political scene by ending dominance of state legislatures by rural minorities in favor of urban and suburban majorities. It also has had a direct impact on national politics, since state legislatures draw congressional district lines. Efforts to overturn the decision by constitutional amendment failed. In the *Reynolds* case and subsequent decisions, the Court has not insisted on absolute equality of representation, requiring only "substantial" equality of representation. But "one person, one vote" remains firm as the basic principle governing the American system of representative government. The *Reynolds* case was a logical outgrowth of the 1962 *Baker v. Carr* decision.

United States v. Harriss   347 U.S. 612 (1954): Upheld the constitutionality of the Federal Regulation of Lobbying Act of 1946 against charges that it violates due process, freedom of speech, press, and petition. *See also* LOBBY-IST, page 86; REGULATION OF LOBBYING ACT, page 181.

Significance   The Court narrowly construed the application of the Lobbying Act in the *Harriss* case by holding that it applies only to lobbyists who directly seek to influence members of Congress concerning pending or proposed federal legislation. Lobbyists who seek to influence federal legislation indirectly through public opinion do not fall within the scope of "lobbying activities" regulated by the Act. The Court emphasized that the intention of the Lobbying Act was to enable Congress to discover "who is being hired, who is putting up the money, and how much." This is information that Congress is entitled to know.

Watkins v. United States   354 U.S. 178 (1957): Established that a person may refuse to answer a question put to him by an investigating committee of Congress if the question is not pertinent to the inquiry. The Court upheld Watkins' refusal to answer questions of the House Committee on Un-American Activities regarding certain persons who had at one time been members of the Communist party. For refusing to answer, Watkins was cited for contempt of Congress. The Court reversed his conviction on the ground that the Committee had failed to demonstrate that the questions were pertinent. *See also* INVESTIGATING COMMITTEE, page 152.

Significance   Many rights guaranteed in the Constitution apply to congressional investigations as well as to judicial proceedings. In the same way that an individual is entitled to know the precise charges when charged with a crime, a person also has the right to know how any particular question asked at a legislative investigation pertains to the matter under investigation. Congress may not conduct a "fishing expedition" in the hopes of uncovering information. This case illustrates one of the limitations of the investigatory powers of Congress.

Wesberry v. Sanders   376 U.S. 1 (1964): Held that congressional districts must be substantially equal in population. The Court based its *Wesberry* ruling on Article I, section 2 of the Constitution, which provides that the House of Representatives shall be chosen "by the People of the several States." While mathematical precision is impossible, said the Court, the Constitution requires that, as nearly as practicable, each person's vote in a congressional election is to be worth as much as any other person's vote. *See also* REDIS-TRICTING, page 162.

Significance   The *Wesberry* case provided the legal basis for ending overrepresentation of rural areas in the House of Representatives. In a pre-*Wesberry* Congress, for example, a representative from one district represented eight times as many constituents as another congressman. This kind of disparity resulted from redistricting patterns established by state legislatures that were themselves malapportioned in favor of rural minorities. By the 1980s, the gross inequities of representation among House seats had been corrected.

IMPORTANT STATUTES

Congressional Budget and Impoundment Control Act of 1974   A major law that revises old procedures and establishes new ones by which Congress considers the annual federal budget. Procedures provided by the Budget Reform Act include (1) adoption by Congress of an annual budget resolution that provides target figures for total appropriations and spending and for needed tax and debt limits; (2) creation of new House and Senate budget committees to study budget data, analyze options, and write budget resolutions; (3) a detailed timetable that sets deadlines for floor action on budget proposals; (4) a change in the national government's fiscal year from the period July 1 to June 30 to the period October 1 to September 30, thus providing an additional three months for congressional action; (5) limits on "backdoor spending" (that is, off-budget spending programs not included in the regular budget) and presidential impoundment (refusal to spend appropriated funds) powers; and (6) creation of a Congressional Budget Office to provide Congress with the fiscal experts and computers essential to study and analyze the tremendous amount of data found in the President's annual budget message. The new budget process required that all congressional spending conforms to the limits established by a budget resolution adopted each year by Congress. *See also* BUDGET COMMITTEES, page 133; CONGRESSIONAL BUDGET OFFICE, page 139; FISCAL YEAR, page 401; PERFORMANCE BUDGET, page 411.

Significance   The Congressional Budget and Impoundment Control Act of 1974 was an attempt by Congress to regain from the President some of the "powers of the purse" that the Constitution assigns to Congress but that Congress has increasingly delegated to the President. The Act tried to reassert congressional powers over government spending by forcing Congress to undertake a better organized, more careful examination of the annual budget package and to reduce or refrain from certain related actions that have weakened congressional authority in the past. Previous efforts by Congress, such as in the Legislative Reorganization Act of 1946, to strengthen the congressional power of the purse have met with little success. The effectiveness of the new Budget Act will be tested over a period of years under increasingly difficult budgetary conditions. By the 1980s, it appeared that the new system had not brought the budget under control; in fact, the federal government established new records of budget deficits in the years following the Act's implementation, despite vast cuts in social programs pushed by the Reagan administration.

Legislative Reorganization Act of 1970 An act to improve the operations of Congress and make its members more responsive to the public will. Provisions of the Act include: (1) modification of the teller vote system (whereby members of the House voted by filing anonymously past a "yes" or "no" recording clerk) so that at the request of one-fifth of a quorum (20 members in Committee of the Whole, 44 in House sessions) each member's vote is now recorded and made public; (2) House committee hearings may be broadcast and televised with the agreement of witnesses and a majority of the committee; (3) votes taken in executive sessions of committees must be made public; (4) a majority of the members of any congressional committee may convene a meeting of the committee over the objection of its chairman; (5) the Legislative Reference Service was renamed the Congressional Research Service and reorganized to provide increased assistance to members of Congress; and (6) installation of an electronic voting device in the House that eliminates the time-consuming roll call of 435 names by the Clerk in record votes. The 1970 Act supplemented and updated changes that were provided in the Legislative Reorganization Act of 1946. *See also* VOTING (LEGISLATIVE), page 174.

Significance   The Legislative Reorganization Act of 1970 constitutes the first substantial legislative reform act in 24 years, since the enactment of the Legislative Reorganization Act of 1946. The 1946 Act had provided for structural and procedural changes, including: (1) reducing the number of committees; (2) strengthening the operations of the committees; (3) providing for a legislative budget system; (4) reducing the work load of Congress; (5) increasing the professional assistance available to each member of Congress; (6) increasing congressional salaries and fringe benefits; and (7) regulating lobbying activity. Although some of these provisions worked well, others failed or were never implemented. The 1970 Act focused most changes on the procedures of the House of Representatives. The key congressional problems of seniority and the filibuster were not affected by the Act, however, and in its efforts to achieve greater responsiveness to the public will, Congress failed to find means for developing party responsibility in legislative matters. Following passage of the Act, Congress continued to operate with most of the critical power held by small groups in key power positions, especially committee chairs.

Regulation of Lobbying Act (Title III, Legislative Reorganization Act of 1946)   The first attempt by Congress to control interest groups, lobbyists, and lobbying activities through legislation. The Act provides for a minimum of *regulation* and a maximum of *publicity.* Specific provisions include that (1) persons or organizations receiving money to be used principally to influence passage or defeat of legislation before Congress must register; (2) persons or groups registering must, under oath, give their name and address, employer, salary, amount and purpose of expenses, and duration of employment; (3) each registered lobbyist must report quarterly full information on his or her activities, which is then published in the *Congressional Record;* and (4) failure to comply with any of these provisions will result in severe penalties prescribed, ranging up to a $10,000 fine and a five-year prison term and including a three-year ban against further lobbying. *See also* FEDERAL ELECTION CAMPAIGN ACT OF 1974, page 123; LOBBYIST, page 86; *United States v. Harriss,* page 179.

Significance   The Lobbying Act has been criticized on the ground that its language is confusing and vague, resulting in much noncompliance. No enforcement agency has been created by Congress. The public generally has ignored the publicity given in quarterly reports. It is doubtful whether the Act has had any appreciable effect on lobbyists or their activities. Congress must be careful in enacting lobby-control legislation to avoid regulations that might abridge freedom of speech, press, or petition. Disclosures in the Watergate investigations of the 1970s of widespread corruption and violations of lobby and campaign laws by corporations and their lobbyists led to the enactment of several laws to tighten federal control, especially in the field of campaign financing. In recent years, thousands of individuals and organizations have registered under the Act and reported spending millions of dollars to influence legislative action. Congress sought to deal with these kinds of problems in enacting the Lobbying Reform Act of 1989, but the problems remain.

5

The Executive: Office and Powers

Amnesty Power exercised by the President to grant a blanket pardon to all members of a group who have violated national law. Amnesty may be full and complete, or it may be conditional, in that those granted a general pardon must perform certain acts to qualify. *See also* PARDON, page 195.

Significance Amnesties have been used generally to absolve groups from legal accountability for political offenses. President Thomas Jefferson, for example, granted a general amnesty to all persons convicted under the Alien and Sedition Acts. The best-known amnesties in American history were those granted by Presidents Abraham Lincoln and Andrew Johnson to all Confederates who had participated in rebellion against the United States. An attempt by Congress to limit the effect of Johnson's amnesty proclamation was found by the U.S. Supreme Court to be invalid interference with the President's constitutional pardoning powers (*Ex parte Garland,* 4 Wallace 333 [1867]). Whether amnesty should be granted to thousands of draft evaders became a major national issue following the end of American troop involvement in the Vietnam War. In 1974, President Gerald R. Ford offered conditional amnesty to all draft evaders, deserters, and others who had avoided service during the Vietnam War, with each person's case considered individually as to how amnesty could be won. In most cases, amnesty required a period of alternative service in the Peace Corps, VISTA, or some other volunteer service.

Appointment Power The authority vested in a public official to fill a vacancy in a governmental office or position. The appointment power is usually shared by the chief executive, who nominates the candidate, with the legislative body, which confirms the appointee. In the national government, the President possesses the full appointing power for some positions but must obtain the Senate's "advice and consent" for others. Positions filled by presidential appointment include those in the executive branch, the federal judiciary, commissioned officers in the armed forces, and members of the independent regulatory commissions. Governors and most mayors share a limited appointment power with their state senates and city councils, respectively. The President and governors may make recess appointments between Senate sessions. *See also* CONFIRMATION, page 138; RECESS APPOINTMENT, page 205; REMOVAL POWER, page 206.

Significance   The appointment power permits an executive to select persons sympathetic to the policies of his or her administration. Through patronage appointments, the executive may control his or her political party. The key difference in executive authority between the President and most governors—and between a "strong" and a "weak" mayor—lies in the substantial appointing power of the former in each case. The kinds of individuals appointed—their ideological convictions, political backgrounds, loyalty to the "boss"—can greatly affect the nature of the decisions made on public issues. Gross misconduct by many appointed officials in the Nixon administration, for example, led to congressional and court actions and to a weakening of the President's leadership. The trend at all levels of government, however, is toward reducing the executive appointing power in favor of merit selection. The ability of the chief executive to use appointing power may be severely weakened when different parties control the executive and legislative branches. This occurred in 1995, when the Republicans gained control of Congress for the first time in 40 years and sought to use the checks and balances system to thwart the Democratic presidential leadership.

Budget Power   The ability to affect political decisions concerning the income and spending of public money. The budgetary powers of the presidency lie in the initiatory role, in the ability to influence Congress during its consideration of the budget, in the threat and use of the veto on appropriations acts, and in the discretion exercised in spending funds appropriated by Congress. Each year, receipt and expenditure estimates are recommended by the President to the Congress for the next fiscal year. In January of each legislative session, the President sends an annual budget message to Congress as required by the Budget and Accounting Act of 1921. Unlike the State of the Union message, which precedes it, the budget message is not usually delivered in person by the President but is sent to Congress in writing to be read to each chamber by its clerk. Many governors, especially of those states that have undergone recent reorganization, also deliver or send to the legislature annual or biennial budget messages. *See also* BUDGET, page 390; BUDGET AND ACCOUNTING ACT OF 1921, page 426; BUDGET COMMITTEES, page 133; CONGRESSIONAL BUDGET AND IMPOUNDMENT CONTROL ACT OF 1974, page 180; PERFORMANCE BUDGET, page 411; PRESIDENTIAL-CONGRESSIONAL BUDGET NEGOTIATION, page 198.

Significance   The importance of the President's budget power is that it places responsibility for the initiation of the financial plan for government on the executive. Legislative bodies begin their consideration of financial matters only after the budget message, with its detailed itemization of fiscal recommendations, has been presented to them. Although Congress or a state legislature is free to modify or reject the proposals found in a budget message, its size and specificity tend to reduce legislative discretion. The executive may also use budget power as a means of arousing public support for certain programs, even though immediate enactment is unlikely. President Richard M. Nixon's broad use of *impoundment* powers—that is, his refusal to spend funds as authorized and appropriated by Congress for specific programs—led to judicial and congressional actions that have reduced but not eliminated the President's impoundment powers. The size—currently substantially more than $1 trillion—and complexity of the national budget have led to the development of a summarized "Budget in Brief" for congressional use. In 1974, Congress passed budget reform legislation under which, for example, the fiscal year was changed from the period July 1 to June 30 to the period October 1 to September 30, and House and Senate Budget Committees were created in an attempt to increase congressional budget powers. In 1990, in a desperate effort to reduce the annual budget deficit for future fiscal years, President Bush and his staff met with congressional leaders for several months to negotiate a "new taxes plus budget cutting" agreement. Congress subsequently voted down the leadership-approved agreement, but efforts to reach agreement through negotiations continued. Finally, after Congress had several times voted to delay the Gramm-Rudman-Hollings sequestration, agreement was reached on a package of tax increases and spending cuts that provided a five-year deficit-reduction measure that allegedly would reduce the national governmental budget by $492 billion, even though annual budget deficits would continue, with estimates in the $200 to $300 billion range. In addition, Congress provided that some spending programs, such as that involving the massive savings and loan crisis, would be "off-budget." When the budget power is divided between a President of one party and a Congress of another party, as happened in 1995, reconciling differences can be extremely difficult. The problems become almost insurmountable when the officials seeking agreement are also divided by ideologies. The 73 members of the freshman class added still another obstacle—no compromise! At the end of 1995, the only agreement reached was that the budget should be balanced in seven years, leaving cuts in entitlement programs and tax reduction for future negotiation, or for voters to decide in the 1996 elections. This budgetary impasse led to gridlock, with the government partially shut down for one week and later for a three-week period.

Cabinet   An advisory group selected by the President to aid him in making decisions. President Washington instituted the Cabinet idea when he regularly called together the heads of the four executive departments and the Vice President to consult on matters of policy. The Cabinet remains an informal group, with its membership determined by tradition and presidential discretion. By custom, the heads of the major departments (State, Treasury, Defense, Justice, Interior, Agriculture, Commerce, Labor, Health and Human Services, Education, Housing and Urban Development, Energy, Transportation, and Veterans Affairs) are members of the Cabinet, and the President may also invite the Vice President and other officials to sit in on Cabinet meetings. *See also* DEPARTMENT, page 224.

Significance   The Cabinet may be a highly influential or relatively insignificant agency, whichever the President decides to make it. The members of the Cabinet individually are often far more influential in advising the President than is the Cabinet as a body. Some presidents, such as James Buchanan and Warren G. Harding, placed great reliance on their cabinets; others, such as Woodrow Wilson and both Theodore and Franklin D. Roosevelt, assigned their cabinets an insignificant role. Abraham Lincoln once illustrated the *advisory* nature of Cabinet decisions when he announced the outcome of a vote on a important issue: "The ayes 7, the nays 1. The nays have it." In making Cabinet appointments, presidents typically seek to obtain broad geographic and interest-group representation and to give some representation to the different political wings of their party. To promote bipartisanship, especially during periods of national crisis, presidents have appointed members of the opposition party to Cabinet posts. For these reasons, presidents usually prefer to seek advice elsewhere and to confine Cabinet meetings to general discussions of administration policy.

Chief Diplomat   The role of the President as the nation's highest-level negotiator and administrator of policies and programs with other nations. The President as chief diplomat constitutes the official spokesman for the government of the United States with all foreign countries. The President's powers are enumerated and implied from Article II of the Constitution and from the Supreme Court's recognition of the inherent powers vested in the presidency. As chief diplomat, the President can negotiate and conclude executive agreements, negotiate and ratify treaties approved by the Senate, grant or withhold recognition of new states and governments, send and receive ambassadors and ministers, and sever diplomatic relations. As chief diplomat, the President depends heavily upon the secretaries of State and Defense and informal advisers to help him in making decisions. *See also* DIPLOMACY, page 546; *United States v. Curtiss-Wright Export Corp.*, page 600.

Significance   The President as chief diplomat plays the key role in making and implementing the nation's foreign policy. The primacy of this role has been recognized and usually supported by Congress and the federal courts since the adoption of the Constitution. The Supreme Court summarized the President's diplomatic role in the famous case *United States v. Curtiss-Wright Export Corp.*, 299 U.S. 304 (1936), in deciding that "the President alone has the power to speak or listen as a representative of the nation." In recent years, however, the Congress has sought to rein in the foreign policy powers of the President and enlarge the role of Congress in the process. In the Case Act of 1972, for example, the Congress required the President to submit the text of all executive agreements to Congress within 60 days; in the War Powers Act of 1973, Congress limited the President's authority to commit American troops to military action abroad by providing for the participation of Congress in such actions. Presidents since 1973 have declared these acts to be unconstitutional limitations on presidential powers, although several have complied with some of the provisions.

Chief Executive   The President's role as head of the government of the United States and its main decision maker. The Constitution, in Article II, vests "the" executive power (meaning *all* of it) in the President and provides that "he shall take care that the Laws be faithfully executed." These grants of power give the President the authority and assign the President the responsibility to run the executive branch of government. As chief executive, the President functions (1) as the initiator of broad programs of action to cope with the nation's main problems; (2) as chief administrator, responsible for the functioning of the federal establishment that he heads; (3) as chief enforcement agent, charged with enforcing all federal laws; and (4) as the nation's chief financial officer, charged with responsibility for formulating and expending annual federal budgets. *See also* GOVERNOR, page 191; PRESIDENT, page 196.

Significance   The President in his role of chief executive makes extensive use of advisers and administrators who act in his name and under his authority. A host of staff and housekeeping agencies, for example, gives the President the help he needs to direct and supervise the federal bureaucracy of several million civil servants. Basically, as chief executive, the President's main challenge is that of trying to persuade members of the bureaucracy to carry out his policies and programs. He also has the power to appoint (in many cases with the approval of the Senate) and to remove executive officials, although in the case of the independent regulatory commissions and with civil service personnel, he can remove only for cause as specified by Congress. The success of a President in his role as chief executive depends to a great extent on his ability to wield power and influence effectively in the executive branch. In a related role, the President also functions as "chief communicator," utilizing press conferences, speeches, newspapers, radio, and television to keep the public aware of issues and administration policies and programs.

Chief Legislator   The role of the President in the making of laws. Constitutional powers available to the President to affect legislation include recommending legislative programs through messages to the Congress, the veto, and some control over sessions. Informal methods of influencing legislation include the President's personal contacts with congressional leaders, his use of patronage, his ability to arouse public opinion in support of his program, his efforts to influence the election of representatives sympathetic to his views, and the continuing efforts of executive officials acting as a "presidential lobby" before congressional committees. In addition, the President's legislative powers include issuing rules and executive orders having the effect of law under powers delegated to him by the Constitution or by Congress. *See also* EMERGENCY POWERS, page 189; EXECUTIVE ORDER, page 190; PRESIDENT, page 196.

Significance   An evaluation of a President's administration is based considerably upon his success or failure in his role as chief legislator. Presidents who have initiated broad legislative programs and successfully pushed them through Congress, using a variety of constitutional and informal political methods and weapons, are generally classified as "strong" presidents; those who have failed to provide effective legislative leadership, through unwillingness or inability, have generally been relegated to the category of "weak" presidents. Congress, because of its size and diffusion of interests, lacks the means of formulating broad legislative programs and of enacting them into law without the continuing leadership of the President in determining legislative outcomes within their political systems. Sometimes a change in conditions can weaken the power of a president to influence legislation. This situation occurred for President Bill Clinton when the Republicans in the election of 1994 took control of Congress for the first time in 40 years.

Chief of Party   The role of the chief executive as the nation's partisan political leader. As chief of party, the President (1) influences the voters on behalf of his party, (2) makes patronage appointments to high executive positions and to federal judgeships, (3) grants "pork barrel" favors, (4) campaigns for party members, (5) plays an important—sometimes decisive—role in decision making within the party's organizations, and (6) frequently consults with party leaders throughout the nation. *See also* PRESIDENT, page 196.

Significance   The President's role as chief of party determines to a considerable extent how effectively he can function in many of his other major roles. His success as chief legislator, for example, depends largely on his ability to gain the active support of key members of his party in Congress. Above all, he must be able to function in a *political* context, practicing the art of the possible while sensitive to the processes of change that characterize politics. Some presidents, such as Franklin D. Roosevelt and John F. Kennedy, relished their political roles, whereas others, such as Dwight Eisenhower and Calvin Coolidge, tried to remain aloof. In any case, under the American political system, a President performs functions as chief of party whether or not he enjoys that partisan role. The role of chief of party is, typically, the most time-consuming of all presidential roles during campaign and election periods.

Chief of State   The role of the President as ceremonial head of the government of the United States. Duties of the chief of state include greeting foreign dignitaries, acting as host at state dinners, throwing out the first baseball at the start of the season, and bestowing honors. American chief executives at all governmental levels function in similar ceremonial roles as part of their executive duties. *See also* PRESIDENT, page 196.

Significance   The President serves in a dual capacity as chief of state and as chief executive. In most countries, these roles are split, as in Britain, where the Queen is the ceremonial head of state, and the Prime Minister and Cabinet head the government and formulate policies. Many students of government believe that the role of chief of state detracts from the ability of the President to give sufficient time and energy to the many other responsibilities. In addition, his role as chief of state has blended with his political and executive roles, with the result that many Americans reject the President as a symbol of national unity and increasingly involve him in the center of conflict during national crises. Yet, if he plays the chief of state role skillfully, the President may reap considerable advantage in increased public confidence and support for him in his other roles.

Commander in Chief   The role of President, as provided in Article II, section 2 of the Constitution, as supreme commander of the military forces of the United States and of the state National Guard units when they are called into federal service. As commander in chief, the President exercises a vast array of "war powers." During periods of war or threat of war, he exercises both military and civilian powers related to defense. *See also* PRESIDENT, page 196; WAR POWERS, page 591; WAR POWERS ACT, page 603.

Significance   Under his war powers, the President can deploy U.S. forces anywhere in the world and, as has happened many times in American history, order them into action against a foreign foe without a declaration of war by Congress. American military interventions—in Korea in 1950; in

Indochina during the 1960s and 1970s; in Central America, Grenada, Libya, Lebanon, and Panama in the 1980s; and in the Persian Gulf region, Somalia, Haiti, and the Balkans in the 1990s—without congressional declarations of war illustrate the extent to which a President can commit the nation to a course of military action under his powers as commander in chief. In a reaction against presidents' foreign military initiatives, the Senate in 1969 passed a "national commitments" resolution requiring congressional approval for any commitment to use American troops abroad. In the War Powers Act of 1973, Congress declared its intent to participate with the President in making decisions to use American armed forces abroad. In Operation Desert Shield in 1990 and Desert Storm in 1991, President George Bush consulted with Congress about the Persian Gulf War but claimed it was voluntary on his part and not required of the President under the Constitution. In recent years, issues involving financial considerations, the end of the Cold War, and the downsizing of military operations have led to the closing of many military bases. In *Dalton v. Specter,* 114 S. Ct. 1719 (1994), the Court ruled that the exercise of presidential discretion in the closing of a military base is not subject to federal court challenge.

Economic Message   The annual economic report submitted each January by the President to Congress, as required by the Employment Act of 1946. The economic message is concerned with employment levels, production, purchasing power, inflation and deflation, trends of the nation's economy, and recommendations to Congress on maintaining or improving economic activity. The economic report is prepared by the President's Council of Economic Advisers, comprised of three leading economists. A joint congressional Committee on the Economic Report, consisting of seven members from each house, studies the message and makes recommendations for implementing it. Ultimately, it is up to the President to initiate specific actions. *See also* COUNCIL OF ECONOMIC ADVISERS, page 422; EMPLOYMENT ACT OF 1946, page 427; KEYNESIANISM, page 407; MONETARISM, page 409.

Significance   The President's annual economic message reflects an acceptance by the national government of responsibility for maintaining stability in the nation's economy through monetary and fiscal policies. This approach, called Keynesianism, substitutes decisions made by the President and his advisers in pursuit of specific social goals for the undirected interplay of market forces. Like other messages, it adds to the President's role as chief legislator by enabling him to initiate and recommend legislative programs and to give them nationwide publicity through the message. When a serious economic crisis arises, as in the stock market "crash" in October 1987, or in the longest post–World War II recession in the early 1990s, the American people tend to look to the President as the chief of the nation's economy to provide the necessary leadership.

Emergency Powers   Powers exercised during a period of crisis by the national government, or those powers conferred by Congress upon the President for a limited period of time. The President's exercise of inherent powers in the field of foreign affairs provides an additional source of power during emergencies. *See also* INHERENT POWERS, page 43; WAR POWERS, page 591; *Youngstown Sheet and Tube Co. v. Sawyer,* page 217.

Significance   The Constitution does not recognize the need for additional national powers during an emergency. The Supreme Court has made this clear in stating that "emergency does not create power" (*Home Building and Loan Association v. Blaisdell,* 290 U.S. 398 [1934]). Yet emergencies have helped to develop the use of otherwise dormant powers and the novel application of ordinary powers. Today, presidents exercise vast emergency powers initially delegated to Franklin D. Roosevelt during the 1933 banking crisis and expanded during World War II, the Korean War, the Cold War, the Vietnam War, the Persian Gulf War with Iraq, and several domestic crises. Congress has repealed some of these emergency grants of power in its effort to restore equilibrium to the separation of powers—check and balances system.

Executive Agreement   An international agreement, reached by the President with foreign heads of state, that does not require senatorial approval. Such agreements are concluded under the President's constitutional power as commander in chief and his general authority in foreign relations, or under power delegated to him by Congress. Executive agreements may be weakened by congressional action and may be rejected by future presidents. The Supreme Court's 1937 action holding that executive agreements are legally equal to treaties and thus enjoy the status of "supreme law of the land" remains in effect (*United States v. Belmont,* 301 U.S. 324). *See also* CHIEF DIPLOMAT, page 186; EXECUTIVE AGREEMENT, page 548; RATIFICATION, pages 161, 205; TREATY, page 583.

Significance   Executive agreements contribute to the President's position of leadership in foreign affairs. Quick, decisive action can be taken during a crisis without having to follow the difficult and time-consuming route of treaty making. Secrecy can be maintained through executive agreements when open debate in the Senate would be dangerous or provocative or doomed to failure. For example, in 1940, before American entry into World War II, President Franklin D. Roosevelt traded 50 over-age destroyers to British Prime Minister Winston Churchill for air bases in British Western hemispheric possessions, a critical action but one for which Senate approval was unobtainable. By possessing the executive agreement alternative, the President is placed in a better bargaining position with Congress on foreign policy matters. In the 1950s, Senator John Bricker of Ohio introduced a constitutional amendment proposal aimed at strengthening the role of Congress in treaty making by limiting the President's power to conclude executive agreements and by ensuring that all treaties and agreements conform to the Constitution. The proposed Bricker Amendment was killed by the Senate by a one-vote margin, but the idea of limiting presidential powers remains and was embodied in the Case Act of 1972 and the War Powers Act of 1973.

Executive Order   A rule or regulation, issued by the President, a governor, or some administrative authority, that has the effect of law. Executive orders are used to implement and give administrative effect to provisions of the Constitution, to treaties, and to statutes. They may be used to create or modify the organization or procedures of administrative agencies or may have general applicability as law. Under the national Administrative Procedure Act of 1946, all executive orders must be published in the *Federal Register. See also*

DELEGATION OF POWER, page 143; FEDERAL REGISTER, page 225; QUASI-LEGISLATIVE, page 232.

Significance   The use of executive orders has greatly increased in recent years as a result of the growing tendency of legislative bodies to leave many legislative details to be filled in by the executive branch. The President's power to issue executive orders stems from precedents, custom, and constitutional interpretation, as well as from discretionary powers given to the President by the Congress in legislation. This trend will likely continue as government involves itself further with highly complex and technical matters. Examples of important executive orders include President Franklin Roosevelt's executive order that created a Committee on Fair Employment Practices to ensure that defense contractors do not discriminate on the basis of race, creed, or national origin; President Harry Truman's executive order that integrated the military services; President John F. Kennedy's executive order that instituted an affirmative action program in federal employment; and President Bill Clinton's executive order that returned abortion counseling to federally funded clinics and allowed the use of fetal tissue from abortions in federally funded research. However, a rider attached to a budget bill then removed all funding for any research using fetal tissue.

Executive Privilege   The right of executive officials to refuse to appear before or to withhold information from a legislative committee or a court. Executive privilege is enjoyed by the President and those executive officials accorded the right by the President. No legal means by which executive privilege could be denied to executive officials existed for many years, but in 1974 the Supreme Court established a landmark precedent (*United States v. Nixon,* 418 U.S. 683 [1974]) by unanimously ordering President Richard M. Nixon to release recorded tapes with allegedly criminal information on them that eventually led to his resignation. *See also* CHECKS AND BALANCES, page 32; INVESTIGATING COMMITTEE, page 152; SEPARATION OF POWERS, page 50; *United States v. Nixon,* page 216.

Significance   Executive privilege in the American system is claimed as an inherent executive power under the constitutional separation of powers and on time-honored tradition. Although the right of the President to refuse to appear before congressional committees is generally unchallenged, the issue remains as to whether his major advisers should enjoy the same privilege. The right of Congress to obtain information for the lawmaking process and to investigate for possible impeachment actions and the right of the courts to hear and decide cases involving executive officials clash with the President's right to function as the head of a coordinate branch of the national government. Critics charge that executive privilege is often invoked to deny the American people information critical of executive policies. Executive privilege, however, has been moderated by the action of President Bill Clinton and his wife, Hillary Rodham Clinton, who voluntarily submitted themselves to be questioned under oath at the White House concerning their conduct in the Whitewater Development Corporation investigation.

Governor   The chief executive officer of a state. The governor is elected by the people and serves for four years except in the states that have two-year terms—Arkansas, New Hampshire, Rhode Island, and Vermont. About half the states limit the governor to one or two terms in office. A governor's executive powers include the power of appointment and removal (although this is severely restricted in most states), preparation and execution of the budget, the power to issue executive orders, and general law enforcement. In the legislative field, governors enjoy considerable power through exercise of the veto power (in all states but North Carolina), and in all but seven states the governor may veto or reduce items in appropriation bills subject to legislative override. A governor may call the legislature into special session and, in several states, may limit the special session to specified subjects. Like the President, the governor may exercise influence over the legislature through party leadership. Most may grant reprieves and pardons to convicted persons. Each also serves as commander in chief of the National Guard of the state, except when it is called into national service. Governors may be removed from office by impeachment and, in a few states, by recall. *See also* CHIEF EXECUTIVE, page 186; LINE-ITEM VETO, page 194.

Significance   The office of governor is one of considerable prestige and political power and has been steadily growing in influence. One of the major difficulties of the office is the requirement in many states that the governor share executive authority with several other elected officials. In this respect, the governor is a weaker executive than the President, since the governor may not have control over many high executive officials. Reorganization movements have sought to strengthen the appointive and removal powers of the governor by reducing the number of elected officers and eliminating many of the boards and commissions that characterize state government. Recent trends also include increasing the governor's terms of office, and expanding the budgetary, management, and personnel powers of the office.

Honeymoon Period   The period of time, usually quite brief, when a newly elected president takes office and provides effective leadership in transforming some of his electoral promises into law. In a honeymoon period, opposition forces in Congress, in the opposing party, in the media, and in the general public either respect the President's electoral mandate or are not yet organized or willing to function as an effective opposition. The honeymoon period typically comes to an end when public support fades, when the President begins to lose key votes in Congress, and when the media begin to engage in carping criticism. *See also* PRESIDENT, page 196; PRESIDENTIAL LEADERSHIP, page 201.

Significance   One of the most effective presidential honeymoons occurred in 1933 when, in the first 100 days of his administration, President Franklin D. Roosevelt was able to push through Congress a series of liberal policies and programs known as the New Deal that amounted to a veritable social and economic revolution. In one of the longest honeymoons on record, President Ronald Reagan in the 1980s in his first six years in office succeeded in carrying out much of his mandate for a conservative revolution. His successes in policy changes came often with the active support of the Democratic party opposition in the Congress. As a result of the Iran-contra revelations in 1987, however, President Reagan was frequently attacked by Congress, the media, and various pressure groups, and his high rating in national polls dropped substantially. His honeymoon was finally over. In an unusual case of leadership without presidential support, Speaker of the House Newt Gingrich in 1995 pushed through his Contract with America action program in the 100-day period that he had promised. The inaction of the Senate on many of these issues brought an end to the legislative honeymoon.

Imperial Presidency   Misuse or abuse of the powers of office by the President and his administration. The term "imperial presidency" is often used by opposition leaders in their attempts to discredit the policies and actions undertaken by an incumbent administration. Frequently the term is used in Congress by members who feel that the President has usurped powers rightfully assigned to the legislative branch. Many constitutional and presidential scholars argue that presidential powers have been so increased and misused—especially in the Vietnam War—as to threaten the American constitutional system. Questionable powers exercised by allegedly imperial presidents such as Lyndon B. Johnson, Richard M. Nixon, and Ronald Reagan have included excessive secrecy, foreign commitments concluded by the President without consulting or informing Congress, and—in the case of President Nixon—use of an extralegal investigative group supported by public funds but used for personal purposes. *See also* STEWARDSHIP THEORY, page 203.

Significance   In American politics, it is often difficult to determine objectively if power is being misused and abused by an imperial president. Supporters of an incumbent president prefer to describe the president's policies as "decisive" and "effective" actions undertaken by a strong president with a vibrant, supportive administration. Such strong actions are regarded by supporters as essential for achieving the national interest. In most cases, charges of an imperial presidency have emerged from conflict between Congress and the executive branch or between liberals and conservatives and usually involve those legislators who support an active foreign policy and those who are inclined to go slow and maintain congressional control over presidential initiatives.

Impoundment   Refusal by a chief executive to expend funds appropriated by the legislative branch. Presidents have often used impoundment as a means for controlling the budget execution process. However, the Budget and Impoundment Control Act of 1974 severely reduced the President's impoundment powers. Under this law, a President who seeks to cut back on expenditures already approved by Congress can either try to cancel programs or postpone them. To cancel, he must send Congress a "recision" message that repeals his authority to spend funds previously authorized. To postpone spending, he must send Congress a "deferral" message. In both cases, the President must be very specific in indicating programs to be repealed or deferred, by how much, and for how long. Although the President's recision message requires approval by both houses, the President is authorized to impound the funds for 45 days without action by Congress. If Congress does not act during that period, the President must give up the impoundment and spend the money. By contrast, deferrals can stand for a year or more but can be "vetoed" at any time by the action of either house. *See also* BUDGET, page 390; CONGRESSIONAL BUDGET AND IMPOUNDMENT CONTROL ACT OF 1974, page 180; LEGISLATIVE VETO, page 155.

Significance   Impoundment is used to prevent expenditures for programs that the President does not support or to call public attention to a "spendthrift" Congress. The actions by Congress in 1974 to limit the President's impoundment powers grew out of the battles between President Richard M. Nixon and the Democratic-controlled Congress. To cut the federal budget substantially, a president would have to flood Congress with recision and deferral messages. Congress, however, retains the ultimate power to determine spending. President Ronald Reagan used the procedures under the 1974 act extensively in his efforts to reduce and balance the federal budget. In *Train v. City of New York*, 420 U.S. 35 (1975), the Supreme Court limited the President's impoundment discretion but left the broader question of impoundment powers unresolved.

Kitchen Cabinet   An informal group of close friends and personal advisers to the President. Members of a kitchen cabinet may supplement or substantially replace the formal Cabinet as the President's chief source of advice on domestic and foreign policies. The kitchen cabinet may, however, include several members of the formal Cabinet. *See also* CABINET, page 185.

Significance   The term "kitchen cabinet" originated during the presidency of Andrew Jackson. President Jackson was strongly influenced by the advice of a group of close friends he met with, sometimes in the kitchen of the White House. Often, he preferred their views to those of his formal Cabinet. Most presidents, like Jackson, have placed primary reliance on advice secured from such relationships, leading frequently to subdued outrage on the part of Cabinet members whose advice is not sought or heeded. President George Bush's kitchen cabinet of unofficial advisers played a major role in helping him develop policy and programs. President Bill Clinton put his friends in the Cabinet and expected them to make the "right" decisions and to accept the blame for those that failed.

Line-Item Veto   The power exercised by the President and the governors in all but a few states to veto sections or items of an appropriation bill while signing the remainder of the bill into law. Governors in several states can reduce appropriation items and in a few states may veto sections of nonfinancial bills. The legislature may override the vetoed items. The President was granted this line-item veto power in 1996 as part of the Contract with America, to take effect in January 1997. With this new power, known as "enhanced recission," the President can strike individual items from spending and revenue bills as well as targeted tax breaks that benefit 100 or fewer taxpayers. He can also remove provisions that entitle certain groups of people to specific benefits. In this process, the President's veto would take effect unless Congress, within 30 days, passed a bill to overturn the President's action. The President can then veto these bills, and Congress can override the veto by a two-thirds vote of both houses. *See also* PORK BARREL LEGISLATION, page 158; RIDER, page 165; VETO, page 209.

Significance   Efforts to give the line-item veto power to the President began in the 1870s and continued sporadically thereafter. In 1996, as a result of efforts to find the means to balance the budget, Congress, in a historic shift in the checks and balances of the American constitutional system, gave the

President the line-item veto power. Proponents argue that it provides a powerful new tool for fiscal discipline that empowers the President to cut out wasteful spending that Congress lacks the will to turn down. Critics describe it as a blow to the constitutional requirement for separation of powers—checks and balances within the government. Moreover, as a practical political maneuver, it will encourage Congress—especially when controlled by a different party than the executive—to engage in political gamesmanship in efforts to embarrass the President. Both Republican and Democratic presidents have long wanted this power. They have said that it will give the President a potent check on Congress's free-spending tendencies and cut back on pork barrel legislation. However, a court test of the constitutionality of the bill is virtually certain.

Minority President   An elected president who has received less than 50 percent of the total *popular* votes cast for all candidates, although obtaining a majority of the *electoral* votes. A winning candidate is most likely to be a minority president when several fairly strong minor party candidates are in the presidential contest. *See also* ELECTORAL COLLEGE, page 74.

Significance   Although the Constitution does not recognize such a status, many American presidents have been "minority presidents," including Abraham Lincoln, Woodrow Wilson, Harry S Truman, John F. Kennedy, Richard M. Nixon, and Bill Clinton. Two presidents, Rutherford B. Hayes in 1876 and Benjamin Harrison in 1888, won election, even though in each case their major opponent polled more popular votes. So long as more than two candidates run for the office and so long as the Electoral College continues to operate, there will always be the possibility of electing a minority president. The concept of minority president also relates informally to the problem of nonvoting. In 1980, for example, Ronald Reagan received 43.9 million votes—50.7 percent of the total vote cast—but those who voted for him constituted only about 27 percent of the eligible voters.

Pardon   An executive grant of a release from the punishment or legal consequences of a crime before or after conviction. The President exercises the complete pardoning power for federal offenses except for convictions in impeachment cases. An "absolute pardon" restores the individual to the position he or she enjoyed prior to conviction for commission of a crime. A "conditional pardon" requires that certain obligations be met before the pardon becomes effective. Pardons are administered for the President by the Office of the Pardon Attorney in the Department of Justice. Thirty states entrust the governor with the full authority for granting pardons. In the remainder, the governor typically shares the power with a pardon board or with the state senate. Pardons are granted usually to provide a remedy for mistakes made in convictions or to release offenders who have been properly rehabilitated. The President and most state governors also have the power to grant *reprieves*, which postpone the execution of a sentence for humanitarian reasons or to await new evidence. The President may also commute sentences, thereby mitigating punishment, but, unlike a pardon, this action does not remove the conviction from the individual's record. *See also* AMNESTY, page 183; *Ex parte Grossman*, page 215.

Significance   The President's pardoning power extends to all offenses against the United States, including contempt of Congress or of a federal court (*Ex parte Grossman,* 267 U.S. 87 [1925]). Most governors regard the pardoning power as among their most bothersome and distasteful tasks. Relatives and friends of offenders besiege governors with applications and pressures for pardons. The trend in the states is toward vesting greater responsibility in recommending or deciding pardons in full-time boards staffed by correctional experts. One of the most controversial presidential pardons in American history was that extended by President Gerald R. Ford to former President Richard M. Nixon. In that case, President Ford granted a blanket pardon for any crimes that Nixon may have committed during his years in office. The pardon was granted before any specific charges had been made. In a 1974 decision, the Supreme Court held that the President's power to pardon comes directly from the Constitution and that limitations, if any, must also be found in the Constitution (*Schick v. Reed,* 419 U.S. 256 [1974]). In 1977, President Jimmy Carter granted a blanket pardon to Vietnam draft evaders, but not to military deserters, and in 1992 President George Bush granted pardons to six individuals, all of whom were involved in the Iran-contra affair.

Pocket Veto   A special veto power exercised at the end of a legislative session whereby bills not signed by a chief executive die after a specified time. Under the Constitution, if the President holds a bill for ten days without signing or vetoing it, the bill becomes law if Congress is in session and is pocket vetoed if Congress adjourns during the ten days. In about a third of the states, governors exercise a similar pocket veto power if they do not approve the measure during a stated period after legislative adjournment. This period varies in these states from 3 to 30 days. *See also* VETO, page 209.

Significance   The pocket veto provides a chief executive with a major legislative power. Unlike the ordinary veto, which is merely suspensive in nature and can be overridden, the pocket veto is absolute. A bill that is pocket vetoed can, of course, be reintroduced in the next legislative session as a new bill. Whereas the regular veto requires an explanation from the chief executive, the pocket veto does not, although presidents usually defend their position in Memorandums of Disapproval. Most significantly, the pocket veto is available at the crucial period at the end of the legislative session, when large numbers of bills are enacted in a last-minute legislative rush. In some states, the practice of the legislature is to recess rather than adjourn when work is completed. It then reassembles briefly to adjourn officially after the pocket veto is no longer effective, thereby preventing its use by the governor.

President   The chief executive of the United States and the key official in the American system of government. The Constitution, in Article II, vests the complete executive power in the President. The President is elected every four years through the Electoral College machinery and is eligible under the Twenty-second Amendment for one additional term. His chief advisers are found in the Executive Office of the President and in the Cabinet. Much of his help in reaching decisions comes from an unofficial and informal "kitchen cabinet" of close friends and advisers. The President exercises a broad array of powers, some provided by the Constitution, some based on custom and tradition, some delegated by Congress, and others that are simply inherent in the nature of the office. Foremost are those broad and largely undefined powers that the President exercises in his role as chief of foreign policy. These include the leadership of the armed forces, the recognition of foreign states and governments, the conduct of diplomacy, the making of international agreements and treaties with the Senate's approval, the initiation of new foreign programs, and the providing of leadership for the United States in the world. In his role of chief administrator, the President exercises broad appointing and removal powers, directs and supervises the operations of the executive branch, directs the formulation of the annual budget, and sees that the laws are faithfully executed. As chief legislator, the President initiates comprehensive legislative programs, delivers regular and special messages to Congress, summons Congress into special sessions, wields a broad veto power, and influences the course of much legislation in his relations with legislative leaders and by arousing public opinion to support his programs. As chief of his party, the President dispenses patronage, influences the direction and nature of party policies, provides leadership to his party's delegation in both houses of Congress, and generally influences and determines party actions and policies. In his role as chief of state, the President maintains relations with other nations and performs numerous ceremonial functions in the United States. The prestige of the office contributes much to the effectiveness of the President in his many roles. Easy access to the mass media of communication aids him in molding public opinion. His many sources of information keep him well-informed on the complex problems facing the nation. *See also* CHIEF LEGISLATOR, page 187; CHIEF OF STATE, page 188; PRESIDENTIAL ELECTION PROCESS, page 102; PRESIDENTIAL LEADERSHIP, page 201; STEWARDSHIP THEORY, page 203; TAFTIAN OR CONTRACTUAL THEORY, page 203.

Significance   The office of President has been shaped by the experiences of the various presidents who have held the office during American history. Much has depended upon the personalities of the individual presidents, their political, economic, and social philosophies, and their conceptions of the office itself. Often, the person and the office have been shaped by the temper of the times—quiet and peaceful or hectic and crisis-filled. Some presidents, such as William H. Taft and Calvin Coolidge, have viewed the office largely in terms of administration and law enforcement. Others, like Abraham Lincoln, Woodrow Wilson, and the two Roosevelts, have regarded the presidency as a position that allows and demands strong leadership and the exercise of broad, undefined powers, whenever they are necessary for the security and well-being of the country. The former group has been labeled as "weak" and the latter as "strong" presidents. All indications are that the nation is moving in the direction of stronger executive leadership, toward what has often been called "presidential government." One fact emphasizes this trend: The President alone has the power to undertake a nuclear war. No other world political leader is that powerful. In recent years, political scientists have tried to evaluate individual presidents by typecasting them as "active" or "passive," with each category divided into several subgroups. Time must pass for an evaluation based on historical perspectives for a president to be judged strong or weak, active or passive.

President-Elect   The candidate selected by the Electoral College to be the next President. Following the November popular election, the winning candidate is unofficially called the "President-designate" until the electors are able to ratify the people's choice when they meet in their respective state capitals in December and cast their Electoral College ballots. These ballots are counted by Congress early in January and the winners are then certified "President-elect" and "Vice President-elect." Under the Twentieth Amendment, the President-elect is sworn into office at noon on the twentieth day of January, and if the President-elect fails to qualify at that time, the Vice President-elect then acts as president until a president qualifies. If the President-elect dies, the Vice President-elect is then sworn in as President. *See also* TWENTIETH AMENDMENT, page 208; TWENTY-FIFTH AMENDMENT, page 208.

Significance   The status of President-elect is an important one because it enables the new chief executive to prepare for assumption of the duties and responsibilities of the office. From the November election until the inauguration on January 20, the President-elect may meet periodically with the outgoing President to be briefed on special continuing problems, especially those in foreign affairs. The President-elect may also begin unofficially to select his top appointees, prepare some legislative messages, study the new budget he inherits, and make other preparations. This transition period can be critical to the future success of a chief executive.

Presidential Commission   A bipartisan ad hoc group, usually composed of experts in the field under investigation who are appointed by the President to study a particular problem area and make recommendations to the President regarding possible governmental actions.

Significance   The presidential commission has been modeled after the royal commission in Great Britain, which has been used for many years to study various problems of public interest. Royal commissions have an enviable reputation because of the completeness and impartiality of their work. Presidents have established commissions on a variety of issues, for many reasons. Often a commission is created to study an issue that has become politicized to such an extent that rational analysis carried on through normal political channels is all but precluded. Commissions attempt to study problems in a politically neutral atmosphere so that their recommendations are likely to be accepted by Congress. The normally bipartisan nature of the commission is supposed to add credibility to its work. Recent commissions have been formed to deal with such politically charged issues as the MX missile, Social Security reform, U.S. policy in Central America, and problems associated with Acquired Immune Deficiency Syndrome (AIDS).

Presidential-Congressional Budget Negotiation   Recognition of the problem of balancing the nation's budget led to the entirely new approach, with the President meeting personally with the congressional leaders. In the past, there had been little or no involvement by the President, with most of the negotiating involving the leaders of the two chambers of Congress. This approach of presidential-congressional budget negotiating began in 1990 when President George Bush and his staff reached agreement for coping with the budget deficit with congressional leaders at Andrews Air Force Base, far removed from the influences of Capitol Hill. First judged a failure because the Congress refused to implement the plan, agreement on a five-year deficit-reduction measure was finally reached after a government shutdown of several days. *See also* BUDGET, page 390; PRESIDENTIAL LEADERSHIP, page 201.

Significance   This new presidential-congressional budget-negotiating approach was continued in 1995 and 1996 by President Bill Clinton after apparent gridlock on a method of balancing the budget. A series of budget-balancing sessions were held at the White House, involving President Clinton, Speaker of the House Newt Gingrich, and Senate Majority Leader Bob Dole. There were two partial government shutdowns, the first for one week, the second for a three-week period. Agreement was reached on balancing the budget in seven years but not on the nature and size of tax cuts and entitlement program reductions.

Presidential Doctrines   Enunciations made by American presidents that relate to potential American foreign policy actions. Presidential doctrines are aimed at putting potential enemies and friendly allies on notice of American intentions to cope with certain situations that may arise as a result of actions undertaken by other states. Often, the press and other media have converted presidential statements into full-fledged "doctrines" merely by labeling them as such. *See also* MONROE DOCTRINE, page 564; PRESIDENTIAL DOMESTIC POLICIES AND PROGRAMS, page 200; TRUMAN DOCTRINE, page 584.

Significance   The Monroe Doctrine was the first enunciated foreign policy program. It stated that there would be no European intervention in the affairs of the American continents and reaffirmed our intention not to interfere in European affairs. Recent presidential doctrines have included the Nixon Doctrine, the Carter Doctrine, and the Reagan Doctrine. President Richard M. Nixon, in a press conference on Guam in 1969, announced a new policy of national restraint in the defense of free nations, such as Vietnam, by limiting American support to those peoples who contributed energetically to their own defense. This Nixon Doctrine proclaimed American national interest as the key ingredient in making intervention decisions. President Jimmy Carter, in his State of the Union address to Congress in 1980, announced that if outside forces sought to gain control of the Persian Gulf region, this action "will be regarded as an assault on the vital interests of the United States of America, and such an assault will be repelled by any means necessary, including military force." The media immediately began to refer to this statement as the Carter Doctrine, and some characterized it as a reversal of the Nixon Doctrine. President Ronald Reagan, in a variety of speeches and statements, declared that the nation was prepared to lend support to guerrilla insurgencies against Soviet-supported governments in Third World countries. The Reagan Doctrine, as the media called it, was used to justify Reagan Administration support for rebel groups (or "freedom fighters" as President Reagan designated them) in Afghanistan, Nicaragua, Angola, and Cambodia. Often, presidential doctrines are weakened by the negative attitude of Congress that reflects the failure of the President to include Congress in the initiation stage of doctrine development. Conversely, when Congress lends its full support to a presidential doctrine, it can become a major instrument of national policy. For example, the 1947 Truman Doctrine of giving military and economic aid to countries resisting communist aggression, such as Greece and Turkey, became a cornerstone of post–World War II policy. Similarly, the Eisenhower Doctrine proclaimed in 1957 that the United States would use force to protect the independence of any country in the Middle East if so requested by that country. The doctrine was supported by Congress through adoption of a joint resolution and remains a critical guide to Middle East policy. In 1990, President George Bush updated the Eisenhower Doctrine with his New World Order, under which aggression would be punished with collective security forces representing the world community. He launched Desert Shield, a massive American military buildup in the Middle East aimed at restoring the independence of Kuwait after an Iraqi invasion and conquest. Operation Desert Storm followed in 1991, during which the Iraqi military forces were conclusively defeated by the United States and its allies.

Presidential Domestic Policies and Programs   Means by which presidents have defined policies and developed programs that were aimed at solving major domestic problems. These policies were often given descriptive names or titles to help call attention to the unified nature of the established program. *See also* PRESIDENTIAL DOCTRINES, page 199.

Significance   Every president has had a set of goals or objectives aimed at strengthening the country's economy and social climate. The first program of note in the twentieth century was Theodore Roosevelt's policy of New Nationalism, which accepted large business combinations but wanted them regulated by the federal government. President Woodrow Wilson's New Freedom favored breaking up large industrial combinations by antitrust actions. Then, in the period of the Great Depression of the 1930s, President Franklin Roosevelt engineered a massive social and economic revolution that he called the New Deal. It became the era of "big government" and greatly influenced the relationship between government and people. A whole new approach to dealing with national problems started with the first 100 days after his inauguration, which became the most productive legislative period in congressional history. Under the New Deal, a regulatory network was implemented. Banks, savings and loans, and stock markets; railroad, bus, trucking, and airplane transportation; labor-management relations—these and many more operations by the private sector were brought under the regulatory oversight and control of new governmental agencies created during the New Deal period. New Deal programs continued to influence the role of government and politics in the American system for more than 50 years before succumbing to major campaigns for deregulation, privatization, and downsizing. Some other programs begun under the New Deal were the Civilian Conservation Corps (CCC), the Tennessee Valley Authority, and the Social Security system. The New Deal was followed by President Harry Truman's Fair Deal, which attempted but failed to fill in the gaps left by the major policy battles of the Roosevelt years. These had become more virulent as the nation recovered from the Depression and war years of the 1940s. In the early 1960s, President John Kennedy offered a New Frontier approach, whereby he challenged the Amrican people, especially the young, to "ask not what your country can do for you, but what you can do for your country." As part of his dream, he created programs such as the Peace Corps and enhanced the space program. Following the assassination of President Kennedy, President Lyndon Johnson, in his Great Society, believed that social and economic problems could be solved by new governmental programs. Under the banner of the Great Society, many programs were created in civil rights, education at all levels, and health and welfare. Although these programs were all attempts at creating a better society, they were weakened by the realization that catchy phraseology alone would not produce the needed support. An extensive legislative program is essential if progress is to be achieved. This lesson should be learned by the President of the United States, whatever his party and ideology.

Presidential Leadership   The key ingredient for success that relates to the sum of the President's many official and unofficial roles. Leadership means that the President has the responsibility of initiating broad action policies and programs. It means that he has the responsibility of "selling" these policies and programs to Congress and to the public, building the support needed to convert them successfully into laws, executive orders, and other forms of decisions. Leadership in substantive areas must be supplemented by his role as a leader in his party, in budgetary and financial matters, and in building a strong, viable economy. In foreign policy, the President must take the lead in developing productive relations with more than 180 other nations. Negative leadership is also vested in the President in the form of such political weapons as the veto and impoundment powers. *See also* BUDGET POWER, page 184; STATE OF THE UNION MESSAGE, page 207; STEWARDSHIP THEORY, page 203.

Significance   In the American system, only the President can provide the kind of leadership needed to cope with problems facing the nation. Congress on occasion has sought to take over the leadership role when a President has been unwilling or unable. Congress, however, has a variety of leaders and lacks the leadership mystique imbued naturally in the presidency. Although important policy decisions have been rendered by the federal courts in such key areas as civil rights and school integration, successful implementation has depended on presidential leadership. When a presidential leadership vacuum occurs, the nation faces great dangers. Critics, for example, have blamed the Reagan and Bush administrations for failure to provide leadership in such critical problem areas as balancing the budget, instituting environmental programs, and developing a coherent program to deal with the savings and loan debacle and bank problems.

Presidential Power   The vast array of foreign and domestic executive powers exercised by the President in carrying out the duties of his office under Article II of the Constitution of the United States. Presidents have differed greatly in their definitions of these powers, and when and how they should be used. They include (1) delegating to the President "The executive Power..." (Art. II, Section 1); (2) designating the President as "Commander in Chief of the Army and Navy of the United States, and of the Militia of the several States, when called into the actual Service of the United States..." (Art. II, Section 2); (3) stipulating that the President may "require the Opinion, in writing, of the principal Officer in each of the executive Departments..." (Art. II, Section 2); (4) empowering the President to "grant Reprieves and Pardons...except in Cases of Impeachment..." (Art. II, Section 2); (5) delegating to the President the power "with the Advice and Consent of the Senate, to make Treaties..." (Art. II, Section 2); (6) empowering the

President to "nominate, and by and with the Advice and Consent of the Senate...appoint Ambassadors, other Public Ministers and Consuls, Judges of the Supreme Court, and all other Officers of the United States, whose Appointments are not herein otherwise provided for, and which shall be established by Law...but the Congress may by Law vest the Appointment of such inferior Officers...in the President alone..." (Art. II, Section 2); (7) granting the President power to "fill up all Vacancies that may happen during the Recess of the Senate..." (Art. II, Section 2); (8) providing for the President to "give to the Congress Information of the State of the Union, and recommend to their Consideration such Measures as he shall judge necessary and expedient..." (Art. II, Section 3); (9) assigning the President the authority "on extraordinary Occasions, (to) covene both Houses, or either of them..." (Art. II, Section 3); (10) granting the President the power "in Case of Disagreement between (the two chambers)...he may adjourn them..." (Art. II, Section 3); (11) authorizing the President to "receive Ambassadors and other public Ministers..." (Art. II, Section 3); (12) assigning the President responsibility to "take Care that the Laws be faithfully executed..." (Art. II, Section 3); (13) granting the President the power, when a vacancy occurs in the office of the Vice President, to "nominate a Vice President who shall take office upon confirmation by a majority vote of both Houses of Congress" (Amendment XXV); and (14) empowering the President to approve, before it becomes law, every bill passed by the House and Senate, but if he disapproves of the bill "he shall return it (veto), with his objections..." (Art. I, Section 7). *See also* PRESIDENTIAL LEADERSHIP, page 201; TWENTY-FIFTH AMENDMENT, page 208.

Significance   American history has been punctuated by interval periods in which strong and weak presidents have served. In many ways, the man has made the office, defining his powers and roles with few legal or political restraints by the other two branches. The key ingredient, or lack of same, that has led to characterizations of "strong" and "weak" is that of leadership. A strong president tends to initiate action programs, cultivate public support for them, and effectively pressure Congress into lending its support for them. Examples include Theodore Roosevelt and his New Nationalism program, Woodrow Wilson's New Freedom, Franklin Roosevelt's New Deal, Harry Truman's Fair Deal, John Kennedy's New Frontier, Lyndon Johnson's Great Society, and George Bush's New World Order. Strong political and legal leadership can result in a decisive role that historians and political scientists refer to as "presidential government." Conversely, other presidents have tended to reject the concentration of power in the hands of the chief executive. Calvin Coolidge, Warren Harding, and Herbert Hoover typified the exercise of power restraint and the absence of strong presidential leadership. Hoover, for example, refused to use government actively to overcome the Great Depression catastrophe, preferring to let private initiatives in the free enterprise system do the job, despite their failure to restore prosperity.

Presidential Power: Prerogative Theory   A theory, first enunciated by John Locke, which holds that the chief executive can exercise extraordinary power if needed to protect and preserve the nation. The idea of unspecified prerogative powers first developed in Britain, where the royal prerogative included not only immunity from prosecution but also the authority to initiate and exercise those powers considered necessary for the security of the state. *See also* INHERENT POWERS, page 43; PRESIDENTIAL POWER, page 201.

Significance   Prerogative powers are one of the many conceptualizations developed by presidents over the past two centuries to justify actions undertaken against domestic and foreign enemies. President Abraham Lincoln, for example, invoked prerogative powers, defining them as "necessary actions undertaken by a president to preserve the nation." For Lincoln, this meant not only taking actions not specifically provided by the Constitution but also directly violating the Constitution. During World War II, President Franklin Roosevelt took the initiative in the exchange with Great Britain of 50 American destroyers for bases in the Western Hemisphere. Though he admittedly violated several laws, he justified the action as essential for the nation's security. The prerogative power concept remains highly controversial. Critics argue that under a democratic system based on rule of law, the chief executive must not exercise dictatorial powers under the fallacious assumption that he knows what is best for the nation. Despite vehement criticism of the prerogative powers theory, no provisions exist in the American system of government that prevent a president from invoking and implementing the doctrine. The possibility of impeachment by Congress or defeat by the voters in the next presidential election, however, does offer means for potential restraint.

Presidential Power: Stewardship Theory   A view of presidential powers that holds that the President has not only the right but also the duty to do anything needed to safeguard the nation and to protect the American people, unless such action is specifically forbidden by the Constitution. The stewardship theory is usually ascribed to Theodore Roosevelt, although other strong presidents, such as Abraham Lincoln, Woodrow Wilson, and Franklin Roosevelt, followed the basic principle on which the stewardship theory rests. *See also* EMERGENCY POWERS, page 189, PRESIDENT, page 196; TAFTIAN OR CONTRACTUAL THEORY, page 203.

Significance   The stewardship theory is one of several conceptions of the President's powers that has contributed to the shaping of that office. Strong presidents have often acted on the stewardship assumption without theorizing. The theory is closely related to, but is an expansion of, the doctrine of inherent powers. Many presidents have rejected the stewardship view and emphasized the contractual and limiting nature of our constitutional system. Those following the stewardship approach are often regarded as "active" presidents, whereas those who use a more restrained, Constitution-limiting approach are categorized as "passive."

Presidential Power: Taftian or Contractual Theory   A view of presidential powers that holds that the President is limited by the specific grants of power authorized in the Constitution and by statute. Supporters of the contractual or Taftian theory, sometimes called "literalists," hold the view that no undefined residuum of power for the office of President exists and that every executive power must be traced to some specific grant of power or reasonably implied from such a grant. The theory was argued explicitly by President William Howard Taft, who regarded it as the only approach compatible with the separation of powers—checks and balances system of the American government. *See also* CONSTITUTIONAL CONSTRUCTION, page 35; MADISONIANISM, page 18; STEWARDSHIP THEORY, page 201.

Significance   The Taftian or contractual theory is one of several conceptions of the President's powers that have contributed to the shaping of that office. In addition to William Howard Taft, presidents who followed the theory's basic guidelines include Rutherford B. Hayes, Chester A. Arthur, Warren G. Harding, and Calvin Coolidge. Their presidencies were largely periods of legislative dominance of the national government. Those who follow the restrained, Constitution-limiting Taftian or contractual approach are usually described as "passive" presidents, whereas those who follow the stewardship approach are regarded as "active" presidents.

Presidential Succession   The order of eligibility for filling a vacancy in the office of President, as specified in the Constitution and statutes. The Constitution, in Article II, section 1, stipulates, "In case of the removal of the President from office, or of his death, resignation, or inability to discharge the powers and duties of the said office, the same shall devolve on the Vice-President..." Congress is empowered by the same section of Article II to provide for the officer to act as President in case both the President and Vice President are unable to serve. Congress has from time to time provided by statute for the line of succession, with the present order based on the Presidential Succession Act of 1947. This law provides for succession after the Vice President by the Speaker of the House, President pro tempore of the Senate, and members of the Cabinet in the order of the establishment of their departments, with the Secretary of State first in line. Cabinet members serve only until a Speaker or President pro tempore is available. The Twentieth Amendment provides that the Vice President-elect shall become President if the President-elect is unable to assume office on inauguration day. In addition, the Twenty-fifth Amendment provides for the temporary succession of the Vice President to the presidency in cases of presidential disability and for the President to fill a vacancy in the vice presidency with the consent of Congress. *See also* TWELFTH AMENDMENT, page 115; TWENTIETH AMENDMENT, page 208; TWENTY-FIFTH AMENDMENT, page 208; VICE PRESIDENT, page 210.

Significance   Nine vice presidents have succeeded to the office of President, eight as a result of the deaths of presidents in American history, and one—Gerald R. Ford—who succeeded to the office following the resignation of President Richard M. Nixon. No President, however, has been removed or been incapacitated to the extent of turning the office over to the Vice President. The question of disability arose on several occasions, but the Constitution made no provision for making such a determination other than for the disabled President to step down voluntarily. As a result of serious illnesses suffered by President Dwight D. Eisenhower, attempts were made to establish a statutory remedy to this problem, but to no avail. Following his illness, Eisenhower entered into a pact in 1958 with Vice President Richard M. Nixon, which provided that the Vice President could determine presidential inability if the President were unable to communicate with the Vice President. Presidents John F. Kennedy and Lyndon B. Johnson entered into similar agreements with their vice presidents. The knotty problems of determining inability led to the adoption in 1967 of the Twenty-fifth Amendment, which spells out procedures for determining presidential disability, permits the Vice President to become acting President under certain conditions, and provides for filling a vacancy in the office of the Vice President. The last provision was first invoked in 1973, when Gerald R. Ford was appointed by President Richard M. Nixon to fill the vacancy created when Vice President Spiro T. Agnew resigned. Then, in 1974, when President Nixon resigned as a result of Watergate disclosures, President Ford again invoked the Twenty-fifth Amendment in appointing Nelson A. Rockefeller as Vice President.

Ratification The approval by the President of the version of a treaty that has received Senate consent by a two-thirds vote. Ratification may involve the problem of whether a President will accept amendments and reservations to the treaty affixed by the Senate. Amendments would—and reservations might—entail reopening of negotiations with other signatory nations. *See also* ADVICE AND CONSENT, page 127; RATIFICATION, page 574; TREATY, page 583.

Significance Ordinarily, presidential ratification of a treaty requires the exchange of ratification documents with other signatories to the treaty and an official proclamation putting the treaty into effect. When amendments or reservations are made by the Senate, the President must decide whether to try to gain their acceptance by the other parties to the treaty or to drop the matter, which kills the treaty as far as the United States is concerned. In a classic case, President Woodrow Wilson refused to accept crippling amendments and reservations to the Versailles Treaty in 1919. The standoff between the President and the Senate resulted in the eventual defeat of the treaty and the refusal of the United States to join the League of Nations. The ratification power serves to enhance the President's role in foreign affairs by leaving the last word with him so far as American approval of treaties is concerned. Although there is a popular misconception among the American people that the Senate ratifies treaties, actually that chamber can only give or refuse to give its consent to the President's authority to ratify.

Recess Appointment An appointment of a federal official made by the President to fill a vacancy while the Senate is not in session. To prevent the President from postponing appointments until the Senate has adjourned, Congress has by statute prohibited the payment of salary to an officer appointed to fill a vacancy that existed but was not filled while the Senate was in session. Recess appointments expire at the end of the next congressional session, unless the Senate has confirmed the appointed official by a majority vote. Most state constitutions provide for recess appointments by the governor. *See also* APPOINTMENT POWER, page 183; CONFIRMATION, page 138.

Significance Recess appointments have often been a matter of contention between the President and the Senate. The provision denying salary to an official who was given a recess appointment, although the position became vacant while the Senate was in session, is an obvious attempt to limit the President's use of recess appointments to circumvent the Senate's approval power. Presidents usually refrain from straining relations with the Senate by not giving recess appointments to highly controversial persons or to those previously rejected by the Senate. In the states, recess appointments may be more contentious because of the typical lack of harmony between governors and state senates and because such appointments are often for long durations, owing to the sizable interims between legislative sessions.

Recognition   The power exercised exclusively by the President to establish diplomatic relations with foreign states. Recognition powers are vested in the President by the Constitution, which grants him the authority in Article II, section 2 to send and receive ambassadors. The President's recognition power applies to new states as well as to new governments. *See also* RECOGNITION, page 574.

Significance   The President's recognition power involves the ability to refuse to recognize a new state or government as well as to grant recognition. Thus, the act of accrediting foreign diplomats, perhaps intended to be a mere ceremonial function, has become a significant discretionary power in the day-to-day conduct of foreign relations. In deciding whether to recognize a new state or government, the President may be influenced by his advisers, by Congress, and by public opinion, but the final decision is his alone. Important recognition controversies in American history have involved the question of whether revolutionary regimes or states created by conquest should be recognized. In the case of China, for example, the President for many years faced a dilemma: recognize the communist regime and thereby strengthen its international standing or refuse it and hope thereby to weaken its diplomatic position. In 1974, President Richard M. Nixon straddled the issue by agreeing to a limited form of diplomatic exchange with the People's Republic of China, but in 1979, President Jimmy Carter granted full diplomatic recognition. Also involved in such recognition controversies has been the question of whether the President considers it advantageous to maintain direct communication with, and observation of, the regime. Presidents have used their discretion in such cases, and no consistent American recognition policy has been developed. In the case of China, American recognition, along with the granting of most-favored-nation status in trade, was one of several factors that contributed substantially to the liberalization of the regime and to the opening of China to Western trade and investment. A difficult problem relating to China is that of Taiwan, which China considers to be part of the mainland and not subject to recognition. In 1995, President Clinton permitted the President of Taiwan to attend his college reunion in the United States and thereby created a recognition controversy between the United States and China. Another of the contemporary recognition problems is that of the Castro regime in Cuba, which American presidents since Dwight D. Eisenhower have refused to grant.

Removal Power   The authority of an executive official to dismiss appointed officials from office. Although the Constitution is silent on the subject, the President has always exercised the power to remove executive and administrative officials. As a general rule, executive officials appointed by the President serve at his pleasure. Federal judges, however, have life tenure, on good behavior, while members of "independent commissions" and merit system employees can be removed only for cause. The removal power of state governors generally compares unfavorably with that of the President because of the number of elective officials and the sharing of the governor's removal power, in many states, with the state senate. *See also Humphrey's Executor [Rathbun] v. United States,* page 216; *Myers v. United States,* page 216; SEP- ARATION FROM SERVICE, page 233.

Significance The ability of the President to get the vast national ad- ministration to follow his leadership and direction depends to a considerable degree on his authority to dismiss those who disobey his orders, are unsym- pathetic toward his program, or neglect their duties. Unless the President can surround himself with loyal subordinates who will strive to carry out his pro- gram, the system of democratic accountability, focused in the President as the elected national executive official, breaks down. Congress has, on occa- sion, sought by statute to gain a share of the power to remove executive offi- cials, but the matter was finally decided by the Supreme Court in favor of unrestricted presidential removal power (*Myers v. United States,* 272 U.S. 52 [1926]). This decision, however, was modified by the Supreme Court in hold- ing that members of independent regulatory commissions can be dismissed by the President only for cause as specified by Congress (*Humphrey's Ex- ecutor [Rathbun] v. United States,* 295 U.S. 602 [1935]). In the states, the recent trend has been toward strengthening and expanding the governors' re- moval powers, and increased removal authority has been given to some may- ors and city and county managers as well. Although unionization and collective bargaining are rights enjoyed by approximately 35 percent of fed- eral employees, President Ronald Reagan in 1982 affirmed the illegality of strikes by federal employees and the power of the President to remove strik- ing federal employees when he fired striking air traffic controllers who had refused to accept a presidential ultimatum to return to work.

State of the Union Message An annual message to Congress in which the President proposes his legislative program. It is based on the constitutional directive that the President "shall from time to time give to the Congress in- formation on the state of the Union, and recommend to their consideration such measures as he shall judge necessary and expedient..." (Art. II, sec. 3). Although the President may choose his time for the message, it has become customary to transmit it in January at the beginning of a legislative session. "State of the state" and "state of the city" messages are typically delivered by governors and mayors to their state legislatures and city councils. *See also* CHIEF LEGISLATOR, page 187.

Significance The importance of the State of the Union message lies primarily in its placing the initiative for developing a broad, comprehensive legislative program in the hands of the President. At the opening of a new leg- islative session, members of Congress busy themselves with routine organi- zational matters and minor legislative proposals until the President presents them with his legislative program. In his message, the President discusses the major problems facing the nation and recommends statutory solutions. His message is followed up in subsequent months by scores of bills drawn up in the executive departments and introduced in Congress by "administration" congressmen. Presidents usually deliver their State of the Union messages in person. Radio and television have greatly increased the importance of these messages, and the President now speaks not only to Congress but to the American people. Some presidents have delivered a second "State of the World" message to Congress to focus on foreign policy problems. It has now become customary for the opposition party to seek to reduce the importance of the president's message by having one of its leaders present the other party's view on the State of the Union and its own legislative agenda. A special situation arose in January 1995, when the Republicans won control of both houses of Congress and used their legislative power to push through the House their own legislative program, the Contract with America. The media offer an opportunity to dramatize policies and objectives and to gain support for them by arousing public opinion.

Twentieth Amendment   The "lame duck" Amendment to the Constitution, adopted in 1933, which changed the date for beginning the presidential and vice-presidential terms from March 4 to January 20, and for beginning congressional terms from March 4 to January 3. Other provisions are: (1) if the President-elect dies before taking office, the Vice President-elect shall become president; (2) if a president-elect has not been chosen or fails to qualify by January 20, the Vice President-elect shall act as president until a president is chosen; (3) if neither qualifies, the Congress shall decide who shall act as president until a president or vice president qualifies; and (4) if the election of a president and vice president is thrown into the House and the Senate and a candidate dies, Congress shall determine by law what shall be done. *See also* PRESIDENT-ELECT, page 197; PRESIDENTIAL SUCCESSION, page 204; TWENTIETH AMENDMENT, page 172.

Significance   The Twentieth Amendment reduced the "lame duck" period for the outgoing President. The change reflects a disposition to make the office more responsive to democratic influences and enables a newly elected President to proceed to develop his policies and programs with little delay. The provisions in the Amendment regarding the inability of the President-elect and Vice President-elect to serve are designed to close a gap in the original Constitution, which failed to provide for these eventualities.

Twenty-fifth Amendment   An amendment to the Constitution, adopted in 1967, that establishes procedures for filling vacancies in the two top executive offices and makes provision for situations involving presidential disability. The Twenty-fifth Amendment specifically assigns to the President the power to fill a vacancy in the office of Vice President, with the approval of a majority of both houses of Congress. In case of presidential disability, the Amendment provides: (1) when the President believes that he is incapable of performing the duties of office, he informs the Congress in writing, and the Vice President thereupon serves as acting President until the President can resume his duties; (2) when the President is disabled and unable to communicate, the Vice President and a majority of the Cabinet declare that fact to Congress, and the Vice President then serves as acting President until the President recovers; and (3) when a dispute arises over whether the President is capable of discharging the powers and duties of his office, Congress by a two-thirds vote decides whether the Vice President should continue as acting President or the President should resume his office. *See also* PRESIDENTIAL SUCCESSION, page 204; VICE PRESIDENT, page 210.

Significance   The Twenty-fifth Amendment continues the provision incorporated in the original Constitution for the succession of the Vice President to the presidency upon the death of the latter, but it also recognizes that other situations may arise that were not provided for. The problems of succession to the presidency and vice presidency were brought to the attention of the American public by such events as the sudden death of President Franklin D. Roosevelt, the serious illnesses suffered by President Dwight D. Eisenhower, and the assassination of President John F. Kennedy. The Twenty-fifth Amendment replaced the informal agreements that had been worked out between presidents and their vice presidents since President Eisenhower's major illness. The Twenty-fifth Amendment has already been used on several occasions. In the first case, it was used to fill the office of Vice President following the resignation of Spiro T. Agnew in 1973. Agnew's successor, Gerald R. Ford, assumed the presidency in 1974 following the resignation of President Richard M. Nixon. Then, President Ford appointed Nelson A. Rockefeller to be Vice President.

Twenty-second Amendment   An amendment to the Constitution, adopted in 1951, limiting presidential tenure to two terms for an individual. A vice president who succeeds to the office may serve as long as ten years as president, provided he has not served more than two years of the uncompleted term of his predecessor. The incumbent President, Harry S Truman, was excluded from the limitations of the Amendment, but he chose not to run for a third term. *See also* PRESIDENT, page 196; TERM LIMITATION, page 114.

Significance   The Twenty-second Amendment was proposed by the Republican-controlled Eightieth Congress in reaction to the four terms of Franklin Roosevelt. Roosevelt had shattered the strong "no-third-term" tradition started by George Washington and followed until 1940. The Amendment was also a reaction to the growth of executive power that had resulted from war and depression crises and reflected a yearning to return to the "normalcy" of congressional domination of weak presidents. Supporters of the Amendment defend it as a useful safeguard against the dangers of executive tyranny and self-perpetuation in power. Opponents argue that it tends to reduce further a second-term President's already weak position as political leader and exhibits a fundamental distrust of the democratic process.

Veto   A legislative power vested in a chief executive to return a bill unsigned to the legislative body with reasons for his objections. The Constitution provides that every bill, both public and private, that passes the House and the Senate must be sent to the President before it becomes law. When the President receives a bill, he may (1) sign it, whereupon it becomes law; (2) not sign it, whereupon it becomes law after ten congressional working days; (3) veto it, and send it back to the house of its origin; or (4) not sign it, whereupon if Congress adjourns within ten days the bill is killed (pocket veto). The President vetoes a bill by writing "veto" (I forbid) across the face of the bill; he then sends it back to Congress with a message setting forth his objections. Congress may amend the bill according to the President's demands and then repass it, or it may reject the President's objections and override the veto by repassing the bill with a two-thirds roll-call vote of those present and voting in each house. Finally, the President's veto may be sustained, which occurs more often than a direct override of the veto. Governors, too, exercise the veto power and, in all but a few states, may line item veto individual parts of appropriation bills—a power denied to the President, until January 1997. In the states, the number of votes needed to override a gubernatorial veto varies from a simple majority in each house to a two-thirds vote of all members elected to the legislature. *See also* LINE-ITEM VETO, page 194; POCKET VETO, page 196.

Significance   Presidents employed the veto power infrequently and with great caution until the post–Civil War administration of Andrew Johnson. Since 1865, the veto power has been used with increasing vigor by most presidents; Grover Cleveland, with 414 regular and pocket vetoes, and Franklin Roosevelt, with 631, have been its most persistent users. The scope of the veto power has also expanded since 1865. The earlier view that the veto should be used to block unconstitutional or technically imperfect laws has been supplemented by its employment to express disapproval of any kind. Although the veto is merely suspensive in effect, few vetoes are overridden by Congress, since if one-third plus one of the members voting in *either* house support the President's view, the veto prevails. The *threat* of the veto can also be used effectively by a chief executive to shape and change legislation while it is still in the hands of the legislature. In the 101st and 102nd Congresses (1989–1992), President George Bush compiled an unbroken string of more than thirty vetoes and threatened Congress with a future avalanche of vetoes. President Bill Clinton exercised the veto and the threat of veto extensively in shaping his relations with the 104th Republican-controlled Congress.

Vice President   The constitutional officer assigned to preside over the Senate and to assume the presidency in case of the death, resignation, removal, or disability of the President. The Vice President is elected on the same ballot with the President and, if no candidate receives a majority of the electoral vote, the Senate chooses the Vice President from the two candidates for that office with the highest number of electoral votes. Although President of the Senate, the Vice President is not considered to be a member, participating only informally, if at all, in its deliberations, and voting only when a tie occurs. *See also* PRESIDENTIAL SUCCESSION, page 204; TWENTY-FIFTH AMENDMENT, page 208; VICE PRESIDENT, page 174.

Significance   During most of American history, the vice presidency has been regarded as an insignificant office and as a political graveyard to be avoided by promising politicians. The low repute of this potentially significant office perhaps resulted mainly from the method of selecting vice-presidential candidates—to balance the party ticket or to reward or appease party wings. Recent presidents have sought to make more effective use of their vice presidents as intermediaries between the President and Congress and as roving ambassadors of good will in foreign affairs. Vice Presidents customarily attend Cabinet meetings, and Presidents Eisenhower, Kennedy, Johnson, Nixon, Ford, Carter, Reagan, Bush, and Clinton have assigned their vice presidents additional responsibilities in the executive branch. The trend has been toward developing the office into an assistant presidency. Nine vice presidents have succeeded to the office of President, eight upon the death of the President, and one—Gerald R. Ford—when the President resigned, thereby leaving the office of Vice President vacant. In addition, seven vice presidents died in office and two (John C. Calhoun, 1832, and Spiro T. Agnew, 1973) resigned. The Twenty-fifth Amendment, adopted in 1967, permits the President with the consent of Congress to appoint a Vice President when the office is vacant, a process first used in 1973 when President Richard M. Nixon appointed Gerald R. Ford to complete Agnew's term. When President Nixon resigned in 1974, Ford assumed the presidency and appointed Nelson A. Rockefeller to fill the office of Vice President.

Watergate   A number and variety of illegal acts perpetrated by high officials in the Nixon administration, and subsequent "cover-up" efforts that led ultimately to the resignation of President Richard M. Nixon and the succession to the presidency of Vice President Gerald R. Ford. The term "Watergate" relates to the break-in by a group of seven men—under direct orders from the White House—of the Democratic national party headquarters located in the Watergate building complex in Washington, D.C. Other illegal acts included generically within the term were bribery of high officials, illegal use of the CIA, FBI, and other government agencies for personal and partisan purposes, income tax fraud, establishment and use by the White House staff of an unofficial "plumbers group" for carrying on espionage against private citizens, the use of "dirty tricks" during the 1972 election campaign, illegal campaign contributions, and use of campaign contributions for personal purposes. *See also* BOLAND AMENDMENTS, page 535; *United States v. Nixon,* page 216; WHITEWATER INVESTIGATION, page 212.

Significance   The crimes and scandals of the Nixon administration collectively referred to as "Watergate" constituted the most extensive and serious violations of public trust of any administration in 200 years of American history. Corruption, bribe-taking, and income tax evasion charges led to the resignation of Vice President Spiro T. Agnew in 1973. Charges of cover-up of criminal activities by subordinates, obstruction of justice, misuse of the CIA and FBI, and other charges led to the resignation of President Richard M. Nixon on August 9, 1974. In addition, many cabinet officers, presidential assistants, and other administration officials were convicted of various crimes and misdemeanors. Watergate revelations increased disharmony and disunity among the American people and produced a general suspicion of and distaste for politicians of both major parties. Yet the American system as a government of laws, not men, along with the system of separation of powers—checks and balances, proved itself by toppling the two highest elective officials and bringing many others to justice. Public demands for more effective controls over political activity and corrupt practices in government led to the enactment of a spate of new laws. Watergate also produced a Supreme Court decision that for the first time limited the doctrine of executive privilege by holding that the privilege cannot be used to prohibit disclosure of criminal misconduct (*United States v. Nixon,* 418 U.S. 683 [1974]). In a 1982 case, brought by a federal employee who had lost his job because he testified about cost overruns, the Supreme Court held that the President enjoys absolute immunity from civil damage suits for all official actions taken while in office, invoking the principle that "the king can do no wrong" (*Nixon v. Fitzgerald* 457 U.S. 731). In a related case in 1982, the Court held that White House aides enjoy a qualified immunity related to their knowledge of the wrongful nature of an act (*Harow v. Fitzgerald,* 457 U.S. 800). In 1987, Congress again became involved in investigating allegedly illegal actions by executive officials in the Iran-contra affair, also known as Irangate because of some similarities to Watergate. In these hearings, evidence indicated White House staff members sold sophisticated weapons to Iran in exchange for release of American hostages and that the funds from this transaction were placed in a secret Swiss bank account and were used to support the Nicaraguan contra rebel forces in violation of the Boland Amendments. "Watergate" has come to describe the abuse and misuse of political power, especially presidential power.

Weekly Compilation of Presidential Documents   An official publication of executive branch activities and decisions. The *Weekly Compilation of Presidential Documents* has been published regularly since Lyndon B. Johnson's presidency. It includes appointments, nominations, communications to Congress, proclamations, press releases, acts approved or vetoed by the President, and all White House announcements and remarks. *See also Congressional Record,* page 140.

Significance   The *Weekly Compilation of Presidential Documents* is a primary source for information concerning the role of presidents in American life. It is a public record in the same sense that the *Congressional Record* publicly reports the activities of Congress and the *U.S. Reports* is a public record of the United States Supreme Court. The *Weekly Compilation* is especially useful for presidential research scholars.

White House Chief of Staff   The assistant to the President who heads the White House Office. The President's chief of staff typically provides the link between the President and Congress, the press, members of the Cabinet, and other high-level administrators. Although the President carries the legal responsibility for all decisions made in the executive branch, most presidents have delegated much of their decision power to their chiefs of staff. *See also* WHITE HOUSE OFFICE, page 215.

Significance   Presidents in recent years have depended heavily on their chiefs of staff in making decisions and in implementing policy. Typically, a president's chief of staff is a close personal friend and a leading member of the President's party, a person who has the full trust and support of the President. Chief of Staff John Sununu, for example, was selected by President Bush because of his major contributions to Bush's election in his role as campaign director in the 1988 presidential election. (Sununu was later removed by the President when he became a political liability in 1991.) In many ways, the chief of staff functions as a de facto president, making many decisions in the President's name and based on his authority. To a considerable extent, the success or failure of a president is determined by how effectively the chief of staff functions in his capacity as the President's top adviser.

Whitewater Investigations   Hearings before special committees in the House and Senate seeking to find violations of law relating to President Bill Clinton and his wife, Hillary Rodham Clinton, and their dealings in Arkansas in the late 1980s, with the Whitewater Land Development Company and the Madison Guarantee Savings and Loan, owned by James B. McDougal. *See also* GRAND JURY, page 264; INVESTIGATING COMMITTEE, page 152; WATERGATE, page 211.

Significance   Whitewater first surfaced as a potential scandal during the 1992 presidential campaign. The Clintons insisted that they were merely passive participants in the Whitewater Co.; that they had lost money on the deal; and that they never gave McDougal or his business special treatment. At that time Hillary Rodham Clinton was a partner in the Rose Law Firm that represented the McDougals. In addition to the congressional hearings, there have been grand jury investigations in Arkansas and in Washington, D.C. For the first time in American history, a First Lady was required to appear before a grand jury to answer questions in the disappearance—and then rediscovery—of her long-sought law firm billing records. Some say the hearings are nothing more than political theater or get-even politics on the part of the Republicans; others regard the charges, if proved, as serious ethical misbehavior on the part of the Clintons, similar to Watergate.

IMPORTANT AGENCIES

Executive Office of the President (EXOP or EOP)   The top staff agencies that give the President help and advice in carrying out his major duties. President Franklin D. Roosevelt established the Executive Office by executive order under the Reorganization Act of 1939. The components of the Executive Office have changed over the years, and today the major staff agencies include the Office of Management and Budget, the White House Office, the National Security Council, the Council of Economic Advisers, the Office of Science and Technology Policy, the Office of Policy Development, the Office of United States Trade Representative, the Office of Administration, and the Council on Environmental Quality. Special offices concerned with trade negotiations, telecommunications policy, international economic policy, consumer affairs, intergovernmental relations, and drug abuse prevention also have been established within the Executive Office of the President. (For specific agencies, *see* Index.)

Significance   The objective in the creation of the Executive Office was to provide the President with a "general staff" to give him the help needed to direct the far-flung activities of the executive branch. The President has been hampered, however, by the refusal of Congress to place some key agencies within the Executive Office, such as the Office of Personnel Management and the General Accounting Office. The White House Office, in particular, contains the close confidential advisers on whom the President leans for day-to-day operations of the executive branch. Conflict, however, can and often has arisen between the President's staff in the Executive Office and other decision makers, especially in the Cabinet. In the Iran-contra investigation conducted by Congress in 1987, for example, the President's National Security Adviser in the White House Office and the Secretaries of State and Defense engaged in acrimonious disagreement over policies and actions undertaken toward Iran and Nicaragua. Despite the need for greater efficiency in the executive branch, a process of downsizing most governmental operations for budgetary reasons was begun in the 1990s that resulted in a cutback of operations in the Executive Office.

Office of Science and Technology Policy (OSTP)   A staff agency established within the Executive Office of the President in 1976 to serve as a source of scientific, engineering, and technological analysis and judgment for the President with respect to major policies, plans, and programs of the federal government. It evaluates the scale, quality, and effectiveness of the federal effort in science and technology, provides advice and assistance to the Office of Management and Budget, and assists in providing leadership and coordination for the research and development programs of the federal government. *See also* EXECUTIVE OFFICE OF THE PRESIDENT, page 213.

Significance   Despite the creation in 1993 of a National Science and Technology Council chaired by the President, which gives the OSTP science adviser unprecedented power to coordinate the science activities of 22 departments and agencies of the federal government, advocates charge that OSTP still does not have the clout within the White House that was originally intended, especially in protecting programs against excessive and poorly designed cuts in an era of declining government expenditures. There even have been recent calls to replace the office with a cabinet-level Department of Science. Others have complained that the council has been ineffective in setting priorities, with nine separate committees providing equal attention to matters of health, environmental quality, economic growth and job creation, education and training, information technology, national security, international science and technology cooperation, world leadership and cooperation in science, and space and aeronautics. This latter criticism of production of varied and often tardy reports with little coordination led to the dismantlement in 1995 of the congressional counterpart to OSTP, the Office of Technology Assessment (OTA), which was created in 1972 to help Congress resolve uncertainties and conflicting claims coming from what they perceived to be biases of institutions offering scientific advice.

Secret Service   A law enforcement division of the Treasury Department, which has full responsibility for protecting the life and security of the President and Vice President and their families, former presidents and their families, and major party presidential candidates. The Secret Service also performs security functions concerned with Treasury matters, and in 1970 it was assigned new responsibilities for protecting foreign dignitaries visiting the United States and for guarding foreign embassies in Washington, D.C. *See also* DEPARTMENT OF THE TREASURY, page 422.

Significance   Secret Service agents are carefully selected and rigorously trained. Each year agents check out thousands of "crank" and threatening letters sent to the President and investigate numerous threats made against the life of the President or members of his family. Whenever the President travels at home or abroad, security arrangements are handled by the Secret Service, with the cooperation of the police of the area or country that the President is visiting. Following the assassination of President John F.

Kennedy and the Warren Commission Report on the assassination, the Secret Service force was increased, and closer cooperation with the FBI in safeguarding the President was undertaken. Again, following the attempted assassination of President Ronald Reagan, the Secret Service took new precautionary actions to protect the President.

White House Office A staff agency in the Executive Office of the President that provides the chief executive with information and assistance in major areas of policy development. The President depends on the White House Office staff to provide him with the personal guidance and expertise he needs in carrying out the duties of his office. His most trusted and most powerful adviser is typically the White House chief of staff. In assisting the President, the staff maintains two-way communication with Congress, with individual members and committees of Congress, with departments and agencies in the executive branch, with the public information media, and with the general public. Staff members are appointed by the President not only because they are able but also because of their loyalty. Senate approval is not needed, and all staff members serve at the pleasure of the President and may be removed by him at any time. *See also* BOLAND AMENDMENTS, page 535; EXECUTIVE OFFICE OF THE PRESIDENT, page 213; WATERGATE, page 211; WHITE HOUSE CHIEF OF STAFF, page 212.

Significance The White House Office, sometimes referred to as the "invisible presidency," is typically the staff on which the President depends most in carrying out many of the critical tasks of his office. A president may turn to his cabinet or some of its individual members for advice, but in the modern era presidents have come to depend increasingly on their readily available staffs in the Executive Office and in the White House Office in particular. Jurisdictional conflicts have often arisen between Cabinet members and White House Office staff members in the development of policy and in gaining the ear and support of the President. Such conflict has been particularly evident between the Secretary of State and the President's National Security Adviser in the White House Office.

IMPORTANT CASES

Ex parte Grossman 267 U.S. 87 (1925): Upheld a pardon granted by the President to Grossman, who had been convicted of contempt of court. It was alleged that the independence of the judiciary depends upon the authority of judges to try without jury individuals who violate court orders and to sentence them for contempt of court free from interference by other departments of government. The Supreme Court rejected this argument and upheld the President, holding that he "can reprieve or pardon all offenses after their commission, either before trial, during trial or after trial, by individuals, or by classes, conditionally or absolutely, and this without modification or regulation by Congress." *See also* PARDON, page 195.

Significance The effect of the *Grossman* case was to extend the President's pardoning power to all federal cases regardless of which branch of government is involved. Only conviction of a public official through impeachment proceedings is beyond the President's pardoning power.

Humphrey's Executor [Rathbun] v. United States   295 U.S. 602 (1935): Upheld the provision of the Federal Trade Commission Act that members of the Commission may be removed from office only for causes specified in the Act. President Franklin D. Roosevelt had removed Humphrey for political reasons, and in this case, decided after Humphrey's death, the Supreme Court held that Congress clearly had the authority to limit the President's removal power to instances of "inefficiency, neglect of duty, or malfeasance in office." The Court pointed out that the broad removal powers accorded to the President in *Myers v. United States,* 272 U.S. 52 (1926), pertained only to purely executive officers, whereas members of the Federal Trade Commission exercise legislative and judicial powers as well. *See also Myers v. United States,* page 216; REMOVAL POWER, page 206.

Significance   The *Humphrey* case emphasized the distinction between independent regulatory commissions, such as the Federal Power Commission (FPC), the Federal Trade Commission (FTC), and Securities and Exchange Commission (SEC), and agencies of the executive branch. The Court, in recognizing the validity of statutory requirements for tenure of commissioners, cited the character of their work, the need to develop expertness through experience, the legislative intention to keep them free from political domination or control, and the threefold nature of their duties—administrative, quasi-legislative, and quasi-judicial.

Myers v. United States,   272 U.S. 52 (1926): Upheld the President's removal from office of a postmaster without securing the approval of the Senate to the removal. The Court held that Congress cannot limit the President's power to remove executive officials, and the provisions of the Tenure of Office Act of 1876 requiring the Senate's concurrence in presidential removals was held to be unconstitutional. *See also Humphrey's Executor [Rathbun] v. United States,* page 216.

Significance   The *Myers* case, with the Court's majority speaking through Chief Justice (former President) William H. Taft, asserted a broad presidential removal power that had been in some doubt during much of American history. In *Humphrey's Executor [Rathbun] v. United States,* 295 U.S. 602 (1935), however, the Court upheld the power of Congress to limit the President's authority to remove members of the independent regulatory commissions.

United States v. Nixon   418 U.S. 683 (1974): Held that the President's claim of executive privilege to preserve the confidentiality of his conversations with members of his staff or others cannot justify withholding of information bearing on a pending criminal trial. The case grew out of a refusal by President Richard M. Nixon to release tape recordings and documents involving conversations relating to the trials of his former aides for Watergate offenses. "Watergate" was the collective term that described a variety of illegal acts perpetrated in the early 1970s by high officials in the Nixon administration, and subsequent "cover-up" efforts that led to the resignation of President

Nixon. The Court rejected claims that either the doctrine of the separation of powers or the need for confidentiality—in the absence of a legitimate claim of national security interests—could sustain an absolute privilege of immunity from judicial process. *See also* EXECUTIVE PRIVILEGE, page 191; PRIVILEGED COMMUNICATION, page 275; WATERGATE, page 211.

Significance   The *Nixon* case was the first court test of the scope of executive privilege. The Supreme Court acknowledged the importance of executive privilege as a means of protecting the process of presidential decision making and as a vital ingredient of the separation of powers doctrine. Nevertheless, the Court insisted that the claim of executive privilege must yield to the nation's commitment to the rule of law so that the integrity of the judicial process and the criminal justice system would be preserved.

Youngstown Sheet and Tube Co. v. Sawyer   343 U.S. 579 (1952): Struck down the President's Executive Order that had authorized seizure of steel mills and their operation by the national government. President Harry S Truman acted under his inherent power as chief executive and commander in chief to safeguard the nation's security during the Korean War, when a strike in the steel mills threatened the supply of weapons. The Court held that the President has no authority under the Constitution to seize private property unless Congress authorizes the seizure and that the Constitution does not permit the President to legislate. *See also* EMERGENCY POWERS, page 189; INHERENT POWERS, pages 43, 591; WAR POWERS, page 553.

Significance   The immediate result of the *Youngstown* case was the return of the steel mills by the government to their private owners and the resumption of the strike by the United Steelworkers Union. More fundamentally, the case established for the first time that limits exist in the exercise of the President's inherent powers in seeking to safeguard the security of the nation. It reaffirmed the importance of private property rights under the Fifth Amendment, and it emphasized that only Congress can exercise legislative powers.

6

Public Administration: Organization and Personnel

Administration   The procedure by which public policy is developed, interpreted and enforced. *Public* administration, as distinguished from *private* or *business* administration, is largely the function of the executive branch of government. It performs its functions under broad guidelines established by the legislative branch, subject to the oversight and review of both the legislative and judicial branches. Orthodox views of public administration treat it as the art or science of managing public affairs, with emphasis on such factors as organization, personnel, and finance, summarized by the acronym POSDCORB for *P*lanning, *O*rganizing, *S*taffing, *D*irecting, *C*oordinating, *R*eporting, and *B*udgeting. Contemporary theory takes account of the vast discretion exercised by administrative agencies through rule making, adjudicating, and informal persuasion.

Significance   All organizations are faced with the problem of efficient administration. Public administration, however, is increasingly complex because of the tremendous range of domestic and foreign responsibilities that modern government has undertaken, the need for organizing and directing millions of employees, and the problem of controlling the expenditure of huge (and even difficult to comprehend) sums of money. The traditional view that administration and policy formation are separate has given way to recognition of the policy-making aspects inherent in administration. Much scholarly attention has been paid to the search for sound principles and practices of administration in order to secure responsibility and accountability of administrative personnel to the people.

Administrative Law Judge   An official who conducts hearings for a regulatory agency and makes recommendations to the heads of the agency on issuance of administrative orders. Under the Administrative Procedure Act of 1946, hearing examiners (renamed "administrative law judges" in 1978) are appointed under civil service rules and are protected against arbitrary dismissal and loss of salary. About 1,200 administrative law judges serve in 32 federal departments and agencies, many dealing with actions arising under the Social Security Act. State governments also utilize administrative law judges. *See also* ADMINISTRATIVE PROCEDURE ACT OF 1946, page 240; QUASI-JUDICIAL, page 232.

Significance   The post of administrative law judge was created in response to the pre-1946 concern that regulatory agencies were both prosecutor and judge of those accused of violating their rules. By giving a degree of independence to administrative law judges, Congress sought to overcome the major weaknesses of administrative adjudication of private rights. Decisions of the judges are presented to the agency heads, who may hear appeals from the judges' recommendations. If no appeal is made, the decision is final. Several states use a central panel system under which administrative law judges are not attached to specific agencies.

Administrative Order   A directive, issued by an administrative agency, that has the force of law. An order is generally distinguished from a "rule" or "regulation" in that an order is specifically directed to an individual or group to correct infractions of a rule. Typically, it takes the form of a "cease and desist order." An example would be an order of the National Labor Relations Board to a union or to an employer to cease a labor practice that the board had found to be inconsistent with the law or a board regulation. Orders are issued after a hearing conducted by the agency that resembles the procedures of a court of law. Appeals may be brought to the regular courts. Orders of federal agencies are published in the *Federal Register. See also* ADMINISTRATIVE LAW, page 248; ADMINISTRATIVE LAW JUDGE, page 218; ADMINISTRATIVE PROCEDURE ACT, page 240; HEARING, page 227; *Immigration and Naturalization Service v. Chadha,* page 177; LEGISLATIVE VETO, page 155; *Opp Cotton Mills v. Administrator of Wage and Hour Division,* page 239.

Significance   Administrative orders are part of the overall development of the administrative process. Legislative bodies have vested control over complex economic and social problems in various administrative agencies that have been granted broad powers to prescribe rules and regulations and to enforce these rules through orders. In this way, the legislature is saved the impossible job of determining in advance all the aspects of complex matters, and the courts are freed from deciding disputes over technical subjects in which they lack competence. The administrative agency can develop the necessary expertness to handle specialized cases. An increasing number of businesses and individuals are subject to administrative orders. As a consequence, Congress sought to exercise control through the use of a legislative veto to void unacceptable administrative orders, but the Supreme Court declared the practice unconstitutional as a violation of the separation of powers (*Immigration and Naturalization Service v. Chadha,* 462 U.S. 919 [1983]). In 1987, Congress acted to control the "race to the courthouse" by those appealing federal agency rules and hoping to file first with a presumably favorable court. Congress provided that parties have ten days for appeal. If multiple appeals are filed, a special judicial panel will designate, by lottery, the court to hear the case.

Administrative Reorganization   The reform of administrative agencies and procedures to improve efficiency, economy, accountability, and responsiveness. Reorganization movements have generally had as their major purposes the concentration of authority and accountability by (1) integrating agencies with similar functions to eliminate overlapping and waste, (2) fixing responsibility in some hierarchical arrangement, (3) establishing advisory and centralized housekeeping agencies to aid the chief administrator, (4) eliminating multiheaded boards or commissions and elective officers engaged in purely administrative work, and (5) improving personnel, budget, and auditing procedures. More recent reorganization efforts have stressed the application of private business practices that enhance personal initiative and customer satisfaction and tend to deemphasize hierarchy and other traditional forms of accountability. *See also* CIVIL SERVICE REFORM ACT OF 1978, page 241; REORGANIZATION ACT OF 1949, page 246.

Significance   Administrative reorganization at all levels of American government has resulted in increased authority for the President, governors, and mayors, the shortening of the ballot, and the adoption of the council-manager plan at the municipal level. Official reorganization studies are continuously carried on, and the President and some governors have been given authority to reshuffle agencies. Budgetary and personnel practices have been improved. Reorganization movements frequently meet resistance from legislatures that fear executive power, from interest groups that seek to protect the position of agencies serving them, and from public employee unions and agency personnel who fear loss of status. In 1993, the Clinton administration inaugurated a National Performance Review under the direction of Vice President Albert Gore. That study seeks to "reinvent" or "reengineer" government by cutting unneccessary spending, empowering employees, delegating authority, using incentives rather than regulation, and emphasizing competition and customer satisfaction.

Auxiliary Agency   A governmental unit that services other governmental agencies. Typical auxiliary agencies include central purchasing, personnel, and accounting. They perform what is sometimes called "housekeeping" or "technical services." *See also* GENERAL SERVICES ADMINISTRATION, page 237; OFFICE OF PERSONNEL MANAGEMENT, page 238.

Significance   Auxiliary agencies not only provide a centralized and less expensive means of dispensing technical services but also give the department head or the chief executive an important control mechanism. For example, each agency can do its own hiring or purchasing, but improved, less costly, and more consistent administration generally results from the assignment of such functions to centralized auxiliary units.

Board   A group of persons, usually three or more, who are charged with responsibility for directing a particular governmental function. The term "commission" is frequently used interchangeably with "board."

Significance   Multiheaded versus single-headed directorship is one of the most controversial problems of administrative organization. Both forms are found at all levels of government. A board is generally agreed to be more desirable than one head when the agency has quasi-legislative and quasi-judicial functions, particularly in the area of regulation of the economy. A board permits the use of bipartisan personnel for controversial matters and, where terms of board members overlap, continuity of policy. A board makes it difficult, however, to fix responsibility, and conflict may develop within the board itself. A single head makes for well-defined responsibility and unity of purpose. Administrative experts recommend the single director for purely administrative tasks, but boards or commissions are frequently used for this purpose. A compromise proposal that has found favor is to retain plural bodies for regulatory and adjudicatory functions but to assign administrative responsibility to the chairman of the board.

Bureau   A major working unit of a department or agency. Bureaus are generally assigned specific functions, and their heads are responsible to the head of the entire department. Well-known examples include the Federal Bureau of Investigation (FBI) in the Department of Justice and the Census Bureau in the Department of Commerce. Bureaus are usually subdivided into various divisions, branches, or sections, each with responsibility for specialized activities.

Significant   Although the nomenclature assigned to various parts of an agency is not uniform, it is considered useful for the development of scientific principles of administrative organization. The Hoover Commission, which studied the organization of the federal executive branch in 1949, and the "little Hoover commissions" in the states suggested a standard nomenclature for all administrative units. In this way, responsibility is more clearly fixed within a major department, and persons working within a department better understand their roles.

Bureaucracy   Any administrative system, especially of governmental agencies, that carries out policy on a day-to-day basis, uses standardized procedures, has a hierarchy, and is based on a specialization of duties. To many critics of government, bureaucracy connotes a system with excessive growth of administrative agencies, accompanied by concentration of power in administrative officials, excessive red tape, dedication to routine, and resistance to change. The term "the bureaucracy" is often used simply to designate the administrative or executive branch of government.

Significance   All modern governments have extensive administrative units. The problem in a democracy is to keep governmental employees responsive to the law and to the elected representatives of the people. Safeguards against the development of irresponsible bureaucracy include legislative oversight of administrative agencies through investigations and the power of the purse, executive direction of the administration, and judicial review of administrative actions. The increased growth and power of administrative agencies makes imperative strong control over their actions, lest administrative officials obstruct rather than further the policies established by the people's representatives.

Career Service   A professional civil service in which employment is based on merit, opportunity is afforded for advancement, and guarantees are provided against arbitrary dismissal. *See also* MERIT SYSTEM, page 230; MERIT SYSTEMS PROTECTION BOARD, page 238; ROGERS ACT, page 602; SENIOR EXECUTIVE SERVICE, page 233.

Significance   Employment by merit has made large inroads on the spoils system, with stress placed on a career service that emphasizes the opportunity to spend a satisfying lifetime in government service and to reach positions of honor and prestige. In recent years, the national government and some states have attempted to recruit talented college graduates for governmental careers. The concept of a career service has also been successfully applied in the Foreign Service, which has its own personnel system. The attractiveness of public service as a career tends to vary with the times and the nation's leaders. An administration that emphasizes governmental programs, such as that of Franklin D. Roosevelt in the 1930s, attracted many intellectual and technical leaders. The administration of Ronald Reagan in the 1980s, by contrast, was openly critical of public servants and sought an end to many established programs, resulting in morale problems and a decrease in the size of the applicant pool. The experiences of the 1990s have not been favorable for career civil servants because of growing public distrust of governmental programs and resultant major cuts in personnel.

Centralized Purchasing   Vesting authority in one agency to purchase and handle supplies and materials for governmental agencies. It is now done for the national government by the General Services Administration, and the practice has been adopted by most states and many local units of government. *See also* GENERAL SERVICES ADMINISTRATION, page 237.

Significance   Centralized purchasing has replaced the system in which each department or agency purchases its own supplies. The advantages include savings through large purchases, competitive bidding, standardization of equipment and record keeping, reduction of the possibilities of corruption, and centralization of responsibility. The major disadvantage is that standardized purchases may not meet the specialized needs of specific agencies and may result in delays, red tape, and high cost. Such problems can be solved by mutual arrangements or by exempting certain items from central purchase. In 1994, Congress authorized agencies to purchase commonly used items "off the shelf" to reduce excessive cost and red tape.

Certification of Eligibles   The practice by which a civil service commission provides a hiring officer of an agency with the names of persons who have qualified for a position. It usually ranks these individuals based on test scores. The practice in most jurisdictions is to certify the top three names, often called the "rule of three."

Significance   Certification is the initial step in the hiring process. The rule of three is designed to give the hiring officer a chance to weigh intangible factors, such as personality, in making a final decision. In some jurisdictions, only the name at the top of the list may be certified; in others, five or more are required. Personnel experts differ over what constitutes the best practice. Certification rules may be further complicated by limiting certain positions to veterans or by the availability of two or more suitable lists from which a position might be filled. A person whose name is certified but who is not selected is returned to the eligible list.

Civil Service   A collective term for most persons employed by government who are not members of the military services. It is more generally understood to apply to all those who gain governmental employment through a merit system. Elective officials, high-ranking policy-making officers who are appointed by elected officials, and members of the judiciary are not considered civil servants. *See also* CAREER SERVICE, page 221; HATCH ACT, page 244; MERIT SYSTEM, page 230; OFFICE OF PERSONNEL MANAGEMENT, page 238; PENDLETON ACT, page 245; SPOILS SYSTEM, page 234.

Significance   The civil service and the merit system in particular have made substantial headway in the national government and in some states and cities. Most county and township governments, however, still retain the spoils system. Marked interest has arisen in professionalizing civil service employment and in applying sound principles of personnel management. In the United States, civil servants are restricted in the scope of their political activities and, though permitted to join labor organizations, may not strike. One of the essential ingredients of modern civil service is the loyalty of the civil servants to whatever administration is in power. In 1994 full-time federal civilian employment exceeded 2 million, most of whom were involved in national defense, health services, and veterans' affairs (but excluding postal services). Congress and the President are committed to reducing the federal work force by 272,900 by the year 2000. In addition, more than 4 million people are employed by state governments and more than 10 million by counties, cities, and school districts.

Classified Service   Positions of governmental employment that are under the jurisdiction of a civil service commission and that are filled by merit. Congress has permitted some agencies to establish their own personnel systems outside the classified service, such as the Foreign Service, the Nuclear Regulatory Commission, and the Tennessee Valley Authority. *See also* GENERAL SCHEDULE, page 226; MERIT SYSTEM, page 230.

Significance   Most classified positions are filled by competitive exam, but many are exempt from examination. The latter categories include technical or professional positions such as attorneys or doctors and positions for which there is no suitable examination procedure, such as laborers or part-time employees. Under federal law, the President may exempt certain positions from the classified service, including top-ranking administrators as well as persons holding confidential or highly technical positions. In the states, exemptions may be determined by statute or by a civil service agency. Agencies outside the regular classified service have specialized personnel needs but may still use a merit system.

Clientele Agency   A governmental unit organized to serve or regulate a social or economic group. Although all agencies have some characteristic of this sort, a clientele agency's function is specifically directed toward its clients' interests. Examples include the Department of Labor, the Farm Credit Administration, and the Bureau of Indian Affairs in the Department of the Interior. *See also* ORGANIZATION, page 231.

Significance   A clientele agency constitutes recognition by the government of the importance of a group, its need for governmental support or regulation, and assurance that funds will be provided to carry on programs of interest to clients. Clients who approve of the agency resist efforts at reorganization or any other changes that may diminish the power or visibility of the agency. Clients who disapprove act either to abolish the agency or to secure a change in personnel to people more closely identified with their interests; this reaction can be particularly troublesome when the function of the agency is to regulate the client in the public interest.

Decentralization   An administrative concept applied by large organizations or departments in assigning decision-making responsibility to subunits on a geographical or subject-matter basis. Decentralization usually takes the form of field-service operations or division of tasks through specialization. *See also* FIELD SERVICE, page 225.

Significance   Decentralization encourages responsible participation by lesser officials and permits adaptation to local needs. The head of a large department cannot make every decision concerning the operations or services of a particular agency. Major policy decisions, however, should be made by top officials.

Delegation of Authority   The assignment of decision-making responsibility to subordinate officials. The heads of large agencies find it essential to delegate some of their authority to others, but it must be done within clearly defined standards, subject to review by the head. *See also* HIERARCHY, page 228.

Significance   In establishing a public agency, legislative bodies often assign a wide range of power to the agency head. The head, in turn, must delegate some of his or her authority in order to maintain adequate control over the agency and not have to handle every detail alone. Successful administration requires that delegations of authority be made ungrudgingly and that authority be commensurate with responsibility. Many top officials overburden themselves out of fear of losing power or fear that others will make the wrong decisions. Proper delegation of authority, under standards of policy established at the top, enables many matters to be settled at lower levels of the administrative hierarchy. Personnel and administrative experts point out that departmental morale is improved by delegation of authority, through giving others a sense of participation.

Department   A major administrative unit with responsibility for the conduct of a broad area of government operations. In the national government, the departments are headed by officers who comprise the permanent members of the President's Cabinet. The Cabinet departments are Agriculture, Commerce, Defense, Education, Energy, Health and Human Services, Housing and Urban Development, Interior, Justice, Labor, State, Transportation, Treasury, and Veterans Affairs. Heads of other major units may be invited to be part of the Cabinet at the President's invitation. State and local governments also departmentalize major functions. Departments are generally subdivided into bureaus, divisions, sections, and other units. (For specific departments, *see* Index.)

Significance   Most of the work of government is conducted through major departments. Departmental status generally indicates a permanent interest on the part of the government to promote a particular function. The

Departments of the Army, Navy, and Air Force retain the title but have been incorporated into the Department of Defense. A number of major functions are vested in agencies outside the regular departments, such as independent regulatory commissions and corporations, in order to remove them from direct presidential supervision. Many administrative authorities feel that all functions should be assigned to one of the major departments to prevent diffusion of responsibility.

Ex Officio   A Latin term for "by virtue of office." Many persons hold a position on a board or agency by virtue of their holding some related position. For example, a governor, typically, is a member of numerous state boards and commissions because of his or her position as governor.

Significance   The ex officio principle is designed to involve appropriate officials in the decisions of major agencies and serves to coordinate the efforts of related agencies. An ex officio assignment clarifies responsibility by assigning it to a position irrespective of the individual who occupies it.

Federal Register   A U.S. government publication initiated by the Federal Register Act of 1935, which requires that presidential proclamations, reorganization plans, and executive orders be published. The Administrative Procedure Act of 1946 requires every public agency to publish a statement of its organization, authority, methods of operation, and statements of general policy in the *Federal Register*. Notice of proposed rules and regulations and administrative orders resulting from the adjudicatory functions of the agency must also be published. The *Federal Register* is published five times each week. The documents are codified in the *Code of Federal Regulations* (CFR). Some states have similar publications. *See also* PAPERWORK REDUCTION ACT OF 1980, page 244.

Significance   The increasing growth of executive orders and administrative rules and regulations makes the *Federal Register* one of the most important and widely read government publications. Prior to its publication, citizens and business interests in particular had difficulty knowing what and how new rules applied to them. Publication of proposed rules and regulations assures interested parties an opportunity to be heard prior to the regulations' enforcement. The extent of administrative rules and regulations is evidenced by the growth of the *Federal Register* from 20,000 pages in 1970 to more than 70,000 by 1977. Some decrease in size was realized during the Reagan administration as regulatory activity diminished considerably. In 1990, the *Federal Register* had 53,500 pages but had increased to 68,100 by 1995.

Field Service   Decentralized administration typified by local or regional branch offices of a federal or state agency. Operations, personnel, and finance are under the control of the central office in Washington, D.C., or the state capital.

Significance   Most governmental work is conducted through field offices. Only about 15 percent of federal employees work in the Washington, D.C. area; the remaining 85 percent are assigned to field service offices around the nation and abroad. Field-headquarters relationships pose a continuing problem for sound administration in securing coordination of activity and responsibility. Field offices provide the citizen with close-to-home services and make possible settling most problems where they arise. The national government's major programs are divided into 10 standard federal regions to coordinate local offices and several federal-state-local programs. In addition, Federal Executive Boards have been established in 28 major metropolitan areas, composed of the heads of field offices in those areas to facilitate interagency projects and to disseminate information.

Functional Consolidation   Combining several administrative units that do related work into one major department. *See also* ADMINISTRATIVE REORGANIZATION, page 219; FUNCTIONAL CONSOLIDATION, page 617; IRON TRIANGLE, page 82.

Significance   Functional consolidation is a basic principle of administrative organization. The tendency of legislative bodies to create new agencies to meet new problems often results in diffusion of responsibility and the existence of too many agencies for the chief executive to direct and control effectively. Administrative experts suggest that, on the state level, all agencies should be consolidated into from 10 to 20 departments. The constitutions of Idaho, Louisiana, Michigan, Missouri, and New Jersey place a limitation on the number of departments in the state's executive branch (20 or fewer). In 1949, the Commission on Organization of the Executive Branch (known as the Hoover Commission) suggested that some 1,800 federal agencies could be consolidated into 22 major departments. Most proposals to make administrative structure more manageable through functional consolidation meet with failure because they are apt to upset existing political arrangements among pressure groups, governmental agencies, and legislative committees concerned with the agencies (the "iron triangle").

General Schedule   (GS) The designation of rank and salary in the classified civil service. Ranks range from GS 1 to GS 15 with 1996 salaries from about $12,400 to $90,000 per year. Clerical and subprofessional grades are those under GS 5. College graduates usually begin at GS 5 or 7, and those with graduate degrees or extensive experience at GS 7, 9, or 11; starting salaries for these categories range from $23,600 to $35,000. Agency management personnel ordinarily are at GS 13 to 15 with starting salaries ranging from $49,900 to $64,300. Top-level civil servants involved in management positions are part of the Senior Executive Service with salaries from $92,900 to $115,700. Each step in the General Schedule has pay rates established by law, as well as in-grade increments. Blue-collar pay rates are determined by local private blue-collar scales. Recent legislation authorizes adjustments in all grades to meet local market conditions, known as "locality pay." *See also* CLASSIFIED SERVICE, page 223; FEDERAL PAY COMPARABILITY ACT OF 1970, page 242; POSITION CLASSIFICATION, page 231; SENIOR EXECUTIVE SERVICE, page 233.

Significance   The General Schedule is in keeping with the principles of position classification, in which jobs are classified according to required skills and duties rather than the individuals holding them and an attempt is made to provide equal pay for similar work. Civil service career opportunities and pay tend to be competitive at lower levels with private enterprise but fall substantially behind comparable positions at higher management levels. The nation is divided into 32 localities, and pay and annual raises may vary several percentage points from city to city. For example, the adjustment for New York City may be 8 or 9 percent while Kansas City receives 4 or 5 percent. At issue is the practice of assigning one percentage to each locality, which may underpay or overpay classes of workers.

Government Corporation   An agency of government that administers a business enterprise. The corporation form is used when an activity is primarily commercial in nature, produces revenue for its continued existence, and requires greater flexibility than Congress normally permits regular departments. Corporations are used at the national level for such enterprises as electric power distribution (Tennessee Valley Authority), bank deposit insurance (Federal Deposit Insurance Corporation), and mail service (United States Postal Service). At the state level, corporations (often called "authorities") operate airports, turnpikes, and harbors, the best known being the Port Authority of New York and New Jersey. Another form of corporation is the quasi-government corporation known as a "government-sponsored enterprise" (GSE). They are privately managed, shareholder-owned operations performing a public purpose. An example is the Federal National Mortgage Association (Fannie Mae) established to make loans more available to home buyers. It is chartered by Congress but owned by private stockholders who trade shares on public stock exchanges.

Significance   The corporation device enables government to operate diverse business services with flexibility similar to that of private enterprise. Prior to 1945, Congress permitted corporations a great degree of independence, but the Government Corporation Control Act of 1945 subjects them to budgetary and auditing controls and to civil service laws. Corporations are generally run by boards of directors, and many are attached to one of the major departments for administrative purposes. The problem of how to balance a corporation's need for flexibility with the democratic requirements of legislative and executive controls remains, especially with regard to GSEs. About twenty government corporations have been established by Congress.

Hearing   Adjudication by an administrative or regulatory agency of alleged violations of the laws or of the rules and regulations administered by it. Hearings are also held to give interested parties an opportunity to be heard prior to the promulgation of a rule. *See also* ADMINISTRATIVE LAW JUDGE, page 218; ADMINISTRATIVE ORDER, page 219; HEARING, page 264; QUASI-JUDICIAL, page 232.

Significance   Hearings may be initiated by the agency itself or by any aggrieved party. They are conducted in a manner similar to, but less formal than, a court of law, under rules established by the Administrative Procedure Act of 1946. Decisions result in the issuance of administrative orders that have the force of law. Appeals may be made to the courts, which generally limit themselves to a review of the overall fairness of the hearing and to whether the record substantiates the findings of the agency. The quasi-judicial power of agencies is one of the major administrative developments of the twentieth century. The requirement of a hearing prior to the promulgation of a rule permits parties likely to be affected by a rule to have a part in its formulation.

Hierarchy   A principle of administrative organization in which each person or office is under the control of and responsible to the next-highest level. In turn, the higher level is responsible to its superior for the conduct of those below. *See also* DECENTRALIZATION, page 224; DELEGATION OF AUTHORITY, page 224; UNITY OF COMMAND, page 235.

Significance   All large organizations are arranged according to the principle of hierarchy. The military is the prototype of hierarchical organization. Students of administration recognize, however, that strict heirarchical organization can be both inefficient and undersirable, particularly in a free society. Rigid hierarchy demands conformity, impersonality, and centralization of power rather than initiative, flexibility, and decentralization. Informal relations in any organization also tend to weaken strict hierarchical authority. Some contemporary critics of hierarchy urge a collegial or participatory model of organization. Yet, in order for responsibility to be fixed in a democratic society, the huge governmental bureaucracy must adhere to the general principle of hierarchy in order to coordinate productivity, structure choices, and identify leadership.

Independent Agency   A federal agency that is not part of the Cabinet-level executive departments. The term may include independent regulatory commissions but is generally used to describe agencies that perform service rather than regulatory functions. Examples of independent agencies are the Office of Personnel Management, the Small Business Administration, and the General Services Administration. Many independent agencies are organized like regular departments and headed by persons responsible to the President.

Significance   A large number of agencies have independent status. Some do not fit into any particular major department, and others serve all departments. In other cases, Congress has wanted to keep a tighter rein on an agency than departmental status would permit or has responded to the pressures of interest groups that seek autonomy for a given function. A few have been given independent status to shield them from partisan politics. Terms of officials frequently overlap to avoid control by any one President, and the removal power of the President may be limited. The existence of large numbers of independent agencies complicates the organizational pattern and lines of responsibility of the executive branch.

Independent Counsel   A special prosecutor appointed under the Ethics in Government Act of 1978 to probe allegations against high-ranking government or campaign officials. The Act requires the appointment of an independent counsel by a special three-judge court whenever the Attorney General determines that allegations of misconduct are serious enough to warrant further investigation and possible prosecution. The scope of the independent counsel's jurisdiction is drafted by the Attorney General but is determined in final form by the special court. *See also* ETHICS IN GOVERNMENT ACT OF 1978, page 242.

Significance   The independent counsel idea rests on the assumption that the executive branch is not likely to investigate itself adequately. The Ethics in Government Act was passed in the wake of the Watergate scandals of the Nixon administration, when President Nixon fired the special prosecutor appointed by the Attorney General to investigate Watergate. Several independent counsels have been selected to investigate allegations of cocaine use by high officials, to investigate former or sitting officials for alleged conflict-of-interest violations, and, most notably, to investigate potential abuse of power by the Reagan administration (Iran-contra scandal) and the Clinton administration (Whitewater real estate and banking scandal). Critics of the law contend that the law is unconstitutional because it allows the judiciary to appoint a prosecutor, which is an executive function. Supporters note that the Constitution permits Congress to vest appointment of "inferior officers" in courts of law (Art. II, sec. 2). In 1988, the Supreme Court upheld the law, ruling that the independent counsel is an "inferior officer" and that the law does not violate the separation of powers principle by unduly interfering with executive power (*Morrison v. Olson,* 487 U.S. 654).

Independent Regulatory Commission   An agency outside the major executive departments charged with the regulation of important aspects of the economy. The commissions include the Federal Trade Commission, Securities and Exchange Commission, Federal Communications Commission, National Labor Relations Board, Commodity Futures Trading Commission, Federal Reserve Board, Federal Maritime Commission, Consumer Product Safety Commission, and the Nuclear Regulatory Commission. All of these agencies are empowered to establish rules for the particular industries they regulate and to prosecute violators. All are multiheaded, with five or seven members. (For specific commissions, *see* Index.)

Significance   The independent regulatory commissions possess vast authority to determine individual and property rights. They have been established because of the sheer complexity of modern economic problems and the desirability of having agencies that could develop expertness and continuity of policy with regard to these problems. Neither Congress nor the courts have the talent or the time. The agencies are independent of the President to remove their quasi-legislative and adjudicatory functions from partisan politics. Members of the commissions are appointed by the President with the Senate's consent but may be removed only for cause. Terms of office are lengthy and overlapping in order to avoid dominance by the appointees of one President, though turnover is quite frequent. No more than a simple majority of commissioners—such as three of five or four of seven—may be members of one political party. Problems arise from the tendency of commissions to become captives of the industries they are supposed to regulate; many officials are necessarily drawn from the regulated industries. Further, the independence of the commissions may result in policies that are contrary to those of the party in power. These commissions have often been called "the headless fourth branch" of government because of their peculiar place in the organization of the government and lack of continuing supervision from the President or Congress. Most are targets of those seeking to "deregulate" the economy, which in some sectors, notably transportation and communications, has been substantially accomplished.

Inspectors General   Independent review offices established by Congress in 1978 for major federal agencies. Inspectors general are appointed by the

President with the advice and consent of the Senate. Unlike many presidential appointees, they are prohibited from participating in partisan political activities. Inspectors general conduct independent audits and investigations within their agencies and prepare semiannual reports, which are transmitted to Congress and made public. *See also* CHIEF FINANCIAL OFFICERS ACT OF 1990, page 422.

Significance   The establishment of the Offices of Inspectors General is a step toward increasing the efficiency and accountability of major federal agencies through the use of independent and objective evaluation and review of agency programs and practices. Before such offices were established, agency reviews were often processed by the same people who were being evaluated. Although the independence of the inspectors general and their staffs was meant to provide better reporting, critics charge that they have become isolated and get minimal cooperation from agency personnel. In 1996, there were 56 inspectors general across the government.

Line and Staff   An administrative concept that categorizes the work of an agency as an operating or supportive function. The line carries out legislative programs and deals directly with the people. The executive departments such as Agriculture or Labor are typical line departments. The staff serves in a supportive capacity, aiding the chief executive and the line officials through such activities as planning, coordinating, and budgeting. The Office of Management and Budget is a major staff agency of the federal government. *See also* AUXILIARY AGENCY, page 220.

Significance   The distinction between line and staff prescribes the division of labor in large organizations. The distinction is, however, by no means precise. Line officials may engage in staff or advisory work, as members of the Cabinet generally do, and some staff agencies may engage in operating tasks, as some budgeting or planning offices do.

Merit System   The selection, retention, and promotion of government employees on the basis of ability, knowledge, and skills after fair and open competition. Though the term is often used interchangeably with "civil service," the merit system emphasizes positive programs of sound personnel management rather than the mere placing of restraints upon the spoils system. *See also* CERTIFICATION OF ELIGIBLES, page 222; CIVIL SERVICE, page 222; CIVIL SERVICE REFORM ACT, page 241; CLASSIFIED SERVICE, page 223; POSITION CLASSIFICATION, page 231; VETERANS' PREFERENCE, page 235.

Significance   The merit system has not been universally adopted in the United States, particularly as a thoroughgoing personnel program. While much headway has been made at the national level, much remains to be done on the state and local levels, particularly in counties and townships. Originally, the concept of civil service was limited to keeping unfit persons out of government service. The merit system represents a more positive approach, looking toward the development of a career service and toward in-service training, position classification, merit pay, and retirement programs. Obstacles to a complete merit system include the perseverance of political patronage and widespread use of veterans' preference. In 1993, for example, veterans (who are given extra points on exams) comprised more than 30 percent of federal government hires. The questionable reliability of competitive tests, which may discriminate against minorities, has also caused concern, resulting in the abandonment of some tests that had low passage rates by minorities and the use of special hiring procedures for minorities during the 1980s. New examinations are more specifically job-related and, in keeping with the Civil Rights Act of 1991, are not "race-normed," a practice used for some tests to rank blacks and Hispanics only against members of their own race. In 1994, minorities held about 28 percent of federal positions but only 10 percent of the Senior Executive Service. Comparable figures for women are 44 percent and 17 percent respectively.

Organization   The arrangement of persons and the assignment of their responsibilities for the most effective achievement of a purpose or objective. Public administration experts are concerned with the problem of the best way to organize the government or a particular agency to eliminate friction and to accomplish the task assigned. The decisions involve the nature of line, staff, and auxiliary agencies, the location of responsibility, and the overall coordination of efforts. Activities may be organized according to major purpose (for example, the Department of Agriculture), process or skills (central purchasing), area (fire and police protection), or clientele (Small Business Administration). The use of a single head or a board is another concern of organization. *See also* ADMINISTRATIVE REORGANIZATION, page 219; CLIENTELE AGENCY, page 223; HIERARCHY, page 228.

Significance   Organizational concepts and techniques are mainly the concern of administrative specialists but are also important to all citizens who seek to understand the nature of administrative organization and the problems of reorganization. Organizational structure may well determine the effectiveness of an agency. Much depends on the purposes to be served and, in government in particular, on the desires and influence of legislative bodies and pressure groups.

Position Classification   The grouping of government employment positions on the basis of duties, responsibilities, and qualifications. A position is classified in accordance with the nature of the job rather than the person holding the position. *See also* GENERAL SCHEDULE, page 226; MERIT SYSTEM, page 230.

Significance   Position classification is regarded as an essential ingredient of a sound merit system. The benefits include (1) simplification of recruitment and selection of personnel through administration of similar tests for similar positions; (2) equal pay for equal work, an important goal of public personnel administration and essential for high morale; (3) established performance standards, with merit pay based on quality of performance; (4) well-defined lines of responsibility for the individual worker and top management; and (5) clear avenues of promotion and transfer. The overall objective of position classification is equitable treatment of government employees, which benefits both the employee and the public. Classification schemes must be reviewed from time to time, however, lest they act as a straitjacket on effective administration and optimum utilization of employees. Position classification is used in the national government and in several state and local governments.

Quasi-judicial   Powers exercised by administrative agencies that have the characteristics of a judicial act. Independent regulatory commissions, as well as other administrative agencies, exercise quasi-judicial powers when they conduct hearings and make decisions having the force of law. *See also* AD-MINISTRATIVE LAW JUDGE, page 218; HEARING, page 227.

Significance   Under the doctrine of the separation of powers, only courts and judges may exercise judicial power. The highly technical nature of modern economic regulation has necessitated the delegation of "quasi-" (Latin for "seemingly" or "resembling") judicial power to expert administrators. For example, Congress has empowered the Federal Trade Commission to determine what constitutes an unfair trade practice and to adjudicate alleged violations. Concern over the inherent violation of the separation of powers led to the passage of the Administrative Procedure Act of 1946, which requires the use of administrative law judges and more judicial-like procedures and expands the power of judicial review of administrative adjudications.

Quasi-legislative   Rule-making powers, exercised by administrative agencies, that have the characteristics of a legislative act. Numerous administrative agencies are authorized to issue rules and regulations having the force of law. They include not only the independent regulatory commissions but also a host of other agencies, such as the Department of Agriculture, which issues rules relative to crop quotas and other agricultural practices. *See also* ADMIN-ISTRATIVE ORDER, page 219; *Opp Cotton Mills v. Administrator of Wage and Hour Division,* page 239.

Significance   Under the doctrine of the separation of powers, all legislative power is vested in the legislative body. Congress and the state legislatures, however, cannot legislate in sufficient detail to cover all the problems that arise in a complex society. Thus, the legislature delegates power to administrative agencies to "fill in the details" under the standards established by the legislature. The Administrative Procedure Act of 1946 requires administrative agencies to give notice and hold hearings on proposed rules and regulations and to publish all rules and regulations in the *Federal Register.* Congress retains a check on "quasi-" (Latin for "seemingly" or "resembling") legislation by being able to change the basic law of the agency. The courts, too, maintain a check over abuse of powers delegated to agencies but tend to be very supportive of agency interpretation of their delegated authority. A substantial number of rules that govern the individual originate in administrative agencies rather than in the legislature.

Secretary   The title of the heads of the major executive departments in the national government (with the exception of the Attorney General) and a title used by a few major state officials. *See also* CABINET, page 185; DEPARTMENT, page 224.

Significance   The secretaries of the federal executive departments are part of the President's Cabinet and serve at the pleasure of the President.

They are the legal and administrative heads of their departments and have broad powers over expenditures and personnel. Several have quasi-legislative and quasi-judicial powers. They set the tone for their departments and act as advisers to the President. Generally, they are chosen more for their political acumen and acceptability than for their training in the subject area of the department. State government secretaries may have similar powers and duties but are generally elected; the title is most commonly used in the states for the office of secretary of state.

Senior Executive Service (SES)   An elite cadre of governmental managers outside the regular merit system, established by the Civil Service Reform Act of 1978. It covers about 6,000 senior supervisory and policy-making executive branch positions formerly in the classified service, plus executive levels that do not require Senate confirmation. People in this gradeless system are held personally accountable for program accomplishment based on agency goals. Highly successful senior executives, as judged by agency review boards, receive bonuses that vary according to level of achievement. Failure to achieve adequate levels of performance is grounds for removal from SES. Criteria by which SES performance is judged include improved efficiency, productivity, quality of work, reduction of paperwork, timeliness of performance, and achievement of affirmative action goals. As of 1991, SES personnel must undergo review and recertification every three years. Annual salary levels for SES in 1996 ranged from $98,000 to $122,000. *See also* CIVIL SERVICE REFORM ACT OF 1978, page 241.

Significance   The SES was established to utilize some of the management techniques of private enterprise and to provide a reward incentive to top managers by making them accountable for agency performance. The Civil Service Reform Act increases both management flexibility and control over the people at the highest levels of management, particularly by the President, agency heads, and top appointed officials. Senior executives, in turn, give up much of their job security and are vulnerable to transfers, dismissals, or demotion and return to the classified service.

Separation From Service   Termination of employment in the civil service. Separation may be voluntary, as by resignation, or the result of retirement laws, a reduction in force, or disciplinary action for conduct unbecoming a public employee. *See also* TENURE, page 235.

Significance   A public employee may resign at any time without prejudice. Liberal retirement allowances are provided for those who serve twenty years in the federal service. When a reduction in force (RIF) is ordered because of a cut in appropriations or less need for employees, due weight is given to such factors as seniority, performance, and veterans' preference. Terminations may take place during a probationary period (about 5,200 per year), but thereafter dismissal from service is permitted "for such causes as will promote the efficiency of said service," and procedures are established by law. Dismissals or resignations in lieu of adverse action (about 7,500 per year) result from charges of misconduct or poor performance. The department head must inform the employee in writing of the causes for dismissal and give him or her an opportunity to respond. The employee may appeal the case to the Merit Systems Protection Board (MSPB) and then to the Court of Appeals for the Federal Circuit. Those in sensitive positions may also be discharged as "security risks," and all government employees are given security checks. Similar procedures are followed in many states with formal appeal procedures to a commission or court. Although economic security motivates many who choose public service, critics allege that the high level of job security leads to indolence and that discharge procedures are too cumbersome. The MSPB data for 1994 shows that 78 percent of federal supervisors had encountered poor performance but only 23 percent had taken corrective action and only 364 individuals were fired for poor performance in a workforce of about 2 million.

Span of Control   An administrative concept concerned with the number of agencies or subordinates that one person can supervise effectively. Experts have different opinions about what constitutes a manageable span of control, but most agree that no person can direct more than twenty agencies or persons. *See also* FUNCTIONAL CONSOLIDATION, page 226.

Significance   The President and almost all governors have too many agencies under their supervision. The same is true for many persons with top-level jobs in government. Most reorganization plans reduce the span of control by drawing many functions into as few departments as possible. In this way, a hierarchy of responsibility can be developed in which no supervisor has more than a few persons reporting directly to him or her.

Spoils System   The award of government jobs to political supporters and friends. The term derives from the expression "to the victor belong the spoils." The spoils system is generally associated with President Andrew Jackson. *See also* PATRONAGE, page 94; *Rutan v. Republican Party of Illinois,* page 239.

Significance   The spoils system is usually defended on the grounds that it is essential for the maintenance of a party system, in that people are not likely to work for a party without some reward, and that victorious candidates should have as employees those who are loyal to them and to their policies. President Jackson took the view that government work is so simple that anyone could handle it and that rotation in office is necessary and healthy for vigorous administration. Few people today consider government work simple, but many still support the principle of rotation in office because civil service tenure may result in an administration having unsympathetic employees. Though the merit system has made large inroads on the spoils system, vestiges of the spoils system remain at the local government level, and many federal jobs are still filled by patronage. In 1976, the Supreme Court cast doubt upon the continuing viability of the spoils system by holding impermissible the firing by a sheriff of non-policy-making or nonconfidential employees simply because of their political party affiliation (*Elrod v. Burns,* 427 U.S. 347). A 1980 ruling (*Branti v. Finkel,* 445 U.S. 507) held that under the First and Fourteenth Amendments, county assistant public defenders could not be discharged solely because of their political affiliation or belief unless pertinent to the performance of their duties. This reasoning was applied to promotions, transfers, and recalls in *Rutan v. Republican Party of Illinois,* 497 U.S. 62 (1990). In 1996 the Court extended these constitutional protections to independent government contractors (*O'Hare Truck Service v. Northlake,* 116 S. Ct. 2353; *Board of County Commissioners v. Umbehr,* 116 S. Ct. 2342).

Tenure   The right to hold a position or office free from arbitrary dismissal. Public employees in the civil service and teachers achieve tenure after serving a probationary period. *See also* SEPARATION FROM SERVICE, page 233.

Significance   Tenure encourages freedom of thought and action on the part of employees and frees them from fear of dismissal for purely personal or political reasons rather than for poor performance. Safeguards have been established by law to assure tenure for most government employees and public school teachers, including requirements of notice and hearing prior to disciplinary action. Critics of tenure allege that it destroys initiative and protects the incompetent because it is difficult to dismiss any public servant.

United States Government Manual   The official organization handbook of the three branches of the federal government. It lists all federal departments and agencies with detailed descriptions of their powers, duties, and activities. The *Manual* is published annually in July.

Significance   The *Manual* is a useful resource for students of government and citizens generally. It includes major agencies of government, various units within the agencies, names of key personnel, lists of governmental publications, and organization charts of the more complex agencies. A list of agencies that have been discontinued in recent years is also provided. Similar information about state agencies can be found in state manuals.

Unity of Command   An administrative concept that no person should be subject to the orders of more than one superior. It is related to the idea of "chain of command," which is common to the military services. *See also* HIERARCHY, page 228.

Significance   Unity of command is difficult to put into practice in the public service because of the variety of tasks that government undertakes and the large number of persons employed. The problem is most acute in areas of technical specialization, where a clash may occur between general administrators and specialists. Informal chains of command may develop in an agency if subordinate individuals command more respect than the actual head. Government agencies also may be independent of the chief executive and more responsive to the legislature or a pressure group. To achieve meaningful unity of command, agencies with similar functions would have to be integrated, a hierarchical arrangement of responsibility established, and authority for final decisions vested in one individual in order to avoid irresponsibility and confusion.

Veterans' Preference   Special consideration given to veterans in various aspects of the civil service. They include (1) the addition of five points to the test scores of veterans and ten points to disabled veterans; (2) the waiver of age, physical, and education requirements in some instances; (3) the limitation of competition for some positions to veterans; (4) the provision for special rights with regard to layoffs and dismissals; and (5) the extension of veterans' preference to wives, widows, and mothers of disabled or deceased veterans. These preferences are provided by almost all civil service jurisdictions in the United States. Under the Veterans Education and Employment Assistance Act of 1976, persons entering the military after October 1976 will not receive veterans' preference in the federal service unless they become disabled during military service or as a result of it. The Civil Service Reform Act of 1978 eliminates federal veterans' preference for those who retired at the rank of major or lieutenant commander or above, unless they are disabled. In the past, it was easy for these "double dippers" to get a federal job and collect a government salary in addition to a military pension. *See also* MERIT SYSTEM, page 230.

Significance   Veterans' preference has resulted in filling about a third of civil service positions with veterans and, in some jobs, a substantial majority. The preference has been held by the courts not to discriminate against women, even though women are adversely affected (*Personnel Administration of Massachusetts v. Feeney*, 442 U.S. 256 [1979]). These special considerations are based on the idea that the country owes a debt to veterans, especially those who have become disabled, and veterans' preference is vigorously supported by veterans' interest groups. Nevertheless, recent legislation has deemphasized veterans' preference in the federal civil service and has virtually eliminated it for peacetime military service. Personnel experts view veterans' preference as a derogation of the merit principle and an obstacle to nonveterans seeking a government career. The 1991 war in the Persian Gulf qualified 750,000 men and women for veterans' preference, the largest group since 1975.

IMPORTANT AGENCIES

Administrative Conference of the United States   An independent agency established in 1964 to study and develop procedures by which federal agencies involved in regulatory and benefit programs might improve their services. Its authority was essentially advisory. It was terminated by Congress in 1995.

Significance   The Administrative Conference of the United States was a small but influential body that developed studies and recommendations on its own initiative or upon request, on such subjects as adjudication, regulation, rule making, and judicial review. The vast network of governmental operations was believed to require an agency such as this to gather data, publish studies, and encourage agencies to share information so that administrative practices may be evaluated and improved, but it was a casualty of budget reductions in 1995.

Federal Labor Relations Authority (FLRA)   An agency that administers federal service labor-management relations under provisions of the Civil Service Reform Act of 1978. The FLRA consists of three members appointed by the President, with Senate consent, for five-year terms. It supervises the creation of bargaining units and oversees labor organization elections. The FLRA also contains the Federal Service Impasses Panel (FSIP), for resolution of bargaining disputes, and an Office of General Counsel to investigate and prosecute unfair labor practices. It also provides similar services for Foreign

Service employees. The Civil Service Reform Act of 1978 codifies federal labor-management relations, which have existed under executive order since 1962, into law for the first time. It affirms the right of federal employees to form labor organizations and bargain collectively. It forbids strikes, picketing, or slowdowns that interfere with government operations, requires the use of negotiated grievance procedures, and defines the scope of permitted collective bargaining for federal employees. *See also* CIVIL SERVICE REFORM ACT OF 1978, page 241.

Significance   The strengthening of the FLRA by placing it under statute reflects the federal government's awareness of the growing importance and strength of public employee unions. Public employee unions have experienced an increase in membership while private-sector unions have had losses. The first public-sector unions appeared in the Postal Service during the 1880s and 1890s, gradually spreading to other agencies. Efforts to organize public workers met with resistance from critics, who claimed that public employee unions would demand too great a role in the decision-making process, thus interfering with the efficient conduct of public business and with governmental responsibility to the people as a whole. Strong action by the Reagan administration in 1981 (firing and replacing striking air controllers) has reinforced the no-strike requirements for public employee unions. Supporters of public-sector unions pointed out that, with the proper limitations, such unions could increase the efficiency of the public sector by improving morale, attracting better-qualified people, and performing a "watchdog" function. Acceptance of public employee unions at the state and local level has grown as well but lagged behind that of the federal government, due in part to the strength of the spoils system in many local governmental units. Prominent broad-coverage federal employees' unions include the American Federation of Government Employees (AFGE), the National Federation of Federal Employees (NFFE), and the National Association of Government Employees (NAGE). For state and local public employees, the AFL-CIO–affiliated American Federation of State, County, and Municipal Employees (AFSCME) is the most prominent.

General Services Administration   An independent agency established in 1949 to centralize purchasing, property management, and records management for the national government. The General Services Administration, headed by an administrator appointed by the President with Senate approval, is assigned responsibility for the procurement, supply, and transportation of property and services for the executive agencies, the acquisition and management of federally owned or leased property, disposal of surplus property, and records management. Its Office of Enterprise Development promotes contracting with small businesses and minority and women business owners, and the Office of Emerging Technology promotes the use of new technologies in government services.

Significance   The General Services Administration gathers under one agency a number of functions formerly performed by separate units. The administration was created upon the suggestion of the Hoover Commission, which noted the need for centralized purchasing and property management in order to avoid waste and duplication in the worldwide operations of the national government. With its varied fields of activities and its heavy involvement with the private business and industrial sector, the General Services Administration resembles a huge corporate conglomerate. In 1994, as part of the "reinventing government" program, Congress altered federal procurement policies to facilitate low-cost contracts and to permit off-the-shelf purchase of routine items such as pens and notepads.

Merit Systems Protection Board (MSPB)   An agency established under the Civil Service Reform Act of 1978 to oversee the administration of the federal civil service merit system. The MSPB consists of three members appointed for seven-year terms by the President with the consent of the Senate. It protects the merit system and federal employees from arbitrary agency decisions and prohibited personnel practices. The board rules on employee appeals and orders appropriate corrective and disciplinary actions as needed. Actions involving allegations of discrimination may be appealed to the Equal Employment Opportunity Commission. Final orders of the MSPB may be appealed to the Court of Appeals for the Federal Circuit. A special counsel is empowered to investigate prohibited personnel practices, bring charges involving employees and agencies in violation of established merit system rules before the MSPB, and recommend to the MSPB that it order a halt to such practices. The Office of Special Counsel is also designated as the unit to receive information from, and give protection to, "whistleblowers"—employees of any federal agency who reveal unethical or illegal activities. In 1989 the Office of Special Counsel became an independent agency, though it still maintains close ties to MSPB, mainly to strengthen its whistleblower protection role. *See also* CIVIL SERVICE REFORM ACT OF 1978, page 241; MERIT SYSTEM, page 230.

Significance   The MSPB is the main watchdog agency of the merit system. As such, the effectiveness and diligence of this body determine the effectiveness of the merit system to a large degree. Maintenance of independence and impartiality are the vital necessities of this body. The MSPB separates the quasi-judicial functions from the management functions, now held by the Office of Personnel Management, but formerly combined in the Civil Service Commission prior to the 1978 reform legislation.

Office of Personnel Management (OPM)   Established by the Civil Service Reform Act of 1978, OPM provides leadership in managing the federal work force. The OPM is headed by a director appointed for a four-year term by the President and confirmed by the Senate. It is the primary organization involved in developing the rules, regulations, and policies for federal personnel management. Responsibilities include central examining and employment operations, personnel investigations, personnel program evaluation, recruitment and affirmative action, executive development and training, and administering the retirement and insurance programs for federal workers. The OPM delegates certain personnel functions to agency heads and provides guidelines and advice to agencies about establishing performance appraisal and other personnel systems. It also supervises affirmative action programs and administers the Ethics in Government Act as it pertains to federal employees. *See also* CIVIL SERVICE REFORM ACT OF 1978, page 241; ETHICS IN GOVERNMENT ACT OF 1978, page 241; MERIT SYSTEMS PROTECTION BOARD, page 238.

Significance   As the central personnel agency, OPM helps the President carry out his responsibilities for management of the federal work force. Through its leadership responsibilities, OPM largely determines the direction of the development of the merit system. The OPM assumed most of the functions of the Civil Service Commission, which was abolished by the 1978 reform, except for quasi-judicial functions, which were transferred to the Merit System Protection Board.

IMPORTANT CASES

Opp Cotton Mills v. Administrator of Wage and Hour Division   312 U.S. 126 (1941): Declared that the provisions of the Fair Labor Standards Act of 1938 authorizing an administrative determination of minimum wages in a particular industry do not constitute an unconstitutional delegation of legislative power. *See also* DELEGATION OF POWER, page 143; QUASI-LEGISLATIVE, page 232.

Significance   The *Opp* case was one of the last in a long series that challenged the right of Congress to vest rule-making power in an administrative agency. The Court pointed out that, in a complex society, Congress could not be expected to fill in the details of all public policies. So long as a standard is established within which the administrative agency must operate, the delegation of authority is permissible. The Court noted further that the Constitution does not demand the impossible, and Congress could not be expected to set every wage rate, every railroad rate, or every other rule that a business must follow. The *Opp* case put an end to the delegation of power issue in American constitutional law.

Railroad Commission of Texas v. Rowan and Nichols Oil Co.   311 U.S. 570 (1941): Refused to overturn a ruling of the Railroad Commission relating to the amount of oil that could be taken from wells in Texas. The Court noted that the issue was too complex for judges to determine and that the commission's order must stand in the absence of a showing that it was based on insubstantial evidence. *See also* ADMINISTRATIVE ORDER, page 219.

Significance   In this case, as in numerous others challenging specific rulings of state and national administrative agencies, the Court has taken the view that administrative decisions stand if they are supported by "substantial evidence." Otherwise, the Court would be substituting its judgment for that of an expert administrative agency. Congress, in the Administrative Procedure Act of 1946, has supported the Court's stand by providing that the scope of judicial review of administrative rulings be limited to determining relevant questions of law and by approving the substantial evidence rule. In 1984, the Supreme Court reinforced this principle by holding that the Court should defer to an agency's construction of its enabling statute (*Chevron U.S.A. Inc. v. Natural Resources Defense Council, Inc.,* 467 U.S. 837).

Rutan v. Republican Party of Illinois   497 U.S. 62 (1990): Ruled that promotions, transfers, and recalls based on political affiliation or support are impermissible infringements on public employees' First Amendment rights. *See also* SPOILS SYSTEM, page 234.

Significance   The *Rutan* decision was the third in a series of cases seriously weakening the patronage system in American politics. In 1976 the Supreme Court had held in *Elrod v. Burns,* 427 U.S. 347, that a sheriff may not fire employees in non-policy-making positions based simply on their political affiliation. In 1980 the Court again ruled in *Branti v. Finkel,* 445 U.S. 507, that county assistant public defenders could not be dismissed because of their political beliefs unless those beliefs were related to their duties. In each case, the Court held that the dismissals violated the employee's First Amendment rights, as well as the due process requirements of the Fourteenth Amendment. The Court noted in *Rutan* that while patronage did help maintain the two-party system and stabilize the political structure, these benefits were not enough to outweigh the infringements on First Amendment freedom. A government job may not be burdened by unconstitutional conditions even if the deprivation is less harsh than dismissal. These principles were extended to independent government contractors in 1996, the Court holding that contracts could not be denied because of failure to demonstrate political loyalty or for speaking out on public issues (*O'Hare Truck Service v. Northlake,* 116 S. Ct. 2353; *Board of County Commissioners v. Umbehr,* 116 S. Ct. 2342).

United Public Workers v. Mitchell   330 U.S. 75 (1947): Ruled that Congress may prohibit federal employees from participating in political activities. The Court upheld the Hatch Act of 1939, which authorizes the removal of a person from civil service employment for taking an "active part in political management or political campaigns." The Court reaffirmed its ruling in 1973 in *United States Civil Service Commission v. National Association of Letter Carriers,* 413 U.S. 548. *See also* HATCH ACT, page 244.

Significance   The Court found no invasion of the constitutional rights of public employees in the Hatch Act. In another case, the Court applied this ruling to state government employees working on projects financed by federal grants-in-aid (*Oklahoma v. United States Civil Service Commission,* 330 U.S. 127 [1947]; reaffirmed in *Broadrick v. Oklahoma,* 413 U.S. 601 [1973]). Critics of these rulings claim that they bar millions of persons from active participation in the democratic process. The Court, however, agreed with Congress that the Hatch Act contributes to the efficiency of the public service and prevents the growth of bureaucratic political machines. In the Federal Election Campaign Act of 1974, Congress removed Hatch Act restrictions on voluntary activities by state and local employees in federal campaigns if not otherwise prohibited by state law. Restrictions on off-duty federal employees were eased in 1993.

IMPORTANT STATUTES

Administrative Procedure Act of 1946   A major law governing the procedures of regulatory agencies and providing for standards of judicial review of administrative determinations. The Act requires that every agency publicize its operations, give advance notice of proposed rules, and permit persons to testify, to be accompanied by counsel, and to cross-examine witnesses. The Act provides further that the same official may not act as both prosecutor and judge and that persons may appeal decisions of these agencies to the courts. The courts are authorized to set aside any agency ruling that is arbitrary or unsupported by substantial evidence. *See also* ADMINISTRATIVE LAW JUDGE, page 218; ADMINISTRATIVE ORDER, page 219; HEARING, page 227.

Significance The Administrative Procedure Act was passed in response to growing criticism of the lack of procedural safeguards in administrative legislation and adjudication. Because so many private rights are now affected by administrative agencies, Congress sought to regulate the internal procedures by which rights are determined and to provide broad standards for judicial review. A 1990 amendment to the Act authorizes federal agencies to use alternative dispute resolution techniques such as arbitration.

Civil Service Reform Act of 1978 A major reform of the civil service system that abolished the Civil Service Commission and divided its main functions between the Office of Personnel Management (OPM), which administers the civil service employment rules, and the Merit Systems Protection Board (MSPB), which adjudicates alleged violations of lawful personnel practices. The Act also established and codified the role of the Federal Labor Relations Authority (FLRA) and the scope of federal labor-management relations. Other provisions of this law require federal departments to establish a Senior Executive Service for top managers. The Act requires federal agencies to inform employees of the critical elements and performance standards of their jobs and to develop, in consultation with their employees, performance appraisal standards within guidelines established by OPM. Federal service middle-level managers also depend on the quality of their performance under these developed standards for the size of any pay increase they receive. The Civil Service Reform Act provides special protections for federal employees who report on waste, fraud, and corruption through the Office of Special Counsel. Such employees, termed "whistle-blowers," are protected from any form of reprisal in return for information on agency abuses. *See also* FEDERAL LABOR RELATIONS AUTHORITY, page 236; MERIT SYSTEMS PROTECTION BOARD, page 238; OFFICE OF PERSONNEL MANAGEMENT, page 238; SENIOR EXECUTIVE SERVICE, page 233.

Significance The Civil Service Reform Act of 1978 represents the most comprehensive overhaul of the federal bureaucracy since the civil service system was established in 1883. It places great emphasis on improving the public service by increasing management flexibility, rewarding efficiency, fixing accountability for agency performance, and encouraging the exposure of fraud, abuse, and corruption. At the same time, the Act provides safeguards for employees through a system of appeal and review, through the MSPB, for those who dispute adverse agency personnel decisions. Under the former Civil Service Commission, responsibility for both administration and adjudication was combined in one agency. The 1978 reform divides these responsibilities and moves the civil service closer to the forms of employment conditions common in the private sector.

Ethics in Government Act of 1978   An act to require financial disclosure by top governmental officials and to regulate the activities of former officials. It requires financial reporting by senior officials, their spouses, and dependent children and restricts the outside earned income of presidential appointees to 15 percent of their salary. Limitations are placed on the acceptance of gifts and other perquisites by officials. In addition, the Act places four restrictions on former governmental employees: (1) a permanent restriction on all employees that prohibits them from serving as another person's representative to government on a case, contractual matter, or similar proceeding in which the former employee was personally or substantially involved while under government employment; (2) a two-year restriction basically the same as the first, which applies to all matters pending under the former employee's official responsibility during the last year of government employment; (3) a two-year restriction on senior employees that prevents them from assisting in the representation of another person in connection with an appearance before the government or with any matter in which the former employee could not act as a personal representative under the first two restrictions; and (4) a one-year restriction on senior employees that prohibits attempts to influence their former agency on a matter pending before the agency or of substantial interest to it, representing either themselves or another person. Under the Act, the Attorney General is required to seek the appointment of a special prosecutor (title changed to "independent counsel" in 1982) by a special judicial panel whenever preliminary investigation reveals potential violations of the law by high-ranking officials. The Act is administered by the Office of Government Ethics in the Office of Personnel Management. *See also* ETHICS CODES, page 144; GOOD BEHAVIOR, page 263; INDEPENDENT COUNSEL, page 228.

Significance   The passage of the Ethics in Government Act reflects a growing concern for ethics in the government service and disclosure of information by public managers. Critics claim that the Act discourages qualified people from joining the public work force because they object to the reporting requirements as an invasion of privacy and to the postemployment restrictions, which limit one of the major "fringe benefits" enjoyed by former governmental officials. Actual experience under the law, especially during the massive personnel changes that occurred when the Reagan administration replaced the Carter administration, illustrates that the restrictions did affect many who declined an opportunity for governmental service. Nevertheless, the legacy of the Watergate scandals and evidence of "influence peddling" by former officials appear to sustain public support for such legislation. Congress has also enacted ethics codes for its own members and provided procedures for disciplining judges guilty of ethical violations.

Federal Pay Comparability Act of 1970   An act that established the principle that public-sector pay scales should match those of similar jobs in the private sector and that placed responsibility for pay adjustments in the executive branch. The law replaced the Federal Salary Reform Act of 1962, under which Congress exercised the authority to set and maintain civil service pay scales. *See also* CAREER SERVICE, page 221; CIVIL SERVICE, page 222; GENERAL SCHEDULE, page 226; SENIOR EXECUTIVE SERVICE, page 233.

Significance   The Federal Pay Comparability Act was designed to make it easier to adjust pay scales for civil servants to keep government service an attractive option. In 1970, a 6 percent pay disparity existed between most government jobs and similar positions in the private sector. Congress felt it could not keep track of the statistical data needed to make informed judgments about pay comparability and that a yearly adjustment was beyond its legislative capabilities. So the act transferred the responsibility for adjusting federal pay rates to the executive branch beginning in 1972. The act created a Federal Employees Pay Council comprised of presidentially appointed members representing the federal workers unions and labor relations experts. The council recommends pay raises to a three-member Advisory Committee on Federal Pay composed of the heads of the Office of Personnel Management, the Office of Management and Budget, and the Secretary of the Treasury. Congress has 30 days to approve the pay raises. Presidents have consistently recommended less of an increase than the council and the committee have advised. In 1990, Congress estimated that federal pay rates were an average of 28 percent behind those of their private-sector counterparts and directed that federal employees' pay raises be linked to local labor markets.

Freedom of Information Act of 1966   An act requiring federal agencies to provide citizens access to public records upon request. Exemptions are permitted for national defense materials, confidential personnel and financial data, and certain law enforcement files. Persons denied access to requested materials may sue for disclosure, and a court may determine whether information is improperly classified and, therefore, improperly withheld. *See also* GOVERNMENT IN THE SUNSHINE ACT, page 243; PRIVACY, page 329.

Significance   Public access to public information is essential if public servants are to be held accountable for their actions. While the necessity for confidentiality in some areas is recognized, early experience under the Act showed that too many things were classified as confidential and that requests for material were often met with bureaucratic delay and excessive charges. A 1974 amendment to the Act requires agencies to expedite release of information, facilitates citizen access to courts to compel disclosures, and empowers judges to determine the propriety of any exemptions. Resultant disclosures of substantial illegal activities on the part of such agencies as the Federal Bureau of Investigation and the Central Intelligence Agency, involving invasions of privacy and violations of constitutional rights of individuals, have demonstrated the need and justification for the Freedom of Information Act. The tendency of the executive branch to seek limitations to the scope of available materials has met resistance from Congress.

Government in the Sunshine Act of 1977   A law requiring that all multi-headed federal agencies conduct their business in public session. The Sunshine law applies to about 50 executive agencies, regulatory commissions, advisory committees, and independent offices, but not to Cabinet departments. Closed meetings are permitted for discussion of specified subjects, such as national defense, personnel issues, confidential commercial or monetary matters, and court proceedings, though minutes of such meetings must be kept. Unofficial contacts between agency officials and persons involved in agency matters are banned. *See also* FREEDOM OF INFORMATION ACT, page 243.

Significance   The Government in the Sunshine Act represents a reaction to excessive secrecy in government and to increasing criticism of the relationships between government agencies and the various publics they regulate or serve. It extends the democratic concept of the public's "right to know" to the right also to know the processes by which decisions are reached. Court challenges to any determination to close a meeting are authorized by the Act. Many states have similar laws.

Hatch Act (Political Activities Act of 1939)   A law enacted by Congress to limit contributions to and spending by political parties. The most important provisions of the Hatch Act sought to prohibit political parties from pressuring federal employees to make contributions or otherwise actively participate in politics. Under the Act, individuals and companies under contract to the federal government may not contribute to political parties or their candidates, and the welfare system may not be used for political purposes. A second Hatch Act (Political Activities Act of 1940), repealed in 1974, imposed similar restrictions on state and local employees working on projects supported by federal funds. *See also* CORRUPT PRACTICES ACTS, page 69; FEDERAL ELECTION CAMPAIGN ACT OF 1974, page 123; *United Public Workers v. Mitchell,* page 240.

Significance   The Hatch Act limitations on the political activities of federal employees have been effectively applied. Prior to the Act, many thousands of federal employees were pressured into making contributions and participating actively in national campaigns as a condition of job security or promotion. On two occasions, the Supreme Court has upheld the key provisions of the Hatch Act. In 1947, in *United Public Workers v. Mitchell* (330 U.S. 75), the Court upheld those provisions of the Act that authorize the removal of a person from civil service employment for taking an "active part in political management or political campaigns." In 1973, the Court again upheld the Act, stating: "It is in the best interest of the country, indeed essential, that federal service should depend upon meritorious performance rather than political service..." *United States Civil Service Commission v. National Association of Letter Carriers,* 413 U.S. 548). Critics of the Court rulings claim that they bar millions of people from active participation in the democratic process and thus deny them their basic political rights. In 1993, the Act was amended to ease restrictions on the off-duty behavior of federal workers, permitting greater participation in political parties and campaigns. The initial restrictions were maintained, however, for high-level employees and certain security-sensitive agencies.

Paperwork Reduction Act of 1980   An Act to reduce paperwork requirements for citizens and businesses. The Act created an Office of Information and Regulatory Affairs (OIRA) within the Office of Management and Budget (OMB) and empowered OMB to oversee all government information management activity, recommend legislation, and establish guidelines for computer and telecommunications systems. The Act also required all agencies to create an information management officer. Special exemptions were included for independent regulatory agencies. The goal was to reduce the public paperwork burden by 25 percent in three years. *See also* FEDERAL REGISTER, page 225.

Significance   The Paperwork Reduction Act was primarily designed to reduce the paperwork burden that had become increasingly oppressive as regulation of the economy, environment, and government benefits grew. In 1980, Congress estimated that paperwork costs alone accounted for over $100 billion. The Act created OIRA, which was supposed to review all agency requests for information made to the public. It applied three rules that all paperwork burdens had to pass: (1) The information was essential to the task at hand, (2) the information was not available elsewhere, and (3) the information was collected in the most efficient manner possible. President Ronald Reagan issued executive orders in 1981 and 1985 empowering OIRA to review all major regulatory actions and established a cost-benefit standard that all such regulations had to meet before becoming effective. Angry that Reagan had used OIRA to further his antiregulatory goals, Congress allowed the Act's authorization to lapse between 1983 and 1986. In 1986, Congress made the head of OIRA subject to Senate confirmation and restricted OIRA's activities to oversight of paperwork burdens. The OIRA also agreed to allow Congress access to its documentation process and to provide reasons for why it made certain decisions. In 1990 in *Dole v. United Steelworkers of America*, 494 U.S. 26, the Supreme Court ruled that OIRA could not prevent reporting requirements but could only reduce the burden such paperwork imposed on the public. The Act's authorization lapsed again in 1989, but OMB continued to fund OIRA. In 1995, Congress reauthorized OIRA for six years and overturned the *Dole* ruling to extend OIRA's authority to paperwork that business produces for a third party. The 1995 amendments also set a governmentwide paperwork reduction goal of 10 percent for 1996 and 1997 and 5 percent from 1998 through 2001.

Pendleton Act (Civil Service Act of 1883)   A law that forms the basis for the personnel policies of the national government. The law established the principle of employment on the basis of open, competitive examinations and created a Civil Service Commission to administer the personnel service. The Pendleton Act extended the merit principle to only 10 percent of national employees, but later laws and executive orders have extended coverage to more than 90 percent of employees. *See also* CIVIL SERVICE REFORM ACT OF 1978, page 241.

Significance   The Pendleton Act was a direct result of the assassination of President James Garfield by a disappointed office seeker. The Act brought to a close the period of Jacksonian spoils, which made governmental employment a reward for political activity. The Pendleton Act turned the tide in favor of employment by merit, which, despite occasional lapses, has spread to all levels of government.

Ramspeck Act (Civil Service Act of 1940)   Authorized the President to place, by executive order, nearly all federal positions under the civil service system. Exemptions include those positions filled by presidential appointment requiring the Senate's approval and certain special agencies, such as the Tennessee Valley Authority and the Federal Bureau of Investigation, which have merit systems of their own. *See also* CLASSIFIED SERVICE, page 223.

Significance The Ramspeck Act is considered to be the culmination of the civil service reforms initiated in 1883 by the Pendleton Act. Presidents since 1940 have used this authority to broaden the coverage of the civil service laws. As a result, most national government positions are covered. Although this power often was used to "freeze" political appointees into their positions, the long-term effect has been to increase coverage of the civil service system. In 1995, Congress, as part of a lobbying reform bill, repealed the Ramspeck Act's provisions under which congressional and judicial employees could claim civil service jobs without competitive examination. This had been done by many Democratic legislative employees after the Republican victory of 1994.

Reorganization Act of 1949 A grant of power to the President to reorganize the executive branch of government. Plans for reorganization must be submitted to Congress. Until 1983, either house of Congress could veto the President's plans. When such legislative vetoes were declared invalid by the Supreme Court in 1983 (*Immigration and Naturalization Service v. Chada,* 462 U.S. 919), Congress, in 1984, affirmed all prior reorganizations. Furthermore, Congress provided that it subsequently must approve, by joint resolution, any reorganization proposed by the President. *See also* LEGISLATIVE VETO, page 155.

Significance A vast enterprise needs continuing reorganization to ensure efficiency of operation. The Reorganization Act places the initiative in the hands of the President, who bears major responsibility for administration. Congress's role enables it to prevent any reshuffling that may threaten the status of any "pet" agencies of members of Congress or major pressure groups. Through reorganization, an agency's status can be enhanced or seriously diminished.

7

The Judicial Process: Courts and Law Enforcement

Access to Courts   The availability of judicial power to resolve disputes. The major issue involves the access to federal courts. Among the issues raised are (1) the ease with which one may transfer a case from a state to a federal court, (2) the ability of social action groups to bring class action suits, (3) the right of taxpayers to challenge public expenditures, and (4) the right to sue state and local governments and their officials in federal courts. Although many legal technicalities are involved in such questions, the basic issues are *who* may bring *what* political or constitutional issues to the federal courts when state and local governments do not respond. *See also* CIVIL RIGHTS ACTS OF 1866, 1870, 1871, AND 1875, page 376; CLASS ACTION, page 253; DIVERSITY OF CITIZENSHIP, page 260; ELEVENTH AMENDMENT, page 261; HABEAS CORPUS, page 319; JURISDICTION, page 267; JUSTICIABLE QUESTION, page 269; *Maine v. Thiboutot,* page 288; POLITICAL QUESTION, page 274; TAXPAYER SUIT, page 281.

Significance   The issue of access to courts ripened during the 1970s as critics argued that the Supreme Court seriously limited access of litigants to federal courts. In 1965, in the case of *Dombrowski v. Pfister* (380 U.S. 479), the Court liberalized the right of litigants to transfer cases from state to federal courts when constitutional rights were being challenged. This ruling resulted in a large growth of transfers involving First Amendment and criminal procedure cases. Eventually, the Court placed restrictions on transfer of such cases unless extraordinary circumstances demanded federal intervention (*Younger v. Harris,* 401 U.S. 37 [1971]) or the state failed to provide full and fair litigation of constitutional claims (*Stone v. Powell,* 428 U.S. 465 [1976]). Strict limits were also placed on federal class action suits (*Eisen v. Carlisle & Jacquelin,* 417 U.S. 156 [1974]) and on federal court intervention into cases in which direct individual injury could not be shown. The latter provoked opposition from consumer, environmental, and other public interest groups. In the late 1970s, the Supreme Court began liberalizing the right to sue state and local governments and officers and sustained payment of attorney fees to winning plaintiffs. But in the late 1980s, the Court began to limit suits against local governments and officers and sharply restricted the use of habeas corpus claims by state prisoners. Congress, in the Antiterrorism and Effective Death Penalty Act of 1996, placed substantial limits on habeus corpus appeals to federal courts. The restrictions were upheld in a death penalty case in *Felker v. Turpin,* 116 S. Ct. 2333 (1996). Supporters of reduced access argue that the federal courts are overburdened and understaffed, that federal intervention destroys the power of state and local governments, that it prolongs resolution of issues, and that some issues are better left to the political process. Proponents of increased access claim that state and local courts are frequently insensitive to civil liberties and too tied to local politics.

Activism Versus Self-restraint   Two approaches to judicial decision making in the American political system. Activists hold that a judge should use his or her position to promote desirable social ends. Proponents of self-restraint counter that in deciding cases a judge should defer to the legislative and executive branches, which are politically responsible to the voters, and not indulge his or her personal philosophy. Both schools of thought recognize the policy-making nature of judicial decisions on major social questions, but they differ on how that power should be used. *See also Eakin v. Raub,* page 287.

Significance   The activism versus self-restraint dichotomy is most clearly evidenced in the United States Supreme Court. This division underscores the policy-making role of the Supreme Court in its decisions on questions of broad policy that are framed in legal terms. Most observers take the view that judges cannot help but inject their personal views into decisions and that one is apt to accept or reject the Court's role, depending upon how it affects the outcome of particular cases. For example, during the New Deal period of the 1930s, liberals opposed the "activism" of the Court in striking down social welfare programs, whereas many liberals today favor Court "activism" on behalf of civil rights.

Administrative Law   That branch of law that creates administrative agencies, establishes their methods of procedure, and determines the scope of judicial review of agency practices and actions. The term also describes the rules and regulations made by administrative agencies. Administrative law deals with rate making, operating rules, the rights of persons and companies regulated by administrative agencies, and the power of the courts to review such actions. *See also* ADMINISTRATIVE ORDER, page 219; ADMINISTRATIVE PROCEDURE ACT, page 240.

Significance   The widespread use of administrative agencies to regulate important aspects of economic and social life results in their producing a great flow of law governing individual conduct. Correspondingly, a body of law controlling operations of administrative agencies has evolved to assure fair procedures that protect the rights of persons affected by these operations. Increasingly, more people are affected by administrative rules than by legislative statutes. The courts have been supportive of these rules due to the expertise of the bureaucracy.

Admiralty Jurisdiction   Authority vested in federal courts by Article III, section 2 of the Constitution to hear cases involving shipping and commerce on the high seas and on the navigable waters of the United States. It is a highly technical body of law based on tradition, congressional statutes, and international law. Typical cases involve maritime contracts, collisions, and crimes committed on vessels. *See also* JURISDICTION, page 267; NAVIGABLE WATERS, page 450.

Significance   The federal courts have exclusive jurisdiction over admiralty and maritime cases. This authority assures maintenance of national supremacy over foreign and interstate commercial water routes.

Adversary System   A concept underlying judicial procedure in the United States that assumes that justice will emerge from the contest of opposing views. Each side in a civil or criminal trial is expected to press its point of view with vigor and do all it can to refute the opposition's witnesses, evidence, and arguments.

Significance   An adversary system of justice assumes that judges act as passive arbiters of conflict and that the truth emerges out of genuine controversies. Some critics argue that the result is to make a trial a contest between lawyers, that judges are overly restrained from direct participation in the resolution of disputes, that the truth is not in fact revealed, and that the administration of justice suffers.

Advisory Opinion   An opinion given by a court, though no actual case or controversy is before it, on the constitutionality or legal effect of a law. No advisory opinions are rendered by federal judges. A few states, however, do authorize the highest state court to give such opinions upon the request of the legislature or governor. An advisory opinion is not generally binding, but it is influential.

Significance   The advisory opinion avoids the confusion that might result from a declaration of unconstitutionality after a law has been in effect for a long period of time. Such an opinion serves as a guide to the legislature, particularly when a statute appears to break new ground, and to governors in deciding whether to sign or veto legislation. When rendering an advisory opinion, however, a court lacks the benefit of opposing arguments by adverse parties over a specific application of the legislation.

Amicus Curiae   A legal term meaning "friend of the court." As *amicus curiae,* individuals or groups who are not parties to a lawsuit may aid or influence the court in reaching its decision. The court may at its discretion give permission to or request persons to appear as *amicus curiae.* Often parties will seek to appear as *amicus curiae* when the decision in the case will affect their rights as well as the rights of those directly involved. In some states, a friend of the court is permanently attached to a court to help it reach decisions in cases involving minors, divorce, or criminal offenders.

Significance   Many lawsuits have implications reaching far beyond the interests of the litigants involved in the case. For example, in a case involving civil rights, several interest groups may seek permission to testify or file documents to demonstrate to the court the implications of the case. The federal government, acting through the Solicitor General, frequently exercises its right to appear as *amicus* before the Supreme Court on matters involving federal policies.

Appeal   Taking a case from a lower court to a higher tribunal by the losing party. A person bringing an appeal is called the "appellant" and the party called upon to answer is the "appellee" or "respondent." The term also identifies those types of cases brought to the U.S. Supreme Court as a matter of right, though such mandatory reviews were virtually eliminated by Congress in 1988. An appeal is generally a complex and costly process. Simplified provisions are made for filing of appeals *in forma pauperis* by indigent appellants in criminal cases. *See also* APPELLATE JURISDICTION, page 250.

Significance   An ordinary appeal is designed to serve as a check upon any errors committed in lower tribunals. When the Supreme Court reviews cases "on appeal," it ensures that specific issues defined by Congress are decided in the highest court in the land. The Court may, however, decide that the issue lacks significance and simply dismiss it. An appeal is limited to questions of law and is not a review of the facts determined in a trial.

Appellate Jurisdiction   Authority of a court to review decisions of an inferior court. In the federal court system, the courts of appeals and the Supreme Court have power to review decisions of district courts and other tribunals. All states have courts of appellate jurisdiction to review decisions of lower state courts. The losing party in a lawsuit generally has the right to appeal the decision to an appellate court. *See also* JURISDICTION, page 267.

Significance   Courts of appellate jurisdiction serve mainly as a check upon errors of law, rather than fact, that might arise in the course of trials in lower courts. They also serve to give the losing party a second chance to win the case. The scope of appellate jurisdiction—that is, the types of cases and questions that may be appealed—is determined by rules of procedure established by the courts or by the legislative body.

Arbitration   A method of settling a dispute in which the parties to the dispute select the arbitrators and agree to accept their decision as binding. About half the states authorize arbitration and make decisions enforceable by the courts. *See also* ARBITRATION, pages 430 and 532; CONCILIATION, page 254.

Significance   Arbitration provides an informal forum for settlement of disputes, saves the time and expense of court action, and relieves the burden of crowded court dockets. Technical matters can be arbitrated by experts in the field of the dispute. The American Arbitration Association, a private organization, provides a panel of available arbitrators. Arbitration is an important part of a growing movement toward alternative methods of dispute resolution that can avoid costly lawsuits.

Attorney General   The head of the Department of Justice and a member of the President's Cabinet. The Attorney General serves as legal adviser to the President and to the executive branch on the scope of their authority, and as the chief law enforcement officer of the United States. The Attorney General has been a member of the Cabinet since 1789, but the Department of Justice was not established until 1870. The Attorney General directs the work of federal district attorneys, U.S. marshals, and federal penal institutions. Criminal investigations and the conduct of lawsuits involving the United States fall under the charge of the Attorney General. An attorney general, frequently an elected official, is also found in each of the states, also serving as a legal

adviser and law enforcement officer. *See also* ATTORNEY GENERAL, page 605; DE-
PARTMENT OF JUSTICE, page 285.

Significance   The office of attorney general is one of the most powerful
in government. The Attorney General's opinions on legal matters, published
as *Opinions of the Attorney General,* have the force of law unless overturned
by a court. The emphasis given to enforcement of particular laws, such as antitrust or civil rights laws, depends largely on the discretion of the Attorney
General. At the national level, broad discretion is vested in the Attorney General in the areas of immigration, citizenship, and subversion.

Brief   A document prepared by an attorney for presentation to a court, containing arguments and data in support of a case. The brief will embody points
of law, precedents, and, in a case involving major social issues, relevant economic, sociological, and other scientific evidence. Despite its name, a brief
may be quite lengthy.

Significance   A well-prepared brief is often used by judges in preparing
their opinions. A brief containing substantial nonlegal data is known as a
"Brandeis Brief," named after former Supreme Court Justice Louis D.
Brandeis. As an attorney, Brandeis first used such data, in addition to strict
reliance on legal precedents, in a case involving regulation of working hours
for women (*Muller v. Oregon,* 208 U.S. 412 [1908]).

Certiorari   An order issued by a higher court to a lower court to send up the
record of a case for review. Most cases reach the U.S. Supreme Court through
the writ of certiorari, as authorized by the Judiciary Act of 1925. The writ is
issued at the discretion of the Court when at least four of the nine justices
agree that the case should be reviewed. *See also* JURISPRUDENCE, page 267;
SUPREME COURT, page 279.

Significance   Though it is commonly assumed that anyone may bring
his or her case to the Supreme Court, only a limited number of cases may be
appealed as a matter of right. In all other cases, the party must petition the
Court to issue a writ of certiorari. Few petitions for certiorari are granted,
thereby leaving the lower court's decision as final. Only cases of importance
reaching far beyond the interests of the parties to the suit tend to be heard.
Often the Court limits its grant of certiorari to specific questions, rather than
reviewing all elements of the trial or of lower court decisions. Petitions
granted have rarely exceeded 200 cases a year, but in recent years fewer than
2 percent of approximately 6000 petitions for certiorari are granted, about
100 per year.

Challenge   Objection to having a prospective juror serve on a jury. A juror
may be challenged by either party. A challenge may be either for "cause" or
"peremptory." An unlimited number of challenges may be made for cause
with approval of the presiding judge. Peremptory challenges, for which no
reason need be given, are limited to a specific number, which varies from
state to state and depends upon the nature of the offense involved. For crimes
punishable by death, as many as 40 peremptory challenges may be allowed;
as few as 5 may be permitted for minor offenses. But a peremptory challenge

may not be used by a prosecutor or defendant to exclude a person because of race in a criminal case (*Batson v. Kentucky,* 476 U.S. 79 [1986]; *Georgia v. McCollum,* 505 U.S. 42 [1992]) or by a private litigant in a civil case (*Edmonson v. Leesville Concrete Co.,* 500 U.S. 614 [1991]). Challenges based on gender are also prohibited (*J.E.B. v. Alabama ex rel. T.B.* 114 S. Ct. 1419 [1994]). *See also* JURY, page 268; *Norris v. Alabama,* page 364.

Significance Both parties to a case are entitled to a trial by an impartial jury. The challenge permits counsel to remove prospective jurors who show bias or who, for any reason, appear unfit to sit in judgment. The limit placed on peremptory challenges prevents unreasonable delay in filling the jury panel. Denial of peremptory challenges based on race or gender is intended to ensure a jury that is representative of the community but is difficult to monitor unless overdone.

Charge A statement by the judge to the jury at the conclusion of a trial to aid the jury in reaching its verdict. The judge instructs the jury in the law governing the case and reviews the evidence. The authority of the judge to comment on the facts of a case, as distinguished from the law involved, varies from state to state; federal judges have wide latitude. *See also* JURY, page 268.

Significance The charge to the jury serves to refresh the minds of the jurors, particularly after a lengthy trial. It is for the jury to weigh the truth or falsity of the evidence, but the jury is bound by the law as interpreted by the judge. If the judge is careless in the charge or demonstrates bias, the case may be overturned by a higher court. Nevertheless, the charge to the jury may play a major role in the verdict the jury eventually reaches.

Chief Justice The highest judicial officer of the United States or of a state. The Chief Justice of the United States, who is appointed for a life term by the President with the consent of the Senate, presides over sessions of the U.S. Supreme Court, assigns the writing of opinions, and performs a variety of administrative duties as head of the federal court system. In the states, the chief justices are chosen in a variety of ways—appointment, election, seniority—usually for a limited term. Their duties are similar to those of the Chief Justice of the United States, although in many states they lack control over lower court administrative matters.

Significance Aside from administrative duties and a slightly higher salary, chief justices have no more power than other members of the high court in deciding cases. The position does carry considerable prestige, however, and the chief justice may be in a position to use the post as presiding officer to influence the course of decision making.

Circuit Court A general trial court in the states, sometimes called a "district court" or a "superior court." In many states, the court serves several counties and the judges go on "circuit" from one county to another, according to a schedule. In most states, the judges of these courts are elected by the voters of a particular county or circuit, with terms varying from two to six years. These are courts of "original jurisdiction," where important civil and criminal cases begin, trials are held, and juries are frequently used. Cases from minor courts, such as justices of the peace or municipal courts, may be appealed to circuit courts.

Significance   For most people, the circuit court represents their main contact with the judicial branch of the government. This includes not only parties to a suit but witnesses and jurors as well. Hence, it is vital that trial courts be efficiently administered in order to maintain respect for the law. Competent judges and juries and simplified procedures, frequently lacking in these courts, are goals of proponents of state judicial reform.

Civil Law   The code regulating conduct between private persons. It is to be distinguished from criminal law, which regulates individual conduct and is enforced by the government. Under civil law, the government provides the forum for the settlement of disputes between private parties in such matters as contracts, domestic relations, business relations, and auto accidents. The government may be plaintiff or defendant in a civil suit, but, in a criminal case, the government is always the prosecutor. Most civil cases in both state and federal courts are tried without jury. Where juries are used, some states authorize trial by a jury of fewer than twelve persons, and decision by less than unanimous vote. *See also* CRIMINAL LAW, page 259; TORT, page 282.

Significance   Civil law provides stability in private arrangements. Thus, a person who enters into a legal contract can seek the aid of the civil law and the courts to enforce the contract. Civil law provides a substitute for private duels as a means of settling private disputes. The government not only provides an impartial tribunal but also will see that any judgment reached (a money award, for example) is enforced.

Class Action   A lawsuit in which one or more persons sue or are sued as representatives of a larger group similarly situated. The class action makes it possible for persons with small individual claims and inadequate financial resources to represent others, so as to make a lawsuit financially viable. The Court's decision in such cases may be more sweeping in application than is usually the case. Class action suits have made it possible for litigants to overcome the general rule that a plaintiff in a suit must have an interest at stake beyond that of the general public. The courts have thus been able to entertain suits on major social issues in which the plaintiff was not the only person subject to possible injury, such as in the case of legislative apportionment. *See also* ACCESS TO COURTS, page 247; DIVERSITY OF CITIZENSHIP, page 260; JUSTICIABLE QUESTION, page 269.

Significance   Although class action suits have been possible for many years, their number has increased substantially since the 1940s as vehicles that involve civil rights, legislative apportionment, welfare, consumer protection, and environmental problems. Class actions involving medical claims, for example, are increasingly common. Two Supreme Court decisions during its 1973–1974 term, however, stemmed the tide of some class action suits. In one case, the Court refused to permit a class action suit brought to a federal court under diversity jurisdiction against a corporation for pollution damage to property because each person in the class did not have a claim for the $10,000 or more then (now $50,000) required for federal court jurisdiction

(*Zahn v. International Paper Co.,* 414 U.S. 291 [1973]). In the other, the Court ruled that persons initiating a class action suit against stock brokerage houses for alleged overcharges of more than 2 million people must notify, at their own expense, all other persons in the class (*Eisen v. Carlisle & Jacquelin,* 417 U.S. 156 [1974]). The Supreme Court's limiting rules sharply decreased the use of class action suits except by well-organized groups. In 1976, Congress authorized state attorneys general to bring class action antitrust suits on behalf of state citizens.

Code   A compilation of laws in force, classified according to subject matter. Federal laws currently in force are collected in the *United States Code,* which is kept up-to-date with annual supplements and is revised every six years. Many states have collected and classified their statutes, including pertinent judicial decisions, under the title *Compiled Laws. See also* STATUTE, page171.

Significance   Without a code, one would have to search through the annual statute books for laws relating to a particular subject. Codes collect all related laws under a subject heading for easy reference use. The failure of some states to keep their codes up-to-date creates a hardship for professional legal personnel and laypeople who want to know "what the law is."

Common Law   Judge-made law that originated in England from decisions shaped according to prevailing custom. Decisions were reapplied to similar situations and, thus, gradually became common to the nation. Common law forms the basis of legal procedures in American states, except in Louisiana, where certain French legal traditions are preserved. There is no federal common law because the national government is one of delegated powers; however, federal judges apply state common law in cases involving citizens of different states, where there is no applicable federal statute. A statute overrides the common law, but many statutes are based upon the common law and are interpreted according to the common law tradition. *See also* EQUITY, page 262; *Erie Railroad v. Tompkins,* page 287; PRECEDENT, page 274; STARE DECISIS, page 278.

Significance   Many important matters, such as the idea of a twelve-member jury, are part of the common law. Reliance on precedents (previous judicial decisions) in determining legal rights and duties characterizes the common law tradition. The common law permits judges great flexibility to adjust the law to community needs, thereby enhancing judicial power.

Conciliation   A method by which a third party attempts to settle a controversy between disputants outside the courtroom. It is similar to arbitration except that the decision is not binding upon the parties or enforceable in court. A number of large cities have established a conciliation branch in their judicial structure. *See also* ARBITRATION, page 250.

Significance   Conciliation looks toward less formal proceedings for settlement of disputes in the hope of easing the burden on courts and lessening expenses for litigants. Conciliation has proved to be particularly effective in divorce proceedings and labor disputes. The Dispute Resolution Act of 1980 provides federal aid to the states to strengthen and develop procedures for resolving minor disputes out of court.

Concurrent Jurisdiction   Authority vested in two or more courts to hear cases involving the same subject matter. The term is generally used to indicate those instances in which both federal and state courts may hear the same kind of case. For example, Congress has conferred concurrent jurisdiction upon state and federal courts in suits between citizens of different states where the amount in controversy exceeds $50,000. The parties to such a suit may choose to have their case heard in either a federal or state court. Suits involving less than $50,000 must be heard in state courts. See also DIVERSITY OF CITIZENSHIP, page 260; JURISDICTION, page 267.

Significance   Concurrent jurisdiction may serve to ease the burden on a court if a certain type of case tends to crowd the court dockets. For example, auto accidents between citizens of different states have become quite common. By sharing this kind of case with state courts, federal courts have been freed from a potentially severe caseload.

Constitutional Court   A federal court established under the provisions of Article III of the Constitution. Constitutional courts are limited to the jurisdiction conferred by Article III, and their judges are protected as to tenure and compensation. They are to be distinguished from "legislative courts," which are created by Congress under its delegated powers in Article I. The major constitutional courts are the district courts, courts of appeals, and the Supreme Court. Congress has conferred constitutional status upon certain specialized courts, including the Court of Appeals for the Federal Circuit and the Court of International Trade. See also LEGISLATIVE COURT, page 269.

Significance   Constitutional courts enjoy a greater degree of independence than do legislative courts. Congress has somewhat confused the distinction by conferring constitutional status upon judges of certain specialized or legislative courts while not giving these courts jurisdiction under Article III. In effect, constitutional status today refers mainly to the selection and tenure of judges. In 1982, the Supreme Court struck down the Bankruptcy Reform Act of 1978 because the judges of the new courts created in it did not have the constitutional status under Article III that their assigned duties required (*Northern Pipeline Construction Co. v. Marathon Pipe Line Co.*, 458 U.S. 50).

Constitutional Law   Law that involves interpretation and application of the Constitution. It is concerned largely with defining the extent and limits of governmental power and the rights of individuals. Final decision as to the meaning of the Constitution of the United States rests with the U.S. Supreme Court. In the case of state constitutions, the highest court of the state renders final decisions, with appeal possible to the U.S. Supreme Court if conflict with the national Constitution, laws, or treaties can be shown.

Significance   Constitutional law represents the highest law, and the Constitution, as interpreted by the Supreme Court, is the supreme law of the land. American constitutional law is noted for its flexibility, with the judiciary acting to maintain its vitality to meet changing social and economic conditions. Typically, constitutional law involves interpretation of such vague phrases as "interstate commerce" or "due process of law." Judges wield their greatest power when they are called upon to interpret the Constitution.

Contempt of Court   Disobedience of a court order, or any action that operates to impair the authority of a court or to interfere with its proper functioning. Contempt may be civil or criminal. Civil contempt involves a refusal to honor a court judgment in a civil case. Criminal contempt involves any interference with court proceedings. Both may be punished by fine, imprisonment, or both. Usually, contempt is punished summarily (without trial), when it is committed in the presence of the court, but if a severe sentence is imposed, a separate trial before a different judge may be ordered. A defendant who flagrantly disrupts a trial may be bound and gagged while in court or even removed from the courtroom (*Illinois v. Allen,* 397 U.S. 337 [1970]) while the trial proceeds.

Significance   If a court order is to have any meaning, the court must have power to enforce its order and to punish disobedience. Similarly, judges need authority to maintain order in their courtrooms so that justice may be served. The power to punish criminal contempt may be abused when a judge too hastily censures overemotional lawyers or observers. Equally serious is the conflict with freedom of speech and press that may arise when a judge cites a person for contempt for verbal or published remarks made outside the courtroom that, in the judge's view, obstruct the administration of justice. The Supreme Court has imposed due process hearing requirements upon contempt proceedings involving an extended jail sentence (*Codispoti v. Pennsylvania,* 418 U.S. 506 [1974]).

Coroner   A county official who investigates deaths that occur by violent means and certifies the cause of deaths unattended by a physician. In the case of violent death, the coroner may conduct an investigation, called an "inquest," to determine if death resulted from a criminal act. A jury of six persons hears evidence presented by the county prosecutor. If the verdict is death by criminal act, the coroner may order the arrest of suspected persons. Most coroners are elected, although a number of states have substituted an appointed medical examiner to perform the duties of the coroner and have transferred the inquest function to the prosecutor.

Significance   The office of coroner requires extensive medical knowledge, as well as knowledge of criminal investigation and judicial proceedings. Often, however, the coroner is a layperson with no medical or legal training and, in some cases, is a mortician who may profit personally from the position. Most students of government oppose the election of coroners. The trend is toward the appointment of physicians as medical examiners, the abolishment of the coroner's jury, and the use of the prosecutor for the legal aspects of the office. Coroner or medical examiner offices in large cities employ investigative staffs of persons known as "criminalists."

Court of Appeals   In the national court system, the appellate court below the Supreme Court. A few states also have an intermediate court of appeals, although in Maryland and New York the highest state court is called the Court of Appeals. On the national level, the country is divided into twelve "circuits," including the District of Columbia, each with a court of appeals with 6 to 28 judges, for a national total of 179. Prior to 1948, these courts were known as the Circuit Courts of Appeals. The U.S. Courts of Appeals have only appellate jurisdiction, being empowered to hear appeals from the district courts in their particular circuits and appeals from decisions of independent regulatory commissions, such as the Federal Trade Commission. Each court normally hears cases in panels of three judges but, on occasion, a full court (*en banc*) will sit. Judges are appointed for life by the President with the Senate's consent. *See also* COURT OF APPEALS FOR THE FEDERAL CIRCUIT, page 257.

Significance   In most appeals, decisions of the courts of appeals are final because few cases reach the Supreme Court. Hence, judges of those courts wield considerable power and influence in American law. Review of decisions of independent regulatory commissions gives the Washington, D.C., circuit, in particular, an important role in the development of administrative law. A decision of one court of appeals is binding only within that circuit, but conflicts among circuits are generally resolved by the Supreme Court. Since 1969, case filings in the Courts of Appeals have grown from 11,000 to about 50,000 per year.

Court of Appeals for the Armed Forces   A court established by Congress in 1950 (as the Court of Military Appeals and renamed in 1994) to review court-martial decisions. It is composed of five civilian judges appointed for fifteen years by the President with consent of the Senate. The court is obligated to review decisions affecting top military personnel, as well as those imposing the death penalty; it has discretion to review certain other cases upon petition, such as bad conduct discharges or those involving lengthy prison terms. The court applies military law, a special body of rules developed by Congress, rather than ordinary federal criminal law. Appeals may be made to the Supreme Court by writ of certiorari. *See also* COURT-MARTIAL, page 543; MILITARY LAW, page 563.

Significance   Military service for millions of Americans has caused great concern over the standards and procedures of military justice. The Uniform Code of Military Justice, passed by Congress in 1950, attempts to strengthen the rights of persons in court-martial proceedings while meeting the needs of military discipline. The Court of Appeals for the Armed Forces is part of this reform effort. By requiring that its judges be civilians, Congress has assured civilian control over military justice.

Court of Appeals for the Federal Circuit   A special court established by Congress in 1982 to be on the same footing as the existing twelve Courts of Appeals but with nationwide jurisdiction based on subject matter rather than geographic area. The Court of Appeals for the Federal Circuit consolidates the former Court of Customs and Patent Appeals with the appellate division of the former Court of Claims. Its jurisdiction includes (1) patent, trademark, and copyright cases; (2) appeals from district courts in contract and Internal Revenue cases in which the United States is a defendant; (3) appeals from the Federal Court of Claims, the Court of International Trade, and the Court of Veterans Appeals; and (4) review of administrative rulings by the Patent and Trademark Office, the International Trade Commission, the Secretary of Commerce, rule making of the Department of Veterans Affairs, agency boards of contract appeals, the Merit Systems Protection Board, and certain discrimination cases involving congressional and presidential staff. The Court is a constitutional court of twelve judges appointed for life terms by the President with the Senate's consent. Cases are heard by panels of three or more judges and occasionally by all *(en banc)*. It holds court in Washington, D.C., and wherever a Court of Appeals sits. Its decisions may be reviewed by the Supreme Court.

Significance   The Court of Appeals for the Federal Circuit represents a major reorganization of judicial functions, particularly as related to certain issues in business, trade, and civil service. Prior to 1982, many of the cases within the Court's jurisdiction could be heard in any of the various federal courts, resulting in conflicting rulings. It is the first court of appeals to have specialized subject matter jurisdiction from all over the nation, which takes an immense burden from the regular federal appellate courts and establishes a locus of expertise on critical legal issues.

Court of Federal Claims   A court renamed in 1992 as successor to the Court of Claims (established 1855) and the Claims Court (renamed 1982) to hear claims of private individuals against the government for breach of contract, for injuries caused by negligent behavior of government employees, or for recovery of other claims, such as back pay. It also determines claims referred by Congress and the executive departments. The Court of Federal Claims has sixteen judges appointed for fifteen-year terms by the President, with Senate consent, each of whom holds court individually in Washington, D.C., or anywhere in the United States as needed. Its decisions may be appealed to the Court of Appeals for the Federal Circuit.

Significance   The national government may not be sued without its consent, but it would be grossly inefficient if Congress had to consider each claim. The Court of Federal Claims relieves Congress of this burden and provides aggrieved citizens with access to a specialized court outside the regular federal court system.

Court of International Trade   A special court established by Congress in 1980 (known as the Customs Court from 1926 to 1980) to decide disputes that arise over tariff laws and duties levied on imported goods. Its jurisdiction includes suits involving eligibility for governmental assistance under the Trade Acts of 1974 and 1979 for economic injury to American industry from imports. The Court consists of nine judges appointed for life terms by the President with the Senate's consent. It sits in divisions at principal ports of entry, with its main office in New York City. In 1956, the Court was given constitutional status by Congress. Its decisions may be appealed to the Court of Appeals for the Federal Circuit and ultimately to the Supreme Court.

Significance   The Court of International Trade relieves regular courts of the burden of hearing the many disputes arising over classifications and valuations placed by customs officers on imported goods. The court has developed the competence necessary to deal with the problems raised by the increased volume of international trade.

Court of Veterans Appeals   A court created in 1988 to hear benefits appeals brought by veterans against rulings of the Board of Veterans Appeals in the Department of Veterans Affairs (DVA). The Court of Veterans Appeals is composed of three to seven judges appointed to 15-year terms by the President with the advice and consent of the Senate. Its decisions are reviewable by the Court of Appeals for the Federal Circuit. The Court's principal office is in Washington, D.C., but may meet elsewhere. *See also* DEPARTMENT OF VETERANS AFFAIRS, page 518.

Significance   The Court of Veterans Appeals affords the nation's veterans the opportunity to seek judicial review of their benefits claims. Prior law has prevented veterans from bringing suit over benefits, a prohibition that particularly angered many Vietnam veterans. Nearly 3.5 million veterans and their families receive monthly benefits from the DVA. The Court came into existence largely because critics alleged that the Board of Veterans Appeals ignored due process and rewarded expediency over just claims. Congress also removed a Civil War–era cap on the amount a veteran may pay a lawyer for help with a DVA claim—namely, $10—which was enacted to protect Civil War widows from unscrupulous attorneys but had actually denied veterans the skilled legal help they needed.

Criminal Law   The code that regulates the conduct of individuals, defines crimes, and provides punishment for violations. In criminal cases, the government is always the prosecutor because all crimes are against public order. The major body of criminal law is enacted by states, although the list of federal crimes is growing. Criminal law falls into two categories, felonies and misdemeanors, the former being the more serious. *See also* CIVIL LAW, page 253.

Significance   Criminal law reflects the mores of society and protects the public against wrongdoing. Laws that define criminal acts must be clear so that people are put on notice as to what they may or may not do. Violators are prosecuted under procedures established by the Constitution or other law to assure fair treatment. Government prosecution and punishment for crime serve as a civilized substitute for personal vengeance.

Declaratory Judgment   A court procedure used to declare the rights of parties under a contract, will, or other dispute, before any damage occurs but without ordering any specific action. It is a method of preventive justice contrary to the traditional procedure of suing for damages after the damage results. The national government (since the enactment of the Declaratory Judgments Act of 1934) and most of the states permit the use of this procedure.

Significance   Declaratory judgments provide access to the courts to prevent the doing of a wrong as well as to redress a wrong. They differ from advisory opinions in that the parties must have an actual controversy in which loss or injury is likely to occur. Expensive legal entanglements are often forestalled. A declaratory judgment is a statement of rights, not a binding order, though an order could follow if sought by one of the parties.

District Attorney   A county official, elected in all but five states (Alaska, Connecticut, Delaware, New Jersey, and Rhode Island) for two- or four-year terms, who represents the state in prosecutions against violators of criminal laws. In some states, this official is called the "county attorney," "county prosecutor," or simply "prosecutor." Prosecutions for the national government are handled by United States Attorneys. District attorneys also conduct proceedings before grand juries. In states where grand juries are not used, the district attorney brings charges in the form of an "information." In addition, the district attorney acts as legal adviser to the county and represents the county in lawsuits. *See also* PLEA BARGAINING, page 273; UNITED STATES ATTORNEY, page 283.

Significance   District attorneys wield great power in local government. Decisions of whether to prosecute alleged violators are within their discretionary powers, often conditioned by their political ambitions. Their recommendations to a court regarding bail or sentences are generally given serious consideration. The office has been used as a political stepping-stone by many young attorneys. The conduct of the office may well depend upon the political climate of a given county, resulting in an uneven application of criminal law within the state.

District Court   The federal court of "original jurisdiction," where most federal cases begin. It is the only federal court of general jurisdiction where trials are held, juries are used, and witnesses are called. Both criminal and civil cases arising under federal law are heard. Each state has at least one federal district court; a few have as many as 4, for a total of 89 in the 50 states and a total of 610 authorized judgeships. District courts are also found in Washington, D.C. (15 judges), Puerto Rico (7 judges), Guam (1 judge), the Northern Marianas (1 judge), and the Virgin Islands (2 judges). Each of the 89 courts has from 2 to 28 judges, depending on the volume of business, but each judge holds court separately. Certain cases are heard by a three-judge panel. All judges are appointed for life terms by the President with the Senate's consent, except those serving in Guam, the Northern Marianas, and the Virgin Islands, who have 10-year terms. *See also* BANKRUPTCY, page 431; FEDERAL MAGISTRATE, page 263; TERRITORIAL COURT, page 281.

Significance   The bulk of judicial work in federal courts is conducted by the district courts, mostly civil cases involving such matters as admiralty law, bankruptcy proceedings, torts, civil rights, and postal laws. A small proportion of cases are appealed to courts of appeals, and a few reach the Supreme Court. Thus, for most people, contact with federal justice is limited to district courts. Since 1969, case filings in district courts have grown from 110,000 to nearly 285,000 per year.

Diversity of Citizenship   Lawsuits involving citizens of different states. The Constitution (Art. III, sec. 2) confers jurisdiction in such cases on the federal courts, which, generally, apply relevant state law. Congress has conferred exclusive jurisdiction on state courts for suits between citizens of different states involving no federal question if the amount in controversy is less than $50,000; concurrent jurisdiction is conferred if more than $50,000 is involved. *See also* ACCESS TO COURTS, page 247; CLASS ACTION, page 253; CONCURRENT JURISDICTION, page 255; *Erie Railroad v. Tompkins,* page 287; JURISDICTION, page 267.

Significance A very complicated body of law has developed in diversity of citizenship cases. Originally, the purpose of the constitutional provision was to prevent bias by state courts against out-of-state litigants. Today, federal court dockets are filled with such cases due to the increasing mobility and interrelationships of the American people. Automobile accidents between citizens of different states, for example, can be cause for a federal case. Congressional action giving state courts jurisdiction over diversity of citizenship cases is aimed at reducing pressures on the federal courts. In turn, the federal courts have tried to cut the number of these cases by applying relevant state law, so that litigants will not "shop around" for more favorable treatment under federal law. Moreover, the Supreme Court has held that a class action suit can be brought to a federal court in a diversity of citizenship case involving no federal question only if each person in the class has a claim of $50,000 or more (*Zahn v. International Paper Co.,* 414 U.S. 291 [1973]).

Docket A record of proceedings in a court of justice. It is usually used to indicate the list of cases to be tried in a specific term of court and may also be known as the calendar of cases. *See also* ADMINISTRATIVE OFFICE OF THE UNITED STATES COURTS, page 284; JUDICIAL COUNCIL, page 266.

Significance Dockets in criminal cases must be current and cleared with dispatch in order to meet the constitutional guarantee of a speedy trial in criminal prosecutions. Civil case dockets have become a national scandal, since one may have to wait several years to have a case heard. More judges and courts are necessary to handle the court business generated by a growing population, complex legislation, and increased use of the courts by individuals and groups. Some courts have much more crowded dockets than others. State judicial councils and the Administrative Office of the United States Courts conduct studies to improve the handling of dockets. The U.S. Supreme Court virtually controls its own docket through its discretionary power to determine which cases it will hear.

Eleventh Amendment An amendment to the Constitution, adopted in 1798, that provides that federal courts do not have authority to hear cases brought against a state by an individual citizen of another state or of a foreign state. The Amendment overruled a decision of the Supreme Court in *Chisholm v. Georgia,* 2 Dallas 419 (1793), which had upheld the right of a citizen of one state to sue another state in federal court. *See also* ACCESS TO COURTS, page 247; CIVIL RIGHTS ACTS OF 1866, 1870, 1871, AND 1875, page 376; *Cohens v. Virginia,* page 286; *Maine v. Thiboutot,* page 288.

Significance Although Article III did confer jurisdiction upon federal courts to hear cases between a state and citizens of other states, the states were alarmed by the *Chisholm* decision, which denied the necessity for the traditional requirement of a state's consent to be sued. The states feared the possibility of many suits against them for defaulting on their debts, as well as the loss of "states' rights." The Eleventh Amendment applies to suits against the state itself or against an officer of the state acting in an official capacity (*Will v. Michigan Department of State Police*, 492 U.S. 58 [1989]). In interpreting the Eleventh Amendment, the Supreme Court has sustained the Amendment's principle of sovereign immunity, establishing that a state is immune to suits brought in federal court by its own citizens as well as by citizens of another state. A state may consent to be sued. A state's consent must be explicit or clearly implicit. In 1991, the Court held that the Eleventh Amendment bars suits by Indian tribes against states in federal court without the state's consent (*Blatchford v. Native Village of Noatak*, 501 U.S. 775). Until 1996, it was believed that Congress could abrogate a state's immunity, but legislation authorizing suits against states by Indian tribes with regard to gambling casinos was struck down by the Court in *Seminole Tribe of Florida v. Florida*, 116 S. Ct. 1114 (1996); this dramatic shift in interpretation of the Eleventh Amendment does not, however affect the immunity of a state to federal suit without its consent for persons claiming infringement of rights in violation of the Fourteenth Amendment (*Fitzpatrick v. Bitzer*, 427 U.S. 445 [1976]) or to violations of federal law (*Maine v. Thiboutot*, 448 U.S. 1 [1980]); it does protect state officials from federal suit for failure to carry out state law (*Pennhurst State School and Hospital v. Halderman*, 465 U.S. 89 [1984]). Further, it does not protect a state from being sued in the court of another state (*Nevada v. Hall*, 440 U.S. 410 [1979]).

Equity   A branch of law that provides a remedy if the common law does not apply. The common law is concerned largely with granting of damages after a wrongful action. Equity is designed to provide justice where damages may come too late to be meaningful. In an equity case, the court may order that something be done (specific performance) or forbid certain actions (injunction). In a typical case, the court may order a person to fulfill a contract or forbid a union to go on strike under certain conditions. Equity procedures are less formal than regular court procedures, and juries are seldom used. *See also* COMMON LAW, page 254; DECLARATORY JUDGMENT, page 259; INJUNCTION, page 265.

Significance   Equity is a legal inheritance from England that grew out of petitions to the king to redress wrongs for which the law provided no remedy. It was based largely on abstract principles of justice but has developed its own body of rules and precedents. A few states have separate courts for equity proceedings, sometimes called "chancery." The courts have a wide area of choice in equity cases to provide solutions to impending conflicts. Irreparable damages may thereby be avoided.

Ex Parte   A judicial proceeding by or for one party without contest by an adverse party. In an ex parte proceeding, there may be no adverse party, or a possible adverse party has had no notice of the case. The term "in re" is sometimes used in place of "ex parte."

Significance   Individuals frequently bring actions in their own behalf seeking the aid of the court. A typical ex parte proceeding may involve an uncontested divorce or a case brought by a prisoner seeking a writ of habeas corpus. Such cases are reported under the name of the person bringing the suit preceded by the term "ex parte": *Ex parte Milligan,* for example.

Federal Magistrate   A minor judicial official who holds preliminary hearings in federal criminal cases, issues arrest warrants, sets bail, and, if the parties consent, holds jury and nonjury trials in civil cases or criminal misdemeanor cases and supervises the selection of jurors in felony cases (*Peretz v. United States,* 501 U.S. 923 [1991]). The position was created in 1968 and given enhanced status in 1979. Magistrates are attorneys appointed under a merit selection system by federal district court judges for eight-year terms. About 345 full-time and 150 part-time magistrates are in service. They serve in various locations, making it unnecessary to bring federal cases to the district court immediately; this is essential because some district courts serve an entire state or a large portion thereof. *See also* MAGISTRATE, page 270.

Significance   Federal magistrates were created in 1968 to replace the United States Commissioner system, which had not been reformed for more than 100 years. Commissioners were not necessarily attorneys and were paid by fees; thus, they resembled justices of the peace. The Federal Magistrates Act professionalizes and expands the routine but essential functions of federal district courts.

Felony   A serious crime punishable by death or by imprisonment in a penitentiary for a year or more. The precise character of a felony varies from state to state and is defined by law. Less serious violations of law are called "misdemeanors." Felonies generally include murder, arson, robbery, aggravated assault, and forgery. *See also* JURY, page 268; MISDEMEANOR, page 271.

Significance   Persons accused of felonies are accorded the full protection of constitutional guarantees, such as indictment by grand jury or information and trial by jury. Misdemeanors are generally tried by "summary process," without indictment or trial by jury. Minor state courts rarely have jurisdiction to try felonies, which usually are heard by district or circuit courts. On the national level, felonies are tried in the district courts.

Good Behavior   The term used in Article III, section 1 of the Constitution to indicate that judges of federal courts are to hold their offices "during good behavior" or, in effect, for life. The independence of the federal judiciary is further secured by the provision that their compensation may not be diminished during their continuance in office. A federal judge may be removed only by impeachment, though in 1980 Congress provided for the first time a procedure for disciplining judges, short of impeachment, which includes suspension or certification of disability. *See also* IMPEACHMENT, page 150.

Significance   The life tenure of federal judges is assumed to promote independence and is generally considered among legal scholars as a major reason for the sound reputation of the federal courts. The constitutional guarantee against reduction in compensation was applied by the Supreme Court in *United States v. Will,* 449 U.S. 200 (1980), holding that Congress could not rescind a cost-of-living salary adjustment for federal judges once it has been implemented. Over the years, however, concern has arisen over the question of limiting the term of office, either because of partisan dissatisfaction with the trends of decisions or because of the difficulty of dealing with the occasional instances of judges who are physically or mentally incompetent or who conduct themselves in unethical but not impeachable ways. The judicial discipline legislation enacted in 1980 does provide a mechanism that allows any citizen to bring a complaint and, through the chief judges and conferences of federal courts of appeals and the Judicial Conference chaired by the Chief Justice of the United States, for complaints to be heard and discipline enforced. The sanctions may include request for voluntary retirement, suspension, or any other action considered appropriate under the circumstances, including a recommendation for impeachment.

Grand Jury   A body of from 12 to 23 members who hear evidence presented by the prosecuting attorney against persons accused of a serious crime and who decide whether to present a "true bill" that "indicts" the accused. If indicted, the accused is bound over for trial; if not, he or she goes free. The Fifth Amendment requires that this procedure be done for any capital or infamous crime, generally those for which death or imprisonment may result. Unlike a petit or trial jury, a grand jury does not determine guilt or innocence but only whether the evidence warrants bringing the accused to trial; it meets in secret and decides by a majority rather than a unanimous vote. The grand jury may also conduct investigations on its own when a prosecutor is lax or when official misconduct is suspected. In such cases, any resulting accusation is called a "presentment." The grand jury exercises vast powers under the common law, being empowered to subpoena witnesses and records and to compel testimony under oath. A grand jury is generally unrestrained by the technical procedural rules applicable to criminal trials but "fishing expeditions" are prohibited. A few states permit persons being questioned to have counsel present. More than half of the states have abolished or limited grand jury indictment to capital cases, replacing it with the "information" that permits the prosecutor alone to bring charges. *See also Hurtado v. California,* page 356; INDICTMENT, page 265; INFORMATION, page 265.

Significance   The grand jury procedure is time-consuming and expensive, and the grand jury tends to follow the dictates of the prosecutor. It has been abolished in England, its place of origin, as well as in many states. It does, however, serve as a protection against overzealous prosecutors and as a watchdog against official wrongdoing. It originated with the idea that before an individual could be subjected by capricious prosecutors to the costs and humiliation of a public trial, sufficient evidence to justify such action must be shown and be acceptable to a majority of a grand jury.

Hearing   In an equity case, a hearing is a trial. In a criminal case, a hearing is an examination of the evidence or issues of law to determine if the accused should be held for trial; it is generally referred to as a "preliminary hearing" or "preliminary examination." If a preliminary hearing is held in an equity case, it is called an "interlocutory hearing." *See also* HEARING, page 227.

Significance   The term "hearing" has a technical meaning in law. Whereas in an equity case it is technically the trial of the case, in a criminal proceeding, the hearing is not a trial to determine guilt or innocence but a procedure to protect the accused from unwarranted detention.

Indictment   The formal accusation, drawn up by the prosecutor and brought by a grand jury, charging a person with the commission of a crime. *See also* GRAND JURY, page 264; INFORMATION, page 265.

Significance   Indictment is a procedure to avoid arbitrary accusations and to inform the accused of the precise charges so that he or she can prepare a defense. A faulty or vague indictment justifies dismissal of the case. The cumbersome nature of this procedure, however, has resulted in its widespread replacement by the "information."

Information   An accusation made under oath by a prosecuting attorney before a court, charging a person with a crime. Though regularly used for minor offenses, more than half the states have substituted the information for indictment by grand jury in serious cases as well. The national government is making increased use of the information for noncapital offenses. *See also* GRAND JURY, page 264; INDICTMENT, page 265.

Significance   The trend has definitely been in the direction of substituting the information for the grand jury indictment. Thus, the prosecuting attorney bypasses the grand jury, and final determination of whether the evidence justifies a trial is placed in the hands of the judge. Use of the information instead of the grand jury results from considerations of both efficiency and economy.

Injunction   An order issued by a court in an equity proceeding to compel or restrain the performance of an act by an individual or government official. A "mandatory" injunction demands that something be done, although the term "injunction" generally refers to a restraining order. Violation of an injunction constitutes contempt of court, punishable by fine or imprisonment. *See also* EQUITY, page 262; WRIT, page 284.

Significance   The injunction prevents irreparable damage to an individual's personal or property rights through the power of courts to issue orders without the necessity of a lawsuit after damages are done. Judges enjoy a great deal of discretion to determine the scope of an injunction.

Intermediate Court   A court of appeals below the level of the highest court. It is found in most states except for a few with small populations. In about half the states, county courts function as intermediate courts as well as trial courts by hearing cases de novo (a new trial) appealed from decisions of municipal and justice of the peace courts. "Intermediate" refers to the fact that these courts exercise appellate jurisdiction, with further appeal possible to a higher court.

Significance   The use of the term "intermediate" by students of government reflects the great variety in court organization, structure, nomenclature, and jurisdiction found in the several states. Intermediate courts of appeals serve to lighten the burden on state supreme courts and provide at least one appeal from decisions of minor courts.

Judicial Council   An investigative and advisory agency composed of judges, lawyers, and laypeople to promote efficient administration in state courts. Though their composition and authority vary from state to state, they are generally charged with collecting statistics on court operations and recommending changes in court organization, court procedure, assignment of judges, and other matters to improve the handling of court business. *See also* ADMINISTRATIVE OFFICE OF THE UNITED STATES COURTS, page 284; UNIFIED COURT SYSTEM, page 282.

Significance   Little attention has been paid to the efficient administration of court business compared with the amount of concern over the outcome of particular cases. The judicial council is a relatively recent innovation, recognizing the importance of applying sound administrative techniques to the operations of courts. The judicial council acts as a unifying force to counteract the decentralization of most state court systems and the independence of locally elected judges. On the national level, the Administrative Office of the United States Courts performs duties similar to those of a judicial council. In 1984, Congress established an independent State Justice Institute to assist in the improvement of state court administration.

Judicial Review   The power of the courts to declare acts of the legislative and executive branches unconstitutional. All courts, both state and national, may exercise this authority, though a final decision is usually made by the highest state or federal court. Though the U.S. Constitution is silent on this matter, the Supreme Court asserted the power of judicial review in the famous case of *Marbury v. Madison,* 1 Cranch 137 (1803). Judicial review is based on the assumptions that the Constitution is the supreme law, that acts contrary to the Constitution are void, and that the judiciary is the guardian of the Constitution. *See also Ashwander v. TVA,* page 286; CONSTITUTIONAL LAW, page 255; *Dred Scott v. Sandford,* page 287; *Eakin v. Raub,* page 287; *Marbury v. Madison,* page 289; SUPREME COURT, page 279.

Significance   Judicial review is one of the basic principles of the American system of government. It places in the judiciary and, in particular, the Supreme Court vast power to determine the meaning of the Constitution and to act as final arbiter over questions involving the power of governmental officials at both the state and national levels. Several hundred state laws and about 115 federal laws have been declared unconstitutional by the Supreme Court. Though the number is small compared with the total number of laws passed, a declaration of unconstitutionality may deter a long line of similar legislation. Courts are reluctant to exercise this vast power because due respect must be accorded the other branches of government and because the Constitution is susceptible to varying interpretations. A court decision on the Constitution can be changed only by amending the Constitution or by a change of view by the court itself. The exercise of judicial review invariably generates widespread comment from those satisfied or dissatisfied with the decision, particularly when the court is divided in its decision and the issue has major social or economic implications. Throughout American history, courts have played a major role in the development of public policy by the exercise of this power. Prior to 1937, the Supreme Court used judicial review authority mainly to protect property rights. Since then, judicial review has been used most often in defense of civil liberties.

Judiciary   A collective term for courts and judges. In the United States, the judiciary is divided into the national and state judiciary. Each is independent of the other, with the exception that the U.S. Supreme Court may, under special circumstances involving federal questions, review a state court decision. Jurisdiction of particular courts or judges is determined by either the national or state constitutions and laws.

Significance   An independent judiciary, coequal with the legislative and executive branches, is one of the cornerstones of the American system of government. The judiciary maintains the appropriate allocations of authority among the three branches of government and between the national and state governments. In addition, the judiciary protects the people against excessive exercise of power by the legislature and the executive and provides an impartial forum for the settlement of civil and criminal cases. The selection of judges by political appointment or by election and an increasing reliance upon courts for the settlement of public policy disputes assure a key role for the judiciary in the American political system.

Jurisdiction   Authority vested in a court to hear and decide a case. The term literally means power "to say the law." The jurisdiction of national courts is controlled by the Constitution and by Congress. State court jurisdiction is similarly determined by state constitutions and statutes. Jurisdiction may be assigned according to such factors as the amount of money involved or the type of case. Courts may exercise original or appellate jurisdiction, or both. *See also* ACCESS TO COURTS, page 247; ADMIRALTY JURISDICTION, page 248; APPELLATE JURISDICTION, page 250; CONCURRENT JURISDICTION, page 255; DIVERSITY OF CITIZENSHIP, page 260; *Ex parte McCardle,* page 288; ORIGINAL JURISDICTION, page 272.

Significance   Lawsuits must be brought to the court that has authority "to say the law" in such a case. A case brought to the wrong court will either not be heard or be overruled by an appellate court. It is common practice in lawsuits for the attorney to show immediately that the court has authority to hear the case. The separate jurisdiction of state and national courts helps preserve the federal system because each government maintains control over the application of its law. Within any court system, specialized jurisdiction tends to promote expertness in the courts.

Jurisprudence   The science or philosophy of law. Jurisprudence involves the study of the origins and functions of law, the place of law in society, and the likely consequences of particular courses of legal action. *See also* JUDICIAL REVIEW, page 266; STATUTORY CONSTRUCTION, page 279.

Significance   Jurisprudence would appear to be the province of legal scholars, but no important piece of legislation or lawsuit is free of jurisprudential implications. Judicial opinions, particularly in appellate courts, ordinarily take into account the effect that a given line of reasoning will have beyond the immediate parties to the suit. The U.S. Supreme Court, in the exercise of its discretion to select the cases it will hear (writ of certiorari), tries to limit itself to those cases and issues apt to have the most far-reaching impact on society. In this way, the Court can either give new direction to the law or bring the law into line with actual practice.

Jury   An impartial body that sits in judgment on charges brought in either criminal or civil cases. A trial jury is also known as a "petit jury," to distinguish it from a grand jury. Under the common law, a trial jury must consist of twelve persons, and their decision must be unanimous. The national government and many states authorize trial by less than twelve in certain cases and a decision by less than a unanimous vote. Jury trials may be waived by the accused. Generally, the jury is the judge of the facts, though some states permit the jury to determine the law and the punishment as well as the facts. The jury is assumed to be impartial, and no persons may be deliberately and systematically excluded from jury service because of class, race, or gender. The Supreme Court has ruled that due process requires that persons accused of serious crimes are entitled to a trial by jury (*Duncan v. Louisiana,* 391 U.S. 145 [1968]), defined a serious crime as one for which imprisonment for more than six months is possible (*Baldwin v. New York,* 399 U.S. 66 [1970]), and authorized states to provide juries of less than twelve (but a minimum of six) for the trial of serious offenses (*Williams v. Florida,* 399 U.S. 78 [1970]; *Ballew v. Georgia,* 435 U.S. 223 [1978]). Verdict by less than unanimous vote is permissible, except in the case of a six-person jury (*Johnson v. Louisiana,* 406 U.S. 356 [1972]; *Burch v. Louisiana,* 441 U.S. 130 [1979]). In federal criminal trials, a jury of twelve and a unanimous verdict is still required. Jury selection proceedings must be open to the public (*Press-Enterprise Co. v. Superior Court of California, Riverside County,* 464 U.S. 501 [1984]). Trial by jury is provided for in Article III, section 2 and by the Sixth and Seventh Amendments of the U.S. Constitution. *See also* CAPITAL PUNISHMENT, page 296; CHALLENGE, page 251; CHARGE, page 252; GRAND JURY, page 264; *Norris v. Alabama,* page 364; PANEL, page 273.

Significance   The right to be judged by a jury of one's peers is a long-standing tradition of the common law. The competence of the average jury and the motivations that may lead it to a particular verdict are frequently questioned. Yet, the jury system brings the common sense of the community to bear upon the laws of the state or nation. It permits the citizen to participate in the administration of justice and gives the people more confidence in the application of the law.

Justice of the Peace   A judicial officer empowered to try minor civil and criminal cases, such as traffic violations or breaches of peace. In some areas, the justice of the peace conducts preliminary hearings to determine whether a person should be held for trial in a higher court. The justice of the peace is usually elected in rural areas and small towns for a two-year term and is generally paid through fees and fines. Not many justices of the peace are learned in the law, although a few states require a law degree. *See also* MAGISTRATE, page 270.

Significance   The office of justice of the peace has a long tradition but the fee system, it is charged, leads to corruption and biased judgment.

Supporters argue that the justice of the peace provides an inexpensive method of dispensing justice in petty cases. In many urban areas, the office of justice of the peace is being replaced by municipal courts. The Supreme Court has held that a nonlawyer judge may hear a case, provided an appeal is available to a lawyer judge (*North v. Russell*, 427 U.S. 328 [1976]).

Justiciable Question   A dispute that can be settled through the exercise of judicial power. For a controversy to be justiciable, (1) it must be an actual case, not a trumped-up suit; (2) the person bringing the suit must have a direct interest at stake and have standing to sue; (3) the case must be ripe for adjudication, other remedies having been exhausted; and (4) the court must have jurisdiction over the subject. A question may be ruled "political" rather than justiciable if the court believes that the other branches of the government are better equipped or constitutionally responsible to handle the matter. *See also* ACCESS TO COURTS, page 247; CLASS ACTION, page 253; *Frothingham v. Mellon,* page 288; JURISDICTION, page 267; POLITICAL QUESTION, page 274.

Significance   The rules regarding justiciable questions help preserve the separation of powers by confining courts to their proper functions. While a court may exercise considerable discretion to determine justiciability, careful adherence to the rules assures that courts will not become embroiled in issues over which they lack competence or that will weaken the judiciary vis-à-vis the other branches. The wide use of "class actions" has somewhat altered the rule of standing to sue by permitting a person not solely liable to sustain a direct injury to bring a suit on behalf of himself or herself and others similarly situated. This has enabled the courts in recent years to entertain several important issues, such as integration and legislative apportionment, involving questions in which litigants did not have an interest beyond that of the general public.

Law   A rule of conduct prescribed by or accepted by the governing authority of a state and enforced by courts. The law may derive from a constitution, legislative acts, and administrative rules or may develop through custom, as have common law and equity. The law controls relations among people and between them and their government. Penalties are imposed for violation of law. *See also* ADMINISTRATIVE LAW, page 248; CIVIL LAW, page 253; COMMON LAW, page 254; CONSTITUTIONAL LAW, page 255; CRIMINAL LAW, page 259; EQUITY, page 262; INTERNATIONAL LAW, page 557; ORDINANCE, page 622.

Significance   Democracy is distinguished from totalitarian government largely in terms of the place of law in society. A totalitarian system operates by the whim of the rulers. In a free society, law provides advance notice of what legally is right and wrong. Conflicts are resolved by application of pre-existing rules. Law must emanate from and be enforced only by duly constituted authority.

Legislative Court   A court established by Congress under its delegated powers rather than under the authority granted in Article III of the Constitution. The judges of legislative courts need not have life tenure, may be assigned nonjudicial functions, and have only that jurisdiction that Congress assigns. For example, the Territorial Courts of Guam and the Virgin Islands were created under congressional power to govern the territories. The judges have limited terms, and the courts have regular federal jurisdiction, as well as jurisdiction over matters that ordinarily belong in state courts. Another example is the Court of Appeals for the Armed Forces created under the power to make rules for the armed forces. *See also* CONSTITUTIONAL COURT, page 255; UNITED STATES TAX COURT, page 424.

Significance   By establishing legislative courts, Congress provides flexibility to the federal court system and relieves the regular courts, and Congress itself, of some burdens. Legislative courts introduce a degree of specialization into the judicial system but are distinguished mainly by the limited terms assigned to the judges. In 1982, the Supreme Court struck down a law establishing a new bankruptcy court system as a legislative court because, in the Court's view, the duties assigned to the judges required status as defined by Article III of the Constitution (*Northern Pipeline Construction Co. v. Marathon Pipe Line Co.,* 458 U.S. 50).

Magistrate   A minor judicial officer, usually elected in urban areas, with jurisdiction over traffic violations, minor criminal offenses, and civil suits involving small amounts of money. Magistrates may also conduct preliminary hearings in serious criminal cases and commit the offender for trial in a higher court. In some areas, the magistrate court is called a "police court," and its authority is similar to that of a justice of the peace serving in a rural area. Juries, though rarely used in magistrate courts, may consist of only six jurors. *See also* FEDERAL MAGISTRATE, page 263; JUSTICE OF THE PEACE, page 268.

Significance   Magistrate courts have been established to handle the large number of cases that arise in urban communities. Unlike the justice of the peace, a magistrate is usually paid a salary rather than a fee per case. The magistrate can dispose of large numbers of petty offenses, thereby relieving the burden on higher courts and facilitating matters for offenders. Increasingly, cities are turning to specialized courts, such as traffic courts and domestic relations courts, to handle the large volume of work.

Mandamus   An order issued by a court to compel performance of an act. A writ of mandamus may be issued to an individual or corporation as well as to a public official. In the case of public officers, a writ will be issued only to compel performance of a "ministerial" act—one that the officer has a clear legal duty to perform. If the officer has discretion to determine whether he or she will perform an act, the court will not order its performance. *See also* WRIT, page 284.

Significance   The authority of the court may be brought to bear upon anyone who fails to perform an act that someone has a legal right to expect. Thus, a contract must be fulfilled as agreed upon, or a court order will be issued. Similarly, a public officer who refuses to issue a license to someone authorized to have one may be ordered to do so by the court. Failure to obey the court order is contempt of court.

Marshal   An official of the federal Department of Justice attached to each federal district court. The duties of U.S. marshals correspond to those of sheriffs in county governments. They make arrests in federal criminal cases, keep accused persons in custody, secure jurors, serve legal papers, keep order in the courtroom, and execute orders and decisions of the court. Marshals are appointed by the President, subject to the Senate's confirmation, for four-year terms.

Significance Marshals are part of the executive, not the judicial, branch and perform federal police duties. Although the job is not quite as glamorous as portrayed on television westerns, modern-day United States marshals perform important functions in enforcement of federal law. Deputy marshals are also attached to most district courts.

Misdemeanor A minor criminal offense. The precise nature of a misdemeanor varies from state to state, where it is defined by law. It may include such offenses as traffic violations, petty theft, disorderly conduct, and gambling. Punishment is usually limited to light jail terms of less than one year or to fines. Minor courts such as justices of the peace or municipal courts usually hear such cases without a jury. *See also* FELONY, page 263.

Significance Most violations of law are misdemeanors, which constitute the bulk of judicial business in the United States. Many such cases are handled by "summary process," without indictment or trial, and are settled by payment of a fine. Misdemeanors are distinguished from felonies, more serious violations of law, which require more formalized proceedings in arrests and trials.

Missouri Plan A method of selecting state judges that combines both appointment and election. In Missouri, judges of the Supreme Court, of courts of appeals, and of courts in St. Louis and Kansas City are appointed by the governor from a list of three names prepared by a commission composed of lawyers and laypersons. The judge serves one year and then stands for election on the basis of his or her record. There is no opposition candidate. If the voters approve, the judge serves for six to twelve years, depending on the court. If the candidate is defeated, the procedure is started anew. Other communities in the state may come under the plan if the voters approve. A similar plan exists in California; here, however, the governor nominates the candidate subject to approval of the commission, rather than from a list prepared by it.

Significance The issue of appointment versus election of judges is one of the "great debates" of American politics, though most state judges are elected. The Missouri Plan has been hailed as a satisfactory compromise in that it retains power in the electorate while reducing the pressure on judges from the consequences of specific rulings and from the necessity of campaigning for office. At least 24 states use the Missouri Plan for some of their courts.

Obiter Dictum A statement in a court opinion on an issue not precisely involved in the case. Because such statements are not relevant to the conclusions reached in the decision, they are not binding as precedents. *See also* OPINION OF THE COURT, page 272.

Significance   Obiter dicta provide clues to the thinking of the court on issues related to the case at hand and may influence the decisions of the court in similar cases.

Opinion of the Court   A written statement, usually of an appellate court, announcing the court's decision and the reasoning on which it is based. The opinion of the Court represents the views of the majority of the judges and, especially on the U.S. Supreme Court, is often accompanied by concurring or dissenting opinions. The majority opinion will announce the rules of law pertinent to the decision, instruct the lower court on next steps, and also serve as a public justification for the ruling. A *concurring* opinion supports the conclusion but offers different reasons for reaching that conclusion. A *dissenting* opinion disagrees with the decision and, often in strong terms, the reasoning. An unsigned decision *per curiam* (by the court) is written at times, usually to dispose of an uncomplicated issue, without assigning responsibility for developing an extended opinion. *See also* OBITER DICTUM, page 271; UNITED STATES REPORTS, page 283.

Significance   The opinion of the court must satisfy a majority of the judges, often a delicate task. On the Supreme Court, the Chief Justice assigns the opinion if he or she is part of the majority; if not, assignment is made by the senior justice who votes with the majority. Too many concurring opinions can weaken the force of a majority opinion or result in a plurality rather than a clear majority opinion, while a strong dissenting opinion can challenge the logic of the decision and cast public doubt on its validity. At times concurring or dissenting views have eventually become the law. Thus, the crafting of opinions often involves subtle but important considerations of legal thought and public policy.

Original Intent   An approach to constitutional interpretation that would limit the meaning of the Constitution to its clearly stated words or clearly discernible intentions. Jurists who employ this doctrine try to determine the original meaning of the Constitution by examining the writings of the framers, Constitutional Convention debates, and the grammatical structure of the document itself. If the language of the Constitution and historical documents do not provide guidance on modern problems, the doctrine of original intent holds that judges should seek ways to uphold rather than abrogate legislative actions involving constitutional interpretation. *See also* CONSTITUTIONAL CONSTRUCTION, page 35.

Significance   Original intent gained prominence in the 1980s as Reagan administration officials and Reagan judicial appointees used it as a means of promoting judicial restraint and to express dissatisfaction with prior expansive decisions of the Supreme Court. This method of constitutional interpretation rejects the idea of a "living Constitution," which has guided judicial interpretation throughout most of American history and has made it possible to adapt the Constitution to changing circumstances without extensive use of the amending process.

Original Jurisdiction   The authority of a court to hear a case in the first instance. Generally, courts of original jurisdiction are minor courts or trial courts. They are to be distinguished from courts of appellate jurisdiction, which hear cases on appeal from courts of original jurisdiction. A court that is primarily appellate may have some original jurisdiction. The U.S. Supreme Court, for example, has original jurisdiction over suits involving ambassadors and those to which a state is a party. *See also* JURISDICTION, page 267.

Significance   Original jurisdiction is often "final" jurisdiction because few cases are heard on appeal by higher courts. Even if a case is appealed, the determination of the facts in the case by the judge or jury in the court of original jurisdiction is generally considered to be final, with only questions of law heard by the appellate court.

Panel   The list of persons summoned for jury duty. A trial jury is "impaneled" when the parties to the case have agreed to the selection of the jurors from the panel. Panels are selected in a variety of ways in different states, by jury commissioners or county or township clerks, or by other officials. Names are usually selected from voting or taxpayer lists. A 1968 law requires random selection from voter lists for federal juror panels. In 1972, Congress lowered the age requirement for federal jury service to eighteen. *See also* CHALLENGE, page 251; JURY, page 268.

Significance   The major problem in selecting jury panels is to assure fair trials by impaneling a representative cross-section of the community. State laws may exempt public employees, professional persons, and those who will suffer financial hardship while serving. As a result of these exemptions, it may be difficult to get a representative panel to enable an accused person to be tried by a jury of his or her peers. No persons may be systematically excluded from jury panels because of sex, race, religion, or color.

Parole   Release from prison prior to the expiration of a sentence. The release is based on the good behavior of the prisoner, who may be returned to prison if he or she violates the conditions of the parole. In 1984, Congress abolished the parole system for federal prisoners in the Comprehensive Crime Control Act and established the use of fixed sentences (reduced for good behavior), effective November 1, 1987. In the states, paroles are generally administered by parole boards or by the governors. *See also* SENTENCE, page 277.

Significance   The possibility of parole encourages prisoners to be on their good behavior and to demonstrate fitness to return to a normal life. The parole system emphasizes rehabilitation rather than punishment. Major criticisms of parole practice are that parole boards are often composed of political appointees rather than properly qualified persons and the lack of sufficient numbers of qualified parole officers to supervise the parolee. Increased use of fixed rather than indeterminate sentencing in most states has led to a decline in the use of the parole system based largely on the failure of parole to decrease the number of repeat offenders and on the theory that a fixed punishment may deter criminals. About 700,000 adults were on parole in 1995.

Plea Bargaining   Negotiations between a prosecutor and an accused person or his or her counsel to secure a guilty plea from the accused in exchange for a lesser charge or promise of leniency. *See also* DISTRICT ATTORNEY, page 260.

Significance   Plea bargaining takes place in the majority of criminal cases in the United States. The accused is often willing to bargain to avoid a harsher charge and sentence and to avoid the humiliation and cost of a trial. The prosecutor, in turn, is eager to secure a conviction and also to avoid the time and rigors of a trial. The procedure is criticized because of its obvious potential for abuse, political or otherwise; the extensive discretion it places in the hands of prosecuting attorneys; and the resultant failure to determine the merits of individual cases in open court. Yet, without considerable plea bargaining, chaos would be likely to result in the criminal justice system because of the high rate of crime combined with the lack of adequate numbers of law enforcement and judicial personnel. The Supreme Court has upheld the practice of plea bargaining, even though recognizing that it generally involves a form of self-incrimination made under considerable pressure. Such discretion in the hands of the prosecutor is proper, however, provided the accused is free to accept or reject the offer (*Bordenkircher v. Hayes,* 434 U.S. 357 [1978]).

Political Question   A doctrine enunciated by the Supreme Court holding that certain constitutional issues cannot be decided by the courts but are to be decided by the executive or legislative branches. The doctrine has generally been invoked when the issue would place the courts in serious conflict with other branches, involve the courts in political controversies, or raise serious enforcement problems. Examples of "political questions" include presidential power to recognize foreign governments, congressional power to determine whether constitutional amendments have been ratified within a reasonable time, and congressional and presidential power to determine whether states have a republican form of government. *See also* ACCESS TO COURTS, page 247; *Baker v. Carr,* page 176; JUSTICIABLE QUESTION, page 269; *Luther v. Borden,* page 55.

Significance   The doctrine of the political question is a self-imposed restraint on the Court's power of judicial review. Thus, it is for the Court to decide which issues are "political" and which are "justiciable." Few cases have involved "political questions," and it is impossible to predict with certainty what issues will be considered to be "political." Much depends upon the political climate of the day and the viewpoint of the majority of the Supreme Court. The most dramatic example of the political question doctrine involved the Supreme Court's decisions on legislative apportionment. After holding that courts could not intervene, the Court changed its mind and dramatically altered the nature of legislative representation (*Baker v. Carr,* 369 U.S. 186 [1962]).

Precedent   A court ruling bearing upon subsequent legal decisions in similar cases. Judges rely upon precedents in deciding cases. The common law is based primarily upon reasoning from precedents. *See also* COMMON LAW, page 254; STARE DECISIS, page 278.

Significance   Legal disputes in the United States are fought out largely over the application of precedents to a particular controversy. A lawyer will try to convince the court that the precedents serve to prove his or her case. Judges, in turn, must decide between competing precedents in reaching a decision. If a precedent appears to be unreasonable or dated, a court may specifically overrule it and establish a new precedent.

Privileged Communication   A discussion between specified individuals that neither can legally be compelled to divulge. This privilege usually extends to communications between husband and wife, attorney and client, priest and penitent, and, with some limitations, physician and patient and psychotherapist and patient.

Significance   Privileged communication is one of the major rules for exclusion of evidence in a trial. Though jurisdictions vary on the precise application of what may be excluded as privileged, the general rule is in support of the complete confidentiality of conversations with one's spouse, lawyer, clergyman, physician or psychotherapist. The protection of the desired relationship between those categories of persons is deemed to be more important than the need to use those particular sources of information in the administration of justice. Because of a Supreme Court ruling that the press has no special right to withhold evidence received in the course of gathering news (*Branzburg v. Hayes,* 408 U.S. 665 [1972]), several states have enacted "shield laws" that extend the concept of privileged communication to journalists and their confidential sources.

Probate Court   A court, used in about half the states, with jurisdiction over wills, estates, guardians, and minors. Probate courts are found at the county level; in states without separate probate courts, such matters are handled by regular county courts. In some areas, probate courts are called "surrogate courts." Much of the work connected with probate courts is administrative in nature, concerned largely with proper handling of estates by guardians and administrators and the care of minors. Juries are rarely used. Probate judges are generally elected.

Significance   Probating, or proving the authenticity of a will, and the subsequent administration of an estate are important elements of American law, reflecting concern with property rights. The rights of minors, too, are protected. Probate courts exist, in the main, to help people, rather than to punish wrongdoers. One major problem is that separate probate courts tend to proliferate an already complicated court system.

Probation   Suspension of the sentence of a person convicted of a crime, permitting him or her to remain free, subject to good behavior. Persons on probation are subject to supervision by an agent of the court. If the person's conduct justifies it, he or she will be released from probation after a period of time determined by the court. Failure to observe the terms of probation subjects the offender to possible imprisonment. *See also* RECIDIVISM, page 276.

Significance   Imprisonment may do more harm than good to numerous offenders. Probation permits offenders to demonstrate to the court that they can become good citizens. This technique has been particularly effective with juvenile delinquents. A competent probation office staff is essential for successful administration of probation. Probation is also encouraged because of overcrowding of jails and prisons. Nearly 3 million adults were on probation in 1995.

Public Defender   An official whose duty it is to act as attorney for persons accused of crime who are unable to secure their own counsel. Since the Supreme Court ruled in *Gideon v. Wainwright,* 372 U.S. 335 (1963) that indigent defendants must be furnished counsel, many state and local governments have established public defender systems. In 1970, Congress authorized the appointment of federal public defenders by federal courts of appeals or, as an alternative, the establishment of community defender organizations financed by federal grants. *See also* LEGAL SERVICES CORPORATION, page 519; RIGHT TO COUNSEL, page 333.

Significance   The use of a public defender is considered to be superior to assignment of counsel by the court or by a private legal aid association. Assigned counsels vary not only in ability but also in willingness to devote attention to the defendant's interests. Moreover, private counsel frequently lack the resources available to the public prosecutor. The public defender tends to equalize the differences between the public prosecutor and the defendant by assuring the latter adequate counsel regardless of financial resources. In short, the public defender system is designed to assure greater justice for the poor.

Recidivism   Relapse into criminal behavior. Recidivism describes the tendency of the habitual criminal who, after conviction and punishment for crime, commits crime again and is returned to prison. *See also* PAROLE, page 273; PROBATION, page 275.

Significance   Recidivism is a major problem in the United States. More than 60 percent of the persons arrested are likely to be repeat offenders. In certain types of crime, such as robbery, the rate of recidivism is above 70 percent. In effect, prison becomes a "crime school" for "career criminals" who view imprisonment as part of the cost of doing business. This calls into question the purposes and results of prison confinement and intensifies the need for research into why people commit crimes after having received corrections treatment. The high rate of recidivism allegedly makes judges reluctant to send first-time offenders to prison. However, increased requirements for mandatory sentences, especially for drug-related violations, are now forcing them to do so.

Referee   A person, ordinarily an attorney, appointed by the court to conduct a hearing on a particular matter and then report back to the court. In federal courts, referees (known as "special masters") are used often in complex financial proceedings to collect information and to present it to the court for final disposition of the case.

Significance   The referee, who is usually a subject matter expert, relieves the judge of attention to complex matters or matters of detail. Preliminary consideration is given to questions that eventually require judicial decision. This is particularly useful when accounting or administrative detail is involved, as in a bankruptcy case.

Sentence   The punishment inflicted upon a convicted criminal. An "indeterminate" sentence of imprisonment involves minimum and maximum limits set by a judge or by statute. Once the prisoner serves the minimum sentence, release may result upon approval of a parole board or special commission. Increasingly, however, most states are utilizing the "fixed" sentence, which is stipulated by statute for conviction of a specific crime. In the Comprehensive Crime Control Act of 1984, Congress required federal judges to follow specific sentencing guidelines established by a sentencing commission, effective November 1, 1987, and abolished parole. *See also* COMPREHENSIVE CRIME CONTROL ACT OF 1984, page 380; PAROLE, page 273; RECIDIVISM, page 276; U.S. SENTENCING COMMISSION, page 285.

Significance   The sentence reflects society's attitude toward specific crimes and is usually assigned by statute. The law may give more or less discretion to judges, and in some instances to juries. The indeterminate sentence reflects a policy to reform and rehabilitate criminals by providing hope of early release for proper behavior. Increased recidivism and increased crime rates have led to widespread adoption of fixed sentences, on the theory that clearly established punishment upon a finding of guilt will act as a deterrent to crime. In addition, fixed sentencing laws erase the considerable discrepancies in sentencing by different judges for similar offenses. One result of fixed sentencing, however, has been an overcrowding of prisons. In 1995, more than 1.6 million persons were imprisoned in state and federal prisons, more than double the number in 1985. By the end of 1995, 1 out of 167 Americans was incarcerated, compared to 1 out of 320 in 1985. Fixed sentencing can also result in the assignment of more time for repeated minor offenses (e.g., drugs) than for serious violent crimes. A majority of federal inmates are serving time for drug offenses. A significant recent development is the adoption by at least twenty-four states by 1996 of "three strikes and you're out" laws, which impose sentences up to life imprisonment for three felony convictions, irrespective of the specific crimes. This discourages plea bargaining by third-time offenders, adding to already crowded court dockets.

Sheriff   The chief law enforcement officer of a county. The sheriff is an elective position in all the states except Alaska, Rhode Island, and Hawaii, and in four counties: Denver, Colorado; Dade, Florida; St. Louis, Missouri; and King, Washington. The sheriff's duties pertain to both civil and criminal actions. In addition to general law enforcement, the sheriff, as an officer of the court, serves papers, enforces orders, maintains the jail, and collects taxes, with particular functions varying from state to state. In many jurisdictions, the sheriff is paid through fees for each job performed rather than on a regular salary basis. Law enforcement activities are generally limited to areas outside cities and to patrol on county highways.

Significance   The office of sheriff has had a long history, dating back to ninth-century Anglo-Saxon England. Though the office has declined in power and prestige, it remains strongly entrenched as part of American law enforcement. In many areas, the office has proved to be highly lucrative because of the fee system, but it rarely excels as a police agency. With the growth of population in suburban areas, sheriff's offices are faced with increased responsibilities that untrained sheriffs and appointed deputies are not able to meet. Critics advocate the substitution of a professional, countywide police system.

Small Claims Court   A court found in many large cities to expedite minor cases at low cost. Disputes over such issues as fuel or grocery bills or wages are quickly settled by a judge.

Significance   Thousands of small claims are settled each year in small claims courts without cluttering the dockets of regular courts and without need for the parties to hire attorneys or go to other great expense. Where small claims courts are not found, such cases are generally heard by justices of the peace, who receive a fee for their service. The Dispute Resolution Act of 1980 provides funds to states to develop procedures for settling minor disputes out of court.

Solicitor General   An important official in the Department of Justice who conducts cases on behalf of the United States before the Supreme Court. In addition, the approval of the Solicitor General is necessary before any appeal may be taken on behalf of the federal government to any appellate court.

Significance   As chief counsel for the national government, the Solicitor General's conduct of cases may decide the fate of many important programs. As supervisor of appeals, he or she is in a position to affect the administration of federal criminal and civil law by determining which issues or cases are worthy of appeal. The decisions and the general conduct of this office may be important keys to the policies of the administration in power in Washington, as reflected in the types of cases appealed and in the arguments made before the Supreme Court. Care in the selection of cases and continuing working relations contribute to substantial success for the Solicitor General in cases argued before the Supreme Court.

Stare Decisis   A legal term meaning "let the decision stand." It is an important element of the common law whereby a decision applies in similar cases and is binding upon lower courts. Precedents thus established stand until overruled. *See also* PRECEDENT, page 274.

Significance   The rule of stare decisis lends stability to the law and to legal arrangements among individuals. Thus lawyers, judges, and the public at large are bound by what has gone before unless compelling reasons call for establishing new precedents.

Statute of Limitations   A state or federal legislative act that establishes a time limit within which lawsuits may be brought, judgments enforced, or crimes prosecuted. The time limit varies among different jurisdictions and with the nature of the case, although for certain major offenses, such as murder, no limits are placed on prosecution.

Significance   Statutes of limitations compel timely legal action and prevent endless harassment of individuals by other persons or by the government. Though certain violations of law may go unchallenged, it is considered desirable that at some point the threat of prosecution be ended and a case be closed.

Statutory Construction   Judicial interpretation of legislative enactments. The application of a statute is not always clear from the words of the statute. Judges seek "legislative intent" by consulting legislative committee hearings, floor debates, and legislative journals. If these sources do not reveal the legislature's objectives, the court must then discern the meaning of the law. *See also* CONSTITUTIONAL CONSTRUCTION, page 35; JURISPRUDENCE, page 267.

Significance   Statutory construction is one of the most difficult tasks of the judiciary. In a complicated society, most laws can be stated only in the most general terms, with specific application to wide varieties of situations left to judges as disputes arise as a result of some executive or administrative action. Although the legislative history of an act may produce needed information, it often fails to reveal how the legislature intended the law to fit a specific situation. It is this lack of clarity that often leads to lawsuits. Legislative bodies may deliberately leave statutes vague so that details can be worked out by judges on a case-by-case basis. The net effect of statutory interpretation is to strengthen greatly the power of the courts. Some legal theorists and many judges disdain the search for legislative intent, holding that the law must speak for itself or be clarified by additional legislation.

Subpoena   An order of a court, grand jury, legislative body or committee, or any duly authorized administrative agency, compelling the attendance of a person. A *subpoena duces tecum* requires the person to produce specific documents. Failure to honor a subpoena may subject the person to prosecution for contempt. *See also* WITNESS, page 343.

Significance   Public agencies could not properly perform their functions without the power of subpoena. Persons called may refuse to testify or to reveal certain documents if they validly claim that such action may result in self-incrimination. The power of subpoena is of special importance in judicial proceedings, in which both sides of a case have the right to compel testimony of witnesses. The subject of a subpoena must fall within the legal authority of the agency issuing the subpoena and be relevant to the inquiry involved (that is, no "fishing expedition" is permissible).

Summons   A complaint made by an individual or a police officer and signed by a judicial officer requiring a person to appear in court to answer charges made against him or her.

Significance   The summons is usually the first step in civil suits or minor criminal cases. It gives formal notice to the defendant of the charges made against him or her. In serious criminal matters, charges are made through indictment by grand jury or through a prosecutor's information. The summons satisfies the requirement that a person not be brought to trial without formal complaint and proper notice of the charges.

Supreme Court   The court of last resort in the federal and most state judicial systems. In a few states, the highest court is called by another title. The Supreme Court of the United States is composed of the Chief Justice of the

United States and eight associate justices. The number of justices is established by Congress; it has varied from five to ten, but has been set at nine since 1869. Cases are decided by majority vote. The Supreme Court is the only court specifically provided for in the Constitution, and its original jurisdiction is set therein to include cases affecting ambassadors, public ministers, and consuls and those to which a state is a party. Its appellate jurisdiction is determined by Congress. Certain cases involving federal questions may be appealed to the Supreme Court from the highest state court. With few exceptions, the Supreme Court determines which cases it will hear through the writ of certiorari. The Court sits from October to July. Its decisions are reported in the *United States Reports.* State supreme courts vary in size (five, seven, or nine judges) and jurisdiction in accordance with state constitutions and laws, but, except for cases that may be brought to the U.S. Supreme Court, they are the courts of last resort in each state. Justices of the U.S. Supreme Court are appointed by the President, with the Senate's consent, for life terms, subject to impeachment. Most state supreme court judges are elected. The U.S. Supreme Court and some state supreme courts oversee their respective court systems in matters of procedure and administration. *See also* ACTIVISM VERSUS SELF-RESTRAINT, page 248; *Ashwander v. TVA,* page 286; JUDICIAL REVIEW, page 266; JUDICIARY ACT OF 1789, page 290; UNITED STATES REPORTS, page 283.

Significance   Courts of last resort, particularly the Supreme Court of the United States, wield tremendous power and play a major role in the development of public policy. In the final analysis, these courts determine the meaning of the Constitution and of statutes, the scope of legislative and executive power, and the scope of their own power. Decisions as to the meaning of constitutional phrases have lasting impact, unless overruled by the court itself (as in the racial segregation cases) or overturned by constitutional amendment (as in the case of the income tax). Decisions are binding upon all lower courts, assuring uniformity of judgements. Because of the importance of the questions that reach it, the U.S. Supreme Court has often been involved in major economic, political, and social controversies. Appointments to the Court are watched with avid interest to ascertain in which way the new justices may influence the interpretation of the Constitution and laws. Presidential nominees to the Supreme Court are carefully scrutinized by the Senate, and 20 percent of the nominees have either withdrawn or been rejected by the Senate. Approximately 6,000 appeals are filed annually with the Supreme Court, but only about 100 receive a full review and full opinion.

Supreme Court Packing Plan   A proposal made in 1937 by President Franklin D. Roosevelt that the President be authorized to appoint an additional justice of the Supreme Court for each justice over the age of 70 who did not retire after 10 years of service. The maximum number of appointments was to have been six, thereby possibly increasing the size of the Supreme Court from nine to fifteen. The President claimed that this plan would increase the efficiency of the Court, but it was defeated in the Congress on the ground that Roosevelt was trying to "pack" the Court to overcome unfavorable decisions on New Deal programs.

Significance   The idea of packing the Court so as to affect the nature of decisions is not novel in American history. The size of the Court was altered on six different occasions by Congress, either to prevent appointments by a President or to affect decisions. These instances, but especially the Roosevelt plan, point up the significance of the Supreme Court in the formulation of public policy. Roosevelt's plan met with strong resistance from members of the Court and Congress, as well as from the public at large, demonstrating general support for the Court as an institution that should not be tampered with. In the course of the debate, the Court reversed its previous position, handing down new interpretations of the Constitution that gave free rein to the New Deal. It is said that President Roosevelt "lost the battle but won the war."

Taxpayer Suit   A suit brought by a taxpayer to prevent the expenditure of public funds for a given purpose. Such suits are permissible in most states but rarely in federal courts. *See also* ACCESS TO COURTS, page 247; *Frothingham v. Mellon,* page 288.

Significance   The taxpayer suit is based on the theory that each taxpayer has an interest in how public funds are spent, regardless of the amount of the individual's contribution. Such suits are not heard in federal courts because the Supreme Court has held that no taxpayer has a sufficient personal interest in the vast expenditures of federal funds (*Frothingham v. Mellon,* 262 U.S. 447 [1923]). However, in 1968, in *Flast v. Cohen,* 392 U.S. 83, the court modified its position to authorize suits that involve a possible breach of a specific constitutional limitation on the power to spend or tax, in this instance a challenge to federal aid to parochial schools.

Territorial Court   A court established by Congress in a territory of the United States. Under its power to govern the territories, Congress has established district courts in Guam, Puerto Rico, the Northern Mariana Islands, and the Virgin Islands. Congress has also authorized minor courts in the territories to hear cases ordinarily heard in state courts. The federal district court judges in Puerto Rico hold life terms; those in the other territorial courts are appointed for ten-year terms. *See also* DISTRICT COURT, page 260; LEGISLATIVE COURT, page 269; TERRITORY, page 51.

Significance   Residents of Guam, Puerto Rico, the Northern Marina Islands, and the Virgin Islands are citizens of the United States. Though statehood is not in the offing, Congress has provided these areas with regular district courts, thereby establishing the American legal tradition.

Test Case   A lawsuit initiated to assess the constitutionality or application of a legislative or executive act. Since federal courts and most state courts do not give advisory opinions, it is necessary to institute a suit to obtain a judicial ruling on the act. This may require the deliberate violation of the act to compel a prosecution or a suit seeking to restrain enforcement. The term "test case" also refers to any landmark case that is the first test of a major piece of legislation.

Significance   The role of the judiciary in the American system is underscored by the common use of the test case. Interest groups that lose in the legislative or executive arena will turn to the courts for satisfaction. Great care is exercised in the selection of test cases to increase chances for a favorable decision. Often similar cases are initiated in several jurisdictions at one time in the hope that varied interpretations will more likely assure Supreme Court review.

Tort   A wrongful act involving injury to persons, property, or reputation, but excluding breach of contract. The injured party may bring suit against the wrongdoer. This is an important and often-used branch of law. A major tort problem concerns the responsibility of governmental units for torts committed by government employees against individuals. *See also* CIVIL LAW, page 253; *Maine v. Thiboutot,* page 288.

Significance   Tort law serves as a substitute for private duels and assures that for most wrongs there will be a remedy. The issue of the tort liability of government has not been definitively resolved. Generally, no one may sue the government without its consent. Many states and the national government have authorized suits for certain kinds of torts. At the municipal level, the law varies from state to state, but as a general rule, municipalities are not responsible for torts committed by their employees who are engaged in purely "governmental" functions. There may, however, be liability for torts committed in the course of "proprietary" functions (gas supply, transportation, and other businesslike functions) or in violation of federal law. The Federal Tort Claims Act of 1946 permits certain claims against the national government to be settled by administrative officials.

Trial   The examination of a civil or criminal action in accordance with the law of the land before a judge who has jurisdiction. A trial must be public, conducted fairly before an impartial judge, and, in the case of criminal trials, started without unreasonable delay. *See also* JURY, page 268; *Moore v. Dempsey,* page 361; PUBLIC TRIAL, page 330; SIXTH AMENDMENT, page 338; SPEEDY TRIAL, page 338.

Significance   A speedy, impartial, and public trial conducted in conformity with established procedures of the law is one of the major hallmarks of a free and civilized people. Knowledge that disputes will be settled in this manner gives the people confidence in the law and makes private feuds unnecessary for settlement of grievances. American trial procedures give adequate opportunity to each side to present its case for examination by the judge or jury.

Unified Court System   An integrated statewide or areawide court system, organized into divisions for more efficient distribution of case load and judges. A chief judge, aided by a judicial council or business manager, supervises the operations of the courts, shifts judges about to meet caseload demands, and, through collection of significant data, promotes the efficient administration of justice. *See also* JUDICIAL COUNCIL, page 266.

Significance   Most proponents of judicial reform endorse the unified court plan. Most state and local court systems are organized on a geographic basis, with many types of cases heard in each jurisdiction by the same judge.

The unified plan, its proponents claim, will encourage specialization among judges, relieve the situation in which some court dockets are crowded while others are not filled, and promote uniformity in decision making. Overall supervision by a chief judge can result in more efficient use of personnel and money and expedite the business of the courts. While progress has been made toward a unified plan in a few states, notably Connecticut, the administration of state court systems remains largely fragmented and under local political and fiscal controls.

United States Attorney   A federal official whose principal function is to prosecute violations of federal law. A United States Attorney, appointed for a four-year term by the President with the Senate's consent, is assigned to each district in which a federal district court is located and is under general supervision of the Department of Justice and the Attorney General of the United States. *See also* DISTRICT ATTORNEY, page 260.

Significance   The functions of the United States Attorney underscore the divided nature of American law enforcement. Though he or she may cooperate with local law enforcement officials, the United States Attorney is responsible only for violations of federal law. The position is frequently a step toward appointment to the federal judiciary or to elective office.

United States Reports   The official record of cases heard and disposed of by the U.S. Supreme Court, including the full opinions of the justices. The volumes are issued at the conclusion of the term of the Court, but opinions are available in "advance sheets" prior to issuance of the volumes. Three or four volumes of the *Reports* may emerge each year, depending on the volume of business and length of opinions. The volumes are numbered consecutively now, but, prior to 1874, at which time the *Reports* totaled 90 volumes, they were identified by the names of the official court reporters. These include Dallas, Cranch, Wheaton, Peters, Howard, Black, and Wallace. Thus, a case cited as 1 Cranch 137 (1803), means that the case, decided in 1803, can be found on page 137 of the first volume compiled by Cranch. Since 1874, the volumes are simply numbered, beginning with 91. A case cited as 345 U.S. 123 (1953) will be found on page 123 of volume 345 of the *United States Reports* and was decided in 1953. All recorded legal decisions in any court may be found in similar fashion by locating the title, volume, and page of the *Report* in which it is given. Reports are available from federal courts of appeals *(Federal Reporter)*, district courts *(Federal Supplement)*, and highest state courts. State reports are identified by the name of the state, for example, 156 Michigan 124. Commercial companies also put out volumes reporting Supreme Court cases: *The Supreme Court Reporter* (cited as 57 S. Ct. 234) and the *Lawyer's Edition* (cited as 57 L. Ed. 234). Headnotes, which summarize the important points of each case and serve as a reference to similar legal issues, are written by the editors and placed ahead of the opinion of the court. These helpful guides to the law are not part of the decision. *See also* OPINION OF THE COURT, page 272.

Significance   The reports of cases are available for use by lawyers, legal scholars, and all persons. The reports of Supreme Court cases, in particular, provide some of the best material available on American political and legal thought and practice. Major social and political issues are apt to find their way to the Supreme Court and the opinions are important social documents.

Venue   The county or district in which a prosecution is brought for trial and from which jurors are chosen. Venue refers to a particular area, not to the court that has jurisdiction.

Significance   Under American law, trials are held in the area in which the wrong is done. The Sixth Amendment to the Constitution provides that, in federal criminal prosecutions, trials are to be held in the state and district in which the crime was committed. Similar provisions are found in state constitutions. This gives the defendant the benefit of a court and a jury familiar with the problems and people of the area. A defendant may, however, ask for a "change of venue," a transfer of the trial to another locality, on the grounds that the people of the locality or, particularly, the media are prejudiced against him or her and that an impartial jury could not be drawn. The judge determines whether a change of venue is justified.

Writ   An order in writing issued by a court ordering the performance of an act or prohibiting some act. A wide variety of writs exists, ranging from orders to appear in court to orders regarding the execution of the court's judgment. *See also* CERTIORARI, page 251; HABEAS CORPUS, page 319; INJUNCTION, page 265; MANDAMUS, page 270.

Significance   Courts exercise their power largely through the issuance of writs, which are essential for the orderly progress of judicial functions. The right to enforce a decision is as necessary as the right to hear and decide cases. Failure to honor a writ may subject a person to a fine or imprisonment for contempt of court, or both.

IMPORTANT AGENCIES

Administrative Office of the United States Courts   An agency that handles administrative matters for all federal and territorial courts except the Supreme Court. The Office, established in 1939, is headed by a director who is appointed by the Chief Justice. Its functions include supervision of administrative personnel of the courts, the fixing of compensation of such personnel, preparation of the budget for the operations of the court system, and care of court funds, books, equipment, and supplies. The Office also gathers statistics on dockets and supervises administration of bankruptcy, federal probation, the federal magistrates, and the federal public defenders. *See also* JUDICIAL COUNCIL, page 266.

Significance   The Administrative Office of the United States Courts has established centralized control over court administration. In the past, little attention was paid to the administrative problems involved in maintaining an effective judiciary. A Federal Judicial Center was established in 1967 to conduct research on court management and to develop continuing educational programs for judges and court personnel. A 1970 law authorized court executives to handle administrative duties for each federal judicial circuit. Since 1972, an administrative aide has been appointed to assist the Chief Justice of the United States with administrative duties pertaining to the operation of the Supreme Court. The governing body for the administration of the federal judicial system is the Judicial Conference of the United States. It is chaired by the Chief Justice of the United States and includes the chief judge of each federal circuit, district court judges from each circuit, and the chief judge of the Court of Appeals for the Federal Circuit. In 1984, Congress established the State Justice Institute to further the development and improvement of state court administration.

Department of Justice   A major department of the executive branch concerned with the enforcement of federal laws. The Justice Department is headed by the Attorney General, who is a member of the President's Cabinet. The department furnishes legal counsel in cases involving the national government, interprets laws under which other executive agencies operate, supervises federal penal institutions, directs U.S. attorneys and marshals, and supervises immigration laws. Its major divisions include Antitrust, Civil, Civil Rights, Criminal, Land and Natural Resources, and Tax. The department includes the Federal Bureau of Investigation (FBI), which is the major police agency for the national government. *See also* ATTORNEY GENERAL, page 250; DEPARTMENT OF JUSTICE, page 344; SOLICITOR GENERAL, page 278.

Significance   The Department of Justice maintains a close relationship with all other units of the national government because of its widespread responsibility for law enforcement. Its functions also put it into frequent contact with the judicial branch at all stages of judicial proceedings, from the apprehension of suspected law violators to their imprisonment. The department is not, however, a part of the judicial branch, as is sometimes erroneously thought; this would constitute a violation of the separation of powers because it would unite prosecutor and judge.

United States Sentencing Commission   An independent advisory commission within the judicial branch, established by Congress in the Comprehensive Crime Control Act of 1984, to design guidelines ensuring greater certainty and uniformity in federal criminal sentencing. The Commission has seven members made up of three federal judges, three law professors, and a former parole officer, all of whom are appointed by the President. The Commission's purpose is to research and establish sentencing rules for all federal crimes (effective November 1, 1987) on a continuing basis. Every federal crime is assigned a sentence with points added or subtracted for mitigating or aggravating circumstances, age, prior convictions, amount of money involved in the crime, use of weapons, and so on. Deviations from the guidelines require an explanation by the judge and may be appealed. The commission's authority extends to ordinary criminal violations as well as to white-collar crimes. The commission's guidelines become mandatory six months after release if Congress does not act to overturn or amend them.

Significance   The Sentencing Commission is designed to reduce the discrepancies existing from jurisdiction to jurisdiction and case to case in sentences imposed on individuals committing similar crimes. The 1987 law also eliminated parole in the federal penal system, which lends certainty to sentencing and the time actually to be served. The commission studies the effects of mandatory sentencing and continually evaluates sentencing practices. Critics argue that the rules are too complex and that "determinate" sentencing eliminates the opportunity for the judge to take extenuating or mitigating circumstances into account. A more serious criticism is that the system results in a greater transfer of sentencing decisions to the prosecutors and accused persons who negotiate a plea bargain. In 1989, the commission was challenged in *Mistretta v. United States* (488 U.S. 361) as a violation of the separation of powers doctrine and for having too much authority delegated to it, but the Supreme Court upheld the commission's authority. Public disputes emerge from time to time over disparate sentencing requirements for similar crimes and over concern with increasing crowding of prisons as a result of mandatory sentencing.

IMPORTANT CASES

Ableman v. Booth   21 Howard 506 (1859): Established that a state court may not issue a writ of habeas corpus to a prisoner in federal custody.

Significance   The *Ableman* case underscores the independence of state and federal courts from each other in their proper spheres of authority. No judicial order can have any effect outside the lawful jurisdiction of the court. Neither the states nor the federal courts can intrude into the domain of the other unless the nature of the case demands the exercise of the supreme federal authority.

Ashwander v. TVA   297 U.S. 288 (1936): Upheld the right of the TVA to sell surplus electric power. The case is well known for the concurring opinion by Justice Louis D. Brandeis in which he attempted to sum up the rules that the Court had developed in considering the constitutionality of the acts of the legislative and executive branches. Among these were: (1) The Court will not decide questions of a constitutional nature unless absolutely essential to disposal of the case; (2) the Court will not pass on a constitutional question if the case can be disposed of on some other ground; (3) the Court will not formulate a constitutional rule broader than is required by the precise facts of the case; and (4) the Court will try to construe a statute so as to avoid ruling on constitutional questions, even if serious doubts exist as to its constitutionality. *See also Ashwander v. TVA*, page 495; JUDICIAL REVIEW, page 266.

Significance   The Court's self-denying rules, as summarized by Justice Brandeis, for handling constitutional issues have generally governed its course. It remains reluctant to rule on the constitutionality of federal legislation and has sought to avoid controversy with the legislative and executive branches. Nevertheless, the Court has acted on numerous historic constitutional issues, especially in times of dramatic social and political change.

Cohens v. Virginia   6 Wheaton 264 (1821): Ruled that state court decisions are subject to review by the Supreme Court if the case involves a question of federal law, treaties, or the Constitution, even though a state is a party to the suit. An appeal brought to a federal court by a defendant who has been convicted in a state court does not constitute a suit against the state, contrary to the Eleventh Amendment. *See also* ELEVENTH AMENDMENT, page 261.

Significance   The question of whether the Supreme Court had appellate jurisdiction over cases appealed from state courts was crucial to the development of federal judicial power. Prior to the *Cohens* decision, the Supreme Court held, in *Martin v. Hunter's Lessee,* 1 Wheaton 304 (1816), that it has the right to review state court decisions involving suits between private individuals when a federal question is involved. The *Cohens* decision extended this principle to cases in which a state is a party. In both cases, the Court pointed out that federal jurisdiction is essential to establish uniformity of decision throughout the United States on the interpretation of the Constitution, federal law, or treaties. Otherwise, each state, rather than the national government, would be supreme.

Dred Scott v. Sandford   19 Howard 393 (1857): Held, in a famous case, that blacks could not become citizens of the United States and were not entitled to the rights and privileges of citizenship. The Court also ruled that the Missouri Compromise, which had banned slavery in the territories, was unconstitutional.

Significance   The *Dred Scott* decision is considered to be one of the most disastrous handed down by the Supreme Court. The Court itself was badly divided and muddled in its views. The case failed to resolve the slavery issue and contributed to the inevitability of the Civil War. Both the Civil War and the provisions of the Fourteenth Amendment on citizenship were needed to overcome the *Dred Scott* ruling. The *Dred Scott* case is also noted for being the second in which a federal law was declared unconstitutional, following the Supreme Court's exercise of judicial review in *Marbury v. Madison,* 1 Cranch 137 (1803). The crucial role of the Supreme Court in American life and politics is underscored by the *Dred Scott* case.

Eakin v. Raub   12 S. & R. 330 (1825): Decided by the Supreme Court of the State of Pennsylvania, this case is famous for an opinion by Judge John B. Gibson against the principle of judicial review. Judge Gibson disagreed with the logic of Chief Justice John Marshall's opinion in *Marbury v. Madison,* 1 Cranch 137 (1803), in which Marshall argued that judges had a special duty to interpret the Constitution and to declare any law in conflict with the Constitution null and void. Judge Gibson argued that judges had no such duty. Rather, the legislature bore responsibility for unlawful acts, and the people should hold them responsible. *See also* ACTIVISM VERSUS SELF-RESTRAINT, page 248; *Marbury v. Madison,* page 289.

Significance   Judge Gibson's opinion is the best-known argument by a judge against the principle of judicial review. Although it never overthrew that principle, the position he took is still held by many persons. The student of government may find the complete opinion of Judge Gibson reproduced in many casebooks or textbooks on constitutional law.

Erie Railroad v. Tompkins   304 U.S. 64 (1938): Ruled that, in diversity of citizenship cases heard in federal courts, the law to be applied is the state law as declared by the state legislature or courts. There is no general federal common law. *See also* DIVERSITY OF CITIZENSHIP, page 260.

Significance   The *Erie* case overruled *Swift v. Tyson,* 16 Peters 1 (1842), which had held that, in the absence of a state statute controlling a case, the federal courts could apply their own principles of the common law. After almost a century of confusion resulting from several versions of the common law, particularly in commercial cases, the Court declared in the *Erie* case that the *Tyson* rule was not only incorrect but unconstitutional as well because there is no general federal common law.

Ex parte McCardle   7 Wallace 506 (1869): Declared that the Supreme Court may not exercise appellate jurisdiction over a case when Congress prohibits such jurisdiction. This case arose when Congress repealed an 1867 law that had authorized appeals to the Supreme Court in certain cases involving enforcement of the post–Civil War Reconstruction Acts.

Significance   The *McCardle* case demonstrates the veto power of Congress over the appellate jurisdiction of the Supreme Court. The Constitution, in Article III, section 2, provides that the Supreme Court has appellate jurisdiction in all cases heard in federal courts "with such exceptions, and under such regulations as the Congress shall make." Congress does not grant appellate power but may make exceptions to its exercise. Congress withdrew jurisdiction from the Supreme Court in this case for fear that the Court would declare the Reconstruction Acts unconstitutional. Nevertheless, the Court dismissed the case on the ground that it lacked jurisdiction.

Frothingham v. Mellon   262 U.S. 447 (1923): Held that a taxpayer may not bring suit in a federal court to restrain the expenditure of federal funds. The case involved a protest against a federal grant-in-aid to the states for maternity benefits. The Court has since modified the rule to permit taxpayer suits where a specific breach of constitutional power is alleged (*Flast v. Cohen,* 392 U.S. 83 [1968]). *See also* ACCESS TO COURTS, page 247; *Massachusetts v. Mellon,* page 56.

Significance   An important element of judicial procedure is that a party to a suit must have standing to sue. That is, a party must be able to show "some direct injury...and not merely that he suffers in some indefinite way in common with people generally." Although taxpayer suits are common in state and local courts, the Supreme Court has taken the view that an individual's interest in federal taxation and expenditures is too minute. In *Flast v. Cohen,* the Court ruled that an exception could be made by which a taxpayer could establish a link between himself or herself and the taxing or spending law and could point to a specific constitutional limitation on the right to tax and spend. Thus the Court authorized a challenge to public expenditures for parochial schools in that a violation of the First Amendment was possible. The Court reaffirmed the *Frothingham* rule that a taxpayer suit cannot be brought because the taxpayer believes the tax unwise or an interference with the reserved powers of the states.

Maine v. Thiboutot   448 U.S. 1 (1980): Expanded the right of individuals to sue state and local governments for denial of rights under any federal law rather than only for claims involving constitutional or civil rights. The decision involved a suit against the state of Maine for denying benefits under the Social Security Act. In addition, the Court held that the state could be ordered to pay attorney fees. *See also* ACCESS TO COURTS, page 247; CIVIL RIGHTS ACTS OF 1866, 1870, 1871, AND 1875, page 376; ELEVENTH AMENDMENT, page 261.

Significance   *Maine v. Thiboutot* was the most far-reaching of a series of decisions liberalizing the rights of individuals to sue state and local governments and their officials for denials of federally guaranteed rights or programs. Earlier, states and cities had been presumed to be immune to suit without their consent. In *Owen v. City of Independence, Mo.,* 445 U.S. 622 (1980), the court ended any notion of immunity of city officials to suit by denying that officials could argue that they acted in good faith. These and similar rulings were made under the Civil Rights Act of 1871, which prohibits any person acting "under color" of law to deny rights secured by the Constitution or laws and makes such persons "liable to the party injured." The award of attorney fees is authorized by the Civil Rights Attorney's Fee Act of 1976, which allows such awards for suits brought under the 1871 law, thereby encouraging plaintiffs who might otherwise not pursue their claims. Some narrowing of the right to sue state and local governments and officials occurred in the late 1980s and during the 1990s as the Supreme Court gave more credence to state immunity under the Eleventh Amendment.

Marbury v. Madison   1 Cranch 137 (1803): Struck down, for the first time in American history, an act of Congress as unconstitutional. The Court, speaking through Chief Justice John Marshall, held unconstitutional a portion of the Judiciary Act of 1789 that had added to the original jurisdiction of the Supreme Court, as specified in Article III of the Constitution. Marshall argued that the Constitution was the supreme law and that judges were bound by their oath and the nature of their positions to act as guardians of the Constitution. Any law in conflict with the Constitution cannot be enforced in the courts. *See also Eakin v. Raub,* page 287; JUDICIAL REVIEW, page 266.

Significance   Few cases have had the impact upon American governmental development as has *Marbury v. Madison,* in which Chief Justice Marshall struck a decisive blow for judicial supremacy. The case was essentially a political controversy between the defeated Federalist party and the incoming Jeffersonian party over last-minute Federalist party appointments to the federal courts. Marshall used the occasion to write a strong, logical defense of the role of the judiciary under the separation of powers doctrine, which is generally assumed to reflect the views of the framers of the Constitution. Although the Constitution fails to mention judicial review, the American people have accepted its exercise by the courts as an integral part of the American constitutional system. In 1974, in rejecting President Richard M. Nixon's claim that the separation of powers doctrine precluded judicial review of his claim of executive privilege, the Supreme Court relied heavily on the statement from *Marbury v. Madison* that "it is emphatically the province and duty of the judicial department to say what the law is" (*United States v. Nixon,* 418 U.S. 683). In 1995, the Court declared that Congress had violated the separation of powers by enacting legislation instructing federal courts to reopen certain decisions made with respect to securities fraud (*Plaut v. Spendthrift Farm,* 115 S.Ct. 1447).

IMPORTANT STATUTES

Judiciary Act of 1789   A law passed by the first Congress to establish the federal court system. The Act determined the organization and jurisdiction of the courts. Over the years, the Judiciary Act has undergone numerous changes, adding and deleting courts, changing jurisdiction of courts, establishing rules of procedure, and providing for a variety of court officers and employees.

Significance   The Judiciary Act of 1789 and its subsequent amendments demonstrate congressional authority over federal court organization, jurisdiction, and procedure. The only constitutional limit placed on Congress is that a Supreme Court must exist with specified original jurisdiction. A portion of the Judiciary Act of 1789 was declared unconstitutional in the famous case of *Marbury v. Madison,* 1 Cranch 137 (1803), because, in it, the Congress had unconstitutionally added to the original jurisdiction of the Supreme Court. Changes of significance include the Act of 1891, which ended "circuit riding" by Supreme Court justices and established the courts of appeals; the Act of 1925, which gave the Supreme Court discretionary authority to issue writs of certiorari; and the Act of 1988, which gave the Supreme Court virtually complete control over its docket by eliminating most mandatory review requirements. In 1982, Congress established the Court of Appeals for the Federal Circuit, the first court of appeals to have specialized subject matter jurisdiction from all over the nation on specified matters of business, international trade, and civil service.

8

Civil Liberties, Civil Rights, Immigration, and Citizenship

Abortion   Termination of a pregnancy. In 1973, the Supreme Court ruled that the right of a woman to voluntarily terminate a pregnancy prior to viability of the fetus was protected by the constitutional right to privacy (*Roe v. Wade,* 410 U.S. 113). That decision unleashed a controversy that has since dominated the political landscape in the United States. Subsequently, the Supreme Court rendered about a dozen decisions supportive of the right to an abortion and overturned state legislation aimed at restricting access to such a medical procedure. In 1989, however, the Court, reflective of the antiabortion perspective of the Reagan and Bush administrations, sustained state limitations on liberal abortion policies, holding the issue to be not one of privacy but of a state's interest in preserving human life without unduly burdening women's rights (*Webster v. Reproductive Health Services,* 492 U.S. 490). In Congress, proponents of *Roe v. Wade* were successful for many years in providing support for family-planning measures, including abortion in medical, military, welfare, and international aid programs. This support eventually fell victim to the veto power of President Bush, however, who opposed all legislation supportive of abortion. The *Webster* decision and congressional inaction transferred the issue to 50 state legislatures and governors, thereby considerably broadening the battleground. In 1992, the Court confirmed *Roe v. Wade* but accepted the imposition of state restrictions deemed not to place a substantial obstacle to a woman's choice (*Planned Parenthood of Southeastern Pennsylvania v. Casey,* 505 U.S. 833). See also *Roe v. Wade,* page 367.

Significance   Abortion, with its strong religious and moral undertones, is an unlikely "political" issue that has, nevertheless, affected all branches and levels of government. Prior to 1973, abortion law was a patchwork. Only four states (Alaska, Hawaii, New York, and Washington) allowed abortions for any reason. Three (Louisiana, New Hampshire, and Pennsylvania) prohibited all abortions. Thirty permitted abortion only to save the life of the mother, and thirteen had somewhat less restrictive rules, permitting abortion for mental or physical health reasons. It is estimated that prior to 1973, about 500,000 abortions were performed legally each year. Each year since 1973, an average of 1.5 million pregnancies (25 percent of total pregnancies) have ended in abortion. *Roe v. Wade* gave rise to numerous lawsuits, legislative activity, and unusually active interest groups on all sides of the issue. Whichever position "wins," it is certain to stimulate a countercampaign for new laws, new political leaders, new judges, and a constitutional amendment. For students of government, the issue highlights, better than most, the critical role played by each of the "players"—from voters to the President—in determining the outcome of an issue that is of great emotional interest to almost everyone, though not a typical political question.

Academic Freedom   The principle that teachers and students have the right and the duty to pursue the search for truth wherever the inquiry may lead, free of political, religious, or other restrictions except those of accepted standards of scholarship. Important corollaries to the principle are that alleged violations of academic freedom will be investigated under procedures consonant with due process and that the tenure of teachers will not depend upon adherence to any orthodoxy.

Significance   Academic freedom is not a constitutionally enforceable right, although it is commonly recognized as a major element of freedom of speech in a free society. Academic freedom is continually under stress, its degree and nature varying with the political, religious, and social values of a community. Problems of academic freedom traditionally involve community fears of alien political or religious ideas and result in loyalty oaths for teachers, investigations into educational programs, and attempts to control the private political or social activities of teachers and students. The courts have generally been protective of the values underlying academic freedom and have resisted imposition of conditions that stifle the freedom to teach and learn.

Acquittal   Formal release by a court of a person charged with a crime. Ordinarily it occurs after a trial and a finding of "not guilty" by a judge or jury. An acquittal may also take place before or during a trial because of procedural violations, improper charges, or insufficient evidence.

Significance   Once a person is acquitted of a charge, he or she can never be tried again on that charge. To do so would constitute double jeopardy. An acquittal should not be confused with a pardon, which frees one from punishment but is not a declaration of innocence.

Affirmative Action   A plan or program to remedy the effects of past discrimination in employment, education, or other activity and to prevent its recurrence. Various federal and state statutes require affirmative action to redress past discrimination against or promote the employment of racial or religious minorities, women, the handicapped, disabled veterans, veterans of the Vietnam era, and, to some extent, the aged. Affirmative action usually involves a workforce utilization analysis, the establishment of goals and timetables to increase use of underrepresented classes of persons, explanation of methods to be used to eliminate discrimination, and establishment of administrative responsibility to implement the program. Good faith and a positive effort to remedy past discrimination must also be shown. Affirmative action is required by law or regulation for all governmental agencies and for recipients of public funds, such as contractors and universities. Affirmative action is to be distinguished from antidiscrimination or equal opportunity laws, which forbid unequal treatment rather than requiring positive corrective measures. In 1978, the Supreme Court held that affirmative action programs are valid but that explicit racial quotas are prohibited (*Regents of the University of California v. Bakke,* 438 U.S. 265). *See also Adarand Constructors v. Pena,* page 347; EQUAL RIGHTS, page 309; FAIR EMPLOYMENT PRACTICES LAWS, page 311; *Regents of the University of California v. Bakke,* page 366; REVERSE DISCRIMINATION, page 332.

Significance   Affirmative action is supported by those who argue that some form of preferential treatment is essential to break down long-standing patterns of discrimination against minorities and women so that employment patterns will more accurately reflect the pluralistic nature of American society. Such action, it is believed, will strengthen confidence in public and private institutions. Critics of affirmative action claim that it constitutes "reverse discrimination" and that, whatever the merits of preferential treatment, the result will be to deny equality of opportunity based on merit. The Supreme Court has endorsed affirmative action if the plans are voluntary, do not violate established seniority systems, do not unduly harm others, and do not involve quotas. The use of quotas has been upheld, however, where justified to remedy the effects of demonstrated past discrimination. Open hostility to affirmative action grew during the 1990s, largely as a result of downturns in economic growth and employment, resulting in reversals or weakening of affirmative action programs in universities and governmental contracting. In addition, court decisions on the issue tended to reject racial classifications, absent clear discrimination. In *Adarand Constructors, Inc. v. Pena,* 115 S. Ct. 2097 (1995), the Supreme Court held that all racial classifications are to be held to "strict scrutiny" and must be narrowly tailored to further a compelling governmental interest.

Alien   An individual who is neither a citizen nor a national of the state in which he or she is living. Aliens generally owe allegiance to a foreign power but may acquire citizenship by following prescribed procedures. *See also* ALIEN REGISTRATION ACT, page 374; DEPORTATION, page 305; IMMIGRATION REFORM ACT OF 1986, page 382; *Truax v. Raich,* page 371.

Significance   In the United States, aliens enjoy many of the civil rights that the Constitution accords to "persons" as distinguished from citizens. They include most provisions of the Bill of Rights and freedom from arbitrary discrimination. Aliens are subject to the laws of the United States, must pay taxes, and may be drafted. Military service and other duties and rights of aliens are generally in accord with treaties between the United States and other nations. An alien who does not have permanent resident status can refuse to be drafted but in so doing forfeits the right ever to become a citizen. Under the laws of most American states, an alien may not engage in certain professions, own firearms, hold government employment, or, in some states, own real estate. However, the Supreme Court has taken a dim view of restrictions that deny aliens economic rights or opportunities. In no case may an alien enjoy such political rights as voting or holding public office. The most serious disability imposed upon an alien is the continuing possibility of deportation. Because an alien has no *right* to live in the United States, he or she may be deported for illegal entry, for moral turpitude, for affiliation with the Communist party, or for terrorist activities. In time of war, aliens who are subjects of enemy states may be severely restricted. Under present law, all aliens must register with the Immigration and Naturalization Service every year. Over the years, the number of aliens illegally entering the United States increased dramatically, bolstered by the lack of penalties for employers hiring illegal aliens. In 1986 Congress acted to end this "shadow society" by making it illegal to hire undocumented aliens and by offering amnesty to such aliens who have resided in the United States prior to January 1, 1982; nevertheless, illegal immigration continues to be high.

Arraignment   A stage in criminal proceedings in which the accused is brought before the court to hear the formal charges against him or her as prepared by a grand jury or prosecutor. The accused is then asked to plead guilty or not guilty. The Supreme Court has ruled that there must be no unnecessary delay between arrest and arraignment. A confession or other evidence obtained as a result of such delay will be barred as evidence (*Mallory v. United States,* 354 U.S. 449 [1957]). In the Speedy Trial Act of 1974, Congress provided that an accused person must be arraigned within ten days of being charged. *See also McNabb v. United States,* page 359; SPEEDY TRIAL, page 338.

Significance   A major factor in fair criminal procedure is that the accused be informed of the charges so that he or she can prepare a defense. Speedy arraignment acts as a safeguard against arbitrary arrest, prolonged detention, and unsavory police tactics. Police officials across the country argue that too stringent application of the *Mallory* rule handicaps law enforcement. The Omnibus Crime Control and Safe Streets Act of 1968 permits a voluntary confession to be used as evidence in a federal court if obtained within six hours following arrest.

Arrest Warrant   An order issued in writing by a court or magistrate authorizing the detainment of a person. The Fourth Amendment to the Constitution specifies that such warrants are to be issued only upon "probable cause," supported by oath, describing the person to be seized. All state constitutions have similar provisions. *See also* FOURTH AMENDMENT, page 314.

Significance   The arrest warrant requirement has the effect of protecting persons against overzealous officers. Arrests may be made without a warrant if the law officers have "probable cause" for making the arrest. For example, an officer who witnesses a crime need not secure a warrant. Prompt judicial determination of probable cause for a warrantless arrest is required. This determination must be made within 48 hours (*County of Riverside v. McLaughlin,* 500 U.S. 44 [1991]). Several states have authorized police to enter a home without a warrant to arrest a person charged with a felony, but in 1980 the Supreme Court ruled that in the absence of exigent circumstances, police must obtain an arrest warrant in order to enter a house to arrest its occupant (*Payton v. New York,* 445 U.S. 573). Even with a warrant, police are expected to knock and announce their presence (*Wilson v. Arkansas,* 115 S. Ct. 1914 [1995]). Whether an arrest has been properly made is a matter for judicial determination. An arbitrary or illegally executed arrest may void any subsequent conviction.

Bad Tendency Rule   A test used by the Supreme Court to determine the permissible bounds of free speech. The bad tendency rule, first applied by the Court in *Pierce v. United States,* 252 U.S. 239 (1920), holds that speech or other First Amendment freedoms may be curtailed if there is a possibility that their exercise might lead to some evil. Judges who hold this view feel that it is the legislature's duty, not the Court's, to determine what kind of speech has a bad tendency. It is to be distinguished from the "clear and present danger" doctrine, which holds that an individual's liberty may not be curtailed unless it presents some imminent danger of illegal action. *See also* CLEAR AND PRESENT DANGER RULE, page 300; *Dennis v. United States,* page 352.

Significance   The bad tendency test, like the clear and present danger test, proceeds from the search for some formula to solve the problem of balancing individual freedom against the rights of society. Both tests have been used by the Supreme Court over the years, with results determined by the nature of the times and the ideas of the justices. In the years from 1948 to 1952, known as the "era of McCarthyism," the bad tendency rule prevailed against alleged subversives. More liberal majorities on the Court have since rejected the bad tendency rule in favor of the clear and present danger doctrine or other approaches that give special weight to free speech interests.

Bail   Funds provided as assurance that a person will appear in court at the proper time. Bail is permitted after arrest and before trial, as well as after conviction pending appeal or sentencing. Bail is usually denied in capital cases. The Eighth Amendment to the Constitution forbids excessive bail; wide discretion is left the courts to determine the amount in relation to the severity of the offense, the record and resources of the defendant, and the likelihood of his or her reappearing in court. A defendant may appeal a denial of release on bail or the amount of bail.

Significance   Bail rests on the theory that one is innocent until proven guilty and should not have punishment inflicted by unnecessary internment until guilt is established. Bail permits a defendant freedom to prepare a case before trial and to continue a normal work and family life. Because the poor have difficulty raising bail, many jurisdictions now release defendants on their own recognizance when it appears likely that the defendant will not flee to avoid prosecution. This practice is permitted in federal courts under the Bail Reform Act of 1966. However, in the Comprehensive Crime Control Act of 1984, Congress authorized federal judges to deny bail before trial and after conviction, pending appeal, if the defendant poses a danger to the community (preventive detention). The act also requires revocation of bail of a person arrested while on pretrial or postconviction release. The Supreme Court upheld the preventive detention provision in *United States v. Salerno,* 481 U.S. 739 (1987).

Balancing Doctrine   A concept used by judges to weigh the competing interests or values in a case. Typically it involves striking a balance between the interests that society seeks to preserve and the rights of the individual. For example, balancing the government's interest in national security against the free exercise of speech, or traffic control on a busy street against the right of assembly, are common problems. *See also* POLICE POWER, page 328.

Significance   Controversy over the balancing doctrine has emerged on the Supreme Court with some regularity, particularly in civil liberty cases. One viewpoint holds that the limits placed on government by the Bill of Rights should not be "balanced away" with rationalizations based on contemporary problems. Another view holds that constitutional rights are not absolute and may be limited when outweighed by society's needs.

Bill of Attainder   A legislative act that declares the guilt of an individual and metes out punishment without a judicial trial. The state legislatures and Congress are forbidden to pass such acts by Article I, sections 9 and 10 of the Constitution. *See also United States v. Lovett,* page 372.

Significance   A legislative body may not exercise the judicial function of ascertaining guilt and pronouncing sentence. Rather, the legislature is limited to passing general laws, with specific applications left to the courts. This is an important ingredient of the separation of powers and of freedom itself.

Bill of Rights   The first ten amendments to the United States Constitution. Bills of rights, sometimes called "declarations of rights," are also found in all state constitutions. They contain a listing of the rights a person enjoys that cannot be infringed upon by the government. Many important rights, such as trial by jury and the guarantee of habeas corpus, are stated in other parts of the U.S. Constitution. All bills of rights contain provisions designed to protect the freedom of expression, the rights of property, and the rights of persons accused of crime. No rights are absolute, however, and all are subject to reasonable regulation through law. *See also* CIVIL LIBERTIES, page 299.

Significance   Bills of rights are restrictions on government rather than on individuals or private groups. History teaches that unchecked governmental powers can lead to the decay of freedom. A bill of rights provides the legal mechanism through which the individual can challenge the oppressive acts of government officials in courts of law. Without guarantees for individual freedom, democracy would become meaningless and unworkable. Some state bills of rights antedate the federal Bill of Rights, which was added to the Constitution as a condition for its ratification, on the insistence of people who feared an unchecked central government. Although these rights were intended to restrain only the national government, since 1925 the Supreme Court has gradually extended them as restraints upon state action through the due process clause of the Fourteenth Amendment.

Capital Punishment   The death penalty for the conviction of a serious crime, now generally limited to murder. Electrocution and lethal injection are the most commonly used methods of execution; lethal gas, hanging, and firing squad are also employed. In 1972, the Supreme Court declared the death penalty, as then applied in the United States, to be cruel and unusual punishment, in violation of the Eighth Amendment (*Furman v. Georgia,* 408 U.S. 238). The Court found that capital punishment was assigned in an apparently arbitrary manner, for a variety of crimes, and mainly to blacks and the poor. All but thirteen states have since reinstated the death penalty, as has Congress, using a two-stage process in which sentence is determined in a second trial after a finding of guilt, wherein specified legislative guidelines are used to determine whether mitigating circumstances justify a sentence other than death. *See also* ANTITERRORISM AND EFFECTIVE DEATH PENALTY ACT OF 1996, page 375.

Significance   Capital punishment has long been debated on both moral and legal grounds. Many authorities question its utility as a deterrent to crime; others abhor it for religious or moral reasons. The number of executions had decreased dramatically since the 1960s, due in part to the reluctance of judges and juries to assign the death penalty and in large measure to pressures from civil rights groups, who pointed to the extraordinarily high proportion of blacks sentenced to death compared to whites guilty of similar offenses (53 percent of all persons executed from 1930 to 1965 were blacks). In the decade of 1930 to 1939, 1,666 persons were executed; 716 in the decade 1950 to 1959; fewer than 200 in the decade 1960 to 1969, with only 1 execution in 1967, and then none until 1977. When the Court decided *Furman v. Georgia* in 1972, more than 600 convicts were awaiting execution, over half of whom were members of minority groups. In 1976, the Supreme Court declared that capital punishment was not inherently cruel and unusual punishment and upheld a sentence of death where the two-step process was used (*Gregg v. Georgia,* 428 U.S. 153). At the same time, it struck down the application of mandatory death sentences (*Woodson v. North Carolina,* 428 U.S. 280) and, a year later, declared the death penalty invalid for rape (*Coker v. Georgia,* 433 U.S. 584 [1977]). Executions were renewed with the shooting of Gary Mark Gilmore at the Utah State Prison in 1977. From 1977 through the 1980s about 150 persons were executed, and by 1996 the number exceeded 320. The Supreme Court continued to monitor sentences of death with great care, insisting on clearly defined statutes and on a trial record of careful consideration of possible mitigating circumstances by judges and juries (*Beck v. Alabama,* 447 U.S. 625 [1980]; *Godfrey v. Georgia,* 446 U.S. 420 [1980]). As the pace of death sentences picked up, the Court began to receive and disapprove of repeated appeals and last-minute delays accompanying each scheduled execution. In 1984, in *Pulley v. Harris,* 465 U.S. 37, the Court resolved a major issue by holding that a state court need not review a death sentence to ensure its "proportionality" to the punishment imposed upon others for similar offenses. A 1986 decision, *Lockhart v. McCree,* 476 U.S. 162, permits exclusion of jurors who oppose the death penalty from serving in two-stage capital trials. In other cases, the Court held that an insane person may not be executed (*Ford v. Wainwright,* 477 U.S. 399 [1986]) and that a state may not mandate the death penalty for any crime (*Sumner v. Shuman,* 483 U.S. 66 [1987]). The death penalty may not be imposed for a crime committed when under the age of 16 (*Thompson v. Oklahoma,* 487 U.S. 815 [1988]) but is permissible for those committing crimes at age 16 or 17 (*Stanford v. Kentucky,* 492 U.S. 361 [1989]). Furthermore, a mentally retarded defendant, if competent to stand trial, may be executed (*Penry v. Lynaugh,* 492 U.S. 302 [1989]). Debate over the validity of capital punishment virtually ended in 1987, when the Court ruled in *McClesky v. Kemp,* 481 U.S. 279, that, in the absence of clear proof of purposeful discrimination, the death penalty is valid despite clear statistical evidence that blacks are more likely to receive the death penalty than are whites and that those convicted of slaying whites are more likely to receive the death penalty than those who murder blacks. More than 3000 inmates, almost all male and about half members of minority groups, were on death row in 1996. In 1991, the Court overturned previous rulings to hold in *Payne v. Tennessee,* 501 U.S. 808, that a capital sentencing jury may hear "victim impact" evidence, that is, evidence relating to the murder victim's character and the impact of the crime on the victim's family. During the 1990s the pace of executions accelerated, running at the 1950s levels of one or more a week. Thousands of women have been convicted of murder but very few executed. Approximately 30 people have been executed during this century who were later proven to have been innocent. Since the 1970s about 60 death-row inmates have been released after their innocence was established.

Censorship   The curbing of ideas either in speech or in writing *before* they are expressed. Accountability *after* expression is provided by laws regulating libel and slander, obscenity, incitement to crime, contempt of court, or seditious utterance. Except in time of war or other national emergency, any prior restraint upon freedom of speech or of the press is forbidden. *See also* INTERNET, page 81; *Freedman v. Maryland,* page 354; FREEDOM OF THE PRESS, page 315; *Miller v. California,* page 360; *Near v. Minnesota,* page 362; *Nebraska Press Association v. Stuart,* page 363; *New York Times v. United States,* page 364; *Roth v. United States,* page 368.

Significance   The rights of freedom of speech or of the press would be meaningless if prior censorship could be exercised. Although a person must bear the consequences of any expression, no governmental official may determine in advance what may be said or written. The Supreme Court has authorized exceptions in the case of motion pictures, holding that a city may require submission of films to a censor (*Times Film Corporation v. Chicago,* 365 U.S. 43 [1961]), provided prompt judicial review is available (*Freedman v. Maryland,* 380 U.S. 51 [1965]), and in the case of school-sponsored student publications that are inconsistent with the school's mission (*Hazelwood School District v. Kuhlmeier,* 484 U.S. 260 [1988]). In recent years, unusual censorship efforts have been directed at the National Endowment for the Arts (NEA) and its funding of allegedly obscene art. Congress has imposed a "decency" standard upon the NEA and requires grantees to return any funding should their work be found to be obscene by a court. Concern with censorship has heightened dramatically during the 1990s as a consequence of worldwide access to computers and internet services, and with congressional imposition of decency standards on such communication tools as well.

Citizen   An individual who is a native or naturalized member of a state, owes allegiance to that state, and is entitled to the protection and privileges of its laws. Citizenship in the United States is defined in the Fourteenth Amendment to the Constitution: "All persons born or naturalized in the United States, and subject to the jurisdiction thereof, are citizens of the United States and of the state wherein they reside." Citizenship is based mainly on one's place of birth (*jus soli*) but may be acquired through naturalization and, under circumstances defined by Congress, through blood relation (*jus sanguinis*). *See also* JUS SANGUINIS, page 322; JUS SOLI, page 322; NATIONAL, page 325; *United States v. Wong Kim Ark,* page 372.

Significance   Two basic citizenship issues were raised prior to the Civil War: (1) Should blacks born in the United States be considered citizens? (2) Is state citizenship secondary and incidental to national citizenship? The Fourteenth Amendment provides affirmative answers to both questions. Subsequent developments include the extension of citizenship by birth to American Indians and to the people of Guam, Puerto Rico, the Virgin Islands, and the Northern Marianas. Prior to 1922, a married woman took the citizenship of her husband, but under the Cable Act of 1922 women are treated the same as men. An alien spouse of an American citizen may be naturalized after a shorter period of residence. Children of foreign diplomatic agents who are born here are not citizens because they are not "subject to the jurisdiction" of the United States.

Civil Disobedience   Refusal to obey a law, usually on the ground that the law is morally reprehensible. An individual or group practicing civil disobedience seeks to call attention to a situation considered unjust and willingly suffers community ostracism and even imprisonment for such disobedience.

Significance   Civil disobedience is to be distinguished from direct or revolutionary attacks upon constituted authority. Rather, civil disobedience takes the form of nonviolent resistance and is aimed at arousing public opinion against the law. Contemporary examples include the leadership of the Rev. Martin Luther King Jr. against racial segregation laws, the refusal of anti–Vietnam War groups to honor draft regulations, the activities of antiabortion groups in attempting to close birth control clinics, and the resistance of environmentalists to nuclear power plants or other threats to the environment.

Civil Liberties   Those liberties, usually spelled out in a bill of rights or a constitution, that guarantee the protection of persons, expression, and property from the arbitrary interference of governmental officials. Restraints may be placed upon the exercise of these liberties only when they are abused by individuals or groups and when the public welfare requires them. *See also* BILL OF RIGHTS, page 296.

Significance   Civil liberties are basic to a free society as contrasted with a totalitarian society, which makes no such guarantees. They are a restraint upon the government rather than upon individuals. Civil liberties may be distinguished from "civil rights" in that the latter is generally understood to refer to positive policies of government to protect individuals from arbitrary treatment both by government and by other individuals. However, the terms are often used interchangeably.

Civil Rights   Positive acts of government designed to protect persons against arbitrary or discriminatory treatment by government or individuals. Civil rights guarantees are sometimes written into constitutions but frequently take the form of statutes. Though the term is often used interchangeably with "civil liberties," the latter generally refers to restraints upon government as found in bills of rights. The term "civil rights" is also to be distinguished from "political rights"—the right to participate in the management of government through such practices as voting—and "equal rights," used mainly in connection with the movement to achieve equality between men and women. *See also* CIVIL RIGHTS ACTS, pages 376–380; EQUAL RIGHTS, page 309; POLITICAL RIGHT, page 328.

Significance   Since 1940, there have been extensive attempts by government at all levels to secure civil rights for blacks and other minorities in such areas as employment, housing, and public facilities. Traditional constitutional civil liberty provisions have not always proved workable to meet the challenges of governmental discrimination, and especially private discrimination, against minority groups. The precise role and permissable extent of government action to secure civil rights remain a controversial question. Examples of civil rights legislation include the Civil Rights Acts of 1957, 1960, 1964, 1968, and 1991 and the civil rights laws enacted in many states and local communities.

Civil Rights Organizations   Groups organized to promote observance of the Bill of Rights and related constitutional provisions. These include organizations concerned with civil rights as well as those with broader interests and goals. The major black civil rights groups include the National Association for the Advancement of Colored People (NAACP), which concerns itself mainly with legislative and legal matters; the National Urban League, which concentrates on economic improvement for blacks; and the Southern Christian Leadership Conference (SCLC), which concentrates on mass demonstrations, boycotts, and sit-ins. Among the leading general civil rights and liberties groups are the American Civil Liberties Union (ACLU), the National Council of Churches of Christ, most labor unions, and ethnically oriented groups such as the American Jewish Congress. *See also* PRESSURE GROUP, page 104.

Significance   Civil rights organizations differ from most American pressure groups in that they are not primarily concerned with promoting the economic interests of their members. The ACLU, for example, supports court tests and in other ways protects First Amendment freedoms of expression and the rights of persons accused of crime. Few organizations are blatantly against civil rights, although the Ku Klux Klan, black separatist groups, and certain right-wing extremist groups oppose the efforts of civil rights organizations.

Clear and Present Danger Rule   A test used by the Supreme Court to measure the permissible bounds of free speech. The test was formulated by Justice Oliver Wendell Holmes in *Schenck v. United States,* 249 U.S. 47 (1919): "The question in every case is whether the words used are used in such circumstances and are of such a nature as to create a clear and present danger that they will bring about the substantive evils that Congress has a right to prevent. It is a question of proximity and degree." The application of this test has varied a good deal since 1919. *See also* BAD TENDENCY RULE, page 295; *Schenck v. United States,* page 369.

Significance   The clear and present danger rule is one attempt to establish a criterion for the protection of the individual's right to speak in light of society's right to protection. Freedom of speech is not absolute, particularly when its exercise has a close relationship to some unlawful act, such as the violent overthrow of the government. Yet, the relationship between mere speech or the advocacy of a doctrine on the one hand and the performance of an illegal act, on the other, is not easy to determine.

Commercial Speech Communication by a business enterprise. First Amendment issues arise from the conflict between the right of companies to advertise their products or take sides on public issues, and the right of government to protect consumers or the integrity of the political process. Although the underlying purpose of the First Amendment is to protect political expression, the Supreme Court has recognized a right to commercial speech as vital to a free enterprise system. This was established in *Virginia State Board of Pharmacy v. Virginia Citizens Consumer Council, Inc.*, 425 U.S. 748 (1976), in which the Court struck down a state law banning the advertising of prescription drugs, and *Bates v. State Bar of Arizona*, 431 U.S. 85 (1977), which upheld the right of lawyers to advertise. Despite these rulings, however, the Court has upheld restrictions where a substantial governmental interest is demonstrated, as in the 1990 case of *Austin v. Michigan Chamber of Commerce*, 494 U.S. 652, barring the use of corporate funds on behalf of political candidates. *See also Virginia State Board of Pharmacy v. Virginia Citizens Consumer Council, Inc.*, page 372.

Significance Commercial speech in an age of media dominance puts special stress upon the concept of free speech as traditionally perceived. In the case of marketing of products, the government's major interest lies in protecting consumers against fraud or unhealthful products. Cigarette and liquor businesses, for example, project controversial images that, in the view of some people, should be prohibited. Regulating the political side of commercial speech is far more complicated because of First Amendment protection and the ability of large corporations to overwhelm the political process with corporate funds. Thus, while several laws regulating the financing of political campaigns and lobbying activities by businesses at both the national and state levels exist, the degree of permissible regulation is unclear. In 1978 in *First National Bank of Boston v. Bellotti*, 435 U.S. 765, the Supreme Court invalidated a state law prohibiting corporations from spending money on a ballot referendum, though it later made a distinction with regard to support for a candidate in the 1990 *Austin* case. And although corporations may and do participate in the political process through political action committees, funds must come voluntarily from shareholders and employees and not from corporate accounts. Advertising by lawyers and physicians, once frowned upon or forbidden, has become commonplace.

Comparable Worth A concept, advanced by the women's movement for equal rights, which holds that certain occupations, though different in nature, are of equal value and should be equally compensated. Questions of comparable worth usually arise in reference to wage inequalities that are perceived to exist as a result of the traditional roles of men and women in American society. Thus, certain occupations thought to be "women's work" (nurses, librarians, schoolteachers, secretaries) are paid less than male-dominated jobs (mechanics, truck drivers, janitors, gardeners) though clearly of equal if not more worth to a business or society. *See also Craig v. Boren*, page 352; EQUAL RIGHTS, page 309; WOMEN'S LIBERATION MOVEMENT, page 120.

Significance   Comparable worth has emerged as a major issue in the women's movement. Working women earn only about 70 percent of the average annual income of working men. Women's rights advocates use such figures to argue that discrimination in the workplace still exists. Opponents argue that income differentials between men and women are the result of factors such as job seniority, educational background, individual job preferences, and women's life choices in childbearing and intermittent labor force participation, which are unrelated to employer discrimination. Comparable worth is to be distinguished from "equal pay for equal work"; the latter covers similar jobs requiring similar skills, and the former involves comparing the value of different jobs and resultant wage inequalities.

Confession   An admission of guilt by one accused of a crime. A confession must be voluntary and not induced by force, "third-degree" methods, prolonged interrogation, threats, psychological coercion, or promise of leniency. A confession must be corroborated with evidence that a crime has actually been committed. *See also Ashcraft v. Tennessee,* page 349; *McNabb v. United States,* page 359; *Miranda v. Arizona,* page 361; PLEA BARGAINING, page 273.

Significance   A confession exacted by illegal means is not admissible in a trial and may result in the release of the accused. Corroboration prevents the conviction of persons who confess to crimes they have not committed. The courts have been strict in demanding proof that a confession was made voluntarily and, preferably, in the presence of counsel. But in 1991, the Supreme Court held that an involuntary confession may, when assessed in the context of other evidence, be considered to be a "harmless error" and therefore admissible in a trial (*Arizona v. Fulminante,* 499 U.S. 279).

Confrontation Clause   The part of the Sixth Amendment to the Constitution that guarantees that, in criminal prosecutions, the accused shall have the right "to be confronted with the witnesses against him." An important corollary is the right to cross-examine such witnesses. In 1965, the Supreme Court ruled that the right of confrontation of witnesses also applied in state trials under the due process clause of the Fourteenth Amendment (*Pointer v. Texas,* 380 U.S. 400). *See also* WITNESS, page 343.

Significance   The confrontation clause safeguards defendants against faceless and nameless informers, permits defendants to hear the testimony and to see the evidence, and through an attorney, enables them to fully challenge the witness by cross-examination. Conversely, those who testify against an accused must be ready to face the defendant in open court and withstand cross-examination. In a case involving the use of a screen in court to protect children from having to face a defendant accused of sexually assaulting them, the Supreme Court held that the defendant's right to confront witnesses against him had been violated (*Coy v. Iowa,* 487 U.S. 1012 [1988]). But the Court authorized a child abuse victim to testify on closed-circuit television rather than in open court (*Maryland v. Craig,* 497 U.S. 836 [1990]). Along with other provisions of the Sixth Amendment, the confrontation clause is vital to a fair trial.

Conscientious Objector   A person who refuses to render military service because of religious training and belief. While the right to religious freedom does not extend to refusal to serve in the military service, Congress has, as an act of grace, authorized noncombatant service or exemption from military service for conscientious objectors. Even aliens who are conscientious objectors may still become citizens (*Girouard v. United States,* 328 U.S. 61 [1946]). The law does not exempt persons who oppose military service because of "political, sociological, or philosophical views or a merely personal moral code," but the Supreme Court has interpreted this liberally to include nontraditional conscientious objection held with the fervor of religious conviction. *See also* SELECTIVE SERVICE, page 577.

Significance   A conscientious objector does not have the right to refuse military duty. A high regard for those whose beliefs make them unable to participate in a war effort has led Congress to a policy of leniency. In effect, Congress gives such people preferred treatment when it excuses them from actual combat or requires them to do other service. Whether a person is a true conscientious objector and not a "draft dodger" is a question to be determined by draft boards and, at times, the courts. In 1965, the Supreme Court held in *United States v. Seeger,* 380 U.S. 128, that persons without formal or traditional religious affiliation or belief could qualify as conscientious objectors if their beliefs occupy a "place parallel to that filled by the God of those admittedly qualifying for the exemption." The standard was further broadened in 1970 to include one whose beliefs are rooted in moral or ethical grounds if they are held "with the strength of more traditional religious convictions" (*Welsh v. United States,* 398 U.S. 333). Conscientious objector status for objection to a specific war (for example, Vietnam), however, has been denied (*Gillette v. United States,* 401 U.S. 437 [1971]).

Conspiracy   Any agreement between two or more persons to commit an unlawful act. Conspiracy is a crime under numerous criminal statutes; in the realm of business and labor activities, the law forbids conspiracies in restraint of trade. A controversial conspiracy law in the field of civil liberties is that found in the Smith Act of 1940, which makes it a crime to conspire to teach, advocate, or organize groups that advocate the overthrow of government by force. *See also* ENTRAPMENT, page 308; GUILT BY ASSOCIATION, page 318.

Significance   Conspiracy laws are designed to punish persons who participate in the planning of a criminal act. In the areas of speech, press, and association, conspiracy laws pose the danger that persons who do not have actual plans to do evil may be punished for simple conjecture.

Cruel and Unusual Punishment   Any lingering torture, wanton infliction of pain, mutilation, or degrading treatment, or any sentence too severe for the offense committed. The Eighth Amendment to the Constitution forbids such punishment, leaving the scope of the ban to be determined by the courts. *See also* CAPITAL PUNISHMENT, page 296.

Significance   The idea of humane treatment for criminals, a relatively modern concept, holds that even the undesirable elements of the community should have their individual dignity preserved. Whether a particular punishment is cruel depends upon community standards as determined by the courts. Changing attitudes are reflected by Supreme Court decisions holding as cruel and unusual punishment the deprivation of citizenship for wartime desertion (*Trop v. Dulles,* 356 U.S. 86 [1958]) and a state law making it a crime to be addicted to the use of narcotics (*Robinson v. California,* 370 U.S. 660 [1962]). In 1972, the Supreme Court held that the death penalty as then imposed in the United States constituted cruel and unusual punishment (*Furman v. Georgia,* 408 U.S. 238). The penalty has since been restored in most jurisdictions. In 1976, the Court upheld death penalty laws that provide for careful consideration of mitigating factors that might affect a sentence (*Gregg v. Georgia,* 428 U.S. 153). In 1977, the Court rejected a claim that corporal punishment in public schools violated the Eighth Amendment (*Ingraham v. Wright,* 430 U.S. 651). The Court has held that the denial of medical care to a prison inmate is cruel and unusual punishment (*Estelle v. Gamble,* 429 U.S. 97 [1976]), as is confinement of a nonsmoking prisoner with a chain smoker (*Helling v. McKinney,* 509 U.S. 25 [1993]), but not the double celling of prisoners in cells designed for one person (*Rhodes v. Chapman,* 452 U.S. 337 [1981]). Claims that prison conditions constitute cruel and unusual punishment must show deliberate indifference by prison officials (*Wilson v. Seiter,* 501 U.S. 294 [1991]) or use of excessive physical force (*Hudson v. McMillan,* 503 U.S. 1 [1992]). In 1983 the Court held that a sentence must be proportionate to the offense and struck down as cruel and unusual a life sentence without possibility of parole for a nonviolent multiple offender (*Solem v. Helm,* 463 U.S. 277). But the Court cast doubt upon the viability of *Solem v. Helm* when in 1991 it upheld a mandatory sentence of life imprisonment without parole for drug possession in *Harmelin v. Michigan,* 501 U.S. 957.

De Facto Segregation   The existence of racially segregated facilities that are, however, not required by law (*de jure*). *De facto* segregation refers especially to school systems in typical northern communities, in which neighborhood racial patterns result "in fact" in predominantly black and white schools similar to those in the South that, in the past, were segregated by law. *See also* ELEMENTARY AND SECONDARY EDUCATION ACT, page 523; *Milliken v. Bradley,* page 360; *Swann v. Charlotte-Mecklenburg Board of Education,* page 370.

Significance   *De facto* segregation has been a difficult if not impossible problem leading to protest demonstrations, violence, and numerous complex lawsuits. Minority groups demanding integrated schools charge that segregation results from housing discrimination and from deliberate policies of school officials. White parents often resist integration efforts, demanding retention of neighborhood schools. Some school districts have tried or have been compelled by court orders to integrate schools by "busing" children to distant schools or by a variety of school mixing plans, notably establishment of magnet schools built around special interest curricula. Current law does not require elimination of *de facto* segregation, and Congress has restricted positive action, including busing, to achieve racial balance in schools. The massive ghettos in major cities may make it virtually impossible to eradicate *de facto* segregation in schools, leading to increasing demands for equality in financing school districts by the states. In an important 1992 decision, *Freeman v. Pitts,* 503 U.S. 467, the Supreme Court held that schools were under no obligation to remedy racial imbalance caused by demographic forces where resegregation is a product of private choices.

Denaturalization   The revoking of citizenship that has been acquired by naturalization. This may be done only by court order in accordance with due process of law.

Significance   The most common ground for denaturalization is fraud or willful misrepresentation during naturalization. Lengthy residence abroad by a naturalized citizen, once a ground for denaturalization, may no longer, under Supreme Court ruling, result in termination of citizenship (*Schneider v. Rusk,* 377 U.S. 163 [1964]). Legislation permits denaturalization of those who affiliate with subversive organizations within five years after naturalization, as well as those who are convicted of contempt of Congress for refusal to testify in an investigation into subversive activities within ten years after naturalization. Many observers charge that such provisions make "second-class" citizens of naturalized persons because native-born citizens are not affected by such laws. A commonly held assumption, that one loses citizenship when convicted of a serious crime, is not true. One may lose certain privileges of citizenship, such as the right to vote or hold certain jobs, but citizenship is retained.

Deportation   Compulsory expulsion of an alien from a state to his or her country of origin. Deportation is a civil proceeding rather than a criminal proceeding under American law; hence, various constitutional safeguards do not apply. With the exception of naturalized citizens who lose their citizenship, a citizen may not be deported. *See also* ANTITERRORISM AND EFFECTIVE DEATH PENALTY ACT OF 1996, page 375; *Fong Yue Ting v. United States,* page 354; IMMIGRATION AND NATURALIZATION SERVICE, page 346; IMMIGRATION REFORM ACT OF 1986, page 382.

Significance   Aliens remain in the United States at the sufferance of Congress, which has virtually unlimited power to establish grounds for deportation. Illegal entry is the most common cause of deportation. The Immigration and Naturalization Service estimates that about 8 million illegal aliens reside in the United States and that 800,000 to 1.5 million are apprehended and deported each year. Calls for stricter enforcement against illegal entry, particularly along the Mexican border, have met with resistance because of the monetary as well as social costs associated with increased border patrols, identity cards for all Americans, or other costly or undesirable practices. Congress resolved this in part through the Immigration Reform Act of 1986, making it illegal to employ illegal aliens and granting amnesty to millions of illegal aliens who had resided in the United States prior to January 1, 1982. In recent years Congress has considerably increased the number of grounds for deportation, particularly for illegal aliens, political undesirables, terrorists and aliens convicted of serious crimes. Constitutional safeguards with regard to bail and ex post facto laws, for example, do not apply to deportation proceedings, and great discretion is vested in the Attorney General. The courts have been reluctant to interfere because the issue involves the plenary powers of the national government in international affairs. The Refugee Act of 1980, however, grants asylum to those seeking refuge from persecution and provides for a hearing before an immigration judge for those facing deportation for failure to prove a persecution claim.

Double Jeopardy   The guarantee in the Fifth Amendment to the Constitution that one may not be twice put in jeopardy of life or limb for the same offense. Thus, a person who has been tried may not be tried again for the same crime or subjected to multiple punishments. The guarantee does not, however, apply to trials by both the national government and a state, or by two different states, for offenses growing out of a single criminal act. A person is put in jeopardy once the jury is sworn or the first witness is sworn. Trial following a mistrial is not double jeopardy unless the prosecution has deliberately forced a mistrial in order to get better evidence or a more favorable jury. The government may not appeal an acquittal or appeal a reversal of a guilty verdict due to insufficient evidence. In 1969, the Supreme Court held the protection against double jeopardy applicable to the states through the Fourteenth Amendment (*Benton v. Maryland,* 395 U.S. 784). *See also Bartkus v. Illinois,* page 349.

Significance   Although considerable confusion exists as to what constitutes double jeopardy in specific instances, this guarantee does afford protection against continual harassment of accused persons. Also, the courts and the accused are spared endless costs and time-consuming litigation.

Drug Testing   A procedure, usually performed by chemically testing the urine or hair—but sometimes breath or blood—for the presence of illegal narcotics. Drug testing, a controversial and important tool in the "drug war," has become especially pervasive in the federal government. Drug tests are usually conducted once a job applicant has tentatively been selected for employment, when an employee has applied for transfer to a sensitive or dangerous job, or, in the case of employees in jobs that may affect the public safety or trust, randomly. The controversy surrounding drug testing largely concerns the invasion of privacy that accompanies the administration of the test and the accuracy of the test results themselves. *See also* FOURTH AMENDMENT, page 314; OFFICE OF NATIONAL DRUG CONTROL POLICY, page 346.

Significance   Drug testing was mandated by President Reagan in 1986 by executive order for all federal government jobs involving special public trust, law enforcement, or public safety. The Department of Transportation and the Department of Defense issued regulations in 1988 requiring several private industries and contractors to conduct drug tests under certain circumstances. As of 1991, about 40 federal agencies were requiring drug tests, largely at the hiring stage. Supporters of drug testing argue that it serves a strong governmental interest and that the tests are not nearly as physically invasive as searches of clothing or personal effects are. Critics point to the emotional trauma that drug tests cause, note that the tests are often inaccurate or sloppily processed, and suggest that probable cause should be required to force an individual to take a drug test. Drug testing has been upheld by the Supreme Court. The leading cases involve the testing of postaccident railroad employees in *Skinner v. Railway Labor Executive Association,* 489 U.S. 602 (1989), the testing of customs officers applying for promotion to sensitive and high-security positions in *National Treasury Employees Union v. Von Raab,* 489 U.S. 656 (1989), and the testing of student athletes in *Vernonia School District v. Acton,* 115 S. Ct. 2386 (1995). In those cases the Court found a compelling government interest in protecting the public that outweighed the individual's right to privacy and freedom from unwarranted searches guaranteed in the Fourth Amendment. Drug testing by private firms is commonplace. To interdict the flow of drugs and to promote drug-free communities and institutions, Congress has appropriated funds to the Customs Service, the Coast Guard, Housing and Urban Development, the Drug Enforcement Administration in the Department of Justice, and various health agencies. The Office of National Drug Control Policy, headed by a "drug czar," was established in the Executive Office of the President in 1988 to develop a national drug control policy and strategy and to coordinate all federal programs.

Dual Citizenship   Holding citizenship in two or more countries. This may occur because most countries recognize as citizens those born within their boundaries as well as children of their subjects born abroad. Thus, a person born abroad of American parents is an American citizen (*jus sanguinis*) and may also be a citizen of the country in which he or she was born (*jus soli*).

Significance   Dual citizenship has become widespread because of increasing mobility. It may cause hardship when, for example, conflicting claims are made over the right to require military service. Under American law, a person who, after reaching the age of twenty-two, lives for three years in another country that also claims him or her as a citizen forfeits American citizenship unless he or she takes an oath of allegiance to the United States before a diplomatic official.

Due Process of Law   Protection against arbitrary deprivation of life, liberty, or property. The Fifth and Fourteenth Amendments forbid the national and state governments, respectively, to deny any person life, liberty, or property without due process of law. While no precise definition of this term has ever been made, it establishes the principle of limited government. Two types of due process—procedural and substantive—have emerged in the course of litigation. Though used sparingly in recent years, substantive due process has been used by the judiciary to strike down legislative and executive acts that, in their view of the term "liberty," are arbitrary or lacking in reasonableness or that cover subject matter beyond the reach of government. Procedural due process was defined by Daniel Webster as procedure "which hears before it condemns, which proceeds upon inquiry, and renders judgment only after trial." The Supreme Court, in a long series of cases, has marked out the general meaning of the phrase so as to forbid any procedure that is shocking to the conscience or that makes impossible a fair and enlightened system of justice for a civilized people. Increasingly, due process concepts are being extended by the courts to noncriminal issues such as the confinement of the mentally ill or the withdrawal of governmental benefits. *See also Addington v. Texas,* page 347; *Goldberg v. Kelly,* page 521; *Moore v. Dempsey,* page 361; *Palko v. Connecticut,* page 364; *Wolff v. McDonnell,* page 373.

Significance   Protection against arbitrary treatment is basic to the American system of government. Due process functions both as a limitation on public officials and as a power in the hands of the judiciary, which has wide latitude in applying it. Judges may, but infrequently, determine that a law bears no reasonable relationship to a proper governmental function. But judges constantly evaluate whether procedures used are fair and reasonable.

Eighth Amendment   That part of the Bill of Rights that prohibits excessive bail, excessive fines, or cruel and unusual punishments. All are binding on the states through the due process clause of the Fourteenth Amendment. *See also* BAIL, page 295; CRUEL AND UNUSUAL PUNISHMENT, page 303; FINE, page 312.

Significance   The Eighth Amendment's provisions are obviously subject to substantial and varying interpretation. The protection against cruel and unusual punishments, for example, enables the courts to modify penalties that are no longer consistent with social mores. The Supreme Court has used the constitutional provision to make dramatic changes in the imposition of the death penalty. The Court has guarded against excessive bail or fines, especially when used to penalize indigent persons.

Eminent Domain   The power inherent in all governments to take over private property, provided that it is taken for a public purpose and that just compensation is awarded. The Fifth Amendment prohibits the taking of private property for public use without just compensation. Disputes as to purpose or price are generally settled in the courts in suits referred to as "condemnation proceedings." A "taking" of property requiring compensation may also occur when restrictions are placed upon the uses of property through land use or zoning regulations. *See also* TAKINGS CLAUSE, page 340.

Significance   The right to own and use private property ranks high in the American scheme of values. Yet, without the power of eminent domain, projects that benefit many persons, such as slum clearance or highway projects, would be impossible. Individual rights, however, are recognized by the provision for equitable compensation, resulting often in lawsuits.

Entrapment   Action by an agent of the government to lure someone into self-incrimination by inducing performance of an illegal act. The Supreme Court has held that entrapment may not be used as a defense if it can be shown that the accused was predisposed to commit the act anyway (*Hampton v. United States*, 425 U.S. 484 [1976]). *See also* CONSPIRACY, page 303; SELF-INCRIMINATION, page 335.

Significance   The widespread use by federal, state, and local police of infiltrators and informers often results in their urging, aiding, or even initiating criminal behavior as, for example, when arrangements are made for the supply and sale of drugs through undercover agents. Critics of this practice (often referred to as a "sting operation") charge that the government's duty is to prevent crime, not to promote it, even for allegedly good reasons. Nevertheless, claims of entrapment are rarely successful unless it can be shown that the criminal act was not seriously contemplated, until induced by the sting.

Equal Protection of the Law   A requirement of the Fourteenth Amendment that state laws may not arbitrarily discriminate against persons. Identical treatment is not required. Classification of persons is permitted provided that the classification is reasonable and bears some relationship to the end sought. Hence, taxation in accordance with ability to pay has been held to be a reasonable classification, whereas classification according to color, religion, sex, or social class has been held to bear no reasonable relationship to the functions of government. Current interest in the application of equal protection centers on racial discrimination, equal justice for the poor, inequality in state legislative apportionment, and equal treatment for women, the aged, handicapped persons, and homosexuals. Though the Constitution does not contain a similar restriction on the national government, the courts have read the equal protection concept into the meaning of the due process clause of the Fifth Amendment. *See also Baker v. Carr,* page 176; *Bolling v. Sharpe,* page 350; *Brown v. Board of Education of Topeka,* page 350; CIVIL RIGHTS, page 299; *Craig v. Boren,* page 352; FINE, page 312.

Significance   Equal protection of the law emanates from the democratic concepts of the equality of persons under the law and their right to equality of opportunity. Arbitrary or irrelevant barriers to full enjoyment of rights are forbidden. Although the constitutional prohibition does not extend to private discrimination, both the national and many state governments have acted to forbid private discrimination against persons based on color, creed, sex, national origin, age, handicap, and, increasingly, sexual orientation. Such "civil rights" laws have evoked resistance from those who see them as "reverse discrimination" violative of the equal protection clause.

Equal Rights   The movement to equalize the rights of men and women. Traditionally in American law, women have not enjoyed the same rights as men, which has manifested itself in many areas of American life, including property rights, education, and employment opportunities. State laws vary widely, although many are protective of women rather than directly discriminatory. Women's suffrage led to a gradual narrowing of legal differences but, with increasing intensity since the 1960s, an extensive body of new laws and administrative regulations, as well as court decisions, has provided protection against gender discrimination. In March 1972, Congress proposed to the states a constitutional amendment that provided that "equality of rights under the law shall not be denied or abridged by the United States or any state on account of sex." The seven-year time limit for ratification expired in March 1979, and Congress, in an unprecedented move, extended the deadline to June 1982. Still, the proposal failed to receive the 38 state legislative approvals necessary for ratification. *See also* AFFIRMATIVE ACTION, page 292; *Arizona Governing Committee for Tax Annuity and Deferred Compensation Plans v. Norris,* page 348; COMPARABLE WORTH, page 301; *Craig v. Boren,* page 352; FREEDOM OF ASSOCIATION, page 315; *Meritor Savings Bank, FSB v. Vinson,* page 359; WOMEN'S LIBERATION MOVEMENT, page 120.

Significance   The concept of equal rights has had a dramatic impact upon American life, equal to, if not greater than, the impact of changing race relations. Many constitutional authorities believe that changes already brought about in behalf of women's rights as well as liberal application of equal protection of the law concepts diminish the need for an equal rights amendment. Others note that an amendment will give rise to a host of constitutional problems relating to the traditional roles of men and women. The equal rights movement achieved two major victories in the 1960s: the passage of the Equal Pay Act of 1963, which requires equal pay for men and women doing similar work, and the Civil Rights Act of 1964, which forbids discrimination against women in hiring and other personnel policies. An end to sex discrimination in education was ordered by Congress in 1972, and the Equal Credit Opportunity Act was adopted in 1974. A 1978 enactment prohibits discrimination against pregnant women in any area of employment. Pension rights of widowed homemakers and of working mothers who temporarily leave jobs to raise families were put under protection in 1984. In 1986, the Supreme Court declared sexual harassment to be unlawful sexual discrimination under the Civil Rights Act of 1964 (*Meritor Savings Bank, FSB v. Vinson,* 477 U.S. 57). Congress strengthened this concept by enactment in 1994 of the Violence Against Women Act, which defines gender-motivated crime as a deprivation of civil rights and subjects violators to a civil suit for damages under the Civil Rights Act of 1964. The Supreme Court has tended to reject legal distinctions based on sex as contrary to equal protection of the law, with the notable exception of its 1981 ruling in *Rostker v. Goldberg,* 453 U.S. 57, that women may be excluded from the military draft.

Establishment of Religion   The close, legal alliance between a state and a church marked by the enforcement of particular religious beliefs and doctrines and the use of public funds to support clergy and maintain churches. Nine of the original thirteen colonies in America had established churches, and six still had them at the time of the framing of the Constitution in 1789. Thomas Jefferson and James Madison led the fight to legally separate the church from the state and were successful in the state of Virginia. The opening words of the Bill of Rights' First Amendment read "Congress shall make no law respecting an establishment of religion, or prohibiting the free exercise thereof." Much contemporary American concern over the establishment clause revolves around education, namely, the constitutionally permissible public support of religious education and the validity of religious observances in public schools. *See also* FREEDOM OF RELIGION, page 316; SEPARATION OF CHURCH AND STATE, page 336.

Significance   The establishment of religion is still commonplace in many parts of the world, and religious conflicts abound between groups seeking to control governments. In the United States, the multicultural nature of the population makes any traditional establishment both impossible and unwise. Nevertheless, strong emotions evoked by religious beliefs do erupt from time to time, posing a challenge to governmental attempts to play a neutral role, as in the case of prayer in schools or support for parochial schools. Controversy also emerges over displays of religious objects on public property. The American people are still divided over the question of whether the establishment clause requires a "wall of separation between church and state" or merely a nondiscriminatory attitude on the part of government in support of all religions.

Expatriation   Voluntary withdrawal of allegiance or residence from the country in which citizenship is held. Since 1865, Congress has expressly recognized the right of expatriation and has set forth specific grounds.

Actions that may constitute expatriation include naturalization in a foreign state, taking an oath of allegiance to another state, serving in a foreign army without consent, taking a job open only to citizens of another state, and conviction of treason or attempt to overthrow the government by force. The Supreme Court has taken a dim view of expatriation laws, holding that citizenship is a constitutional right that can be given up only by a truly voluntary act. A citizen living abroad may voluntarily renounce his or her citizenship before a diplomatic officer, but renunciation is permitted within the United States only during wartime with the consent of the Attorney General. *See also Afroyim v. Rusk,* page 348.

Significance   Congress recognized the right of expatriation as a "natural and inherent right of all people," essential for the rights to life, liberty, and the pursuit of happiness. The major purpose of this declaration was to justify before the world the great number of people from foreign lands who were emigrating to the United States. The expatriation laws assume that the persons committing certain acts, whether or not they intend them to be acts of expatriation, act voluntarily and with full knowledge of the consequences. Supreme Court decisions, however, have declared unconstitutional several statutory provisions on expatriation, including (1) leaving the United States to avoid military service (*Rusk v. Cort,* 372 U.S. 144 [1963]); (2) conviction for wartime desertion, a decision based on the ground that expatriation for desertion is cruel and unusual punishment (*Trop v. Dulles,* 356 U.S. 86 [1958]); and (3) voting in a foreign election (*Afroyim v. Rusk,* 387 U.S. 253 [1967]) because such acts do not necessarily indicate an intention to renounce citizenship. Intention to expatriate oneself may be evaluated in a trial.

Ex Post Facto Law   A criminal law that is retroactive and that has an adverse effect upon one accused of a crime. Thus, an *ex post facto* law is one that makes an act a crime that was not a crime when the act was committed, that increases the penalty for a crime after its commission, or that changes the rules of evidence to make conviction easier. Neither the state nor the national government may enact such laws under provisions of Article I, sections 9 and 10 of the Constitution. The prohibition does not extend to civil laws, such as retroactive taxation, or laws favorable to an accused person.

Significance   The *ex post facto* prohibition emphasizes that each individual is free to do those things not specifically forbidden by existing criminal law without fear of future punishment. This is pertinent to the concept of "a government of laws and not of men," for it prevents abuse of power by governmental officials, who might otherwise retrospectively apply new laws for vindictive purposes.

Fair Employment Practices Laws   Laws that forbid private or public employers, labor unions, or employment agencies to discriminate in hiring or in other personnel policies on the grounds of race, color, creed, or national origin. Most states have enacted such laws. In the Civil Rights Act of 1964, Congress provided for equal employment opportunities in businesses and labor unions engaged in interstate commerce. Equal treatment in employment for women is also required by the Act. Later legislation forbids discrimination in employment because of age (Age Discrimination Act of 1967) or handicap (Rehabilitation Act of 1973 and Americans with Disabilities Act of 1990). *See also* AFFIRMATIVE ACTION, page 292; AMERICANS WITH DISABILITIES ACT OF 1990, page 375; CIVIL RIGHTS ACT OF 1964, page 378; CIVIL RIGHTS ACT OF 1991, page 379; EQUAL EMPLOYMENT OPPORTUNITY COMMISSION, page 345; REVERSE DISCRIMINATION, page 332.

Significance   Fair employment laws represent positive governmental action in the field of private rights, in contrast to the traditional concept of civil liberties as a restraint against government. Both the national and state laws stress education and conciliation, although several state laws provide criminal sanctions. The national law encourages state action in this field. For a number of years, presidential executive orders had prohibited racial discrimination in public employment and by government contractors. Increasingly, challenges to racial and sexual discrimination have made their way through administrative agencies and courts. Where discrimination is found, awards of back pay and seniority have been made (*Albermarle Paper Co. v. Moody*, 422 U.S. 405 [1975]; *Franks v. Bowman Transportation Co.*, 424 U.S. 747 [1976]).

Fifth Amendment   A part of the Bill of Rights that imposes a number of restrictions on the national government with respect to the rights of persons accused of crime. It provides for indictment by grand jury, protects against double jeopardy and self-incrimination, and forbids denial of life, liberty, or property without due process of law. In addition, the Fifth Amendment prohibits the taking of property without just compensation. The Amendment's due process clause is treated as embodying the concept of equal protection of the law. *See also* DOUBLE JEOPARDY, page 306; DUE PROCESS, page 307; EMINENT DOMAIN, page 308; EQUAL PROTECTION OF THE LAW, page 308; GRAND JURY, page 264; IMMUNITY, page 321; SELF-INCRIMINATION, page 335; TAKINGS CLAUSE, page 340.

Significance   The Fifth Amendment gathers in a few words a wide range of procedural and substantive rights. It is a significant source for protection of individual and property rights. Its famed due process clause was also placed in the Fourteenth Amendment as a limitation on state power. The Amendment is popularly known in connection with persons who refuse to testify before congressional committees or courts by "taking the Fifth," a shorthand phrase for claiming the privilege against self-incrimination.

Fine   A sum of money paid as a penalty for an illegal act. The Eighth Amendment to the Constitution forbids the imposition of excessive fines. A fine may constitute the total penalty, or it may be levied in addition to or as a substitute for imprisonment. The Supreme Court has held it to be a denial of equal protection either to extend a jail sentence for inability to pay a fine (*Williams v. Illinois*, 399 U.S. 925 [1970]) or to put an indigent person in jail for an offense punishable by only a fine (*Tate v. Short*, 401 U.S. 395 [1971]). *See also* EQUAL PROTECTION OF THE LAW, page 308.

Significance   Fines are common penalties for minor offenses, such as traffic violations, but are also levied for major offenses, especially when funds have been accumulated as a result of violation of law. Fines serve as both a painful penalty and a source of governmental revenue. Recent decisions of the Supreme Court assure equal justice for the poor, who otherwise would be jailed for longer periods than those able to pay fines. The court has also voided excessive forfeitures of property, as in the case of seizure of property (e.g., a car or home) used in commission of drug-related crime (*Austin v. United States,* 509 U.S. 602 [1993]). The excessive fine prohibition has been held not to apply to large awards of punitive damages in suits between private parties (*Browning-Ferris Industries of Vermont v. Kelco Disposal Co.,* 492 U.S. 257 [1989]) unless punitive damages are grossly excessive (*BMW of North America, Inc. v. Gore,* 116 S. Ct. 1589 [1996]).

First Amendment   The opening passage of the Bill of Rights and the source of those substantive rights fundamental to a free society—freedom of conscience and expression. The First Amendment prohibits Congress to establish a religion, to prohibit the free exercise of religion, or to abridge the freedoms of speech, press, assembly, or petition. While the Amendment is specifically directed at Congress, all of its provisions have been made binding upon the states through Supreme Court interpretation of the due process clause of the Fourteenth Amendment. *See also* FREEDOM OF ASSEMBLY, page 314; FREEDOM OF ASSOCIATION, page 315; FREEDOM OF THE PRESS, page 315; FREEDOM OF RELIGION, page 316; FREEDOM OF SPEECH, page 317; PETITION, page 328; SEPARATION OF CHURCH AND STATE, page 336.

Significance   The First Amendment is viewed by most civil libertarians as containing the very essence of a free society. The surest limitation on potential or real tyrants is the exercise of the free conscience through the medium of religious expression, speech, and press. All other provisions of the Bill of Rights are more secure so long as people are free to speak or write about them and to seek redress of grievances through peaceful assembly and petition. Potentially harmful exercise of these freedoms may be curtailed but the courts have generally resisted limitation by encouraging "more" expression of various views.

Fourteenth Amendment   A post–Civil War Amendment (1868) that defines citizenship, restricts the power of the states in their relations with their inhabitants, requires reduction of a state's representation in Congress for denials of suffrage, disqualifies former officeholders who participated in the rebellion, and invalidates any war debts of rebellious states. The most important provisions are those that forbid a state to deprive any person of life, liberty, or property without due process of law or deny to any person the equal protection of the law. *See also Barron v. Baltimore,* page 349; CITIZEN, page 298; DUE PROCESS OF LAW, page 307; EQUAL PROTECTION OF THE LAW, page 308; INCORPORATION DOCTRINE, page 321.

Significance   Since its enactment, the Fourteenth Amendment has produced extensive controversy over the intentions of its framers and in its specific applications by the Supreme Court. Whatever the intent of the framers may have been, the uses of the Fourteenth Amendment have altered the federal system. The due process clause and the equal protection clause have been prominent in constitutional disputes for many years. Both have made possible federal intervention against alleged state encroachment on the rights of the people. For a time, the due process clause was used mainly to limit the states in the exercise of their taxing and police powers in business regulation. Since 1925, the due process clause has been interpreted by the courts to forbid state denials of First Amendment freedoms as well as of essential procedural rights found in the Fourth, Fifth, Sixth, and Eighth Amendments. The equal protection clause has been invoked to restrain racial segregation practices, to maintain fair legislative apportionment by state governments, to gain equal justice for the poor, and to gain equal treatment for women.

Fourth Amendment   A part of the Bill of Rights that prohibits "unreasonable" searches and seizures. Under ordinary or "reasonable" circumstances, a search warrant must be secured from a judge or magistrate upon a showing of "probable cause." This written order, issued under oath, describes the place to be searched and the person or things to be seized. A warrant is not essential if it can be shown that time or circumstances did not reasonably permit securing it. Under the "exclusionary rule," evidence gathered through illegal or unreasonable means is not admissible in federal trials or, under the Fourteenth Amendment, in state trials (*Weeks v. United States,* 232 U.S. 383 [1914]; *Mapp v. Ohio,* 367 U.S. 643 [1961]). Such evidence may be used, however, if it "inevitably" would have been discovered anyway (*Nix v. Williams,* 467 U.S. 431 [1984]) or even if obtained as a result of a defective warrant if the police acted with "objective good faith" (*United States v. Leon,* 468 U.S. 897 [1984]). *See also* ARREST WARRANT, page 294; DRUG TESTING, page 306; *Mapp v. Ohio,* page 358; PRIVACY, page 329; WIRETAPPING, page 342.

Significance   The Fourth Amendment has proved to be one of the more troublesome provisions of the Bill of Rights. What constitutes an "unreasonable" search and seizure? No precise definition can be made, and the courts have treated the issue on a case-to-case basis, considering all the circumstances involved. In recent years, the Supreme Court has eased restrictions on searches and arrests with liberal interpretations of "reasonableness" to provide greater flexibility for police and other agencies. Serious contemporary problems include the reasonableness of searches through electronic devices, aerial surveillance, the search of movable vehicles, or computer networks. The increasing use of "regulatory" or "administrative" searches (such as inspections of persons or property for health or safety reasons) or blanket searches (as at airports) pose additional problems. Individualized suspicion and search underlie the meaning of the Fourth Amendment, but it can be abused in the name of "emergency" or "national security." Increasingly, the courts are weighing the extent of "probable cause" for a search against the individual's "legitimate expectations of privacy." Evidence obtained through an unreasonable search and seizure is inadmissible on the ground that it constitutes self-incrimination—forcing the accused to reveal what he or she has a right to conceal.

Freedom of Assembly   The right of the people to congregate for the discussion of public questions and to organize into political parties or pressure groups for the purpose of influencing public policy. The right of assembly does not authorize meetings designed to accomplish an illegal purpose or those that lead to a breach of the peace or resistance to lawful authority.

Freedom of assembly is guaranteed by the First Amendment and state constitutions. In addition, the Supreme Court has ruled that the due process clause of the Fourteenth Amendment protects the individual's freedom of assembly against infringement by state governments. *See also Hague v. CIO,* page 355.

Significance In a democratic society, the people must have the right to meet freely in peaceable assemblage to consider public questions. This right is closely related to freedoms of speech and of petition. All act as a restraint upon legislators and other public officials. Civil rights protest movements and mass demonstrations for peace, disarmament, environmental safety, and other issues of major public controversy such as abortion have put the right of assembly to severe tests because of the potential for violence and civil disobedience in any large gathering.

Freedom of Association The right to organize for political, religious, or other social purposes. The Constitution makes no mention of freedom of association, but it is implicit in guarantees of freedom of speech, assembly, and religion. *See also* GUILT BY ASSOCIATION, page 318; *NAACP v. Alabama,* page 362; *Scales v. United States,* page 369.

Significance The American people are noted for being organization-minded; many Americans belong to several organizations. The right to associate received much attention during the 1950s because of laws passed to curtail the activities and rights of alleged subversive organizations and their members and various efforts to impede the activities of civil rights groups promoting desegregation. Such laws tend to impute guilt by association; members of a group may not necessarily subscribe to all its beliefs or actions. Persons do not, however, have the right to organize in order to accomplish illegal aims. The courts have generally not permitted any limitations to be placed upon lawful association. The right to associate is recognized as essential in a democratic society because generally an individual can accomplish more with a group than by acting alone. In the social and economic arenas, the Supreme Court has held that when women are denied access to the business contacts and civic activities that characterize membership in male-only private clubs, states and cities may ban sex discrimination by such clubs without violating the right of association of men (*Board of Directors of Rotary International v. Rotary Club of Duarte,* 481 U.S. 537 [1987]; *New York State Club Association, Inc. v. City of New York,* 487 U.S. 1 [1988]).

Freedom of the Press The right to publish and disseminate information without prior restraint, subject to penalties for abuse of the right. Abuses include libel, obscenity, incitement to crime, contempt of court, and sedition. Freedom of the press is protected by the First and Fourteenth Amendments to the Constitution and by all state constitutions. Major contemporary problems have involved censorship of books, art, and movies for alleged obscenity; restraints on political publications; governmental secrecy; and the difficulty of safeguarding both freedom of the press and a fair trial. *See also Miller v. California,* page 360; *Near v. Minnesota,* page 362; *Nebraska Press Association v. Stuart,* page 363; *New York Times v. Sullivan,* page 363; *New*

York Times v. United States, page 364; PUBLIC TRIAL, page 330; *Roth v. United States,* page 368.

Significance   A free press is essential to a free society, particularly as it relates to the dissemination of political information. The Supreme Court has narrowly restricted any efforts at political censorship and has permitted wide latitude to criticize public officials. In dealing with obscenity, the courts have had difficulty in developing a formula to identify this abuse. The conflict between a free press and a fair trial involves a clash between two essential rights. The problem arises from the difficulty of holding a trial free from bias when press, radio, and television publicize details of the crime and the trial. In 1980, Congress enacted legislation (to reverse the Supreme Court's decision in *Zurcher v. Stanford Daily,* 436 U.S. 547 [1978]) to prohibit unannounced searches of newsrooms or other organizations engaged in First Amendment–protected activities.

Freedom of Religion   Freedom of worship and religious practice. The national government under the First Amendment and the states under their constitutions and the Fourteenth Amendment may not abridge this right of worship. Government may not compel or punish affirmation or rejection of religious beliefs, impose any disability on the basis of religious status, or take sides in controversies over religious authority. Any religious practice that is contrary to public peace or morality may be outlawed, such as snake-handling or polygamy. *See also* JEHOVAH'S WITNESSES CASES, page 357; *Reynolds v. United States,* page 367; SEPARATION OF CHURCH AND STATE, page 336.

Significance   In a nation with such diversity of religious groups, the free exercise of religion and the separation of church and state are essential. This was foremost in the minds of the Founding Fathers, who also provided that there be no religious test for public office. Religious freedom is the first item in the Bill of Rights, reflecting the need for freedom of conscience in a free society. Any interference of state with church or of church with state constitutes a danger to both. Although the free exercise of religion has not proved to be as controversial a matter in American life as has the concept of the separation of church and state, various civil rights laws now include prohibitions against religious discrimination, thereby extending the scope of religious liberty. An issue emerging with increasing frequency is the right of religious exercise as it affects one's employment. The Supreme Court has held that an employer has the duty under the Civil Rights Act of 1964 to make a reasonable accommodation to an employee's religious practices but need not adopt the worker's plan for the accommodation (*Ansonia Board of Education v. Philbrook,* 479 U.S. 60 [1986]). The Court also ruled that a person discharged for refusal to work on the Sabbath may not be denied unemployment benefits (*Hobbie v. Unemployment Commission of Florida,* 480 U.S. 136 [1987]). In a controversial decision in 1990 (*Employment Division, Department of Human Resources of Oregon v. Smith,* 494 U.S. 872), the Court upheld the denial of unemployment benefits to Native American Indians who used an illegal drug, peyote, for sacramental purposes. In that case, the Court rejected previous doctrine that required the state to show a compelling governmental interest in limiting a religious practice and held that the law in question was valid because it applied to everyone and was not directed at a specific religion. Critics alleged that the decision failed to sustain the basic purpose of the First Amendment to protect the aberrant minority. In the Religious Freedom Restoration Act of 1993, Congress overrode the "peyote case." The Act restores the principle that a law of general applicability may not burden the exercise of religious liberty unless it furthers a compelling governmental interest and uses the least restrictive means to further that interest.

Freedom of Speech   The right to speak without prior restraint, subject to penalties for abuse of the right. Abuses include slander, obscenity, incitement to crime, contempt of court, and sedition. By virtue of the First and Fourteenth Amendments and state bills of rights, neither the national government nor the states may abridge the right of freedom of speech. *See also* ACADEMIC FREEDOM, page 292; BAD TENDENCY RULE, page 295; CENSORSHIP, page 298; CLEAR AND PRESENT DANGER RULE, page 300; COMMERCIAL SPEECH, page 301; FREEDOM OF THE PRESS, page 315; LIBEL AND SLANDER, page 323; LOYALTY OATH, page 324; PUBLIC TRIAL, page 330; *Texas v. Johnson,* page 371; *Virginia State Board of Pharmacy v. Virginia Citizens Consumer Council,* page 372.

Significance   Freedom is impossible without the right to disseminate ideas. Generally, the courts have treated the guarantee liberally. With regard to the advocacy of allegedly subversive doctrine, the courts have distinguished between mere advocacy of abstract doctrine and conspiratorial advocacy. Antiwar protests and the civil rights movement have also tested American tolerance for dissent. For the most part, the courts have protected the peaceful expression of unpopular ideas, including the right to "symbolic speech" such as picketing or wearing protest insignia. Freedom of expression has also been extended to commercial advertising and to the arts. In placing limitations on freedom of speech, the courts have attempted to apply such concepts as "clear and present danger" to determine whether a given situation justifies restriction.

Gay Rights   The movement to end discrimination against homosexuals. Since the 1970s, gay and lesbian individuals and groups have "come out of the closet" to publicly identify themselves as homosexuals and to demand that their lifestyles and sexual orientation be legitimized and protected. Gay rights laws, similar to those prohibiting discrimination because of race, sex, religion, or national origin, have been adopted in seven states (California, Connecticut, Hawaii, Massachusetts, New Jersey, Vermont, and Wisconsin) and in more than 50 cities including New York, San Francisco, and Washington, D.C. The Supreme Court ruling in 1986 in *Bowers v. Hardwick,* 478 U.S. 186, that there is no constitutionally protected right to engage in homosexual conduct stunned the gay community. In 1992, Colorado voters passed a constitutional amendment prohibiting passage of state or local gay rights laws but the Supreme Court struck it down as a violation of the equal protection clause (*Romer v. Evans,* 116 S. Ct. 1620 [1996]). During the 1990s, the gay rights movement focused on ending discrimination against homosexuals by the military services, which adopted a "don't ask, don't tell" policy but prohibits homosexual behavior. Gay rights activists also fought for the recognition of the right to same-sex marriages or, as an alternative, recognition of "domestic partners" who would be accorded the same rights (such as dependent health insurance) as married couples. The domestic partner concept has been adopted by some local governments and private businesses. In 1996, however, Congress enacted the Defense of Marriage Act which, for the first time, defined marriage in federal law as the "legal union between one man and one woman," authorized states to deny recognition to same-sex marriages approved elsewhere, and denied eligibility for federally authorized spousal benefits to same-sex couples.

Significance   Antipathy toward homosexual conduct has deep historical and religious roots. All of the original thirteen states and, subsequently, all states prohibited sodomy. In recent years, due to liberalizing of attitudes spurred by the gay rights movement, such laws have either been repealed or declared void in more than half the states. The Supreme Court decision in *Bowers v. Hardwick* was viewed by the gay rights community as a potential rationale for discriminatory action against homosexuals in employment, housing, and other social needs. The only previous gay rights opinion of the Supreme Court was in 1967, when the Court held in *Boutilier v. Immigration and Naturalization Service,* 387 U.S. 118, that homosexual aliens could be excluded from entry, as "psychopathic personalities." The status of homosexuals remains cloudy. They have received confusing public signals but their recent openness and use of public demonstrations and other activist tactics have gained greater tolerance for them as citizens entitled to be protected against unreasonable discrimination.

Guilt by Association   Attribution of criminal or wrongful behavior or beliefs to a person because of association with certain people or organizations. *See also Elfbrandt v. Russell,* page 353; FREEDOM OF ASSOCIATION, page 315; INTERNAL SECURITY ACT OF 1950, page 383; *Scales v. United States,* page 369.

Significance   Guilt by association is a denial of the concept underlying American justice that guilt is personal and that an individual should not suffer any disabilities because of conduct or ideas attributed to his or her associates. The problem relates to those who lose their jobs or suffer other penalties as a result of membership in an alleged subversive or unpopular group. The issue is whether mere membership or association is presumptive of illegal behavior or proves agreement with all the tenets of the group. The Supreme Court has at times sustained the power of national, state, and local governments to impose disabilities upon members of particular groups or exponents of certain ideas, notably Communists. However, recent decisions have overturned this position, with the Court striking down most laws that penalize people for mere membership in an organization. Guilt by association should not be confused with conviction for conspiracy to commit a crime, which involves actual and deliberate participation in the planning of a wrongful act.

Gun Control   The regulation of the sale and possession of firearms by private individuals. Contemporary national gun control legislation followed the assassinations of the Rev. Martin Luther King Jr. and Senator Robert F. Kennedy with the passage of the Omnibus Crime Control and Safe Streets Act of 1968. That law barred mail order or interstate shipment of firearms, established licensing procedures for dealers and collectors, and required dealers to keep records. In 1986, Congress lifted the ban on interstate shipment of rifles and shotguns, limited the licensing requirements for dealers, and barred the establishment of any firearms registration plan. The ban on interstate shipment of handguns was retained, but other provisions limited federal authority over state laws on firearms. In 1993, the Brady Bill was enacted. Named after former White House Press Secretary James S. Brady, who was seriously wounded in an assassination attempt on President Reagan in 1981, the bill provided for a five-day waiting period and a background check to purchase a handgun. A 1994 crime bill banned 19 assault weapons. *See also* BUREAU OF ALCOHOL, TOBACCO AND FIREARMS, page 343; SECOND AMENDMENT, page 334.

Significance   Controversy over gun control legislation stems from the Second Amendment's provision, "A well regulated militia, being necessary to the security of a free state, the right of the people to keep and bear arms, shall not be infringed." Court decisions support the view that individual possession of firearms is related to the collective militia provision and that whatever limits may exist on the national government to control guns, state and local government regulations are valid, including outright ban (*Lewis v. United States,* 445 U.S. 55 [1980]). Both expansions and limitations on the right to bear arms tend to be viewed as victories or defeats for the National Rifle Association, which opposes gun control laws. Proponents of gun control believe that regulation will reduce violent crime. Opponents argue that criminals are less likely to commit crimes if they know that law-abiding citizens may be in possession of a firearm. More important, perhaps, is the argument of the pro-gun lobby that possession of firearms is essential to defend against a tyrannical government, should such a situation emerge. The status of gun control in the late 1990s was very mixed across the nation, with strong bans or regulations of firearm ownership in some states and cities and encouragement to own guns and even carry concealed weapons in others.

Habeas Corpus   A court order directing an official who has a person in custody to bring the prisoner to court and to show cause for his or her detention. The Constitution guarantees the right to a writ of habeas corpus, but Congress may suspend it in cases of rebellion or invasion (Art. I, sec. 9). Though President Lincoln suspended the writ on his own volition, Congress subsequently affirmed his action. A number of state constitutions absolutely forbid its suspension. *See also* ANTITERRORISM AND EFFECTIVE DEATH PENALTY ACT OF 1996, page 375.

Significance   Habeas corpus is generally considered to be the most important guarantee of liberty in that it prevents arbitrary arrest and imprisonment—the frightening knock at the door and the disappearance of the seized person. A prisoner must be released unless sufficient cause to detain him or her can be shown. Today, habeas corpus is typically used by persons serving sentences in state and federal prisons to reopen their cases on the ground of illegal detention because of rights denied before or during their trials. Controversy exists over the extent to which state prisoners may challenge their imprisonment through a federal writ of habeas corpus. The writ has been a major instrument for federal judges to reform state criminal procedure. Recent Supreme Court decisions, however, have narrowed the availability of federal habeas corpus relief for state prisoners. Such was the case of the 1991 ruling in *McClesky v. Zant,* 499 U.S. 467, which imposed restrictions on filing more than one petition. In the Antiterrorism and Effective Death Penalty Act of 1996, Congress sharply restricted the opportunities for state or federal prisoners to file habeas corpus petitions in federal district courts. The law places time limits on such appeals after state procedures are exhausted. Federal judges are to defer to any reasonable state court rulings on the cases. In order to get a second round of federal habeas corpus review, an inmate must first get clearance from a panel of appellate judges. The Supreme Court upheld these new limits on habeas corpus after an expedited hearing in *Felker v. Turpin,* 116 S. Ct. 2135 (1996). The Court ruled that the limitations placed by Congress did not constitute a "suspension" of the writ contrary to Article I, section 9 of the Constitution or affect the Supreme Court's own authority to grant the writ under its original jurisdiction in Article III, section 2.

Immigration Admittance of a person to a country of which he or she is not a native for the purpose of establishing permanent residence. Early attempts by seaboard states to regulate immigration into the United States were invalidated by the Supreme Court, which declared immigration an exclusive function of the national government, incidental to its power over foreign affairs. Immigration into the United States was unlimited until 1882, when Congress began to impose restrictions on the admission of criminals, mentally ill or diseased persons, paupers, illiterates, anarchists, advocates of violent governmental change, and the Chinese. In 1924, Congress barred Asians and established the "national origins quota" system, which limited annual immigration and assigned a quota to each country based on the numerical contribution it had made to the national stock as of 1920. In 1952, Congress erased racial exclusions but retained the quota system and the annual limit. Restrictions against the admission of Communists or other suspected subversives were increased. In 1965, Congress abolished the national origins quota system and established a new annual limit of 170,000, with preference given to relatives of citizens and persons with special skills. Immigration from the Western Hemisphere was restricted (to 120,000) for the first time. In the Refugee Act of 1980, Congress raised the total annual limit from 290,000 to 320,000. Legislation enacted in 1986 attempts to control the large flow of illegal immigration by making it unlawful to employ undocumented aliens. In the first major revision of immigration law since 1965, Congress, in 1990, set a new annual level of 675,000 immigrants. The 1990 law broadens the diversity of the immigrant pool by favoring Europeans, who have been disadvantaged by the existing system that gave preference to families of recent immigrants, about 85 percent of whom came from Asia and Latin America. Recent debate over immigration has centered on the growing problems of controlling illegal immigration and the issue of withholding welfare benefits from both legal and illegal immigrants. Immigration laws are administered by the Departments of State and Justice, which have been given extensive discretion to determine who may enter the United States. *See also* ANTITERRORISM AND EFFECTIVE DEATH PENALTY ACT OF 1996, page 375; DEPORTATION, page 305; IMMIGRATION ACT OF 1965, page 381; IMMIGRATION ACT OF 1990, page 381; IMMIGRATION AND NATURALIZATION SERVICE, page 346; IMMIGRATION REFORM ACT OF 1986, page 382; PASSENGER CASES, page 365.

Significance   About 50 million people have come to the United States from all over the world. Congress has relaxed quota restrictions by admitting large numbers of refugees and displaced persons from war-torn or totalitarian countries. Pressures for limiting immigration have come largely from labor organizations, from those who fear the introduction of alien ideologies, and from those who, though immigrants or descendants of immigrants themselves, look down upon new groups seeking admission. During the first decade of the 1900s and during the 1980s, the United States absorbed more new legal immigrants than in any other decades in its history—approximately 9 million people, in addition to huge numbers of illegal immigrants. The United States has a proud record of achievement in absorbing millions of immigrants, and, in turn, the nation has benefited immeasurably from the contributions of many people of varied backgrounds and talents.

Immunity   A privilege granted to exempt a person from prosecution for any self-incriminating testimony given before a court, grand jury, or investigating committee. Immunity involves an enforced waiver of the constitutional right against self-incrimination, so that an individual can be compelled to give testimony or be punished for contempt. No evidence revealed by a witness who has been granted immunity may be used against him or her in any criminal prosecution, state or federal. (*Murphy v. Waterfront Commission,* 378 U.S. 52 [1964]). *See also* SELF-INCRIMINATION, page 335.

Significance   A grant of immunity is designed to compel testimony from persons who refuse to answer questions on the grounds that their answers would tend to incriminate them and subject them to prosecution. Some legal scholars question the propriety of this procedure because it forces an individual to waive a constitutional right. Immunity will not be granted unless the information likely to be secured is of great public importance. Care must be taken not to make immunity a loophole for notorious criminals to escape punishment. The Immunity Act of 1954 may be used to compel testimony from witnesses in cases involving national security. The Organized Crime Control Act of 1970 provided that immunity extends to use of a witness's testimony against him or her but not to freedom from prosecution for acts mentioned, provided that any evidence is derived from sources independent of the person's testimony. The Supreme Court upheld this narrowed "use" or "testimonial" immunity in *Kastigar v. United States,* 406 U.S. 411 (1972).

Incorporation Doctrine   The legal concept under which the Supreme Court has "nationalized" the Bill of Rights by making most of its provisions applicable to the states through the Fourteenth Amendment. The court has interpreted the due process clause of the Fourteenth Amendment to require states to adhere to safeguards and procedures essential to a scheme of ordered liberty. As a consequence of decisions in a series of cases, the Court has made binding upon the states most provisions of the Bill of Rights, except for the Second, Third, and Seventh, Amendments and the requirement of indictment by grand jury found in the Fifth Amendment. *See also Barron v. Baltimore,* page 349; FOURTEENTH AMENDMENT, page 313; *Gideon v. Wainwright,* page 354; *Gitlow v. New York,* page 355; *Hurtado v. California,* page 356; *Palko v. Connecticut,* page 364.

Significance   The incorporation doctrine ranks among the most significant developments in American constitutional history. It overcame (but did not overrule) the decision in *Barron v. Baltimore* (7 Peters 243 [1833]) that the Bill of Rights limits only the national government. The incorporation process made possible national involvement in protection of individual rights against state and local officials and has had the effect of equalizing the rights of the people regardless of residence. The concept of national protection of individual rights has now been extended beyond traditional Bill of Rights concerns of free expression and criminal procedures to protection of minorities, the lower economic classes, and women.

Involuntary Servitude   Slavery, peonage, or forcing a person to work to fulfill a contract or work out a debt. The Thirteenth Amendment provides that neither slavery nor involuntary servitude, except in punishment for crime, may exist anywhere in the United States. *See also* Pollock *v. Williams,* page 366; SELECTIVE SERVICE, page 577; THIRTEENTH AMENDMENT, page 340.

Significance   Though aimed primarily at putting an end to slavery, the Thirteenth Amendment serves as a guarantee of free and voluntary labor, which may be threatened by situations less drastic than outright slavery. Congress has supplemented this Amendment by passage of the Antipeonage Act of 1867, which is still vigorously enforced to protect debtors. Inferior working and living conditions of many migrant farm workers and exploitation of illegal immigrants in some industries have been likened to slavery, especially when financial indebtedness to employers places the worker in virtual involuntary servitude. The Supreme Court has held that psychological coercion in the absence of physical restraint or other coercion does not constitute involuntary servitude (*United States v. Kozminski,* 487 U.S. 931 [1988]).

Jus Sanguinis   "Law of the blood"—a principle by which citizenship is determined by parentage rather than by place of birth (*jus soli*).

Significance   The Fourteenth Amendment recognizes only birth and naturalization as bases for citizenship, but Congress has adopted the rule of *jus sanguinis* to apply in special circumstances. Thus, one may be a citizen of the United States if born abroad, provided that either or both of one's parents are citizens. If only one parent is a citizen, that parent must have lived in the United States or one of its possessions for 10 years, 5 of them after the age of 14; and the child, in order to remain a citizen, must live in the United States continuously for 5 years between the ages of 14 and 28. The latter provision was upheld by the Supreme Court as not violating the rights of a person claiming citizenship since the person was not born or naturalized in the United States (*Rogers v. Bellei,* 401 U.S. 815 [1971]).

Jus Soli   "Law of the soil"—the basic rule under which American citizenship is determined by place of birth rather than by parentage (*jus sanguinis*). *See also* United States *v. Wong Kim Ark,* page 372.

Significance   The Fourteenth Amendment's provision that all persons born in the United States are citizens (with minor exceptions, as, for example, children born to foreign diplomats who are not under American jurisdiction) is far-reaching. Anyone born here is a citizen whether his or her parents are legal or illegal immigrants or merely visitors. For purposes of citizenship, Congress has declared that the soil of the United States includes Puerto Rico, Guam, the Virgin Islands, and the Northern Mariana Islands.

Juvenile Delinquent   A child whose behavior is unlawful and who is subject to governmental custody. The definition of a delinquent child is determined by law and usually applies to persons under sixteen or eighteen years of age. All states have developed special courts to process juvenile cases. Juvenile courts have operated under informal procedures, but recent court decisions have imposed basic constitutional due process requirements upon them. *See also In Re Gault,* page 356.

Significance   Child delinquency status has been viewed as a civil rather than a criminal matter on the theory that a child is not fully responsible for unlawful acts. Juvenile courts are usually closed to the public, cases are handled under flexible procedures, and, theoretically, the emphasis is on redemption rather than punishment. In 1967, however, the Supreme Court held in *In Re Gault,* 387 U.S. 1, that constitutional standards of notice, right to counsel, protection against self-incrimination, and the right to confront witnesses apply to juveniles accused of crime. Further, the Court held that in juvenile cases, as in adult cases, conviction must be based on proof beyond a reasonable doubt (*In Re Winship,* 397 U.S. 358 [1970]). Yet, the Court refused to require jury trials for juveniles (*McKeiver v. Pennsylvania,* 403 U.S. 528 [1971]) and has authorized pretrial detention of juvenile delinquents (*Schall v. Martin,* 467 U.S. 253 [1984]). In 1988 the Court ruled that the death penalty may not be imposed for a crime committed when the defendant was under age 16 (*Thompson v. Oklahoma,* 487 U.S. 815). Increasing juvenile crime rates have led to extensive changes in numerous state laws including (1) authorizing prosecution of juveniles as adults in certain cases, (2) opening juvenile courts to the public, and (3) holding parents responsible for the crimes of their children, including victim restitution.

Libel and Slander   Defamation of character, written, in the case of libel, and oral, in the case of slander. Both include statements that expose a person to hatred, contempt, or ridicule; that injure his or her reputation by imputing to him or her a criminal act; or that harm the person in his or her trade or profession. Libel and slander usually involve suits for civil damages, but they may also be punished under criminal laws. Libel is generally considered more serious than slander because the written word is more durable than a passing remark. The reputation of those involved, the nature of the audience, and the conditions under which the words were written or spoken may prove pertinent in a suit for damages. Truth of a statement is generally an absolute defense. *See also New York Times v. Sullivan,* page 363.

Significance   Libel and slander are limitations on the freedoms of speech and press, and many state constitutions expressly make this distinction. Libel and slander do not apply to comments made about public officials or newsworthy people unless malicious intent is proved, since such comments are considered to be in the public interest (*New York Times v. Sullivan,* 376 U.S. 255 [1964]). Proof of malice is subject to special judicial scrutiny to protect First Amendment rights (*Bose Corp. v. Consumers Union of United States, Inc.,* 466 U.S. 485 [1984]). Major recent problems concern (1) determining who falls under the definition of "public figure" and, therefore, may be without protection against libel and slander; (2) the harm done to private reputations by legislative or executive officials who enjoy immunity from suit for remarks made in the line of duty; and (3) "group libel" or "hate speech" laws, which make it illegal to impugn the reputation of a minority group.

Loyalty Oath   An oath that requires an individual to disavow or abjure certain beliefs and associations. Such oaths were exacted during the Revolutionary War, the Civil War, the "red scare" of the 1920s, and the Cold War of the 1940s and 1950s. Cold War loyalty oaths were generally required of public employees, teachers, attorneys, defense workers, and recipients of governmental benefits; they generally required persons to swear that they did not advocate the violent overthrow of government or belong to any organization advocating it. The courts struck down most loyalty oath laws after earlier acceptance, usually on the grounds that the oaths did not excuse those whose associations were innocent of illegal intent or because the oath was totally unrelated to any governmental purpose. In 1970, the United States Civil Service Commission dropped the loyalty oath requirement for federal employees. Test oaths for students receiving federal aid, for Job Corps members, and for recipients of Medicare have also been dropped. *See also Elfbrandt v. Russell,* page 353; LOYALTY-SECURITY PROGRAMS, page 324.

Significance   Few people object to taking an ordinary oath of allegiance declaring loyalty to the United States and swearing to uphold the Constitution. However, loyalty or "test" oaths have met numerous objections based largely on the reversal of the presumption of innocence because individuals may be considered disloyal unless they swear that they are not. It is also charged that such oaths abridge freedoms of speech and assembly by the discretion vested in the imposer of the oath to determine suitable beliefs and associations. Moreover, many doubt the utility of oaths as a weapon against subversives, who would undoubtedly swear falsely to the oath. The major utility of loyalty oaths lies in making the oath taker aware of possible illegal activities or associations and in bringing perjury charges against those who swear falsely.

Loyalty-Security Programs   Programs carried on by national and state governments to rid the public service of disloyal persons or persons suspected of being security risks. The national government's loyalty program had its inception in 1947, when President Truman ordered that governmental employees be dismissed if grounds existed to doubt their loyalty. President Eisenhower extended the program to include all "security risks"—disloyal as well as generally untrustworthy people. The programs have also been applied to the armed forces, defense plants, maritime workers, and other government-connected activities. Appeal procedures are provided for discharged persons but do not always permit confrontation with informers. Many persons have been denied jobs without knowing the precise reasons, and the programs have resulted in numerous dismissals. Although the courts have sustained these programs, they have, in recent years, limited their application to persons holding sensitive positions and those whose activities encompass illegal aims. Similar programs have been undertaken in the states, although most states have limited their loyalty requirements to the taking of a loyalty oath. *See also* LOYALTY OATH, page 324; MCCARTHYISM, page 325.

Significance Few people insist that disloyal persons should work for the government. Many people, however, have protested the procedures used in the loyalty-security programs, preferring normal police work to uncover dangerous persons. The use of unidentified informers raises much criticism. Many persons are concerned with the effects on the morale of government employees, who are subject to investigation of all their activities and beliefs. Loyalty-security programs will undoubtedly be part of the American scene as long as the international situation continues to be perceived as threatening to national security.

Magna Carta   The Great Charter of freedom granted in 1215 by King John of England by demand of his barons. The Magna Carta contained such ideas as trial by a jury of one's peers and the guarantee against loss of life, liberty, or property, except in accordance with law.

Significance The sources for many of the basic freedoms found in American law are traceable to the Magna Carta. Although originally limited to privileged classes, the major concepts of the Magna Carta eventually spread to all free people.

McCarthyism   Unsubstantiated accusations of disloyalty and abuse of legislative investigatory power that engender fear over real or imagined threats to the security of the nation. The term was derived in the early 1950s from the actions of Senator Joseph R. McCarthy of Wisconsin, who made repeated charges of pro-Communist sympathies or activities against public officials and private individuals under the protection of his senatorial immunity. *See also* POLITICAL TRIAL, page 329.

Significance McCarthyism was a post–World War II phenomenon that fed on the fears generated by the Cold War between the United States and the Soviet Union. The period was marked by loyalty-security investigations into the lives of public employees, surveillance of scientists and teachers, the imposition of loyalty oaths, and passage of anti-Communist legislation. Many vestiges of the period remain. McCarthyism utilizes the catchwords of "loyalty" and "security" as justification for limitations on civil liberties. McCarthyism fosters suspicion among neighbors, distrust of public officials, and the idea of "guilt by association."

National   A person who owes allegiance to a country, though not a citizen thereof. The term is used at times, however, in the same sense as the term "citizen." Under American law, a national is an inhabitant of an outlying possession of the United States to whom Congress has not granted citizenship. Residents of the Philippine Islands were considered nationals until independence was granted, whereas the people of Puerto Rico were granted citizenship in 1917 after a period as nationals. Residents of American Samoa are nationals.

Significance   The term "national" is basically a concept of international law. American nationals are accorded most of the protections that citizens have, but the actual distinction is hazy. By granting the status of nationals to a people, Congress identifies them as belonging to and entitled to the protection of the United States, particularly for purposes of international relations.

Natural-born Citizen   A native of the United States. The term is used in Article II, section 1 of the Constitution, which stipulates that "no person except a natural-born citizen" may be president.

Significance   The language of Article II is the only place in the Constitution where a distinction is drawn between a natural-born and a naturalized citizen. Whether or not a person born abroad of American parents and, therefore, a citizen under the rule of *jus sanguinis* is eligible for the presidency has never been resolved. Although the Constitution makes no other distinctions between natural-born and naturalized citizens, the former cannot be denaturalized or deported.

Naturalization   The legal procedure by which an alien is admitted to citizenship. Congress is authorized by Article I, section 8 of the Constitution to establish uniform rules for naturalization. Naturalization may be individual or collective. Collective naturalization confers citizenship upon entire populations by statute or treaty, as was done in the cases of Alaska, Hawaii, Texas, Puerto Rico, Guam, the Northern Marianas, and the Virgin Islands. An individual over eighteen years of age may be naturalized after meeting certain qualifications, including (1) residence in the United States for five years; (2) ability to read, write, and speak English; (3) proof of good moral character; (4) knowledge of the history and attachment to the principles of American government; (5) neither advocacy of subversive doctrine nor membership (unless involuntary) in any subversive or totalitarian organization; and (6) taking an oath of allegiance to the United States and renunciation of allegiance to the former country. Detailed administration of naturalization is handled by the Immigration and Naturalization Service of the Department of Justice, with final examination and administration of the oath by a judge of a federal court or a state court of record. The residence requirement is lowered for spouses of citizens and for aliens who serve in the armed forces. Minors become citizens when their parents are naturalized. *See also* IMMIGRATION AND NATURALIZATION SERVICE, page 346; IMMIGRATION REFORM ACT OF 1986, page 382; WELFARE REFORM ACT, page 528.

Significance   Millions of people have met the requirements established by Congress and have become American citizens. An average of about 300,000 people are naturalized each year. In 1995 and 1996, however, about 1 million immigrants were naturalized, spurred by the 1986 amnesty for many illegal immigrants, growing anti-immigration sentiment due to economic instability, and the 1996 welfare reform which limits most benefits to citizens. The procedure is designed, however, to foster the "Americanization" of aliens, many of whom become more knowledgeable and appreciative citizens than some of the native born. Through collective naturalization, the United States has demonstrated to the world its desire to give equal rights to all people under its control and, in some cases, to prepare its territories for eventual statehood.

Natural Rights   An underlying assumption of the American political creed that persons are endowed by their Creator with certain rights that may not be abridged by government. *See also* NATURAL LAW, page 20; NINTH AMENDMENT, page 327.

Significance   The doctrine of natural rights assumes that human beings had rights in a "state of nature" and create government to protect those rights. As embodied in the American creed, the doctrine assumes the inviolability of basic human rights. This idea contrasts with another widely held belief, that the individual has only such rights as the government decides to grant.

Ninth Amendment   A part of the Bill of Rights that reads, "The enumeration in the Constitution, of certain rights, shall not be construed to deny or disparage others retained by the people." This provision reaffirms the tradition of the natural rights philosophy, supported by those who feared that a listing of rights in the Bill of Rights might be interpreted to mean that no other rights were held by the people. *See also* NATURAL RIGHTS, page 327; PRIVACY, page 329; *Roe v. Wade,* page 367.

Significance   The "other" rights that the people retain have not been extensively defined, and the Ninth Amendment has not been a major source of litigation. In the case of *Mitchell v. United States,* 313 U.S. 80 (1941), the Supreme Court noted that the Amendment protected the right to political activity by the people. In *Griswold v. Connecticut,* 381 U.S. 479 (1965), the Court struck down a law that forbade counseling married couples to use contraceptives as an invasion of the right of privacy protected by the First and Ninth Amendments. In striking down state laws regulating abortions (*Roe v Wade,* 410 U.S. 113 [1973]) as violating the right to privacy guaranteed by the Ninth and Fourteenth Amendments, the Court brought the Ninth Amendment to new prominence by making it the cornerstone of the developing right to privacy.

Passport   A certificate, issued by an official government agency, that identifies a person as a citizen of a country and authorizes him or her to travel abroad. Passports are granted to Americans by the Passport Office of the State Department, by territorial governors, and by diplomatic officials abroad. *See also* VISA, page 342.

Significance   No American citizen may leave the country without a passport (except for trips to Canada, Mexico, and certain other nearby areas), and few countries will admit a traveler without a valid passport. A passport entitles a person to the privileges accorded travelers by international custom and various treaties. In 1958, the Supreme Court ruled that the Secretary of State could not deny a passport to a citizen because of political beliefs or associations without explicit authorization from Congress (*Kent v. Dulles,* 357 U.S. 116). The Court also struck down a section of the Internal Security Act of 1950 that forbade issuance of passports to members of Communist organizations, on the ground that such denial constitutes a violation of the right to travel (*Aptheker v. Secretary of State,* 378 U.S. 500 [1965]). The Supreme Court has upheld limits on the right to travel to specific countries if it is likely to prove detrimental to the foreign policy interests of the United States (*Zemel v. Rusk,* 381 U.S. 1 [1965]). It has also upheld the revocation of the passport of a person likely to damage the national security or foreign policy of the United States (*Haig v. Agee,* 453 U.S. 280 [1981]). However, a person holding a valid passport is not guilty of a crime if he or she travels to a restricted area (*United States v. Laub,* 385 U.S. 475 [1967]).

Petition   A request to a public official that seeks to correct a perceived wrong or to influence public policy. The First Amendment guarantees to the people the right to "petition the government for a redress of grievances." This provision, like all provisions of the First Amendment, is applicable to the states through the Fourteenth Amendment, although most state constitutions contain a similar provision. The right of petition, closely related to freedoms of speech, press, and assembly, is generally exercised through letter writing to public officials and through pressure-group activity.

Significance   It is vital in a free society that persons be able to call the attention of their representatives to their grievances. In this way, government can remain continually responsive to the people and can be made aware of their opinions at times other than at elections. The right of petition is most effectively exercised through the lobbying activities of interest groups. Mass demonstrations and picketing are useful petitioning tactics used by groups having limited access to the political power structure.

Police Power   The power inherent in state governments to protect the health, safety, morals, and welfare of the people. In the area of civil rights and liberties, a lawful exercise of the police power may justify abridgment of personal or property rights. For example, through use of the police power, a state may destroy property that endangers public health or may limit freedom of speech or assembly when the public safety is jeopardized. *See also* BALANCING DOCTRINE, page 295; POLICE POWER, page 47.

Significance   The police power rests on the assumption that rights are not absolute. The extent of the power is generally determined by the courts when they are faced with concrete situations in which the police power comes into conflict with personal liberties. In a typical civil liberty–police power case, the courts must strike a balance between the needs of society and the rights of the individual, as in the case, for example, of a mass demonstration that blocks the flow of traffic on a busy street.

Political Rights   The right to participate in the management of government and to influence public policy. Typical political rights include the right to vote, to form a political party, and to participate in pressure-group activity.

Significance   Political rights are essential for the operations of a free government. Citizens must be given the opportunity not only to speak out on public issues but also to take positive action to influence or control the government. So long as these rights remain inviolate, regardless of the party in power, dictatorship cannot take hold. Any group denied these rights is left with the recourse of civil disobedience or violent revolution to accomplish its goals. In recent years, emphasis has been placed on securing political rights for minority groups who may be denied access to the polls either as candidates or as voters.

Political Trial   Prosecution directed against alleged enemies of the government or the political system. Sedition laws and other loyalty-security measures are common legislative acts that define political crimes. Prosecutions resulting from such laws are often referred to as "political trials," designed to expose rather than punish. *See also* MCCARTHYISM, page 325; SEDITION, page 334.

Significance   All nations define political crimes and have experienced political trials. In times of tension or alleged threats to national security, sedition laws are actively enforced against leaders of groups in opposition to the government. Political trials direct national attention to security threats. Conversely, those opposed to the system are often eager to use the forum of a sensational trial to propagate their ideas. The nine-month trial of the Communist leadership for violation of the Smith Act in 1948 is a leading American example of such a trial. Many prosecutions of civil rights leaders and those who led Vietnam War protests during the 1960s may be characterized as political trials.

Privacy   The right to determine one's personal affairs free of governmental interference and to control dissemination of information about oneself. The Constitution makes no mention of a right of privacy, but the Supreme Court has recognized it as falling within the "penumbra" (borderline) of the First, Fourth, Fifth, Ninth, and Fourteenth Amendments. In the Privacy Act of 1974, Congress provided, for the first time, that individuals may inspect information about themselves in public agency files and challenge, correct, or amend materials. Agencies may not make their files on an individual available to other agencies without that individual's consent. Exempted from the law, however, are law enforcement agencies, the Central Intelligence Agency, the Secret Service, and certain files pertaining to federal employment. *See also* FOURTH AMENDMENT, page 314; FREEDOM OF INFORMATION ACT, page 243; NINTH AMENDMENT, page 327; *Roe v. Wade,* page 367; WIRETAPPING, page 342.

Significance   In a free society, a large measure of personal privacy must be assumed for each individual. At the same time, demands for governmental service create situations that intrude upon privacy. A welfare or medical care system, for example, requires the acquisition of detailed personal information about citizens, which when stored in computers may be easily retrieved for illegitimate uses. Technological developments, such as eavesdropping devices, may help to curb crime but are dangerously subject to abusive intrusions on privacy. Changes in lifestyle have diminished tolerance for governmental intrusion in such matters as contraception, abortion, homosexuality, and pornography. A guideline used by courts in determining the validity of a search, for example, is whether the situation is one in which an individual would have "legitimate expectations of privacy."

Privilege   An advantage, benefit, exemption, exception, or opportunity granted to an individual or group who has no right to it. The range of privileges bestowed by government is very broad and includes government employment, Medicare, public housing, tax exemptions, welfare programs, professional licenses, and veterans' benefits. The government may attach qualifications or demands before a privilege is granted, but these must pass the test of reasonableness. Any withdrawal of a privilege from an individual must be done under procedures that afford minimal due process rights, such as notice and hearing. *See also Goldberg v. Kelly*, page 521; PRIVILEGED COMMUNICATION, page 275.

Significance   The distinction between a right and a privilege has narrowed considerably. In the past, an individual could lose a privilege under procedures and circumstances that would not be permissible if a right was abridged. This enabled the government to control behavior by the threat of withholding a benefit. The courts have held, however, that neither the granting nor the withholding of a privilege may be conditioned upon the surrender of constitutional rights. For example, government employment cannot be conditioned on standards of belief or association that violate First Amendment rights; recipients of government aid may not be subjected to arbitrary treatment.

Procedural Rights   The means by which individuals or groups are protected against arbitrary actions by public officials. Under American constitutional law, no person may be deprived of life, liberty, property, or any other guaranteed right, except under well-defined procedures, including a fair hearing before a judicial tribunal. American procedural rights are generally considered to be those listed in the Bill of Rights, particularly in the Fourth, Fifth, Sixth, and Eighth Amendments. *Procedural* rights are to be distinguished from *substantive* rights. The latter include those elements that are considered to be of the very essence of freedom, such as freedom of speech, whereas the former are concerned with the methods by which rights are protected. *See also* DUE PROCESS OF LAW, page 307; EIGHTH AMENDMENT, page 308; FIFTH AMENDMENT, page 312; FOURTH AMENDMENT, page 314; SIXTH AMENDMENT, page 338; SUBSTANTIVE RIGHTS, page 339.

Significance   A crucial difference between a free society and an authoritarian society lies in the procedures guaranteed citizens to protect them against arbitrary treatment. Under American law, one may not be tried and condemned except in conformity with due process of law, and any errors in procedure may render a conviction void.

Public Trial   A provision found in the Sixth Amendment that states that in all criminal prosecutions, the accused has a right to a trial open to the public. The Supreme Court has held that the Sixth Amendment is for the benefit of the accused and does not assure access to the public or the press (*Gannett Co. v. DePasquale*, 443 U.S. 368 [1979]). The right of the press and the public to attend criminal trials arises out of the First Amendment guarantees of freedom of speech, press, and assembly, which protect communication on matters relating to the functioning of government (*Richmond*

Newspapers, Inc. v. Virginia, 448 U.S. 555 [1980]). *See also* FREEDOM OF THE PRESS, page 315; *Nebraska Press Association v. Stuart,* page 363.

Significance   Public trials serve as a check on the criminal justice system, promote public confidence, provide an educational function, and protect both the accused and the general public against secret and abusive judicial power. The 1979 ruling in the *Gannett* case led to much confusion and concern, particularly on the part of the press. In the *Richmond* decision, the Court recognized that open trials had been the historical practice since the nation's founding and that the First Amendment makes implicit the right of the press and public to attend criminal trials. This reasoning was later extended to jury selection proceedings and to preliminary criminal proceedings (*Press-Enterprise Co. v. Superior Court of California, Riverside County,* 464 U.S. 501 [1984], 478 U.S. 1 [1986]). Moreover, in the *Richmond* case, the Court recognized for the first time that the press has a right to acquire as well as to disseminate public information. Subsequently, the Court held that state courts are free to permit television coverage of trials unless conducted in a manner that would deny a fair trial (*Chandler v. Florida,* 449 U.S. 560 [1981]).

Racism   A belief that differences among people are rooted in ethnic stock. These differences include color, religion, bloodline, or national origin. Racism usually involves the assumption that one's own race is superior and that social and political organization should reflect that superiority. Nazi persecution of Jews prior to and during World War II on the theory that German Aryans constituted a superior race is a leading example of racism. In the United States the term "white racism" is used to describe discrimination against black people in social and political institutions. *See also* REVERSE DISCRIMINATION, page 332.

Significance   "White racism" was cited by the President's National Advisory Commission on Civil Disorders (the Kerner Report, so named after the Commission Chairman, Governor Otto Kerner of Illinois) in 1968 as the underlying cause of racial disorder in the United States. "What white Americans have never fully understood—but what the Negro can never forget—" wrote the Commission, "is that white society is deeply implicated in the ghetto. White institutions created it, white institutions maintain it, and white society condones it." The most bitter fruit of white racism, said the commission, was the exclusion of blacks from the benefits of economic progress, and it called for a massive national commitment to reform. The concept of racism is rejected by many Americans, who find the charge to be insulting. Nevertheless, contemporary history makes it difficult to refute the Kerner Report's warning that the nation "is moving toward two societies, one black, one white—separate and unequal." Congressional legislation, executive action, and court decisions since the 1950s demonstrate American commitment to eradication of racism as official policy in the United States. Nevertheless, the existence of white racism intensifies the race problem in America and, according to reports of the United States Commission on Civil Rights, extends to other nonwhite Americans as well, such as Chicanos and Native Americans. A 1989 study by the National Research Council, an arm of the National

Academy of Sciences, found little change since the 1968 Kerner Report, with blacks "separated from the mainstream of national life" as a result of continuing racial discrimination.

Reasonable Doubt   The standard for determining the guilt of a person charged with a criminal offense. The prosecution must persuade the judge or jury that the evidence proves guilt beyond a reasonable doubt. Though long accepted as part of the common law tradition, it was not until 1970 that the Supreme Court held "lest there remain any doubt about the constitutional stature of the reasonable doubt standard, we explicitly hold that the Due Process Clause protects the accused against conviction except upon proof beyond a reasonable doubt of every fact necessary to constitute the crime with which he is charged" (*In Re Winship,* 397 U. S. 358 [1970]). The standard applies to both adult and juvenile criminal cases.

Significance   The reasonable doubt standard is to be distinguished from the "preponderance of evidence" standard used in civil cases. In criminal cases, it is especially important that the accused be safeguarded against a dubious conviction and that the judge or jury be as certain of the decision as is humanly possible. The high standard of proof beyond a reasonable doubt enhances respect for the law and protects the innocent.

Religious Test   A requirement that one profess belief in a particular religious faith or in a Supreme Being as a condition for holding public office. Article VI of the Constitution prohibits such tests. Several state constitutions required that public officials profess a belief in God, but in 1961 the Supreme Court held such a Maryland provision unconstitutional (*Torcaso v. Watkins,* 367 U.S. 488). *See also* SEPARATION OF CHURCH AND STATE, page 336.

Significance   The prohibition against religious tests for office is a necessary component of the separation of church and state. Until the election of John F. Kennedy, a Catholic, to the presidency in 1960, there appeared to be an "unofficial" religious test for the office of President, since it was widely believed that only a mainstream Protestant could be elected. The Supreme Court decision in the *Torcaso* case was extended to strike down a Tennessee constitutional provision that disqualified clergymen from membership in the state legislature or in a state constitutional convention (*McDaniel v. Paty,* 435 U.S. 618 [1978]).

Reverse Discrimination   Preferential treatment that favors a previously victimized minority to the disadvantage of the majority. Specifically, reverse discrimination refers to programs designed to redress past discrimination against women, blacks, or other minorities that result in depriving white men and sometimes women of benefits or opportunities they would otherwise obtain. In 1978, the Supreme Court held in *Regents of the University of California v. Bakke* (438 U.S. 265) that affirmative action programs are valid but that explicit racial quotas are prohibited. Race-based "set-aside" programs under which a proportion of state or local governmental construction projects were allocated to minority-owned firms have been held void under the equal protection clause of the Fourteenth Amendment (*City of Richmond v. J. A. Croson Co.,* 488 U.S. 469) and, for federal set-asides, under the due process clause of the Fifth Amendment (*Adarand Constructors, Inc. v. Pena,* 115 S. Ct. 2097 [1995]). *See also Adarand Constructors v. Pena,* page 347; AFFIRMATIVE ACTION, page 292; *Regents of the University of California v. Bakke,* page 366.

Significance   Proponents of preferential treatment for minorities argue that the attainment of socially desirable goals (such as more black doctors, more women lawyers) is more important than the application of criteria that the minority cannot meet because of past discrimination. Opponents fear any classification based on race or sex or the setting of quotas to meet affirmative action goals; such policies or programs, they argue, are tantamount to the racism and sexism that contemporary society seeks to overcome and punishes the present generation for the acts of their forebears. Although the Supreme Court has upheld voluntary or court-ordered affirmative action plans that remedy the effects of demonstrated past discrimination, it has not approved plans that place a "reverse discrimination" burden on a specific individual, as may result, for example, when an affirmative action plan affects a valid seniority system.

Right to Counsel   The guarantee in the Sixth Amendment to the Constitution that a defendant in a criminal case have the assistance of an attorney. The Supreme Court has ruled that the national government (*Johnson v. Zerbst,* 304 U.S. 458 [1938]) and state governments (*Gideon v. Wainwright,* 372 U.S. 335 [1963]) must furnish counsel for indigent defendants. An accused must be permitted to confer with counsel prior to interrogation by the police and at any other critical stage in proceedings against him or her, such as a preliminary hearing, lineup, or appeal. The accused person may waive the right to counsel, but the waiver must be an intelligent one in which the defendant recognizes the consequences of this action. *See also Gideon v. Wainwright,* page 354; *Miranda v. Arizona,* page 361; PUBLIC DEFENDER, page 276.

Significance   Right to counsel is based on the assumption that the average person is unable to understand the intricacies of the law or know the full extent of his or her rights. In the *Gideon* case, the Court sought to overcome the advantages of those able to afford counsel by providing "equal justice for the poor." The Supreme Court's insistence that indigent defendants be furnished counsel has led to extensive use of the public defender system.

Right to Die   Freedom from unwanted medical attention, even to the point of death. The right to die should be distinguished from the right to commit suicide, which is not recognized; that is, the state may act to prevent a suicide but may not under certain circumstances force medical care to prolong life. In the first major case on this issue, *Cruzan v. Director, Missouri Department of Health,* 497 U.S. 261 (1990), the Supreme Court recognized that a competent person has a constitutional right to refuse lifesaving medical treatment. But in the *Cruzan* case, involving a comatose person in a persistent vegetative state, the Court held that the state may require clear and convincing evidence that the patient would wish to have lifesaving equipment withdrawn, irrespective of the wishes of the patient's family, parents, or guardians. Some states have authorized withdrawal of medical care in specific instances, but the Supreme Court recognizes the state's legitimate interest in the protection and preservation of human life. In recent years, much attention has been drawn to physician-assisted suicide, whereby a deathly ill person clearly seeks the assistance of a physician to induce death. States vary as to the legal status of such action.

Significance   The issue of the right to die has taken on major proportions as it becomes more and more common for science to prolong the lives of persons who would not survive without artificial support. Several states now authorize persons to execute "living wills" in order to clarify the nature of treatment desired or appoint a health care proxy should the patient's condition render him or her unable to make the decision. Federal law (effective in December 1991) requires medical facilities that participate in Medicare and Medicaid programs to inform patients of their rights, under state law, to accept or refuse medical treatment. Furthermore, patients are encouraged to prepare a living will or some form of directive concerning their wishes regarding medical decisions should they be unable to communicate competently. The *Cruzan* case and the issue of the right to die highlight the increasing involvement of the government in the life—and death—of people.

Second Amendment   A part of the Bill of Rights that guarantees the right to bear arms because "A well regulated militia [is] necessary to the security of a free state." Similar provisions are found in many state constitutions. The right to bear arms is an implicit recognition of the right of revolution, stemming from the idea that a tryrant could not be overthrown if the people were denied the means. In addition, this guarantee was included in the Bill of Rights to assure the states that the national government would not disarm the state militias. *See also* GUN CONTROL, page 318.

Significance   The assassination of prominent political leaders, widespread use of weapons in civil disturbances, and an increasing crime rate have aroused nationwide concern over the ease of securing firearms and produced pressures for national legislation to control their sale and use. Counterpressures from the National Rifle Association, sportsmen, and some fearful citizens have been successful in preventing enactment of effective gun control laws. Possession of certain types of weapons, such as machine guns or sawed-off shotguns, is prohibited, and registration of some weapons is required. Nevertheless, effective regulation has proved impossible because firearms regulation remains largely a state and local responsibility. The result is a patchwork of laws and practices varying from bans on ownership to outright encouragement of the carrying of concealed weapons.

Sedition   Actions that incite rebellion or discontent against duly established government. Espionage, sabotage, or attempts to overthrow the government constitute sedition, as does advocacy by publication or speech to accomplish these goals. The Sedition Acts of 1798 and 1918 put severe limitations on mere criticism of the government. Sedition legislation of the 1940s and 1950s has been aimed at outlawing Communist conspiracies and advocacy of doctrines aimed at overthrow of government by force. *See also* ALIEN AND SEDITION LAWS, page 374; ALIEN REGISTRATION ACT, page 374; *Dennis v. United States*, page 352; INTERNAL SECURITY ACT, page 383; TREASON, page 341.

Significance   Though closely akin to treason, sedition does not require the precise standard of proof that the Constitution requires for treason convictions. Few people question the legality or wisdom of outlawing and punishing seditious actions. Punishment for seditious *speech,* however, resulted in severe restrictions on nonconformists in postrevolutionary America and during World War I. The Supreme Court has sustained convictions of Communists but has drawn a distinction between mere advocacy of abstract doctrine and conspiracy to advocate concrete action (*Yates v. United States,* 354 U.S. 298 [1957]). A law that makes mere criticism of government a crime makes free government impossible; a citizen may criticize and be loyal at the same time. State sedition acts, common during the 1940s and 1950s, are preempted by national laws (*Pennsylvania v. Nelson,* 350 U.S. 497 [1956]).

Segregation   The separation of the white and black races in public and private facilities. Laws requiring the segregation of the races (Jim Crow laws) have been on the statute books of several states. In 1896, the Supreme Court upheld such laws under the "separate but equal" doctrine, whereby blacks could be segregated if they were provided with equal facilities (*Plessy v. Ferguson,* 163 U.S. 537). Under this doctrine, a wide pattern of segregation developed in schools, transportation, recreation, and housing. Beginning in the 1940s, the Court began to weaken the separate but equal doctrine by insisting that the facilities provided for blacks, particularly in education, be indeed equal. Finally, in 1954, the Court struck down the separate but equal formula, holding that segregation based on color denied the equal protection of the law (*Brown v. Board of Education of Topeka,* 347 U.S. 483). *See also Brown v. Board of Education of Topeka,* page 350; CIVIL RIGHTS ACTS, pages 376–380; DE FACTO SEGREGATION, page 304; *Milliken v. Bradley,* page 360; *Plessy v. Ferguson,* page 365; *Swann v. Charlotte-Mecklenburg Board of Education,* page 370.

Significance   Segregation had been legally required and was part of the pattern of life in seventeen southern states and the District of Columbia for many generations. The Supreme Court's 1954 decision has simultaneously strained and improved the status of the American black. Since 1954, with the law no longer permitting separate treatment, blacks have sought to make the ruling a reality by sit-ins, political action, marches, and mass demonstrations. Moreover, Congress has passed civil rights measures in 1957, 1960, 1964, 1965, 1968, and 1991 to increase black political and civil rights. Unofficial patterns of segregation still exist on a wide scale in both the North and the South and are likely to continue for many years.

Self-incrimination   Testimony by a person that reveals facts that may result in a criminal prosecution against him or her. The Fifth Amendment to the Constitution provides that no person "shall be compelled in any criminal case to be a witness against himself." Though originally applied to persons on trial, the concept has been extended to cover testimony before legislative committees and executive agencies. Persons may not refuse to testify in order to protect other persons or because their answers might bring disgrace upon themselves. The guarantee extends only to testimony that might involve the person in a criminal prosecution. Persons who have been given immunity or a pardon, or who have already been convicted of a particular offense (so that they may not be tried again), may not refuse to testify. No unfavorable inferences may legally be drawn from proper use of the Fifth Amendment guarantee against self-incrimination. It applies with equal force to both state and federal proceedings (*Malloy v. Hogan,* 378 U.S. 1 [1964]). *see also* ENTRAPMENT, page 308; FOURTH AMENDMENT, page 314; IMMUNITY, page 321; *Malloy v. Hogan,* page 358; *Miranda v. Arizona,* page 361.

Significance   In a criminal case, the burden of proof is on the prosecution. The right against self-incrimination is designed to prevent the shifting of the burden to the defendant by forcing him or her to reveal incriminating facts. It also prevents use of torture or inquisitorial procedures to coerce confessions, as well as use of evidence illegally obtained. A major problem involves the question of whether the witness has waived the right by answering questions directly or indirectly related to a matter that might incriminate him or her. A witness who has begun to answer a line of questions may have unknowingly waived the right; for this reason, many concerned witnesses have refused to answer any questions. A person, however, may be found in contempt if he or she uses the right as a mere dodge and refuses to answer proper questions. Although one may not suffer any legal penalty for invoking the Fifth Amendment, the impact on a jury cannot be known, and loss of reputation or employment may result.

Separation of Church and State   A basic principle of American government that prohibits the mingling of church and state. The principle rests on the First Amendment clause forbidding the passage of any law "respecting an establishment of religion." In a series of controversial cases, the Supreme Court has held that the state must be committed to a position of neutrality. In 1971, in *Lemon v. Kurtzman* 403 U.S. 602, the Court established a three-pronged test for applying the establishment clause, holding that any action must (1) have a secular purpose, (2) neither advance nor retard religion, and (3) avoid excessive government entanglement with religion. No public funds may be expended on behalf of any church, and the government may not favor one church over another. Public schools may not be used for sectarian religious observances, and official requirements for Bible reading or prayer recitals are forbidden. Laws that have a predominantly secular effect, such as public bus transportation for parochial schools or Sunday closing laws, have been upheld. The permissible extent of public aid to church-related schools remains, however, unresolved. The national government, under the Elementary and Secondary Education Act of 1965, and many state governments provide aid to parochial schools. The Supreme Court has struck down state programs that paid the salaries of teachers in church-related schools for instruction in nonreligious subjects as "excessive entanglement between government and religion." On similar grounds, the Court voided programs of tuition aid through reimbursement or tax relief to families of children attending nonpublic schools, except where such relief was available to public school children as well. At the same time, however, the Court upheld federal and state construction grants to church-related colleges. The distinction was made by the Court on the grounds that precollege parochial schools are more involved in religious indoctrination and that the state programs would involve continuing controversy over public support. The display of religious objects on public property has aroused much controversy, too. *See also Committee for Public Education and Religious Liberty v. Nyquist,* page 351; ELEMENTARY AND SECONDARY EDUCATION ACT, page 523; ESTABLISHMENT OF RELIGION, page 310; *Everson v. Board of education of Ewing Township,* page 353; FREEDOM OF RELIGION, page 316; HIGHER EDUCATION ACT, page 524; *Mueller v. Allen,* page 362; RELIGIOUS TEST, page 332; *School District of Abington Township v. Schempp,* page 369; *Zorach v. Clauson,* page 374.

Significance   The principle of the separation of church and state is most controversial when applied to the role of religion in the public schools and to the use of public funds for parochial schools. In most cases, the Supreme Court has supported Thomas Jefferson's idea that the establishment clause was intended to erect "a wall of separation between church and state" toward the end that official government support not be placed behind the tenets of any religious orthodoxy and that public institutions not become embroiled in sectarian controversy. A 1984 decision, however, that a city's inclusion of a Nativity scene in its annual Christmas display did not violate the establishment clause (*Lynch v. Donnelly,* 465 U.S. 668) was based on the view that "accommodation" of religious expression is also important. Subsequently the Court rejected the display of a Nativity scene in a county courthouse as conveying an impermissible endorsement of a specific religion but upheld the display of various seasonal objects, including religious items, as conveying secular recognition of different traditions (*County of Allegheny v. American Civil Liberties Union, Greater Pittsburgh Chapter,* 492 U.S. 573 [1989]).

Seventh Amendment   A part of the Bill of Rights that guarantees the preservation of the right to a jury trial in a federal suit at common law if the value in controversy exceeds twenty dollars. It also provides that facts tried by the jury may not be reexamined in any court except in accordance with common law rules. A jury of six persons may be used in such suits.

Significance   The Seventh Amendment is a rarely litigated item that applies only to cases in which Congress permits common law rules to be used. It does not apply to cases arising out of statutory law or in equity proceedings. The Seventh Amendment is an example of a portion of the Bill of Rights that is not made applicable to the states by the Fourteenth Amendment because it involves no right that is basic to fairness or that is so important as to be ranked as fundamental. It was made part of the Bill of Rights to preserve the right to a jury trial in civil cases.

Sexual Harassment   Unwelcome sexual conduct, particularly in the workplace or in an educational institution, that creates a hostile work environment. The Supreme Court has held that sexual harassment is sex discrimination prohibited under the Civil Rights Act of 1964 (*Meritor Savings Bank, FSB v. Vinson,* 477 U.S. 57 [1986]). In its most direct form, sexual harassment involves demands for sexual favors as a condition of employment or academic success. More often, harassment takes the form of unwelcome use of sexual language, jokes, displays of suggestive materials, or touching. *See also Meritor Savings Bank, FSB v. Vinson,* page 359.

Significance   Sexual harassment has emerged as a major issue of the 1990s. The women's equal rights movement, lawsuits, and highly publicized incidents of sexual harassment have sensitized both men and women to the nature of their behavior that might, even inadvertently, result in creating an offensive work or educational environment. Surveys reveal that about half of working women and about 15 percent of working men claim some form of sexual harassment on the job, though most claims refer to subtle forms of harassment from coworkers rather than demands for sexual favors from supervisors. The Civil Rights Act of 1991 authorizes suits for damages by women claiming sexual discrimination. It is likely that the Act will stimulate even greater awareness of the issue, numerous lawsuits, and modification of behavior patterns. In 1992, the Supreme Court held that monetary damages are available to students who are sexually harassed by school officials, under Title IX of the Education Amendments of 1972, which does not explicityly authorize monetary damages (*Franklin v. Gwinnett County Public Schools*, 503 U.S. 60). A 1993 decision (*Harris v. Forklift Systems, Inc.*, 114 S. Ct. 367) declared that sexual harassment does not require a showing of severe psychological injury but only a work environment perceived to be hostile or abusive.

Sixth Amendment   A part of the Bill of Rights that stipulates the basic requirements of procedural due process in federal criminal trials. They include a speedy and public trial, an impartial jury, trial in the area where the crime was committed, notice of the charges, the right to confront witnesses and to obtain favorable witnesses, and the right to counsel. All have been made binding on the states through the due process clause of the Fourteenth Amendment. *See also* CONFRONTATION CLAUSE, page 302; JURY, page 268; PUBLIC TRIAL, page 330; RIGHT TO COUNSEL, page 333; SPEEDY TRIAL, page 338; TRIAL, page 282; VENUE, page 284; WITNESS, page 342.

Significance   The brief but highly important Sixth Amendment sums up the essential procedures of a fair and impartial trial. An improper denial of any of these ingredients may be sufficient to void a conviction.

Speedy Trial   A requirement found in the Sixth Amendment that criminal prosecutions must be undertaken without undue delay. The requirement of a speedy trial is also binding in state cases (*Klopfer v. North Carolina*, 386 U.S. 213 [1967]). In a 1972 decision (*Barker v. Wingo*, 407 U.S. 514), the Supreme Court recognized the difficulty of a precise definition of "speedy" but suggested four criteria: the length of the delay, the reasons for the delay, whether the delay was prejudicial to the defendant, and whether the defendant had demanded a speedy trial. In the Speedy Trial Act of 1974, Congress provided that, by 1980, the permissible period between arrest and trial for a federal offense cannot exceed 100 days. The arrested person must be charged within 30 days, arraigned within 10 days of being charged, and tried within 60 days thereafter. Discretion is vested in judges to determine when delay is essential, as in the case of need for a mental examination, and whether delay is to result in dismissal of charges with or without possibility of reprosecution. *See also* ARRAIGNMENT, page 294.

Significance   The speedy trial requirement is designed to protect a suspect against the harsh uncertainties of a criminal prosecution and to assure that testimony of witnesses will be available and reliable. The neglect or avoidance of the constitutional requirement has become a national scandal, though both the defendant and the prosecutor may be at fault. For example, in *Barker v. Wingo* the Court held that a five-year delay in a murder case was not a violation, since in the given circumstances the delay did not prejudice the defendant, who had not pressed for trial. Crowded court dockets due to increased crime rates and inadequate court facilities and staffs are also a cause of delay. Congressional adoption of some minimal time requirement after which a suspect must be freed is in keeping with the philosophy of the speedy trial requirement that "justice delayed is justice denied."

State Action   An official act by a state or local government agency or officer. The term usually refers to any abridgement of individual rights by state or local governmental agencies, laws, or officials, which is forbidden by the Fourteenth Amendment to the Constitution. Invasions of individual rights by private individuals are not within the purview of the Amendment. For example, a law imposing racial segregation is state action, whereas an individual's discriminatory act does not violate the Fourteenth Amendment, although the individual action may be forbidden by statute. *See also* FOURTEENTH AMENDMENT, page 313.

Significance   The state action concept has been crucial to the legal assault on racial segregation. Discrimination based on segregation ordinances or on official support by elected officials or police officers has been held by the courts to be state action. In one of its early civil rights decisions, the Supreme Court held state judicial enforcement of racially restrictive real estate covenants to be illegal state action (*Shelley v. Kramer*, 334 U.S. 1 [1948]). The major contemporary problem is whether private discrimination becomes state action if an individual seeks governmental support to protect his or her private interests. A 1991 case, *Edmonson v. Leesville Concrete Co. Inc.*, 500 U.S. 614, held it to be state action when private parties in a civil suit were permitted to use peremptory challenges to exclude potential jurors on account of race. The present tests of state action appear to be (1) whether the public interest is strong enough to transform private actions into matters of state concern and (2) the degree of official involvement in the discriminatory act.

Substantive Rights   Constitutional guarantees essential for personal liberty. These generally include those rights listed in the First, Thirteenth, and Fourteenth Amendments—freedoms of speech, press, religion, assembly, and petition; freedom from involuntary servitude; and the right to equal protection of the law. *Substantive* rights are to be distinguished from *procedural* rights, which are concerned with the manner in which the substantive rights are protected, as by due process and fair trial. *See also* PROCEDURAL RIGHTS, page 330.

Significance   No precise listing of substantive rights is possible; they include those personal liberties essential to a free society. No person can be considered free who does not have liberty of expression in speech, press, or prayer, or who is enslaved or arbitrarily discriminated against. Necessary limitations, however, may be placed on substantive rights. Thus, a person may be confined to jail or have his or her expression limited, but only in accordance with due process of law.

Takings Clause   Another name for the "eminent domain" provision of the Fifth Amendment, which prohibits the taking of private property for public use without just compensation. Ordinarily, eminent domain suggests the confiscation of property for such purposes as highway construction or public housing and the payment of the value of the property. In recent years, the clause has increasingly been applied to encompass governmental regulatory activiity on land use that has a negative impact upon the value of property, hence, a "taking" without actual confiscation. In 1994, the Supreme Court ruled that the government must show "rough proportionality" between environmental purposes and the potential harm to be caused by any use of property (*Dolan v. City of Tigard,* 114 S. Ct. 2039). *See also* EMINENT DOMAIN, page 308; ZONING, page 631.

Significance   Recent developments in "takings" suggest a return to an emphasis on private property rights, which, the Court suggested in the *Dolan* case, had become a "poor relation" to the remainder of the Bill of Rights. The urbanization of the nation, technological developments, and environmental concerns have had dramatic impacts on both the use of and regulation of property. The issue is certain to loom large in the years ahead.

Third Amendment   A part of the Bill of Rights prohibiting the quartering (housing) of soldiers in private homes during time of peace without consent of the owner. In wartime, quartering of soldiers may be done under conditions prescribed by law. *See also* CIVILIAN CONTROL, page 537.

Significance   The Third Amendment was a reaction against the practice of the British, during the colonial era, of quartering soldiers in private homes. This has never been done in the United States, and no cases have arisen concerning this provision. It is one of the elements of civilian control over the military.

Thirteenth Amendment   An amendment to the Constitution, adopted in 1865, forbidding slavery or involuntary servitude anywhere in the United States or any place subject to its jurisdiction. It applies to individuals as well as to government. The Amendment is a guarantee against forced labor and, under Supreme Court rulings, gives Congress power to legislate against any acts that impose a "badge of slavery" on anyone. *See also* INVOLUNTARY SERVITUDE, page 322; *Jones v. Mayer,* page 358.

Significance   The Thirteenth Amendment closed a sad chapter in American history. Though the Amendment has been viewed essentially as outlawing slavery, the Supreme Court in 1968 upheld an 1866 law, passed under authority of the Thirteenth Amendment, that outlawed racial discrimination in the sale or rental of property (*Jones v. Mayer,* 392 U.S. 409). The Court ruled that the Amendment gives Congress authority well beyond that of forbidding slavery. This decision, along with another upholding an 1871 law authorizing private suits against persons who conspire to violate the rights of others (*Griffin v. Breckenridge*, 403 U.S. 88 [1971]), gives added vitality to the Thirteenth Amendment.

Treason   A disloyal act, which, as defined by Article III, section 3 of the Constitution, "shall consist only in levying war against [the United States], or in adhering to their enemies, giving them aid and comfort." The Constitution further provides that one may not be convicted of treason "unless on the testimony of two witnesses to the same overt act, or on confession in open court." *See also* SEDITION, page 334.

Significance   Treason is the only crime precisely defined in the Constitution, as a safeguard against irresponsible charges for this most serious of crimes. Levying war or adhering to enemies of the United States are the only grounds for bringing a prosecution and, unless the suspect confesses, two witnesses must testify that they saw the same act. Acts of disloyalty that do not fall within the constitutional definition may be prosecuted under sedition laws. Many state constitutions contain treason provisions, but it is questionable whether one could commit treason against a state and not against the United States. John Brown, hanged in 1859 for his raid on Harpers Ferry, Virginia, is believed to be the only person executed in this country for treason against a state. Treason trials have not been numerous and no one has been executed for treason by the national government.

Victims' Rights   Provision of compensation, services, and information to victims of crime. Victims' rights are designed to protect and compensate victims of crime in a manner similar to the rights of the defendant, which are constitutionally protected. Victims' rights, now available in varying degrees under national and state laws and by constitutional provisions in nearly half the states, include access to counseling and medical care for victims and their families; financial compensation for lost property, wages, or other damages; free access to legal advocates to advise the victim about the court system, legal proceedings, and legal actions to take, as well as to protect the victim from abusive or indifferent practices engaged in by defense counsel and the police; improved legal mechanisms to make it easier to file civil suits and win damages; access to state funds to pay damages when destitute assailants cannot; the right to be informed of plea bargains with the defendant; the right to be informed of the defendant's release on bail or parole; the right to be informed about where and when bail hearings, trials, and other legal proceedings will be held; and prohibitions against publication of the victim's name in the press.

Significance   The concept of victims' rights emerged strongly in the 1980s as the number of violent crimes soared and as public concern grew over increasing judicial protection for defendants' rights. Many jurisdictions realized that few social services were available to the victim and that little information about the court system or proceedings against the accused was available. Private-sector groups such as the National Victim Center were established to lobby government, provide information, and support victims of crime. A majority of states and many local jurisdictions also acted to ensure many victims' rights. As part of the Comprehensive Crime Control Act of

1984, the federal government created an Office for Victims of Crime within the Department of Justice, victims' advocates were placed in every U.S. Attorney's Office, victim and witness protection legislation was enhanced, and a special fine was levied on convicted persons to pay for a federal victims' compensation fund. In 1991, the Supreme Court permitted the use of victim impact statements in capital punishment cases in *Payne v. Tennessee,* 501 U.S. 808. In 1992, the Supreme Court struck down laws that required that a convicted criminal's income from publications or movies describing his or her crime be made available to victims who obtain a civil judgment against the criminal. The Court found the financial disincentive to publish with particular content to be a violation of free speech (*Simon and Schuster v. New York State Crime Victims Board,* 502 U.S. 105). Major arguments against victims' rights are that official compassion on behalf of the victim tends to presume the guilt of the person on trial, and that such laws impose time consuming and expensive delays on prosecutions.

Visa   A permit to enter a country. Persons seeking admission to the United States must get a visa from a U.S. consul located abroad. Many countries require visas as well as passports. Visas are usually stamps of approval affixed to the passport by an official of the country to be visited or entered permanently. *See also* IMMIGRATION ACT OF 1990, page 381.

Significance   The visa procedure is an instrument of national policy that enables a country to screen applicants prior to their departure for that country. In the United States, before 1924, screening was done at ports of entry, causing great hardship to those rejected. Consular officers stationed abroad have unlimited discretion to grant or refuse visas. A controversial issue had involved denial of visas to visiting foreign dignitaries or scholars who may have suspect political beliefs or associations. Congress suspended use of this authority in 1987 and permanently repealed it in 1990.

Wiretapping   The use of any electronic device to intercept private conversations. After years of confusion over the permissible bounds for the gathering and use of electronic eavesdropping, the Supreme Court ruled that the requirements of the Fourth Amendment's protection against unreasonable searches and seizures must be met (*Berger v. New York,* 388 U.S. 41; *Katz v. United States,* 389 U.S. 347 [1967]). Congress, in the Omnibus Crime Control and Safe Streets Act of 1968, authorized use of telephone taps and bugging devices if a warrant is secured from a judge with exceptions for emergency cases involving national security or organized crime. The Supreme Court, however, has drawn a distinction between domestic security cases and foreign intelligence operations, requiring a warrant for electronic surveillance of domestic suspects (*United States v. United States District Court,* 407 U.S. 297 [1972]); this distinction was supported by Congress in the Foreign Intelligence Surveillance Act of 1978. A secret Foreign Intelligence Surveillance Court consisting of seven federal district court judges decides whether to allow electronic surveillance of persons in the United States suspected of espionage or terrorism. During the mid 1990s, warrants for national security wiretaps averaged more than 600 per year. *See also Berger v. New York,* page 350; FOURTH AMENDMENT, page 314; PRIVACY, page 329.

Significance   Technological refinements of electronic listening devices, which have vastly complicated traditional rules of search and seizure, illustrate the difficulty of keeping the Bill of Rights abreast of modern developments. In 1986, for example, Congress extended privacy protection to cover new electronic devices such as cellular phones and electronic mail. Electronic eavesdropping presents special problems not generally involved in searches and seizures: A search warrant ordinarily is used at one time, not for an extended period; innocent people involved in conversations with a suspect lose their privacy; and the suspect is completely unaware of the intrusion. Wiretapping and its rapidly developing related technology have consumed and will continue to consume considerable judicial and legislative attention.

Witness   A person who presents information or evidence in a trial or investigation. Under the Sixth Amendment and most state constitutions, a person accused of a crime is entitled to confront the witnesses against him or her and to compel the attendance of witnesses in his or her favor. In 1965, the Supreme Court ruled that the right of confrontation of witnesses applies in state trials under the due process clause of the Fourteenth Amendment (Pointer v. Texas, 380 U.S. 400). The right to compel the attendance of witnesses was similarly applied to the states in 1967 (*Washington v. Texas,* 388 U.S. 14). *See also* CONFRONTATION CLAUSE, page 302; SUBPOENA, page 279.

Significance   In a criminal case, the government must permit cross-examination of any witness it uses. If it wishes to conceal the identity of an informant, then that person may not be put on the stand, nor may testimony be introduced. In addition, the defendant is entitled to see any reports made to the police by a witness, unless the judge rules otherwise. The right to compel the attendance of favorable witnesses is an important corollary to the right of confrontation, and the defendant has the right to the aid of the government to subpoena any reluctant witness. Though these rights are fairly well established in criminal trials, attention has been directed from time to time to the lack of these rights in congressional investigations; in hearings on subversion or crime, persons are usually permitted to testify, but they are not permitted to confront and cross-examine accusers or to compel the attendance of favorable witnesses.

IMPORTANT AGENCIES

Bureau of Alcohol, Tobacco and Firearms (ATF)   A part of the Department of the Treasury, established in 1972, to assume responsibilities (then held by the Internal Revenue Service) to monitor both legal and illegal trafficking in alcohol, tobacco, and firearms. The ATF's objectives are to maximize compliance with federal laws governing the production, taxation, and distribution of these products and to enforce criminal violations of those laws.

Significance   The ATF, like other units of the Treasury Department (Secret Service, Customs Service), holds specialized law enforcement functions. The widely dispersed law enforcement authority in the United States is underscored by the prominence of such agencies. The ATF has attracted notice in recent years largely due to the controversies generated by gun control issues, particularly widespread use of weapons by criminals and the accumulation of weapons by private "militia" groups. Numerous laws govern tobacco and alcohol sales and usage, adding to ATF's prominence. The agency has been involved in a number of highly publicized raids, is often caught in jurisdictional disputes with the FBI and other police agencies, and is closely watched by civil rights and civil liberties groups. Efforts in Congress to abolish ATF or assign its duties elsewhere have failed.

Civil Rights Commission   Established by the federal Civil Rights Act of 1957 as a bipartisan commission to investigate the broad area of civil rights. In 1983, its membership was changed from six persons appointed by the President to eight (four chosen by Congress and four by the President) and removable only for cause. Its official title was changed to United States Commission on Civil Rights in 1994. It has conducted investigations and published reports on such matters as voting rights, education, housing, employment, and the administration of justice. The Civil Rights Act of 1964 strengthened the commission's investigatory power and established it as a clearinghouse for civil rights information. In 1972, its jurisdiction was expanded to include sex discrimination and, in 1978, discrimination due to age or handicap was added to the commission's responsibilities.

Significance   The Civil Rights Commission has uncovered evidence of abuses of civil rights in all areas of its investigations. Its findings and recommendations played a vital role in the enactment of the Civil Rights Acts of 1960, 1964, 1965, and 1968. The commission has taken the initiative in issuing extended reports on civil rights, thereby calling attention to the great gap between the promise of the law and the plight of minorities, and it has not hesitated to criticize Congress, the President, and specific agencies for inaction. The 1983 change in membership occurred after President Reagan sought to replace members who were openly critical of his administration's civil rights policies. Sharp declines in the commission's programs and prestige did take place subsequently, as a result of discord within the commission and drastic cuts in its budget.

Community Relations Service   Established by the Civil Rights Act of 1964 to help communities resolve civil rights problems growing out of race, color, or national origin. The service is part of the Justice Department, headed by a director appointed by the President and responsible to the Attorney General. The facilities of the service are made available either on request or through its own initiative. It is directed by law to seek the cooperation of state and local agencies and to carry on its work without publicity.

Significance   The Community Relations Service is patterned after the human relations or community relations agencies found in numerous state and local governments that make available conciliatory services to temper dangerous community tensions. Though its activities do not receive publicity, indications are that the service has been involved in a large number of cases, including resettlement of refugee immigrants.

Department of Justice   A major department of the executive branch concerned with the enforcement of federal laws. The Department of Justice has three divisions that are particularly concerned with civil liberty matters. The Federal Bureau of Investigation (FBI), the department's best-known agency, is responsible for investigation of violations of federal law. The Criminal Division prosecutes violations of federal law and bears responsibility for internal security matters. The Civil Rights Division is responsible for the enforcement of all statutes affecting civil rights, including the civil rights acts, antipeonage laws, election frauds, and obstructions of justice. Other units concerned with civil liberties include the Bureau of Prisons, the Drug Enforcement Administration, the United States Parole Commission, the Community Relations Service, and the Immigration and Naturalization Service. *See also* COMMUNITY RELATIONS SERVICE, page 344; DEPARTMENT OF JUSTICE, page 285; FEDERAL BUREAU OF INVESTIGATION, page 345; IMMIGRATION AND NATURALIZATION SERVICE, page 346.

Significance   The Department of Justice is playing an increasingly large role in the field of civil liberties. An increasing crime rate and an intensification of racial conflict have expanded the activities of the FBI, the Criminal and Civil Rights Divisions, and related units. As the scope of federal law enforcement grows, so does the influence of the Justice Department. Despite substantial cuts in many federal programs and a tradition of local law enforcement, the Department of Justice, since 1980, has nearly doubled its workforce and has had its budget increased by 600 percent.

Equal Employment Opportunity Commission (EEOC)   Established by the Civil Rights Act of 1964 to investigate and conciliate disputes involving discrimination by employers, unions, and employment agencies because of race, color, religion, national origin, or sex. In 1978, its jurisdiction was extended to cover federal employment, the Equal Pay Act of 1963, discrimination because of age or handicap, and, as of 1992, the Americans with Disabilities Act of 1990. The EEOC consists of five members appointed for five-year terms by the President with Senate consent. It stresses confidential persuasion and conciliation to achieve its objectives. Though given authority in 1972 to institute legal action if conciliation fails, the EEOC lacks authority to issue cease-and-desist orders. Activity by state fair employment practices agencies is encouraged by the Act. *See also* FAIR EMPLOYMENT PRACTICES LAWS, page 311.

Significance   The EEOC represented a major victory for civil rights proponents who had sought fair employment practice legislation from Congress for many years prior to 1964. For some years, racial discrimination had already been forbidden by executive order in the military services, government employment, and in private companies filling governmental contracts. Although most states have established fair employment commissions with varying degrees of enforcement power, the EEOC represents a national commitment to equality of opportunity throughout the nation in both public and private employment. During the 1990s, the agency has had a growing backlog of cases, fueled largely by sex discrimination and disability discrimination complaints, but has suffered from funding and personnel cuts.

Federal Bureau of Investigation (FBI)   The principal criminal investigative arm of the federal government, established in 1908 in the Department of

Justice. The FBI is charged with investigating most violations of federal law. Its jurisdiction extends to criminal activities such as kidnapping, bank robbery, and interstate transportation of stolen goods, to civil matters such as civil rights law enforcement, and to domestic security cases such as espionage and sabotage. It is also engaged in nationwide police-training activities and is well known for its crime laboratory and fingerprint identification services. Generally, FBI agents are required to have degrees in law, accounting, engineering, science, or appropriate work experience.

Significance   The FBI is probably one of the best-known and most highly publicized federal agencies, though it is only a "bureau" in a major department. Its reputation grew largely under the directorship of J. Edgar Hoover, who headed the FBI from 1924 until his death in 1972, during which time the FBI's "G-men" hunted celebrated criminals, communists, and real and imagined threats to domestic peace and security. After Hoover's death, and as part of post-Watergate investigations, the FBI was revealed to have been involved in numerous illegal activities and violations of individual rights in pursuit of its functions. As a result, both houses of Congress have established oversight committees to monitor FBI (and other intelligence agencies') activities, and in 1976 Congress placed a ten-year, single-term limit on the FBI director.

Immigration and Naturalization Service   The part of the Department of Justice that administers the laws regarding the admission, naturalization, and deportation of aliens. The service investigates the credentials of immigrants at ports of entry. Immigration and Naturalization Service officers also patrol the Canadian and Mexican borders to prevent the illegal entry of aliens. Aliens seeking to become citizens are investigated by agents of the service, who recommend to the courts whether the alien should be naturalized. *See also* ANTITERRORISM AND EFFECTIVE DEATH PENALTY ACT OF 1996, page 375; DEPORTATION, page 305; IMMIGRATION, page 320; NATURALIZATION, page 326.

Significance   Agents of the Immigration and Naturalization Service exercise considerable discretion in determining whether persons may enter the United States, become citizens, or be subject to deportation. Their decisions may be appealed to the Executive Office for Immigration Review in the Department of Justice, which includes the Office of Immigration Judges and the Board of Immigration Appeals.

Office of National Drug Control Policy   An agency in the Executive Office of the President, established by the National Narcotics Leadership Act of 1988, to coordinate nationwide strategy to control both the supply and demand for illegal drugs. The office is headed by a director (informally known as the "drug czar") appointed by the President with Senate consent. *See also* DRUG TESTING, page 306.

Significance   The establishment of a "drug czar" at the highest levels of government emphasizes the national concern with a "war on drugs." Numerous national, state, local, and even international agencies are involved in enforcement of laws on narcotics, and about half the prisoners in the United States are drug offenders. In 1993, President Clinton invited the director to meet regularly with his Cabinet. The problem of illegal drug trafficking and use has proved intractable, but suggestions for decriminalization or more lenient policies have not been favorably viewed by political leaders.

IMPORTANT CASES

Adarand Constructors v. Pena   115 S. Ct. 2097 (1995): Held, in a major statement on affirmative action, that all racial classifications, imposed by federal, state, or local governmental action, are to be reviewed under "strict scrutiny" and are lawful only if "narrowly tailored" to further a "compelling governmental interest." The *Adarand* case involved a federal Department of Transportation construction contract, which, under department policy, was awarded to a business owned and controlled by "socially and economically disadvantaged individuals," defined as persons subject to racial, ethnic, or cultural bias. The Court ruled that the policy violated the due process clause of the Fifth Amendment. *See also* AFFIRMATIVE ACTION, page 292; *Bolling v. Sharpe*, page 350; *Regents of the University of California v. Bakke*, page 366; REVERSE DISCRIMINATION, page 332.

Significance   The *Adarand* decision marked an important turning point in Supreme Court attitudes on affirmative action. Many earlier cases supporting affirmative action were indecisive or decided by plurality opinion. In 1989, in *City of Richmond v. J. A. Crosson*, 488 U.S. 469, the Court struck down a city set-aside plan for minority-owned businesses as a violation of the equal protection clause of the Fourteenth Amendment. In *Adarand*, the Court held that in the absence of an equal protection limitation on the national government, racial classification was barred by the Fifth Amendment and subject to the strict scrutiny test.

Addington v. Texas   441 U.S. 418 (1979): Held that civil commitment for mental illness constitutes a "significant deprivation of liberty that requires due process protection." The standard of proof necessary for commitment should be "clear and convincing evidence," rather than the standard of "beyond a reasonable doubt" used in criminal cases or the looser "preponderance of the evidence" rule used in civil suits. *See also* DUE PROCESS, page 307.

Significance   *Addington v. Texas* was a major step toward the recognition of the rights of the mentally ill, who, under the laws of most states, could otherwise be confined indefinitely without the routine protections accorded a person accused of a minor crime. With respect to minor children, the court held in *Parham v. J. R.*, 442 U.S. 584 (1979), that an adversary hearing is not necessary when parents want to have a child committed but that adequate medical and procedural safeguards must be provided. In *Vitek v. Jones*, 445 U.S. 480 (1980), the court held that prison inmates cannot be involuntarily placed under psychiatric treatment without some opportunity for a hearing. A 1992 decision, *Foucha v. Louisiana*, 504 U.S. 71, established that a criminal defendant found not guilty by reason of insanity but who later regains sanity may not be confined indefinitely out of fear that he or she might pose a danger to society. Earlier, the court held it to be a violation of due process for a state to confine a person indefinitely, without treatment, because of alleged mental illness (*O'Connor v. Donaldson,* 422 U.S. 563 [1975]) and subsequently held that mentally retarded persons in state institutions have a constitutional right to safe conditions, freedom of movement, and sufficient training to enjoy those rights (Youngberg v. Romeo, 457 U.S. 307 [1982]). A 1996 decision (*Cooper v. Oklahoma,* 116 S. Ct. 1373) held that in a criminal case a defendant claiming incompetence to stand trial need only prove it by a preponderance of the evidence.

Afroyim v. Rusk   387 U.S. 253 (1967): Declared unconstitutional a law providing that native-born citizens automatically forfeit their citizenship by voting in a foreign election. The Court stressed that in the United States, where the people are sovereign, the citizen has a constitutional right to remain a citizen unless the right is voluntarily relinquished. *See also* EXPATRIATION, page 310.

Significance   The Court had earlier upheld the law regarding voting in a foreign election on the grounds that it was a matter of foreign affairs (*Perez v. Brownell,* 356 U.S. 44 [1958]). The *Afroyim* decision calls into question the validity of all laws on expatriation except for actual naturalization in a foreign state. Ordinarily, a person who expatriates himself or herself becomes a citizen of another state, but American expatriation laws could leave a person stateless. In 1980, the Court held that while Congress may not expatriate anyone, it may set the standard of proof necessary to demonstrate voluntary expatriation in a trial, namely, preponderance of evidence (*Vance v. Terrazas,* 444 U.S. 252).

Arizona Governing Committee for Tax Annuity and Deferred Compensation Plans v. Norris   463 U.S. 1073 (1983): Held that an employer-sponsored retirement plan that provides lower monthly retirement benefits to women than to men who made the same contribution discriminates on the basis of sex in violation of the Civil Rights Act of 1964. In 1978, in *Los Angeles Department of Water and Power v. Manhart,* 435 U.S. 702, the Court held that the Civil Rights Act of 1964 prohibited an employer from requiring women to make larger contributions in order to obtain the same monthly benefits as men. In holding sex distinctions invalid at either the pay-in or pay-out stage of a retirement plan, the Court rejected the argument that women as a class live longer than men. That argument, said the Court, did not predict an individual's life expectancy and results in employers treating employees not as individuals but as components of a class—racial, religious, national, or sexual. *See also* CIVIL RIGHTS ACT OF 1964, page 378; COMPARABLE WORTH, page 301; CRAIG V. BOREN, page 352; EQUAL RIGHTS, page 309.

Significance   The *Arizona* case lent strong support to the women's rights movement's emphasis on economic equity issues in the wake of the defeat of the Equal Rights Amendment proposal in 1982. Growing evidence that a disproportionate share of poor people are women and that the proportion of female-headed families is growing led women's groups to turn their attention to issues related to jobs, insurance, pension plans, and tax reforms. The *Arizona* and *Los Angeles* cases apply to employer-sponsored plans, but the impact of those decisions on other forms of insurance—auto, life, health, and disability—where differentials between sexes do exist remains to be determined. The Arizona decision adds important weight to the Civil Rights Act of 1964 as applied to sex discrimination in the workplace. This was further enhanced in a 1991 ruling that an employer may not exclude a female employee from certain jobs because of concern for any fetus the woman might bear; a fetal protection policy is not a bona fide occupational qualification (BFOQ) (*International Union, UAW v. Johnson Controls, Inc.,* 499 U.S. 187). A 1984 law protects retirement plans of women who leave their jobs temporarily to raise their families.

Ashcraft v. Tennessee   322 U.S. 143 (1944): Ruled that a confession obtained from a suspect after prolonged interrogation under hot lights by a relay of officers is not admissible in a state trial. Such coercive methods to obtain confessions violate the Fourteenth Amendment. *See also* CONFESSION, page 302.

Significance   Earlier, in *Brown v. Mississippi,* 297 U.S. 278 (1936), the Supreme Court announced for the first time that a confession extracted through brutality and torture violated the Fourteenth Amendment. In the *Ashcraft* case, the Court extended this rule to confessions acquired as a result of psychological rather than physical maltreatment. The Court has since carefully examined convictions based on confessions in order to ensure that the confessions have been wholly voluntary. A 1991 case, however, authorized the application of the "harmless error" trial rule to the admission of an involuntary confession whereby the "error" is assessed in the context of other evidence (*Arizona v. Fulminante,* 499 U.S. 279). Thus, an involuntary confession, usually considered sufficient to void a prosecution, may be used if other evidence is sufficient to sustain a verdict.

Barron v. Baltimore   7 Peters 243 (1833): Held that the Bill of Rights limits only the national government and not state governments. This decision is still operative today, although its impact has been greatly modified in practice through interpretations of the Fourteenth Amendment. The Supreme Court has incorporated most of the provisions of the Bill of Rights into the due process clause of the Fourteenth Amendment, thus making them applicable to state governments. *See also* FOURTEENTH AMENDMENT, page 313; *Gitlow v. New York,* page 355; INCORPORATION DOCTRINE, page 321.

Significance   *Barron v. Baltimore* illustrates the application of the federal principle to civil liberties. The Bill of Rights was clearly designed to limit the power of the national government and not the states. Subsequent interpretation of the Fourteenth Amendment to incorporate most of the Bill of Rights and make it binding on the states has all but eliminated the strong impact that the *Barron* decision had for almost 100 years.

Bartkus v. Illinois   359 U.S. 121 (1959): Denied a claim of double jeopardy appealed from a conviction in a state court for bank robbery following acquittal by a federal court for the same bank robbery. *See also* DOUBLE JEOPARDY, page 306.

Significance   The Bartkus case underscores the rule that double jeopardy refers only to repeated trials on the same charge by the same jurisdiction. A person may, therefore, be tried by both the national and state courts for a single offense. One may not, however, be tried by a state and a city within that state for the same offense (*Waller v. Florida,* 397 U.S. 387 [1970]) or for robbery of one victim after acquittal of the charge of robbing another victim in the same incident (*Ashe v. Swenson,* 397 U.S. 436 [1970]), or be tried as an adult after a finding of guilt for the same offense in a juvenile court proceeding (*Breed v. Jones,* 421 U.S. 519 [1975]). A 1996 ruling (*United States v. Ursery,* 116 S. Ct. 2135) held that it is not double jeopardy to prosecute for a crime and then seize property in a civil forfeiture.

Berger v. New York   388 U.S. 41 (1967): A decision in which the Supreme Court brought wiretapping within the protection of the Fourth Amendment search and seizure provisions. The Court declared unconstitutional a New York law that authorized a judge to issue an eavesdrop order but that did not require indication of any specific offense, conversation, or special circumstance. *See also* WIRETAPPING, page 342.

Significance   By holding that the use of an electronic device to capture conversations is a search within the meaning of the Fourth Amendment, the Court clarified one of the more puzzling aspects of the permissible use of electronic eavesdropping. Prior to the *Berger* case, the Court had treated the problem as a matter of statutory rather than constitutional law unless an actual physical invasion of property took place. In another important ruling shortly after the *Berger* decision (*Katz v. United States,* 389 U.S. 347 [1967]), the Court held that federal officials conducted an unlawful search and seizure by eavesdropping on conversations in a public telephone booth. Even though there was no physical invasion of property, such an intrusion into privacy without judicial safeguards afforded by the Fourth Amendment could not stand. It can now be said that "words" as well as "things" are protected against unreasonable searches and seizures, including, under a 1986 law, words transmitted by such new devices as cellular phones and electronic mail. Congress has provided for wiretapping and bugging by state and national officials in the Omnibus Crime Control Act of 1968, requiring warrants under most, but not all, circumstances.

Bolling v. Sharpe   347 U.S. 497 (1954): Declared that segregation in the public schools of the District of Columbia violated the due process clause of the Fifth Amendment. *See also Brown v. Board of Education of Topeka,* page 350; EQUAL PROTECTION, page 308; FIFTH AMENDMENT, page 312.

Significance   The Constitution contains no requirement that the national government afford "equal protection of the laws." The "equal protection" clause is found in the Fourteenth Amendment and is a limitation on the states. Nevertheless, the Court held that segregation of the races by the national government is an arbitrary denial of liberty without due process of law, thereby equating liberty with equal protection.

Brown v. Board of Education of Topeka   347 U.S. 483 (1954); 349 U.S. 294 (1955): Established in a major decision that segregation of the races in public schools violates the equal protection clause of the Fourteenth Amendment. The Supreme Court in 1954 overruled the "separate but equal" doctrine that had been in effect since 1896, noting, "Separate educational facilities are inherently unequal." In 1955, the Court ordered desegregation to proceed "with all deliberate speed," leaving it to the federal district courts to determine implementations of the ruling in specific cases brought before them. *See also Bolling v. Sharpe,* page 350; DE FACTO SEGREGATION, page 304; *Plessy v. Ferguson,* page 365; SEGREGATION, page 335.

Significance   The *Brown* decision ranks among the most important in American constitutional history. Other racial segregation practices have also been declared unconstitutional following this decision. The *Brown* case created a crisis in national-state relations and helped spur the civil rights movement. The decision initiated a social revolution, since supported by major national civil rights acts and by state and local legislation. Nevertheless, most minority students still attend schools with predominantly minority enrollments.

Committee for Public Education and Religious Liberty v. Nyquist   413 U.S. 756 (1973): Struck down, as a violation of the First Amendment's establishment of religion clause, a New York law providing for maintenance and repair grants to nonpublic schools, tuition reimbursement for low-income families with children in parochial schools, and tax relief for families not qualifying for tuition reimbursement. The Court found the primary effect of these provisions was to advance religious rather than secular interests and to produce excessive entanglement between church and state (the "*Lemon* test" based on the formula adopted by the Court in *Lemon v. Kurtzman,* 403 U.S. 602 [1971], holding invalid state payment of salaries of teachers of secular subjects in parochial schools). *See also Everson v. Board of Education,* page 353; *Mueller v. Allen,* page 362; SEPARATION OF CHURCH AND STATE, page 336.

Significance   Soaring educational costs, dissatisfaction with public schools, and increasing interest in parental choice of schools have put parochial schools under considerable economic pressure, resulting in persistent and increasing demands for public subsidy. Nevertheless, the Supreme Court has taken a dim view of direct or indirect financial aid that is clearly designed to sustain church schools rather than aid the pupil, as shown by the *Lemon* and *Nyquist* decisions, or to lend instructional equipment (other than books), or provide auxiliary services such as counseling (*Meek v. Pettinger,* 421 U.S. 349 [1975]; *Wolman v. Walter,* 433 U.S. 229 [1977]). Sending publicly paid teachers into parochial schools to teach secular subjects, including remedial and enrichment classes, was held invalid (*School District of the City of Grand Rapids v. Ball,* 473 U.S. 373 [1985] and *Aguilar v. Felton,* 473 U.S. 402 [1985]). A special school district created for the handicapped children of an orthodox Jewish sect was held to violate the establishment clause because it allocated political power based on a religious criterion in *Board of Education of Kiryas Joel Village School District v. Grumet,* 114 S. Ct. 2481 (1994). A 1983 ruling in *Mueller v. Allen,* 463 U.S. 388, however, upheld a state tax deduction for parents for educational costs of all children in either private or public schools, though the bulk of the deductions went to parochial school parents. Aid to church-related colleges and universities has received judicial support on the grounds that colleges are less religiously oriented and the students less impressionable than at lower educational levels

(*Tilton v. Richardson,* 403 U.S. 672 [1971]; *Hunt v. McNair,* 410 U.S. 952 [1973]; *Roemer v. Maryland Board of Public Works,* 426 U.S. 736 [1976]). The degree of continuing political controversy apt to be generated by a given form of aid appears to be crucial to the Court in making decisions in the area of aid to nonpublic schools.

Craig v. Boren   429 U.S. 190 (1977): Struck down a state law that established different alcoholic drinking ages for men and women. In holding a different drinking age for men (21) than women (18) a violation of the equal protection clause of the Fourteenth Amendment, the Supreme Court established the test for any law classifying persons by sex. To pass the test, the law "must serve important governmental objectives and must be substantially related to achievement of those objectives." *See also Arizona Governing Committee for Tax Annuity and Deferred Compensation Plans v. Norris,* page 348; EQUAL RIGHTS, page 309; *Meritor Savings Bank, FSB v. Vinson,* page 359.

Significance   *Craig v. Boren* is illustrative of the Court's tendency to treat gender distinctions as unconstitutional when based on nothing more than sexual stereotypes. In another case striking down a law setting different ages at which men and women are considered adults, the court noted that "no longer is the female destined solely for the house and the rearing of family and only the male for the marketplace and the world of ideas" (*Stanton v. Stanton,* 421 U.S. 7 [1975]). Although the Court has never asserted that gender is an unacceptable or "suspect" classification, it has viewed with "heightened scrutiny" state and national laws based on sexual assumptions. Thus it struck down a state minimum height and weight requirement for prison guards that few women could meet (*Dothard v. Rawlinson,* 433 U.S. 321 [1977]), provisions under the Social Security Act that assume female dependency on the male and hence favor widows over widowers in survivor benefits (*Califano v. Goldfarb,* 430 U.S. 199 [1977]), laws that authorize women, but not men, to receive alimony (*Orr v. Orr,* 440 U.S. 268 [1979]), and a state university's refusal to admit men to its school of nursing (*Mississippi University for Women v. Hogan,* 458 U.S. 718 [1982]). The Court did uphold a law excluding women from registration for the military draft (*Rostker v. Goldberg,* 453 U.S. 57 [1981]). In 1996, however, the Court strengthened the standard by which gender distinctions must be justified and struck down state-supported exclusion of women from the Virginia Military Institute (*United States v. Virginia,* 116 S. Ct. 2264). Gender-based government action requires "exceedingly persuasive justification."

Dennis v. United States   341 U.S. 494 (1951): Sustained, in a major decision, the conviction of eleven top Communist party leaders for conspiring to teach and advocate the violent overthrow of the government. The decision upheld the Smith Act of 1940. *See also* ALIEN REGISTRATION ACT OF 1940, page 374; *Scales v. United States,* page 369.

Significance   The *Dennis* case attracted wide notice because of the sharp conflict between freedom of speech guaranteed by the First Amendment and the indictment against the Communist leaders for advocating their doctrine. The Supreme Court narrowed the interpretation of the clear and present danger rule by holding that, in the interest of self-preservation, the government need not wait until the conspiracy ripened into action. This decision led to numerous prosecutions of other Communist leaders. In 1957, however, in *Yates v. United States,* 354 U.S. 298, the Supreme Court modified its ruling in the *Dennis* case by holding that a distinction must be drawn between urging people to *believe* in something and urging people to *do* something. In the *Yates* case, the Court found that the defendants were merely preaching Communist doctrine in the abstract and were neither teaching nor advocating unlawful conduct. The *Yates* case has restored the clear and present danger rule to some extent and made it more difficult for the government to prosecute Communists without proving some measure of concrete action to overthrow the government by force. The *Yates* ruling was extended to state laws in 1969 in *Brandenburg v. Ohio,* 395 U.S. 444, in which the court reversed the conviction of a Ku Klux Klan leader for advocating violence.

Elfbrandt v. Russell 384 U.S. 11 (1966): Struck down a state loyalty oath requirement that bound state employees not to become members of the Communist party. The Court held that a law that applies to membership without specific intent to further illegal aims rests on the unacceptable doctrine of guilt by association. A statute touching First Amendment rights must be narrowly drawn. *See also* GUILT BY ASSOCIATION, page 318; LOYALTY OATH, page 324.

Significance The *Elfbrandt* case was one of several in which the Supreme Court struck down loyalty oaths after having sustained their imposition in 1951 in *Garner v. Board of Public Works,* 341 U.S. 716. In the *Garner* case, the Court upheld a non-Communist affidavit as a reasonable requirement for public employment. Thereafter, the Court tended to find some infirmity in test oaths, holding that they must include knowledge of the illegal aims of proscribed organizations (*Wieman v. Updegraff,* 344 U.S. 183 [1952]) and not be unduly vague (*Baggitt v. Bullitt,* 377 U.S. 360 [1964]). The Court has been especially suspicious of the use of test oaths as a condition of securing a public benefit, such as a tax exemption (*Speiser v. Randall,* 357 U.S. 513 [1958]). In 1972, an oath requiring state employees to swear opposition to forceful overthrow of government was upheld (*Cole v. Richardson,* 405 U.S. 676).

Everson v. Board of Education of Ewing Township 330 U.S. 1 (1947): Decided that it is not a violation of the First Amendment's establishment of religion clause for a state to pay for the transportation of children to parochial schools. The Court found this to be a benefit to the children rather than an aid to the church. *See also Committee for Public Education and Religious Liberty v. Nyquist,* page 351; *Mueller v. Allen,* page 362; SEPARATION OF CHURCH AND STATE, page 336.

Significance The *Everson* case was the first major test of the establishment of religion clause. In its decision, the Court emphasized that the First Amendment was designed to "erect a wall of separation between church and state." Nevertheless, it found that in this instance the wall had not been breached. The *Everson* case serves as a precedent supporting a variety of state and federal aids, including textbooks for parochial schools (*Board of*

Education v. Allen, 392 U.S. 236 [1968]), tax exemptions for churches (*Walz v. Tax Commission,* 397 U.S. 664 [1970]), and tax deductions for tuition, textbooks, and transportation for all schoolchildren, including those in sectarian schools (*Mueller v. Allen,* 463 U.S. 388 [1983]).

Fong Yue Ting v. United States   149 U.S. 698 (1893): Supported the authority of the national government to deport aliens under its sovereign power in the field of international affairs. The Court upheld a federal law that authorized the deportation of Chinese laborers who had failed to get certificates of residence. Furthermore, the Court held that deportation is not criminal punishment and, therefore, does not require a judicial trial. Administrative and judicial hearings are available to aliens facing deportation under specifically defined circumstances such as questions regarding refugee status. *See also* DEPORTATION, page 305.

Significance   The major points of the case—that Congress has full power to deport aliens and that such action is not considered to be punishment—remain basic to American law. A 1984 decision held that the exclusionary rule, which prohibits use of illegally seized evidence in a criminal trial, does not apply to a civil deportation proceeding (*Immigration and Naturalization Service v. Lopez-Mendoza,* 468 U.S. 1032).

Freedman v. Maryland   380 U.S. 51 (1965): Held that motion picture censorship is permissible, provided the procedure followed assures prompt judicial review of the censor's decision. By this decision, the Court affirmed its ruling in *Times Film Corporation v. Chicago,* 365 U.S. 43 (1961), that initial submission of a motion picture to a censoring board may be required, but that the board's decision could not be final. *See also* CENSORSHIP, page 298.

Significance   The *Freedman* case raised motion pictures to a level more closely approximating the protection from prior restraint that other forms of expression have. In 1952, movies had been brought within the protection of the First and Fourteenth Amendments' guarantees of freedom of speech and press (*Burstyn v. Wilson,* 343 U.S. 495). Films, however, still do not enjoy the same degree of freedom as books because, under the *Times Film* rule, some form of prior submission to a censor is permitted. In the *Freedman* ruling, the Court sought to promote adequate safeguards against undue inhibition of lawful expression but was not willing to forbid censorship of movies altogether. A similar approach was applied to stage plays in 1975 in *Southeastern Promotions Ltd. v. Conrad,* 420 U.S. 546. No official movie or theater censorship boards were known to exist in the United States in recent years.

Gideon v. Wainwright   372 U.S. 335 (1963): A landmark ruling that state courts are required by the due process clause of the Fourteenth Amendment to provide counsel to indigent defendants in criminal cases. This had been required in *federal* criminal trials since the 1938 decision in *Johnson v. Zerbst,* 304 U.S. 458. State courts, however, were required to furnish counsel to needy defendants only in capital cases (*Powell v. Alabama,* 287 U.S. 45 [1932] known as the First Scottsboro Case) or when special circumstances, such as youth, mental incompetence, or inexperience, necessitated the furnishing of counsel to assure a fair trial (*Betts v. Brady*, 316 U.S. 455 [1942]). In *Gideon*, the Court held that defense by counsel is a fundamental right available to all. *See also* RIGHT TO COUNSEL, page 333.

Significance   The *Gideon* case was a major step in the nationalization of the Bill of Rights through the Fourteenth Amendment because it applied to state cases the guarantee of the assistance of counsel found in the Sixth Amendment. The case was also a forerunner of nationwide concern with equal justice for the poor. The *Gideon* decision not only overcame an illogical distinction between federal and state criminal proceedings but also recognized that most defendants lack the knowledge and skill to defend themselves against prosecutors. Since the *Gideon* case, the Court has extended the right to counsel from arrest to appeal. Defendants may, however, reject appointed counsel and conduct their own defense (*Faretta v. California*, 422 U.S. 806 [1975]). Some erosion of the *Gideon* rule has taken place as the courts refine and, in some cases, limit the circumstances under which an attorney must be provided, particularly in cases in which no sentence of imprisonment is imposed (*Scott v. Illinois*, 440 U.S. 367 [1979]).

Gitlow v. New York   268 U.S. 652 (1925): Established, in a landmark case, that the freedoms of speech and press are protected against state impairment by the due process clause of the Fourteenth Amendment. Nevertheless, in this case, the Court upheld a conviction for publishing and circulating materials advocating the overthrow of government by force.

Significance   Prior to the *Gitlow* decision, the Court had consistently held that the Fourteenth Amendment did not incorporate any part of the Bill of Rights. Since the *Gitlow* decision, the Court has applied the entire First Amendment, as well as most other portions of the Bill of Rights, to the states under the due process clause of the Fourteenth Amendment. The impact of this decision has been an increasing involvement of the national government in the protection of the people against any violations of their liberties by the states.

Hague v. CIO   307 U.S. 496 (1939): Declared unconstitutional under the Fourteenth Amendment an ordinance of Jersey City, New Jersey, that required permission to hold a meeting in or upon public streets, parks, or buildings. Under the ordinance, the officials of Jersey City had molested union organizers of the CIO and denied them permission to hold meetings and to circulate handbills. *See also* FREEDOM OF ASSEMBLY, page 314.

Significance   The *Hague* case established that the right to assemble applies not merely to private meetings of groups but to public meetings in public places. The Court has, in other cases, frowned on prior restraints by governmental officials on public meetings unless some reasonable standards are established for any required permits. These standards must in some way be related to the health, safety, and welfare of the people, not the content or purposes of the assembly. For example, one might legally be required to secure a permit in order to hold a parade (*Cox v. New Hampshire*, 312 U.S. 569 [1941]), and the government is not obliged to permit use of all public property, such as courthouses and jails, for demonstrations of protest (*Adderly v.*

Florida, 385 U.S. 39 [1966]). However, a law barring demonstrations on the sidewalks around the Supreme Court building in Washington, D.C., was struck down by the Supreme Court in *United States v. Grace,* 461 U.S. 171 (1983), as was a law prohibiting the display of hostile signs within 500 feet of a foreign embassy (*Boos v. Barry,* 485 U.S. 312 [1988]). But a ban on sleeping in tents erected in a park across from the White House as a form of protest was upheld in *Clark v. Community for Creative Non-Violence,* 468 U.S. 288 (1984).

Heart of Atlanta Motel v. United States   379 U.S. 241 (1964): Upheld the constitutionality of Title II of the Civil Rights Act of 1964, a provision barring discrimination in restaurants, hotels, and other places of public accommodation, on the ground that it is a valid exercise of the power to regulate interstate commerce. In 1883, the Supreme Court struck down a similar federal law (*Civil Rights Cases,* 109 U.S. 3) on the ground that private acts of discrimination could not be forbidden by the national government. In the *Heart of Atlanta* case and its companion case, *Katzenbach v. McClung,* 379 U.S. 294 (1964), the Court found ample power in the commerce clause for the national government to prohibit discrimination against persons in accommodations that serve substantial numbers of interstate travelers or that rely upon interstate commerce for a substantial part of their supplies and materials. *See also* CIVIL RIGHTS ACT OF 1964, page 378; COMMERCE POWER, page 33.

Significance   The *Heart of Atlanta Motel* case underscored the determination of the Supreme Court to accord Congress the necessary constitutional tools to meet the crisis in racial discrimination. Many scholars believe that Congress has power under the Fourteenth Amendment to deter discrimination in privately owned public accommodations but, because of the 1883 *Civil Rights Cases,* considerable doubt existed. The commerce power has long been used by Congress to enact social welfare legislation and to control individual behavior. Racial integration in public accommodations has been one of the more successful results of the Civil Rights Act.

Hurtado v. California   110 U.S. 516 (1884): Established that a state is not required by the due process clause of the Fourteenth Amendment to provide for indictment by grand jury in felony cases. Indictment by information is consistent with fair procedure. *See also* GRAND JURY, page 264.

Significance   The *Hurtado* case was the first major test of the meaning of the due process clause of the Fourteenth Amendment. In this case, the Court made it clear that the Fourteenth Amendment did not make the Bill of Rights applicable to the states, and that merely because indictment by grand jury is required by the Fifth Amendment, the states are not thereby bound. While the Supreme Court has since made most provisions of the Bill of Rights that relate to criminal procedures binding on the states, the *Hurtado* rule still applies. Few states use the grand jury today.

In Re Gault   387 U.S. 1 (1967): Held that the due process clause of the Fourteenth Amendment requires the essentials of fair treatment in cases involving juveniles accused of crime. The Court reversed a decision committing a child to an industrial school for six years, holding that in juvenile proceedings (1) adequate notice of a hearing must be given (2) the child must be informed of his or her right to counsel and the privilege against self-incrimination, and (3) opportunity must be given to confront and cross-examine witnesses. *See also* JUVENILE DELINQUENT, page 323.

Significance   Prior to the *Gault* ruling, juvenile court proceedings had been informal and confidential. The Court did not insist that *all* requirements of a criminal trial be observed in juvenile cases. It noted, however, that compassion and benevolence did not always mark juvenile proceedings and that, in fact, juveniles faced severe sentences in "schools" rather than prisons. In 1970, the Court held that juveniles, like adults, must be proven guilty beyond a reasonable doubt (*In Re Winship*, 397 U.S. 358) but held in 1971 that juries need not be used in juvenile cases (*McKeiver v. Pennsylvania*, 403 U.S. 528). The Court has tried to maintain some of the flexibility necessary in juvenile cases while guarding essential constitutional rights. Rising juvenile crime rates are leading to more "adult" procedures for prosecution and punishment of youthful offenders.

Jehovah's Witnesses Cases   Involved, in a series of cases, the religious sect known as Jehovah's Witnesses, testing the scope of religious freedom under the First and Fourteenth Amendments. Among the various decisions were those that held unconstitutional (1) laws requiring prior official approval to solicit funds for religious purposes (*Cantwell v. Connecticut*, 310 U.S. 296 [1940]), (2) laws levying license taxes on peddlers of religious tracts (*Murdock v. Pennsylvania*, 319 U.S. 105 [1943]), (3) laws prohibiting door-to-door distribution of religious handbills (*Martin v. Struthers*, 319 U.S. 141 [1943]), (4) laws requiring official approval to hold public worship meetings in public parks (*Niemotko v. Maryland*, 340 U.S. 268 [1951]), (5) a requirement that one display a statement on an automobile license plate that violates one's beliefs (*Wooley v. Maynard*, 430 U.S. 705 [1977]), (6) a denial of unemployment compensation for refusal to work with weapons (*Thomas v. Review Board of the Indiana Employment Security Division*, 450 U.S. 707 [1981]), and (7) an official requirement that children be compelled to salute the flag, contrary to their religious beliefs (*West Virginia State Board of Education v. Barnette*, 319 U.S. 624 [1943]). On the other hand, the Court had held that the sect may not, under the guise of religious freedom, (1) hold a parade without permission (*Cox v. New Hampshire*, 312 U.S. 569 [1941]); (2) have a young child sell magazines on a street corner late at night, contrary to state child welfare laws (*Prince v. Massachusetts*, 321 U.S. 158 [1944]); or (3) create a breach of peace in the course of a public meeting (*Chaplinsky v. New Hampshire*, 315 U.S. 568 [1942]). *See also* FREEDOM OF RELIGION page 316; *Reynolds v. United States*, page 367.

Significance   Through these and other cases, Jehovah's Witnesses have forced the courts to consider the constitutional scope of, and limitations on, the practice of religion. For the most part, the Supreme Court has been sympathetic with the proselytizing activities of the sect, except when their actions were in conflict with reasonable measures designed to protect the public welfare. In 1982, in refusing to uphold the right of a member of the Amish religion to refuse to pay Social Security taxes because of religious objections, the Court noted that "not all burdens on religion are unconstitutional" (*United States v. Lee*, 455 U.S. 252).

Jones v. Mayer   392 U.S. 409 (1968): Held that all racial discrimination, private as well as public, in the sale or rental of property, is outlawed by an 1866 act passed under the authority of the Thirteenth Amendment. The 1866 law provides that black citizens have the same rights enjoyed by white citizens "to inherit, purchase, lease, sell, hold, and convey real and personal property." The Court held that Congress has authority "to abolish all badges and incidents of slavery." *See also* CIVIL RIGHTS ACT OF 1866, 1870, 1871, and 1875 page 376; CIVIL RIGHTS ACT OF 1968, page 378; PUBLIC HOUSING, page 511.

Significance   *Jones v. Mayer* is noteworthy on two major counts. First, the Court resurrected the antislavery Thirteenth Amendment to renewed importance, thereby giving Congress an important weapon with which to combat racial discrimination. Second, it gave strong underpinning to blacks' fight for open and fair housing opportunities, which is probably the most sensitive civil rights issue facing the nation. The decision was rendered just two months after the enactment of the Civil Rights Act of 1968, which bans discrimination in the sale or rental of about 80 percent of the nation's housing. The Court held that its decision did not diminish the significance of the 1968 Act inasmuch as it was a detailed law, applicable to a broad range of discriminatory practices and enforceable by federal authority, whereas the 1866 law was general, applicable only to racial discrimination and enforceable only by private suit. The Supreme Court's strong commitment to open housing is also demonstrated by its decisions that struck down a California constitutional amendment permitting private discrimination in housing (*Reitman v. Mulkey*, 387 U.S. 369 [1967]) and a city charter amendment requiring a referendum on fair housing ordinances (*Hunter v. Erickson*, 393 U.S. 385 [1969]). Standing to sue discriminatory landlords and realtors has been granted by the Court to villages and individuals (*Gladstone Realtors v. Village of Bellwood*, 441 U.S. 91 [1979]) and to "testers" who seek evidence of housing discrimination (*Havens Realty Corp. v. Coleman*, 455 U.S. 363 [1982]).

Malloy v. Hogan   378 U.S. 1 (1964): Held that the protection against self-incrimination found in the Fifth Amendment to the Constitution applies to the states through the Fourteenth Amendment in the same manner that it limits the national government. *See also* SELF-INCRIMINATION, page 336.

Significance   The *Malloy* case overturned a long-standing ruling that states were not bound by the Fifth Amendment's guarantee against self-incrimination (*Twining v. New Jersey*, 211 U.S. 78 [1908], a decision reaffirmed in *Adamson v. California*, 332 U.S. 46 [1947]). The Malloy decision was part of a pattern of the 1960s, in which the Supreme Court largely abolished the double standard between federal and state criminal procedures. Formerly, state procedures were held to violate the Constitution only when they were shockingly unjust.

Mapp v. Ohio   367 U.S. 643 (1961): Ruled that a state may not use illegally seized evidence in criminal trials (the "exclusionary rule"). This decision overruled *Wolf v. Colorado,* 338 U.S. 25 (1949), which held that a state could use evidence secured through an illegal search and seizure. *See also* FOURTH AMENDMENT, page 314.

Significance   Prior to the *Mapp* decision, about half the states admitted illegally seized evidence in criminal trials, although in federal criminal trials such evidence is not admissible (*Weeks v. United States,* 232 U.S. 383 [1914]). In *Mapp v. Ohio,* the Court declared that the *Wolf* rule made the constitutional protection against unlawful search and seizure meaningless. The *Mapp* decision is a major example of national supervision of state criminal procedures through the Fourteenth Amendment and of the Supreme Court's nationalization of the Bill of Rights so as to equalize the rights of accused persons in state and federal criminal trials. Nevertheless, the "exclusionary rule" is a source of continuing controversy because it appears to handicap the police and to protect guilty persons who are "caught with the goods" but freed on a technicality of search procedure.

McNabb v. United States   318 U.S. 332 (1943): Held that the federal courts may not convict a person of a crime on the basis of a confession secured while the person was unlawfully detained. The Court ruled that a prisoner must be taken before a judicial officer for arraignment without delay. *See also* ARRAIGNMENT, page 294; SPEEDY TRIAL, page 338.

Significance   The *McNabb* rule prohibits police officials from unduly detaining a suspect in order to secure a confession. The Court reaffirmed this in *Mallory v. United States,* 354 U.S. 449 (1957), which released a confessed criminal because of a delay in arraignment. In the Omnibus Crime Control and Safe Streets Act of 1968, Congress provided for modification of the rule by permitting admission of voluntary confessions in federal cases involving a brief delay in arraignment.

Meritor Savings Bank, FSB v. Vinson   477 U.S. 57 (1986): Held that sexual harassment constitutes discrimination based on sex. In holding that Title VII of the Civil Rights Act of 1964 banning sex discrimination in the workplace protects against sexual harassment, the Court emphasized that employees have a right to be free of a hostile work environment involving intimidation, ridicule, and insult. The key element in sexual harassment, said the Court, is not provocative behavior or the perceived voluntary nature of response, but whether the advances are "unwelcome." Even if management of a company is unaware of the harassment, the company may still have liability. *See also* SEXUAL HARASSMENT, page 337.

Significance   The *Meritor* case was the first sexual harassment case to be heard by the Supreme Court. Numerous studies show that half or more of working women and about 15 percent of working men claim to have been subjected to sexual harassment. The Equal Employment Opportunity Commission defines sexual harassment under Title VII as "unwelcome or unsolicited verbal, physical or sexual conduct that is made a term or condition of employment, is used as the basis for employment or advancement decisions, or has the effect of unreasonably interfering with work or creating an intimidating, hostile or offensive work environment." The *Meritor* decision resulted in both an increase in harassment complaints and behavior changes in the workplace. The Civil Rights Act of 1991 greatly strengthened the power of women claiming sexual discrimination in the workplace by authorizing suits for money damages and by making clear that an employer may not base an employment decision on sex, even if other factors are involved.

Miller v. California   413 U.S. 5 (1973): Established a major reformulation of the legal test for determining obscenity. The Supreme Court reaffirmed its earlier rulings that obscene material was not protected by the First Amendment but limited the scope of regulation to works depicting or describing sexual conduct as specifically defined by state law. The basic test is to be whether the average person, applying contemporary community (local, not national) standards, would find that the work, taken as a whole, appeals to prurient interest in sex, portrays sexual conduct in a patently offensive way as defined by law, and, taken as a whole, does not have serious literary, artistic, political, or scientific value. *See also Roth v. United States,* page 368.

Significance   Miller v. California was the first case since the 1957 decision in *Roth v. United States* (354 U.S. 476) in which a majority of the Court could agree on guidelines intended to isolate "hard-core" pornography from protected expression. Since 1957, the Court considered numerous cases under the *Roth* test, but its application to concrete issues caused much confusion. Critics fear that the *Miller* formula has not clarified the issue. Most concern is directed at permitting localized determinations of obscenity and of the standards to be applied to determine whether an allegedly obscene film, art exhibit, musical recording, magazine, or book has serious literary, artistic, political, or scientific value. In reaching its decision in the *Miller* case, the Court specifically rejected the view formerly held by some justices that a work, to be judged obscene, must be "utterly without redeeming social value." Also rejected was the position taken by others that the entire problem could be eliminated by limiting access to pornographic materials to consenting adults. In 1982, the Court held that pornographic depictions of children under age sixteen are not protected by the Constitution and the standards of *Miller v. California* do not apply (*New York v. Ferber,* 458 U.S. 747). A 1987 decision, *Pope v. Illinois,* 481 U.S. 497, held that the standard of the "reasonable man" and not a local standard is to be used to determine what constitutes serious literary, artistic, political, or scientific value.

Milliken v. Bradley   418 U.S. 717 (1974): Ruled that a federal court could not order busing of schoolchildren across school district boundary lines to achieve racial integration unless each school district affected had been found to practice racial discrimination, or the school district lines had been deliberately drawn to provide for racially segregated schools. The decision overturned a major cross-country busing order involving the city of Detroit, Michigan, and 53 surrounding suburban schools. The Supreme Court gave strong support to the concept of the neighborhood school, even if substantial de facto racial segregation existed. *See also* DE FACTO SEGREGATION, page 309; SEGREGATION, page 335; *Swann v. Charlotte-Mecklenburg Board of Education,* page 370.

Significance   Milliken v. Bradley represented a major reversal of a trend established in 1954 to favor all efforts made to integrate schools. In the

Milliken case, the Court drew a distinction between state-imposed de jure segregation and de facto segregation existing as a result of residential patterns without legal restraints. In holding that school district lines could not ordinarily be ignored, the Court effectively put an end to the likelihood of extensive integration of schools in major metropolitan areas where, typically, black students are concentrated in inner-city schools and whites are clustered in surrounding suburbs. The *Milliken* decision came at a time when Congress began taking a strong stand against busing of students to achieve racial integration. Where segregation results from the proven intentional action of public officials, however, the Supreme Court has stipulated an "affirmative duty" to undertake integrative action, including busing (*Columbus Board of Education v. Penick*, 443 U.S. 449; *Dayton Board of Education v. Brinkman*, 443 U.S. 526 [1979]). Similarly, a state that once operated segregated public universities must do more than merely declare them open to any race (*United States v. Fordice*, 505 U.S. 717 [1992]).

Miranda v. Arizona   384 U.S. 436 (1966): A major ruling on criminal procedure to secure the privilege against self-incrimination. The Court held that "prior to any questioning, the person must be warned that he has a right to remain silent, that any statement he does make may be used against him, and that he has a right to the presence of an attorney, either retained or appointed." The defendant may "knowingly" waive these rights. *See also* SELF-INCRIMINATION, page 335.

Significance   The *Miranda* case followed the highly controversial 1964 decision of *Escobedo v. Illinois*, 378 U.S. 478, which held that when an investigation begins to focus upon a person, the police must inform the person of his or her right to remain silent and honor his or her request to consult counsel. The *Miranda* case extended these rights to persons taken into custody, and the requirement applies no matter how minor the charge, except for ordinary roadside traffic stops (*Berkemer v. McCarty*, 468 U.S. 420 [1984]). The Miranda rule assumes that criminal law enforcement is more reliable when it is based on independently secured evidence than when it is based on confessions secured through prolonged interrogation in the absence of counsel. The Supreme Court reaffirmed and extended the *Miranda* rule in *Rhode Island v. Innis*, 446 U.S. 291 (1980), by defining "interrogation," at which time a person has a right to have an attorney present, as going beyond direct questioning in a police station to "any words or actions on the part of the police that the police should know are reasonably likely to elicit an incriminating response." In *New York v. Quarles*, 467 U.S. 649 (1984), the court authorized an exception to the *Miranda* warning when "overriding considerations of public safety" are at stake.

Moore v. Dempsey   261 U.S. 86 (1923): Declared that a trial conducted under the influence of a mob, in which public passion dominates the judge, jury, witnesses, and defense counsel, is a denial of due process of law. In this case, the trial of five blacks was conducted under the duress of a mob, making the outcome a certainty. *See also* DUE PROCESS OF LAW, page 307.

Significance   The *Moore* case emphasizes that it is not enough that the mere forms of a trial be observed. The proceedings must be fair and provide the defendant with the full measure of his or her rights. Although the Court is usually concerned with specific aspects of a case, it will, as it did here, insist that the entire proceedings be conducted in an atmosphere that will assure a fair trial.

Mueller v. Allen   463 U.S. 388 (1983): Held as consistent with the First Amendment establishment of religion clause a Minnesota law providing income tax deductions for the cost of tuition, textbooks, and transportation for elementary and secondary school children in public or private (including parochial) schools. The Court found the state law to have a secular purpose that did not advance religion or involve an excessive entanglement of state and church. The Court distinguished the Minnesota law from other parochial school aids it had invalidated because the tax benefit was available to all parents, including those whose children attended public and nonsectarian private schools. *See also Committee for Public Education and Religious Liberty v. Nyquist,* page 351; *Everson v. Board of Education of Ewing Township,* page 353; SEPARATION OF CHURCH AND STATE, page 336.

Significance   Until *Mueller v. Allen,* the Supreme Court had invalidated a number of state laws aimed at assisting parochial schools facing increasing costs. Most of the other cases had involved direct assistance in the form of direct grants to parochial schools and teachers or tax credits to parents. The Minnesota law applies to all parents, although the bulk of the tax deduction goes to parents of parochial school children. The decision reflected the policies of the Reagan administration, which vigorously advocated tax benefits for parents of children in nonpublic schools.

National Association for the Advancement of Colored People v. Alabama 357 U.S. 449 (1958): Established that a state may not compel the disclosure of the membership lists of an organization that is pursuing lawful ends, if members are likely to suffer physical, economic, and other hostile reprisals from such disclosure. *See also* FREEDOM OF ASSOCIATION, page 315.

Significance   The racial integration movement in the South led to an effort on the part of some states to harass and impede the activities of the NAACP and other organizations active on behalf of black people's rights. In this case, the Court stressed the importance of the freedom to associate.

Near v. Minnesota   283 U.S. 697 (1931): Defined freedom of the press to mean that the press is to be free from prior restraint or censorship. A state may not, under the due process clause of the Fourteenth Amendment, permanently enjoin a newspaper from being published. If a newspaper abuses its privilege, it may be tried subsequently. The Court held unconstitutional a Minnesota statute that authorized officials to forbid publication of "malicious, scandalous and defamatory" newspapers. *See also* FREEDOM OF THE PRESS page 315; *Nebraska Press Association v. Stuart,* page 363; *New York Times v. United States,* page 364.

Significance   The *Near* case was the first important decision of the Supreme Court on censorship. The Court admitted that under exceptional circumstances, such as war, a paper might be prevented from publishing certain information, but it stressed that freedom of the press means freedom from government censorship or ban. Otherwise, government officials would be in a position to suppress news, as in the *Near* case, because it was critical of them.

Nebraska Press Association v. Stuart   427 U.S. 539 (1976): Held, in a major test of the free press–fair trial conflict, that a trial judge could not issue a "gag order" restricting what the press could report about a case prior to trial. The Supreme Court did not say that a gag order was never permissible but ruled that prior restraint of the press could not stand when less drastic means are available (for example, change of venue or postponement) to assure a fair trial. *See also* FREEDOM OF THE PRESS, page 315; *Near v. Minnesota,* page 362; PUBLIC TRIAL, page 330.

Significance   Nebraska Press Association v. Stuart was the first case in which the Court squarely faced the issue of prior restraint to protect the right of a defendant, in a highly publicized case, to a fair trial. Past cases have presented such questions as whether too much publicity had an impact upon the selection of an impartial jury or whether the conduct of a trial had been affected by a continuing glare of publicity. Contrary to popular belief, it is not essential that jurors be completely ignorant of news accounts of a crime (*Murphy v. Florida,* 421 U.S. 794 [1975]). Codes of conduct have been developed between press and bar associations, but such agreements are always put to a difficult test when a trial involves notorious persons or heinous crimes.

New York Times v. Sullivan   376 U.S. 254 (1964): Held that a public official could not recover civil libel damages for criticism of his official conduct by a newspaper or other persons. The rule applies even if the criticism is exaggerated or false, unless deliberate malice and reckless disregard for the truth or falsity of the statement can be shown. This principle was extended to suits for criminal libel in *Garrison v. Louisiana,* 379 U.S. 64 (1965). *See also* LIBEL AND SLANDER, page 323.

Significance   The New York Times case gives the widest latitude to the freedoms of speech and of the press when they are used to criticize public officials. The Court maintained that the limitation on libel suits was necessary to ensure free discussion of public affairs, one of the major purposes of the First Amendment guarantees. Later decisions have extended the ruling to newsworthy people engaged in public controversy (*Associated Press v. Walker,* 388 U.S. 130 [1967]) and with some limitations to ordinary private citizens involved in events of general interest (*Rosenbloom v. Metromedia, Inc.,* 403 U.S. 29 [1971]; *Gertz v. Robert Welch, Inc.,* 418 U.S. 323 [1974]). In *Hutchinson v. Proxmire,* 443 U.S. 111 (1979), and *Wolston v. Reader's Digest Association,* 443 U.S. 157 (1979), the Court narrowed the definition of "public figure" to exclude persons who do not thrust themselves into the public eye or who are simply involved in a matter that attracts public attention by events outside their control. To determine deliberate malice or reckless disregard for the truth, the Court has authorized scrutiny of prepublication thoughts and conversations of reporters and editors by those claiming libel (Herbert v. Lando, 441 U.S. 153 [1979]), but proof of malice is held to strict judicial scrutiny (*Bose Corp. v. Consumers Union of United States,* 466 U.S. 485 [1984]). The *New York Times* rule prohibits a public figure from recovering damages for infliction of emotional distress by an unfavorable article (*Hustler Magazine v. Falwell,* 485 U.S. 46 [1988]).

New York Times v. United States   403 U.S. 713 (1971): Held that any prior restraint of freedom of expression by the government carries a heavy presumption of unconstitutionality. In this case, the Court held that the Nixon administration could not forbid newspaper publication of classified documents on the Vietnam War because the government had failed to bear the heavy burden of justification for censorship. *See also* FREEDOM OF THE PRESS, page 315; *Near v. Minnesota,* page 362.

Significance   The *New York Times* case, also known as the "Pentagon Papers" case, involved publication of secret documents on the history of American policy in Vietnam that had been leaked to the press. The case was the first involving an effort by the national government to restrain newspaper publication of material in its possession. Although the Court permitted publication in this instance, the opinions of the justices left unclear the question of whether the government could enjoin publication of information that presents a serious threat to national security.

Norris v. Alabama   294 U.S. 587 (1935): Held, in what is popularly known as the Second Scottsboro case, that blacks could not be systematically excluded from jury service. *See also* CHALLENGE, page 251; JURY, page 268.

Significance   Under the *Norris* rule, a black defendant does not have a right to have members of his race serve on the jury in his trial. Blacks may not, however, be deliberately excluded. In this case, the Court found that no blacks had ever served on juries in the counties involved and showed that it would look behind the nondiscriminatory wording of the state law to see what the actual practice was with regard to jury selection. Jury discrimination has been a continuing problem, leading to reversals of many convictions of black defendants and to national legislation in 1968 requiring random selection from voting lists in federal juror selection. The Court has held that the use of peremptory challenges (requiring no explanation) by a prosecutor or by a criminal defendant to exclude blacks from a jury violates the equal protection clause of the Fourteenth Amendment (*Batson v. Kentucky,* 476 U.S. 79 [1986]; *Georgia v. McCollum,* 505 U.S. 42 [1992]). The Court held too that a white defendant could object to a prosecutor's exercise of peremptory challenges to exclude black jurors under the equal protection clause of the Fourteenth Amendment (*Powers v. Ohio,* 499 U.S. 400 [1991]). The Court has also extended this prohibition against racial exclusion to civil suits holding in *Edmonson v. Leesville Concrete Co.,* 500 U.S. 614 (1991), that a private litigant may not use peremptory challenges to exclude jurors on account of race because doing so would constitute state action in support of a denial of equal protection of the law.

Palko v. Connecticut   302 U.S. 319 (1937): Ruled that the double jeopardy provision of the Fifth Amendment does not apply to the states through the Fourteenth Amendment. In the *Palko* case, the Supreme Court permitted the state to appeal a conviction of a defendant in order to ask for a more severe sentence. The *Palko* case was overruled in 1969 in *Benton v. Maryland,* 395 U.S. 784. *See also* INCORPORATION DOCTRINE, page 321.

Significance   The *Palko* case is noteworthy because of the Court's opinion, written by Justice Benjamin N. Cardozo, setting forth the criteria by which the Court determines whether a state violates the rights protected by the due process clause of the Fourteenth Amendment. These include those rights "implicit in the concept of ordered liberty," which are "so rooted in the traditions and conscience of our people as to be ranked as fundamental" or "essential to a fair and enlightened system of justice," or those rights whose denial would be "shocking to the sense of justice of the civilized world." Within this framework, Justice Cardozo indicated that the freedoms of speech, press, religion, and assembly were essential for liberty and hence covered by the Fourteenth Amendment but that variations in criminal procedures were permissible so long as they violated no fundamental principles of justice. On a case-to-case basis, the Court has marked out the limits of the due process clause, permitting the states, for example, to abolish the grand jury, but forbidding states to conduct unreasonable searches and seizures or to permit cruel and unusual punishment. In the 1960s, the Court moved toward an equalization of rights for state and federal defendants through incorporation of most of the Bill of Rights provisions into the due process clause of the Fourteenth Amendment.

Passenger Cases   7 Howard 283 (1849): Declared that immigration is the exclusive concern of the national government and not subject to state control. The seaboard states had sought to regulate the heavy flow of immigrants to their shores by levying a tax on ships carrying immigrants. *See also* IMMIGRATION, page 320.

Significance   The *Passenger* decision helped to promote a uniform immigration policy prior to the great influx of immigrants in the late nineteenth and early twentieth centuries. Not, however, until 1882 did the national government assume full responsibility for regulating immigration. Recent concern with illegal immigration has led to some state efforts to control immigration, especially in California, but courts have restrained such programs.

Plessy v. Ferguson   163 U.S. 537 (1896): Upheld, in a famous decision, a state law requiring segregation of the races in public transportation. The Court held that under the equal protection clause of the Fourteenth Amendment, a state could provide "separate but equal" facilities for blacks. This case was overruled in *Brown v. Board of Education of Topeka,* 347 U.S. 483 (1954). *See also* SEGREGATION, page 335.

Significance   The *Plessy* case served as justification for the segregation policies of many states until 1954. Although it is no longer effective, its impact was enormous. The decision demonstrates the great power of the Supreme Court in giving direction to the law. Until the case was overturned, the Court limited itself to considering whether facilities provided for blacks were, indeed, equal though separate.

Pollock v. Williams   322 U.S. 4 (1944): Decided that a state lends support to slavery or peonage, contrary to the Thirteenth Amendment, when it requires that a person must work to discharge a debt or go to jail. The Court held unconstitutional a law that made it a crime to take money in advance and then refuse to perform the required labor. A state may punish fraud, but it cannot make failure to work a crime. *See also* INVOLUNTARY SERVITUDE, page 332.

Significance   A surprisingly large number of persons appear to be forced into labor because they are ignorant of their rights. The Justice Department gets numerous complaints of involuntary servitude involving persons who are forced to work through indebtedness to their employers. Frequently the victims are illegal aliens or migratory farm workers. The Court's decision makes clear that it will outlaw practices that are just short of slavery.

Regents of the University of California v. Bakke   438 U.S. 265 (1978): Held invalid a state medical school admissions program based on a specific racial quota but upheld the use of race as a factor in admissions decisions. In the *Bakke* case, the Court ruled (1) that where no previous racial discrimination has been found, a special admissions program setting aside a specific number of places for disadvantaged minority students violated both the equal protection clause of the Fourteenth Amendment and the Civil Rights Act of 1964, which bars exclusion of persons because of race from participation in federally financed programs; and (2) that it is constitutionally permissible for admissions officers to consider race, among other factors, in order to promote affirmative action programs. *See also Adarand Constructors v. Pena,* page 347; AFFIRMATIVE ACTION, page 292; REVERSE DISCRIMINATION, page 332.

Significance   The *Bakke* case is considered to be the most politically sensitive decision involving race since the 1954 ruling in *Brown v. Board of Education of Topeka,* 347 U.S. 483, which struck down state-imposed segregation of races in public schools. Most observers viewed the *Bakke* decision as a satisfactory compromise between supporters and opponents of affirmative action programs. The majority opinion vindicated the use of racial considerations in university admissions decisions while proscribing the more extreme aspects of reverse discrimination. A voluntary quota system to promote minority employment was upheld in *United Steelworkers of America v. Weber,* 443 U.S. 193 (1979). Similarly, in *Johnson v. Transportation Agency, Santa Clara County, California,* 480 U.S. 616 (1987), the first case involving affirmative action for women, the Court upheld a voluntary plan to correct an imbalance in traditionally segregated job categories. In *Fullilove v. Klutznick,* 448 U.S. 448 (1980), the Court ruled that Congress could use racial quotas to remedy past discrimination by setting aside a portion of federal public works funds for minority businesspeople. The Court has drawn a distinction between affirmative action goals in hiring and promotion that diffuse the burden and layoff according to a valid seniority system, which places a burden on specific individuals (*Firefighters Local Union No. 784 v. Stotts,* 467 U.S. 561 [1984]; *Wygant v. Jackson Board of Education,* 476 U.S. 267 [1986]). Moreover, where past discrimination is clear, the Court has upheld court-ordered quota systems, such as requiring one black firefighter or police officer to be promoted for every white person promoted (*Local No. 93,*

International Association of Firefighters, AFL-CIO C.L.C. v. City of Cleveland, 478 U.S. 501 [1986]; *United States v. Paradise*, 480 U.S. 149 [1987]). Statistical evidence of employment practices may be used to demonstrate disparate treatment of minorities or women in the use of objective tests that may not be related to performance (*Griggs v. Duke Power Co.*, 401 U.S. 424 [1971]) or in the use of subjective criteria, such as personality traits, which result in unfavorable disproportionate results for employment or promotion of minorities or women (*Watson v. Fort Worth Bank and Trust*, 487 U.S. 977 [1988]). The affirmative action debate and the Bakke case continue to challenge American decision makers. Recent political developments and Supreme Court decisions have, however, marked a retreat from affirmative action programs and race-based classifications.

Reynolds v. United States   98 U.S. 145 (1879): Established that claims of religious freedom cannot protect a person who commits a crime or an act contrary to accepted public morals. In this case, the Court upheld the enforcement of antipolygamy laws against Mormons who practiced polygamy as a religious doctrine. *See also* FREEDOM OF RELIGION, page 316; JEHOVAH'S WITNESSES CASES, page 357.

Significance   The *Reynolds* case established one of the clearest legal principles involving the free exercise of religion. A person is free to believe and worship as he or she pleases so long as his or her conduct violates no laws that validly protect the health, safety, or morals of the community. In 1983, the Court upheld a denial of tax exemption status to racially discriminatory schools that base their policies on religious belief, declaring that the government's interest in ending racial discrimination overrides the religious liberty involved (*Bob Jones University v. United States*, 461 U.S. 574). A 1990 decision held that the free exercise clause does not prohibit the application of drug laws to the sacramental use of peyote by Native American Indians (*Employment Division, Department of Human Resources of Oregon v. Smith*, 494 U.S. 872). But Congress overrode the "peyote" case with the Religious Freedom Restoration Act of 1993, which requires that any law that burdens religious liberty must serve a compelling governmental interest and be narrowly tailored to address that interest.

Roe v. Wade   410 U.S. 113 (1973): Held that criminal laws that prohibit abortions except to save the life of the mother are unconstitutional violations of the right to privacy embraced within the personal liberty protected by the due process clause of the Fourteenth Amendment. Specifically the Court held that (1) prior to the first trimester, abortion must be left to medical judgment; (2) during the second trimester, the state may, if it chooses, regulate abortion to protect maternal health but may not prohibit abortion; and (3) during the third trimester, the stage subsequent to viability, the state may regulate or even prohibit abortion except where necessary, in medical judgment, to preserve the life of the mother. *See also* PRIVACY, page 329.

Significance   *Roe v. Wade* illustrates the rise of the concept of privacy in American law, particularly as it relates to marriage and procreation. Growing concern for the rights of women is also reflected in the ruling. The case stirred extensive controversy, touching as it does on sensitive and emotional issues with strong religious undertones. Subsequently, the Court held that a state may not require the consent of a spouse or parent prior to an abortion or prescribe surgical procedures for abortions (*Planned Parenthood of Central Missouri v. Danforth,* 428 U.S. 152 [1976]). However, the Court also held that a state is not required to provide public funds for abortions and that a public hospital is not required to provide abortion services (*Maher v. Roe,* 432 U.S. 464, and *Poelker v. Doe,* 432 U.S. 519 [1977]). A congressional ban on federal funding of abortions, largely affecting women on welfare or Medicaid, unless the life of the mother is endangered or in promptly reported cases of rape or incest, was upheld in *Harris v. McRae,* 448 U.S. 297 (1980). The Court strongly reaffirmed *Roe v. Wade* in 1983, holding in *Akron v. Akron Center for Reproductive Health,* 462 U.S. 416, that women have a constitutional right to an abortion free of all but the most essential governmental interference, which must be clearly related to the state's interest in health and maintenance of medical standards. Again, in 1986 in *Thornburgh v. American College of Obstetricians and Gynecologists,* 476 U.S. 479, the Court rebuffed a Reagan administration effort to have *Roe v. Wade* overturned, declaring that a state may not intimidate a woman into continuing a pregnancy by requiring that she be informed of all detrimental physical and psychological effects of abortion. In 1989, following changes in Supreme Court justices reflective of the strong antiabortion position of the Reagan administration, the Court, in *Webster v. Reproductive Health Services,* 492 U.S 490, upheld a Missouri law prohibiting public employees from performing abortions unless the mother's life is at stake, barring the use of public buildings to perform abortions, and requiring doctors to perform viability tests on a fetus at twenty or more weeks of pregnancy (thereby rejecting the trimester formula of *Roe v. Wade*). The Court's new standards appear to rest not on the privacy issue but in balancing the state's interest in furthering human life and in not imposing an undue burden on women seeking an abortion. The *Webster* case was followed by decisions in 1990 that upheld parental notification requirements for minors seeking an abortion, provided that a procedure is available for a minor who is fearful of informing her parents to obtain consent from a judge (*Hodgson v. Minnesota,* 497 U.S. 417; *Ohio v. Akron Center for Reproductive Health,* 497 U.S. 502). In 1992, in *Planned Parenthood of Southeastern Pennsylvania v. Casey,* 505 U.S. 833, the Court reaffirmed the essence of both the *Roe* and *Webster* decisions, upholding the right to an abortion but permitting state restrictions that do not unduly burden that right. The issue continues to be a vital one in Congress, state legislatures, and election campaigns, with polls showing strong public support for abortion rights.

Roth v. United States   354 U.S. 476 (1957): Excluded obscenity from the area of constitutionally protected speech and press. The Court held that the proper standard to determine obscenity is "whether to the average person, applying contemporary community standards, the dominant theme of the material taken as a whole appeals to prurient interest." The Court reformulated this standard in 1973 in *Miller v. California,* 413 U.S. 5. *See also* CENSORSHIP, page 298; *Miller v. California,* page 360.

Significance   The *Roth* decision was the first effort by the Supreme Court to define obscenity, a matter that has long puzzled American courts. In denying constitutional protection to obscene publications, the Court expressed the view that obscenity was without the "redeeming social importance" of the kinds of speech that the First Amendment is designed to protect. In a companion case, *Alberts v. California,* 354 U.S. 476 (1957), the Court applied the same rule to state obscenity laws. Whether a particular publication is obscene is determined on a case-to-case basis. In 1964, the Court defined the "community standards" rule of the *Roth* case to mean national rather than local standards (*Jacobellis v. Ohio,* 378 U.S. 184). In all censorship cases, the Court has insisted that prompt judicial review be made available, but continued confusion led to a redefinition that would confine obscenity to offensive sexual conduct as defined by state law within guidelines established by the Court in *Miller v. California.*

Scales v. United States   367 U.S. 203 (1961): Sustained that portion of the Smith Act of 1940 that makes it a crime to be a member of an organization that advocates overthrow of the government by force if the member knows this to be the purpose of the organization. The Court drew a distinction between active membership and mere membership, noting that only active membership in a party that has illegal aims is not constitutionally protected. *See also* ALIEN REGISTRATION ACT, page 374; *Dennis v. United States,* page 352; GUILT BY ASSOCIATION, page 318.

Significance   In the *Scales* decision, the Court sought to avoid imputing guilt by mere association by insisting that the government must prove that an individual was an active participant in illegal activities. This formulation has been applied to most loyalty legislation, forcing both the national and state governments to use greater restraint in imposing penalties upon persons for their associations.

Schenck v. United States   249 U.S. 47 (1919): Upheld a conviction against Schenck, who had circulated materials urging men to resist the call to military service during World War I. The Court held that this was a justified infringement upon the freedoms of speech and press in view of the wartime emergency. *See also* FREEDOM OF SPEECH, page 317.

Significance   The *Schenck* case is noteworthy because of the Court's opinion, written by Justice Oliver Wendell Holmes, which established the clear and present danger doctrine. Justice Holmes wrote that "the question in every case is whether the words used are used in such circumstances and are of such a nature as to create a clear and present danger that they will bring about the substantive evils that Congress has a right to prevent." With these words, Justice Holmes provided the formula that has been used in many free speech cases since that time. The *Schenck* case is also noted for the distinction drawn between speech that may be permissible in peacetime but not when the nation is at war.

School District of Abington Township v. Schempp   374 U.S. 203 (1963): Held devotional Bible reading and/or the recitation of the Lord's Prayer in public schools to be an unconstitutional violation of the establishment clause of the First Amendment as applied to the states through the Fourteenth Amendment. The Court reasoned that the study of religion could be part of a school curriculum but that an organ of government (the public school) could not be used for essentially religious purposes. The Court held that the fact that students could excuse themselves from the devotional exercises was irrelevant because the exercises in themselves constituted an establishment of religion. "In the relationship between men and religion," said the Court, "the state is firmly committed to a position of neutrality." *See also* SEPARATION OF CHURCH AND STATE, page 336; *Zorach v. Clauson,* page 374.

Significance The *Schempp* decision ranks among the most controversial rendered by the Supreme Court. In 1962, in *Engel v. Vitale,* 370 U.S. 421, the Court struck down a nondenominational prayer written by the New York Board of Regents for public school recitation on the ground that it was improper for public officials to write or sanction official prayers. In 1980, a Kentucky statute requiring the posting of the Ten Commandments in public school classrooms was held invalid (*Stone v. Graham,* 449 U.S. 39). A 1985 case, *Wallace v. Jaffree,* 472 U.S. 38, held unconstitutional an Alabama law authorizing a one-minute period of silence in public schools for "meditation or voluntary prayer." And, in 1987, the Court struck down a Louisiana law requiring the teaching of "creation science" (the biblical story of creation) alongside the teaching of the theory of evolution (*Edwards v. Aguillard,* 482 U.S. 578). The *Schempp* rule was extended to exclude prayer at public school graduation ceremonies in *Lee v. Weisman,* 505 U.S. 577 (1992). These decisions have led numerous political leaders to demand a constitutional amendment to permit school prayers. The practice of opening legislative sessions with prayer was upheld by the Court in 1983 (*Marsh v. Chambers,* 463 U.S. 783) because of the long and unique history of the practice in the United States. An act of Congress requiring public high schools to permit student religious groups to meet on the same basis as other extracurricular activity groups was upheld in *Board of Education of the Westside Community Schools v. Mergens,* 496 U.S. 226 (1990).

Swann v. Charlotte-Mecklenburg Board of Education 402 U.S. 1 (1971): Held that all vestiges of state-imposed racial segregation in schools must be eliminated at once and that federal district courts have wide authority to fashion remedies to accomplish such changes. Among the remedies approved were busing, racial quotas, and pairing and grouping of noncontiguous school zones. School boards must eliminate racial distinctions in the assignment and treatment of students and faculty and in school construction decisions. *See also* DE FACTO SEGREGATION, page 304; *Milliken v. Bradley,* page 360; SEGREGATION, page 335.

Significance Dissatisfaction with the pace of school desegregation since the Supreme Court's historic decision in 1954 in *Brown v. Board of Education of Topeka,* 347 U.S. 483, led the Court to uphold strong positive action on the part of district courts or school boards in the *Swann* decision. In the *Brown* case, the Court had said that desegregation should proceed with "all deliberate speed" but found that this formula did not work. The *Swann* case strongly reaffirmed prior holdings that dual school systems must be replaced with unitary school systems in which race is not a factor. The decision applies only to state-imposed, not de facto, segregation, and though it appeared to strike a blow at the concept of the neighborhood school as the only basis for pupil assignment, the Court supported that concept where de facto segregation exists (*Milliken v. Bradley*, 418 U.S. 717 [1974]). However, faced with increasing resegregation of schools, the Court held in *Board of Education of Oklahoma City Public Schools v. Dowell*, 498 U.S. 237 (1991), that desegregation decrees issued to a formerly segregated school district are not intended to operate in perpetuity and can be dissolved if a school board has operated in good faith and has eliminated past vestiges of discrimination to the extent practicable. Further encouragement to lower courts to disengage from detailed supervision of school districts emerged in *Missouri v. Jenkins*, 115 S. Ct. 2038 (1995), in which the Supreme Court held that remedial directives issued by a lower court were excessive.

Texas v. Johnson   491 U.S. 397 (1989): Held that a conviction for burning the American flag during a political protest rally violates the First Amendment. The Court ruled that the government's interest in preserving the flag as a symbol of national unity could not justify a criminal prosecution for flag desecration. "If there is a bedrock principle underlying the First Amendment," said the Court, "it is that the Government may not prohibit the expression of an idea simply because society finds the idea itself offensive or disagreeable."

Significance   *Texas v. Johnson* evoked an enormous emotional response across the nation in protest of the decision. After extended debate in Congress over whether to amend the Constitution to overturn the case, Congress instead adopted the Flag Protection Act of 1989. Though the Act was designed to be content-neutral while still prohibiting desecration of the flag, it was nevertheless struck down in *United States v. Eichman*, 496 U.S. 310 (1990). Shortly thereafter, an attempt to adopt a constitutional amendment failed in Congress, and the issue appeared to lose much of its energy until 1995, when, once again, Congress considered but failed to enact a constitutional amendment. In striking down a city "hate crimes" ordinance in 1992, the Court stressed that speech or symbolic speech may not be curtailed on the basis of its content (*R.A.V. v. City of St. Paul*, 505 U.S. 377).

Truax v. Raich   239 U.S. 33 (1915): Declared unconstitutional an Arizona law requiring that at least 80 percent of the employees of any private business must be citizens, as a denial of equal protection of the law. The Court held that a state may not deny a person the right to earn a living, regardless of race or nationality. *See also* ALIEN, page 293.

Significance   The *Truax* case and others that have followed it underscore the fact that an alien is entitled to most of the rights of a citizen because the Constitution speaks of "persons" rather than citizens with regard to most rights. Examples include the rulings in *Graham v. Richardson*, 403 U.S. 365 (1971), that states may not deny welfare benefits to resident aliens; *Sugarman v. Dougall*, 413 U.S. 634 (1973), and *Hampton v. Mow Sun Wong*, 426 U.S. 67 (1976), that aliens may not be barred from state or federal civil service jobs; *In Re Griffiths*, 413 U.S. 717 (1973), that aliens may not be denied admission to the bar; and *Plyler v. Doe*, 457 U.S. 202 (1982), that children of illegal aliens may not be denied a free public education. The Supreme Court has held, however, that citizenship may be required for certain governmental functions such as police officers (*Foley v. Connelie,* 435 U.S. 291 [1978]), schoolteachers (*Ambach v. Norwick,* 441 U.S. 68 [1979]), and "peace officers," defined to include park rangers, correctional and probation officers, welfare investigators, and drug enforcement agents (*Cabell v. Chavez-Salido,* 454 U.S. 432 [1982]).

United States v. Lovett   328 U.S. 303 (1946): Declared unconstitutional, as a bill of attainder, an act of Congress that named three individuals as ineligible for continued governmental employment, in that the act punished the individuals without judicial trial. *See also* BILL OF ATTAINDER, page 296.

Significance   Few cases have arisen in American constitutional history involving bills of attainder. After the Civil War, the Supreme Court found certain laws imposing disabilities upon all persons who participated in the rebellion to be bills of attainder (*Cummings v. Missouri,* 4 Wallace 277; *Ex parte Garland,* 4 Wallace 333 [1867]). Some legislation designed to keep Communists out of public service has been upheld by the Court on the ground that it established general qualifications for employment rather than naming specific individuals (*Garner v. Board of Public Works,* 341 U.S. 716 [1951]). In *United States v. Brown,* 381 U.S. 437 (1965), however, the Court held that the Landrum-Griffin Labor Act section making it a crime for Communists to hold office or employment in a labor union was a bill of attainder.

United States v. Wong Kim Ark   169 U.S. 649 (1898): Established that all persons born in the United States are citizens of the United States, even if the person's parents are aliens ineligible for citizenship. The only major exceptions are children born to foreign diplomats stationed here. The Court held that a Chinese person born in California who went to China for a visit could not be denied readmission to the United States. *See also* JUS SOLI, page 322.

Significance   The *Wong Kim Ark* case involved a major interpretation of the meaning of the Fourteenth Amendment, which confers citizenship upon "all persons" born in the United States and subject to its jurisdiction. The Court made it clear that citizenship by birth, regardless of parentage, is the basic rule of American citizenship.

Virginia State Board of Pharmacy v. Virginia Citizens Consumer Council, Inc.   425 U.S. 748 (1976): Extended the protection of the First Amendment to commercial advertising. The Supreme Court struck down a state law banning advertising the prices of prescription drugs as an infringement on the rights of both the dispenser and the receiver of the information. *See also* COMMERCIAL SPEECH, page 301.

Significance   The *Virginia State Board of Pharmacy* case represents a major extension of the free speech concept to include "commercial speech." Many authorities have considered the protection of the expression of political ideas as the basic assumption underlying the First Amendment, and the courts have generally assumed that purely economic interests were not protected by the First Amendment. The Supreme Court held in this case, however, that in a free enterprise system, the formation of intelligent opinions on how that system is to be regulated depends on the free flow of commercial information. The Court emphasized that its decision did not mean that advertising could never be legally regulated as to time, place, or manner. Subsequently, the Court upheld the right of lawyers to advertise (*Bates v. State Bar of Arizona,* 433 U.S. 350 [1977]) and of homeowners to place "for sale" signs on their property, even though the purpose of a restrictive ordinance was to prevent panic selling in racially changing neighborhoods (*Linmark Associates, Inc. v. Township of Willingboro,* 431 U.S. 85 [1977]). The Court also struck down a state law forbidding advertising of contraceptives (*Carey v. Population Services International,* 431 U.S. 678 [1977]) and another banning the advertising of liquor prices (*44 Liquormart v. Rhode Island,* 116 S. Ct. 1495 [1996]). But in *Posadas de Puerto Rico Associates v. Tourism Company of Puerto Rico,* 478 U.S. 328 (1986), the Court held that advertising may be banned even for a legal product (in this case, casino gambling) if the government can show a substantial interest in doing so. The Court also held in *Austin v. Michigan Chamber of Commerce,* 494 U.S. 652 (1990), that a state may bar use of corporate funds on behalf of political candidates.

Wolff v. McDonnell   418 U.S. 539 (1974): Established the right of prison inmates to due process in prison disciplinary proceedings that might result in an inmate's loss of good behavior credits. The Supreme Court held that prisoners should have advanced written notice of charges, a chance to have witnesses on their behalf, and a statement of findings. However, the Court ruled that the right to counsel, confrontation of witnesses, and cross-examination were not in keeping with the necessities of prison discipline. *See also* DUE PROCESS OF LAW, page 307; PAROLE, page 273; RECIDIVISM, page 276; SENTENCE, page 277.

Significance   *Wolff v. McDonnell* represents an important extension of due process rights into the prison system itself and provides some safeguards to the otherwise arbitrary authority held by prison officials. Prisoners must be assisted in pursuit of legal claims by having access to law libraries or to legal assistance (*Bounds v. Smith,* 430 U.S. 817 [1977]) and be provided medical attention when needed (*Estelle v. Gamble,* 429 U.S. 97 [1977]). However, the Court did not uphold the right of inmates to form a prisoners' labor union (*Jones v. North Carolina Prisoners' Labor Union, Inc.,* 433 U.S. 119 [1977]), to enjoy "contact visits" (*Block v. Rutherford,* 468 U.S. 576 [1984]), or to protect against searches of prison cells (*Hudson v. Palmer,* 468 U.S. 517 [1984]). With respect to First Amendment rights such as censorship of mail or publications, the Court has adopted the standard that regulations be reasonably related to legitimate penological interests (*Thornburgh v. Abbott,* 490 U.S. 401 (1989). More than one million persons were incarcerated in state and federal jails and prisons in 1996. Some states were sending prisoners to other states and many had, or were considering, privatization of prisons. Excessive crowding of prisons, coupled with heightened prisoner expectations of due process and First Amendment rights, have led to increasing turbulence in the nation's prisons. Congress, in the Prison Litigation Reform Act of 1996, placed restrictions on prisoner suits and the extent of judicial supervision of prison systems. The Supreme Court, in Lewis v. Casey (116 S. Ct. 2174 [1996]), placed limits on prisoner access to law libraries and legal assistance, and set stricter standards for hearing prisoner suits.

Zorach v. Clauson   343 U.S. 306 (1952): Supported New York's released-time program in public schools, under which students are released from classes to attend religious exercises in their respective churches. The Court found no conflict between this practice and the establishment of religion clause in the First Amendment. *See also School District of Abington Township v. Schempp,* page 369; SEPARATION OF CHURCH AND STATE, page 336.

Significance   The teaching of religion in public schools is one of the most controversial questions in public education, going to the heart of the issue of the separation of church and state. The Zorach decision attracted wide notice because it followed the Court's decision in *McCollum v. Board of Education,* 333 U.S. 203 (1948), in which the Court declared unconstitutional a program of released time under which children attended religious classes on school grounds. The *Zorach* ruling rested largely on the fact that the religious classes were not held on school property.

IMPORTANT STATUTES

Alien and Sedition Laws   Acts passed in 1798 authorizing the President to deport undesirable aliens and making it a crime to criticize the government or its officials. Through these Acts, the Federalist party sought to silence opposition. About 25 persons were jailed or fined for criticizing President John Adams. These Acts were a major reason for the defeat of the Federalist party in the election of 1800. Thomas Jefferson, the winner of that election, pardoned those convicted under the Acts.

Significance   The Alien and Sedition Laws were undoubtedly unconstitutional, but they were never tested in the Supreme Court. They serve as a reminder that civil rights are under constant threat and subject to varying interpretations. But, free government is not possible unless it is understood that one may be loyal to the nation and, at the same time, critical of those who make its policies. Sedition laws were not enacted again until World War I in 1918, when they were aimed at interference with the war effort rather than at mere criticism of officials.

Alien Registration Act of 1940 (Smith Act)   A major sedition law requiring the annual registration of aliens and prohibiting the advocacy of violent overthrow of the government. Its major provisions make it unlawful to teach, advocate, or distribute information advocating the forcible overthrow of government or knowingly organize or join an organization that so advocates. Other provisions outlaw activities designed to create disloyalty in the armed forces or encourage participation in a violent revolution or in the assassination of public officials. *See also* ALIEN, page 293; *Dennis v. United States,* page 352; *Scales v. United States,* page 369.

Significance   The Smith Act was the first law passed in peacetime since the Alien and Sedition Laws of 1798 that outlaws particular forms of speech and writing. It is also the first act to make it a crime to be a member of an organization; this provision, some critics claim, imputes guilt by association. The advocacy and membership provisions of this Act have been upheld by the Supreme Court (*Dennis v. United States,* 341 U.S. 494 [1951]; *Scales v. United States,* 367 U.S. 203 [1961]). Though the Act does not mention the Communist party by name and was also intended to apply to Nazi and fascist groups, it has been applied only against Communist party leadership. The alien registration requirement is designed to control the activities of aliens in times of crisis. Large numbers of aliens, however, reside illegally in the United States.

Americans with Disabilities Act of 1990   An act to provide protection against discrimination in employment, public services and accommodations, transportation, and telecommunications for disabled persons. A disabled person is defined as one having a physical or mental impairment that substantially limits one or more major life activities, has a record of such impairment, or is regarded as having such an impairment. The employment discrimination rules went into effect in 1992 for businesses with 25 or more employees and in 1994 for those with 15 employees. The act requires "reasonable accommodations" to the disabled by employers unless "undue hardship" results. Although AIDS patients are covered by the law, the ADA does exclude from its protection homosexuality, bisexuality, current users of illegal drugs, and various sexual disorders such as pedophilia. Existing public accommodations are to be made accessible if readily achievable; new construction is to be built in compliance with the needs of the handicapped. Similarly, new public transportation equipment must immediately comply with the Act's provisions; existing trains, stations, and subways are to be made accessible within three to five years. Telecommunication companies have three years to develop systems for speech- and hearing-impaired persons. *See also* REHABILITATION ACT OF 1973, page 526; CIVIL RIGHTS ACT OF 1991, page 379.

Significance   The Americans with Disabilities Act of 1990 is a major step forward in federal efforts to "mainstream" handicapped citizens. The legislation is the capstone of a variety of efforts in the past three decades to enable the physically impaired to participate more fully in society. Other major acts, such as the Rehabilitation Act of 1973, provided for grants and services for the handicapped and extended protection against discrimination, though they were somewhat limited in scope and penalties. In the Civil Rights Act of 1991, Congress included the ADA and the 1973 Rehabilitation Act, under which workers may recover compensatory and punitive damages in cases of intentional discrimination. An estimated one-fifth of the nation's population may be covered by the ADA's broad definition of a disabled person, resulting in substantial monetary costs. Nevertheless, the ADA represents a national commitment to enable all persons to have access to jobs, restaurants, stores, transportation, and communications media. The Act has become a major source for grievances filed against employers before the Equal Employment Opportunity Commission (EEOC).

Antiterrorism and Effective Death Penalty Act of 1996   A multifaceted law designed to control international and domestic terrorism, tighten immigration and deportation rules, expand victims' rights, and limit use of the writ of habeas corpus in federal courts by state and federal prisoners. Among its major provisions, the Act broadens federal jurisdiction and enhances penalties for crimes linked to terrorism, here and abroad, and increases controls over explosives. Immigration and visa controls are enhanced to monitor potential terrorists, and deportation procedures are expedited through establishment of a special deportation court for aliens suspected of terrorism. The law bans aid to nations aiding terrorist activity and prohibits fundraising by terrorist groups in the United States. Victim restitution laws are expanded for all serious federal crimes and special provisions are made for victims of terrorist violence. The limits on federal habeas corpus were quickly upheld by the Supreme Court in *Felker v. Turpin,* 116 S. Ct. 2135 (1996); these place a time limit on such writs, make second appeals more difficult, and require federal judges to defer to state court rulings unless such rulings are unreasonable. *See also* ACCESS TO COURTS, page 247; ALIEN, page 293; DEPORTATION, page 305; DOMESTIC TERRORISM, page 73; HABEAS CORPUS, page 319; IMMIGRATION, page 320; INTERNATIONAL TERRORISM, page 558.

Significance   The Antiterrorism and Effective Death Penalty Act brings together a variety of provisions that respond to increasing American concern with crime, court decisions, death penalty delays, crime victims, and the frustrations of seemingly random violence and terrorism. Originally intended to address heightened concern with domestic terrorism growing out of major bombings in New York City's World Trade Center and Oklahoma City's federal building (the former the result of international terrorism, the latter domestic in nature), the legislation became a vehicle to deal with a number of related issues in immigration and criminal punishment. Because the legislation touches on many sensitive civil liberties issues, it is likely to be a source of continuing legislative and judicial attention for many years.

Civil Rights Acts of 1866, 1870, 1871, and 1875   Laws passed by Congress after the Civil War to guarantee the rights of blacks. The public accommodation provisions of the 1875 law were declared unconstitutional by the Supreme Court in the *Civil Rights Cases,* 109 U.S. 3 (1883), as a federal invasion of private rights. Other provisions of these laws were struck down by the courts or repealed by Congress. Today, a few major provisions remain from the Acts of 1866 and 1871. One makes it a federal crime for any person acting under the authority of a state law to deprive another of any rights protected by the Constitution or by laws of the United States. Another authorizes suits for civil damages against state or local officials by persons whose rights are abridged. Others permit actions against persons who conspire to deprive people of their rights. *See also* ELEVENTH AMENDMENT, page 261; *Jones v. Mayer,* page 288; *Maine v. Thiboutot,* page 288.

Significance   The failure of the post–Civil War Acts reflected the general attitude of the time that the national government had a limited role to play in the enforcement of individual rights. The remaining provisions served occasionally as a weapon in the hands of national officers to restrain state officials who violated the constitutional rights of persons in their charge. As the national government expanded its role in the protection of individual rights, particularly in the area of race relations, these laws have taken on new importance. Of particular significance are (1) the Supreme Court's ruling in *Jones v. Mayer,* 392 U.S. 409 (1968), holding that the 1866 law, enacted under authority of the Thirteenth Amendment ban on slavery, bars public and private racial discrimination in the sale or rental of housing, and a subsequent ruling that a private school may not, under the 1866 law, deny admission to black students (*Runyon v. McCrary*, 427 U.S. 160 [1976]); (2) the Court's virtual elimination of restrictions on the right of individuals to sue state and local governments and their officials under the Act of 1871 for alleged violations of constitutional rights or of federal laws in *Maine v. Thiboutot*, 448 U.S. 1 (1980); and (3) the Court's 1987 rulings that open the right to sue under the 1866 law to a wide variety of ethnic groups, including Arabs and Jews (*Saint Frances College v. Al-Khazraji*, 481 U.S. 604; *Shaare Tefila Congregation v. Cobb*, 481 U.S. 615). However, in 1989, an increasingly conservative majority of the Supreme Court began narrowing the scope of the 1866 and 1871 provisions. It held that the 1866 law cannot be used to sue state and local governments for racial discrimination absent a showing of an official policy of racial bias (*Jett v. Dallas Independent School District*, 491 U.S. 701 [1989]). Similarly, it held that a municipality could be held liable for violation of civil rights only if the violation was the result of deliberate indifference (*City of Canton, Ohio, v. Harris*, 489 U.S. 378 [1989]). The Court also held that states and state officials, acting in their official capacities, are not "persons" within the scope of the 1871 law and are thereby immune from suit under the Eleventh Amendment (*Will v. Michigan Department of State Police*, 491 U.S. 58 [1989]). But state officials may be sued in their personal capacities for violations of rights under authority of state law (*Hafer v. Melo*, 502 U.S. 21 [1991]).

Civil Rights Act of 1957   The first civil rights law passed by Congress since Reconstruction, designed to secure the right to vote for blacks. Its major feature empowers the Department of Justice to seek court injunctions against any deprivation of voting rights, and it authorizes criminal prosecutions for violations of an injunction. In addition, the Act established a Civil Rights Division, headed by an assistant attorney general in the Department of Justice, and created a bipartisan Civil Rights Commission to investigate civil rights violations and to recommend legislation. *See also* VOTING RIGHTS ACT, page 124.

Significance   The Civil Rights Act of 1957 marked a major breakthrough in positive federal action in the field of civil rights. The Act is based on the theory that if blacks are protected in their voting rights, they will be in a better position to seek reform in other areas of discrimination. It is supplemented by voting provisions in the Civil Rights Acts of 1960 and 1964 and by the Voting Rights Act of 1965.

Civil Rights Act of 1960   A law designed to further secure the right to vote for blacks and to meet problems arising from racial upheavals in the South in the late 1950s. The major provision authorizes federal courts to appoint referees who will help blacks register after a voter-denial conviction is obtained under the 1957 Civil Rights Act and after a court finding of a "pattern or practice" of discrimination against qualified voters. Other provisions (1) authorize punishment for persons who obstruct any federal court order, such as a school desegregation order, by threats or force; (2) authorize criminal penalties for transportation of explosives for the purpose of bombing a building; (3) require preservation of voting records for 22 months and authorize the Attorney General to inspect the records; and (4) provide for schooling of children of armed forces personnel in the event that a school closes because of an integration dispute. *See also* VOTING RIGHTS ACT, page 124.

Significance Continuing the pattern established in the 1957 Civil Rights Act, Congress sought to strengthen the voting rights of citizens and reached out into other problem areas. The Civil Rights Act of 1964 and the Voting Rights Act of 1965 supplement the Acts of 1957 and 1960.

Civil Rights Act of 1964 A major enactment designed to erase racial discrimination in most areas of American life. Major provisions (1) outlaw arbitrary discrimination in voter registration and expedite voting rights suits; (2) bar discrimination in public accommodations, such as hotels and restaurants, which have a substantial relation to interstate commerce; (3) authorize the national government to bring suits to desegregate public facilities and schools; (4) extend the life and expand the power of the Civil Rights Commission; (5) provide for withholding federal funds from programs administered in a discriminatory manner; (6) establish the right to equality in employment opportunities; and (7) establish a Community Relations Service to help resolve civil rights problems. The Act forbids discrimination based on race, color, religion, national origin, and, in the case of employment, sex. Techniques for gaining voluntary compliance are stressed in the Act, and the resolution of civil rights problems through state and local action is encouraged. Discrimination in housing is not covered by the law but is prohibited by the Civil Rights Act of 1968. *See also* CIVIL RIGHTS ACT OF 1991, page 379; CIVIL RIGHTS COMMISSION, page 344; COMMUNITY RELATIONS SERVICE, page 344; EQUAL EMPLOYMENT OPPORTUNITY COMMISSION, page 345; *Heart of Atlanta Motel v. United States*, page 356.

Significance The Civil Rights Act of 1964 is the most far-reaching civil rights legislation since Reconstruction. It was passed after the longest debate in Senate history (83 days) and only after cloture was invoked for the first time to cut off a civil rights filibuster. Compliance with the Act's controversial provisions on public accommodations and equal employment opportunity has been widespread. Title VI of the Act, which authorizes the cutoff of federal funds to state and local programs practicing discrimination, proved to be the most effective provision of the Act. For example, a dramatic jump in southern school integration took place when the national government threatened to withhold federal funds from schools failing to comply with desegregation orders. All agencies receiving federal funds are required to submit assurance of compliance with the 1964 act. Hundreds of grant-in-aid programs are involved, amounting to 15 percent of all state and local revenues. The Supreme Court upheld the public accommodations provisions of the law as a legitimate exercise of the commerce power by Congress (*Heart of Atlanta Motel v. United States*, 379 U.S. 241 [1964]).

Civil Rights Act of 1968 A law that prohibits discrimination in the advertising, financing, sale, or rental of housing, based on race, religion, or national origin and, as of 1974, sex; the Act, however, provided limited and ineffective enforcement powers. A major amendment of the Act in 1988 extended coverage to the handicapped and to families with children and added enforcement machinery through either administrative enforcement by the

Department of Housing and Urban Development (HUD) or by suits in federal court, with the choice of forum left to either party in the dispute. The law covers about 80 percent of all housing. Major exclusions are owner-occupied dwellings of four units or less and those selling or renting without services of a broker. Other provisions of the 1968 act provide criminal penalties for interfering with the exercise of civil rights by others, or for using interstate commerce to incite riots. *See also Jones v. Mayer,* page 358.

Significance   Residential segregation was the last and most sensitive civil rights issue faced by Congress. The 1968 Act was passed in the wake of the assassination of Dr. Martin Luther King Jr. and after a filibuster was overcome in the Senate. Discrimination in housing isolates minorities, intensifies school segregation problems, and deprives even economically successful blacks from full enjoyment of housing opportunities. Most housing discrimination results from the private acts of bankers, real estate agents, and individual landowners rather than governmental action. Shortly after enactment of the Civil Rights Act of 1968, the Supreme Court ruled in *Jones v. Mayer,* 392 U.S. 409 (1968), that the Civil Rights Act of 1866 outlawed all racial discrimination in housing. The Court reconciled the 1968 law with the 1866 law by noting that the 1968 law covers religion and national origin in addition to race and provides for enforcement machinery. Housing remains among the most segregated areas of American life.

Civil Rights Act of 1991   A reaffirmation and expansion of protection against discrimination in employment. The main purpose of the legislation was to overturn several 1989 Supreme Court decisions that made it harder for employees to challenge or prove discrimination, which narrowly interpreted the scope of civil rights laws and limited access to the courts. Major provisions of the Civil Rights Act of 1991 (1) establish the concepts enunciated by the Supreme Court in 1971 in *Griggs v. Duke Power Co.,* 401 U.S. 424, that hiring practices must be related to job performance and business necessity, with the burden of proof placed on the employer in "disparate impact" cases (that is, employment practices that cause a disproportionate impact on protected groups); this overrules the controversial decision in *Wards Cove Packing Co. v. Atonio,* 490 U.S. 642 (1989), which put the burden of proof on the employee; (2) clarify that rights established by a post–Civil War law prohibiting racial discrimination in the making and enforcement of contracts applies not only to the act of hiring but also to all aspects of the contractual relationship; (3) extend the right to sue for damages for intentional discrimination to women, religious minorities, and the disabled (previously limited to racial minorities under the post–Civil War law); the right to sue extends coverage of Title VII of the Civil Rights Act of 1964, the Americans with Disabilities Act of 1990, and the Rehabilitation Act of 1973; (4) authorize jury trials for intentional discrimination suits, with limits placed on awards depending on the size of the firm; (5) make clear that an employer may not base an employment decision on race, sex, religion, or national origin even if other factors motivate the decision; (6) extend protection to Americans working abroad for American-based companies unless it violates the laws of the other country; (7) bar "race norming" on tests (that is, adjusting test scores according to race or ethnicity to compensate for alleged bias in tests); (8) bar most lawsuits challenging settlements in affirmative action programs

but expand the time frame for bringing suits challenging a discriminatory seniority system; (9) establish a "Glass Ceiling Commission" to study barriers
to the advancement of women and minorities; and (10) establish a procedure
to protect Senate employees and extend coverage of Title VII of the Civil
Rights Act of 1964, the Americans with Disabilities Act of 1990, the Rehabilitation Act of 1973, and the Age Discrimination in Employment Act of 1967
to most presidential appointees and to employees of elected state officials.

Significance   The Civil Rights Act of 1991 was enacted after a two-year
struggle between President George Bush and Congress. Bush had labeled the
bill a "quota" bill and had vetoed a similar enactment in 1990. The reversal
of eight Supreme Court decisions in one statute is extraordinary and represented a rejection of the conservative majority of the Court's restrictive attitudes toward long-standing civil rights laws. The key issue was raised in the
Wards Cove case, which had shifted the burden of proof to workers to challenge employment practices. It is left to the courts to determine the meaning
of a "business necessity" for practices adversely affecting protected groups,
but the law directs the judiciary to follow the standards of the *Griggs* case
and rulings flowing from it. The provision giving victims of employment discrimination the right to sue for damages, and to recover legal and expert witness costs, greatly expands the likelihood of a suit and, conversely, adherence
to the Act's purposes. Enforcement rests with the Equal Employment Opportunity Commission and the Justice Department. The extension of antidiscrimination in employment requirements to the previously uncovered
political leadership was an important step in correcting the practice, common in Congress, of exempting itself and other top officials from the laws applicable to everyone else.

Comprehensive Crime Control Act of 1984   A far-reaching anticrime package covering a broad range of social concerns. Its major provisions (1) permit
the pretrial detention of dangerous defendants, (2) overhaul federal sentencing procedures to reduce disparity in punishments and abolish parole for federal crime, (3) limit the insanity defense to those unable to comprehend the
wrongfulness of their acts and shift the burden of proof of insanity to the defendant, (4) give federal prosecutors authority to seize the business and personal assets and profits of organized crime and drug traffickers, (5) prohibit
computer and credit card fraud, and (6) create an Office of Justice Programs
to improve criminal justice systems and to administer block grants to state
and local governments. In addition, the Act strengthens federal laws pertaining to violent crime, juvenile justice, missing children, labor racketeering,
foreign business violations, trademark abuses, witness protection, and terrorism and establishes a crime-victims' fund financed through fines of convicted persons. *See also* BAIL, page 295; SENTENCE, page 277; OMNIBUS CRIME
CONTROL AND SAFE STREETS ACT OF 1968, page 384; PAROLE, page 273; UNITED
STATES SENTENCING COMMISSION, page 285.

Significance   The Comprehensive Crime Control Act of 1984 illustrates the need to keep the criminal justice system current with experience
and technology. The Supreme Court upheld the preventive detention provision in 1987 in *United States v. Salerno,* 481 U.S. 739. Sentencing guidelines
were established by a special sentencing commission created by the Act. Its

authority was upheld in *Mistretta v. United States,* 488 U.S. 361 (1989). The new system, effective November 1, 1987, has 43 levels of punishment based on a point system derived from the nature of the offense and the record of the defendant. The 1984 Act, following the Omnibus Crime Control and Safe Streets Act of 1968 and the Organized Crime Control Act of 1970, deeply involves the federal government in nationwide crime-control activities.

Immigration Act of 1965   A major revision of American immigration policy that eliminated the national-origins quota system. Under the quota system, in effect since 1924, American immigration policy discriminated against Asians, Africans, and southern and eastern Europeans. The overall quota was set at less than 157,000 immigrants per year, with nearly 127,000 assigned to northern and western Europe. It was often criticized as racist in philosophy and detrimental to the American international position. The 1965 law ended the quota system, established an annual limit of 170,000 immigrants (no more than 20,000 from one country), and gave preference to relatives of citizens and persons with special skills. For the first time, a limit (120,000) was placed on immigrants from the Western Hemisphere. The total limit was raised from 290,000 to 320,000 (including 50,000 refugees) by the Refugee Act of 1980. Additional refugees may be admitted by the President in consultation with Congress. *See also* IMMIGRATION, page 320; IMMIGRATION ACT OF 1990, page 381.

Significance   The Immigration Act of 1965 climaxed a 40-year effort by ethnic groups to eliminate race and ancestry as bases of American immigration policy. The stress on reuniting families and admitting skilled persons regardless of ancestry reflects growing national concern with domestic racial problems and foreign policy considerations. The 1980 amendments were a response to a rising tide of persons seeking asylum from Vietnam, Cambodia, Cuba, and other strife-torn regions. The Act resulted in huge increases in Asian and Latin American immigrants and a decrease in Europeans.

Immigration Act of 1990   The first comprehensive overhaul of immigration law since 1965, increasing the number of persons allowed to enter the United States and adjusting the mix of immigrants to favor Europeans and specially trained workers. The new law permits immigration to rise to over 675,000 per year, reflecting changing policies, and creates a new "diversity" visa to benefit nationals of countries adversely affected by the Immigration Act of 1965. The Act also establishes special classes of nonimmigrant, temporary visas for certain technical workers, artists, entertainers, and religious workers. It permits special immigration status and expedited naturalization procedures for certain aliens who served honorably in American forces in World War II or have enlisted to serve in the U.S. armed forces for a period of at least twelve years. The Act also strengthens the sanctions on aliens who commit crimes while in the United States and increases the number of officers in the Border Patrol. Although the Act states that members of Communist or other totalitarian political parties may still be denied visas, several exceptions now apply, and nonimmigrants may no longer be prohibited entry for political reasons. The Act grants the Secretary of Health and Human Services the authority to determine which diseases and health problems constitute enough of a threat to deny a visa, a determination previously made by

Congress. *See also* ANTITERRORISM AND EFFECTIVE DEATH PENALTY ACT OF 1966, page 375; IMMIGRATION, page 320; IMMIGRATION ACT OF 1965, page 381.

Significance   The Immigration Act of 1990 is a major revision of the immigration and citizenship laws of the United States. The 1965 law favored immigrants with immediate families in the United States, with the effect that in recent years about 85 percent of immigrants came from Asia or Latin America. The 1990 Act still gives immediate family members preference but also puts increased emphasis on specially trained workers with exceptional abilities or talent, and on Europeans. Remnants of Cold War–era restrictions on Communists and others were removed to reflect the decreased fear of foreign subversion. Overall, the distinctive features of the Act are the increases in the number of visas to be granted, the broadening of the diversity of the immigrant pool, and the emphasis on admitting more specially trained and skilled immigrants who will serve the nation's economic interests.

Immigration and Nationality Act of 1952 (McCarran-Walter Act)   A major revision and restatement of the immigration and citizenship policies of the United States. The Act maintained the quota system for immigration and placed restrictions upon the immigration and naturalization of Communists and other totalitarians. All racial barriers to immigration were eliminated by the Act, but Asians, Africans, and southern and eastern Europeans were assigned small quotas. (The Immigration Act of 1965, however, eliminated the quota system.) Communists or other persons advocating violent overthrow of the government were denied admission to the United States. Further, such persons residing in this country could not be naturalized, and citizenship could be taken from naturalized persons who joined the Communist party or refused to testify before a congressional committee investigating subversive activities. *See also* DENATURALIZATION, page 305; IMMIGRATION, page 320; NATURALIZATION, page 326.

Significance   The Immigration and Nationality Act of 1952 is a comprehensive collection of the immigration and citizenship laws of the United States. Many of its provisions reflect the harsh anticommunist sentiment of the time. Most opponents of the Act protested its retention of a discriminatory immigration policy and its continuation of the policy of making naturalized citizens subject to loss of citizenship on grounds not applicable to native-born citizens. In 1965, Congress, in response to extensive ethnic group pressures and foreign policy considerations, eliminated the discriminatory national origins quota system. The Supreme Court has moved in the direction of ending the "second-class citizenship" of naturalized citizens. In 1987, Congress suspended a portion of the Act under which even temporary entry into the United States could be denied to persons because of their political beliefs or associations and made the suspension permanent in the Immigration Act of 1990.

Immigration Reform Act of 1986   A major addition to the immigration laws designed to stem the tide of illegal immigrants and to provide amnesty to those already in the United States. Key features of the law (1) make it illegal for an employer to hire illegal aliens and require employers to verify the legal status of their employees; (2) enable aliens who entered the United States illegally prior to January 1, 1982, to achieve residential status and eventual citizenship; (3) make special arrangements for seasonal agricultural migrant workers to achieve residential status; and (4) create an Office of Special Counsel in the Justice Department to protect minorities against discrimination by employers fearful of hiring persons who look or sound foreign.

Significance   Illegal immigration reform faced numerous obstacles over the years in spite of a continuing increase in illegal aliens. Employers resisted the imposition of responsibility for verifying legal status, though in many cases employers were exploiting the "shadow society" of illegal aliens. Conversely, Hispanic and Asian Americans feared employment discrimination against legal residents and citizens would result. Agricultural areas feared loss of seasonal workers to harvest crops, labor that Americans tend to reject. Illegal aliens feared the necessity of proving their residency prior to 1982 because their lifestyle demanded false identities in many cases, and the status of family members was uncertain under the Act. Nevertheless, passage of the measure was viewed as a major achievement in meeting most concerns and as a humane resolution of a festering problem. In the course of the year ending May 4, 1988, during which time the amnesty program was in effect, about 1.7 million aliens applied, substantially less than the 2 to 3 million anticipated. Illegal immigration continues to be a major problem, with an estimated 1 million or more illegal immigrants entering the United States each year. More recent efforts to control illegal immigration have concentrated on enhancing border patrols and denying governmental benefits.

Internal Security Act of 1950 (McCarran Act)   An act designed to place the Communist party and other totalitarian groups under rigid controls. The Act outlaws any conspiracy, peaceful or violent, that has as its purpose the establishment of a foreign-controlled dictatorship in the United States. A Subversive Activities Control Board (now abolished) had been established to designate Communist "action" groups, "fronts," or Communist-"infiltrated" organizations and require action and front groups to register with the Attorney General, listing their officers and members, financial records, and any printing equipment under their control. Publications of these organizations were to be labeled as Communist propaganda. Infiltrated trade unions lost all rights under national labor laws. Individual members of any of these groups could not hold office in a labor union, obtain a passport, or work in any public office; members of action groups were also barred from defense plants. The law also strengthened espionage and sedition laws and immigration requirements and provided for the deportation of Communist aliens. Another provision established procedures for detention of suspected saboteurs in an emergency but was repealed in 1971. Judicial rejection of most key provisions of the Act has weakened its force considerably. *See also* MCCARTHYISM, page 325.

Significance   Many serious constitutional questions are raised by the McCarran Act, and, to date, the Supreme Court has upheld only the organizational registration requirement (*Communist Party v. Subversive Activities Control Board,* 367 U.S. 1 [1961]). An order that individual Communist party leaders register was, however, declared invalid by the Supreme Court as an invasion of the right against self-incrimination (*Albertson v. Subversive*

Activities Control Board, 382 U.S. 70 [1965]). The Court also struck down the passport provision as a denial of the right to travel (*Aptheker v. Secretary of State,* 378 U.S. 500 [1964]) and the restrictions on defense plant workers as a violation of the right of association (*United States v. Robel,* 389 U.S. 258 [1967]). A 1967 amendment to the Internal Security Act eliminated the self-registration requirement and empowered the Subversive Activities Control Board to register individuals. Finally, the board itself was abolished in 1973. The McCarran Act provides concrete evidence of the fears generated by the Cold War and Communism, and of the dangers to liberty inherent in the administration of such laws.

Omnibus Anticrime Bill of 1994   A major extension of federal involvement in fighting crime. The 1994 law establishes a trust fund of $30.2 billion, which is to be secure through the year 2000. Major provisions provide funds to the states for 100,000 police officers, new prison construction, and crime prevention programs. The bill also authorizes the death penalty for about 50 federal offenses, adopts a "three strikes and you're out" policy that mandates life imprisonment for repeat offenders, permits juveniles of 13 and older to be tried as adults in federal courts for certain crimes, and bans manufacture and possession of 19 varieties of assault weapons. A Violence Against Women Act makes crimes motivated by gender a federal civil rights violation. *See also* COMPREHENSIVE CRIME CONTROL ACT OF 1984, page 380; OMNIBUS CRIME CONTROL AND SAFE STREETS ACT OF 1968, page 384.

Significance   The increasingly prominent role of the federal government in crime control is emphasized by the 1994 crime bill. It has become quite commonplace for both major political parties to demonstrate their intention to be tough on crime prior to an election. A substantial part of the debate in 1994 concerned the issue of how best to fund state and local programs so as to enhance or minimize federal control. The ban on assault weapons was also very controversial, and efforts to repeal that ban in 1996 failed. Building prisons will consume substantial resources. Though Americans generally have rejected the concept of extensive national police involvement, the 1994 law, added to others enacted since 1968, puts the national government heavily into crime control.

Omnibus Crime Control and Safe Streets Act of 1968   The first comprehensive national anticrime legislation. Major provisions (1) provide for federal block grants to states to upgrade state and local police forces, (2) authorize wiretapping and bugging by police with and without warrants, and (3) alter federal criminal procedures to modify Supreme Court decisions (*Miranda* and *Mallory* cases) in order to make voluntary confessions admissible irrespective of delay in arraignment or failure to inform a suspect of his or her rights. The law also contained national gun control provisions. *See also* COMPREHENSIVE CRIME CONTROL ACT OF 1984, page 380; GUN CONTROL, page 318; *McNabb v. United States,* page 359; WIRETAPPING, page 342.

Significance   Until 1968, the federal government generally did not participate in local crime control. The concept of a national police force has been abhorrent to most Americans. Extensive violence, rising crime rates, campus unrest, and ghetto riots, along with attacks on Supreme Court rulings, led to passage of the Act. It placed the national government into a new and expanding role in state and local police activity. In 1968, Congress also passed the Juvenile Delinquency Prevention and Control Act, which provides grants to states to prevent delinquency and to rehabilitate youthful offenders.

Organized Crime Control Act of 1970   A comprehensive law designed to strengthen the federal government's ability to combat organized crime. Major provisions (1) authorize special grand juries to investigate organized criminal activities; (2) standardize witness-immunity laws for legislative, administrative, and judicial bodies; (3) limit challenges to illegally seized evidence; (4) forbid use of income from organized criminal activity to establish a legitimate business; (5) extend federal jurisdiction over gambling and use of explosives; and (6) authorize increased prison terms, up to 25 years, for dangerous offenders.

Significance   The existence of an organized national network of crime, as well as the extensive corruptive influence of criminals in some state and local governments, appears to be well established. Under the American system of government, police activity is rigidly localized and often unable to cope with widespread criminal activity that transcends geographic boundaries. The Organized Crime Control Act is designed to cope with this problem by expanding national jurisdiction over some of the more obvious outlets for organized crime. Congress took further aim at organized crime in the Racketeer Influenced and Corrupt Organizations Act of 1970 (RICO), which provides broad powers to prosecute those who use patterns of racketeering activities in conducting a business enterprise. In an unusual application of RICO, the Supreme Court held in *National Organization for Women v. Scheidler*, 114 S. Ct. 798 (1994), that abortion clinics could sue violent antiabortion protestors under RICO inasmuch as RICO is not restricted to activity motivated solely by economic gain.

9

Finance and Taxation

Ability versus Benefit Theory   The belief that taxes should be based on the individual's ability to pay, as indicated by income, property, consumption, and wealth, or, conversely, that taxes should be paid in proportion to the benefits received from governmental services. Taxes based on ability to pay are generally used for whatever purposes government policymakers determine, whereas those based on the benefit theory are often earmarked for special purposes. *See also* EARMARKING, page 396; INCOME TAX, page 405; PROGRESSIVE TAX, page 411; SPECIAL ASSESSMENT, page 418.

Significance   The graduated income tax most nearly approximates the ideal of the ability theory because of its progressive increases in rates as income (and, hence, ability to pay) rises. Although the federal income tax is based theoretically on the ability theory, many exemptions and other favored treatment have grossly reduced its progressive nature. "Luxury taxes" in the form of excises on goods typically purchased by high-income groups also tend to be based on the ability theory. The benefit and cost of services theories have largely been superseded by the ability theory, which is regarded as more equitable and easier to determine in a complex society in which benefits derived from taxes often go unnoticed. The benefit theory is still applied in areas where benefits can be easily assessed. The 1956 Federal Highway Act, for example, provides for financing the vast interstate highway system with federal gasoline excise taxes levied on highway users. On the local level, special assessments on improvements that benefit the property owner, such as sewers and paving, are generally used by cities and other local units. The "cost of government services rendered" approach as a means of determining tax liability is an attempt to apply the benefit theory by levying taxes in proportion to the services rendered to each taxpayer. Recent studies indicate that most Americans pay approximately the same percentage of their income in taxes, whether rich or poor.

Assessed Valuation   Value assigned to property for tax purposes. The general property tax levied by local governments in the United States is based on the valuation placed upon real estate (land, buildings, and other improvements) and personal property, both tangible (machinery, livestock, merchandise) and intangible (stocks, bonds, bank accounts). The tax paid on property is based on the assessed valuation and the mileage or tax rate applied to the assessed value. The assessed valuation is based on a proportion of the actual value of each piece of property assessed within a taxing district, usually 30 to 50 percent of true market value, although some political units currently assess at 100 percent of value. Assessments can be changed by reappraisals, adjustment of individual inequities by a board of review, adjustment of unequal valuations for different assessment districts by a county or state board of equalization, or by a general revaluation of all assessments within a district. *See also* ASSESSOR, page 387; PROPERTY TAX, page 412.

Significance   The assessment of property for tax purposes is a complex process that produces much controversy among taxpayers, many of whom believe their property is assessed too high or unequally as compared with their neighbors' or with those of other taxing districts. The fair assessment of personal property poses the greatest problem because of assessors' difficulty in finding and appraising movable property. When a taxing district crosses assessment boundaries, such as a school district that includes a city and several townships, the danger of disparities in assessed valuation is increased. The key to a fair assessment system may be found in the appointment of professional countywide or statewide assessors.

Assessor   A public official who determines the value of real and personal property for purposes of taxation. Assessors are commonly elected in towns, townships, or counties. In some midwestern townships, the supervisor serves as the assessor. About 10 percent of city assessors are still elected, and the remainder are political or merit system appointees. Many local units hire private assessing specialists in response to taxpayer criticism of elected or appointed governmental assessors. *See also* ASSESSED VALUATION, page 386; PROPERTY TAX, page 412.

Significance   Many students of government challenge the election of assessors. The elective method is unlikely to secure competent assessors, and elected officials may underassess so as not to antagonize the voters. Critics also charge that the town or township is too small a unit for assessment purposes. Many areas have moved in the direction of appointing assessors on a merit basis and making the county the assessment unit. Whether appointed or elected, the assessor is often an important local political official.

Auditor   An official, usually an agent of a legislative body, who checks on the expenditure of appropriated funds to determine that they will be or have been spent for the purposes approved by the legislature in its appropriation acts. The federal auditor, the Comptroller General, is appointed by the President with the Senate's approval; state and local auditors are either appointed or elected by the voters. *See also* COMPTROLLER GENERAL, page 392; GENERAL ACCOUNTING OFFICE, page 423; STATE AUDITOR, page 626.

Significance   Proper auditing of disbursed funds is essential to fiscal responsibility. In many state and local governments, only a preaudit in the form of a spending authorization is required, with no proper postaudit after expenditures to check their validity. In other cases, the same officials who authorize the expenditures are later called upon to check on the authenticity of their own work. Effective auditing procedures require careful examination of the validity of accounts and payments by competent, independent auditors *after* the expenditures have been made by the executive branch.

Banking Systems   The national and state banking systems, which exist side by side in the United States. Congress was not granted the specific power to charter banks, but the power is implied from granted powers that can best be carried on through banks, such as the borrowing and currency powers. Both national and state-chartered banks are privately owned financial institutions, which are regulated and have their accounts audited by the respective chartering government. National banks, chartered by the national government since 1863, are supervised by the Comptroller of the Currency in the Treasury Department and are required to join the Federal Reserve System. Most state banks accept Federal Reserve membership and thereby come under a measure of national as well as state regulation. The citizen can usually distinguish between national and state-chartered banks by their names, such as First National Bank or Industrial State Bank. *See also* FEDERAL RESERVE SYSTEM, page 400.

Significance   Federal and state regulation of banks involves such matters as issuance of stock, stockholder liabilities, assets and investments, organization and management, reserves, loans, and depositor security. The public is protected through periodic inspections and audits by examiners and by deposit insurance, up to $100,000 for each account guaranteed by the Federal Deposit Insurance Corporation. Under banking deregulation, many independent banks have been purchased or have merged with other banks, with the trend toward greater competition among fewer but larger banks. In the early 1990s, an increasing number of banks failed and filed for bankruptcy, resulting in the need for Federal Deposit Insurance Corporation (FDIC) to secure additional funds for insured accounts. The cost of failure of financial institutions has run over $200 billion for the FDIC.

Block Grant   A form of financial aid that involves the transfer of funds from the national government to state and local governments for use in broad policy areas, with discretion remaining with state and local units to develop and implement specific programs. Block grants are intended to provide federal funds in a way that results in the consolidation of previously separate and fragmented grant-in-aid categorical and revenue-sharing programs. Revenue sharing, by which the federal government funneled billions of dollars into state and local governments, was ended in 1986. However, it continues on the state and local level. Common examples of taxes collected by the states and shared with their local governments are motor fuel, license, income, liquor, cigarette, and sales taxes. In the block grant approach, state and local units are given discretionary powers in spending the funds granted, but they must plan how they will use the money and report how the funds have been spent. *See also* GRANT-IN-AID, page 404; MATCHING FUNDS, page 408.

Significance   The block grant system was first used in the Partnership for Health Act of 1966. Other well-known block grant programs include the Comprehensive Employment and Training Act (CETA) and the Housing and Community Development Act of 1974. The latter, for example, consolidated ten separate categorical urban development programs and delegated major decision-making authority to local units of government. In 1981, the Reagan administration's major budget reconciliation produced a consolidation of many programs and a massive changeover from federal control to state and local management via the block grant approach. In those areas in which Congress retained strong federal control over programs, President Ronald Reagan indicated that he would continue to push for removal of federal "strings." Guidelines for transition from federal to state control were included in a special governmental affairs section of the reconciliation bill. By the latter part of the 1990s, block grants became a vehicle by which elective officials downsized the federal government's role and provided for local and state initiatives to spend the funds so appropriated, as they saw the need. These grants have been focused mainly in health and welfare. These changes continue to be fostered by the American public in its voting behavior.

Board of Review   Public officials charged with the duty of reviewing individual tax assessments on property. The review function is to be distinguished from "equalization," which is the comparison and adjustment of assessments between entire tax-imposing units. The board of review may be elected or composed of local government officials serving ex officio. *See also* ASSESSED VALUATION, page 386; PROPERTY TAX, page 412.

Significance   Citizens dissatisfied with their property tax may appeal to a board of review. The board's objective is to tax all citizens equitably, according to the value of their property. Most citizens fail to take advantage of their right to review, not wanting to take the time or trouble, or out of fear that their assessment may be raised. Many taxpayer complaints result from a lack of understanding of assessment and tax-levying procedures. Decisions reached by a local board typically can be appealed to a state review board.

Bond   A certificate of indebtedness, tendered by a borrower to a lender, that constitutes a written obligation for the borrower to repay to the lender the principal plus accrued interest on the loan. A public bond is issued by the national government or by a state or local government as a means of borrowing money for public needs that cannot be financed out of current revenues. *See also* DEBT LIMIT, page 393.

Significance   Various types of bonds, such as savings bonds, are issued by the U.S. government to finance budget deficits and to carry the public debt. State and local governments commonly make use of either serial bonds or sinking fund issues to finance new projects. Sinking fund bonds are paid from a separate fund set aside from revenues over a period of time until the bonds are due for payment. Serial bonds come due at different dates over a period of years, with each series paid off by the borrowing authority from current revenues. Commercial bond rating firms evaluate credit ratings of local governments and thus help to determine the interest rates and marketability of bond issues. General obligation bonds are backed by the "full faith and credit" of the issuing government, whereas revenue or nonguaranteed bonds are financed by income from self-liquidating projects. The attractiveness to the purchaser of many bonds relates to their tax-exempt nature; the interest earned is not taxable by the national government or by state and local governments. These bonds enable local governing units, school districts, colleges, and universities to finance building and operating needs. In the nation's private bond market during the 1980s, high-yield "junk bonds" were sometimes issued to finance takeover actions by which giant corporations bought a controlling interest in many smaller and weaker companies.

Borrowing Power   The authority of a government to finance budget deficits that result when expenditures exceed income. The Constitution (Art. I, sec. 8) provides Congress with full borrowing power, free from restrictions. Most state constitutions, however, severely limit the authority of state governments to incur indebtedness, permitting state borrowing only when authorized by constitutional amendment or by a vote of the people. Local units of government are restricted by state constitutional or statutory limitations on their borrowing power. *See also* DEBT LIMIT, page 393; DEFICIT SPENDING, page 394; PUBLIC DEBT, page 412.

Significance   The borrowing power is essential for governments to meet short- and long-term crises and to finance major projects that cannot be paid for out of current income. The national government, for example, used its borrowing power extensively during World War II and the economic crisis of the 1930s. Deficit spending to counteract economic recessions has become a standard weapon in the arsenal of federal fiscal policy. Most state and local borrowing is used to finance major building projects. Some citizens support borrowing for capital improvements as an investment in the future, similar to borrowing by a family to purchase a home. Others view extensive use of the borrowing power as fiscal irresponsibility. Although economists generally regard the borrowing power as a necessary tool of governmental fiscal policy, political leaders disagree over the extent, timing, and purpose of specific applications of the policy.

Budget   An estimate of the receipts and expenditures needed by government to carry out its program in some future period, usually a fiscal year. The President is responsible for formulating the national budget under the Budget and Accounting Act of 1921, and governors of most states likewise operate under an "executive budget" system. The budget process begins in the executive branch with the lengthy and detailed process of preparing estimates, followed by a central review in which budget officers hold hearings and agency officials defend their estimates. Next, the budget is approved by the chief executive and submitted to the legislative body in a "budget message." After study and hearings in appropriations committees in both houses, the budget is enacted as an appropriation act. This is followed by budget execution, the actual spending of the money during the fiscal period by executive officials. The final step is a postaudit check on the validity of expenditures. Some states and cities use a separate capital budget for financing major public works projects, which are often paid for on a long-term bonding or self-liquidating basis. Budget authority describes the process by which a federal agency is granted the right to make commitments that will result in immediate or future spending. Budget outlays provide the spending authority that is needed to carry on a particular program. Each year Congress passes a general budget resolution that serves as a guide in writing tax and spending bills. To strengthen its fiscal role, Congress in 1974 established budget committees in each house to oversee revenue and spending activities. Also established was a new Congressional Budget Office similar to the President's Office of Management and Budget (OMB). *See also* BUDGET AND ACCOUNTING ACT OF 1921, page 426; BUDGET POWER, page 184; PRESIDENTIAL-CONGRESSIONAL BUDGET NEGOTIATION, page 198; RECONCILIATION, page 414.

Significance   A budget is a work plan that gives direction to the execution of government policies. The budget process has undergone a major change in the twentieth century with the adoption of the executive budget to replace the formulation of budgets by legislative committees. Performance and program budgets are also used for more effective evaluation of spending. The executive budget gives the chief executive—president, governor, or mayor—extensive control over fiscal affairs. The executive budget power, however, is often diminished by the influence of pressure groups on the budget process and by the structure of "built-in" appropriations that are protected by a political linkage involving the administrative agency, its clientele, and the legislative appropriations committees. Zero-based budgeting, implemented by some state and local units, seeks to overcome this problem by forcing each bureaucratic unit to justify its total spending program in each new budget period. The President's control over the federal budget is limited because almost 80 percent of spending involves entitlements that are often uncontrollable. These include Social Security, government employee and military retirement benefits, contractual obligations, Medicare and Medicaid, and categorical welfare aid. Despite campaign pledges to reduce the size of the federal budget, recent presidents have proposed record-high budgets each year, with conservative presidents often outdoing liberals in the size of their budgets. Many ideas to achieve a balanced federal budget have been advanced. These have included the Gramm-Rudman-Hollings Act approach that used a specified annual reduction formula and an automatic sequestering of funds if Congress failed to act, a balanced budget constitutional amendment, and a presidential line item veto power. These approaches, however, have either failed to be adopted or failed to produce the fiscal restraint needed to achieve a balanced federal budget, even though many political leaders give suport to them. The 1989 budget submitted to Congress by President Ronald Reagan was a record $1.1 trillion. Under the Bush administration, large expenditures, such as the estimated $200 billion savings and loan bailout, are increasingly funded by off-budget appropriations. Despite much political talk about "balancing the budget," the last time the nation enjoyed a balanced budget was in the 1960s. In 1995 and 1996, President Bill Clinton, Speaker of the House Newt Gingrich, and Senate Majority Leader Bob Dole met in budget summit negotiating sessions to try to reach agreement on balancing the budget in seven years.

Business Cycles   The rhythmic fluctuation of a free economy as changes occur in business activity. Business cycles, typically, involve movements from prosperity to recession or depression, followed by economic recovery and the completion of the cycle by a return to the previous high point of economic activity. A new cycle then begins. Economists have identified and studied both short-term and long-range cycles of business activity. *See also* FISCAL POLICY, page 400; KEYNESIANISM, page 407; MONETARY POLICY, page 410; RECESSION/DEPRESSION, page 414.

Significance   Business cycles were considered to be natural economic phenomena by classical economists, and their recurrence was regarded as inevitable. Since the 1930s, however, allowing cycles to run their course is no longer considered politically feasible or economically necessary. Policymakers aim at avoiding the heavy costs in unemployment and economic stagnation and the ever-present dangers of inflation. The national government employs countercyclical fiscal and monetary policies to control the extremes of business cycle activity and inactivity in attempts to promote continuing stability for the economy. The problem remains, however, of developing sophisticated applications of fiscal and monetary policy and applying them at the right time with the correct amount of forcefulness. Theories to explain business cycles have focused on psychological factors, under- and over-savings, the impact of politics, and the expansion and contraction of bank credit. Radical groups have tended to explain business cycles as a natural and defective consequence of the capitalistic system.

Comptroller General   The federal official responsible for auditing the accounts of all national government agencies. Functioning as the financial adviser to Congress, the Comptroller General heads the General Accounting Office (GAO) and is appointed by the President with the Senate's approval for a fifteen-year term. The Comptroller General also has power to validate all payments to ensure that they fall within the purposes and limits of congressional appropriations acts and to standardize accounting systems of government agencies. The Comptroller General can be removed from office by impeachment or by joint resolution of Congress. *See also* AUDITOR, page 387; GENERAL ACCOUNTING OFFICE, page 423.

Significance   The Comptroller General acts as an agent of Congress in controlling and auditing the budget execution process in the executive branch. Controversy has developed on occasion when the Comptroller General has been charged with letting his personal views influence the validation of expenditures. For example, President Franklin D. Roosevelt became involved in many controversies with the Comptroller General because the latter's open hostility to the New Deal was regarded as the reason for his holding up many emergency spending programs. Numerous observers, including the first Hoover Commission, have recommended that the Comptroller General's "preaudit" validation of payments be transferred to an executive official, leaving the Comptroller General with responsibility for a "postaudit." In recent years, the Comptroller General has expanded operations by sending GAO investigators abroad to check on foreign aid and other types of overseas spending.

Corporation Income Tax   A national tax levied on corporations, based on their annual net income. The corporation income tax prior to the enactment of the Tax Reform Act of 1986 was a flat 15 percent for the first $25,000 of net income. The rate then increased progressively until it reached the maximum of 46 percent on all net income over $100,000. The 1986 law reduced the tax rate on corporate profits from the maximum of 46 percent to 40 percent in 1987 and 34 percent thereafter. These reductions, however, were more than offset by ending or reducing many corporate tax benefits, with the result of substantial increases in corporation tax payments for most companies. The corporate income tax is, essentially, a tax on the privilege of doing business as a corporation and, as such, was first enacted prior to the adoption of the Sixteenth Amendment. *See also* EXCESS PROFITS TAX, page 399; INCOME TAX, page 405.

Significance   The federal corporation income tax is probably the most complicated tax levied by the national government, involving controversy over what constitutes "net income" and "legitimate expenses" for a corporation. It ranks next to the individual income tax in the amount of its annual yield. The tax has been attacked for fostering "double taxation," that is, taxing corporation income through the corporation income tax, followed by taxing shareholders' dividends through the individual income tax. Others have criticized the corporation income tax for its lenient rates and loopholes, although many of the latter were closed by the 1986 law. As a percentage of total federal revenues, the corporate income tax dropped from 30 percent in 1940 to 7.5 percent in 1982. The Reagan administration had accelerated this process in the Economic Recovery Tax Act of 1981, which considerably reduced tax payments by corporations. The Tax Reform Act of 1986, however, was projected to reduce taxes on individuals by about 6 percent and to offset this reduction by an increase of $120 billion each year in corporate collections. Nevertheless, in 1987 the corporation income tax produced only 10 percent of the federal government's income. In 1994 federal income from corporate taxes remained at 10 percent.

Debt Limit   A constitutional or statutory limitation upon the ability of a government to incur indebtedness. In the national government, the debt limit is fixed by Congress and can be changed to meet new debt needs. All but a few states, however, are restricted by constitutional provisions that limit state indebtedness, usually to a specified figure. Debt limitations on local governments generally take the form of restricting total debt to a percentage of assessed valuation or involve state approval of bond issues. *See also* PUBLIC DEBT, page 412.

Significance   Self-imposed statutory debt limits established by legislative bodies, as by Congress, are useful only psychologically, if at all. Over the past three decades, Congress has altered the public debt limit on numerous occasions. On the state and local levels, cumbersome constitutional restrictions have produced many techniques for evasion. Although state and local debt limits can ordinarily be exceeded by favorable referendum votes, voter apathy or conservatism had made this increasingly difficult. Devices that have been used to incur indebtedness beyond state or local limits include borrowing by state agencies instead of the state per se and borrowing on a self-liquidating basis without state certification of bonds. For example, state toll road authorities borrow large sums to construct highways and repay the debt out of income from tolls. Despite efforts to keep debt limited on the national, state, and local levels, new demands for governmental functions and services beyond the means of current income, as well as the increasing tendency to use federal deficits to stimulate a sluggish economy, keep debt rising in the United States. In 1981, President Ronald Reagan requested Congress to increase the debt limit to nearly $1 trillion as one of his first actions in office, and there have been annual presidential requests for debt limit increases since. In 1990, Congress raised the national public debt limit to nearly $3.5 trillion. It also financed some programs, such as the estimated

$200 billion savings and loan bailout, off-budget to reduce their impact on the debt limit. In Congress, debt limit increases usually are the product of bipartisanship because neither party wants the sole blame for the increases. In his first year in office, President Reagan pushed a large tax cut and huge increases in defense spending through Congress, producing enormous deficits in their wake. To cope with them, he advocated a balanced budget constitutional amendment, line item veto power for the President, and fiscal restraint by Congress, especially in the social welfare field. Among the states, 49 require a balanced budget (Vermont being the lone exception), 44 by constitutional provision and 5 by statute. Many times the President and Congress have become embroiled in controversy over the debt limit and balancing the budget, but despite several partial shutdowns, the U.S. government has never reached the point that it was not able to pay its due bills. By 1996, in efforts to balance the nation's budget, Congress raised the public debt limit to $5.3 trillion and gave the President the line item veto power.

Deficit Spending   A technique of fiscal policy that utilizes government spending beyond its income to avoid or combat an economic slump. The use of deficit financing to "prime the pump" of the free enterprise economy was popularized by the British economist John Maynard Keynes in the 1930s. It has since become generally accepted and used as a tool of federal economic policy. *See also* DEBT LIMIT, page 393; FISCAL POLICY, page 400; KEYNESIANISM, page 407; PUBLIC DEBT, page 412.

Significance   The objective of deficit spending is to inject new purchasing power into the economy to stimulate an upturn in economic activity during a period of stagnation resulting from overproduction or underconsumption. Deficit financing is accepted by most economists and politicians on the assumption that deficits are less troublesome than high unemployment and economic stagnation. Conservatives oppose it on the grounds that it involves fiscal irresponsibility and is ineffectual, and they usually demand government cutbacks in spending as the best means of stimulating the free economy. The national government used deficit financing during the Depression of the 1930s and in World War II and has employed it to combat nine post–World War II recessions. Huge federal budget deficits have become common, with balanced or surplus budgets increasingly rare. Issues tend to involve the magnitude of the deficit, how the deficit will be spent, and its inflationary impact. In the more than 200 years since Congress formulated the first national budget, only 19 had annual budget surpluses, most of which were very small. Most American politicians have committed themselves publicly to the search for a balanced budget and an end to deficit spending. However, recent presidents, such as Richard Nixon, Gerald Ford, Jimmy Carter, Ronald Reagan, George Bush, and Bill Clinton, promised balanced budgets but were unable to produce them. The largest federal deficits have been during the Reagan and Bush administrations, with several annual deficits exceeding $200 billion. Some economists have questioned the Keynesian view that deficits should be utilized only during recession periods, holding that deficits empirically have become essential to help prevent as well as cure recessions. Substantial deficits, however, may actually weaken the economy because the government is forced to compete with private individuals and groups for scarce capital resources, resulting often in a substantial rise in interest rates followed by a weakening of the economy. Since 1940, large-scale deficit spending and huge military budgets have provided the stimulus needed to avoid another Great Depression.

Deflation   An economic condition in which price levels decrease and the value of money in terms of purchasing power is consequently increased. Deflation may result from either a decrease in the amount of money and credit available or an oversupply of consumer goods. *See also* INFLATION, page 406; MONETARY POLICY, page 410.

Significance   Proponents of stable monetary policies regard deflation and inflation, its opposite, as twin evils to be equally avoided. Deflation is characteristically associated with economic depressions, just as inflation tends to accompany prosperity. Most economists believe that deflation can be prevented or controlled through stimulative use of monetary policy by the Federal Reserve Board and the Treasury and by the use of fiscal policy, such as deficit financing. A policy of deflation is sometimes adopted by a nation suffering from an adverse balance of payments, with the objective of reducing prices to make exports more attractive to other countries. The last deflationary period for the American economy occurred during the Great Depression of the 1930s. This situation was caused partly by the gold standard system under which the amount of money available was determined by the amount of gold reserve held by the Federal Reserve system. President Roosevelt, in 1934, sought to end this deflationary activity by going off the gold standard.

Devaluation   A policy undertaken by a nation to reduce the value of its monetary unit in terms of gold or in terms of its exchange ratio with other national currencies. The United States devalued the dollar by about 59 percent in 1934 by increasing the price of gold to $35 an ounce. The price thereafter remained fixed at $35 an ounce until President Richard M. Nixon agreed in late 1971 to devalue the dollar by raising the official price of gold in exchange for agreement by other major nations to realign their currencies by raising their values in relation to the dollar. Subsequently, the United States ended its selling and buying of gold at a fixed price, thereby, in effect, severing the dollar's tie with gold. In 1974, Congress changed a 40-year policy by permitting American citizens to own gold, with the price determined by market conditions. *See also* BALANCE OF PAYMENTS, page 533; GOLD STANDARD, page 403; INTERNATIONAL MONETARY FUND, page 558.

Significance   Although American devaluation of the dollar in 1934 was based largely on domestic reasons, ordinarly the objective of devaluation is to improve a nation's balance of international payments by reducing imports and expanding exports. These results are likely to occur because devaluation decreases the cost of domestic products for foreign buyers and increases the cost of foreign products for domestic consumers. Devaluations are often matched by equal or greater devaluations by competitor states in an effort to maintain their position in international trade. Competitive rounds of devaluations were carried out by many states during the Great Depression. President Nixon's action during the 1970s of divesting the dollar of its gold base resulted from chronic deficits in the American balance of payments with a resulting massive outflow of dollars. One of the major responsibilities of the International Monetary Fund (IMF) is to try to eliminate competitive devaluation as an international trade weapon. In recent years, currencies of the major industrial nations have been permitted to "float," with their values relative to each other determined by supply/demand factors. Most governments, however, continue to support the exchange value of their nation's currency under this flexible exchange rate system unless they want it devalued for economic and trade purposes.

Direct Tax   Any tax paid directly to the government by the taxpayer. An indirect tax, such as sales or excise tax, conversely, is paid to private businesspersons who then remit it to the government. The Constitution, in Article I, section 9, states: "No capitation, or other direct tax shall be laid, unless in proportion to the census of enumeration herein before directed to be taken." This provision meant that, for example, the people in a state containing 10 percent of the nation's population would pay 10 percent of any direct tax levied by the national government. *See also Pollock v. Farmers Loan and Trust Co.,* page 425.

Significance   The question of which taxes are direct and therefore to be apportioned according to the population of the states has been the subject of much legal controversy. In 1796 (*Hylton v. United States,* 3 Dallas 171), the Supreme Court interpreted "direct taxes" to include poll taxes and taxes on land. In 1895 (*Pollock v. Farmers Loan and Trust Co.,* 158 U.S. 601), the Court struck down an income tax as a direct tax that Congress must apportion among the states. This decision was overcome by the Sixteenth Amendment, which granted Congress the power to tax incomes "without apportionment among the several states, and without regard to any census or enumeration." Congress has refused to levy direct taxes because apportionment involves many administrative complications and because inequities would result in that tax-paying ability is not divided equally among the people of the 50 states.

Discount Rate   The interest rate paid by a commercial bank to borrow money from a Federal Reserve Bank. *See also* FEDERAL RESERVE SYSTEM, page 400.

Significance   The Federal Reserve System uses the discount rate as a tool of monetary policy. By lowering the discount rate, the Federal Reserve Board can encourage member banks to liquidate their holdings of commercial paper by having the Federal Reserve banks buy them at a favorable price. This frees up funds for member banks and enables them to make additional loans to the public, thus stimulating purchasing power and, thereby, the nation's economy. By raising the discount rate, the Federal Reserve banks can obtain the opposite result of reducing the availability of credit in the country. Typically, therefore, the discount rate is lowered during a recession to stimulate an upturn in the economy (loose money policy) and raised during a boom period when serious inflation threatens (tight money policy).

Earmarking   Allocation of tax revenues for specific purposes. Earmarking gasoline taxes for highway purposes is the most common example, with about

half the states doing so by constitutional provision and the others by statutory requirement. About half of total state revenue is earmarked for specific
purposes. Earmarked taxes are often based on the "benefit theory" of taxation. *See also* ABILITY VERSUS BENEFIT THEORY, page 386.

Significance   Earmarking tax revenues by constitutional provision reduces legislative and executive control over budgeting and finance. Earmarked programs may be adequately financed while other equally or more
deserving public needs go unfilled. It is often easier, however, for the legislature to secure public consent to an earmarked tax because the people can
clearly see the object of the tax and because powerful interest groups that
stand to benefit use propaganda and lobbying tactics to "sell" the tax to the
public and to members of the legislature. The most commonly earmarked
taxes in the states are those for financing highway building programs and
those that set aside percentages of general sales or income taxes for educational purposes. An example of federal earmarking is the use of gasoline taxes
for building interstate highways. Entitlements, such as Social Security payments, also constitute a form of earmarking by the national government.

Economic Summit   An annual meeting of the leaders of the seven major industrialized countries of the West, aimed at developing common approaches
to current economic and political problems. Initiated in 1975, the early meetings involved the Group of Five (Britain, France, Japan, Germany, and the
United States), but in the 1980s the participation of Italy and Canada
changed it to the Group of Seven, or G-7. Economic summit meetings are not
aimed at writing treaties or agreements but at harmonizing and coordinating
national policies and programs. *See also* SUMMIT DIPLOMACY, page 580.

Significance   Economic summit meetings have given the President
the opportunity to provide leadership in the Western bloc of states. The 1988
Economic Summit Conference that met in Toronto provided an example of
such an opportunity. Participants included British Prime Minister Margaret
Thatcher, Canadian Prime Minister Brian Mulroney, French President
François Mitterrand, German Chancellor Helmut Kohl, Italian Prime Minister
Ciriaco DeMita, Japanese Prime Minister Noboru Takeshita, and President
Ronald Reagan. Major economic issues taken up at the G-7 summit included
the international debt crisis, the need for exchange rate stability, increasing
trade protectionism, and the threat of a global economic recession. Political
issues considered by the group included providing protection in the Iran-Iraq
war for Persian Gulf oil shipments, developing a common approach to Soviet
leader Mikhail Gorbachev's disarmament initiatives, and coordinating national policies in a global attack on the disease AIDS. President Reagan's
main efforts at the conference were directed at developing Western support
to help the United States manage its huge international trade deficit. In 1990
G-7 met in Houston with President George Bush as host. At the same time,
a competitive group, seeking to upstage the Economic Summit, sponsored
a "Summit of Seven of the World's Poorest Peoples," with participants from
such countries as Haiti, Bangladesh, and Nigeria. In 1995, the Economic
Summit was held in Halifax, Nova Scotia. The twenty-first annual meeting
tackled difficult political and economic issues, including the Russian war
with the Chechen rebels, French nuclear weapons testing in the Pacific, the

American-Japanese trade dispute, and general world economic problems. The last of these led to a pledge to attack high unemployment, achieve sustainable growth and low inflation, and reform World Bank and International Monetary Fund operations. In the 1996 Economic Summit in Lyon, France, international terrorism became the priority item following a major bombing of a military base in Saudi Arabia in which 19 Americans were killed and many more injured.

Equalization   The review and adjustment of tax assessments among taxing districts in the state. The equalization function may be exercised at the county level to adjust assessments among the townships, cities, and other units of the county and at the state level to equalize assessments among counties. If property in one area is assessed at 50 percent of its value and in another at 30 percent, some adjustment is necessary to equalize the burdens borne by taxpayers if both areas are involved in a common government program. Equalization differs from local review of assessments in which individual rather than area assessments are reviewed. *See also* PROPERTY TAX, page 412.

Significance   One of the characteristics of local government in the United States is the multiplicity of taxing units. This, combined with variable assessment by popularly elected nonprofessional assessors, often results in unequal distribution of tax burdens. Equalization reduces inequities among units of government but does not eliminate them and does not resolve inequities in assessment of individual properties within the same unit.

Estate Tax   A tax, usually with progressive rates, levied on the property of deceased persons. Estate taxes apply to the total estate, whereas inheritance taxes are levied on the portion of the estate received by each beneficiary. The national government has levied an estate tax since 1916, and all states except Nevada have an estate or inheritance tax, usually the latter. The gift tax, having the same rate structure as the estate tax, is used to plug the loophole by which money was given to relatives and friends before death in order to avoid estate taxes. In 1981, Congress reduced the unified estate and gift maximum tax rate from 70 percent to 55 percent and provided substantial exemptions. Collections have since declined and hit a low of $4 billion in 1991, as contrasted with $8 billion in 1981. American gift and estate tax rates are among the lowest in the world. *See also* PROGRESSIVE TAX, page 411.

Significance   The unified federal estate and gift taxes are a lucrative source of income for the national government. A high percentage of state death taxes may be offset as a credit against payment of the federal estate tax, which has served as an encouragement for the states to enact such levies. State inheritance taxes are also progressive, with rates increasing sharply as the beneficiary's share rises, and as the relationship of the beneficiary to the deceased becomes more distant. Estate and inheritance taxes are aimed at preventing excessive concentrations of wealth in a few families as well as at raising revenue. The use of trusts to avoid the payment of estate and inheritance taxes has become a matter of some concern. Under the federal gift tax, any individual can give up to $10,000 each year to any number of recipients without any tax liability on either the donor or the recipient. Thus the gift tax exclusion can be used to avoid or reduce estate taxes.

Excess Profits Tax   A special tax levied during wartime to supplement the corporation income tax. The excess profits tax is calculated on the difference between business earnings in normal years and earnings during the war years when profits soar. An excess profits tax was levied by Congress during World Wars I and II and during the Korean War from 1951 to 1953. In the last case, the tax was fixed at 30 percent of the excess profits, with the limitation that the combined corporation income tax and excess profits tax should not exceed 70 percent of net income. Failure to levy an excess profits tax during the Vietnam War contributed to the nation's serious inflation and balance of payments problems of the 1970s. *See also* CORPORATION INCOME TAX, page 392.

Significance   The excess profits tax is designed primarily to recapture abnormal profits and to help finance military expenditures. It is also psychologically motivated to quiet public fears of wartime business profiteering. The opposition of business to the tax, usually quiescent during the war period, has always forced an early repeal of the tax at the war's end.

Excise tax   A tax levied upon the manufacture, transportation, sale, or consumption of goods. Federal excise taxes are permitted by the Constitution, and such levies have been placed on a variety of consumer goods. The main excise taxes used by the states are sales and use taxes. Heavy excises on what are regarded as socially undesirable commodities, such as liquor and tobacco, are a form of sumptuary tax. *See also* REGULATORY TAX, page 415; SALES TAX, page 416.

Significance   Federal income from excise taxes is exceeded only by that from the individual and corporation income taxes. Excises on liquor and tobacco provide the greatest yields. State excise taxes, unlike the federal, are often criticized for their regressive character in taxing necessities, with the tax burden falling proportionately heavier on low-income families. Many federal excises were first levied during World War II as emergency income measures.

Federal Reserve Notes   Currency issued by Federal Reserve banks, backed by deposits with the government of discounted commercial paper (such as promissory notes or bills of exchange), government bonds, and gold certificates. *See also* FEDERAL RESERVE SYSTEM, page 400.

Significance   Federal Reserve notes are the most important kind of currency in circulation in the United States today. A small number of silver certificates, treasury notes, federal bank notes, and national bank notes still circulate, but are being retired. Since going off the gold standard in 1934, the United States has had a "managed" currency. Elasticity in the supply of Federal Reserve notes is provided by its commercial paper backing; when borrowing is heavy, more currency can be issued, and when demand for loans shrinks, the issue of currency can be reduced. A symbolic gold backing of Federal Reserve notes is fixed by statute. In recent years counterfeiting problems have led to efforts to develop a paper currency that cannot be easily copied by would-be counterfeiters. The first newly designed Federal Reserve note is the hundred dollar bill with Ben Franklin's likeness off center.

Federal Reserve System The private/public banking regulatory system in the United States, which establishes banking policies and influences the amount of credit available and currency in circulation. The Federal Reserve System was created by Congress in 1913. It consists of twelve Federal Reserve banks, each located in one of the twelve Federal Reserve districts into which the country is divided, and a central Board of Governors of seven members appointed by the President and confirmed by the Senate for staggered terms of fourteen years, with the chairman appointed by the President for a four-year term that overlaps his own term in office. Each of the Federal Reserve banks is headed by a board of nine directors, six of whom are chosen by the member banks in the district and three by the Federal Reserve Board in Washington. In addition, the system includes a Federal Open Market Committee of twelve members—the seven Federal Reserve Board members plus five of the seven Federal Reserve Bank presidents—that makes policy in buying and selling securities and through foreign currency operations, and a Federal Advisory Council—composed of one member from each Federal Reserve Bank—that advises the Board of Governors. Membership in district Federal Reserve banks is required of all national banks and permitted for state banks, and most of the latter have joined. The Federal Reserve banks are actually privately owned "bankers' banks," with all member banks required to hold stock in them. *See also* BOARD OF GOVERNORS, page 421; DISCOUNT RATE, page 396; MONETARY POLICY, page 410; OPEN MARKET OPERATIONS, page 410; RESERVE RATIO, page 416.

Significance The Federal Reserve System determines the nation's general monetary and credit policies through decisions made by the Board in Washington, D.C., and by the regional boards. The Chairman of the Board of Governors wields vast power because of his ability to influence board members in their decision-making roles. Three means for affecting the money supply for the nation are (1) setting the discount rate, that is, determining the rate at which member banks may borrow from a Federal Reserve Bank; (2) open market operations, that is, purchasing and selling government securities on the open market; and (3) reserve requirements, that is, determining the amount of reserve cash banks must hold when making loans. These policies are carried out through the Reserve banks and by the thousands of member banks across the country. The "Fed" has played an increasingly significant role in attacking the nation's major economic problems of inflation and recession. In trying to control inflation, the Fed has carried out "hard" money policies during economic boom periods when inflationary pressures are greatest. In fighting recessions and unemployment, the Fed has carried out liberal monetary and credit policies designed to stimulate investment and purchasing power. When, however, a condition of "stagflation" exists—that is, when both serious unemployment and serious inflation plague the economy simultaneously—the Fed's role becomes more difficult. Stagflation persisted throughout the decade of the 1970s and into the 1980s. "Monetarists"—members of one school of economic thought—believe that the money and credit suppy made available by the Federal Reserve System is the most important factor that determines the state of the nation's economy.

Fiscal Policy The government's use of its taxing and spending powers to influence the nation's economy. Fiscal policy is developed largely on the basis of the monthly measures of growth or decline in the economy. These measures have taken the form of the Leading Economic Indicators, which have been transferred in a cost cutting move from the Bureau of Economic Analysis in the Commerce Department to the New York–based Conference Board, a private research group. These indicators, which are designed to "lead" or predict national economic activity in the short run, include (1) new material prices, (2) new business orders for plant and equipment, (3) average work week, (4) manufacturers' unfilled orders for durable goods, (5) length of delivery time, (6) stock prices, (7) building permits, (8) consumer confidence, (9) money supply, (10) unemployment claims, and (11) unfilled orders for consumer goods. In addition, all of the indicators are fused together into a Leading Indicator Index. Decisions on fiscal policy are made largely by the President and Congress, and are concerned with revenue, expenditure, and debt. John Maynard Keynes, the British economist, was the first to develop the theoretical basis and sophisticated applications of fiscal policy in combating economic slumps through the use of macroeconomic policies. *See also* EMPLOYMENT ACT, page 427; KEYNESIANISM, page 407; MONETARY POLICY, page 410.

Significance   Fiscal policy utilizes governmental financial programs to maintain economic stability by arresting and reversing violent downswings or upswings in the economy. The objective is to maintain a viable economy while steering a middle course between inflation and recession. Fiscal policies available to fight a serious recession and heavy unemployment include deficit spending, public works projects, and tax reductions. Reverse policies of reduced government spending, surplus budgets and debt retirement, and increased taxes are needed to combat inflation. Although the application of governmental fiscal policies to effect changes in the nation's economy is generally accepted as a proper function for government, some opposition exists. Most controversy, however, involves conflicts over the choice and timing of specific policies; it arises, particularly, from groups adversely affected. The most serious challenge to the effective use of fiscal policy occurs when the economy is simultaneously beset with the problems of stagnation and inflation—a condition called "stagflation." Extensive use of fiscal policy to stimulate the economy may then result in increased inflationary dangers. In the 1980s, the Reagan administration utilized monetary policy to control inflation and fiscal policy in the form of reduced taxes, increased government spending in defense, and huge deficit budgets to stimulate the economy. In the Bush administration, however, taxes were increased, inflation worsened, defense spending was decreased, and an effort was made to bring the huge deficits under control. Despite these actions, the threat of a major economic slump remained, with low growth rates, heavy unemployment, increased budget deficits, and other indicators of a recession, which continued until a more favorable fiscal climate developed in the mid-1990s.

Fiscal Year   The twelve-month financial period used by a government for record keeping, budgeting, appropriating, revenue collecting, and other aspects of fiscal management. The traditional fiscal year of the national government, which ran from July 1 to June 30, was changed by Congress in 1974 to run from October 1 to September 30. Some state and local governments use the calendar year from January 1 to December 31, while a few states use a two-year fiscal period. *See also* APPROPRIATION, page 129.

Significance   The student of government must differentiate between those statistics and programs that apply to a calendar year and those that apply to a fiscal year. The national government's fiscal year of July 1 to June 30 was originally selected to conform with the flow of governmental actions involved in budgeting and appropriating. The 1974 change to begin the fiscal year on October 1 recognized the new realities in the budgeting and appropriating functions involving huge budgets and complex processes, which had reduced the effectiveness of Congress.

Flat Tax   A tax based on a single tax rate, with no deductions, credits, or exemptions. The flat tax is an often suggested alternative to the existing federal income tax system. *See also* INCOME TAX, page 405; PROGRESSIVE TAX, page 411; REGRESSIVE TAX, page 415.

Significance   The flat tax is part of the growing controversy over tax reform. The present U.S. Tax Code, on which the federal income tax is based, has grown past 17,000 pages of laws and regulations that confuse Congress, taxpayers, and the IRS. One Republican presidential candidate, Steven Forbes, ran, albeit unsuccessfully, in the 1996 presidential primaries largely by advocating a flat tax. Critics of the flat tax argue that it is regressive in nature, putting the millionaire and the middle-income worker at the same tax rate. They also point out that the nations' economy needs the stimulation produced by deductions and that it undermines charitable giving, destroys the housing market, and bankrupts homeowners. The flat tax, according to its supporters, would bring order out of chaos and simplify the return by eliminating deductions and loopholes. They say it would spur the economy, cut government growth, lower taxes, and raise national wealth. Progressivity can be built into a flat tax by exempting a specified amount of earned income, thus eliminating many lower-income families from payment of any tax. Some proponents prefer a higher flat rate with deductions for home mortgages and charitable contributions. Opponents of both the present income tax system and the flat tax advocate either a consumption tax—taxing people on what they spend rather than on their income—or on a national sales tax. The flat tax is sometimes referred to as a single tax. The single tax concept was originally proposed by the American economist Henry George as a full and complete answer to the budgetary needs of a community. It was a single tax on land, whether it contained improvements or not. The effect would be to encourage growth and modernization by opening new opportunities to capital and increasing the production of wealth. The city of Fairhope, Alabama, is an example of a single tax community; the land is owned by the Fairhope Single Tax Corporation, which leases the land to members and nonmembers, who have complete control of its use as long as the lessee pays the annually appraised rent, or single tax.

General Welfare Clause   The clause in Article I, section 8 of the Constitution that authorizes Congress to levy and collect taxes to provide for the common defense and general welfare of the United States. *See also* CONSTITUTIONAL CONSTRUCTION, page 35; SOCIAL SECURITY CASES, page 522.

Significance   The general welfare clause appears to give Congress an unlimited spending power, but it has been a source of constitutional controversy. The issue is whether Congress can spend tax monies only for purposes authorized in other sections of the Constitution or whether the general welfare clause gives Congress an unlimited power to spend for whatever might contribute to the "common defense and general welfare." The former position has been held by the strict constructionists, the latter by the loose or liberal constructionists. The liberal constructionist view of the interpretation of the general welfare clause has prevailed, and the spending power as such has never been successfully challenged in the courts. The only limitation suggested by the Supreme Court (*United States v. Butler*, 297 U.S. 1 [1936]) was that taxes levied by Congress be spent for *national* welfare and not for the welfare of particular groups. The general welfare clause has enabled the national government to carry on programs in fields not specifically granted to it by the Constitution, as in the Social Security programs.

Gold Standard   A monetary system in which a nation's currency is backed by gold, has a standard of value measured in gold, and can be exchanged for gold. An international gold standard provides for free convertibility of currencies into gold and the unimpeded movement of gold bullion from one nation to another to pay international debts. The gold standard became universally accepted during the nineteenth and early twentieth centuries; the United States adopted it in 1900. In the worldwide Depression of the 1930s, the nations of the world discarded it, with the United States going off the gold standard in 1934. After World War II, much of the world functioned under a gold exchange standard system, through which central banks bought and sold national currencies backed by gold at a fixed price. Under this system, the American dollar became the major reserve and trading currency since it was freely exchanged into gold at a fixed rate. In the early 1970s, the Nixon administration ended the gold exchange standard system whereby foreign governments could no longer exchange dollars for gold at a fixed price. *See also* DEVALUATION, page 395; INTERNATIONAL MONETARY FUND, page 558.

Significance   The gold standard provided stability in domestic monetary systems, an "international currency," and a self-regulating payments system in international trade and finance for many years. The severe Depression of the 1930s, however, forced the major industrial countries, including the United States, to adopt flexible fiscal and employment policies based on "managed" paper currencies that were incompatible with the gold standard. In discarding the gold standard, Congress provided for calling in gold and gold coin in circulation and fixed the price at $35 for a fine ounce. By the late 1960s, the role of the dollar as a substitute for gold as an international medium of exchange was under considerable pressure. The International Monetary Fund tried to meet the crisis by creating "paper gold" in the form of special drawing rights (SDRs), and a two-tier governmental/private gold market was established in which the official American price was maintained in the governmental market but was permitted to fluctuate freely in the private market. In 1971, as a result of domestic inflation and heavy international pressure on the dollar, President Richard M. Nixon devalued the dollar in terms of gold and ended the free convertibility of dollars into gold at a fixed price. Thereafter, major currency values in the 30 industrialized capitalist countries have been adjusted largely by market conditions of supply and demand in a flexible exchange rate system. In 1974, Congress restored the right of American citizens to buy, hold, and sell gold at market prices, denied to them since the monetary crisis of 1933.

Grant-in-Aid   Funds made available by Congress to the state and local governments for expenditure in accordance with prescribed standards and conditions. State legislatures also make such grants to local governments. Some measure of supervision over the expenditure of the funds accompanies the grants. In addition, the receiving government is required to match the contribution dollar-for-dollar or in some other ratio. Highways, airports, agriculture, education, welfare, and health are among the major functions financed through the grant-in-aid device. *See also* BLOCK GRANT, page 388; COOPERATIVE FEDERALISM, page 37; FEDERAL AID HIGHWAY ACT, page 57; *Massachusetts v. Mellon,* page 56; MATCHING FUNDS, page 408.

Significance   Grants-in-aid make available the superior tax resources of the national government for financing activities administered by the state and local governments. This has enabled the national government to enter fields considered to be within the reserved power of the states. The states have accepted some national control because they need federal funds. Often, because state governments have been unwilling or unable to deal with pressing problems, people have turned to Washington for help. In recent years, this has also been true in local areas. This has enabled all sections of the country to benefit from governmental services that otherwise might be available only in wealthier states. In addition, states have been stimulated to undertake needed activities and improve their administrative and technical standards. The major disadvantage of the grant-in-aid system is that it transfers policy-making authority to the national government in areas formerly handled by state and local governments. Recipients have been burdened by the complexity and volume of paperwork involved in applying for, administering, and reporting grant funds. The grant-in-aid system, however, represents an alternative to extreme centralization of the administration of services. As another alternative, the Reagan administration began, in 1981, to emphasize the use of "block grants" that combine several grant-in-aid programs and permit states somewhat greater discretion in the allocation of federal funds. This new trend accelerated after the Republican Revolution of 1994, which signaled inter alia that grant-in-aid programs would continue but largely through block grant programs to state and local governments. This will occur especially in welfare, in which the states will have much greater control over programs and funds. However, budget reductions included in the new approach may result in decreases in all nationally funded programs.

Gross Domestic Product (GDP)   A measurement of a country's total annual output of the goods and services produced within its borders expressed in terms of the market value. Gross domestic product replaced the former analysis tool, gross national product (GNP), which included gross domestic product plus profits earned by American companies from operations of their overseas subsidiaries and other income from abroad. The Department of Commerce gathers GDP data on a quarterly basis and publishes it as an annual figure. The 1990 report marked the first time the government used the GDP to measure the nation's health. Other industrial countries also use the GDP.

Significance   The gross domestic product has become a major analytical tool for measuring a nation's economic well-being and for comparing progress within different countries and economic systems. A more accurate picture of economic progress, however, requires analysis of GDP in terms of constant dollars to avoid inflation- or deflation-caused price changes and also measurement of GDP on a per capita basis to take population changes into account in order to determine standards of living. Comparative economic growth rates are based on annual changes of GDP corrected for price changes. The U.S. GDP has grown from about $300 billion in 1949 to a figure estimated at $7 trillion in 1995, but much of the latter figure represents inflation since 1965. The year 1987 remains the base year the government uses for measuring changes in the GDP. Economists, in general, have praised the change from GNP to GDP as providing a more accurate guide to economic conditions within the United States, but some critics claim the GDP has shortcomings because rapid technological changes and the inability to measure these changes make it difficult to obtain a precise figure of economic growth for comparative analysis. Although the GNP can still be used as an analytical tool, the GDP has become the official economic measurement concept.

Income Tax   A tax levied on profits, salaries, rents, interest, dividends, and other income sources, less deductions permitted by law. The national government's income tax includes a tax on both individual income and corporate income, with different rates applicable to each. Most of the 50 states also levy income taxes, many applicable to both individual and corporate income. Many cities, because of increasing resistance to higher property taxes, have adopted an income tax. *See also* FLAT TAX, page 402; SIXTEENTH AMENDMENT, page 417; UNITED STATES TAX COURT, page 424; WITHHOLDING TAX, page 421.

Significance   The individual income tax is based on ability to pay and provides for progressive or graduated tax-rate increases as income increases. The federal tax rate currently starts at 15 percent and, for most taxpayers, jumps to 28 percent. The top tax rate for those with higher incomes is 39.6 percent. In 1981, Congress provided for an indexing of taxes to inflationary price increases starting in 1985. The income tax's major weakness results from its complicated nature and the successful efforts of various pressure groups to riddle it with exemptions and loopholes. The majority of taxpayers pay through the payroll withholding system. The individual income tax is the major source of revenue for the national government, with the corporate income tax being the next most important source. The two together have provided about 70 percent of total national tax receipts in recent years. A windfall profits tax enacted in 1980 to capture some of the benefits reaped by a tenfold increase in oil prices has provided a substantial supplemental source of income. In the states, the income tax, including individual and corporate, is the third largest source of revenue. Increased use of income taxes by the states or by local governments is hampered by public opposition to additional taxes on incomes. In the Economic Recovery Tax Act of 1981, a huge reduction in federal tax rates was provided, with special reductions for business. Whereas the 1981 tax tended to shift the burden from higher-income to lower-income taxpayers, the Tax Reform Act of 1986 reversed this action by granting relief to millions of low-income people, who are no longer required to file a return, and boosted taxes for corporations and some individuals at the high-income levels. Budget cuts for the IRS in 1995 led to the elimination of the super random audit while increasing the number of general audits.

Indexing   A contractual system by which the amounts of monetary payments or receipts are adjusted periodically on the basis of changes that have occurred in the nation's cost of living index. In the United States, indexation is usually referred to as COLA (cost of living adjustment). Indexing is aimed at avoiding the financial catastrophes or injustices that occur as a result of the impact of heavy inflationary or deflationary factors on the national economy. In a collective bargaining contract, for example, provision may be made that, if the Consumer Price Index (CPI) rises 10 percent annually, all workers covered by the contract will receive an automatic 10 percent increase in their wages in addition to any other benefits owed to them. *See also* DEFLATION, page 395; INFLATION, page 406.

Significance   Indexing systems have developed in the United States largely as a response to heavy inflationary pressures. Brazil and Israel are examples of countries that have attempted—with some measure of success—large-scale national indexing systems in efforts to adjust their economies to major inflation. Inflation rates, however, have continued to skyrocket in both countries. With the advent of double-digit inflation in the United States in the 1970s, indexing became commonly associated with such monetary contractual relationships as labor-management agreements, insurance policies, business contracts for future delivery, and private pension systems. In 1972, Congress applied indexing to the Social Security system and other entitlement programs by providing that pensions and survivor's benefits be increased automatically each year in the same proportion that prices had increased during the prior year. In 1981, Congress applied indexing to income tax payments, so that taxpayers would not have to pay at a higher tax rate on their inflation-boosted incomes after 1985. During a period of deflation, the benefits of indexing would be reversed, and the other party in each contractual arrangement would gain.

Inflation   An economic condition in which the price level is increased and the value of money in terms of purchasing power is consequently decreased. Theories that seek to explain and correct inflation abound. Inflation may result from an increase in the amount of money and credit available or a decrease in the supply of consumer goods, with the result that consumers tend to bid up prices ("demand-pull" inflation). A second source of inflation is rapidly increasing costs of production, such as raw materials, wages, and energy ("cost-push" inflation). A third source ("profit-pull" inflation) occurs when lack of competition permits powerful corporations to seek additional profits by raising prices or by maintaining them at artificially high levels when their costs are going down. Mass psychological factors are also a characteristic ingredient of inflation, regardless of causes. Once under way, inflation is difficult to deal with because reinforcement factors encourage it to "feed on itself." *See also* DEFLATION, page 395; INDEXING, page 406; MONETARY POLICY, page 410.

Significance   Most economists believe that serious inflation—an increase in the price level of more than 5 percent per year—can be prevented through proper use of monetary policy by the Federal Reserve Board and the Treasury Department, and by fiscal policy, such as providing for balanced federal budgets and increased taxes. The trade-offs involved in limiting inflation to 5 percent or less per year, however, may involve such politically undesirable factors as heavy unemployment and economic slowdown. Although the effects of inflation are largely internal, a nation suffering from serious inflation may jeopardize its foreign markets with a resulting disequilibrium in its balance of international payments and a serious threat to the international exchange value of its currency. Within a nation, although debtors find that inflation may make it easier for them to repay their creditors, persons living on fixed incomes and those with little job-bargaining power typically suffer the most. In the early 1970s, the Nixon administration first tried to control the serious Vietnam War–caused inflation by orthodox monetary and fiscal measures, then adopted a new economic policy and imposed a wage-price freeze. Wage-price controls were never fully implemented, and the nation suffered its most serious inflation since the Korean War period. By the mid-1970s, skyrocketing world oil prices and a global food and raw materials shortage made inflation between 10 and 25 percent a worldwide phenomenon. In the United States, the economy suffered simultaneously from a recession (stagnation) and from inflation, an atypical condition dubbed "stagflation" by economists. In the 1980s, though the Consumer Price Index rose 64 percent, inflation was brought under control in the latter half of that decade through a tight monetary policy administered by the Federal Reserve Board. Inflationary pressures were also reduced by a world oil glut that substantially reduced energy prices. The nation, however, failed to reach the goal set by the Humphrey-Hawkins Act of 1978, which called for zero inflation by 1988, a year in which it was 4.4 percent. In 1990, Iraq's seizure of Kuwait and the threat of a major war doubled crude oil prices and sent global inflation rates soaring. These subsided, however, following the successful Gulf War against Iraq in the "Desert Storm" action of 1991.

Keynesianism   A philosophy and practice of utilizing the machinery of government, through fiscal and monetary policies, to guide and direct a free enterprise economy. Keynesianism, based on the principles and analyses propounded by the British economist John Maynard Keynes, seeks to improve rather than replace capitalism by providing an orderly, predictable pattern of economic activity based on economic indicators utilized by policymakers. Techniques used by Keynesians to manage a state's economy, as set forth in Keynes's classic, *The General Theory of Employment, Interest, and Money* (in 1936), include government control and direction of such matters as budgeting, spending, tax policy, interest rates, and credit availability. Keynesianism substitutes rational decisions made by state leaders in pursuit of specific social goals for the undirected free interplay of market forces that characterizes a laissez-faire approach. Keynes recognized oversaving as one of the fundamental problems of a capitalistic system, and Keynesian policymakers tend to prescribe government programs to alleviate the problem by stimulating the movement of savings into investment and mass consumer purchasing. In this way, Keynes focused on the role of government through fiscal policy to correct the imbalance between *potential* output (controlled by supply factors) and *actual* output (determined by the aggregate demand of consumers, investors, and government). *See also* EMPLOYMENT ACT OF 1946, page 427; FISCAL POLICY, page 400; MONETARISM, page 409; MONETARY POLICY, page 410.

Significance Keynesianism, which contains the basic framework of contemporary macroeconomic theory, has been adopted as state policy in most of the advanced, industrial states of the capitalist world. In the United States, the national government began playing a Keynesian role at the end of World War II. Presidents increasingly have made decisions concerning the national economy on the basis of recommendations offered by economic advisers who have been greatly influenced by Keynesian theories. By managing a nation's economy, Keynesians seek to avoid cyclical movements, stagnation, heavy unemployment, and serious inflation, while at the same time encouraging economic growth and general economic well-being. In the United States, fiscal policy with emphasis on deficit spending carried out by the President and Congress and monetary policy with emphasis on easy credit developed by the Federal Reserve System have served as the main tools for implementing Keynesian economic policies. During the 1970s, however, overstimulation produced serious inflation and, simultaneously, a high level of unemployment. This "stagflation" challenged economic policymakers because the Keynesian prescription for stagnation or unused economic capacity is governmental stimulation of the economy, whereas the cure for inflation is substantial destimulation. Nevertheless, Reagan administration deficit spending on a massive scale—along with easier money and credit, lower taxes, and heavy government spending for the military—helped to move the nation's economy out of a major recession in the early 1980s. Some Keynesians believe, based on the experience of the 1980s, that deficit public and private spending provides a means for avoiding or at least postponing a serious economic recession because of its stimulative effect on the nation's economy. In the long run, however, multi-trillion-dollar debt threatens the stability of the entire economic system.

Legal Tender Any medium of exchange that by law must be accepted in payment of a debt. The Constitution gives the national government full control over the nation's money, and it forbids the states to "make anything but gold and silver coin a tender in payment of debts" (Art. I, sec. 10). *See also* LEGAL TENDER CASES, page 425.

Significance A major legal controversy developed during the first century of American history as to whether the national government could issue fiat notes not backed by the precious metals as legal tender. A series of cases was climaxed in 1884 by *Juilliard v. Greenman*, 110 U.S. 421, in which the Supreme Court declared that Congress has full power to issue notes as legal tender in the payment of debts. The states for many years authorized state-chartered banks to issue notes for circulation as currency, but not as legal tender. Although these issuances did not violate the Constitution, Congress regarded them as a danger to monetary uniformity and stability. In 1865, Congress levied a 10 percent tax upon state notes that was sustained by the Supreme Court (*Veazie Bank v. Fenno,* 8 Wallace 533 [1869]) and that drove all state notes out of circulation.

Matching Funds A financial agreement between two levels of government by which one level agrees to provide specific amounts of money for a program, activity, or project if the other will provide specific amounts of money for the same purpose. Matching funds are involved in federal-state, federal-local, and state-local arrangements. For example, if a new city sewage disposal plant will cost $5 million, the national government may encourage the city to build it by offering to pay $4 million of the cost if the city will pay the remaining $1 million. Contributions by a participating state or local government may take the form of "in-kind matching"—that is, may consist of personnel, equipment, or facilities valued at the amount required under the agreement. *See also* BLOCK GRANT, page 388; GRANT-IN-AID, page 404.

Significance   Most state and local projects and activities are currently undertaken through "block grant" and matching funds financial arrangements. Revenue-sharing funds, however, may not be used directly or indirectly to obtain federal money under any matching funds agreement between the national government and state or local units. That means that state and local governments must raise their share of matching funds from their own tax programs. The matching funds technique has successfully encouraged cooperation among many governmental units in the American federal system, and it has provided a means by which higher levels of governments have been able to stimulate lower levels into undertaking new programs or activities. In the 1980s, most federal-state and federal-local matching funds programs were greatly reduced or eliminated by President Reagan's efforts to lower nonmilitary spending. When the Republicans gained control of Congress after the 1994 election, they sought to reduce such outlays further in an effort to achieve a balanced federal budget.

Monetarism   A school of economic thought based on the principles of laissez-faire and the use of monetary policy by government to determine the quantity of money in the system. Monetarists argue that the money supply provided by government is the key variable affecting the performance of the economy. Inflation, monetarists believe, is caused by an explosive growth in the money supply, whereas economic stagnation and high unemployment are caused by a too-rapid shrinkage of the quantity of money available. The monetarist holds that there should be a restrained but steady growth in the money supply, enough to encourage growth and prosperity, but not so much as to encourage inflation. Unlike Keynesianism, which places major emphasis on managing *demand* through government fiscal policy, monetarism seeks to encourage supply or production and rejects huge government budgets and deficit spending as unnecessary and unwise. Manipulation of the economy by Keynesians in efforts to avoid booms and busts adds to the nation's problems, according to monetarists. The latter place their faith in time-tested workings of the marketplace and the interaction of supply and demand. *See also* KEYNESIANISM, page 407; MONETARY POLICY, page 410.

Significance   Monetarism is based on the theories set forth by the "Chicago School" of economists headed by Nobel Prize winner Milton Friedman. Monetarism developed as a reaction against governmental deficit-spending and economy-manipulating policies pursued by Keynesians and neo-Keynesians. Functioning as a new conservatism, monetarism seeks to apply the classical ideas and ideals of laissez-faire to modern economies. The main reason for its emergence as an alternative to Keynesianism was the inability of the Keynesians to deal effectively with the massive wave of inflation that engulfed much of the world in the 1970s and 1980s. By providing for a slow but steady increase in the quantity of money inserted into an economy by the government, monetarists believe that inflation can be slowly but surely brought under control. Keynesians, however, reject the ideas of monetarism on the grounds that severely restricting the money supply will cause great economic hardship, will probably result in a prolonged recession, and will be unlikely to cure inflation. Most of the recent Nobel Prize winners in Economics have been members of the Chicago monetarist school.

Monetary Policy   Government policy that aims at affecting the amount of currency in circulation and the availability of credit. In implementing monetary policy, the Federal Reserve (or "Fed") makes decisions concerning, for example, the operations of the banking system and the rate of interest charged borrowers. The Federal Reserve Board uses "tight money" policies to restrain and prolong boom periods in the nation's economy and to fight inflation. "Loose money" policies are used to check deflation and to fight recessions by making money and credit more freely available. *See also* FEDERAL RESERVE SYSTEM, page 400; FISCAL POLICY, page 400; KEYNESIANISM, page 407.

Significance   In the post–World War II period, Federal Reserve monetary policies have been employed in fighting recessions and restraining economic booms. The use of such policies must be delicately and expertly handled lest a serious deflationary or inflationary spiral be touched off or a downturn in the economy occur. In pursuing a tight money policy, the Federal Reserve Board decreases the availability of money and credit by raising member bank's reserve requirements, by raising the rediscount rate, and by selling government securities through its Open Market Committee. The Federal Reserve Board pursues policies exactly the opposite of these when loose money policies are called for. Monetary policy is particularly effective when harmonized with fiscal policies initiated by the President and Congress and when aimed at the same objectives.

Open Market Operations   Buying and selling governmental securities, bills of exchange, and other commercial paper by the Federal Open Market Committee. The committee is composed of the Board of Governors of the Federal Reserve System and five directors of the Federal Reserve banks chosen annually by the boards of directors. *See also* FEDERAL RESERVE SYSTEM, page 400.

Significance   The Federal Open Market Committee operations facilitate commerce and business and stabilize credit in the United States. Its functions are particularly useful in implementing the monetary policies determined by the Federal Reserve Board. For example, when inflation threatens, the committee sells government securities and commercial paper in the open market to restrict the availability of credit; when deflation or recession threatens, the committee buys so as to make credit more easily available through member banks. The committee's open market operations are supplemented by other instruments of monetary policy, such as fixing the discount rate and reserve requirements for member banks.

Performance Budget   The drawing up of a plan for anticipated expenditures based on the activities, services, and functions (that is, *units* of work) performed by government, rather than allotting funds on the basis of items to be purchased and salaries to be paid by each department and agency. *See also* BUDGET, page 390; OFFICE OF MANAGEMENT AND BUDGET, page 423.

Significance   Based on the recommendations of the Hoover Commission, Congress adopted the principle of the performance budget in the Budget and Accounting Procedures Act of 1950. Since 1951, the Bureau of the Budget (now the Office of Management and Budget) has drawn up much of the budget on a performance basis. The major advantage of the performance budget is that by detailing how and for what government functions funds are expended, it gives a clearer accounting for evaluation than the itemization system. Performance budgeting has been developed by some state and local governments into program budgeting that evaluates expenditures on the basis of their effectiveness in achieving *program* objectives. Performance and program budgeting attempt to evaluate appropriations and expenditures on the basis of how they relate to the larger purposes of an agency or other unit, rather than viewing them as a set of separate expense items.

Personal Property Tax   A tax levied on things of value other than real property. Personal property is usually classified as tangible or intangible. On the one hand, tangibles include valuables of substance such as business inventories, machinery, jewelry, and household goods. Intangible property, on the other hand, includes a right, claim, or interest of value, such as found in bonds, stocks, and bank accounts. *See also* ASSESSED VALUATION, page 386; PROPERTY TAX, page 412.

Significance   Property is usually classified for tax purposes, with the tax on personal property applied at a different rate than that on real property. Personal property tax collection involves considerable administrative work, particularly in getting the owners to declare their property for tax purposes or, if they do not, of finding it. This becomes an almost hopeless task when levying the tax on intangible properties that can easily be concealed from the assessor's eyes. Often, the value of such intangibles as stocks and bonds exceeds the value of real estate and tangibles, yet the taxes levied upon them depend almost entirely on the personal honesty of the individual taxpayer. Most personal property taxes are levied by local governments and are paid mainly by business and industry.

Progressive Tax   Any tax in which the tax *rates* increase as the tax *base* (that is, the amount subject to be taxed) increases. A progressive income tax, for example, might provide for a 10 percent rate on the first $5,000 of income, a 25 percent rate on the second $5,000, and so forth, with, characteristically, a maximum rate for all income over a certain level. It is the opposite of a regressive tax, in which tax rates remain uniform or decline as the tax base increases. A progressive tax, therefore, is one that is based essentially on ability to pay. A progressive tax *system* may incorporate both progressive and regressive types of taxes but on balance tends to place the major tax-paying burden on those most able to pay. *See also* ABILITY VERSUS BENEFIT THEORY, page 386; INCOME TAX, page 405; REGRESSIVE TAX, page 415.

Significance　Progressive taxes levied by the national and state governments include the individual and corporate income taxes and the estate and gift taxes. Progressive taxes are based on the principle of ability to pay, as reflected, for example, in the federal individual income tax, in which percentage rates in the mid-1990s ranged from 15 percent to 39.6 percent on taxable income, with most individuals in the 28 percent bracket. Supporters of progressive taxation regard it as an equitable means of securing necessary government income. Opponents claim that it penalizes initiative and success. Other critics claim that its ostensibly progressive nature is offset by loopholes and special benefits available to individuals and corporations with high incomes.

Property Tax　An ad valorem (according to value) tax levied on real or personal, tangible or intangible property. The general property tax is levied by local units of government throughout the country, and most states make limited use of some form of the tax. The tax process includes assessment of property valuations, determination of tax rates (millage), tax computation, and tax collection. To correct injustices, boards of review on the local level adjust inequalities in assessments. Where the taxing jurisdiction crosses political boundaries, central assessment or equalization is often provided to avoid geographical inequities. *See also* ASSESSED VALUATION, page 386; BOARD OF REVIEW, page 389; EQUALIZATION, page 398.

Significance　The general property tax provides the fiscal foundation for local units of government across the nation. In recent years, it has provided about 85 percent of the tax revenues for cities, counties, school districts, towns, townships, villages, and other local units. For many years, the general property tax was the nation's major source of revenue, exceeding other state and national levies, until the twentieth century's many crises boosted income and sales taxes. The general property tax has come increasingly under attack in recent years because of difficulties and conflicts involved in assessment, equalization, and exemptions. The flexibility of the tax as a source of revenue has nearly reached exhaustion in many localities because of constitutional or statutory limitations, popular rejections of tax increase referendums, and heavy property tax loads resulting from failure to use other tax sources. The Supreme Court has held that the fact that some children's education is more adequately financed than that of others does not serve to invalidate the property tax as the chief means of financing schools (*San Antonio Independent School District v. Rodriguez* 411 U.S. 1 [1973]). The Court in 1969 held that a state law that permits only "property-taxpayers" to vote on local revenue bond issues violates equal protection guarantees (*Cipriano v. City of Houma,* 395 U.S. 701).

Public Debt　The total indebtedness, including accrued interest, of a government or of a country, the latter embracing the indebtedness of all its units of government. The public debt of the United States government is usually referred to as the "national debt." Whenever expenditures exceed revenue during a fiscal year, the deficit is added to the public debt; when revenue exceeds expenditures, the public debt is reduced by the amount of the surplus. Part of the U.S. national debt is carried by the public through the purchase of short- and long-term treasury bonds; the remainder is financed through the Federal Reserve Banking System and by foreign creditors. The Treasury

Department's Bureau of the Public Debt is charged with responsibility for managing the national public debt. *See also* DEBT LIMIT, page 393; DEFICIT SPENDING, page 394; GRIDLOCK, page 79.

Significance   Over a period of four decades of frequently unbalanced budgets, the United States has built up a national public debt of sizable proportions. The national debt rose from about $16 billion ($132 per capita) in 1930 to over $43 billion ($367 per capita) in 1940 as a result of deficit financing to stimulate the stagnated economy of the Great Depression. By 1950, it had risen to $257 billion ($1,697 per capita) through the financing of World War II and part of the Korean War; from that point, it rose to a level of more than $370 billion ($1,806 per capita) in 1970 because of financing defense programs and combating five post–World War II recessions. By 1980, the national debt had soared to over $800 billion ($4,000 per capita) as a result of massive deficits by which the Nixon, Ford, and Carter administrations sought to stimulate the sluggish economy. By 1990, annual deficits—some exceeding $200 billion—pushed the national debt to over $3.2 trillion (more than $13,000 per capita). In the early 1990s, Congress expanded the permanent debt ceiling to $3.444 trillion in expectation of continuing huge budget deficits, and in 1996 Congress raised the debt ceiling to $5.3 trillion. Much controversy has arisen concerning the rapid rise of the national debt in recent years. Some economists view the debt as a useful governmental weapon for stabilizing the economy, adding to it by "pump-priming" (deficit spending) during economic downturns and retiring portions of it through surpluses during periods of prosperity to reduce the threat of inflation. Some students of finance are relatively unconcerned about the size of the debt, pointing out that "we owe it to ourselves." In other words, much of the debt constitutes an investment for the future of the American people, and that the debt has actually not grown excessively in recent years if measured in relation to the gross domestic product. The concerned, however, regard the "owe it to ourselves" argument as specious and contend that future generations of Americans will suffer from our excessive spending and that the size of the debt threatens not only economic solvency but national security as well. During the 1980s, despite cuts in social programs, the Reagan administration's budgets added large amounts to the national public debt, especially because of tax cuts and large increases in defense spending. The Gramm-Rudman-Hollings Debt Reduction Act of 1985 (GRH) sought to require a balanced budget by providing that if the Congress and President did not progressively eliminate the deficit by meeting annual reduction targets, such reductions would occur automatically through a process known as "sequestration." In 1986, however, the Supreme Court ruled unconstitutional the procedure for achieving automatic spending cuts, holding that the assignment of reduction authority to the Comptroller General violated the separation of powers doctrine (*Bowsher v. Synar,* 478 U.S. 714). Thereafter, a revised GRH was passed by Congress that changed the procedure to comply with the Court's objections, reduced the size of the annual reductions, and extended the deadline for achieving a balanced budget from 1991 to 1993. The GRH Act failed to achieve its goals and was not applied after 1990. When in 1994 the Republicans won control of Congress, one of their main objectives embodied in their Contract with America was to achieve a balanced budget in seven years. In the more than 200 years since the first budget was formulated in 1789, only

19 have had surpluses. Some critics claim that deficit spending is a "crutch" for capitalism and that achieving a balanced budget is both politically and economically extremely difficult. During the 1995 budget crisis, President Bill Clinton noted that the U.S. national debt, in relation to the GDP, was smaller than that of any other country in the world with the exception of Norway. Past behavior makes predictions concerning a balanced budget problematical at best.

Recession/Depression   Economists define a "recession" as a short-term decline of at least two quarters in duration in a nation's business cycle; a depression is an economic slump of greater proportions, of longer duration, and having a more serious impact, with massive unemployment, greatly reduced GDP, and a sharply reduced willingness to invest. *See also* BUSINESS CYCLE, page 391; FEDERAL RESERVE SYSTEM, page 400.

Significance   The American economy has experienced numerous recessions of varying severity; nine since the end of World War II. These postwar slumps occurred in the following years: 1948–49, 1953–54, 1957–58, 1960–61, 1969–70, 1973–75, 1980, 1981–82, and 1990–91. Three of these—1957–58, 1973–75, and 1981–82—were particularly severe. All previous downturns in the economy were dwarfed by the Great Depression of the decade of the 1930s, which was global in its scope and impact. Because of its drastic effect on American society, many efforts have been made to understand why the capitalistic–free enterprise economy could tolerate such a massive upheaval in its economic life. Controversy continues over why and how the Depression happened and how we can prevent or cure its happening again. Conservatives believe that the Great Depression was caused by a failure to live within our income, to balance our private and public budgets, and to reduce rather than increase our national debt. For them, payment of debts and living within one's income would contribute to the stability of the nation's economy and avoid serious recessions or depressions. Liberals have a different approach. For them, the Great Depression was a product of oversaving. Needed were policies aimed at stimulating the nation's economy and resolving the overproduction/underconsumption conundrum. Proof could allegedly be found in the way deficit spending on military equipment contributed to the change from the lowest to the highest economic growth rates in American history. Classical economic theory held that recessions are inevitable in a free enterprise economy and that self-correcting economic forces set into motion would, in time, provide adjustments without governmental interference. Today, economic theory and analysis are aimed at preventing a recession, and most economists believe that government monetary and fiscal policies can prevent or quickly remedy a serious downturn if they are wisely used. The nine post–World War II economic recessions have been attacked with monetary and fiscal measures, and the serious downturns in the economy have been arrested and reversed before they could assume depression proportions.

Reconciliation   A legislative process that enables Congress to decentralize responsibility for effecting budget cuts. The reconciliation process begins with the enactment of an omnibus reconciliation savings bill or resolution that requires standing committees to reduce the authorizations for programs under their jurisdictions. The committee in each case determines which programs should be cut or eliminated, and these decisions are reported to its parent body, the House or Senate. All reductions are then lumped together into a megabill on which members can vote only "yes" or "no" but cannot amend. *See also* AUTHORIZATION, page 130; BUDGET, page 390.

Significance   Theoretically, reconciliation can be an effective tool for the Congress when substantial reductions in the budget are needed in most or all programs. Without public support for reducing programs, however, the reconciliation process may fail. In each case, the standing committee having jurisdiction over substantive programs makes the de facto decisions for budget cuts rather than leaving it up to the House and Senate. The process gained acceptance in 1981 when the Reagan administration determined that the country was in a fiscal and inflationary crisis and that substantial reductions must be made in existing and future budgets. Reconciliation resulted in Congress making substantial budget authority cuts on domestic programs each fiscal year during the 1980s. Huge military spending increases, however, offset these cuts, and despite reconciliation tactics, enormous annual budget deficits resulted.

Regressive Tax   Any tax in which the burden falls relatively more heavily upon low-income groups than upon wealthy taxpayers. It is the opposite of a progressive tax, in which tax rates increase as ability to pay increases. *See also* PROGRESSIVE TAX, page 411; SALES TAX, page 416.

Significance   Regressive taxes are used mainly by the state and local governments and include, for example, the sales tax and the uniform or declining rate income tax. Such taxes take a higher percentage of the total income of low-income groups than of high-income groups, even though the rates are uniform. Sales taxes on the necessities of life are probably the most regressive in nature, since a major portion of the expenditures of low-income families is for such commodities. Graduated income taxes, generally regarded as the most progressive type of tax, can also be substantially regressive in their impact as a result of exemptions and deductions favoring high-income groups.

Regulatory Tax   A tax levied for purposes other than the raising of revenue. A protective tariff is a clear example of regulatory tax. More subtle uses of taxing power for nonrevenue regulatory purposes include restricting the marketing of a product (the heavy tax on margarine once levied to maintain the butter market) or adding to the government's arsenal against illegal or undesirable activities (a tax on gambling operations), sometimes called a "sumptuary tax." *See also Veazie Bank v. Fenno,* page 426.

Significance   Most taxes have a regulatory function even when levied primarily for revenue. The income tax, for example, affects the distribution of wealth and is used to promote specific fiscal policies. With rare exceptions, the courts will not question the motives of the legislature in levying a tax. A regulatory tax may be used to reinforce an existing power of government or to reach a problem for which no direct legislative authority exists. For example, a heavy tax on an undesirable commodity may keep it off the market though no power exists to do so directly. Also, a tax levied by one level of government may help another to enforce its laws. The federal tax on gambling devices, for example, helps states enforce antigambling laws. Some have suggested that drugs be legalized but their regulation be continued, with taxes levied on various aspects of the drug trade and income from drug sales taxed at a rate to discourage their use.

Reserve Ratio   The percentage of liquid assets held by a bank as a reserve for its deposits. The *legal* reserve ratio is that percentage set by government to ensure that banks will maintain a safe proportion of ready cash to meet depositors' demands for their money. Under the Federal Reserve System, the legal reserve requirement is set for the member banks within each district by the Federal Reserve Board of Governors. Reserve requirements for state banks are usually set by law in each state. *See also* FEDERAL RESERVE SYSTEM, page 400.

Significance   Legal reserve requirements are set by government to protect the accounts of individual depositors. Through the Federal Reserve System, the government additionally obtains a powerful means of carrying out monetary policy and maintaining stability with flexibility in the monetary system. When deflation or economic recessions threaten, the Federal Reserve Board can free money and credit to stimulate business by lowering the reserve requirements of member banks. When inflation threatens, or it is desirable to restrain an economic boom, the Board reduces the availability of money and credit to business and consumers by raising reserve requirements. Along with its open market operations and its discount function, the setting of reserve ratio requirements is a major monetary tool that helps the Board set the general direction and tone of the American economy.

Revolving Fund   An operational fund established for a governmental agency carrying on proprietary (business-type) functions that make the agency financially self-supporting, or nearly so. Through one form of "backdoor financing," for example, income from the agency's operation is not turned in to the Treasury Department but is spent directly by the agency. The Tennessee Valley Authority (TVA), for example, uses its revenue from electric power sales to finance its continuing operations and its expansion programs. "Backdoor financing" obviously tends to weaken the traditional controls over the purse strings exercised by legislative bodies. *See also* PROPRIETARY FUNCTION, page 453.

Significance   A revolving fund gives a public business enterprise the financial flexibility to carry out long-range programs. Agencies ordinarily cannot plan operations beyond those approved by Congress in its annual appropriations, and a revolving fund frees the agency from this kind of dependence. The revolving fund principle has been followed especially in federal lending agencies. Critics object to the lack of control over agencies that use a revolving fund, and some regard competition from such agencies as a threat to private enterprise.

Sales Tax   A tax levied upon the sale of commodities, usually paid by the purchaser. The sales tax may apply generally to all commodities, or it may be restricted to certain classifications or specific commodities. Typically, the sales tax is levied on retail sales, but in some cases it is imposed on sales by manufacturers and wholesalers as well. Closely related to the sales tax is the "use" tax, which applies to purchases made outside the taxing jurisdiction and is designed to prevent state residents from avoiding the sales tax through out-of-state purchases. Most of the 50 states levy sales taxes from 3 to 7.5 percent, and an increasing number of cities also levy sales taxes. A value-added tax (VAT), imposed by Canada and most European countries, is a special type of sales tax in which each stage of production and distribution of the product is taxed, with the consumer paying the ultimate cost of all the value-added taxes. *See also* REGRESSIVE TAX, page 415; TAX INCIDENCE, page 420.

Significance   Most of the states that levy a sales tax adopted it during the depression of the 1930s, when they were under heavy obligation to meet rising welfare and general government costs. The sales tax has become the single most important source of state revenue. Most opposition to the sales tax centers around its regressive character, which places a heavy tax burden upon low-income groups. Some states have sought to reduce its regressive impact by exempting food, clothing, medicine, or other necessities. Support for the sales tax is based on the idea that all citizens should contribute to the support of government and that the sales tax makes this possible because all persons are consumers. The Tax Reform Act of 1986, however, reduced the appeal of sales taxes by eliminating them as a tax deduction on the federal income tax return. Supporters of a federal VAT for the United States argue that it would reward efficiency and encourage capital formation, savings, and investment. Critics claim that VAT would reduce the purchasing power of American consumers and lead to more frequent and more severe recessions. Moreover, Americans generally are strongly opposed to any new taxes, however logical or necessary they may be. A national sales tax is one of the options being considered as a replacement or supplement to the income tax.

Severance Tax   A tax levied upon natural resources at the time they are taken from the land or water. Severance taxes are used by many states for both revenue and conservation purposes. *See also* CONSERVATION, page 481; REGULATORY TAX, page 415.

Significance   Conservation objectives can be achieved through a severance tax by adjusting tax rates to control the "severing" of timber, minerals, and other resources from the soil. Some states accomplish the same purpose without a severance tax per se by, for example, exempting timberland from the general property tax until the timber has been harvested.

Sixteenth Amendment   A Constitutional amendment, adopted in 1913, granting Congress the power to levy taxes on incomes without apportioning them among the states according to population. The individual income tax levied by the national government is based on the power granted by this amendment. *See also* INCOME TAX, page 405; *Pollock v. Farmers Loan and Trust Co.,* page 425.

Significance   The Sixteenth Amendment resulted from a Supreme Court decision that a federal income tax is a direct tax that, under Article I, section 9, must be appportioned among the states according to population

(*Pollock v. Farmers Loan and Trust Co.,* 158 U.S. 601 [1895]). Although a Civil War income tax levy had been upheld by the Supreme Court as an indirect tax, the 1895 decision reversed this view. The controversy, however, continued. The Sixteenth Amendment put aside the question of whether income taxes are direct or indirect by giving Congress blanket power to lay and collect taxes on income "from whatever source derived," without any apportionment or regard to any census. Without this amendment, income taxes apportioned among the states according to population would have been manifestly unfair because of the vast differences in income among the states, and Congress refused to levy such a tax. Since 1913, the individual and corporation income taxes have become the major sources for federal revenue.

Special Assessment   A charge made by a government against a property owner for that part of the cost of public improvements made adjacent to his or her property that are especially useful or beneficial to this property. Special assessments are different from taxes in that the improvements have been petitioned for by a majority of the landowners concerned. *See also* ABILITY VERSUS BENEFIT THEORY, page 386.

Significance   Special assessments are used mainly by local governments to provide homeowners with facilities such as paved streets, sewers, and sidewalks. A portion of the cost of such improvements is borne by the local government out of taxes. This is a recognition that the improvements are beneficial to the community as well as to the individual landowner. Such projects are financed through special assessment bonds, which are backed by the government's power to assess for public improvements. The property owner typically makes annual payments for a period of ten to twenty years for interest and to retire the assessment debt.

Supply-side Economics   An economic approach that emphasizes the importance of the role played by business and industry in promoting prosperity in the general economy of the nation by increasing production. Supply-side economics typically calls for reducing taxes on business, encouraging savings and investments through positive governmental actions, and generally providing a positive rather than a negative climate for business and industrial operations. These programs are based on the assumption that the increasing productivity and expanded output resulting from supply-side policies will cure unemployment and inflation and generally stimulate the nation's economy to full health. Moreover, it is assumed (using the Laffer curve) that tax reductions to business will stimulate tax revenues because of increased prosperity and thus restore balance to the nation's budget. *See also* KEYNESIANISM, page 407; MONETARISM, page 409.

Significance   Supply-side economics was espoused by President Ronald Reagan and his economic advisers. As a result, it was usually referred to as "Reaganomics." It is another way of expounding the "trickle-down" theory of economics, which holds that policies favorable to business and industry will result in a trickling down of prosperity so that all benefit. It stands in opposition to consumer-based economic theories—sometimes referred to as the "bubble up" or "percolate up" approach to economic stimulation—which seek to increase the purchasing power of low-income groups through government programs, assuming that this will benefit all segments of the economy, including business and industry. In Congress, conservatives have generally supported the supply-side approach, whereas liberals have usually placed their main emphasis on boosting consumption. The huge budget deficits in the 1980s tended to discredit the Laffer curve approach to stimulating tax revenues and raised serious questions about supply-side economics as an approach to solving the nation's economic problems. Politically, however, supply-side economics was a 1980s success, contributing substantially to the elections of President Ronald Reagan and President George Bush. Economically, it failed to deliver on its promise to increase the GDP growth, raise productivity rates, balance the nation's budget, and increase national savings. Studies show that each of these critical economic areas suffered in relation to their performance during the 1970s.

Tax Equity   The question of fairness that arises whenever new taxes or tax rates are considered. Tax equity involves issues over incidence, directness, progressivity, purpose, exemptions, offsets, nature, and type. This means, basically, who pays what, why, when, and how much.

Significance   Issues involving questions of tax equity permeate the political process in every domestic system. In the United States, tax issues are involved in almost every election at all three levels of government—national, state, and local. Frequently, the issue is how to balance the budget, whether through spending reductions or tax increases. Studies have shown that, in the decade of the 1980s, much of the overall tax burden was shifted from the wealthy to the poor. This regressivity has been defended on the ground that lower taxes for the rich provide more capital for investment, which boosts economic growth, thereby creating jobs and prosperity. In 1990, for example, tax reductions under the Tax Reform Act of 1986 barely reduced federal income taxes for the poorest fifth of the nation's taxpayers, whereas the top 1 percent of taxpayers received a very substantial reduction, with the Act's supporters claiming an "equity" victory. Critics claim that under the Reagan and Bush administration policies, the richest fifth of American families increased their after-tax income in 1990 over 1980 an average of almost 32 percent, whereas the poorest fifth's income dropped by 3.2 percent. Social Security taxes tend to be highly regressive because they are levied at a flat percentage rate and apply only up to a certain level of income ($62,700 in 1996). In addition, only employment income is taxed for Social Security purposes and not income from profits, capital gains, interest, and dividends. Today, about 75 percent of Americans pay more in Social Security taxes (after including their employer's share) than they pay in income taxes. State and local taxes are also highly regressive because of heavy dependence on sales taxes, flat-rate income taxes, and property taxes. Critics warn that the lack of equity in these kinds of taxes on all three government levels led to the Great Depression of the 1930s. Supporters of the Reagan and Bush administrations argue that these policies produced unprecedented prosperity and economic growth during the 1980s. In recent years, Republicans have sought to substantially reduce or eliminate the capital gains tax on the grounds that this action would increase investment, create jobs, and generally stimulate the nation's economy. This position has gained support because millions of Americans have invested in the stock markets and in other investment opportunities and receive capital gains income. They resent what many consider double taxation and therefore seek repeal of the capital gains tax.

Tax Exemption   The privilege granted by a government legally freeing certain types of property, sales, or income from general taxpaying obligations. Tax exemptions are government subsidies to special groups. *See also* SUBSIDY, page 457.

Significance   Most states have established constitutional or statutory exemption of educational and religious properties from the general property tax. Income from national, state, or local bonds may be exempted from taxation, and cooperatives from income tax levies. Most state sales taxes exempt certain classes of commodities. Tax exemptions may be used to encourage activities as well as to recognize that exceptions within general taxpaying categories must be acknowledged in the interest of fairness. Often, tax exemptions merely illustrate the political power of special interest groups. Exemptions generally benefit the large taxpayer more than the small. Low-income groups, the aged, and other needy groups, however, may be aided by tax exemptions on food, drugs, and other necessities. Many states and local communities also grant tax exemptions to business and industry as an inducement to commence or to continue operations within their jurisdictions.

Tax Incidence   The point at which the actual burden of paying a tax falls, regardless of whom the tax is formally levied upon. Those taxes in which the burden cannot be shifted to someone else by the taxpayer are sometimes classified as *direct* taxes; those in which the burden can be passed on are *indirect* taxes. *See also* PROGRESSIVE TAX, page 411; REGRESSIVE TAX, page 415.

Significance   The incidence of almost all taxes that are levied at some point in the production and consumption of goods is ultimately shifted to consumers through higher prices for commodities. The price of a loaf of bread, for example, may include scores of national, state, and local taxes that, having been paid by different farmers, processors, distributors, and retailers, are passed on to the ultimate consumer. Direct taxes, for which the burden cannot easily be shifted, include income levies and taxes on land, although when the land is rented the owner can shift the burden of taxation to the renter. The incidence of taxation brings into serious question the fairness of taxes that are indirectly paid by others than those who make the formal tax payments. In 1994, the federal government's income came from the following sources: personal income tax, 37 percent; Social Security and related taxes, 31 percent; borrowing, 14 percent; corporate income tax, 10 percent; and estate, excise, and other taxes, 8 percent.

Tax Offset   Payment of taxes to one level of government that reduces the amount of tax liability to another level. The tax offset has been used by the national government to induce states to adopt certain types of taxes or programs by permitting individuals to deduct such state taxes from the amount of federal tax that they would otherwise pay. Some states permit payment of local property taxes to serve as a partial credit against payment of the state income tax.

Significance   The tax offset has been used effectively by the national government to prod the states into adopting such tax programs as unemployment compensation and state inheritance taxes. To induce the states to adopt unemployment compensation programs, for example, the national government levied a payroll tax on employers but permitted them to offset 90 percent of that tax if they contributed to a state unemployment compensation fund. The effect of this tax offset was to secure a nationwide, state-administered program of unemployment compensation. Some economists regard the tax offset as the best means of inducing all of the states to adopt uniform tax programs to meet growing revenue needs, with none losing ground in the fierce competition among states to attact and hold industry by means of low taxes.

Withholding Tax   Provisions of an income or payroll tax system by which the employer deducts a specified percentage from an employee's wage or salary and remits it to the government's tax bureau. Amounts withheld by employers constitute a credit against the employee's total tax liability. *See also* INCOME TAX, page 405.

Significance   Under the Current Tax Payment Act of 1943, the national government provided for the payment of federal income taxes through employer-withholding of wages and salaries and by the payment of an estimated tax in quarterly installments on income derived from other sources. The individual taxpayer must still file a return by April 15 of each year, at which time he or she must pay any amount owed over the total withholdings or file a refund claim if the tax is less than the withholdings. The withholding system was adopted by Congress during World War II to help finance the military effort. The main advantages of the system are that it makes tax collections more certain and facilitates payment of taxes through relatively "painless" deductions from paychecks, rather than expecting each taxpayer to voluntarily put aside enough from each paycheck so as to be able to make a once-a-year tax payment. It also provides the Department of the Treasury with sizable funds coming in regularly during the year. Most opposition has come from employers, who dislike the extensive bookkeeping involved, and from other groups who oppose the singling out of wage and salary incomes for withholding. Individuals who receive income from nonwithholding sources, such as stock dividends and business profits, must make quarterly estimated tax payments.

IMPORTANT AGENCIES

Board of Governors, Federal Reserve System   A board composed of seven members that determines general monetary and credit policies and oversees the operations of the twelve district Federal Reserve banks and member banks throughout the country. Board members are appointed for fourteen-year terms by the President with the Senate's confirmation, with consideration given to geographical and major business interests in the selection process. The board is, by statute and practice, independent of the President. *See also* FEDERAL RESERVE SYSTEM, page 400.

Significance   The Board of Governors determines monetary policies through its control over the issuance of Federal Reserve notes by Federal Reserve banks, its fixing of the discount rate, its Open Market Committee, and the purchase and sale of government and other securities. These activities have a profound effect on the amount of money in circulation and the credit available through Federal Reserve member banks, which in turn influences general economic conditions in the country. The Board also sets the margin requirements for purchases of securities and conducts periodic examinations of Federal Reserve and member banks. Some students of government and finance would like to have its activities brought under the direct supervision of the President because of the close, important relationship of monetary policies to fiscal policies and the stability of the economy. Others consider it essential that the board retain its independence from presidential control in order that its decisions be free from politics. Because fiscal policy is largely determined by the President, whereas monetary policy is dominated by the "Fed," conflicting policies that may tend to nullify the impact of each are sometimes carried on simultaneously.

Council of Economic Advisers (CEA)   A staff agency in the Executive Office of the President. It consists of three leading economists who advise the President on measures to maintain stability in the nation's economy. The council was established by Congress in the Employment Act of 1946 and was given responsibility by that Act to formulate proposals "to maintain employment, production, and purchasing power." The council's recommendations— if the President agrees with them—are included in the President's annual economic report to Congress, in which are set forth the economic problems facing the nation and recommended legislative solutions. *See also* EMPLOYMENT ACT OF 1946, page 427; KEYNESIANISM, page 407.

Significance   The Council of Economic Advisers' role as a leading staff agency reflects the increasing responsibility of the President to provide leadership in keeping the nation's economy healthy. The council has played a significant role in recommending fiscal policies to help overcome nine post–World War II recessions. Its influence depends upon its acceptance as a professionally competent body of advisers, but it must avoid detachment from political realities. Sometimes the council's lack of a direct liaison with the Federal Reserve Board of Governors has resulted in the pursuit of incompatible fiscal and monetary policies by the two agencies. Today the CEO uses a great variety of indices to keep its finger on the pulse of the national economy, and engages in constant diagnoses and prognoses.

Department of the Treasury   A major department of the national government, responsible for fiscal management and headed by a secretary with Cabinet rank. The Department of the Treasury was one of the original departments established in 1789. Important administrative units include the Internal Revenue Service, Customs Service, Bureau of Accounts, Secret Service, Bureau of Public Debt, and Office of the Comptroller of the Currency. *See also* FISCAL POLICY, page 400; PUBLIC DEBT, page 412; SECRET SERVICE, page 214.

Significance   The Department of the Treasury plays a broad and significant role in formulating both monetary and fiscal policies for the national administration. The Secretary of the Treasury is often regarded as second only to the Secretary of State as a Cabinet adviser to the President. In addition to its duties to collect taxes and customs duties, administer the public debt, keep accounts for the entire government, and coin money, the Department also registers and licenses ships engaged in foreign and interstate commerce, administers the counterfeiting and narcotics control laws, and is responsible for protecting the President and Vice President, their families, and former presidents.

General Accounting Office (GAO)   An independent agency created by the Budget and Accounting Act of 1921 that controls and audits national government expenditures as an agent of Congress. The GAO is headed by the Comptroller General, who is appointed by the President with the Senate's approval for a fifteen-year term and can be removed only through impeachment or a joint resolution of Congress. The major functions carried on by the GAO include (1) prescribing accounting systems for federal agencies; (2) authorizing federal agencies to make specific expenditures (preaudit); and (3) making extensive investigations to determine the validity of the receipt and disbursement of public funds (postaudit). *See also* COMPTROLLER GENERAL, page 392.

Significance   Congress by law determines in general how public money shall be spent, and the GAO acts as an agent of Congress, checking on specific expenditures to ensure that each falls within the intent of Congress. Its investigations may lead to legal action against individuals who have violated federal law in disbursing funds.

Internal Revenue Service (IRS)   A unit in the Department of the Treasury that has major responsibility for the collection of federal taxes except for customs duties. The Internal Revenue Service is headed by a commissioner and operates through district offices, each headed by a director. The IRS collects approximately three-fourths of the total budget receipts of the national government. *See also* INCOME TAX, page 405; WITHHOLDING TAX, page 421.

Significance   The Internal Revenue Service collects more than $1 trillion each year, mostly in individual and corporation income taxes. Because of its discretionary powers in making decisions in specific tax cases, it has become an important agency in the lives of millions of Americans. Taxpayers, however, are entitled to administrative hearings of their cases and may appeal IRS decisions to the United States Tax Court. In 1983, the Supreme Court held in an imporant decision that the IRS has authority to withhold tax-exempt status from racially discriminatory private schools (*Bob Jones University v. United States,* 461 U.S. 574). The IRS computers contain more financial information about American citizens than any other agency or organization. This gives the IRS great potential for abuse.

Office of Management and Budget (OMB)   An agency in the Executive Office of the President, headed by a director who has primary responsibility for efficient and economical conduct of government operations and for budget preparation and administration. The President appoints the director with Senate approval. In addition to budget functions, specific activities carried on by the office include legislative reference, management and organization, statistical standards, and financial management. The Office of Management and Budget was created by Executive Order in 1970 to replace the Bureau of the Budget and perform its statutory functions. The Office of Information and Regulatory Affairs in the OMB negotiates disputes as part of its regulatory review process, as does the Council on Competitiveness, though the Council does so under the shield of executive privilege. The Council—a secret body— was established by President George Bush in 1989 with Vice President Dan Quayle as its head. *See also* BUDGET, page 390; BUDGET AND ACCOUNTING ACT, page 426; COMPETITIVENESS, page 437.

Significance   The director of the Office of Management and Budget is empowered, under the Budget and Accounting Act of 1921, to "assemble, correlate, revise, reduce, or increase" the estimates from executive agencies. Broad fiscal powers flow from this grant, both in the planning and estimating stages and, following congressional approval of the budget, in the budget execution state, when agency heads must obtain approval in financing their programs. In addition to its budgeting function, the office carries on duties directed toward improving organization and management within the executive branch and acts as a powerful clearinghouse for legislative proposals originating in the executive agencies. Since 1939, when the Bureau of the Budget was transferred from the Department of the Treasury to the Executive Office, it has become the President's major staff agency in fiscal, legislative, and administrative management. The office is one of the best perspectives from which to gain an overview of the operations of the entire national government because budget and operations are inextricably linked. The office also has major responsibility for getting the President's legislative program enacted by Congress.

United States Tax Court   A special judicial agency, headed by a chief judge, that hears controversies between taxpayers and the Commissioner of Internal Revenue and has jurisdiction over excess profits proceedings. Under the Tax Reform Act of 1969, the Tax Court was designated a court of record under Article I of the Constitution. Prior to this designation it had functioned as a quasi-judicial administrative agency. The Court consists of nineteen judges appointed by the President, with the Senate's consent, for twelve-year terms. Each judge heads a division and, although the Court and its judges are located in Washington, D.C., trial sessions are held throughout the country. Special trial judges are also used to handle the heavy caseload. In 1991, the Supreme Court held (*Freytag v. Commissioner of Internal Revenue,* 501 U.S. 868) that the Tax Court can appoint special trial judges as "inferior officers," who are subject to provisions of the Appointment Clause, and that the Tax Court is a "court of law" under the Appointment Clause (Art. 2, sec. 2) of the Constitution.

Significance   The Tax Court provides a relatively easy and inexpensive means (a small fee is required to file a petition) for taxpayers to appeal decisions made by tax officials. It relieves the regular courts of the tremendous burden of suits resulting from the far-reaching effects of federal tax programs. "Small tax cases," up to a maximum of $5,000, are decided by a judge in an informal proceeding. The taxpayer does not need to hire a lawyer, and most tax cases are settled by the IRS without going to trial. Decisions rendered in small tax cases cannot be appealed, and the decisions do not set legal precedents. Other decisions of the Tax Court can be appealed to the Court of Appeals and thereafter to the Supreme Court of the United States by writ of certiorari.

IMPORTANT CASES

Legal Tender Cases (Knox v. Lee; Parker v. Davis),   12 Wallace 457 (1871): Recognized the power of Congress to make Treasury notes (paper money) legal tender in place of gold or silver in payment of debt. *See also* FEDERAL RESERVE NOTES, page 399; LEGAL TENDER, page 408.

Significance   The *Legal Tender Cases* grew out of a wartime debt, but, a few years later, the Court also upheld the issuance of paper money as legal tender in time of peace in *Juilliard v. Greenman,* 110 U.S. 421 (1884). In the *Legal Tender Cases* the Court recognized a new category of "resulting powers"—those powers that are not expressly granted by the Constitution or implied from a single enumerated power but which arise from the aggregate powers of government.

Pollock v. Farmers Loan and Trust Co.,   158 U.S. 601 (1895): Held the federal income tax law of 1894 unconstitutional on the ground that it was a direct tax; therefore, Congress should have apportioned it among the several states according to population as provided in Article I, section 9 of the Constitution. *See also* INCOME TAX, page 405; SIXTEENTH AMENDMENT, page 417.

Significance   The *Pollack* decision was a reversal of earlier decisions by the Court in which the validity of income taxes not apportioned according to the population had been upheld. The inequity of levying income taxes on a population basis restrained Congress from enacting a new income tax law until 1913, when the Sixteenth Amendment was adopted. The Amendment sidestepped the dispute of whether an income tax law is a direct or indirect tax simply by eliminating any legal necessity for apportionment.

South Carolina v. United States,   199 U.S. 437 (1905): Upheld a federal tax levied upon wholesale and retail liquor sales by the state of South Carolina on the ground that exemption of states from federal taxes applies only when a state carries on strictly governmental functions, not when it engages in business of a private nature. The state argued unsuccessfully that because all profits from liquor sales went into the state treasury, it was exercising the sovereign power of the state and should be immune from federal taxes. *See also* INTERGOVERNMENTAL TAX IMMUNITY, page 43; PROPRIETARY FUNCTION, page 453.

Significance   The *South Carolina* case laid down the fundamental rule that state immunity from federal taxation does not apply when a state enters a commercial or proprietary field. The case has served to modify substantially the intergovernmental tax immunity rule laid down in *McCulloch v.*

Maryland, 4 Wheaton 316 (1819). Generally, the courts will not intervene when Congress decides to tax a state or local proprietary function.

Veazie Bank v. Fenno,   8 Wallace 533 (1869): Upheld the validity of a 10 percent tax on state bank notes levied by Congress in 1866 for the purpose of driving them out of circulation. *See also* LEGAL TENDER, page 408; REGULA-TORY TAX, page 415.

Significance   The *Veazie Bank* decision gave judicial acceptance to the use of a federal tax primarily for a nonrevenue regulatory purpose, and it sanctioned the action of Congress to provide a uniform currency for the United States. The objective of the tax sustained in this case has been realized, and state bank notes have been out of circulation for many years.

IMPORTANT STATUTES

Budget and Accounting Act of 1921   A law that established a national budget system and created the Bureau of the Budget (now the Office of Management and Budget) and the General Accounting Office. It provides for the formulation of an annual executive budget by the bureau under direction of the President and for the auditing of all government expenditures by the General Accounting Office under the direction of the Comptroller General as an agent of Congress. *See also* GENERAL ACCOUNTING OFFICE, page 423; OFFICE OF MANAGEMENT AND BUDGET, page 423.

Significance   Prior to the enactment of the Budget and Accounting Act of 1921, the budget system was a loose and haphazard process in which various executive agencies submitted requests to as many as 24 different House and Senate committees. No attempt was made to look at the financial picture from an overall viewpoint, and the President had little or no voice in the entire process. Under the Act, a budget is prepared by fiscal experts under the direction of the President and is submitted as a single-package budget to Congress, where it is assigned to revenue and appropriations committees for study. Congress can now consider the budget as a total picture for the fiscal period of proposed expenditures and anticipated income. Execution of the budget by the spending agencies is done under the watchful eyes of the General Accounting Office, which carries on auditing functions. The Budget and Accounting Act of 1921 is probably the most significant piece of fiscal control legislation to come out of Congress and, through a process of development and application over a period of 50 years, has helped to bring some order into the budgetary process. The size of the federal budget and the annual deficits incurred, however, continue to grow at a rapid pace. When Congress is controlled by one party and the President is a member of another party, serious problems are likely to arise in carrying out the budgetary functions. This situation occurred most recently following the election of 1994, in which the Republican party gained control of Congress and the presidency was held by a Democrat, Bill Clinton.

Chief Financial Officers Act of 1990   Legislation establishing financial standards and reporting requirements for the entire federal government. The

Act creates within the Office of Management and Budget (OMB) an Office of Federal Financial Management headed by a deputy director of management. On a graduated schedule, selected agencies and departments are required to develop and issue audited financial statements for revolving funds, trust funds, and commercial functions. The Act also requires the deputy director to implement government-wide accounting principles developed by the Federal Accounting Standards Advisory Board (which was established by the Federal Managers Financial Integrity Act of 1982). Chief financial officers (CFOs) appointed by the President are assigned to most federal agencies to implement the terms of the Act, and a Chief Financial Officers Council coordinates their activities and identifies problems. These agency CFOs will report directly to the agency head or Cabinet secretary. *See also* INSPECTORS GENERAL, page 229; OFFICE OF MANAGEMENT AND BUDGET, page 423.

Significance   The Chief Financial Officers Act was designed to strengthen financial accountability in the wake of the Housing and Urban Development scandal of 1989, in which one person siphoned off millions of dollars of public housing funds. It replaces the Budget and Accounting Procedures Act of 1950, which had required uniform accounting and reporting standards within agencies, but not among them. As budgetary pressures increased, Congress found that these accounting systems were also woefully inadequate. There was no way to know how much money was owed the federal government, what liabilities the government had, how risky certain government investments and loans were, or how much money remained to be spent at any given moment during the fiscal year. The CFOs wield considerable power under the new act, building integrated accounting systems, enforcing financial integrity, linking accounting and budgeting systems, and developing performance measures to evaluate program effectiveness. Critics charge that it places agency CFOs in conflict with inspectors general and information resource managers, that the Act ignores the discretionary funds accounts that comprise the majority of most departments' budgets, and that standard financial statements will prove useless unless in managing federal programs. But proponents say that the Act provides the sort of basic financial and accounting tools needed to improve fiscal accountability.

Employment Act of 1946   An act that establishes responsiblity for the national government to maintain stability in the nation's economy. A Council of Economic Advisers (CEA) was created by the Act and placed in the Executive Office to advise the President on economic matters. The Act requires the President to make an annual economic report to Congress setting forth the major economic problems confronting the nation and recommending appropriate legislation. *See also* COUNCIL OF ECONOMIC ADVISERS, page 422; FISCAL POLICY, page 400; KEYNESIANISM, page 407.

Significance   The Employment Act of 1946 was the first legislation to recognize a continuing responsiblity of government to use its broad economic powers to promote the nation's economic well-being. Specific goals of the Act include the maintenance of high levels of production, employment, and purchasing power. Congress has created a Joint Commitee on the Economic Report to study the President's economic program and to recommend legislative actions. The acceptance by government of responsibility for economic stability has received the approval of the American public. The 1980s and early 1990s provided a new challenge to the government's role under the Employment Act of maintaining stability in the economy despite heavy unemployment and massive budget and trade deficits, and a basic conflict over whether the national government's approach to the economy should be based on Keynesian, supply-side, or monetarist principles.

Tax Reform Act of 1986   A major revision in the Internal Revenue Code that provides for reductions in individual and corporate tax rates that are offset by substantial changes in tax procedures, deductions, and exemptions. For individuals, fifteen individual tax rates have been consolidated by the Tax Reform Act into three rates—15 percent, 28 percent, and 33 percent—with the highest rate levied on a small number of high-income taxpayers. The new law wiped out or substantially reduced many favorable provisions that powerful interest groups had obtained from Congress over many years. These included elimination of many tax shelters, ending the special low-tax treatment for capital gains, and a special minimum tax levied on individuals and corporations that otherwise would pay no tax. Under the new tax system, an estimated 6 million low-income Americans no longer pay income tax, and approximately 80 percent of individual taxpayers pay only the lowest rate of 15 percent. For corporations, the 1986 law reduced the tax rate on corporate profits from a maximum of 46 percent to 40 percent in 1987 and 34 percent thereafter. However, the 1986 law also repealed or reduced many corporate tax benefits, resulting on balance in substantial increases in corporation tax payments for most companies. *See also* INCOME TAX, page 405.

Significance   The Tax Reform Act of 1986 was the most complex and substantial alteration of the income tax since it was adopted in 1913. Supporters of the Tax Reform Act held that, overall, the new tax would be revenue-neutral. Reductions to individuals that would average about 6 percent would be offset by an increase of $120 billion per year in corporate collections. Many loopholes, especially those for business, industry, and investors, were limited or closed out by the new law. A new emphasis on "fairness" was claimed by its supporters. Opponents, however, pointed out that the law did nothing to meet the budget deficit crisis, that a tax increase was likely within several years, and that its antibusiness provisions were likely to lead the country into an early economic recession, which occurred in 1990–1991.

10

Business and Labor

Agency Shop   A labor-management contractual relationship in which workers are not required to join an existing union representing a majority of the employees but must pay the union a sum in lieu of regular union dues in order to hold a job. The payment represents a fee for the services of the union, which acts as the worker's agent in collective bargaining and administration of union contracts. *See also* CLOSED SHOP, page 435; UNION SHOP, page 460.

Significance   The agency shop represents a compromise between the closed shop, now outlawed, and the union shop, wherein all workers must eventually join the union. In an agency shop, the right of a majority to establish a union and the right of an individual not to be forced to join are both preserved without permitting "freeloading" on union-secured benefits. The Supreme Court upheld the agency shop for public employees in *Abood v. Detroit Board of Education,* 431 U.S. 209 (1977) but ruled in 1988 that nonmembers may not be forced to pay full union dues to cover costs of political activities (*Communications Workers of America v. Beck,* 487 U.S. 735).

Amtrak   The national semipublic corporation established in 1970 to operate intercity passenger railway traffic. Amtrak is the popular name for the National Railroad Passenger Corporation, which Congress established as a business seeking to earn a profit but which is infused with a public purpose and is under public control. Under Amtrak, the rails remain owned by the private carriers, but the rolling stock is managed through joint government-business cooperation. The majority of the board of directors are appointed by the President so that government control of policy will be maintained. *See also* GOVERNMENT CORPORATION, page 227.

Significance   Amtrak was a product of increasing financial pressures, especially due to the competition from the trucking industry and the airlines, that severely reduced or threatened to eliminate passenger traffic on most railroad systems and contributed to the bankruptcy of others. Amtrak initially reduced the number of trains by half in its campaign to consolidate intercity passenger traffic. Environmental concerns, the energy crisis of the 1970s, and improved service led Amtrak to expand passenger operations. Yet, extensive federal subsidies have been needed. If Amtrak fails in its mission, nationalization of intercity passenger service may be inevitable. Charges of poor service led to a legal test in which the Supreme Court held that the 1970 law establishing Amtrak does not authorize private persons or groups to try to change train routes and service by civil suit action (*National Railroad Passenger Corp. v. National Association of Railroad Passengers*, 414 U.S. 453 [1974]). Whereas Amtrak is concerned only with passenger service, Congress in 1973 created a federally financed private corporation, the Consolidated Rail Corporation (Conrail), to operate seven bankrupt railroad lines to maintain freight hauling and limited commuter passenger services.

Antitrust Laws   Laws intended to regulate or prohibit unfair competition and combinations in restraint of trade, including monopolies, cartels, trusts, mergers, junk-bond takeovers, and interlocking directorates. The objective of antitrust action by the government is to maintain and strengthen the free enterprise system by requiring competition in business. Responsibility for the enforcement of antitrust laws is vested in the Antitrust Division of the Department of Justice and in the Federal Trade Commission. *See also* CLAYTON ACT, page 474; MERGER, page 448; SHERMAN ANTITRUST ACT, page 478.

Significance   Since the enactment of the Sherman Act in 1890, the national government's antitrust policy has been vigorously enforced at times, and at other times it has been sporadically enforced or ignored. Enforcement has been greatly influenced by Supreme Court decisions limiting or expanding the scope of enforcement authority, by the antitrust philosophy of particular presidents and the "trust busters" of the Antitrust Division, and by the views and pressures of public opinion calling for action or accepting inaction. Much also has depended upon the circumstances of the times, antitrust action having been reduced during periods of war, defense programs, or strenuous foreign competition. During the period 1960 to 1995, American business went through an unparalleled era of mergers and building of huge conglomerates, with little restraining action by the government. This trend has continued in the latter part of the 1990s. For example, mergers, acquisitions, and restructurings accounted for 30 percent more name changes in the first half of 1996 compared to the same period in 1995. Increasingly, giant multinational corporations dominate the marketplace in the United States and abroad.

Arbitration   The submission of the labor-management dispute to an impartial board or individual whose decision is binding upon the parties to the dispute. Many collective bargaining agreements provide for arbitration of unresolved grievances. A few states have passed statutes requiring compulsory arbitration of disputes in public utility enterprises, such as electric, gas, and water. *See also* ARBITRATION, page 532; MEDIATION AND CONCILIATION, page 447.

Significance   A large number of labor disputes are submitted to private professional arbitrators. Many strikes are thereby avoided. Binding arbitration has been used in wartime, but both management and labor fear compulsory arbitration. Both prefer to keep the government out of labor disputes and to pursue their ends through collective bargaining. For example, compulsory arbitration procedures are provided under the Railway Labor Act to supplement, rather than substitute for, collective bargaining. These procedures have not, however, proved successful, and they have often been bypassed during a railroad labor dispute. The American Arbitration Association (AAA), a private organization, provides a panel of technically qualified arbitrators who, at the request of the parties, can hear and decide a dispute. This procedure can save individuals and companies a great deal of time and money that otherwise would be spent in resolving the dispute in the courts.

Bankruptcy   A procedure for discharging unpaid obligations through a court action that frees the litigant from existing debt liability. Bankruptcy proceedings may be initiated either by the insolvent debtor (voluntary bankruptcy) or by a required number of creditors (involuntary bankruptcy). Such cases have been handled by federal district courts under equity jurisdiction. The court appoints an officer who sells the bankrupt's assets and pays the creditors on a prorated basis. In 1978, Congress enacted the first major revision in bankruptcy laws in 40 years. Under that legislation, a new bankruptcy court system was established to loosen federal district court control by providing for presidential appointment of bankruptcy judges for 14-year terms and to modernize bankruptcy law and judicial procedure. In 1982, however, the Supreme Court struck down the bankruptcy court structure established by the 1978 legislation (*Northern Pipeline Construction Co. v. Marathon Pipe Line Co.,* 458 U.S. 50). Congress in 1984 enacted a new bankruptcy law that (1) assigns overall authority for bankruptcy proceedings to federal district judges, who can turn those cases not involving other federal questions over to bankruptcy judges; (2) makes it more difficult for consumers to eliminate their debts through bankruptcy; (3) bars employers from using bankruptcy to unilaterally cancel union contracts; and (4) reduces what debtors may keep and makes it more difficult to file. In 1986, Congress, in the Bankruptcy Judges Act, again amended the basic bankruptcy law to clarify some of the provisions of the 1984 act. In the 1990s, choices for heavy debtors include (1) Chapter 7 of the Bankruptcy Code, which gets rid of all or most of the petitioner's debt with few or no assets given up; (2) Chapter 13, which permits the petitioner to work out a "deal" with his or her creditors; and (3) Chapter 11, which covers businesses as well as individuals and involves negotition with creditors to pay off debts, sometimes at only five cents on the dollar. *See also* EQUITY, page 262, LEGISLATIVE COURT, page 269; REFEREE, page 276.

Significance   Bankruptcy proceedings enable persons, both human and corporate, to wipe clean a slate of hopeless debt and start anew. Some provisions of this kind are indispensable to protect the credit structure of modern business enterprises. Major federal bankruptcy acts have been passed by Congress in 1898, 1933, 1978, and 1984. The 1982 decision of the Supreme Court voiding the 1978 bankruptcy law left the administration of bankruptcy in limbo. The Court's position was that a new bankruptcy court should be established under the judicial powers of Article III rather than under the legislative powers of Article I of the Constitution. Critics of bankruptcy charge that bankruptcy procedures encourage financial irresponsibility. They recommend more restrictive measures concerning voluntary bankruptcy. Labor unions strongly oppose the position taken by the Supreme Court, that bankruptcy may invalidate labor agreements (as it does ordinary business contracts) and wage pacts must therefore be abandoned or renegotiated (*National Labor Relations Board v. Bildisco & Bildisco,* 465 U.S. 513 [1984]). Lobbying by labor leaders led Congress to overturn this decision in the new law. The number of bankruptcies has been steadily increasing each year. The increase is largely due to the fact that a person who files for bankruptcy today often gets to keep a large portion of assets while getting rid of most or all liabilities. Each state has its own bankruptcy statute or allows the federal statute to prevail. Some states—especially California, Florida, and Texas—are very liberal in allowing those who file to keep most of their assets while ridding themselves of most of their liabilities. Studies have shown that three-fifths of those who file bankruptcy double their net worth after filing. The main limitations on declaring bankruptcy are the stigma associated with it and, often, the difficulty in securing credit after filing.

Blue Laws   Laws on the books of many states that prohibit certain business operations on Sundays and on religious holidays. Blue laws often make exceptions for amusements or essential activities and for persons who observe a Sabbath day other than Sunday. The term "blue laws" originated in the seventeenth-century New England colonies, where laws regulating public and private behavior were printed on blue paper to indicate that the content of the laws was not proper for general public reading. *See also* FREEDOM OF RELIGION, page 316; POLICE POWER, page 328.

Significance   Blue laws are religious in origin and have been challenged as violations of religious liberty. They are now supported largely as welfare measures to encourage rest and relaxation. In 1961, the Supreme Court upheld a number of such laws on these grounds (*McGowan v. Maryland*, 366 U.S. 420). Blue laws have not been rigorously enforced, and their many exceptions render them ineffective. Civil libertarians generally oppose blue laws on the ground that they violate the individual's freedom of religion.

Blue Sky Laws   State laws to protect investors in securities from misrepresentation and outright fraud. Blue sky laws commonly require that companies selling securities be certified by a state agency and furnish detailed information concerning their financial position. *See also* SECURITIES AND EXCHANGE COMMISSION, page 469.

Significance   The term "blue sky" refers to the gullible investor who discovers that the securities purchased represent nothing of value but the blue sky above. Blue sky laws have been enacted in almost all states since the early part of the twentieth century. Although most states continue to offer some protection to buyers of securities, most of their functions have been taken over by the Securities and Exchange Commission, created by Congress in 1934.

Boycott   An economic weapon used by labor to curtail the purchase of products from an employer. There are two types of boycotts—primary and secondary. A primary boycott involves withdrawing patronage and urging others to withdraw their patronage from an employer with whom a union is having a labor dispute. A secondary boycott involves a refusal to deal with or patronize anyone who deals with the employer with whom there is a dispute. Secondary boycotts are outlawed by the Taft-Hartley Act of 1947 and, with certain exceptions, by the Landrum-Griffin Act of 1959. Most states also outlaw secondary boycotts. *See also* PICKETING, page 451.

Significance   The primary boycott is lawful but often ineffective for a union. People may continue to cross a picket line to patronize a strikebound store and, in the case of large industrial plants, suppliers may continue to sell to the plant and dealers may continue to sell its products. Labor prefers the secondary boycott, which enables it to bring pressure upon others whose continued dealing with the strikebound plant hinders the successful conclusion of the strike. Secondary boycotts are, however, illegal, because they interfere with the rights of persons not involved in the dispute, and public policy seeks to confine the dispute to the particular parties involved.

Business Affected with a Public Interest   Any privately owned and operated selling or service activity that, as a matter of public policy, has been brought under the regulatory power of government. Businesses affected with a public interest, such as public utilities, are regulated by government boards and commissions in regard to their service and rates. The doctrine of "business affected with a public interest" was developed by the Supreme Court in *Munn v. Illinois,* 94 U.S. 113 (1876). *See also Munn v. Illinois,* page 472; PUBLIC UTILITY, page 453.

Significance   Many regulatory bodies have been created by national, state, and local governments when policymakers have determined that the free competition of the marketplace does not protect the right of the public to obtain satisfactory products or services at reasonable rates. For many years, Americans believed that such businesses as public carriers and gas and electric companies could operate under conditions of monopoly or near monopoly without danger to the public interest so long as they were regulated by government. In the 1990s, however, competition from independent providers of gas and electricity who can sell their product at lower cost are forcing reconsideration of the role of the marketplace as regulator.

Business and Professional Organizations   Groups organized to promote the interest of business and the professions. The leading nationwide business organizations are the Chamber of Commerce of the United States and the National Association of Manufacturers (NAM). The Chamber is a federation of more than 4,000 local chambers of commerce representing 3 million businesspeople. The NAM represents about 12,000 large industrial firms. Another powerful organization, the Business Council, is composed of executives representing approximately 150 of the largest American corporations; it functions as an unofficial adviser to national policy makers. This organization, which usually agrees with Republican policies, has been supportive of President Bill Clinton's trade and inflation issues and has given mixed support to the Republican Contract with America. In addition, businesspeople are organized according to their trade or industry interests in numerous national and local trade associations. Leading professional associations include the American Medical Association (AMA), the American Bar Association (ABA), and the National Education Association (NEA). *See also* POLITICAL ACTION COMMITTEES (PACS), page 96; PRESSURE GROUP, page 104.

Significance   Most business and professional organizations reflect conservative attitudes toward taxes, government spending, and welfare programs. The Chamber of Commerce and NAM spend much effort on public education programs in support of the free enterprise system. The AMA's long battle against a national health program and its involvement in Medicare reform beginning in 1995 are outstanding examples of pressure-group involvement in a major political controversy. Both business and professional organizations are concerned with influencing government policy toward restricting entry and managing competition within their respective fields. To circumvent the Taft-Hartley Act's prohibition against corporations making campaign contributions, the NAM created a Business-Industry Policital Action Committee (BIPAC) that collects and uses voluntary contributions from businesspeople for political purposes. All business and professional organizations are involved in pursuing political objectives compatible with the interests of their members.

Caveat Venditor   A term meaning, literally, "let the seller beware." *Caveat venditor* involves the acceptance by government of a responsibility to regulate business operations for the protection of consumers. It can be contrasted with the philosophy of *caveat emptor,* "let the buyer beware, " that typified the freewheeling business practices of the nineteenth-century period of laissez-faire. Both philosophies continue to exist, but *caveat emptor* is on the decline in today's consumer-based economy. *See also* UNFAIR TRADE PRACTICE, page 459.

Significance   Under the doctrine of *caveat venditor,* government aloofness has given way, in the twentieth century, to numerous national, state, and local laws and enforcement agencies that operate in the interest of consumer protection. Businesses that sell impure foods or drugs, engage in false advertising, give short measure to buyers, sell dangerous items, or misrepresent their products may be subject to civil or criminal action. National agencies that are particularly concerned with safeguarding consumer interests include the Food and Drug Administration, the Office of Consumer Adviser, the Office of Consumer Affairs, the Office of Consumer Litigation, the Consumer Product Safety Commission, and the Federal Trade Commission. Regulation is intended to force businesses to present certain facts about their products for the information of the public, though sound investments and purchases still require careful buying methods. Ralph Nader and his "Nader's Raiders," a group of lawyers and students whose legal approaches and lobbying methods to expand consumer rights and protections, have done much to pressure the national government into taking a more forthright stance in protecting the consuming public. Federal laws, for example, provide for product safety and require disclosure of finance charges and truth in advertising. The Republican-controlled Congress in 1995 tried to reduce government regulation in various business areas.

Certificate of Public Convenience, Interest, and Necessity   Permission granted by a regulatory agency to an individual or group to conduct a particular type of business. The standard of "public convenience, interest, and necessity" has been established by Congress and state legislatures to guide regulatory agencies in issuing licenses and permits to public utlities and communication media. Typical licensees include common carriers, such as airlines, railroads, bus companies, taxicabs, ships, pipelines, and trucking companies. *See also* DEREGULATION, page 440; FRANCHISE, page 443; PUBLIC UTILITY, page 453.

Significance   The public interest is rarely served by the presence of several utility companies in one community or by competing railroads or buses. Limited channels for television and radio make regulation essential, lest the airways be jammed. Thus, the determination of which company will be given the right to a television channel or to engage in a public utility enterprise is a major problem facing regulatory agencies. A company granted such a privilege receives an asset of considerable financial value and influence, and it may be subject to continuing regulation of the quality of its service and rates. In the 1970s, Congress began a program of deregulation aimed at improving service and reducing costs and prices.

Child Labor   The employment of children below the legal age limit. The national government and most states prohibit the employment of children below the age of sixteen and, in certain hazardous occupations, below the age of eighteen. Children are permitted to work outside of school in nonhazardous jobs. *See also* FAIR LABOR STANDARDS ACT OF 1938, page 475.

Significance   Until about 1910, large numbers of children 10 to 15 years of age were regularly employed. State governments then began to impose restrictions, but states that did not do so were at an economic competitive advantage over those that did. Agitation for national regulation led to the passage of legislation. The Supreme Court, however, struck down a law aiming at banning products of child labor from interstate commerce (*Hammer v. Dagenhart*, 247 U.S. 251 [1918]) and another law that taxed such products (*Bailey v. Drexel Furniture Co.*, 259 U.S. 20 [1922]). In 1924, Congress submitted to the states a constitutional amendment that would authorize federal regulation of child labor. Strong opposition prevented its ratification, though, by 1937, 28 states, 8 short of the required three-fourths, had ratified it. A more liberal view of national power, however, resulted in the passage and Supreme Court approval of the Fair Labor Standards Act of 1938 (*United States v. Darby*, 312 U.S. 100 [1941]), which, among other things, prohibited child labor. In 1990, the Department of Labor found widespread violations of federal child labor laws. Under federal law, children 14 and 15 years of age are permitted to work no more than 3 hours on school days, or 18 hours during a 5-day week, and only from 7 A.M. to 7 P.M. Of the thousands of violations reported to the Labor Department, most were in the fast-food business or among children of migrant farm workers.

Closed Shop   An industrial plant that agrees to hire only those persons who are members of a labor union. The closed shop is outlawed by the Taft-Hartley Act of 1947, although later legislation has modified this restriction with regard to the building trades. *See also* AGENCY SHOP, page 429; RIGHT TO WORK LAW, page 455; UNION SHOP, page 460.

Significance   The closed shop is opposed by management because it allegedly places the hiring power in the union rather than in the hands of management. Approximately 30 percent of organized labor, largely in craft industries, was under closed shop agreement prior to 1947. Though forbidden by the Taft-Hartley Act, many establishments continue to operate as closed shops through the mutual agreement of the union and management, who are reluctant to upset customary patterns.

Collective Bargaining Negotiation on the terms and conditions of employment between an employer and a union representing the employees. It is to be distinguished from negotiation between an employer and an individual employee. The right of workers to organize and to bargain collectively through their representatives has been the official policy of the United States since 1935. Collective bargaining imposes upon the employer and labor union an obligation to confer in good faith with respect to working conditions and to execute a written contract embodying the agreements reached. Refusal to bargain by an employer or a duly recognized union may be adjudged an unfair labor practice. *See also* FEDERAL LABOR RELATIONS AUTHORITY, page 236; *NLRB v. Jones and Laughlin Steel Corp.* page 472; STRIKE, page 456; WAGNER ACT, page 479.

Significance Official recognition of the principle of collective bargaining was the culmination of years of industrial strife in which unions sought recognition from employers as legitimate bargaining agents for employees. Both national and state labor-management relations laws were enacted to guarantee the right of collective bargaining in the interest of avoiding continued industrial unrest. The principle of collective bargaining is recognition of the inequality of bargaining power between an employer and an individual employee. National and state laws now extensively regulate the procedures by which agreements are to be reached, the administration of agreements, and the problems attending the breakdown of collective bargaining procedures. In 1977, the Supreme Court upheld the right of public employees to organize and bargain collectively with the government that employs them (*Abood v. Detroit Board of Education*, 431 U.S. 209).

Commerce The buying and selling of commodities, transportation, and commercial intercourse and the transmission of radio, television, and telephonic and telegraphic messages. The commerce clause, Article I, Section 8, of the U.S. Constitution, grants Congress the power to regulate interstate and foreign commerce and commerce with the Indian tribes. The states retain the power to regulate intrastate commerce. *See also* COMMERCE POWER, page 33; *Cooley v. Board of Wardens*, page 471; *Gibbons v. Ogden*, page 472.

Significance The power of Congress to regulate interstate and foreign commerce has, throughout American history, proved to be one of the key powers of the national government. Through successively broader interpretations by Congress and the Supreme Court, the term "commerce" has come to include almost all forms of business activity, including manufacturing since 1937. Although many legal battles have been fought concerning the extent of the commerce power, the issue since 1937 has become largely a political question rather than a legal one, to be settled by Congress and the people and not, ordinarily, by the Supreme Court. Commerce that is intrastate may come under the regulatory power of Congress if it directly or indirectly affects interstate commerce. States may also regulate interstate commerce if such regulation does not impede the free flow of that commerce and has a reasonable relation to the protection of the public safety, health morals, and welfare, and if the activity regulated does not require uniform national treatment.

Competitiveness   A slogan expounded in the 1980s by the Reagan administration and some members of Congress, which conveyed the idea that the nation's trade and unemployment problems can be overcome through more efficient production and expanded foreign markets. Competitiveness assumes that productivity increases will lead to faster economic growth and the creation of many new jobs for American workers. Because the concept of competitiveness is general and imprecise, politicians exploit it for their political advantage. Nevertheless, to encourage competitiveness, many state governments, unlike the national government, have entered into a variety of partnership arrangements similar to those in Japan between the government and industry. The need to compete more effectively in world trade—especially with Japan and Germany—led to the creation of a Competitiveness Council headed by the Vice President. During the Bush administration, it sought to increase American competitiveness mainly by limiting or ending government regulation of the economy. *See also* DEREGULATION, page 440; INDUSTRIAL POLICY, page 444; KEY ELECTION ISSUES, page 85; PRIVATIZATION, page 452.

Significance   Competitiveness as an answer to economic problems relates to the fact that the United States no longer enjoys unchallenged superiority in trade and technology. Massive national budget deficits, trade deficits, and balance-of-payments deficits financed by borrowing abroad have alerted the government and the American people to the dangers of failing to become competitive with the Japanese, South Koreans, West Germans, Chinese, and other efficient producers who have been steadily capturing American markets. In the 1980s, the value of the dollar was substantially depreciated in its exchange value with currencies of most competitor nations. This action was justified on the ground that the lower value of the dollar would tend to make American products less expensive and therefore more competitive in the world market, while at the same time making foreign products more expensive and therefore less competitive in the American market. During the Reagan, Bush, and Clinton administrations, however, huge trade deficits continued. Although the quantity of imports in relation to exports improved, the higher cost of imported items due to the depreciated dollar kept the trade-figure deficit high. In a 1996 International Institute for Management Development report on competitiveness, defined in terms of the mechanisms that help produce wealth in a nation, the United States ranked highest of 46 countries, followed by Singapore, Hong Kong, and Japan.

COMSAT   The joint public-private Communications Satellite Corporation, which was created by the Communications Satellite Act of 1962. It includes several hundred private communications companies as shareholders and a board of directors that is composed of public and private officials. In 1963, 18 nations signed agreements to participate in COMSAT operations, leading to the creation of the International Telecommunications Satellite Consortium (INTELSAT); members include the United States and 170 other nations and territories. It provides for international cooperation in operating a global satellite-relay telephonic, telegraphic, radio, and television communications system. *See also* GOVERNMENT CORPORATION, page 227.

Significance   COMSAT was created to follow up the spectacular achievement in space technology that occurred when the National Aeronautics and Space Administration (NASA) placed the first communications satellite, Telstar, in orbit. Developed by American Telephone and Telegraph, Telstar revolutionized communications by permitting the transmission of television, radio, telephone, and telegraph programs and messages on a global basis. Spectacular news and other events are regularly beamed thousands of miles via a number of satellites now in orbit, tying the world together with a communications network.

Consumerism   The popular movement in the United States that aims at achieving effective protection for consumers. Consumerism has sought to achieve increased safety standards, truthful advertising, proper labeling, full compliance with regulatory laws and rules, control over food additives and dangerous herbicides and pesticides, consumer credit and pricing protection, and regulation of certain practices carried on by the legal and medical professions. One of the leaders of the American consumer movement, Ralph Nader, has built an organization of young professionals and students, known as "Nader's Raiders," who use the courts and lobbying techniques to increase consumer protection. *See also* CAVEAT VENDITOR, page 434; CONSUMER PRODUCT SAFETY COMMISSION, page 462; FEDERAL TRADE COMMISSION, page 467; UNFAIR TRADE PRACTICE, page 459.

Significance   Although Americans historically have tended to organize along *producer* rather than *consumer* lines, consumer protection movements have appeared from time to time. Some of these movements have sought improvement for the consumer through expanded governmental protection, while others have pursued it through cooperatives and consumer credit organizations of their own making. Consumerism has helped to pressure national, state, and local governments into adopting policies to protect consumer rights, although frequently agencies established to administer such policies have been inefficient or captured by powerful producer groups. Recent protective laws enacted by Congress and state legislatures include "truth in lending," "truth in labeling," and "truth in packaging" laws, but proposals for a major Consumer Protection Agency have failed in Congress. The most active—and controversial—federal consumer protection agency is the Consumer Product Safety Commission (CPSC), which seeks to reduce the risk to consumers from products sold to them in the American marketplace.

Contract Clause   Article I, section 10 of the Constitution, which prohibits any state from passing laws impairing the obligation of contracts. This clause applies to contracts between individuals and to contracts made by the states. The state may neither weaken the effect of a contract nor make it more difficult to enforce. All contracts, however, are subject to the limitation that they may not endanger the health, safety, and welfare of the people—the areas of the states' "police powers."

Significance At one time, the contract clause was a major constitutional defense against state regulation of private property. The framers of the Constitution sought to guard against state practices of relieving private persons (such as debtors) of their contractual obligations. The clause was also used to favor corporations receiving charters from the states by making it impossible for the states to change the charters at a later date (*Dartmouth College v. Woodward,* 4 Wheaton 518 [1819]). State constitutions or statutes now make specific provisions permitting revocation or alteration of corporation charters and other state contracts, subject to the limitations of due process of law. This development, along with police power limitations, has modified the restrictive nature of the contract clause. In 1978, the Supreme Court held that a state violated the ban on impairment of contracts when it enacted a pension benefits protection law that increased pension liability for private companies beyond that which they had voluntarily undertaken in agreements with their employees (*Allied Structural Steel Co. v. Spannaus,* 438 U.S. 234).

Cooling-Off Period A period of time, stipulated by the Taft-Hartley Act of 1947, during which parties to a labor-management controversy may not engage in a strike or lockout. Under the Act, an existing collective bargaining contract can be terminated or changed only after 60 days' notice to the other party. If no agreement is reached within 30 days, the Federal Mediation and Conciliation Service must be notified. During the 60-day period no strike or lockout is permitted. In the case of disputes threatening the national welfare, the Taft-Hartley Act authorizes the President to seek an injunction from the courts that maintains the status quo for 80 days. During this time, fact-finding and conciliation efforts are to be made, and the workers given a chance to vote on the employer's last offer. If at the end of the 80-day period no solution is reached, a strike or lockout may take place. Similar procedures are provided for the rail and air transport industries in the Railway Labor Act. *See also* STRIKE, page 456; TAFT-HARTLEY ACT, page 478.

Significance The 60-day and 80-day cooling-off periods are designed to give the parties to the dispute a chance to reach an amicable settlement without resort to disruptive practices. Oftentimes, in practice, the parties "warm up" rather than "cool off" during this period. Both labor and management tend to judge any governmental intrusion into collective bargaining arrangements according to its effect on their respective positions.

Copyright The exclusive right granted by the Copyright Office in the Library of Congress to the creative products of authors, composers, dramatists, photographers, and others. A copyright is issued to anyone who wants one, following publication of the material and its submission to the Copyright Office. In 1976, a new copyright law—the first general overhaul since 1909—was enacted by Congress. Under the new law, a copyright confers an exclusive privilege for the life of the author plus 50 years, or a total of 75 years for a company. Typical copyrighted items include books, cassette tapes, newspapers, magazines, musical compositions, translations, cartoons, sermons, motion pictures, photographs, paintings, maps, charts and computer software. The 1976 law modernized copyright procedures to apply to such technical innovations as photocopying, radio, television, and motion pictures. The copyright power is based on the constitutional grant to Congress to promote science and the arts by granting authors "the exclusive right to their respective writings." Since March 1, 1989, "the use of the copyright notice is the responsibility of the copyright owner and does not require advance permission from, or registration with, the Copyright Office." *See also* PATENT, page 451; TRADEMARK, page 458.

Significance   Copyrights are intended to foster creative efforts and to reward talent. Like patents, they constitute an exception to the laws against monopolies. The Copyright Office makes no effort to enforce the exclusive grant, however, and the individual grantee must take civil suit or injunctive action through the federal courts when he or she believes the copyright has been infringed. The United States has entered into copyright agreements with most foreign states, but a few have refused to participate in reciprocal protection ageements. The most controversial provisions of the 1976 law are those that deal with photocopying and electronic recording of copyrighted materials. In an important 1984 decision, the Supreme Court held that home taping of copyrighted television programs for personal, noncommercial use does not violate copyright laws. (*Sony Corp. of America v. Universal City Studios, Inc.,* 464 U.S. 417). Information about the copyright law, the method of securing a copyright, and registration procedures can be obtained by writing to the Copyright Office, Library of Congress, Washington, D.C., 20559.

Decertification Election   The formal process for removing a labor union as the bargaining representative for a group of workers. A petition signed by the required number of union members leads to the call for an election by the National Labor Relations Board or similar state agency. In such an election, the support of employee members for their union is tested. The union may be retained or voted out.

Significance   Though workers are still voting to join unions in much greater numbers than those who vote to decertify them, it is becoming clear that a union is no longer completely secure once it has been established. The number of decertification elections has grown annually from 154 in 1954 to 856 in 1981. Most of this growth took place in the decade from 1970 to 1980. The union lost most of these elections. Many believe that worker protection laws such as wage and hour laws and health, safety, and pension regulations have accomplished much formerly done for workers by unions. Others believe that the increasing sophistication of management in negotiations has reduced union effectiveness to the point that workers begin to question the expense of union dues.

Deregulation   The elimination of government controls over private companies. The deregulation campaign began in 1976 under the Carter administration with giving the railroads rate-setting authority. The Airline Deregulation Act followed in 1978; it ended government authority over fares, mergers, and other business activities and provided for the elimination of the Civil Aeronautics Board in 1985. Safety regulations, however, remained with the Federal Aviation Administration and the National Transportation Safety Board.

The deregulation process was speeded up under the Reagan administration and continued under the Bush and Clinton administrations. *See also* CONSUMERISM, page 438; FEDERAL DEPOSIT INSURANCE CORPORATION, page 465; TELECOMMUNICATION ACT, page 479.

Significance   The trend in the late 1970s, 1980s, and 1990s has been toward deregulating industries and decontrolling prices. Both major parties support deregulation, but for different reasons. The Republicans have been motivated by philosophical issues favoring free enterprise and the belief that regulatory activity by government stifles initiative and economic progress. The Democrats believe that deregulation will encourage growth through marketplace competition, control consumer prices, and ensure good service. Under the Carter administration, Professor Alfred Kahn provided the sophisticated leadership and economic aplomb that made deregulation feasible. Following the airline deregulation, restrictions on the trucking industry eased. One of the first actions undertaken by President Ronald Reagan was to decontrol crude oil prices in the United States by executive order, and decontrol of natural gas pricing followed. Deregulation has increasingly become a major objective of regulated industries, which claim that it will stimulate the nation's economy and combat inflation and unemployment. Some regulated industries, however, prefer to retain governmental controls over their industry as a means of avoiding price wars and generally anarchic conditions. Price competition, for example, led in the 1980s to the bankruptcy of several airlines, substantial losses for many, and the takeover of numerous small and medium-sized airlines by larger companies. In an effort to reduce government regulation, the Reagan administration determined that any new regulation must be justified by an impact analysis statement. Deregulation involves dramatic changes in the American economy, with its ultimate impact unpredictable. A catastrophic example of the impact of deregulation occurred in the 1980s and 1990s, when the Reagan administration's deregulation of savings and loans (which nonetheless retained federal guarantees for all depositors) led to massive debt accumulation by the federal government at over $200 billion. During the Cinton administration all trucking regulations were removed and one of the most powerful federal regulatory agencies, the Interstate Commerce Commission (ICC), was eliminated effective January 1, 1996. It had been established in 1887 and played a major role in the national government's regulation of substantial sectors of the nation's economy. The jurisdiction of the ICC extended to railroads, express companies, bus and truck companies, intercoastal and inland waterway carriers, and terminal facilities used in transporting goods or people. Deregulation has taken on the aura of a major economic and political revolution. The future of remaining regulatory agencies will depend on the nature and successes of those segments of our economy that have already been partially or wholly deregulated.

Downsizing   An approach aimed at achieving greater efficiency in the functioning of government and business by reducing the level of operations. *See also* CONTRACT WITH AMERICA, page 67; REPUBLICAN REVOLUTION, page 109.

Significance   Downsizing has become the buzzword, used especially by the GOP, to achieve less government at lower cost and with greater efficiency. In the political field, it has involved the devolution of power from the federal government to the various states, especially in the social welfare field. Advanced technology and the computer age have been responsible for reductions in the labor force for many years. Downsizing of government was begun under President Clinton with the Reinventing Government Program and reductions in the number of federal employees. Under the Republican-controlled Congress, it has been linked to budget cutting and balancing, efforts at elimination of departments and agencies, and in the size and mode of government at all levels. Military downsizing has involved closing many bases and reducing the numbers of military personnel. Downsizing is also apparent in the great reduction of grant money available for science and scientific research. In the corporate world, downsizing has resulted in major reductions in the labor force, the scaling back of wages, changes in health and pension benefits, and the loss of job security, causing many members of the working class to fear for their economic future. Conversely, many results of downsizing have been good, at least for the downsizers; homes are larger, more Americans are finishing high school and college, they join the labor force later and retire earlier, they take more vacations, and household income has doubled even with adjustment for inflation. Our economy has become more efficient and competitive in the world, and our nation is now the number one exporter. The overall impact of downsizing, whether good or bad, will probably not be known for at least a decade.

Economic Planning   The establishment by government of economic goals and the means for reaching them. Economic planning may be concerned with providing some protection against violent swings of the business cycle in a capitalistic economy. At the other extreme, it may involve total governmental control and direction of investment, production, consumption, and other economic forces. *See also* COUNCIL OF ECONOMIC ADVISERS, page 422; INDUSTRIAL POLICY, page 444; KEYNESIANISM, page 407; PRIVATIZATION, page 452.

Significance   The national government, since the Depression of the 1930s, has increasingly used economic planning, primarily through the national budget, to fight recessions and to promote full employment. Long-range resources planning was first begun by the National Resources Planning Board, established in 1934, which was charged with studying economic trends and recommending national policies to avoid runaway booms or major slumps in the economy. In the Employment Act of 1946, Congress created a new planning group, the Council of Economic Advisers. The Council is charged with responsibility for short-term planning of recommended governmental policies that will give stability to the nation's economy, promote full employment, and avoid major booms and busts. In Communist and socialist countries, economic planning is based on setting up national goals for a specific period, such as in a five-year plan, and marshalling the nation's workforce and resources, often through authoritarian control, to achieve these goals. Some democratic countries, such as France, place much greater emphasis on long-range government planning to achieve economic and social objectives than does the United States. In the 1980s, many nations followed the lead of the United States in moving away from governmental economic planning toward privatization and laissez-faire economic policies, a trend encouraged by the Reagan administration.

Featherbedding   A labor practice requiring an employer to pay for sevices that are not performed. Featherbedding is considered to be an unfair labor practice and is outlawed by the Taft-Hartley Act. An example of feather-bedding is a requirement that a radio station pay musicians who do not play, because phonograph records, rather than "live" musicians, are used. Feath-erbedding may also take the form of deliberate slowdowns in production or insistence that a job be performed by a particular individual, though others can do it as well.

Significance   The increasing automation of industry has caused con-cern in labor circles. Featherbedding practices are designed to maintain the employment of persons whose jobs are rendered useless by new techniques. Labor leaders defend the practice by comparing it to the businessperson who restricts output to keep prices high, to professions that restrict the licensing of those seeking to join the profession, and to farmers who are paid not to grow crops. Featherbedding practices are likely to be part of the labor scene except in times of full employment.

Franchise   A privilege conferred by government upon a private company to operate a public utility and to use public property for the welfare or conve-nience of the public. Franchises are granted by the national, state, and local governments to bus companies, railroads, telephone and electric power com-panies, pipelines, and other private companies performing public services. *See also* CERTIFICATE OF PUBLIC CONVENIENCE, INTEREST, AND NECESSITY, page 434; PUBLIC UTILITY, page 453.

Significance   A government grants a franchise when a condition of lim-ited competition or natural monopoly exists and competition is not practica-ble. In restricting competition, the government accepts a responsibility to regulate the service and rates of the franchised company to ensure that it op-erates in the public interest. Most franchises are granted by city govern-ments, and franchise fees constitute a sizable source of municipal funds.

Holding Company   A corporation whose assets consist of stocks in operat-ing companies, usually a controlling share in each of several allegedly com-peting companies (subsidiaries). Holding companies, although illegal under the common law, have been legalized by statute in many states. The policies and pricing of subsidiary companies are controlled through stock ownership and the membership of holding company officers on the boards of directors of subsidiaries. *See also* PUBLIC UTILITY, page 453.

Significance   In the late nineteenth and early twentieth centuries, holding companies were used to establish monopoly or near-monopoly pric-ing conditions, especially in electric and gas utilities. By the 1930s, holding companies were recognized as a threat to free enterprise competition and to the welfare of consumers in the gas and electric indutries. Congress enacted the Holding Company Act of 1935 to control the operations of such compa-nies engaged in interstate and foreign commerce. One section of this law, the so-called death sentence provision, halted the pyramiding of holding compa-nies by limiting them to two holding companies beyond the operating level.

The effect of the law in dissolving many holding company structures, along with increasing regulation of rates and services, placed the operations of utilities under a greater measure of public control.

Industrial Policy   An economic strategy that calls for the national government to strengthen the competitive position of American firms through cooperation among management, labor, and the government. The industrial policy approach places great emphasis on reindustrialization—that is, shifting from traditional "smokestack" to "high tech" industries, such as computers and telecommunications. *See also* COMPETITIVENESS, page 437.

Significance   Proposals for the development of a new industrial policy stem from a recognition of the growing industrial might of other nations and the economic competition they present to industries in the United States. Huge deficits in the American balance of trade emphasize the problem. Among supporters of an industrial policy, there is also a recognition that the rapid growth of technology—especially in the computer, communications, and automation fields—is producing a dramatic restructuring of the nation's economy. Political leaders have also become increasingly concerned with the impact of the shift to high technology upon the country's basic industries and workers, such as in steel and autos. A consensus has begun to develop that the nation must achieve a coherent national industrial policy to mitigate the impact of these changes and to take advantage of American strengths. The main thrust of the proposals for a new industrial policy focuses on a larger and more helpful role by government in both the older and the newer sectors of the economy. Supporters of the policy generally admit that the nation must learn from the Japanese, especially in the positive, promotional role played by government in that economy.

Injunction   A court order to compel or restrain the performance of an act. In the field of labor, the injunction became a weapon in the hands of management to restrain the activities of labor unions during their formative period. For many years, the injunction was used to enforce the Sherman Antitrust Act against unions. The Norris-LaGuardia Act of 1932 outlawed the use of the labor injunction when labor pursues lawful ends by legitimate means. The Taft-Hartley Act of 1947, however, empowers the President to seek an injunction when a labor dispute threatens the national welfare. *See also* INJUNCTION, page 265.

Significance   The labor injunction used prior to 1932 was based on the theory that organized labor was a conspiracy in restraint of trade and that, when a union conducted a strike, it threatened the property rights of the employer. The injunctive power exercised by an unfriendly judiciary made it virtually impossible for labor to pursue its goals. From 1890 to 1932, the major political aim of labor was to eliminate the injunction from labor-management disputes, and success was achieved in the Norris-LaGuardia Act. The return to the injunctive device in the Taft-Hartley Act caused resentment among labor leaders, and presidents have been reluctant to use this power. However, under the Taft-Harley Act, the injunction can last only 80 days, after which labor is free to strike.

Jawboning   The role of the President in applying pressure on Congress, on state political leaders, and on business, labor leaders, and other key economic decision makers to make their behavior compatible with the national goals of full employment, economic growth, and price and wage stability. Jawboning has been carried on by most presidents, with its success largely dependent upon the personality of the President and the perception of economic leaders regarding his effectiveness in generating public opinion pressures. *See also* PRESIDENT, page 196.

Significance   The President in his jawboning role acts as spokesman for the American people and as manager of the nation's prosperity. Some presidents, such as Lyndon B. Johnson, have used jawboning with telling effect to limit the freedom of action of private individuals and groups in the public interest. The threat of more stringent government action against affected companies and groups usually increases its effectiveness. Its most frequent use has been in trying to limit price and wage increases during periods of inflation without resorting to government controls. Presidents Richard M. Nixon, Gerald R. Ford, Jimmy Carter, and Ronald Reagan used jawboning sporadically to fight inflationary pressures, with some success. President George Bush sought to use jawboning to avoid tax increases, but failed.

Jurisdictional Strike   A strike involving a dispute between unions rather than between a union and an employer. Jurisdictional strikes may occur over the question of which union has the right to represent the workers or over the question of which workers are to do a specific job. For example, both carpenters and metalworkers may claim the right to install metal-framed windows, or one union may try to "raid" another union's territory. The Taft-Hartley Act and many state laws make the jurisdictional strike unlawful. *See also* STRIKE, page 456.

Significance   Jurisdictional strikes generally are viewed with little sympathy by the public. The consumer and the employer suffer the consequences of a fight in which they are innocent bystanders. Unions, too, recognize that such strikes harm them in the public eye and have tried to reach voluntary agreements on problems likely to lead to jurisdictional disputes. Nevertheless, workers may be vitally affected by problems arising over which group is to do a specific job. Jurisdictional strikes still erupt from time to time, but the number has diminished.

Labor Unions   Organizations of workers that seek to improve the economic status and working conditions of labor through collective bargaining and political action. The largest and most influential labor organization is the American Federation of Labor–Congress of Industrial Organizations (AFL–CIO). The remainder of organized labor is in independent unions, such as the Teamsters, Mine Workers, Longshoremen, Railroad Brotherhoods, and a number of smaller unions. In 1994, union membership was holding steady at 16 percent of the work force or 16.8 million members. More than 37 percent of public employees belong to unions, compared with 11.2 percent in private industry. *See also* FEDERAL LABOR RELATIONS AUTHORITY, page 236; PRESSURE GROUP, page 104; STRIKE, page 456.

Significance   Labor unions are no longer the major force on the American scene that they were following World War II, when 37 percent of the workforce was unionized. The labor movement had been strengthened and its political power increased after the merger of the AFL and the CIO in 1955. However, rivalry among unions and union leaders reduced its full potential. Organized labor's major objectives have been improving wages and hours, working conditions, and social welfare legislation. For the most part, labor unions have been identified with the Democratic party. Smaller portions of the workforce have been represented by unions in the last four decades. In 1953, union members constituted 25.5 percent of the total workforce, whereas in 1994 it was only 16 percent. Membership varies from state to state, with Hawaii and New York having the highest percentage of union workers and North and South Carolina having the smallest share. Membership in unions has been in decline due to improved technology that results in fewer factory-type jobs. However, public employees are unionizing in increasing numbers. In 1962, federal government employees were given the right to organize and bargain collectively, but not to strike. On the state and local levels, however, work stoppages and strikes of teachers, public safety personnel, and other government workers do occur and tend to become highly controversial. Only 31 work stoppages occurred in 1995, one-tenth the number 20 years earlier. Labor unions have had a rocky existence with plant owners and politicians since the 1970s. First, hundreds of unionized factories closed, as manufacturers moved their production facilities to areas of low labor costs. Then in 1981, President Ronald Reagan fired most of the nation's federal air traffic controllers for striking illegally. The North American Free Trade Agreement (NAFTA) passed in Congress, in 1993, despite an organized labor campaign to block its approval. Most recently, in 1994, a bill to prohibit employers from permanently replacing workers was blocked in Congress by a Republican-led filibuster. Some labor scholars believe that as the economy shifts to more service-type industries and more self-employment, legislation will protect workers rather than labor unions, but others feel the opposite.

License   A certificate granted under law by administrative officials, permitting private individuals to engage in certain business or professional activities. Licensing power is exercised primarily by the state and local governments, but the national government also uses it to regulate such fields as atomic materials, securities, market exchanges, and radio and television. Licensing is thus a powerful tool in the hands of government officials at all levels. *See also* CERTIFICATE OF PUBLIC CONVENIENCE, INTEREST, AND NECESSITY, page 434.

Significance   Persons seeking a license must meet the requirements established by law. Discretion is exercised by administrative officials when choosing from among many qualified applicants for a limited number of licenses. The power to grant licenses includes the power to suspend, revoke, or refuse to renew licenses for cause. Licensing by government is often demanded by professional or skilled groups, such as physicians and beauticians, to ensure proper standards and, in some cases, to restrict competition in the field.

Lockout   Action taken by an employer to close down a plant to keep workers from their jobs in order to force them to accept the employer's position in a labor controversy. Lockouts are lawful unless they violate a collective bargaining agreement or seek a goal that the law declares to be an unfair practice. *See also* STRIKE, page 456; UNFAIR LABOR PRACTICE, page 459.

Significance   The lockout is to the employer what the strike is to the union—a major weapon to force agreement. Lockouts are not commonly used, but some labor authorities point out that what the public usually considers to be a strike may also be a lockout, since the employer closes the plant by refusing to meet union demands.

Margin   The cash down payment made by a customer who purchases stocks or bonds on credit. The margin, or minimum down payment required for the purchase of securities, is set by the Board of Governors of the Federal Reserve System. The securities purchased usually constitute the collateral for the loan on the balance owed. Margin requirements set by the Federal Reserve Board relate to the level of the stock market, the demand for credit, and the state of the nation's economy. *See also* BOARD OF GOVERNORS, FEDERAL RESERVE SYSTEM, page 421.

Significance   Margin requirements are set by the Federal Reserve Board because credit purchases of stocks and bonds can have a major impact on inflationary or deflationary monetary policies carried on through the Federal Reserve System. Margin levels are also pertinent to the stability of the securities markets. In 1929, for example, margins were not regulated by government, and great overextensions of credit contributed to the collapse of the stock markets. Margin requirements have ranged from 40 to 100 percent of the purchase price of securities, but have been set at 50 percent in recent years. A near-crash of the market occurred on October 19, 1987, when the market dropped 500 points but rallied in a few days to avert what investors feared might be another major collapse of the market. Following this experience, automatic stops were installed that make a major market upheaval less likely. A limit on trades occurs when the Dow Jones Industrial Average falls by 50 points a day. This limit was imposed 30 times in 1994.

Mediation and Conciliation   Terms used interchangeably to refer to nonadversarial proceedings in which a third party attempts to settle a labor or business dispute by bringing the parties together, clarifying issues, and persuading them to reach a compromise. Unlike arbitration, the mediator or conciliator has no power to make suggested solutions binding upon the parties. *See also* ARBITRATION, page 430; FEDERAL MEDIATION AND CONCILATION SERVICE, page 466; NATIONAL MEDIATION BOARD, page 469.

Significance   Elaborate mediation and conciliation machinery has been established by the national government and most state governments. The Federal Mediation and Conciliation Service, an agency established in 1913 in the Department of Labor but given independent status by the Taft-Hartley Act, may be called into a dispute by either party, or it may offer its services. State mediation services operate on only a part-time basis in most states, but the larger industrial states have established full-time agencies. In the railway and air transport industries a federal agency, the National

Mediation Board, has been established to mediate disputes in those critical areas of industrial relations.

Merger   The pooling of assets of two companies to form a single company. Various kinds of mergers are possible, including those between competing companies (horizontal), those aimed at gaining control of raw material suppliers (vertical-backward), those involving retail outlets (vertical-forward), and those of unrelated businesses (conglomerate). *See also* SHERMAN ANTITRUST ACT, page 478.

Significance   For many years, mergers were regarded as reasonable business combinations not in violation of the antitrust laws. As a result of a rapidly increasing number of business mergers and growing pressure for governmental action, Congress enacted the Celler Antimerger Act in 1950 as an amendment to the Clayton Act. Mergers that reduce competition or that foster the growth of monopoly conditions are prohibited by the law. Many controversies have arisen concerning the application of the Celler amendment because its vague and general language leaves considerable discretion in the hands of enforcement officials. Most such controversies involve the question of whether a specific merger will increase or decrease competition. Companies often seek approval from enforcement officials prior to undertaking a merger. Since the 1960s, there has been a period of unprecedented merger activity leading to fewer and larger corporations, many operating on a multinational basis. Reagan administration policies in the 1980s resulted in megamergers and corporate giantism. This movement toward ever-larger business enterprises was justified as necessary for competing in what has become a gigantic, highly competitive global market, but many of the new, huge corporations are deep in debt as a result of financing mergers with issues of so-called junk bonds. Most mergers today are aimed at lowering the cost of production, achieving greater efficiency, and gaining a competitive edge and lead to large layoffs. Statistics show a record number of mergers in 1995, involving more than $400 billion in more than 8,000 merger deals.

Monopoly   A market condition characterized by absence of competition and artificially fixed prices for services or commodities, unaffected by the supply-demand forces of the market economy. A monopoly holds exclusive control over a product or service in terms of supply to a particular market. *See also* OLIGOPOLY, page 450.

Significance   Monopolies result when business firms establish conditions in which prices are controlled through mergers, holding companies, interlocking directorates, conspiracies to restrain trade, and collusive bidding. Under the Sherman Act of 1890, the Clayton Act of 1914, and the Federal Trade Commission Act of 1914, the national government seeks to break up monopolies and restrain their price-fixing techniques so as to foster competition in the free enterprise system. In some cases, however, the national government has permitted and even encouraged monopolies, as, for example, in granting exclusive franchises to public utilities, in conferring patent and copyright privileges, and in fostering the export trade (Webb-Pomerene Act). A natural monopoly is one bestowed by nature on a geographical area or one that, because of the nature of the enterprise, would make competition wasteful or self-destructive, such as a public utility. In 1975, in the first case of its kind, the Supreme Court held that lawyers and bar associations violate federal antitrust laws against price-fixing by setting minimum fees for legal services (*Goldfarb v. Virigina State Bar,* 421 U.S. 773). Recent administrations have sought to develop competition in fields formerly dominated by a single public utility, as, for example, in the 1984 breakup of American Telephone and Telegraph and the creation of competing companies in the telephone industry.

Multinational Corporation   A large business based in one country that carries on operations in many countries through subsidiaries. Multinationals—also known as transnational corporations—typically carry on a variety of business activities as a result of their acquisitions and diversification. Although they sometimes enjoy oligopoly or near-monopoly market conditions, their expansion is usually aimed at taking advantage of economies of scale (reductions in product cost by increasing the level of output). *See also* THIRD WORLD, page 582; WEBB-POMERENE ACT, page 480.

Significance   Much global economic activity in the form of local sales, trade, investment, and currency exchange is carried on by multinational corporations. Many of the largest are based in the United States, giving an American hue to their global operations. In the nearly 130 countries of the developing world, multinationals often have an advantage because of the stronger demand for their industrial goods and financial services over locally produced manufacturers and primary commodities. These countries of Asia, Africa, and Latin America, acting as a bloc in the United Nations have pushed since 1976 for an International Code of Conduct for Transnational Corporations, but opposition from the West, especially the United States, has been strong. The code would encourage responsible behavior, worker safety, fair taxation, and local investment of profits. Adoption of such a code received much support in 1984 when almost 2,000 people were killed in Bhopal, India, as a result of gas leak in a plant owned by Union Carbide, an American multinational. Multinationals have often been criticized for their manipulation of markets and their involvement in the political affairs of these developing countries. Also, their loyalty to the home country is often suspect, as in the case of oil companies dependent on an international market.

Nationalization   The transference of the ownership and operation of private enterprises to a national government. Nationalization may result from purchase or confiscation (expropriation), with or without compensation, and may apply to properties owned by citizens or foreign nationals. *See also* EMINENT DOMAIN, page 308.

Significance   Although American nationalization has been limited mainly to the seizure of enemy assets during time of war, other democratic nations, such as Britain, have nationalized some of their basic industries and communications, transportation, banking, and health facilities. Nationalization of private business and industry is a goal of the socialists and Communists, and in many countries private assets have been confiscated without compensation to the owners. Fear of expropriation has been a significant factor in limiting American private investments abroad, especially in the developing nations of Latin America, Asia, and Africa. American constitutional guarantees limit the nationalization powers of the national government, although private property may be appropriated by law for a public purpose under the power of eminent domain with the payment of just compensation to the private owners.

Navigable Waters   All waters within the boundaries of the United States that are or may be used as highways for interstate or foreign commerce, such as rivers, streams, lakes, inlets, and intercoastal waterways. The Supreme Court, in its decision in the *Daniel Ball* case (10 Wallace 557 [1871]), declared that the jurisdiction of Congress extends to all natural waterways that can be used for the transmission of commerce among the states and with foreign nations. *See also* ADMIRALTY JURISDICTION, page 248; *Gibbons v. Ogden,* page 472.

Significance   Although the beds of navigable waterways are under state jurisdiction, no state may constitutionally impede the flow of commerce on the waters. Approval for construction of bridges over navigable waters by state or local governments must be obtained from the U.S. Corps of Engineers.

Oligopoly   A market condition wherein the supply of a commodity is controlled by a few companies, consequently limiting competition. Oligopoly is sometimes referred to as a situation of partial or potential monopoly, because market prices can be fixed through collusion or passive competition. In such a market, business enjoys *market power;* that is, pricing policy is set by managerial discretion with little concern for competition, rather than by the competitive market forces of supply and demand. *See also* MONOPOLY, page 448.

Significance   Oligopoly conditions have tended to increase in many areas of the nation's economy in recent years, especially as a result of business mergers. Oligopoly constitutes an especially difficult enforcement problem in the national government's efforts to maintain effective competition in business, because competition appears to exist when it may not in fact exist.

Original Package Doctrine   A limitation on state taxing powers that exempts commodities from state jurisdiction so long as they remain in their original shipping containers. The Supreme Court applied the original package doctrine to products imported from foreign countries (*Brown v. Maryland,* 12 Wheaton 419 [1827]) and to those commodities produced in the United States and shipped in interstate commerce (*Leisy v. Hardin,* 135 U.S. 100 [1890]). *See also Brown v. Maryland,* page 471.

Significance   The Supreme Court's original package doctrine was intended to restrain the states from imposing a burden upon the flow of interstate and foreign commerce. Otherwise, commodities could be subjected to a series of crippling taxes levied by each state that the commodities passed through on their way to their final destination. This rule is still in effect but has been weakened by recent decisions.

Patent   An exclusive grant to an inventor by which the national government extends to an individual or corporation "the right to exclude others from making, using, or selling the invention throughout the United States" for a period of seventeen years. Patent grants are made only for bona fide "discoveries" and not for improvements upon existing inventions. They apply to any new machine, design, process, composition, substance, or plant variety. The Constitution grants Congress exclusive power to grant patents. Patents are granted by the U.S. Patent Office in the Department of Commerce. *See also* COPYRIGHT, page 439; TRADEMARK, page 458.

Significance   The U.S. Patent Office has issued more than 5 million patents since it was established by Congress in 1836. In recent years, patent applications have been made at the rate of more than 3,000 each week, and there is a huge backlog of applications in various stages of processing. In 1993, 189,000 patents were applied for, and during that same period 109,700 patents were issued. As the Founding Fathers intended, the monopoly granted to inventors has served as a major incentive in developing the thousands of useful products that typify the American economy. The United States has entered into patent agreements with most foreign states, although a few have jeopardized inventors' international patent rights by refusing to conclude reciprocal protection agreements.

Picketing   Patrolling the site of a business establishment by workers who are on strike. Peaceful picketing is a form of free speech protected by the First Amendment (*Thornhill v. Alabama,* 310 U.S. 88 [1940]). Under national and state laws, however, picketing may not be used to promote any purpose that is contrary to law or public policy. The Taft-Hartley Act and the Landrum-Griffin Act forbid picketing for such purposes as encouraging secondary boycotts or trying to force employers to recognize a union other than one already lawfully recognized. *See also* BOYCOTT, page 432.

Significance   Picketing by a labor group serves the purposes of both informing the public of the controversy and persuading customers and other workers to refrain from dealing with a business establishment. It is a potent labor weapon since many people will not cross a picket line, out of either sympathy for the strike or fear of retaliation. Labor leaders hailed the 1940 Supreme Court decision that made picketing a free speech right, but subsequent legislation and court decisions have placed numerous restrictions upon the practice.

Ponzi Schemes   Swindle-type operations in which investors are promised quick and large returns on their investments. "Profits" are paid to early investors from monies collected from subsequent investors in a variety of get-rich-quick schemes. The name, *ponzi schemes,* comes from America's most notorious swindler, Charles Ponzi, whose huge fraudulent operations in Boston in 1920 made him part of American lore and his name forever attached to these confidence rackets, where Peter is robbed to pay Paul. The most frequently used forms of ponzi schemes are the chain letter and the pyramid sales scheme. *See also* BABY BOOMERS, page 61.

Significance Ponzi-type schemes have existed throughout the history of the financial world. Charles Ponzi, an Italian immigrant and a charismatic, sweet-talking con artist, created the Security Exchange Company in 1919, supposedly buying and selling International Reply Coupons. As early investors received 50-percent interest payments in only 45 days, the gullible flocked to give Ponzi their life savings to get rich quick until it all collapsed in 1920. Ponzi was sent to federal prison, later deported to Italy, and died in a charity hospital in Rio de Janeiro in 1949. Since 1920, there have been many ponzi games. The best known scandal was the Home-Stake Production Company swindle in which some of the biggest names in industry, finance, law, and show business lost millions. In the 1990s, new ponzi rackets have involved such diverse enticements as supposedly buying Scotch cheap in Scotland and selling for profit in Japan and another that claimed huge profits from buying and selling frequent-flyer coupons. Some people consider both Social Security and the stock market as ponzi schemes. The money paid into Social Security is not invested for your retirement, but is paid out to the elderly who are collecting. The millions of baby boomers are now concerned whether there will be money for their retirement. In the stock market, when investors buy into a bull market, the price continues to rise because subsequent buyers are willing to pay more to get in on the bonanza. The only winners in a ponzi scheme, however, are those who get in, and out, early.

Privatization Private sector involvement in financing and operating businesses and industries that were once governmentally owned and operated. In the United States, the trend toward privatization has included selling, contracting, or leasing various kinds of services and production facilities to private groups by the national, state, and local units of government. In the foreign field, many countries have moved away from socialism to encourage foreign and domestic private investment so as to increase their rates of economic growth. Some of the most successful Third World countries—among them South Korea, Brazil, Singapore, Taiwan, and Hong Kong—have made great economic gains by unleashing private entreprenuers. In the United States, privatization has had its main impact on the local level, where private operators increasingly provide such services as garbage collection, snow plowing, industrial waste removal, and parking—even fire and police protection in several municipalities. *See also* LAISSEZ-FAIRE, page 15; SOCIALISM, page 26.

Significance The privatization movement was encouraged by the Reagan administration and by the public demand not to increase taxes and yet provide a meaningful level of services. Some ideologues support the trend toward privatization on the basis that capitalism in its broadest forms is the hope of the future. Others believe that governmental ownership and operation of basic service functions is essential to protect the public interest. The main opposition to privatization has come from government employee labor unions, which find it a threat to their jobs. The greatest gains for privatization have come in the "sunbelt" states of the South and West. The process of privatization differs from the role of public utilities in that it does not involve governmental regulation of rates and services but does encourage competition by private companies trying to win a contract. The largest ever privatization movement began in 1990 and involves the independent former republics of the Soviet Union and the East European former communist countries, all of which are moving toward free enterprise capitalism and a "market economy."

Proprietary Function   A governmental activity involving business-type operations ordinarily carried on by private companies. Proprietary functions include such activities as supplying electricity and gas, recreational facilities, garbage collection, and transportation and operating a liquor business. Proprietary functions carried on by one level of government may be subject to taxes levied by another level. *See also* INTERGOVERNMENTAL TAX IMMUNITY, page 43; *South Carolina v. United States,* page 425.

Significance   Governments engage in proprietary functions to secure revenue, to provide proper regulation of certain activities, to establish a model operation that private firms can emulate, or to offer services that private companies cannot or will not provide. Neither level of government can tax the other level's purely governmental functions, but the problem of distinguishing between proprietary and ordinary government activities has been a troublesome one for the courts. Supplying water to a city, for example, was held by the courts to be a regular function of government immune from federal taxes, whereas bottling and selling mineral waters by a state were held to be proprietary functions subject to federal taxation.

Public Service Commission   A regulatory agency, found in each of the states, that regulates the rates and services of public utilities operating within the state. Public service commissions vary in size from one to seven members, with most states fixing the number at three. Private utility companies regulated by the commissions include gas and electric suppliers, buses, interurban railway transit systems, taxicabs, oil and gas pipelines, telephone and telegraph services, and in some states, municipal utilities. Some of the larger cities have also established public service commissions, and in many others the city council functions in this role. *See also* PUBLIC UTILITY, page 453.

Significance   Public service commissions regulate utilities in the public interest to provide good service and fair rates for consumers. In most states, their efforts are hampered by complicated, court-imposed valuation formulas for determining rates, by inadequate operating funds, and by politically appointed staffs. In some states, the regulated companies have an inordinate influence over the commissions, which undermines the latter's regulatory role and results in poor service and high rates. Organized consumer groups in some states have successfully exerted political pressure to strengthen the regulatory function of commissions. Public service commissions increasingly are required to hold their hearings and make their decisions in public sessions. In many states, public service commissions are faced with resolving complex financial issues arising out of ballooning costs of nuclear power plant construction and the reduced use of electrical energy as a result of conservation practices.

Public Utility   A privately owned business that performs an essential service for the community and is extensively regulated by government. Congress and the state legislatures establish general criteria for regulation and create government commissions to perform the regulatory function subject to review by the courts. Typical examples of public utilities include transportation facilities, electric and gas suppliers, communication services, and water suppliers. *See also* FRANCHISE, page 443; PUBLIC SERVICE COMMISSION, page 453; RATE-MAKING, page 454.

Significance A public utility is given a licence or franchise by government when noncompetitive conditions are desirable. When government grants franchises to private businesses to carry on operations in the public interest free from competition, it has a resulting responsibility to regulate their services and rates. This involves decisions over the types of businesses that can be regulated as public utilities, the respective regulatory spheres of the nation and the states, and the methods of calculating a fair return for the company in fixing rates. In the 1990s, independent producers of electricity are changing the picture for the government-regulated, privately owned businesses. Competition is most pronounced in areas of large population with many production facilities, where independents are able to sell their energy units at lower cost than the public utilities. The large utility companies are not only beset with competition problems but must also cope with environmental regulations. As a result, government regulation of public utilities has come under a barrage of criticism.

Public Works Improvements in public facilities financed or built by government for the public welfare and convenience. Public works include such projects as parks, bridges, public buildings, roads, sewers, dams, harbors, housing, hospitals, canals, reclamation, irrigation, and navigation. *See also* CORPS OF ENGINEERS, page 490; FISCAL POLICY, page 400; PORK BARREL LEGISLATION, page 158.

Significance Public works projects not only provide facilities for public benefit but also are useful in carrying out countercyclical fiscal policies to combat economic recessions. Economists suggest that public improvements be carefully planned in advance and, during an economic downturn, be quickly put into effect. Governments on all three levels generally cooperate in carrying out public works programs, with major financing usually provided by the national government. In addition to stimulating the economy by increasing purchasing power and reducing unemployment, public works can greatly strengthen the nation by meeting present and future needs. Critics charge, however, that some public works programs are enacted for political reasons (pork barrel legislation) rather than out of need, such as the annual appropriations for rivers, harbors, and flood control. Some critics of the federal-state welfare system have advocated putting welfare recipients to work on public works projects, while others want private business to handle them on a contractual basis. The need for rebuilding much of the nation's basic infrastructure, now tired, worn, and often crumbling, constitutes a major public works challenge. The need is obvious, but financing remains a serious problem.

Rate-Making The determination by governmental regulatory agencies—national, state, and local—of the charges that privately owned public utilities will be permitted to levy for their services to the public. Rate-making agencies usually fix only maximum rates, although minimum rates may be set to avoid rate wars where competition exists. Rate-making approaches to determine fair prices include (1) the *original cost theory,* which is based on ascertaining the total investment made by the stockholders when the corporation was organized, plus subsequent capital expansion, less depreciation; (2) the *prudent investment theory,* in which the original costs of investments in the utility are determined and those investments over the years that have been imprudent or wasteful are deducted from the total; and (3) the *reproduction cost theory,* which is based on ascertaining the cost of reproducing the assets of a utility at current prices, less depreciation over the period of their use. *See also* PUBLIC UTILITY, page 453; *Smyth v. Ames,* page 473.

Significance   Rate-making involves the problems of protecting consumer interest while permitting rates high enough for the utility to earn a fair return. Rates are usually fixed to produce a return of from 7 to 10 percent, but the difficulty remains of determining the base on which this profit is to be calculated. Utilities usually favor the "original cost theory" if most of their investments have been made during the periods of high cost. If made during periods of deflation, "reproduction cost" would probably be favored. The Supreme Court has favored the use of the "prudent investment theory" by federal regulatory agencies, although it has not tried to establish a single formula (*FPC v. Hope Natural Gas Co.,* 320 U.S. 591 [1943]). Utilities often appeal to the courts when they regard their return as too small. With the growth of consumer protection, rate-making agencies have come under increasing criticism for the lenient regulation and liberal rate increases. Members of regulatory commissions are often appointed from the industry subject to their regulation and rate-making, resulting, it is often charged, in decisions that favor the utility and penalize consumers.

Restraint of Trade   The use in the business world of trusts, monopolies, price fixing, collusion, conspiracy, or other practices that hamper or eliminate a market economy based on free competition. The phrase is used in the Sherman Act of 1890, which forbids any "conspiracy in the restraint of trade." *See also* SHERMAN ANTITRUST ACT, page 478.

Significance   Although the laissez-faire theory of free enterprise calls for economic freedom from governmental controls, some measure of regulation of business and commerce has proved necessary to maintain free competition. Major federal statutes that have sought to prevent private actions in restraint of trade and free competition include the Sherman Act of 1890, the Clayton Act of 1914, and the Federal Trade Commission Act of 1914. Despite the historical emphasis on free enterprise, these acts reflect strong common law precedents for antitrust policy.

Right to Work Law   A law that prohibits making union membership a qualification for employment. Twenty states have constitutional or statutory provisions that a person may not be compelled to join a union or to remain a member of a union to hold a job. Right to work laws establish the principle of the "open shop." *See also* CLOSED SHOP, page 435; UNION SHOP, page 460.

Significance   Right to work laws are designed to curtail the closed shop and union shop. Though union shops are permitted by section 14(b) of the Taft-Hartley Act, that Act also permits states to pass right to work legislation. These laws are prompted in part by exposures of union corruption and by concern for workers who are penalized for not holding union membership. Some states seek to attract industry by enacting right to work laws that greatly weaken labor unions. Labor leaders strongly oppose these laws. They argue that nonunion members benefit from the union's efforts and that the laws will destroy unions and the principle of collective bargaining. Right to work laws have helped to attract industry to the "sunbelt" and other states where companies have often been able to remain free of union pressures. Unlike the American concept, the view expressed by many countries in human rights declarations and covenants is that right to work implies an ultimate responsibility of government to provide a job for all persons who seek work.

Strike   A stoppage of work by employees for the purpose of winning concessions from their employer on matters of wages, hours, or working conditions. The right to strike, except for purposes prohibited by law, is considered to be a fundamental right of free workers. Government employees are not legally permitted to strike, but such strikes, particularly by local government employees and teachers, have increased in recent years. National and state laws contain a variety of limitations on the right to strike. For example, strikes may not be used to promote a secondary boycott or other unfair labor practice. Procedures are also provided by law for "cooling-off" periods, injunctions, fact-finding boards, and mediation services in order to avoid strikes. *See also* COOLING-OFF PERIOD, page 439; JURISDICTIONAL STRIKE, page 445; LOCKOUT, page 446; PICKETING, page 451.

Significance   The strike is labor's most effective weapon, but it is often damaging to both sides and to the public. A strike in one industry has an effect on other industries dependent upon the struck plants for supplies. The Taft-Hartley Act of 1947 permits the President to obtain an 80-day injunction if a strike might cause a national emergency. Workers on strike are not considered to have given up their jobs, and a lawful dispute may not be interfered with by "strikebreakers" or "scabs" who replace the striking workers. Many unions provide strikers with subsistence allowances during a strike. Although federal employees have a right to organize and bargain collectively, they do not under the law have a right to strike. In 1982, President Ronald Reagan, in declaring that strikes against the federal government are illegal, fired several thousand air traffic controllers who had refused to accept a presidential ultimatum to return to work. In 1995, President Bill Clinton signed an executive order that forbids large federal contractors from hiring replacement workers during a strike. In 1996, this decision, intended to help striking unions, was ruled invalid by a U.S. Appeals Court on the grounds that it conflicts with federal labor law guaranteeing the right of the employer to hire permanent replacements for economic strikers. President Clinton ordered the Justice Department "to take all appropriate steps to have this decision overturned." The strike, which has been labor's major weapon since unionization began, has today been supplemented by such approaches as public relations campaigns to embarrass large companies, environmental lawsuits, and safety inspectors to pressure employers to grant concessions. Also, many union leaders are promoting cooperation with management as a better system for securing benefits. Some companies have established workplace teams in which management and union representatives work together to improve production techniques and job satisfaction.

Subsidy   Financial or other forms of aid bestowed by government upon private individuals, companies, or groups to improve their economic position and accomplish some public objective. Subsidies may be direct, like sums of money paid to shipbuilders and farmers, or indirect, like the tariff that protects American business, labor, and agriculture from foreign competition. A subsidy may take the form of a grant by one level of government to another level. Subsidies may relate wholly to domestic affairs, or they may be aimed at achieving some foreign policy objective. *See also* FREEDOM TO FARM ACT OF 1996, page 500; PRICE SUPPORT, page 486; TAX EXEMPTION, page 420.

Significance   Although subsidies are granted to private individuals by all three levels of American government, the national government has been the most active. The federal income tax, for example, consists of a maze of subsidies, such as tax exemptions and tax shelters, that are aimed at granting favorable treatment to various groups of taxpayers. Since Alexander Hamilton first proposed subsidies in his financial program and his famous Report on Manufactures, they have been a continuing and significant function of the national government, amounting to billions of dollars annually in recent years. Major beneficiaries of governmental subsidies are or have been railroads, airlines, farmers, businesses, home builders, defense contractors, the unemployed, and veterans. In many cases, subsidies to one group may imperil the economic position of another group, for example, the effect on railroads of extensive subsidies to airlines. In 1979, Congress authorized a subsidy in the form of a $1.5 billion loan guarantee to the Chrysler Corporation to avoid the impending bankruptcy of the large corporation and the massive impact it would have had on the nation's economy. In the mid-1990s, efforts to achieve a balanced budget in seven years led to the reduction and in some cases elimination of subsidies. For example, farm subsidies, which have been in place since the Roosevelt administration in the 1930s, will be progressively reduced until eliminated in 2002 and will be replaced by a free market system in agriculture.

Trade Gap   The difference in the U.S. balance of trade between the value of all exports in relation to the total value of imports. The trade gap is often a key election issue because it indicates the health of the American economy, reflects the problem of trying to maintain good employment levels, and, in general, reveals the nation's competitiveness in the economic world. *See also* BALANCE OF TRADE, page 534; COMPETITIVENESS, page 437; GATT, page 551; KEY ELECTION ISSUES, page 85; NAFTA, page 567.

Significance   For most Americans, the trade gap is of little importance as an election issue until it affects an individual's economic well-being. The trade deficit for the United States has been running most years at over $100 billion annually. One group of Americans believes that open markets and competitiveness should dominate in the world marketplace and that the United States should continue to provide leadership in this endeavor. They argue that although some American companies have lost out in competition, others—such as those manufacturing computers, software, commercial aircraft, and films—have tended to dominate world markets. A rival group holds that the United States has opened its market to all forms of competition, but many countries, especially Japan and Germany, have used questionable means to keep American products out of their markets. In agriculture, for example, they claim that American farmers could dominate the world food markets if a free market system prevailed. If the trade gap widens, causing widespread loss of jobs and income, Americans are likely to demand a restoration of protective tariffs and other devices of economic nationalism, which once dominated world trade.

Trademark   A name, mark, or symbol used by a manufacturer or dealer to identify a product or service to the consuming public. Trademarks are granted by the Patent Office through a procedure similar to that for obtaining patents. Registered trademarks are valid for twenty years, provided registrants file affidavits with the Patent Office every five years attesting to their use, and are renewable for subsequent twenty-year periods. Trademark protection is left up to registrants, who can take civil suit action in the courts when infringements occur. *See also* COPYRIGHT, page 439; PATENT, page 451.

Significance   Like patents and copyrights, a trademark bestows a monopoly right upon an individual or company. Trademarks are significant not only to registrants, whose sales of products may be increased through such identification, but also to consumers, who are protected from a welter of confusion of similar marks and symbols when making purchases. In 1946, Congress enacted the Lanham Trademark Act, which revised and codified the numerous federal statutes relating to trademarks.

Trust   Two or more corporations linked together by assigning the voting rights of a majority of stockholders in each corporation to a single group of trustees. The term is also commonly used to describe any huge corporation or group of corporations that pursues monopolistic policies in the production or supplying of goods and services. *See also* CLAYTON ACT, page 474; SHERMAN ANTITRUST ACT, page 478.

Significance   The trust as a business combination was used extensively to reduce or eliminate competition among previously competing companies until it was outlawed by the Sherman Act of 1890. The Supreme Court, however, subsequently modified the antitrust provisions with its "rule of reason," which applied the Sherman Act only to those combinations that unreasonably restrict competition and in which a clear intention of monopoly can be shown. While most trusts fell to renewed competition after the turn of the century, a few continued to flourish until the 1930s, when the Department of Justice engaged in a vigorous trust-busting campaign. In recent years, the department has turned its attention to mergers and collusive practices that, like the trusts of an earlier period, are substantially reducing competition.

Unemployment Insurance   A program of insurance under the Social Security Act of 1935 that provides for payment of funds for a limited period of time to workers who are laid off or discharged for reasons beyond their control. The program is administered by the states under national supervision. Under the plan, Congress imposes a tax on the payroll of employers of four or more workers. Ninety percent of the revenue from this tax is credited to each state that comes under the act (all do), with the remainder used for administrative purposes. All proceeds of the tax are held by the national Department of the Treasury in separate state accounts to be paid out as needed by each state. Each state determines the amount to be paid to each unemployed person, for how long, and under what conditions. Benefits are available to unemployed persons who register with the proper state agency and are willing to accept suitable employment. Most states penalize employers with poor employment records by raising their payroll tax. Overall supervision of state plans is in the hands of the Unemployment Insurance Service in the Department of Labor. *See also Social Security Cases,* page 522.

Significance   Unemployment insurance is one of the major programs of social insurance in effect today. Unemployment insurance makes public relief unnecessary and puts some purchasing power in the hands of the unemployed. Critics of the plan charge that it encourages laziness, and many oppose the compulsory nature of the plan. Supporters point out that unemployment tends to have a chain effect and that the loss of purchasing power endangers other jobs. In 1976, Congress extended coverage to state and local government employees. In times of high unemployment, funds have been made available for workers not regularly covered, such as farm or household workers.

Unfair Labor Practice   Activity by a labor union or an employer that is defined by law as constituting a threat to industrial peace. Unfair labor practices are defined in the Taft-Hartley Act of 1947. Employers are forbidden to interfere with the rights of unions to organize, to discriminate against union members, or to refuse to bargain collectively. Unions may not discriminate against or coerce employees who are not union members, or engage in such practices as secondary boycotts, featherbedding, jurisdictional strikes, charging excessive dues or fees, or refusing to bargain collectively. *See also* BOYCOTT, page 432; FEATHERBEDDING, page 443; JURISDICTIONAL STRIKE, page 445; TAFT-HARTLEY ACT, page 478.

Significance   By listing unfair labor practices, Congress sought to cope with the more common causes of labor-management unrest. The Taft-Hartley Act represented a departure from previous legislation by listing unfair union tactics as well as unfair employer behavior. The National Labor Relations Board (NLRB) and its General Counsel are charged with the duty of policing unfair activities. Exactly what constitutes an unfair practice is often open to dispute since the law cannot cover every eventuality. Many NLRB decisions on unfair practices are appealed to the federal courts. In 1995, the Supreme Court held that a company may not refuse to hire a worker because the person is a paid organizer for a union trying to unionize that company (*NLRB v. Town and Country Electric,* 116 S. Ct. 450).

Unfair Trade Practice   Any business activity that deceives or misleads consumers and results in their being sold shoddy, dangerous, or overpriced goods or services. Examples of unfair trade practices include false and misleading advertising, misbranding, improper labeling, conspiracies to fix prices, collusive bidding, discrimination against buyers, price cutting to eliminate competition, and other practices in restraint of trade. *See also* CLAYTON ACT, page 474; CONSUMERISM, page 438; FEDERAL TRADE COMMISSION, page 467.

Significance   Unfair trade practices were outlawed by the Congress in two laws enacted in 1914, the Clayton Act and the Federal Trade Commission Act. The former forbids price discrimination, price cutting to restrain trade, and purchases of stock among competitors. The latter seeks to promote fair competition and, through the Wheeler-Lea Act amendments of 1938, outlaws unfair and deceptive practices and false advertising of foods, drugs, cosmetics, and other commodities. Both acts are administered by the Federal Trade Commission. Consumer interests are also protected by the Food and Drug Administration, which safeguards against misbranding, adulteration, and false labeling.

Union Shop   An establishment in which all newly hired workers must join the union after a specified period of time, usually 30 days. Unlike the closed shop, now outlawed, the employee need not be a member of the union in order to be hired. *See also* AGENCY SHOP, page 429; CLOSED SHOP, page 435; RIGHT TO WORK LAW, page 455.

Significance   The union ship is the major form of union security permitted by law. About 75 percent of organized labor works in union shops. The union shop eliminates "free riders" who would benefit from collective bargaining agreements without supporting the union. Many employees object to being forced to join a union, but they must remain members in order to hold their jobs. The Taft-Hartley Act authorizes union shop agreements but permits states to eliminate them through right to work laws.

Usury   Charging interest in excess of the maximum rate permitted by law. State usury laws provide for civil and criminal actions against persons or lending institutions charging illegal interest rates. During periods of inflation and high interest rates, lending institutions circumvent usury laws by charging maximum rates and adding fees that have the effect of increasing the total cost to the borrower. *See also* CONSUMERISM, page 438.

Significance   All states have enacted usury laws, although the legal maximum rates vary considerably. Usury laws are aimed mainly at holding down interest rates charged by small loan companies and pawnbrokers. Usury laws have gained in importance as the American economy has become increasingly dependent on consumer credit. When interest rates exceed those permitted by usury laws, either few loans are made, with a subsequent loss of business activity, or means are found to get around the usury laws.

Workers' Compensation   An insurance program, in effect in all states, that provides compensation for workers injured on their jobs and for dependents of workers who are killed in the course of employment. In most states, the program is financed entirely by the employer, who must take out private or public insurance for this purpose. Occupational diseases are also covered in many states. An administrative agency is generally established to settle claims arising under the law, with appeal to the courts possible. State laws vary with regard to types of employers and occupations covered.

Significance   Workers' compensation has replaced the system that required an injured worker to bring a lawsuit against his or her employer to recover damages. In such lawsuits, the employer could be freed from liability if it could be shown that the injury was the fault of the worker or of another employee. Workers' compensation is based on the theory that whatever the cause, the worker cannot bear the financial burden of a lawsuit and that insurance is to be carried as a regular cost of production. Workers' compensation laws have reduced hardship and have sustained families who might otherwise have to seek welfare aid. They have been especially critical in work fields that are dangerous, such as coal mining.

IMPORTANT AGENCIES

Antitrust Division   A major division of the Department of Justice, which has responsibility for enforcement of antitrust laws. The Antitrust Division investigates, brings charges, prosecutes, negotiates, and enforces final judgments. The division also studies and reports on competitive conditions in the nation's economy. *See also* ANTITRUST LAWS, page 430.

Significance   The forcefulness with which the national government has carried on its antimonopoly programs has depended often on economic conditions and on the person chosen by the President and the Attorney General to head the Antitrust Division. When Thurman W. Arnold, a law professor dedicated to breaking up monopolies, headed the Antitrust Division, almost as many legal proceedings were initiated in the five years of his tenure from 1938 to 1943 as had been started in the preceding half century following the enactment of the Sherman Act. The Antitrust Division carries out its enforcement duties through both civil and criminal actions.

Bureau of the Census   An agency within the Department of Commerce that collects and publishes a variety of statistical data about the people and the social and economic characteristics of the nation. Its best-known and major function is to count the population of the United States every ten years (the decennial census) as required by the Constitution for the purpose of apportioning representatives among the several states. In addition, it compiles information and statistics on housing, state and local government, agriculture, mineral industries, construction, transportation, imports and exports, shipping, manufacturing, retail trades, and other areas. *See also* CENSUS, page 135.

Significance   The Bureau of the Census is a repository and disseminator of information vital to Congress, the executive branch, and the public for the development of public policy. Its continuous flow of studies is available in most libraries in print and on computer tapes. Its *Bureau of the Census Catalog* is a guide to its many publications. The *Statistical Abstract of the United States* and the *Historical Statistics of the United States, Colonial Times to 1970* are useful sources of information. Information collected by the Bureau from individuals or institutions is strictly confidential and may be used only for statistical purposes. Census publications, however, provide information of great use to business and industry in planning their operations. The Bureau of the Census has come under heavy criticism for its 1980 and 1990 counts. It is charged that in 1980 there was a 9 million undercount and that the 1990 count was even further off the mark. There is essentially no way of determining the accuracy of each census, however, despite its importance in apportioning congressional seats and in dividing up federal grant money by population of the states or local units.

Consumer Product Safety Commission (CPSC)   A five-member independent regulatory agency established by Congress in 1972 to reduce the risk of injury to consumers from products sold to them. The commission has primary responsibility for protecting consumers, superseding the role carried out by a number of other agencies of the national government. The Consumer Product Safety Act of 1972 also authorizes the commission to carry on research concerning consumer product standards, to develop uniform safety standards, to minimize conflicting state and local regulations, to engage in various consumer information and education programs, and to establish an Injury Information Clearinghouse. Consumers and consumer organizations can petition the commission to secure the issuance, amendment, or revocation of a consumer product safety rule. *See also* CONSUMERISM, page 438.

Significance   Congress, by the 1972 Act and by creation of the Consumer Product Safety Commission, reacted to growing political pressures from consumer organizations and from many individuals who have been injured or endangered by consumer products. In addition to the commission's broad new powers, it also assumed responsibility for enforcing the Flammable Fabrics Act, the Poison Prevention Packaging Act, the Hazardous Substances Act, and the act that requires safety devices on refrigerators. By forcing enforcement of consumer product safety in one federal agency, the Congress sought to achieve effectiveness and political support. Efforts by Congress to establish a broader, more powerful Consumer Protection Agency during the 1970s met with failure, and in the 1980s and 1990s the nation began to move away from dependence on government for consumer product safety and toward self-regulation.

Department of Commerce   One of the fourteen major departments of the national administration headed by a secretary with Cabinet rank. The Department of Commerce and Labor, founded in 1903, was split in 1913 by Congress into the two separate departments of Commerce and Labor. Major units found in the Department of Commerce and the main responsibility of each are (1) the Bureau of the Census, which conducts the decennial census; (2) the National Oceanic and Atmospheric Administration, which monitors the physical and biological environment, including weather forecasting; (3) the International Trade Administration, which promotes world trade and seeks to strengthen the American trade position; (4) the National Bureau of Standards, which maintains basic units for testing and measuring in business and industry; (5) the Minority Business Development Agency, which seeks to establish, preserve, and strengthen ownership of business by members of minority groups; (6) the Patent and Trademark Office, which examines and grants patents and trademarks; and (7) the Economic Development Administration, which provides aid to areas with substantial and persistent unemployment. *See also* CABINET, page 185.

Significance   The Department of Commerce has major responsibility for providing services for the business community. It promotes and protects the interests of business at home and abroad. It is primarily a service, rather than a regulatory, agency. The Secretary of Commerce is, typically, a businessperson or one who has been identified as friendly to the business community. The department places its main emphasis on "promoting the national interest through the encouragement of the competitive, free enterprise system."

Department of Labor   A major department of Cabinet status that administers laws designed to promote the welfare of wage earners through improved working conditions and employment opportunities. The department, established originally in 1903 as Commerce and Labor and separated in 1913, is headed by the Secretary of Labor and is divided into seven major operational units: (1) Employment and Training Administration, which appraises national manpower requirements to deal with unemployment, underemployment, the impact of automation, apprenticeship training, and aspects of the war on poverty, including the Job Corps, and administers the unemployment compensation program and the United States Employment Service; (2) Labor-Management Services, which administers laws relating to welfare and pension plans, enforces the Labor-Management Reporting and Disclosure Act relative to internal affairs of labor unions, and provides a wide variety of industrial relations services; (3) Labor Statistics, which is the principal fact-finding agency on labor economics issues; (4) Employment Standards Administration, which administers the wage and hour laws and seeks to improve working conditions, with special attention to the needs of women, children, and minority groups; (5) Occupational Safety and Health Administration, which develops and regulates industrial safety and health standards; (6) Mine Safety and Health Administration, which promotes and regulates safe mining conditions; and (7) Veterans' Employment and Training Service, which oversees the implementation of programs for training and employing veterans. *See also* CABINET, page 185.

Significance   The Department of Labor was established to give labor a direct voice at the highest level of government to accord it equal political status with agriculture and business. Increased federal labor legislation and growing American international economic involvement have strengthened the influence and stature of the department in meeting national and international problems related to labor and the economy in general.

Department of Transportation (DOT)   One of the fourteen major departments of the national administration, headed by a secretary with Cabinet rank. The department, established in 1966, brought together more than 30 separate agencies and bureaus dealing with transportation. Its major components include the Federal Aviation Administration, the Federal Highway Administration, the Federal Railroad Administration, the Urban Mass Transportation Administration, the National Highway Traffic Safety

Administration, the Coast Guard, the Maritime Administration, and the Saint Lawrence Seaway Development Corporation. Its major responsibility is to develop the nation's overall transportation policy, focusing on highways, mass transit, railroads, aviation, and safety. *See also* AMTRAK, page 429; CABINET, page 185.

Significance   The Department of Transportation was created to develop national transportation policies and programs to achieve efficient transportation at low cost. Although several important agencies concerned with transportation, such as the Federal Maritime Commission, were not included in the Department, the Secretary of Transportation may suggest policy guidelines to independent agencies. Safety in all forms of transportation is a major concern of the department. The energy crisis of the 1970s and 1980s has placed added responsibility on the department to foster development of effective mass transportation facilities. Whenever a plane crash occurs, the Federal Aviation Administration (FAA) and the National Transportation Safety Board carry out detailed investigations to determine the cause.

Export-Import Bank of the United States (Eximbank)   A government corporation that guarantees private credit and makes direct loans to foreign and domestic businesses to promote the flow of trade. The Export-Import Bank, originally chartered in 1934, is governed by a five-member bipartisan board appointed by the President with Senate consent.

Significance   The Export-Import Bank, also known as Eximbank, was originally created to foster trade between the United States and the Soviet Union and with Latin America, but its operations have become almost worldwide in scope. Its loans must be repaid in American dollars, and capital equipment needed by the party receiving the loan must be purchased in the United States. The bank is an important contributor to aid programs for underdeveloped countries, financing the building of steel mills, roads, dams, manufacturing plants, and other projects. It also encourages private loans by banks and exporters by providing guarantees and insurance. Eximbank is authorized to have a maximum of $40 billion outstanding in loans, guarantees, and insurance. Most of its loans go to corporate giants, such as Boeing and General Electric.

Federal Communications Commission (FCC)   A seven-member independent regulatory commission that controls interstate and foreign communication via radio, television, telegraph, and cable. The FCC was created by and administers the Federal Communications Act of 1934. Under the Act, the FCC grants licenses to broadcasters and enforces regulations prohibiting indecent language and lotteries. The FCC has no power to regulate rates charged sponsors of radio and television programs, but Congress designated telephone, telegraph, and cable services as "common carriers" and, therefore, subject to extensive regulation of rates and services. The Telecommunication Act of 1996, however, ended this regulatory activity and now permits the common carriers to compete in each other's markets. The FCC also implements provisions of the Communications Satellite Act of 1962. *See also,* COMSAT, page 437; DEREGULATION, page 440; EQUAL TIME RULE, page 76;

INDEPENDENT REGULATORY COMMISSION, page 229; TELECOMMUNICATION ACT, page 479.

Significance   A major responsibility of the FCC is that of granting licenses to broadcasters, since only a limited number of radio frequencies and television channels are available. A television license, for example, is granted free by the FCC but may be worth millions of dollars to the licensee. As a result, the FCC has often had to select from a number of applicants who may bring political pressure to bear on the commissioners. Although its regulation of broadcasting has continued, in 1984 it ended regulation of telephone services as part of the deregulation program fostered by Congress in recent years. Because licenses granted by the FCC are for fixed periods and must be renewed, much controversy has centered around renewal hearings on the issue of what constitutes a record of adequate service in the public interest and whether the licensee has achieved such a record. In the 1990s, political battles are being fought concerning the role of the FCC and other federal agencies in the development of new technologies, such as digital radio, high-definition television, and cellular phones. Private companies claim they need government help to compete effectively in developing and marketing such products, especially in competing with Japanese companies.

Federal Deposit Insurance Corporation (FDIC)   A government corporation established in 1933 that insures depositor's accounts in participating banks up to $100,000 for each account. The FDIC insurance system is financed through annual assessments levied on privately owned banks. Member banks of the Federal Reserve System must participate, and nonmember banks may request to join the program. The FDIC is directed by the Comptroller of the Currency and by two directors appointed by the President with Senate consent. *See also* FEDERAL RESERVE SYSTEM, page 400.

Significance   The FDIC program promotes stability by maintaining the confidence of depositors. Prior to the FDIC guarantee, "runs" on individual banks and general bank "panics" were quite common. They were difficult to control because banks do not normally keep enough cash on hand to meet widespread demands from depositors. All but a small fraction of the commercial banks in the United States are insured by the FDIC. The Federal Savings and Loan Insurance Corporation (FSLIC), operating under the supervision of the Federal Home Loan Bank Board, until 1990 insured each depositor's account up to $100,000 in all federally chartered and in most state-chartered savings and loan associations. The National Credit Union Administration continues to insure members' accounts up to $100,000 in all federal and most state-chartered credit unions. In the late 1980s, as a result of deregulation, many savings and loan associations suffered from financial instability. Congress eliminated the FSLIC and placed FSLIC accounts under FDIC management. A national confidence crisis ensued when savings and loans misdeeds, corruption, and thievery were revealed. In the Financial Institutions Reform, Recovery, and Enforcement Act of 1989, Congress provided for payment of billions of dollars to insured depositors and created the Resolution Trust Corporation to oversee, through its RTC Oversight Board, the resolution of this massive debt.

Federal Emergency Management Agency (FEMA)   The central agency within the federal government for emergency planning, preparedness, mitigation, response, and recovery. It was established by executive order in March 1979 to consolidate the nation's emergency-related programs. It works with state and local governments, funds emergency programs, offers technical guidance and training, and deploys federal resources in times of catastrophic disaster. These activities are designed to protect life and property and provide recovery assistance after a disaster. *See also* DOMESTIC TERRORISM, page 73; MOBILIZATION, page 563; STOCKPILING, page 578.

Significance   Ten regional offices are responsible for accomplishing FEMA's national program goals. The Federal Emergency Management Agency reports directly to the White House and manages the President's Disaster Relief Fund, the source of most federal funding assistance after major natural disasters or human-caused emergencies. After all types of national diasters, whether from hurricanes, tornados, other severe weather conditions, earthquakes, floods, fires, riots, or bombings, FEMA steps in. Other activities include planning for emergencies at commercial nuclear power plants and Army chemical stockpile sites, emergency food and shelter funding for the homeless, response to major terrorist incidents, and plans to ensure continuity during national security emergencies. The agency also provides national leadership in fire safety and prevention through the United States Fire Administration (USFA) and manages the National Flood Insurance Program through the Federal Insurance Administration (FIA). Civil Defense, once a part of FEMA, was responsible for providing protection from radioactivity due to nuclear attack by designating shelters stocked with food and establishing warning systems. With the end of the Cold War in the late 1980s, FEMA's efforts were turned toward protection from natural and human-caused disasters.

Federal Maritime Commission (FMC)   A five-member independent regulatory agency that controls rates and services of water carriers engaged in foreign and domestic offshore commerce. Members are appointed by the President with the Senate's approval for four-year terms. The FMC's authority includes approving rates and routes, settling disputes, and prescribing working conditions for seafarers. The FMC works closely with its international counterpart, the International Maritime Organization (IMO), headquartered in London. *See also* INDEPENDENT REGULATORY COMMISSION, page 229.

Significance   The Federal Maritime Commission was established in 1961 to make and enforce regulations relating to the merchant marine. Foreign shippers are freer from governmental controls than are coastal and inland waterway shippers. The Maritime Administration in the Department of Transportation aids shipbuilders and operators through the payment of "construction differentials" and "operating differentials" as subsidies to enable American shippers to compete with foreign companies. The FMC works with the Department of State to eliminate foreign discrimination against American shipping.

Federal Mediation and Conciliation Service   An agency formerly within the Department of Labor, but given independent status under the Taft-Hartley

Act of 1947. The service is headed by a director appointed by the President with the Senate's consent. The service has no law enforcement authority but relies upon persuasion to prevent strikes that will impede the free flow of interstate commerce. Professional mediators employed by the Service assist in the settlement of labor-management disputes and try to promote good relations between labor and management. The Taft-Hartley Act requires that employers and unions must file notice of any dispute not settled 30 days after either side has expressed an intention to terminate an existing contract. The Mediation and Conciliation Service then tries to conciliate the dispute, though neither side is compelled to accept the solution suggested. The service may also offer to enter a dispute on its own motion or at the request of the parties. The service often helps in the selection of arbitrators when both sides accept arbitration. *See also* MEDIATION AND CONCILIATION, page 447.

Significance   The Federal Mediation and Concilation Service reflects government policy to prevent the disruptive influence of strikes whenever possible. The service has been highly successful in carrying on its functions because of the high prestige of its employees and its independent status in the government organization.

Federal Trade Commission (FTC)   A five-member independent regulatory commission established by Congress in 1914 to promote fair competition in business and to restrict unfair business practices in interstate and foreign commerce. Commissioners are appointed by the President with the Senate's approval for seven-year terms. The FTC enforces the Clayton and the Federal Trade Commission Acts of 1914. It seeks to prevent illegal combinations in restraint of trade, deception, price discriminations, price fixing, interlocking directorates, fraudulent advertising of foods, drugs, and cosmetics, and other business activities that reduce competition or endanger or defraud the consumer. The operations of the FTC include making rules and regulations to establish a code of fair competition, holding hearings concerning alleged violations, and enforcing decisions through cease and desist orders and injunctions granted by federal courts. *See also* CAVEAT VENDITOR, page 434; INDEPENDENT REGULATORY COMMISSION, page 229.

Significance   Most of the work of the FTC is carried on by persuading businesspeople to cease some activity of doubtful legality. The FTC plays a relatively minor role in enforcing antimonopoly legislation and directs most of its efforts to protecting consumer interests in preventing deceptive advertising, fraud, and the sale of dangerous products. Although the duties of the FTC are varied, its underlying purpose is to strengthen the free enterprise system by preventing corrupt practices and by keeping competition both free and fair. Yet it has often come under attack from critics who charge it with being probusiness and not energetic enough in protecting the rights of consumers. In 1994, Congress strengthened the FTC's authority to act against deceptive telephone solicitation. State attorneys general can now bring civil suits to seek compensation and damages against the operators.

National Aeronautics and Space Administration (NASA)   An independent agency established in 1958 to conduct research for the solution of problems of flight within and outside the earth's atmosphere and to develop, construct, test, and operate aeronautical and space vehicles. It conducts activities required for the exploration of space with manned and unmanned vehicles and arranges for the most effective utilization of the scientific and engineering resources of the United States with other nations engaged in aeronautical and space activities for peaceful purposes. Directors of NASA centers are responsible for the execution of agency programs, largely through contracts with research, development, and manufacturing enterprises. NASA has seven program offices in the fields of aeronautics; space access and technology; life and microgravity sciences and applications; mission to planet Earth, which focuses on global climate change and integrated functioning of the Earth as a system; space science; space flight; and space communications. While its headquarters is in Washington, DC, the host center for the agency's shuttle program is in Houston, and there are 10 centers in all around the country, including the Jet Propulsion Laboratory.

Significance   Once at the forefront of American pride as the agency that set Neil Armstrong on the moon in 1969, NASA has faced a number of mishaps and operational problems since the Apollo missions. With the explosion of the *Challenger* in 1986, killing all aboard as millions of Americans watched on television, public support diminished. Concern for the national budget deficit made the public increasingly hostile toward multibillion dollar spending for "big science." Nevertheless, many scientists feel that the experiments being conducted and the information from projects, such as the space telescope, are yielding data of such great value for advancement in the fields of technology, physics, and medicine that funding must be continued. Two historic dockings took place in 1995 between the space shuttle *Atlantis* and the Russian space station *Mir*. For the first time an American, Norman Thagard, was launched aboard a foreign space craft, a Russian Soyuz, to a docking with *Mir* and two Russian crewmen returned to earth aboard *Atlantis*. NASA, in 1995, announced plans to privatize space shuttle operations over a three-year period, saving a billion dollars from their $3 billion annual budget. It also endorsed the development of a new generation of reusable rockets that would be built, owned, and operated by private companies as part of the NASA program.

National Labor Relations Board (NLRB)   An independent regulatory commission, established in 1935, which administers the Wagner Act, the Taft-Harley Act, and the Landrum-Griffin Act relative to unfair labor practices and the designation of appropriate bargaining units. The NLRB consists of five members appointed by the President, with the Senate's consent, for five-year terms, and a General Counsel similarly appointed for a four-year term. The Board is authorized to issue cease and desist orders, to hold bargaining representative elections, and to seek court injunctions and other enforcement orders. The General Counsel conducts investigations, issues complaints, and conducts prosecutions before the board. Actual hearings are held by trial examiners, with final orders issuing from the Board. *See also* FEDERAL LABOR RELATIONS AUTHORITY, page 226; *NLRB v. Jones and Laughlin Steel Corp.* page 472.

Significance   The NLRB, like other independent regulatory commissions, reflects the policy of utilizing an independent agency to not only administer policy but also perform quasi-legislative and quasi-judicial functions in important sectors of the economy. It has played a crucial role in the development of broad policies as well as specific rules to meet the complicated problems posed by the growth of labor unions and the increasing problems of labor-management relations in an industrial society. Whereas all of the independent regulatory commissions have been charged with being captives of the businesses they regulate, many critics have charged the NRLB with being labor dominated. However, appointments made in the 1980s by President Ronald Reagan resulted in a strong promanagement posture for the NRLB, an attitude that continued under President George Bush.

National Mediation Board   An independent agency established in 1934, under an amendment to the Railway Labor Act of 1926, to mediate differences between management and labor in the railroad and airline fields and to determine bargaining representatives. The board consists of three members appointed by the President with the Senate's consent. For the settlement of disputes growing out of the application of collective bargaining contracts, the National Railroad Adjustment Board, consisting of representatives of the unions and the carriers, is called into action. In the event of deadlocks in the Adjustment Board, the National Mediation Board appoints a referee. Parties may appeal to the courts for enforcement of any settlements reached through this procedure. If the dispute does not involve a collective bargaining agreement and the National Mediation Board cannot effect a solution, the law authorizes the President to appoint a special fact-finding board and, if this fails, to place the carrier under government operation. *See also* MEDIATION AND CONCILIATION, page 447.

Significance   The National Mediation Board and the related procedures are designed to prevent strikes and lockouts in the crucial areas of rail and air transport. With occasional lapses, these procedures have proved effective and work stoppages in these fields are relatively rare. Every effort is made to avoid government-imposed solutions and to help the parties reach agreement.

Securities and Exchange Commission (SEC)   A five-member independent regulatory commission established by the Securities Exchange Act of 1934 to regulate the buying and selling of securities (stocks, bonds, options, and so forth). Commissioners are appointed by the President, with the Senate's approval, for five-year terms. In addition to the Act of 1934, the SEC enforces the Securities Act of 1933, which compels full disclosure of information concerning new security issues, and the Public Utility Holding Company Act of 1935, under which the SEC tries to limit mergers and combinations of utility companies. To supplement the regulatory activity of the SEC, Congress in 1974 created the Commodity Futures Trading Commission (CFTC) and empowered it to regulate trading in the nation's eleven exchanges that offer futures and options contracts. *See also* MARGIN, page 447.

Significance   The establishment of the SEC and adoption by Congress of the acts of 1933 and 1934 grew out of the shocking disclosures of deception, manipulation, fraud, and dishonesty revealed by a Senate investigation of causes of the stock market crash of 1929. The SEC does not guarantee the financial soundness or money-making possibilities of any security; it merely requires disclosure of all pertinent information to prospective buyers and forbids any attempts to manipulate prices or engage in fraudulent sales practices. Following the stock market "crash" of October 19, 1987, the SEC undertook extensive studies in an effort to determine the causes and possible violations of SEC rules.

Small Business Administration (SBA)   An independent agency, headed by an administrator, established to make loans to small businesses and to assist them in obtaining government contracts. The SBA was given temporary status by Congress in 1953 and was expanded and made a permanent agency in 1958. Some of its operations since 1961 have been carried on through small-business investment companies around the nation. Principal functions of SBA include financing plant expansion and modernization, aiding disaster victims, helping businesses cut through red tape to secure government procurement contracts, and giving managerial advice to small firms. Applicants for loans must show they have been turned down by private banks. *See also* FEDERAL EMERGENCY MANAGEMENT AGENCY, page 466.

Significance   The SBA was the first agency established for the specific purpose of aiding small business. There are approximately 4 million small businesses in the United States today, with an annual turnover rate of about 10 percent. The SBA utilizes a revolving fund that gives it a measure of freedom from dependence on annual budget grants from Congress. Although the agency was criticized in its early operations for mainly granting large loans to sizable businesses, it has increased the number of its loans and reduced the average amount of each loan to about $40,000 in recent years. It also makes disaster loans to victims of floods and other catastrophes, and since 1976, farming enterprises have been included as "small business concerns." In 1987, the SBA became involved in a series of scandals that included bribery of public officials to gain SBA loans.

United States Postal Service   The independent government agency that has the responsibility for operating the U.S. postal system. The U.S. Postal Service was created by the Postal Reorganization Act of 1970 to replace the Post Office Department, which had been a major department of the national government, with Cabinet rank. The Postal Service Board of Governors appoints postmasters and postal employees, controls rates and classes of mail, and makes general postal operating policy free from political and congressional influence. The Postmaster General, appointed by the board, serves as the chief executive officer of the Postal Service. Civil service status and rights of postal workers were retained under the new system. The Postal Service, in addition to carrying the mail, runs a parcel post service; a system of registering, certifying, and insuring mail; sells government bonds; offers money order, C.O.D., and special delivery services; and protects the mail from loss or theft. *See also* DOMESTIC TERRORISM, page 73.

Significance   The Postal Service operates about 40,000 local post offices and is one of the biggest business operations in the world, employing over 700,000 persons and handling several hundred billion pieces of mail annually. The changeover was aimed at correcting some of the major weaknesses of the old system—political influence, senatorial control over all postmasterships, huge second-, third-, and fourth-class subsidies to business and other politically powerful groups, and substantial annual deficits. In 1996, the Postal Service posted its second consecutive year with a profit of over $1 billion. The Postal Service is increasingly facing competition from private carriers and delivery systems that are at the forefront in the use of new communication technologies. In recent years, the Postal Service has received decreased annual subsidies from congressional appropriations, but increased postal rates have helped keep it competitive with private companies. Job pressures have led to violent actions by postal workers. In the 10-year period from 1983 to 1993, for example, 29 postal workers were killed by fired or disgruntled postal employees. Recent acts of terrorism, such as by the Unabomber and explosions in cargoholds of airliners, led the Postal Service in 1996 to announce a new policy requiring that any package weighing over one pound must be hand delivered to the post office by the sender.

IMPORTANT CASES

Brown v. Maryland, 12 Wheaton 419 (1827): Established the "original package" doctrine, which holds that the authority of Congress over foreign commerce does not end until the merchandise arrives at its ultimate destination, the contents of the package are sold or removed for the purpose of selling, and they become mixed together with the general property of a state. The case invalidated a law of Maryland that had required importers of foreign goods to obtain a license before being permitted to sell them. *See also* COMMERCE, page 436; ORIGINAL PACKAGE DOCTRINE, page 450.

Significance The original package doctrine established in the *Brown* case remains a significant factor in restricting state interference with foreign commerce. In *Leisy v. Hardin,* 135 U.S. 100 (1890), the Court expanded the original package doctrine to include products shipped in interstate as well as foreign commerce. Recent decisions have weakened the doctrine where the state tax is nondiscriminatory and the goods have come to rest (*Limbach v. Hooven & Allison Co.,* 466 U.S. 353 [1984]).

Cooley v. Board of Wardens, 12 Howard 299 (1851): Upheld the right of the states to regulate interstate commerce if Congress has not covered the field with its regulations and if the subject regulated by the states is not of a nature to require uniform national regulation. The case involved local regulations for port pilots, which were upheld as a reasonable regulation of interstate commerce by a state since such regulation does not need a uniform national policy. *See also* COMMERCE, page 436; COMMERCE POWER, page 33.

Significance The *Cooley* case established the precedent on which a vast amount of state regulation of interstate commerce is based today. By permitting states to enter the field, the Court recognized that the national government would be unable to provide all regulations needed to control the flow of commerce. Under the *Cooley* rule, the permissible extent of state regulation of interstate commerce in the absence of federal regulation is left to the courts to decide.

Gibbons v. Ogden,   9 Wheaton 1 (1824): Nullified a state grant giving an exclusive right to use navigable waters within the state. The Court held that congressional control over interstate commerce includes navigation. It was the first case involving the commerce clause. Under the clause, the powers of Congress to regulate interstate commerce were broadly interpreted by Chief Justice John Marshall and the Court. They defined interstate commerce to include all commercial intercourse. *See also* COMMERCE POWER, page 33; NAVIGABLE WATERS, page 450.

Significance   The *Gibbons* case opened the door to a vast expansion of national control over commerce through liberal interpretation of the commerce power. The Supreme Court, for example, has held that a farmer could be fined under the commerce power for growing a small amount of wheat for his own consumption in violation of the quota set for him by the Secretary of Agriculture (*Wickard v. Filburn,* 317 U.S. 111 [1942]). Today, the powers of Congress to regulate interstate commerce include the regulation of transportation, communications, buying and selling, and manufacturing. Few areas of economic activity remain outside the regulatory power of Congress.

Munn v. Illinois,   94 U.S. 113 (1876): Held that a state can validly fix maximum rates for a "business affected with a public interest." Regulation of a privately owned grain warehouse by the state of Illinois was upheld on the ground that when a proprietor devotes his or her property to a public use, he or she "must submit to be controlled by the public for the common good." *See also* BUSINESS AFFECTED WITH A PUBLIC INTEREST, page 433; LICENSE, page 446.

Significance   The *Munn* case was a landmark in establishing the power of government to regulate certain other businesses in addition to public utilities. Congress and state legislatures continue to use the flexible criterion of "business affected with a public interest" to regulate many business activities.

NLRB v. Jones and Laughlin Steel Corp.   301 U.S. 1 (1937): Upheld the National Labor Relations Act of 1935, which guarantees labor the right to organize and bargain collectively and establishes the National Labor Relations Board to regulate labor-management relations. The Act was upheld as a valid exercise of Congress' power to regulate interstate commerce. *See also* COLLECTIVE BARGAINING, page 436.

Significance   The *NLRB* case reflected a major shift in attitude by the Supreme Court toward New Deal regulatory legislation. The Court asserted the right of Congress to regulate activities having "a close and substantial relation to interstate commerce" and to prevent strikes and other industrial disputes that might burden or obstruct the free flow of commerce. In its decision, the Court took a broad view of the power of Congress to meet the challenges of an industrial society. The case was a turning point for the American labor movement and has been followed by extensive involvement by the national government in labor-management relations.

Smyth v. Ames, 169 U.S. 466 (1898): Declared, in a historic rate-making case, that government regulatory agencies must consider a number of factors in fixing rates, rather than a single one. The facts in the case involved a dispute over rate-setting for Nebraska railroads, in which the governmental agency based its formula chiefly on "reproduction cost," while the railroads demanded that the rate base be "original cost." The Court held that many factors should be considered in determining fair value, including original cost, cost of improvements, value of securities, reproduction cost, earning capacity, and operating expenses. *See also* RATE-MAKING, page 454.

Significance Because due process requires that rates fixed by government for private businesses be fair and reasonable, the problem of determining the base upon which the fair return will be calculated is a critical one. In recent years, the Court has modified the *Smyth* decision, adopting the "prudent-investment" theory as a guide and using a pragmatic approach to determine whether the rates permit companies to operate successfully (*FPC v. Hope Natual Gas Co.*, 320 U.S. 591 [1943]).

United States v. Darby Lumber Co., 312 U.S. 100 (1941): Upheld the Fair Labor Standards Act of 1938, which imposes wage-and-hour regulations upon businesses engaged in or producing goods for interstate commerce and places restrictions upon the use of child labor. *See also* FAIR LABOR STANDARDS ACT, page 475.

Significance The *Darby* decision climaxed many years of national efforts to regulate wages, hours, and other conditions of employment in the face of hostile judicial decisions. The *Darby* case specifically overruled *Hammer v. Dagenhart,* 247 U.S. 251 (1918), in which the Supreme Court held unconstitutional a statute that barred goods made by child labor from interstate commerce. In the *Darby* case, the Court repudiated long-held notions that Congress could not regulate production or control wages and hours. The decision virtually put an end to legal challenges to the power of Congress to regulate aspects of business that directly or indirectly affect interstate commerce. The decision also made it unnecessary to secure ratification of the proposed child labor amendment to the Constitution.

West Coast Hotel Co. v. Parrish, 300 U.S. 379 (1937): Supported a minimum wage law of the state of Washington. The Court held that a minimum wage law did not violate freedom of contract under the due process clause of the Fourteenth Amendment.

Significance The *Parrish* case put an end to the use by the Court of the due process clause of the Fourteenth Amendment to restrict state regulation of working conditions. It specifically overruled *Adkins v. Children's Hospital,* 261 U.S. 525 (1923), in which the Court had struck down a federal law establishing minimum wages for women in the District of Columbia. In the *Parrish* case, the Court rejected the notion that wages were beyond legislative control. It also rejected the concept of freedom of contract, which the Court had in earlier decisions injected into the due process clause. Such regulation was upheld as a valid exercise of the police power in the interest of protecting the health, safety, morals, and welfare of the people.

IMPORTANT STATUTES

Atomic Energy Acts of 1946 and 1954   The Act of 1946 created the Atomic Energy Commission (AEC) to control and develop the uses of atomic energy. Private mining of fissionable materials was permitted, but all other aspects of atomic energy were kept under strict governmental control. The Act of 1954 modified the public monopoly by permitting private development and operation of atomic power plants and the use of nuclear fuels and sale of by-products by private firms under government licensing. *See also* DEPARTMENT OF ENERGY, page 491; NUCLEAR REGULATORY COMMISSION, page 494.

Significance   These laws served as the base for developing the civilian nuclear energy industry in the United States. The first Atomic Energy Act placed atomic energy, which had been developed by the military, under civilian control. Growing foreign achievements in the atomic field awakened Congress to the need to stimulate more rapid development of atomic energy. As a result, the second Act, which sought to unleash private energies within limits of governmental control, was passed. Because of the extremely high cost of producing electricity in atomic power plants, the government contributes a major portion of the cost in building private facilities. In 1974, Congress abolished the Atomic Energy Commission, transferring its research and development functions to the Energy Research and Development Administration (ERDA) and its licensing and regulatory functions to the Nuclear Regulatory Commission (NRC). In 1977, ERDA was absorbed into the new Department of Energy. The nuclear energy industry, with 109 nuclear power plants now operational, remains a controversial source of electrical energy. Problems of nuclear waste disposal and fears of meltdown, other dangerous accidents, and acts of sabotage encouraged research for safer and cheaper sources of electrical energy. Currently underway at the Lawrence Livermore National Laboratory in California is research on a new fusion device. Whereas fission produces energy by splitting the atomic nucleus, fusion creates energy by combining isotopes under extreme temperature.

Clayton Act of 1914   A major antitrust act, aimed at increasing competition in business. Provisions of the Clayton Act forbid price cutting and other abuses that tend to weaken competition, restrict corporations from acquiring stock in competing firms or building interlocking directorates, make corporation officers individually liable for violations, and facilitate civil suit procedures by injured parties. Labor unions and agricultural organizations not carrying on business for profit are exempted from the provisions of the Act. *See also* ANTITRUST DIVISION, page 461; ANTITRUST LAWS, page 430.

Significance   The Clayton Act was intended to supplement and reinforce the Sherman Act of 1890, which had been weakened by the Supreme Court's interpretation limiting its application to "unreasonable" combinations in restraint of trade. The Act was aimed at reducing the confusion surrounding the Sherman Act by more clearly defining unfair business practices. Enforcement, however, has been weakened through administrative unconcern and judicial tolerance, except for a few periods of vigorous enforcement by the Antitrust Division and the Federal Trade Commission.

Fair Labor Standards Act of 1938   An act establishing minimum wages and maximum hours for employees engaged in interstate commerce and outlawing the use of child labor. An eight-hour day and a minimum wage per hour is established ($4.75 in 1996; $5.15 in 1997) as the basic requirement, with time and a half for work exceeding 40 hours a week. Persons not engaged in interstate commerce are not covered unless state laws make similar provisions. Certain types of work are exempted from coverage, but Congress has progressively increased coverage over the years. *See also United States v. Darby Lumber Co.,* page 473.

Significance   The Fair Labor Standards Act was designed to eliminate substandard working conditions and to minimize competition among the states, which might be inclined to have lower standards in order to attract industry. The Act has also been successful in eradicating the worst aspects of child labor. Responsibility for enforcement of the Act is lodged in the Department of Labor. Earlier, in 1936, Congress passed the Walsh-Healey Act, which established minimum wages and maximum hours, and outlawed child labor for persons working on federal contracts. The Fair Labor Standards Act was patterned on the Walsh-Healey Act, but has broader coverage. The Equal Pay Act of 1963, an amendment to the Fair Labor Standards Act, requires employers to pay equal wages to men and women doing equal work. In 1976, the Supreme Court ruled that federal minimum wage laws are not binding on state and local governments' payment of wages to their own employees (*National League of Cities v. Usery,* 426 U.S. 833). However, in 1985 the court overruled the *Usery* case in *Garcia v. San Antonio Metropolitan Transit Authority,* 469 U.S. 528, which held that the minimum wage provisions of the Fair Labor Standards Act could be applied to employees of a city-owned transit system. The Court made clear that the use of the commerce power was exclusive and can curtail state power. The remedy lies with Congress, not the courts.

Job Training Partnership Act (JTPA)   The major federal job training and education act designed to assist youth, the poor, and the unemployed by providing training, education, and benefits to enable them to enter or reenter the job market. The Act replaced the corruption-ridden and ineffective Comprehensive Education and Training Act (CETA) in 1982. The JTPA funnels large block grants through the states to Private Industry Councils (PICs), which set performance standards and guide training. The Act targets funds to low-income youth and areas with severe unemployment. Matching state funds help retrain the dislocated worker. The Act also focused federal attention for the first time on Native American, migrant, and seasonal workers and seeks to upgrade their job skills to make them more productive. The JTPA is part of the Department of Labor's Employment and Training Administration and includes the Job Corps. *See also* JOB CORPS, page 508.

Significance   The Job Training Partnership Act was a major turning point in the federal approach to job training. Critics of previous efforts such as CETA and the Community Conservation Corps of the 1930s had argued that the federal government often trained workers in skills that were not needed by private industry. The JTPA created Private Industry Councils— half of whose membership comes from private industry and whose chairman is a business executive—to guide training efforts toward productive skills. The program also set up performance standards to allow restructuring or replacement of those state programs that did not work, curbing waste and abuse. In 1986 JTPA was expanded to include farmers and older citizens not yet eligible for retirement, a summer youth program, and educational projects. In 1987 the scope of the program was again enlarged to permit the training of welfare recipients so that they could forgo public assistance, and to retrain workers displaced due to trade fluctuations. In the mid-1990s, under the Republican-controlled Congress, some programs were reduced or curtailed.

Landrum-Griffin Act (Labor-Management Reporting and Disclosure Act of 1959)   Informally known as the Labor Reform Act of 1959, this law strengthens the Taft-Hartley Act's restrictions upon internal procedures of labor unions and provides a "bill of rights" for members of labor unions. The Act requires detailed reports to the Secretary of Labor on union finances and the operations of union constitutions and bylaws, and it makes misuse of union funds a federal crime. Ex-convicts, Communists, and labor officials with conflicting business interests are barred from holding union office. The "bill of rights" provisions secure the secret ballot in union elections, freedom of speech in union meetings, hearings in disciplinary cases, and the right of members to sue the union for unfair practices. The provisions also authorize member access to union records. *See also* TAFT-HARTLEY ACT, page 478; WAGNER ACT, page 479.

Significance   The Landrum-Griffin Act was a direct result of investigations by the Senate Rackets Committee that revealed a variety of corrupt practices by some labor leaders. The Act is designed to protect the integrity of law-abiding labor unions as well as the rights of individual members. The provision barring Communists from union offices was declared unconstitutional as a bill of attainder (*United States v. Brown*, 381 U.S. 437 [1965]). Both the Taft-Hartley Act and the Landrum-Griffin Act reflect a change in governmental policy since the Wagner Act of 1935, from promotion of labor interests to regulation of unions.

Norris-LaGuardia Act of 1932   An act that outlawed "yellow-dog" contracts by which workers agreed not to join unions and limited the use of the injunction in labor disputes. *See also* INJUNCTION, page 444.

Significance   The Norris-La Guardia Act was one of the first pieces of prolabor legislation. Its main purpose was to free labor from two major weapons used against it and to enable labor unions to pursue lawful goals. The Act was instrumental in providing the climate in which labor could develop as an economic power. It led to the passage of the Wagner Act in 1935, which guaranteed the right of labor to organize and bargain collectively.

Occupational Safety and Health Act of 1970 (OSHA)   A comprehensive industrial safety program that requires employers engaged in interstate commerce to furnish a workplace free from hazards to life or health. The Act authorizes the Secretary of Labor to promulgate safety standards, conduct investigations, and to issue citations for noncompliance. An independent agency, the Occupational Safety and Health Review Commission, was established by the Act to adjudicate alleged violations contested by either employers or employees and to assess civil penalties. It is composed of three members appointed by the President, with Senate consent, for six-year terms. Appeals from commission orders may be brought to a federal court of appeals. The Act also authorizes federal grants to states to promote occupational safety.

Significance   The Occupational Safety and Health Act climaxed years of effort by organized labor to gain passage of extensive and enforceable industrial safety legislation. In 1969, the year prior to passage of the Act, more than 15,000 persons were killed at work, and estimates of the number suffering disabling injuries exceeded 2 million. The Act covers environmental as well as mechanical hazards. Much controversy has centered over the extent to which OSHA regulations intrude upon the rights of business and increase production costs, and the agency is targeted for sharp budget reductions by conservatives. The authority of the Occupational Safety and Health Review Commission was upheld by the Supreme Court in *Atlas Roofing, Inc. v. Occupational Safety and Health Review Commission*, 430 U.S. 442 (1977), but a warrant is required for OSHA agents to search work areas of commercial establishments for safety violations (*Marshall v. Barlow's Inc.*, 436 U.S. 307 [1978]). In 1991, the Supreme Court held, in *Martin v. Occupational Safety and Health Review Commission (OSHRC)*, 499 U.S. 144, that courts should defer to the Secretary of Labor when the Secretary and OSHRC are in conflict over the interpretation of an ambiguous regulation under OSHA. The Supreme Court noted that OSHRC is like a court with non-policy-making adjudicatory powers, whereas the Secretary of Labor's authoritative interpretation is a necessary adjunct of the secretary's rule-making and enforcement powers.

Pension Reform Act (Employee Retirement Income Security Acts of 1974 [ERISA])   An act to establish minimum federal standards for private pension plans. In ERISA, Congress created the Pension Benefit Guaranty Corporation (PBGC) to guarantee payments of basic pension benefits in private pension plans. The PBGC is composed of the Secretaries of Labor, Treasury, and Commerce, with the Secretary of Labor serving as chair. The PBGC is a self-financing, wholly owned government corporation. It functions with an advisory committee composed of two labor, two business, and three public members appointed by the President. The Pension Reform Act does not require businesses to establish a pension plan but does require certain standards for those that do. Generally, all employees 25 years of age or older, with one year of experience, must be enrolled in any existing plan. After a period of time, a part of the worker's pension rights "vests" and is guaranteed to the worker whether he or she remains with the same employer or not. In some instances, the vested portion may be transferred to another plan if the worker changes jobs. The Act also establishes minimum funding requirements and provides for insurance against failing retirement plans. Special provisions are made for the self-employed to undertake retirement planning by providing tax incentives to those setting aside funds for retirement.

Significance   The Pension Reform Act is the first effort by the national government to regulate private pension plans. About 30 million workers are covered by private retirement programs. Most required a worker to stay with one employer for many years until retirement. Several pension programs had failed in their investment practices, and most lacked adequate safeguards to ensure workers the retirement security they had envisioned or had been promised. The Pension Reform Act adds an important dimension to social welfare programs, notably as a supplement to Social Security retirement benefits, which have not always proved adequate to support retired persons. The Act is administered by the Department of Labor and the Treasury Department.

Sherman Antitrust Act of 1890   The basic federal antimonopoly law that forbids "every contract, combination . . . or conspiracy in the restraint of trade or commerce." Enforcement of the Act is provided through criminal penalties, civil suit action with triple damages to injured parties, injunction, and seizure of property. Responsibility for enforcement is vested in the Antitrust Division of the Department of Justice. *See also* ANTITRUST DIVISION, page 461; ANTITRUST LAWS, page 430.

Significance   The Sherman Act was a recognition by Congress that, paradoxical as it might appear, governmental intervention in the free economy is essential to preserve competition. Soon after its enactment, the Act was seriously crippled in two major Supreme Court tests. In the first, the Court held that *manufacturing* trusts were not engaged in commerce and, therefore, could be regulated only by the states (*United States v. E. C. Knight Co.*, 156 U.S. 1 [1895]). In the second, the Court laid down the "rule of reason" by which not *every* combination in restraint of trade (as Congress had explicitly stated in the Act) was illegal, but only those *unreasonably* so (*Standard Oil Co. v. United States*, 221 U.S. 1 [1910]). To supplement and reinforce the Sherman Act, Congress adopted the Clayton Act of 1914 and the Federal Trade Commission Act of 1914. The history of the Sherman Act demonstrates the influence of the Supreme Court, the President, the Attorney General, and other high officials in interpreting the language of the Act narrowly or broadly and in vigorously or reluctantly enforcing it.

Taft-Hartley Act (Labor-Management Relations Act of 1947)   A major revision of the Wagner Act of 1935 that seeks to equalize the power of employers and labor unions. The Act places limitations upon labor union practices, regulates certain internal arrangements of unions, and strengthens the position of the individual worker. Provisions of the Wagner Act relative to unfair practices by employers against unions are retained. Among the major limitations placed upon unions by the Taft-Hartley Act are those outlawing the closed shop (but permitting the union shop), jurisdictional strikes, secondary boycotts, political expenditures, and excessive dues. The Act also permits unions and employers to sue each other for contract violations and provides for the use of the injunction and other cooling-off procedures in strikes that threaten the national welfare. Internal affairs of unions are regulated by requiring them to file reports on the use of union funds and organizational procedures. The National Labor Relations Board (NLRB) was increased from three to five members, and the office of General Counsel was established to investigate and prosecute unfair labor charges. *See also* LANDRUM-GRIFFIN ACT, page 476; WAGNER ACT, page 479.

Significance   The Taft-Hartley Act was a reaction to growing union strength, to allegations that the Wagner Act and the NLRB favored unions over employers, and to revelations of Communism and corruption in some unions. Since its enactment, it has been criticized concerning the extent to which it involves the government in labor-management relations and restricts the range of free collective bargaining for both labor and management. Many states have passed "little Taft-Harley" acts. Nineteen states, under section 14(b) of the Act, have passed "right to work" laws that have further limited the power of unions by curtailing the union shop. Both the national and state laws gave great impetus to the merger of the AFL-CIO in 1955 and have intensified the political activity of organized labor.

Telecommunication Act of 1996   A comprehensive law enacted by Congress in early 1996 that seeks to adjust the former highly regulated telecommunication industry to a new world of free enterprise. The 1934 Federal Communication Act had restricted individual carriers such as telephone and wireless from competing in markets outside their own. Competition began in 1984, when federal courts, after charges of anticompetitive practices, forced American Telephone and Telegraph Company (AT&T) to spin off its local telephone companies, creating the "Baby Bells" and established competition in the long-distance market. The new Telecommunication Act of 1996 allows telephone companies, broadcasters, and cable TV operators to enter each other's markets and through competition bring consumers lower prices and better service. The law also requires that television sets be equipped with a "V-chip" for parental control of objectionable violent and sexual programs. *See also* FEDERAL COMMUNICATIONS COMMISSION (FCC), page 464; INTERNET, page 81; MASS MEDIA, page 87.

Significance   The new Telecommunication Act is aimed at deregulating the $500 billion telecommunication industry, which previously was divided into regulated fiefdoms. Supporters of the Act say investments in all aspects of the communication field will be greatly increased, millions of jobs will be created, our aging phone system will be modernized, the U.S. economy will be boosted, and all citizens will have access to the information superhighway. Critics claim that subscribers to telephone and cable service will pay more, that dangerous concentration will develop in the media industry because large broadcasters will be permitted to buy even more stations, and censorship will damage the Internet. The bill passed after presidential candidate and Senate Majority Leader Robert Dole withdrew his demand that new frequencies be auctioned off to private companies, thus providing billions of dollars for deficit budget reduction, instead of being freely given to broadcasters. Dole argued that the airways belong to all the American people and should not be provided to huge telecommunication companies at no cost.

Wagner Act (National Labor Relations Act of 1935)   A major enactment of the New Deal period that guarantees the right of labor to organize and bargain collectively through representatives of its own choosing. The Act established the National Labor Relations Board (NLRB) to administer the Act. The board is authorized to issue cease and desist orders to employers who commit unfair labor practices as defined by the law and to certify bargaining representatives for unions. *See also* FEDERAL LABOR RELATIONS AUTHORITY, page 236; LABOR UNIONS, page 445; *NLRB v. Jones and Laughlin Steel Corp.* page 472.

Significance   The Wagner Act was a boon to the American labor movement. Until the year 1947, when it was amended by the Taft-Hartley Act, union membership grew from 4 to 15 million and the overwhelming majority of manufacturing plants were covered by union contracts. This growth was accompanied by increased economic and political power for unions. Criticism of the Act as being too one-sided in favor of organized labor and discriminatory against employers and individual workers led to the passage of the Taft-Hartley Act in 1947. Nevertheless, the Wagner Act has significantly altered labor-management relations in the United States. "Little Wagner" acts were also passed in many states to cover workers not engaged in interstate commerce. The underlying purposes of the law—to foster and protect the right of collective bargaining—remains basic to public policy in the labor field. In recent years, labor movement membership and political influence have been declining. Whereas about 40 percent of all nonagricultural workers were union members in 1955, membership had fallen to 16 percent by 1994. Since 1983, total union membership has declined by about 2.2 million. Only public employee unions show any significant growth. Although the protections of the Wagner Act remained, economic factors such as trade competition, plant closings, and negotiated pay reductions caused many workers to lose confidence in their unions as guarantors of a good life.

Webb-Pomerene Act of 1918   An act that exempts business associations engaged in export trade to foreign lands from the provisions of the antitrust laws. Such organizations must register with and submit reports to the Federal Trade Commission. *See also* MONOPOLY, page 448.

Significance   The Webb-Pomerene Act was enacted to promote American foreign trade and to put American exporters on a competitive basis with countries that have little or no effective antitrust or anticartel legislation. Although the Act was intended to permit American industries to carry on monopoly operations in the world but not in the domestic market, critics have charged that world monopolistic activities tend to have a "monopoly-like impact" on the domestic market.

11

Agriculture, Energy, and Environment

Conservation   The careful management and wise use of natural resources to prevent depletion and to maximize the long-term production of wealth from their use. Conservation involves the protection, preservation, replenishment, and planned use of land, forests, wildlife, minerals, and water by private individuals and national, state, and local governments. Conservationists include those who wish to conserve resources for economic reasons and those who are mainly concerned with ecological and esthetic considerations. *See also* CONSERVATION AND ENVIRONMENTAL ORGANIZATIONS, page 481; SOIL CONSERVATION, page 489; WATER CONSERVATION, page 489.

Significance   Conservation was recognized as a new problem area at about the turn of the century. Apprehension over the squandering of the nation's natural wealth plus the crusading zeal of President Theodore Roosevelt led to the first national conservation programs in the vast areas of the public domain. These were followed by state efforts, cooperative nation-state programs, and educational and publicly financed efforts in privately owned areas. The major impetus behind the conservation program remains with the national government, although some states have developed extensive programs covering water resources, mineral production, reclamation and irrigation, forest protection and reforestation, and protection of wildlife. Conservation has increasingly come to mean not only the preservation of existing natural wealth but also the planned use of resources to increase wealth and to turn unproductive areas into productive natural assets. This approach, however, has come under increasing attack by environmentalists, who regard the invasion of more and more wild country for such purposes as destructive of basic ecological balances. Major conservation programs of the national government are carried out by the Departments of Agriculture and the Interior, while conservation and agricultural departments in state governments have primary responsibility for implementing state programs. In the 1970s, conservationists joined with the environmental movement to develop a political action program.

Conservation and Environmental Organizations   Groups organized to promote conservation and environmental policies and programs on the national, state, local, and international levels. Conservation and environmental organizations active in the United States include the Sierra Club, the National

Audubon Society, the National Wildlife Federation, the National Parks and Conservation Association, the Scientists' Institute for Public Information, the Wilderness Society, the Conservation Foundation, the International Union for Conservation of Nature and Natural Resources, the Izaak Walton League of America, and Friends of the Earth. About 170 "environmental organizations," ranging from the Alaska Coalition to Zero Population Growth, function as Washington lobbies. Key issues for environmental and conservation organizations include preservation of wild country and endangered species; control of pollution of the air, water, and land; limiting population and the encroachments of urban civilization; the wise and careful use of natural resources and energy supplies; protection of the world oceans; and education of the American public to gain its acceptance of the conservation ethic and the environmental imperative. *See also* ENVIRONMENTALISM, page 483; PRESSURE GROUP, page 104.

Significance   Conservation and environmental organizations have multiplied and become increasingly active in promoting public awareness of ecological dangers and programmatic approaches to their solutions. Such groups differ from most American pressure groups in that they are interested mainly in promoting the general interest rather than that of their individual members and because they are primarily concerned with long-term stabilities rather than solutions to immediate problems. Tactics employed in pursuit of their objectives include litigation in state and federal courts, lobbying and pressure techniques, public education campaigns, and protests, including picketing. Conservation and environmental organizations are often put on the defensive as political leaders and others blame them for current energy or economic problems arising from what they may perceive as unproductive uses of land, water, or minerals.

County Agent   The local official charged with promoting agriculture under the federal, state, and county cooperative extension program. The Smith-Lever Act of 1914 created the modern extension service, under which the county agent program was developed. *See also* FARM ORGANIZATIONS, page 484.

Significance   County agents seek to improve agriculture by encouraging farmers to adopt new methods developed in laboratories and in agricultural research centers. They try to reach the ordinary farmer through advice, demonstrations, and exhibits, and the great increase in farm productivity testifies to their success over the years. The county agent has also been an important factor in many states in the development of the American Farm Bureau Federation, a leading farmers' organization. Although the early integration of the county agent system with the Farm Bureau has ended, the county agent continues to work closely with the organization in some states.

Environmental Impact Statement   A requirement of the National Environmental Policy Act of 1969 that all federal agencies must consider the effect that any federally sponsored or regulated project or policy must have on environmental stabilities. If a federal, state, or local agency using federal funds proceeds with a project or policy that threatens substantial environmental damage, the Act provides that private citizens, members of Congress, or government officials may undertake legal action to challenge its continuation.

Many state and local governments also require environmental impact statements before a government agency or private party can undertake a new project. *See also* ENDANGERED SPECIES ACT OF 1973, page 499; NATIONAL ENVIRONMENTAL POLICY ACT OF 1969, page 501.

Significance   The federal requirement of environmental impact statements relates especially to major engineering projects that may threaten an area's biological balance. Because of pressure resulting from the energy crisis, Congress set the requirement aside as it applied to the Alaskan Pipeline project. The Act has had the effect of preventing some projects, altering others, and encouraging long-range planning that includes ecosystem considerations. In many cases, the controversial nature of a national, state, or local project results in public hearings and prolonged debates that may ultimately be resolved by a decision at the ballot box. In 1976, the Supreme Court ruled in *Kleppe v. Sierra Club,* 427 U.S. 390, that the National Environmental Policy Act does not require a *regional* (Northern Great Plains states) impact statement, but each mining operation in the area must comply. The concept of an "impact statement" has spread widely and become a major tool for public policy analysis. Often, however, a debate over the impact statement is really over property values, industrial development, or jobs rather than over biological or scientific concerns.

Environmentalism   A social and political movement that seeks to warn the public about ecological dangers and to encourage action to achieve basic environmental goals. Environmental politics is aimed at pressuring national, state, and local governments to support policies and programs to end pollution of air, water, and land. Environmentalism starts with the assumption that life-sustaining ecosystems are being rapidly destroyed as a result of technological and economic growth. The movement is working for the adoption of governmental policies to clean up pollution, to preserve wild areas, to protect living species, to meet the problem of depletion of natural resources, to deal with population and urbanization problems, and generally to move toward restoring ecological balance. *See also* CONSERVATION AND ENVIRONMENTAL ORGANIZATIONS, page 481; ENDANGERED SPECIES ACT OF 1973, page 499; NATIONAL ENVIRONMENTAL POLICY ACT OF 1969, page 501.

Significance   Environmentalism, long concerned with fighting battles for conservation and esthetics, suddenly assumed a center-stage position in the American political system in the 1960s and 1970s. Revelations of the extent of pollution of the biosphere by modern industrial societies, the world population explosion, and the dangers of future ecosuicide have enlisted many Americans in the political movement to change the role of government from one of aiding and abetting environmental degradation to one of seeking to reverse the trend. Congress reacted to the growing support for environmental policies by enacting a basic National Environmental Policy Act in 1969 and numerous laws dealing with specific forms of pollution. In addition, Congress created a major administering agency, the Environmental Protection Agency (EPA), and a staff agency in the Executive Office, the Council on Environmental Quality. American initiatives have contributed to the establishment of a United Nations Environmental Program (UNEP) and numerous regional programs of cooperation. Securing environmental protection in the

United States through court processes was given support by the Supreme Court when it held that citizens who allege injury by government action affecting the environment, even though that action might also affect large numbers of other people, have standing in court to sue (*United States v. SCRAP,* 412 U.S. 669 [1973]. By the 1980s, environmentalism received a setback as the nation focused its attention increasingly on energy, defense, and economic problems. In the 1990s, concern over depletion of the ozone layer and consequent global warming led to renewed emphasis on environmental politics and international cooperation. Since 1970, April 22 has been celebrated as Earth Day.

Farm Organizations   Groups organized to promote the interests of the farmer. The oldest and most conservative farmers' organization is the National Grange, which was most effective after the Civil War and now has most of its membership in the New England and Middle Atlantic states. The most powerful and energetic speaker for the farmers in the twentieth century has been the American Farm Bureau Federation, which represents all types of farmers throughout the country. The Farm Bureau, now a private organization, grew out of the promotional activities of county agents sponsored by the Department of Agriculture through the agricultural extension services. Another major group is the National Farmers' Union, representing less prosperous farmers. Two new groups—the National Farmers' Organization (NFO) and American Agriculture—seek to emulate the strike techniques of labor unions by having farmers withhold products from the marketplace to drive up prices. *See also* CONSERVATION AND ENVIRONMENTAL ORGANIZATIONS, page 481; PRESSURE GROUP, page 104.

Significance   Farm organizations have long been a political force, strengthened by rural overrepresentation in legislative bodies. In the 1990s, however, fewer than 5 million people—about 2 percent of the nation's population—live on farms. This decline in the number of farms and farmers in the United States and the trend toward urban-suburban dominance of legislatures pose threats to the continued success of farmers' organizations. The Farm Bureau and the National Farmers' Union represent the major differences among farmers today. While both support governmental research, extension services, and credit facilities for farmers, the Farm Bureau emphasizes free enterprise, while the Farmers' Union supports production controls and government subsidies. In addition to the major farm organizations, farmers who produce specialized crops or products have also become politically active as, for example, the Milk Producers Association. There are about 150 active farm organizations today.

Food for Peace   A special foreign aid program that provides for the disposal of American surplus food to needy countries. Congress established the Food for Peace program by Public Law 480 in 1954 to reduce American farm surpluses, to increase foreign consumption of American products, and to strengthen United States foreign policy abroad. Under the program, surplus products—especially wheat—have been subsidized and sold in huge quantities to many nations for local currencies, which have often been returned to the aid-receiving state. Congress has extended the Food for Peace program periodically since 1954. The program is administered through the joint actions of the Department of Agriculture (sales) and the Agency for International Development (grants and donations).

Significance   The Food for Peace program has helped to adjust demand for surplus agricultural products in the United States and to meet some of the challenges of the population explosion in the developing world. Local currencies received for food shipments have been used to promote educational and cultural exchanges, to pay for development programs in aid-receiving states, to build resistance to internal and external enemies, and to achieve American foreign policy objectives. Under the Act, the President is empowered to provide emergency food aid following natural disasters and during famines. Food aid may be given to friendly governments or to friendly people living under a government that is unfriendly toward the United States. The major recipients of Food for Peace aid include India, Pakistan, Bangladesh, Egypt, and Ethiopia.

Organization of Petroleum Exporting Countries (OPEC)   A group of major oil-producing and exporting states that are joined together in an intergovernmental cartel to limit oil supplies on the world market and to maintain prices at agreed levels. Members include seven Arab states (Algeria, Iraq, Kuwait, Libya, Qatar, Saudi Arabia, and the United Arab Emirates) and five Asian, African, and Latin American states (Indonesia, Iran, Nigeria, Gabon, and Venezuela). Established in 1961, OPEC remained ineffectual during the 1960s. The Middle East war of 1973, however, produced an Arab oil embargo against Western nations that supported Israel, and this new unity, along with a vastly increased world demand for oil, resulted in an expansion in OPEC membership and a growing militancy among oil producers.

Significance   OPEC's significance rises and falls with the international political scene, but it illustrates U.S. dependence on outside energy sources. During the first half of the 1970s, OPEC's price-setting mechanism quadrupled world oil prices. The result was major inflation in most countries, a near-global reduction in economic activity, growing unemployment, and the threat of economic depression in the industrial countries. The United States sought to counter OPEC's cartel pricing by unifying oil-importing countries and developing a common policy approach, by applying diplomatic and economic pressures on OPEC countries, and by threatening military intervention if the West is faced with disaster as a result of OPEC's actions. Other approaches included voluntary cutbacks in oil use, government programs and regulations to reduce oil consumption, and stockpiling supplies such as the Strategic Petroleum Reserve. Efforts to free the United States from dependence on imported energy by developing alternative energy sources—for example, atomic power plants and the Alaskan oil fields—have made little headway. In 1980 the United States established the Synthetic Fuels Corporation (Synfuels) to assist private-sector development of substitutes for imported fuel, but it failed and Congress dismantled it in 1985. Oil prices continue to rise and fall with international crises and economic agreements.

Parity   A government price policy designed to maintain a level of purchasing power for farmers equal to that of a previous base period that was favorable to agriculture. This means, for example, that a farmer who in the period

1910–1914 was able to sell ten bushels of wheat and buy a piece of farm machinery with the receipts should, at full parity, be able to work out the same exchange today. Parity-support price levels are determined by Congress, and actual parity prices for specific crops are determined each year by the Department of Agriculture based on a ten-year moving average. In 1996, Congress dramatically altered the direction of agriculture toward a free market economy. *See also* FREEDOM TO FARM ACT, page 500; PRICE SUPPORT, page 486.

Significance   The concept of parity was an integral part of the national government's farm program, assuming that the agricultural sector of the economy is basic to the well-being of the rest of the nation's economy and that any serious imbalance might result in a slump for the entire economy. Parity does not provide a maximum price, only a minimum, which has often been exceeded on the free market. Government price support programs have generally ranged from 60 to 90 percent of parity, depending on the supply and demand for each basic crop. New legislation establishes a system of fixed and declining payments to farmers.

Price Support   A program of the national government to help stabilize agricultural prices near parity by buying up market surpluses. Price supports, which have been used since 1933, are accompanied by production controls. The program is based on the concept of "the ever-normal granary," whereby in times of short supply, the government sells from its granaries to meet market demand and stabilize prices. The Commodity Credit Corporation (CCC) and the Agricultural Stabilization and Conservation Service (ASCS) administer the price support program through outright purchases and, more commonly, by granting loans to farmers, accepting their stored crops as collateral. The individual farmer can, in effect, turn the loan into a government purchase of the crop by simply not paying it off. If, however, the market price of the commodity goes above support level, the farmer may pay off the loan, redeem the stored crop, and sell it on the free market. A Reagan administration program, "payment-in-kind" (PIK), gives farmers surplus commodities in return for idling cropland. *See also* AGRICULTURAL ACT OF 1977, page 496; FREEDOM TO FARM ACT, page 500; *Mulford v. Smith*, page 496; PARITY, page 485.

Significance   The price support program recognizes the significance of agriculture and demonstrates the extent of agriculture's power in national politics and that of the farm bloc in Congress. The basic problem of agriculture is to bring the supply of farm products into line with the demand for them. As a result of a technological revolution in farming methods, productivity increased to the point where the national government spends billions of dollars annually to manage the surpluses produced, with annual storage costs running into millions of dollars. Various domestic and foreign disposal programs, such as aid to urban poverty groups and the Food for Peace program, help diminish the size of the government's surpluses. In the 1970s and 1980s, a global food shortage led the national government to adopt a policy of "unleashing" agriculture from government controls to encourage greater production, resulting in gross overproduction, lower prices for farm products, and a national farmers' strike. Soaring interest rates combined with high prices for farm machinery served to worsen the economic plight of many

American farmers. The agricultural price support program expanded federal spending more rapidly than defense or social programs in the 1980s. In the first five years of the Reagan administration, defense expenditures increased by 55 percent, whereas outlays for price supports increased by 340 percent. Much of the price support funds go to a relatively few "superfarmers." In 1994, more than 25 percent of federal farm subsidy payments went to 2 percent of all farmers. Congress sought to deal with this problem by limiting each grower to a $50,000 maximum in support each year, but big producers found ways of avoiding this limitation. A politically acceptable plan for stabilizing farm prices—which would gradually end farm subsidies and move toward a market-based program—was finally achieved in the Freedom to Farm Act of 1996. That law replaces market price support programs for most products with fixed, declining payments. The new policy will be evaluated in 2002.

Public Domain   Public lands owned by the U.S. government. The public domain consists of national parks and forests, grazing districts, Indian reservations, and miscellaneous holdings. The Bureau of Land Management in the Department of the Interior has custody over a large portion of the public domain. *See also* HOMESTEAD ACT OF 1862, page 501.

Significance   Most of the land area of the United States today, with the exception of the thirteen original states and Texas, was once under the proprietorship of the national government. Through many programs, including homesteads, state grants, sales, grants to railroads, aids to education, and grants to soldiers and sailors, the national government has divested itself of most of its public lands. The public domain now comprises approximately 900 million acres, about 30 percent of the nation's total land area. Most of these public lands are found in eleven western states; in five of those states, the national government holds more than half of the state's lands. In Alaska, more than 90 percent of the land remains part of the public domain. Political controversy has erupted over the leasing of vast areas of the public domain for exploitation by private parties, especially mining, ranching, and petroleum companies. The Reagan administration moved toward greater state control over federal lands in the West and permitted greater exploitation of mineral and timber resources by private operators. The Supreme Court upheld state regulation of federal lands in the absence of contradictory legislation from Congress (*California Coastal Commission v. Granite Rock Co.*, 480 U.S. 572 [1987]).

Public Power   The production of electrical energy by government-built and operated dams and power plants. Millions of kilowatts are produced and sold by the national government, especially from generating plants on the Colorado, Columbia, and Tennessee rivers. Public power production has become one of the major functions of the huge government dams, along with reclamation, irrigation, navigation, and flood control. Many cities and towns also produce and sell public power. *See also Ashwander v. TVA*, page 495; TENNESSEE VALLEY AUTHORITY, page 495.

Significance   Public power development by the national and local governments was negligible until the Depression years of the 1930s. The case for public power is based on the multipurpose nature of government dams and on the claims that water power is a public resource that should not be used for private gain and that public power is necessary to build up underdeveloped regions. The case against public power holds that it is dangerous to free enterprise, that government facilities do not pay taxes or dividends, and that the taxpayers of the entire nation subsidize the people of the regions with public power. Where multipurpose government dams are necessary, critics believe that a partnership should be worked out, with private business buying wholesale power and selling it to consumers. More than three-fourths of the electric power used in the United States is produced by private public-utility companies.

Recycling   The process of separating reclaimable materials from other trash and refining them into raw materials to be used in new products. Recycling was originally used in wartime, when shortages of cloth, rubber, steel, and other materials important to the war effort forced the civilian population to recycle in order to obtain quantities of these goods. During the 1960s, however, recycling came to be seen as a means of reducing environmental pollution, slowing the use of nonrenewable resources, and solving the nation's problem of waste disposal. Often, laws must be enacted to mandate recycling, as many people are unwilling to bear the costs or bother of separating trash. Also, the cost of recycling is often too high to prove profitable for companies whose competitors use less-costly "first-run" raw materials. *See also* ENVIRONMENTALISM, page 483.

Significance   Recycling became particularly popular in the late 1980s and early 1990s, as landfills and other waste disposal areas rapidly filled up. Worry that plastic and aluminum products were not biodegradable also moved many people to recycle. Estimates show that up to 75 percent of all garbage can be recycled into raw materials or refined into another usable form, but many locales confronted with trash disposal problems also found that recycling had to be mandated in most cases or people simply would not recycle. In other cases, cities have had to subsidize private recycling companies to keep them in business or create publicly owned and operated recycling companies. Several major cities have enacted mandatory recycling laws, although the amount of trash recycled rarely rises above 30 percent. The recycling of certain products such as paper, glass, tin, aluminum, and steel is relatively cheap, but recycling other products such as chemicals, plastics, and tires has proven to be either impossible, too costly, or unhealthy. Many private recycling centers find themselves buried in as much trash as recyclable products, and labor and shipping costs have increased dramatically. Some jurisdictions have abandoned recycling in favor of burning their trash to make it more compact and less prone to generating bacteria that can cause disease. The outlook for recycling is positive, however, because the national problem of disposing of solid waste continues to grow more severe. Increasingly, the federal government has become involved in recycling efforts through clean water, clean air, and solid waste disposal legislation.

Rural Electrification   The government program to bring electric service and telephone lines to rural people not serviced by private enterprise. The Roosevelt administration initiated the electrification program in 1935 with the establishment of the Rural Electrification Administration (REA) by executive order. The REA is now a part of the Department of Agriculture. The telephone program was added by Congress in 1949.

Significance   The REA has encouraged rural electrification by making low-interest loans to farmer cooperatives and local governments to build transmission lines, and to private electrical companies engaged in wiring individual farms. When the program started, only 10 percent of the nation's farms were electrified, whereas today almost all farms have light and power and most have telephone service. Critics of the REA charge that rural electrification and telephone programs involve a considerable subsidy by the nation's taxpayers because of the low-interest loans, high administrative costs, and tax exemptions to cooperatives. Supporters of the REA program defend it on the ground that private enterprise has refused to bring electrical services to the farmers because of lack of profit, and they note that improvement of farm conditions benefits the entire nation.

Soil Conservation   A cooperative program of the national government, states, local units, and individual farmers to preserve valuable topsoil from being washed or blown away through erosion and dust storms. Primary responsibility for developing and carrying out national soil and related water conservation programs is vested in the Soil Conservation Service of the Department of Agriculture.

Significance   Although government can initiate soil conservation programs and provide some financing, their effectiveness depends almost wholly upon the efforts of individual farmers. Soil-conserving methods include proper drainage, crop rotation, terracing, contour plowing, and strip cropping. The national government provides an incentive for individual farmers to cooperate by requiring all farmers participating in price support subsidy programs to use soil conservation methods. The Conservation Reserve Program of 1985 permits eligible farmers to lease fragile land to the government for a ten-year period in order to remove it from production. National programs for many years sought to improve soil conservation and reduce agricultural surpluses by paying farmers to retire overworked cropland by planting soil-conserving grasses and trees. Most of the soil conservation programs are preserved in the Freedom to Farm Act of 1996.

Water Conservation   The planned use and protection of water resources. Water conservation programs include promoting the navigability of streams, flood control, irrigation, river basin development, pollution control, recreation, reclamation, hydroelectric power, and the use of water for home and industrial consumption. The Bureau of Reclamation of the Department of the Interior, the Soil Conservation Service of the Department of Agriculture, and the U.S. Army Corps of Engineers play significant and sometimes competing roles in developing the nation's water resources. Since 1970, the Environmental Protection Agency has also participated in programs to protect water purity. *See also* FEDERAL WATER POLLUTION CONTROL ACT, page 499.

Significance   Because the use of water has increased tremendously in the United States, water conservation and pollution control programs have become increasingly critical. Pollution control is carried on through federal and state programs. Interstate agreements on waterways that flow through several states (such as the Colorado River Compact among seven states and the Columbia River Compact among four states) serve to monitor and preserve water resources and to harness the rivers through huge multipurpose dams. The most pressing problem for the future is that of providing adequate supplies of fresh water for human consumption and industrial use. Although President John F. Kennedy initiated a program to develop practical means for converting saltwater from the oceans into fresh water, the program has faltered as other critical problems diverted attention from it and as budget cuts to fight inflation reduced the scope of research. One of the most important problems of the 1980s and 1990s has involved protection of massive underground water supplies in the United States from pollution and exhaustion. In 1987, Congress enacted a major aid program to state and local governments for improvements of sewage treatment plants and in 1996 authorized funds for drinking water systems and toughened regulations.

IMPORTANT AGENCIES

Corps of Engineers   A branch of the United States Army charged with planning and constructing public works on navigable waterways. It constructs dams and power-generating facilities on many major rivers and develops extensive flood-control projects. In civil projects, the Corps has developed a tradition of autonomy from the Army and the Department of Defense, functioning as engineering consultants to the Congress. The commanding general of the Corps also manages Army and Air Force real estate programs and administers law for protection of navigable waters and related resources such as wetlands and assists in recovery from natural disasters. *See also* WATER CONSERVATION, page 489.

Significance   The construction of government dams and other public projects involving multipurpose river development has often produced jurisdictional battles among the Corps of Engineers, the Department of Agriculture, the Department of the Interior, and valley authorities like the TVA. The Corps of Engineers, with strong congressional support, has been able to maintain its position as a major agency in the development of river programs because of opportunities for "pork barrel" projects. Increasingly, however, the Corps has had to defend its projects from attacks by conservationists and environmentalists, who charge it with being concerned solely with engineering problems and indifferent toward ecological and social needs.

Council on Environmental Quality   A staff agency in the Executive Office that advises the President on measures to control or eliminate air, water, and other forms of pollution and to promote a high quality of life for the American people. The council, created by the National Environmental Policy Act of 1969, assists the President in drawing up an annual environmental quality report, which is transmitted to the Congress with recommendations for appropriate legislative action. Three members appointed by the President with the approval of the Senate comprise the council, with one of the three selected by the President to serve as chairman. *See also* ENVIRONMENTAL PROTECTION AGENCY, page 493; NATIONAL ENVIRONMENTAL POLICY ACT OF 1969, page 501.

Significance   The Council on Environmental Quality's role as an Executive Office staff agency reflects the increasing responsibility of the President to provide leadership in restoring the quality of the nation's environment. The council also reflects public concern and outcry against past and present policies that have permitted the degradation of the nation's environment in the interest of private gain. Because the Act creating the council requires that the individuals appointed to the council be well-qualified environmentalists, the council can function as a powerful advocate of effective federal programs, though it finds itself in competition with the Environmental Protection Agency (EPA) for the President's attention. Environmental pressure groups have demanded that council members be guided by an "environmental ethic," rather than by a "technological ethic" or an "economic growth ethic."

Department of Agriculture   A major department of the national government that provides numerous services for farmers and regulates various aspects of agriculture and related fields in the interest of farmers and the general public. The Secretary of Agriculture is appointed by the President with the Senate's approval and serves as a member of the Cabinet. A variety of activities are carried on by the department's major operational units: Rural Economic and Community Development; Farm and Foreign Agricultural Services; Research, Education and Economics; Natural Resources and Development; Food, Nutrition and Consumer Services; and Food Safety *See also* AGRICULTURE ACT OF 1977, page 496; FREEDOM TO FARM ACT, page 500; PRICE SUPPORT, page 486; SOIL CONSERVATION, page 489.

Significance   The Department of Agriculture is primarily concerned with maintaining stability in the farm economy, expanding agricultural markets, and helping to achieve supply-demand adjustments in the marketplace. During the 1960s and 1970s, the farm economy underwent a scientific revolution in production, resulting in huge surpluses, low prices for farm products, and an increasing need for government assistance. The Department of Agriculture developed various foreign and domestic programs to reduce surpluses and encourage higher prices. Some critics point out that the department is largely responsible for market instabilities as the result of its interference with supply-demand forces. Others have noted the population explosion in the world and a growing dependence by the United States on sales of agricultural products to offset spiraling costs of oil and other necessary imports. Despite the expenditure of huge sums of money in an effort to stabilize farm production, solutions to the "farm problem" have eluded both Congress and the Department of Agriculture. The Freedom to farm Act of 1996 moves the Department of Agriculture in new directions, from depression-era concepts to free market approaches.

Department of Energy   A department established in 1977 that exercises primary responsibility for policies, programs, and administration in the field of energy. The Secretary of Energy has Cabinet status and is appointed by the President with Senate approval. Departmental functions include finding new energy sources, helping to make them operational to meet the needs of industry and the American people, encouraging conservation, and coping with the impact of energy problems. It also manages the nuclear weapons and nuclear space programs. The five federal Power Marketing Administrations that sell electric power from 133 federal dams—Alaska, Bonneville, Southeastern, Southwestern and Western—are also under its authority. *See also* FEDERAL ENERGY REGULATORY COMMISSION, page 494; NUCLEAR REGULATORY COMMISSION, page 494.

Significance   The Department of Energy is responsible to the President for developing new policies and programs to cope with the energy problems besetting the nation. The short-term problem for the Energy Department is to reduce the growing American dependence on imported energy that has resulted in major balance of trade and balance of payments problems. The long-term problem facing the department is coping with steadily increasing production and use of energy and rapidly decreasing world reserves of fossil and nuclear fuels. The Nuclear Waste Policy Act of 1982 gave the department responsibility for disposal of high-level radioactive waste and spent nuclear fuel. In 1987, after much controversy, Congress chose Yucca Mountain, Nevada, as the site for a permanent repository of potentially dangerous waste. Defense-related nuclear waste is slated for storage in underground caverns near Carlsbad, New Mexico. Both Nevada and New Mexico have resisted, filing lawsuits that have resulted in delays and virtually uncontrolled stockpiling of such waste around the country. The disposal of low-level waste (for example, that produced by university research reactors) is generally a state or regional responsibility but has resulted in similar disputes over sites. The entire issue of disposal is complicated by the competing responsibilities of the Nuclear Regulatory Commission (NRC) and the Environmental Protection Agency (EPA).

Department of the Interior   A major department of the national government that has responsibility for a variety of functions concerning the territories and properties of the United States. The Secretary of the Interior is appointed by the President with the Senate's approval and serves as a member of the Cabinet. Some of the major operating units found in the Interior Department are (1) the Fish and Wildlife Service, which oversees endangered species programs and improves commercial and recreational fishing and hunting through research and conservation programs; (2) the Office of Surface Mining Reclamation and Enforcement, which is responsible for protecting the environment from the adverse effects of coal mining while assuring an adequate supply of coal to meet the nation's needs; (3) the Geological Survey, which surveys and classifies public lands and conducts geologic research; (4) the Bureau of Indian Affairs, which promotes health, welfare, and educational facilities for Indians; (5) the Bureau of Land Management, which supervises the exploitation of natural resources of the public domain by private companies; (6) the National Park Service, which develops and administers natural beauty and historic sites for the enjoyment of the American people; (7) the Minerals Management Service, which maintains a continuing inventory and evaluation of leasable minerals on the Outer Continental Shelf; and (8) the Bureau of Reclamation, which constructs and operates public facilities to generate electric power, promote flood control, and provide irrigation. The Department of the Interior also has some budget and program coordination authority for the "Insular areas" (territories): Guam, American Samoa, the U.S. Virgin Islands, the Commonwealth of the Northern Mariana Islands, the Marshall Islands, the Federated States of Micronesia, and Palau.

Significance Most of the agencies in the Department of the Interior are concerned with conservation. Conservation as practiced by the department means not only the preservation of land, water, forests, natural resources, and wildlife but also their wise and systematic use. Not only is the department the custodian of the nation's natural resources but also its jurisdiction extends to islands in the Caribbean and South Pacific and to lands within the Arctic Circle. Expanding demands for energy and raw materials and a growing interest in environmental, conservational, and ecological problems have thrust the department into political controversies.

Environmental Protection Agency (EPA) An independent agency established in 1970 to administer federal programs aimed at controlling pollution and protecting the nation's environment. Headed by an administrator, the Environmental Protection Agency is concerned with air and water pollution, pesticide research and control, radiation dangers, and basic ecological research. The agency administers the National Environmental Policy Act of 1969 and those acts that Congress has passed to deal with specific pollution problems. The Clean Air Acts of 1970 and 1990, for example, require inter alia that auto makers substantially reduce hazardous emissions. The Federal Water Pollution Control Act of 1972 extends pollution control to all waters in the nation, and the Federal Insecticide, Fungicide, and Rodenticide Act of 1972 provides for extensive control over the use of pesticides. Under the Resource Recovery Act of 1970, a major effort is under way to recover useful materials and energy from solid wastes. The Toxic Substance Control Act of 1979 regulates chemical waste, and under the Resource Conservation and Recovery Act of 1976, the EPA is responsible for regulating storage and transportation of hazardous and solid wastes. In 1980, Congress created a "Superfund" to enable the EPA to administer a huge toxic waste cleanup program. The EPA carries on its operations in cooperation with state and local governments through regional offices located in ten major cities. *See also* COUNCIL ON ENVIRONMENTAL QUALITY, page 490; ENVIRONMENTAL IMPACT STATEMENT, page 482; NATIONAL ENVIRONMENTAL POLICY ACT OF 1969, page 501; SUPERFUND, page 501.

Significance The Environmental Protection Agency, along with the Council on Environmental Quality that advises the President on ecological matters, represents part of the federal government's response to the American public's growing concern about pollution. Expanding programs of environmental protection have substantially increased the power and influence of the Environmental Protection Agency. However, conflicts between environmental protection and economic growth and the resulting numerous lawsuits have made it difficult for EPA to meet its obligations.

Farm Credit Administration An independent agency of the national government that supervises and coordinates the operations of the federal land banks and other corporations and cooperatives that provide credit for farmers. The Farm Credit Administration makes decisions through a three-member Farm Credit Board, appointed by the President with Senate consent.

Significance The Farm Credit Administration plays an important role in the agricultural sector of the economy. Farmers are often in dire need of credit because of their heavy investments in land and machinery and their need to purchase seed and fertilizer in the spring following a period of low income. Availability of credit, particularly when agricultural prices slump, may spell the difference between survival and bankruptcy for individual farmers. In recent years, farmers and their associations have borrowed annually in excess of $56 billion from banks and cooperatives that are regulated by the Farm Credit Administration. A growing crisis in the condition of farm banking systems and the farm economy led to passage of a sweeping reform of the farm credit system in 1987. The legislation overhauled the Farm Banking System, restructured delinquent loans, and established a federally supported secondary market, the Federal Agricultural Mortgage Corporation (dubbed "Farmer Mac"), for trading securities backed by farm real estate loans.

Federal Energy Regulatory Commission (FERC)   A five-member independent commission created in 1977 to control the production, interstate transmission, and sale of electrical energy and the transportation and sale of natural gas. Members of FERC are appointed by the President on a bipartisan basis and are subject to Senate approval. The commission, located in the Department of Energy, replaced the Federal Power Commission (FPC), which had licensed hydropower dams and regulated electrical energy and natural gas since 1930. Also transferred to FERC were (1) power to regulate mergers and securities acquisitions under the Federal Power and Natural Gas Acts, (2) authority previously exercised by the Interstate Commerce Commission to set rates for transporting oil by interstate pipelines, and (3) jurisdiction to alter oil price regulations under the Emergency Petroleum Allocation Act of 1973. *See also* DEPARTMENT OF ENERGY, page 491.

Significance   National regulation of electric power and natural gas operations of private utility companies by the FPC and FERC has stemmed largely from the inability of state utility commissions to protect the public interest in these crucial areas. Rather than relying on information supplied by utility companies at formal hearings—a practice that characterizes much state regulation—FERC undertakes extensive studies and detailed investigations to determine fair prices and reasonable service. Major issues in recent years have been whether the national government or private utility companies should develop the few remaining sites for major dams, and whether regulation of natural gas prices should be eased or eliminated as a means of raising prices to encourage exploration and production.

Nuclear Regulatory Commission (NRC)   An independent regulatory body created in 1974 to carry on licensing and regulatory functions in the civilian uses of nuclear power. The five-member Nuclear Regulatory Commission was established to replace the Atomic Energy Commission (AEC) and to carry on the regulatory functions formerly performed by that agency. The research and development functions in the field of atomic energy assigned to the AEC for many years were transferred at that time to a new Energy Research and Development Administration (ERDA), which in 1977 became part of the new Department of Energy. Responsibility for enforcing the Atomic Energy Acts of 1946 and 1954 is vested in the two agencies. The NRC licenses and regulates the uses of nuclear energy by private companies and persons to protect the public health and safety, as well as the environment. *See also* ATOMIC ENERGY ACTS OF 1946 AND 1954, page 474.

Significance   The Nuclear Regulatory Commission has assumed primary responsibility for maintaining scientific and engineering safeguards and environmental control over civilian uses of nuclear power. The NRC, with its extensive regulatory activities concerning private power companies, is supervised by Congress through a Joint Committee on Atomic Energy. To what extent the nation should depend on nuclear energy for its future power needs remains highly controversial.

Tennessee Valley Authority (TVA)   A major corporation established by Congress in 1933 to provide for the development of the Tennessee River and its tributaries. The TVA has responsibility for the generation, transmission, and sale of electric power; flood control; improvement of navigation; production of fertilizers; and reforestation, reclamation, and soil conservation. The TVA operates under a board of three directors appointed by the President with the Senate's approval. Its operations cover an area of more than 40,000 square miles in Alabama, Georgia, Kentucky, Mississippi, North Carolina, Tennessee, and Virginia. Development projects are financed through TVA bonds and through sale of electric power to private companies. *See also Ashwander v. TVA,* page 495; DEPARTMENT OF ENERGY, page 491.

Significance   The TVA, the nation's largest utility, is an outstanding example of regional development fostered by a single independent government corporation. Almost 30 major dams have been constructed, and others are planned. The flood-prone Tennessee River has been tamed. Navigation and farming have been improved, and the cheap power supplied by the TVA has encouraged the industrial development of the entire region. The TVA is also a principal source of electric power for the national atomic energy and space programs. All essential features of the program have been sustained by the Supreme Court. Yet, in spite of its success, opposition remains. Many businesspeople oppose the TVA as unfair subsidized government competition with private power companies. Some critics in other parts of the country oppose the use of government tax money to subsidize industry and consumers in a single region with cheap power, resulting in the movement of industry away from other sections of the country to the Tennessee Valley. Private power companies operating in the area oppose the use of TVA rates as a yardstick to measure the fairness of the rates they charge consumers. Despite the political controversy over TVA, it has contributed significantly to the economic and social development of the region and has provided excellent recreational facilities.

IMPORTANT CASES

Ashwander v. TVA,   297 U.S. 288 (1936): Upheld the construction of major dams by an agency of the national government under the war and commerce powers and upheld the authority of such an agency to build transmission lines and to sell electrical energy generated at the dams. The Court held that Congress could properly build huge dams, if needed for national defense and to improve navigation, and that it could, under the Constitution, sell property belonging to the United States, such as electric power. *See also Ashwander v. TVA,* page 286.

Significance   The *Ashwander* decision sustained the legal basis for the vast complex of the TVA and its multipurpose program. The case emphasizes the broad application of the commerce clause and the domestic implications resulting from a liberal interpretation of the war power.

Mulford v. Smith,   307 U.S. 38 (1939): Sustained the constitutionality of the Agricultural Act of 1938. The Supreme Court held that Congress may limit the amount of a crop sold in interstate commerce and that the delegation of powers to the Secretary of Agriculture by Congress is proper, in that definite standards were laid down in the Act. It also held that Congress may validly exercise its power to regulate interstate commerce through a regulatory tax. *See also* COMMERCE POWER, page 33; REGULATORY TAX, page 415.

Significance   The *Mulford* case sanctioned attempts by Congress and the Department of Agriculture to provide a more orderly marketing system for the basic crops of cotton, wheat, corn, tobacco, and rice. National government procedures under the Act include crop purchases, loans, marketing quotas, storage of crop reserves, and the parity concept aimed at securing fair prices for farmers. This case had the effect of overruling the Supreme Court's earlier decision in *United States v. Butler,* 297 U.S. 1 (1936), in which it held that national regulation of farm prices invaded the reserved powers of the states. Since the *Mulford* decision, the national government's handling of the farm problem has involved primarily political and economic rather than legal problems.

IMPORTANT STATUTES

Agricultural Act of 1977   Major farm legislation that continued the national government's role of providing price supports for major crops that are in substantial surplus. Main provisions of the Act include (1) price support subsidies for surplus crops; (2) an overhaul of the Food Stamp Program to curb fraud and eliminate the requirement that recipients pay cash for some of their stamps; (3) creation of a new subsidy program for sugar producers; (4) provision for a farmer-held grain reserves system by extending normal price support loans from one year to three to five years; (5) a new wheat research and nutrition education program; and (6) an extension of the Food for Peace (Public Law 480) foreign aid program. *See also* FOOD AND NUTRITION PROGRAMS, page 507; FOOD FOR PEACE, page 484; FREEDOM TO FARM ACT OF 1996, page 500; PRICE SUPPORT, page 486.

Significance   The Agricultural Act of 1977 was one of many extensions of farm support legislation that essentially maintained the policies established in the basic New Deal farm legislation, the Agricultural Adjustment Act of 1938. The Agricultural Act of 1977 was noteworthy in that it substantially altered the Agricultural and Consumer Protection Act of 1973, which was based on the assumption that farmers should be "unleashed" from government controls to grow more food to meet rising world demand. Price support and other programs aimed at limiting production and holding up prices were eliminated or reduced by the 1973 Act. The result was that by 1977 a tremendous glut of surplus crops, especially wheat, plagued the farm economy, and the 1977 Act was an effort to cope with the new problems of worldwide bumper crop production, weak demand, and low prices. Angry farmers, reeling under the financial burden of shrinking incomes and growing debts, criticized the new law and demanded 100 percent parity prices guaranteed by the national government. Attempts to pressure Congress into taking corrective actions led to nationwide farmer strikes and boycotts. Under the 1977 law, the "target price system" (whenever the market price falls below an established target price, the Department of Agriculture pays farmers the difference) established in the 1973 law was applied to offer limited aid to farmers for the first time. In 1981, Congress passed an omnibus farm program renewal, which continued many of the features of the 1977 Act for four more years. In 1985 Congress replaced the 1981 Act with a five-year farm bill that allowed a gradual reduction of price supports and target prices, but the problems persisted. In 1990 Congress once again enacted a five-year farm bill that, like most of its predecessors, was patterned after the original 1938 Agricultural Adjustment Act in that it authorized procedures for increases or decreases in commodity price supports, agricultural exports, soil conservation, farm credit, and research and provided sharp increases in food assistance to the needy. A major new feature of the 1990 Act was a plan called "triple base" that provides subsidies for planted crops, subsidies for idled land, and the opportunity for farmers to plant whatever they choose on 25 percent of the land used for regular subsidized crops. The program signaled a modest return to a free market, giving farmers an incentive to grow crops best suited to specific markets. Farm subsidies, however, continued to grow at an alarming rate and resulted in the Freedom to Farm Act of 1996, which ended the restrictions and subsidies that had been in place for 60 years and placed agriculture on the path of a free market economy.

Agricultural Adjustment Acts of 1933 and 1938   Broad agricultural programs sponsored by the Roosevelt administration and enacted by Congress to maintain farm income through parity price supports and production controls for basic crops. After the 1933 Agricultural Adjustment Act (AAA) had been declared unconstitutional by the Supreme Court in *United States v. Butler*, 297 U.S. 1 (1936), a second AAA, very similar to the first program but eliminating or modifying those sections that had failed the constitutionality test, was adopted in 1938. The Court held the 1933 Act to be an invalid use of the taxing power, whereas it upheld the 1938 Act as a valid exercise of the commerce power (*Mulford v. Smith*, 307 U.S. 38 [1939]). *See also Mulford v. Smith*, page 496.

Significance   Most of the procedures for aiding agriculture that were initiated in these two AAA programs remained the basic approach used by the national government for more than 60 years, until substantially modified by the Freedom to Farm Act of 1996. Features of the AAA included direct government payments to individual farmers for reducing acreage by soil conservation, government loans on surplus crops when overproduction drives prices down, support of farm crop prices at a parity level, and establishment of acreage allotments and marketing quotas on basic crops when farmers approve them through a two-thirds majority vote in a national referendum.

Clean Air Act of 1970   Environmental legislation that set standards limiting the amount of pollutants generated by automotive and industrial emissions. Primary standards are designed to protect human health. Secondary standards were devised to protect buildings, crops, and other material goods. Administered by the Environmental Protection Agency (EPA), the Act required that the EPA establish safe concentrations for seven major air pollutants and set a 1975 deadline for states to meet clean air requirements or face severe penalties including loss of millions of dollars of federal aid. Originally drafted as a three-year, $1.1 billion effort, the Act was reauthorized in 1977 and amended to extend deadlines for meeting national air quality standards, pushed back auto and industrial emissions controls another two to eight years, and established a policy of "nondeterioration" designed to protect areas with air quality levels better than those mandated by law. Other provisions of the Act regulate the type and quantity of additives in jet and automotive fuels, prohibit removal of air pollution devices from automobiles, and prohibit the sale of new cars and/or engines not in compliance with emission standards. *See also* CLEAN AIR ACT OF 1990, page 498; ENVIRONMENTALISM, page 483.

Significance   The Clean Air Act, often labeled as one of the most expensive and technically complex pieces of legislation ever passed, has both been lauded as the cornerstone of an effective antipollution policy that has resulted in improved air quality, and decried as a fundamental threat to the economic stability of American industry. The Act affects a wide range of industries including steel, coal, auto, chemicals, petroleum, and electric utilities and has been the focus of many intense legislative battles in Congress, especially over the issue of automobile emission controls. The issue of how to respond to the growing problem of lead pollution and acidic precipitation ("acid rain") is also a major source of controversy. Extensions of deadlines for meeting standards are common.

Clean Air Act of 1990   A major environmental act that set standards for limiting the amount of pollutants emitted into the air. Its major sections established (1) new standards for ozone, carbon monoxide, lead, and particulates; (2) motor vehicle emissions standards, gasoline and diesel fuel requirements, and service station vapor recovery rules; (3) a delineation of hazardous air pollutants and a goal of a reduction in cancers caused by them; (4) acidic precipitation ("acid rain") provisions that seek a substantial reduction in sulfur dioxide emissions by the year 2000; (5) provisions to phase out ozone-depleting chlorofluorocarbons (CFCs); and (6) assistance to workers laid off due to the costs of meeting the Clean Air Act's standards in the form of job searches, relocation, and an extension of their unemployment benefits. The Act is administered by the Environmental Protection Agency (EPA) and provides civil and criminal penalties for noncompliance. *See also* CLEAN AIR ACT OF 1970, page 498.

Significance   The 1990 Clean Air Act was the first clean air legislation since 1977. Earlier versions were criticized for their complexity and cost and because standards were pushed back year after year. The 1990 Clean Air Act is equally complex and costly. The 1990 Act creates a new permit system that provides economic incentives to comply with the law. The 1990 Act also reduces the discretion of the EPA to make rules concerning pollutants by prescribing highly technical standards in the law itself. Whether the Act will overcome the failures of existing legislation may depend upon economic realities. Environmentalists believe that the law will push hope for any major progress on clean air well into the twenty-first century.

Endangered Species Act of 1973   An act to protect species of animals and plant life that are considered to be in danger of biological extinction throughout all or a significant part of their natural habitat. The Act authorizes the Department of the Interior and the Department of Commerce to purchase lands and waters for the purpose of protecting, restoring, or propagating endangered species. It is also declared a federal offense to possess, buy, sell, import, or export endangered species or any products made from them. State governments have primary responsibility for managing programs under the Act through federal assistance. The U.S. Fish and Wildlife Service in the Department of the Interior is the key agency in implementing the Act. *See also* ENVIRONMENTALISM, page 483.

Significance   The Endangered Species Act of 1973 constituted a comprehensive extension of earlier legislation enacted in 1966 to protect the biological diversity of the nation. As species become extinct, potentially valuable medical and nutritional resources may be lost. About 960 species in the United States alone are considered endangered. The law often has engendered controversies when construction projects such as dams endanger marine life or land use threatens birds or predatory animals. Increasingly, disputes have involved regulatory efforts aimed at otherwise lawful uses of private property in order to protect obscure but endangered insects, plants, birds, or rodents. A Supreme Court decision, *Babbitt v. Sweet Home Chapter of Communities for a Great Oregon,* 115 S. Ct. 2407 (1995), strengthened the hand of the Secretary of the Interior to prohibit harm to actual or potential habitats of endangered species and led Congress to suspend further listing of new endangered species. In 1978, Congress established the Endangered Species Committee to grant exemptions to the Act. It is composed of a state representative, the chairman of the Council of Economic Advisors, and the top officials of the Departments of Interior, Agriculture, and Army, the Environmental Protection Agency, and the National Oceanic and Atmospheric Administration. The Committee is known as the "God Squad."

Federal Water Pollution Control Act of 1972 (Clean Water Act)   A major statute administered by the Environmental Protection Agency that mandates a sweeping federal-state campaign to "restore and maintain the chemical, physical, and biological integrity of the Nation's waters." The Water Pollution Control Act established two basic goals: (1) By 1983, water in the United States was to be generally clean enough for swimming and to support fish, shellfish, and wildlife, and (2) by 1985, all discharges of pollutants into the nation's waters would be ended. Specific actions by national, state, and local governments and by industries were called for, with strict deadlines and enforcement provisions in the Act. Special emphasis was placed on solving the problems of industrial pollution and municipal sewage treatment. *See also* NATIONAL ENVIRONMENTAL POLICY ACT OF 1969, page 501; WATER CONSERVATION, page 489.

Significance   The Federal Water Pollution Control Act of 1972 expanded and strengthened earlier water pollution control legislation. Water increasingly has become a major political issue among local and national governmental and private decision makers because of skyrocketing needs for clean water. Conservation and environmental groups have also pressured government on all three levels for positive action. The Act extends national pollution control programs to *all* U.S. waters, rather than only to those interstate waters covered by earlier programs. Since 1972, great amounts of money and effort have been expended in trying to clean up the nation's waters, but many pollution activities have continued apace, and deadlines for compliance have been extended. A 1987 extension of the Act expanded aid to state and local governments for sewage treatment plants, a problem plaguing urban areas. In 1990, Congress, prompted by the massive 1989 Exxon Valdez oil spill in Alaska, strengthened liability rules concerning hazardous substance spills. Allegedly excessive regulatory costs and efforts to return more authority over water resources to the states continued to delay clean water programs. Legislation to improve drinking water cleared Congress in 1996.

Freedom to Farm Act of 1996   A major reform of the agricultural price support system that replaced the New Deal Depression-era formula for subsidizing agriculture with a system that would end most subsidies within seven years. The Act authorizes fixed, declining payments to growers of corn, other feed grains, cotton, rice, and wheat, regardless of market conditions. Farmers may plant any variety of crops while continuing to receive guaranteed payments through 2002. Other provisions of the Act phase down support for some dairy products, retain the major soil conservation program, reauthorize the Food Stamp Program for two years (pending welfare reform), and establish a fund for rural development. The powerful peanut, sugar, and tobacco farms are largely excluded from the Act. *See also* AGRICULTURAL ACT OF 1977, page 496; AGRICULTURAL ADJUSTMENT ACTS OF 1933 AND 1938, page 497; PRICE SUPPORT, page 486.

Significance   The Freedom to Farm Act moves toward the elimination of subsidies to farmers in favor of a free market system. The goals are to boost production in growing markets, increase exports, and end payments to farmers not to farm. The seven-year transition period allows time for experimentation with crop rotation strategies. Opponents fear elimination of a safety net for farmers and allege that the law will help monied grain traders at the expense of small or family farms. To assure needed congressional action by 2002, the Act provides that the price support system will revert to the Agricultural Act of 1949, which sustained the high price supports growing out of World War II and which was based on the basic 1938 Agricultural Adjustment Act. Under the Freedom to Farm Act, the government will no longer determine what crops to plant or how much land to use; the farmer, in turn, should farm with an eye toward the market rather than toward price support funds.

Homestead Act of 1862   A historic act in which Congress offered 160 acres of the public domain to any person who would pay a $10 registration fee and live on the land for five years.

Significance   The Homestead Act opened up the vast areas of the public domain in the Midwest and West to farming. Millions of acres were parceled out to pioneering "homesteaders," and by 1910 restrictions had to be imposed to keep some governmental lands under public ownership. The Homestead Act contributed greatly to the growing strength of the nation by opening the West and encouraging land and home ownership.

National Environmental Policy Act of 1969   The basic declaration of national policy aimed at encouraging "productive and enjoyable harmony between man and his environment" and promoting efforts that "prevent or eliminate damage to the environment and biosphere and stimulate the health and welfare of man." The Act established a Council on Environmental Quality in the Executive Office to advise the President. Each year the President is required by the Act to transmit to Congress an environmental quality report that includes reviews of the current situation and recommendations for legislative programs. The Act in effect recognizes that modern technology and the "growth ethic" of capitalism must be redirected so that they function more in harmony with the natural environment. *See also* COUNCIL ON ENVIRONMENTAL QUALITY, page 490; ENVIRONMENTAL PROTECTION AGENCY, page 493.

Significance   The National Environmental Policy Act of 1969 was passed by Congress with bipartisan support, strong presidential urgings, and broad public demands. Although the Act is phrased in hortatory language, with few specific directives, the Environmental Act explicitly recognizes a new and important role for the national government. Some critics point out, however, that the effort to achieve continuous economic expansion in the interest of full employment and economic stability tends to conflict with the objectives of the Act.

Superfund (Comprehensive Environmental Response, Compensation, and Liability Act of 1980)   An Act of Congress that established a $1.6 billion fund for the purpose of locating and cleaning up hazardous waste sites and other releases of hazardous substances (excluding oil spills) into the environment. Superfund is financed by taxes on both the chemical and petrochemical industries and, to a lesser extent, by the federal government, for the purpose of devising and implementing emergency responses to hazardous waste releases. The Act charges the Environmental Protection Agency (EPA) with the responsibility of identifying hazardous waste sites in the country and instituting measures necessary to clean up sites found to present threats to the health and well-being of individuals and the environment. The Act also assigns liability to those responsible for dumping hazardous wastes. The government tries to compel polluters to clean up sites or cleans up the site itself and then sues those responsible to recover cleanup costs. *See also* ENVIRONMENTAL PROTECTION AGENCY, page 493.

Significance Superfund was the first federally coordinated attempt to address the problems of hazardous waste disposal. The EPA estimates that more than 1.5 billion pounds of hazardous waste are produced every day and that as many as 23,500 hazardous waste sites constitute a threat to the nation's public health and environmental integrity. These include 1,238 sites placed on its "National Priorities List" in 1995 as having high risk to human health and the general environment. Fewer than 200 sites have been cleaned up since passage of the Act, and levels of funding are continuing major legislative battles in Congress. Charges of industry collusion with EPA officials have been leveled, and congressional investigations in 1983 resulted in the resignation of a score of EPA officials charged with administering the Act. The problems of controlling and cleaning toxic waste dumps are extremely complex, and the political and economic stakes are high. Compensation for toxic waste victims has also emerged as a major issue. Congress has appropriated more than $15 billion for the Superfund by mid-1994, but critics claim that more has been spent on administration and litigation than on cleaning up sites. Extensive controversy over "retroactive liability" exists as to which parties are to be held responsible for toxic waste dumped before passage of the Act in 1980. Numerous hazardous waste sites have been discovered on federal lands.

12

Health, Education, and Welfare

Acquired Immune Deficiency Syndrome (AIDS)   An incurable illness (caused by the "human immunodeficiency virus," or HIV), which inhibits the body's ability to resist diseases. Most AIDS patients contract the disease through homosexual or bisexual sex, intravenous drug use through shared needles, infected blood through transfusions, at birth from infected mothers, or in products to treat coagulation disorders. Increasingly, persons have become infected through heterosexual sex. Most victims die within ten years after infection. *See also* AMERICANS WITH DISABILITIES ACT OF 1990, page 375.

Significance   The advent of AIDS has posed significant medical and political problems. Treatment for AIDS is lengthy and expensive, and no cure currently exists. A large national program to find a vaccine and a cure for AIDS is under way, but AIDS activists claim that too little is being done. By mid-1995, nearly 300,000 people had died of AIDS in the United States, and close to a million more have AIDS or are HIV-positive. Moreover, AIDS has turned into a civil rights issue, complicated by the prevalence of AIDS sufferers among members of marginalized groups such as homosexuals and intravenous drug users. Although AIDS is not communicable through casual contact at work or in the home, many people fear contact with AIDS-infected individuals, and discrimination against AIDS patients is common. Though the Americans with Disabilities Act of 1990 and various state antidiscrimination laws provide AIDS sufferers with protection, critics argue that without legislation specifically addressing AIDS discrimination, AIDS sufferers will be unable to effectively use the Constitution's equal protection and due process clauses or other tort laws to obtain redress of their grievances. Debate rages over the issue of forcing certain individuals such as health care workers, prostitutes, and rapists to undergo AIDS testing—a practice that critics view as an invasion of privacy as well as an additional obstacle to eliminating discrimination against AIDS-infected persons. Others contend, however, that such actions are necessary to protect the public and to expose those who knowingly spread the AIDS virus. This disease provides a sad but classic example of the tensions in a free society arising from the conflict of individual rights, protection of afflicted minorities, and the demands on government to provide for and protect the health, safety, and welfare of the community.

Aid to Families with Dependent Children (AFDC)   Financial aid provided under the Social Security Act of 1935 for children who lack adequate support though living with one parent or relative. Aid to two-parent families was later made optional for states, but most AFDC recipients have been in one-parent or foster care households. The program is administered by states with the assistance of federal funds under supervision of the Department of Health and Human Services. As an "entitlement" program, the number of recipients, including parents and children, had grown from less than 3 million in 1955 to more than 14 million in the mid-1990s. After years of controversy, Congress in 1996 ended AFDC (effective July 1997) and established block grants for states with broad discretion to determine eligibility for assistance. *See also* CATEGORICAL ASSISTANCE, page 504; ENTITLEMENTS, page 505; WELFARE REFORM ACT OF 1996, page 527.

Significance   Although but one of several programs of aid to the needy, AFDC was the most controversial and the program that most people associate with the term "welfare." It has been viewed by many as self-defeating—encouraging illegitimacy, inducing men to leave their families in order to make their children eligible, encouraging migration to more generous states, and encouraging recipients to avoid employment. Numerous efforts to reform AFDC by establishing programs of job-training, child care, and enforcement of child-support by absentee fathers failed. Reductions in available AFDC funds led to greater usage of food stamps, another federal entitlement program. During the 1990s increasingly greater discretion was accorded each state to determine requirements for and limits on eligibility. Finally, in the Welfare Reform Act of 1996, Congress ended AFDC in favor of block grants to the states.

Categorical Assistance   Welfare programs provided under the Social Security Act. These programs include (1) old-age assistance for the needy, (2) aid to the blind, (3) aid to dependent children, and (4) aid to the totally and permanently disabled. Persons in these categories not covered by Social Security and in need of financial assistance have received aid from their state from funds supplemented by federal grants. Under the Supplemental Security Income (SSI) program, initiated in 1974, aid to the adult categories—needy aged, blind, and disabled—is assumed by the national government, though states may choose to supplement the basic amount. Responsibility for the categorical aid programs rests with the Department of Health and Human Services and the Social Security Administration. The programs also extend to the District of Columbia, Puerto Rico, Guam, and the Virgin Islands. *See also Goldberg v. Kelly,* page 521; SOCIAL SECURITY ACT OF 1935, page 527; SUPPLEMENTAL SECURITY INCOME, page 513; WELFARE REFORM ACT OF 1996, page 527.

Significance   Categorical assistance establishes a continuing program of aid for major categories of destitute people. In former years, local governments commonly provided poorhouses or almshouses for the care of the needy. Congress requires that any state participating in the program must establish a state agency, staffed by the merit system, to conduct the program or to supervise local units that conduct the program. Persons denied aid must be given the opportunity to appeal to the state supervisory agency. Under the Supreme Court's decision in *Goldberg v. Kelly* (397 U.S. 254 [1970]), termination of aid can take place only after a hearing. The states may establish their own requirements that individuals must meet to receive assistance, but the Supreme Court has outlawed state residence requirements as denying the poor the freedom to travel (*Shapiro v. Thompson,* 394 U.S. 618 [1969]). Supplemental Security Income is designed to guarantee a minimum support level for the needy. More than 15 million individuals were covered by categorical aid programs in the 1990s.

Community Action Program (CAP)   A "War on Poverty" program created by the Economic Opportunity Act of 1964 to stimulate communities to mobilize their resources against poverty. Federal aid was given to local public and private agencies to undertake antipoverty programs that involve the poor themselves in operating the programs. Since 1981, block grants have been given to states for administration by the governors. Possible projects include literacy instruction, job training, vocational rehabilitation, homemaker services, job development, and health services. *See also* ECONOMIC OPPORTUNITY ACT OF 1964, page 522; LEGAL SERVICES CORPORATION, page 519.

Significance   The Community Action Program encourages public and private nonprofit agencies to engage in positive and varied programs to meet and, if possible, conquer the causes of poverty in the community. Many Community Action Programs have stimulated fresh approaches to the poverty problem other than direct handouts to the poor. The program has been very controversial and has had to withstand numerous efforts to curtail its activities or abolish it. Most criticism has been directed at the tendency of local public agencies to use the program for political patronage, the lack of sufficient involvement of poor people in the administration of community projects, the use of programs as centers for the promotion of social activist causes, and evidence of corruption and exploitation of target communities in some areas.

Entitlements   Benefits provided by government to which recipients have a legally enforceable right, based on eligibility criteria such as age, income, or occupation. The largest entitlement programs are Social Security, Medicare, bank deposit insurance, Medicaid, civil service retirement, unemployment compensation, military retirement, food stamps, Supplemental Security Income, family support, veterans' benefits, and farm price supports. Such expenditures consume about 50 percent of government spending, which, when added to other uncontrollable costs (such as long-term contracts and interest on the national debt), leaves Congress with less than a third of the annual budget to allocate through the regular budget process. *See also Goldberg v. Kelly,* page 521; PRIVILEGE, page 530; WELFARE REFORM ACT OF 1996, page 527.

Significance   Entitlements are difficult to control because of the political strength of the groups that benefit from them and because devising formulas to distinguish among individuals receiving entitlements is almost impossible. Moreover, many costs are indexed to inflation, while others are virtually uncontrollable, as in the case of Medicare or interest rates. President Reagan, who campaigned on a platform of making huge budget cuts, was able very early in his administration to make reductions in expenditures for some entitlement programs. In 1990, Congress, as part of budget reform, provided that new entitlements can be enacted only by raising taxes or taking money from existing entitlements. By the mid-1990s much political debate centered on either ending or sharply limiting entitlements through the use of block grants to the states for discretionary use for similar programs.

Federal Aid to Education   Various programs of federal grants-in-aid to the states for educational purposes. Such aid has taken the form of land grants for schools and colleges; grants for vocational education and vocational re-habilitation; school lunch programs; scholarship funds for science, mathe-matics, and other programs in the interest of national defense; grants to veterans to attend school; and grants to areas with a heavy influx of students because of the establishment of a military base or other national facility. In 1965, the first general aid-to-education bill, providing substantial aid to ele-mentary and secondary schools, was passed, and numerous aids to higher ed-ucation have been enacted by Congress. Direct aid to college students from low-income families (Basic Educational Opportunity Grants, renamed "Pell Grants" in 1980) was enacted in 1972. *See also* DEPARTMENT OF EDUCATION, page 516; ELEMENTARY AND SECONDARY EDUCATION ACT, page 522; HIGHER EDUCA-TION ACT, page 523; STUDENT AID PROGRAMS, page 512.

Significance   General federal aid to education has engendered much controversy. Opponents point out that education has traditionally been a state and local concern and that federal aid means federal supervision and control of the school system and curriculum. Supporters point to the wide variety of federal aids to education carried on over a long period of Ameri-can history without undue federal interference. They claim that the states are in no position to finance the increasing need for better educational fa-cilities. Deeply involved in the controversy is the issue of aid for parochial schools. Many persons oppose aid to religious institutions as a violation of the principle of separation of church and state. Others argue that all chil-dren should benefit from such aid, and, hence, no restriction should be placed on the type of school affected. Additional controversy has been aroused over the use of federal aid to education in the enforcement of racial integration, particularly where such aid is withheld as a sanction against continuing segregation. The issue of equal rights for women has also emerged as a factor in administration of federal aid to education, as has equal educational opportunities for the handicapped. During the Reagan and Bush administrations, federal educational efforts focused on the idea of vouchers for parents who could choose any school for their children, an idea that opponents claim threatens the public school system. More specific poli-cies have encouraged the creation of specialized magnet schools, basic skills education, and the establishment of national achievement standards in spe-cific grade levels and subject matter. President Bush called for an "America 2000" plan for educational achievement, under which all children would start school ready to learn, high school graduation rates would increase to 90 percent, competence in core subjects would be achieved, and American children would lead the world in science and mathematics; every adult would be literate and skilled to work, and every school would be safe and free of drugs. Such efforts and programs continue to arouse fears of loss of local control and the establishment of a national curriculum, and they have met with little success.

Food and Nutrition Programs   A variety of food programs, administered by the Department of Agriculture, to provide nutritional assistance to the poor. Among the more notable and costly programs are the Food Stamp Program; the school milk, breakfast, and lunch programs; and the WIC (Women, Infants, and Children) program. In addition, programs are directed at the homeless, the elderly poor, and the various human services agencies that assist the needy. *See also* FOOD STAMPS, page 507.

Significance   Domestic food and nutrition programs consume about 60 percent of the Department of Agriculture's budget, reflecting a serious problem in meeting the needs of the nation's poor. Food stamps, the most costly of the programs, serves more than 26 million people, while the school lunch program serves 25 million children. The WIC program is specifically aimed at about 5 million pregnant or nursing women and small children who potentially suffer from malnutrition. These and similar programs serve the interests of farmers and agricultural businesses as well as meet a social need; thus they find support relatively easily from members of Congress with either rural or urban interests. These programs essentially now amount to entitlements in that any person who qualifies for the aid receives it.

Food Stamps   A welfare program to improve nutrition in low-income households. The Food Stamp Program is administered by the Department of Agriculture through state and local welfare agencies, which establish eligibility, issue stamps, and maintain controls. Stamps may be exchanged for food at retail stores. *See also* WELFARE REFORM ACT OF 1996, page 527.

Significance   The Food Stamp Program has virtually assured that no person suffers from hunger and malnutrition because of low income. Abuse and scandal, however, have marked the program. Uncontrolled inflation, rising food costs, and high unemployment combined to strain the program further. In the 1980s and early 1990s, up to 26 million people—or about one in ten Americans—were using food stamps at a cost of over $30 billion annually, making the Food Stamp Program among the most costly of the federal welfare programs. In the Welfare Reform Act of 1996, Congress cut the allocation for food stamps and restrained its use by unemployed adults without children, and by immigrants.

Head Start   One of several Community Action Programs (CAP) created under the Economic Opportunity Act of 1964. Project Head Start provides educational, health, nutritional, and other social services to about 750,000 disadvantaged preschool children, ages three to five. Administered by the Department of Health and Human Services, more than 1,400 Head Start programs are operated by a variety of local public and private nonprofit agencies. *See also* COMMUNITY ACTION PROGRAM, page 505.

Significance   Head Start is considered to be one of the more effective programs of the Johnson administration's "War on Poverty." It has received consistent bipartisan support and was one of only a few social programs to have been spared budget cuts under the Reagan, Bush, and Clinton administrations. Head Start relies heavily on volunteers and the active participation of parents. Although the long-range impact of the program on the enrolled students is disputed, Head Start is politically popular and expected to more than double in size.

Health Maintenance Organization (HMO)   A medical group that offers health services for a fixed annual fee. Such programs differ from ordinary health insurance (indemnity plans, which provide specified benefits to insured persons suffering from illness) and from individual physician services (in which separate fees are paid for each service) by offering a wide range of services to members, including preventive care, for a preset fee. In 1973, Congress enacted legislation to encourage HMOs by offering financial aid to those establishing HMOs. It also required companies with 25 or more employees to offer HMO membership for their employees as an alternative to health insurance indemnity plans.

Significance   Health maintenance organizations as an alternative to traditional medical care grew slowly. Congress required HMOs to provide liberal benefits, as well as virtual open enrollment to applicants regardless of health, thereby making costs almost prohibitive. Further, opposition from the American Medical Association, coupled with bureaucratic delays in implementing the 1973 law, resulted in little growth in the number of HMOs. In 1976, Congress eased some of its requirements in order to stimulate HMO growth. Since then, the extraordinary increase in medical care costs and more public acceptance of the HMO concept have led to dramatic growth in HMO membership, spurred by employers choosing the HMO alternative as a way of reducing medical costs. By 1994, "physician employees" of HMOs outnumbered traditional solo practitioners. HMOs are now viewed as a major alternative for reform of Medicare as a way of controlling costs.

Job Corps   A program, authorized by the Economic Opportunity Act of 1964, that enables jobless youths from 16 to 21 to work and study at training centers or in conservation camps. Emphasis is placed upon education, vocational training, and work experience. The Job Corps is managed by the Department of Labor, which contracts with local public and private agencies to establish training centers. *See also* ECONOMIC OPPORTUNITY ACT OF 1964, page 522.

Significance   The Job Corps was inaugurated as part of the Johnson administration's "War on Poverty." Its aim is to attack the causes rather than the effects of unemployment. Through the Job Corps program, it is hoped that school dropouts and underprivileged youth will become useful and productive citizens. While learning, corpsmen receive living and travel allowances. In 1995 about 100,000 corpsmen were in training at 110 residential centers. Another major job-training program is the 1982 Job Training Partnership Act (JTPA), which involves federal aid to states to assist private industry to train the disadvantaged, particularly in urban areas.

Land-grant College   An agricultural and mechanical college or the agricultural and mechanical school of a state university, established under the provisions of the Morrill Act of 1862. The Morrill Act provided for a grant of land (amounting to nearly 11 million acres) by the national government to the states for the support of colleges to teach agriculture, engineering, and home economics. Later, several black institutions were also designated as land-grant colleges. Congress has continued to make money grants to land-grant institutions, supplementing funds given by state and private agencies. Experimental stations for agriculture and an extension service that carries education directly to farmers have also been established at land-grant colleges.

Significance Most of the great state universities and agricultural colleges in the United States are a direct result of the land-grant policy. Congress did not exclude the teaching of other subjects from these schools, and all of them provide education in the humanities and scientific fields. The agricultural and mechanical divisions, however, continue to receive special attention from Congress. The farmer has benefited most from the facilities made available through the land-grant college. Efforts to apply the land-grant concept to the support of urban universities and urban needs have not been successful.

Maternal and Child Welfare Program A feature of the Social Security Act of 1935 that provides for grants to the states for maternal and child health services, crippled children's services, and general child welfare programs. Grants are made to the states not for payments to particular persons, as is true under the categorical aid programs, but for support of state welfare programs. Maternal and child health services include care of mothers before and after childbirth and immunization of children against communicable diseases. Another program seeks to provide therapy and rehabilitation for crippled children whose parents lack independent means to care for them. Child welfare activities include counseling and care of neglected, mentally retarded, and emotionally disturbed youngsters and care of delinquent children. *See also* SOCIAL SECURITY ACT OF 1935, page 527.

Significance The maternal and child welfare program has had remarkable success in reducing infant and maternal mortality and has benefited thousands of crippled, neglected, and emotionally disturbed children. All states have established agencies to carry out these functions. Overall administration is in the hands of the Department of Health and Human Services, but, since 1981, states have had substantial autonomy.

Medicare/Medicaid Medicare is a health insurance program enacted in 1965 as an amendment to the Social Security Act to provide medical care for the elderly. Impoverished persons of any age unable to qualify under Medicare who are in need of medical services are assisted under federally supported state programs called Medicaid (first established in 1960 by the Kerr-Mills Act). Two health programs make up Medicare. The first, the Hospital Insurance Trust Fund (known as Part A), is compulsory and financed by increases in the Social Security payroll tax. It covers many hospital and nursing home costs, home health service visits, and diagnostic services for persons aged 65 and older. The second, the Supplemental Medical Insurance Program (known as Part B), is a voluntary program for persons over 65 that covers a variety of health services both in and out of medical institutions as well as a substantial part of physician costs. The supplemental plan is financed by a monthly charge to the person enrolled and by the national government out of general federal revenues. Medicaid is similar to Part A of Medicare, but the rules under which people qualify are set jointly by the states and federal government. Many states have opted to expand Medicaid coverage beyond the minimum coverage set by the federal government.

Significance   The passage of Medicare in 1965 climaxed a twenty-year fight over what the American Medical Association and other opposition groups called "socialized medicine." The programs recognize that many people cannot afford private health insurance and that illness can quickly exhaust the resources of most families, especially elderly persons, who have the most health problems. The programs have been marred by periodic revelations of fraud and abuse, such as kickbacks among physicians and pharmacists, unnecessary medical treatment, and overblown hospital and clinical laboratory billings. Nevertheless, increasing longevity and rapidly rising medical costs make the programs essential, resulting in continuing major political and fiscal strains on Congress. In adopting Medicare and Medicaid, the United States has followed the lead of most democratic and industrial nations, some of which instituted public medical care programs as early as the nineteenth century. Congress has repeatedly expanded Medicare and Medicaid coverage over the last several years, and by 1993 more than 35 million people were on Medicare and more than 30 million were on Medicaid. Medicaid has grown to such an extent, in fact, that it consumes billions of federal dollars and nearly 20 percent of state budgets. Further expansions include regulations recently put in place that govern nursing homes and home care for the frail elderly, mentally ill, and retarded. An emphasis on preventive care evident in the early 1990s shows promise for reducing some of Medicare and Medicaid's expenses in the longer term. The expansion of Medicare to persons of all ages in the form of national health insurance has been one of the major issues of contemporary American politics, but consensus on ways and means appears unlikely. Fear of future uncontrollable pressures on federal and state budgets because of Medicare and Medicaid has consumed the attention of national and state political leaders, but the possibility of a strong voter backlash from cuts in medical spending gives them equal fear.

Old-Age, Survivors, and Disability Insurance (OASDI)   An insurance program, commonly called "Social Security," administered by the national government under the provisions of the Social Security Act of 1935. Its major purposes are to provide a retirement income for elderly persons, income for workers who are totally disabled, income for the spouses and minor children of deceased wage earners, and medical care for the aged (Medicare). Specifically exempted from coverage are federal employees who, prior to 1984, were under the civil service retirement system, members of the clergy (optional), state and local employees not authorized coverage by state law, and some persons whose incomes are not sufficient to qualify. All other persons are required to contribute a certain percentage of their income that is matched by their employer. The amount paid by the employee appears on his or her tax-withholding form as FICA (Federal Insurance Contribution Act). Self-employed persons contribute both the employee share and the employer share. These contributions are credited to each worker's account and, upon death, retirement, or disablement, funds are allocated in accordance with the formulas provided by law for each eventuality. Retirement usually takes place at the age of 65, but one may retire at 62 with reduced benefits. Retired persons may continue to work, but their benefits are reduced for earnings over a designated annual amount. After the age of 70, no limitations are placed on earnings. Beginning in the year 2003 (those born in 1938 and after), the normal retirement age of 65 will be increased gradually over a 21-year period to age 67 beginning in the year 2025. The program is administered directly by the Social Security Administration, formerly in the Department of Health and Human Services but named an independent agency in 1994. *See also* MEDICARE, page 509; SOCIAL SECURITY ADMINISTRATION, page 521; SOCIAL SECURITY CASES, page 522.

Significance   The OASDI is a compulsory savings plan designed to meet the problems of an increasingly aging population. Modern health programs have contributed to a rapid increase in the number of persons over 65. In addition, OASDI provides for the disabled and the families of deceased workers who would otherwise become public charges. Insurance has taken the place of public and private charity and maintains the dignity of those who receive funds from the program. The program is a direct result of the Depression of the 1930s, during which many people became destitute. Some persons object to the compulsory nature of the program and to the amounts spent on its administration. The program has, however, received the endorsement of both major parties, and benefits and coverage have been regularly increased, as has the cost to contributors. Medicare and OASDI now represent a significant portion of both private and public expenditures. Lower birthrates, a longer life span, and the general aging of the American population mean that a shrinking workforce must support a growing number of retirees. This, coupled with expanded benefits, has threatened the solvency of the program, but the political costs of change have prevented significant action. In 1995, about 35 million people were beneficiaries of the various programs. Major revisions of the Act in 1983 and 1988 provided for higher FICA taxes for all participants, including increased charges for Medicare, and levying income taxes on up to half of Social Security payments for those whose income exceeds a certain level.

Public Housing   Government construction and maintenance of dwellings for low-income families. Since 1937, and with increasing emphasis after 1949, the national government has given assistance to local governments to clear slum areas and to construct housing. Local governments need state authorization to participate in the program, and the local community can reject public housing by referendum. A local housing authority must be established to administer the funds provided by the federal government and to float bonds. Rentals are used to repay the federal loan and private bondholders. Rentals are kept very low, and the federal government subsidizes the difference between costs and rental receipts. Only persons with limited incomes are eligible to occupy the housing. Some cities and states have undertaken their own public housing programs without federal aid. In a major revision of housing programs in the Housing and Community Development Act of 1974, Congress continued conventional public housing and increased rental-assistance programs. During the 1980s, the Reagan administration resisted new public housing development, but Congress finally authorized additional programs and funding in 1987. The National Affordable Housing Act of 1990 provided funds for rehabilitation block grants and rental assistance. The Act also added a new plan to sell existing public housing to tenants and to assist low-income people to purchase single-family homes. *See also Goldberg v. Kelly,* page 521; HOUSING ACT OF 1949, page 525; HOUSING AND COMMUNITY DEVELOPMENT ACT OF 1974, page 525; URBAN RENEWAL, page 514.

Significance   The Depression and World War II contributed to a housing shortage and continuing deterioration of slum areas. Rising costs and widespread conversion of city rental units to condominiums during the 1960s and 1970s have made it impossible for many low-income families to secure decent housing. Rising numbers of homeless people marked the 1980s. Poor housing and slums increase delinquency, impair family ties, and are costly to the community in welfare services and police and fire protection. Opponents of public housing object to the government competing with private industry. It is argued, too, that the availability of public housing discourages tenants from earning higher incomes because they may be forced to move if their income rises. Serious controversy has arisen over the role of public housing policy in stimulating or preventing racial and economic integration in city neighborhood patterns. The tendency of much public housing to resemble vertical ghetto prisons has also drawn criticism. The 1974 Housing and Community Development Act attempted to meet some of these objections by encouraging comprehensive community planning and requiring dispersal of low-income rental housing. Such dispersal of public housing throughout a metropolitan area received Supreme Court approval in *Hills vs. Gautreaux,* 425 U.S. 284 (1976), but the Court also upheld the right of a community to refuse to alter its zoning laws to permit low-cost housing, unless the refusal could be shown to be racially motivated, in *Arlington Heights v. Metropolitan Housing Development Corporation,* 429 U.S. 252 (1977). Increased dispersal of low-cost housing into middle and upper class neighborhoods during the 1990s has often led to community racial and ethnic tensions.

Student Aid Programs   Financial assistance to college and university students through grants and/or loans. Major federal programs include (1) Basic Educational Opportunity Grants (BEOG), renamed "Pell Grants" in 1980, which are based on a formula of expected family contributions and student need; (2) Supplemental Educational Opportunity Grants (SEOG), based on special need; (3) National Direct Student Loans (NDSL), renamed "Perkins Loans" in 1989, which are very low-interest loans to needy students; and (4) Guaranteed Student Loans (GSL), renamed "Stafford Loans" in 1988, under which the government subsidizes interest payments and guarantees repayment to banks that lend money to students for educational purposes. In 1993, Congress approved a new loan program whereby students borrow directly from the national government, bypassing commercial lenders. Resistance to direct government loans from conservatives in Congress and from banking interests has resulted in maintaining direct loans as a small percentage of loans. In addition, the College Work Study Program (CWSP) provides generous matching funds to colleges and universities to facilitate employment of students on campus or in nonprofit organizations. Nearly all states have grant and loan programs as well. *See also* FEDERAL AID TO EDUCATION, page 506; HIGHER EDUCATION ACT OF 1965, page 524.

Significance   Student aid programs have made higher education available to millions of students who were not otherwise in a position to pay for the costs of a college education or, in many cases, graduate education. More than one-third of all college students receive some form of aid and, in some colleges, nearly all students are recipients of federal and/or state aid. Some observers argue that the student aid programs are too generous and too freely given to students and families with marginal or no real need. Since 1990, institutions with high default records on repayments of loans by students are penalized. The direct student loan program is politically controversial because of private lender opposition and disputes over the proper role of the Department of Education.

Supplemental Security Income (SSI)   A program adopted by Congress in 1972 and initiated in 1974 that provided for federal assumption of adult categories of public assistance, namely, aid to the blind, aid to the totally and permanently disabled, and old-age assistance. A basic amount of money is made available to needy adults falling within the designated categories according to marital and family status, not individually determined need. States with already existing higher benefits may continue to supplement SSI. *See also* CATEGORICAL ASSISTANCE, page 504; SOCIAL SECURITY ACT OF 1935, page 527.

Significance   The pressures of increased costs and caseloads have intensified the drive for reform of the welfare program. Under the Social Security Act of 1935, each state sets its own standards for aid to the needy and receives grants-in-aid from the national government. This has led to wide variations in payments and criteria for aid, resulting, it is charged, in migration of the poor to areas with high welfare payments. Administrative costs associated with identifying the needy and checking their eligibility for aid have been criticized. The SSI program seeks to simplify welfare programs by establishing income levels as the index of need, eliminating the red tape and confusion of present programs, lessening differences in benefit levels, and reducing the burden imposed on the states by the grant-in-aid matching requirements. This program was a step toward complete federal assumption of all welfare programs, a step favored by many social welfare authorities, but largely rejected by the Reagan administration and subsequent administrations. A 1994 law restricts alcoholics and drug addicts to no more than three years of SSI and in 1996 Congress excluded immigrants from access to SSI. In 1995, more than 7 million people were receiving SSI aid.

Urban Renewal   Programs conducted by cities to prevent the spread of urban blight, to rehabilitate areas that can be restored, and to clear and redevelop slum areas that are beyond repair. The Housing Act of 1949 and subsequent legislation provide for procedures by which cities can submit programs to obtain federal aid. Aid is provided for planning and clearance programs and for public housing. Federal mortgage insurance is made available to private investors in reconstruction and rehabilitation projects. In the Housing and Community Development Act of 1974, Congress undertook a major revision of urban development policy and made urban renewal one aspect of an integrated block grant program for community development. Under the 1974 Act, Urban Development Action Grants (UDAG) provided funds to cities to stimulate and attract private investment. Urban renewal programs received little active support during the Reagan and Bush administrations. Congress authorized some additional activity in 1987, but it ended UDAG in 1988. *See also* HOUSING ACT OF 1949, page 525; HOUSING AND COMMUNITY DEVELOPMENT ACT OF 1974, page 525.

Significance   Urban renewal is designed to restore rapidly deteriorating cities and to make the city an attractive place in which to live and work. The growth of suburbia has cost cities a good deal in tax resources. Slum areas are a blight on a community and a drain on its financial resources. Suitable housing is needed in most large cities to attract residents and to rehabilitate slum dwellers. Downtown areas need restoration to attract business concerns and customers. Industrial areas need to be developed to provide jobs. The urban renewal program represents a major attempt on the part of the national government to gain the cooperation of both local governments and private capital to save the cities. Critics of the urban renewal program charge that it uproots entire neighborhoods and deprives poor people of property in favor of investment capital, and that waste and politics mark the program. Since 1982, 36 states have established "enterprise zones" that provide tax incentives and upgraded public services to businesses that locate in impoverished urban areas. Pressure grew for a national enterprise zone program, which finally found modest support from Congress in 1992. However, few see enterprise zones as a solution absent major social reform. Enterprise zones appear to work best when combined with tax incentives, low-interest loans, youth programs, and improved law enforcement and social services.

Veterans Organizations   Groups organized to promote the interests of former members of the armed forces and their families. The largest and most influential group is the American Legion, with nearly 3 million members, followed by the Veterans of Foreign Wars, with more than 2 million members. Both organizations take firm stands on political issues and are basically conservative in outlook. Numerous other veterans organizations are based on religious, ethnic, specific war experiences, or military unit considerations. *See also* PRESSURE GROUP, page 104; DEPARTMENT OF VETERANS AFFAIRS, page 518.

Significance   Veterans organizations have been successful at all levels of government in furthering the economic interests of veterans. Public benefits for veterans include bonuses and pensions, educational aid, civil service preference, loans and insurance, and even burial allowances. With the heavy military involvement of the United States in the twentieth century, almost every American family has a veteran member. Legislative bodies find it difficult to resist pressure from organized veterans groups. Veterans groups have been particularly active in promoting patriotism and military preparedness. A major victory for veterans' organizations was the 1989 establishment of the Department of Veterans Affairs as a Cabinet-level department to replace the Veterans Administration.

Vocational Rehabilitation   The training of the physically and mentally handicapped for useful work. The national government provides grants-in-aid to the states for such programs under supervision of the Department of Education and the Department of Health and Human Services. Another major program is in the hands of the Department of Veterans Affairs, which cooperates with various state educational agencies for the training of handicapped veterans. *See also* REHABILITATION ACT OF 1973, page 526.

Significance   Vocational rehabilitation is made available to any handicapped person who can become self-sufficient. If the person can pay for the service, he or she is required to do so, but those unable to pay are provided free training. The program has been expanded in recent years on the theory that it is better for the individual and for society to rehabilitate the handicapped than to provide a permanent dole. The restored worker is not only able to sustain himself or herself but also contributes taxes to the community.

Voluntarism   A doctrine that institutions should be supported by voluntary action and contributions, not by the state. Voluntarism is a major factor in American health, education, and welfare and takes a variety of forms. Examples include health and hospital support (American Cancer Society, American Heart Association, Shriners' Children's Hospitals), disaster relief (American Red Cross, volunteer firefighters), aid to the destitute (Salvation Army), aid to the disadvantaged (Big Brothers, settlement houses), church or ethnic groups (Catholic Charities, United Jewish Appeal), and general community charities (United Fund). A large number of persons volunteer their services to aid the disabled, the aged, the mentally ill, and the socially deprived. Many more contribute funds to private charitable causes, supported by generous provisions for tax deductions for such contributions. Official recognition of voluntary action is also taken by government through agencies that embrace a number of government-sponsored volunteer programs. *See also* CORPORATION FOR NATIONAL AND COMMUNITY SERVICE, page 516.

Significance   Voluntarism is rooted in the belief, strongly held by many Americans, that the private, noncoercive sector of society has a major role to play, particularly in the most sensitive areas of human interaction. Growth of population, technological developments, urban density, and rising costs have led to greater demands for governmental involvement in health programs, educational support services, and welfare programs for the needy. Still, any realistic assessment of health, education, and welfare in the United States must take into account the extraordinary amount of voluntarism and the resultant decreases in political involvement for many vital services. Many volunteer agencies resemble quasi-public organizations in the sense that the public expects and relies on their services; this is true, for example, of volunteer firefighters and the American Red Cross, and the numerous hospitals supported by private religious or secular groups. Support for volunteer agencies is encouraged through tax deduction policies. A major hallmark of the Reagan administration and subsequent Republican party policy is the idea that governmental welfare services should be restricted in favor of the provision of such services by the private, voluntary sector. President Reagan often featured successful volunteers in his public appearances. President Bush continued this emphasis through his "Points of Light" Foundation and awards to encourage community service. President Clinton sponsored the National and Community Service Act of 1993, which establishes the Corporation for National and Community Service to engage Americans of all ages and backgrounds to address various social and environmental needs.

IMPORTANT AGENCIES

Corporation for National and Community Service   An independent agency established by the National and Community Service Act of 1993 to support an ethic of voluntary service in America. It is governed by a fifteen-member bipartisan board appointed by the President with Senate consent for a five-year term. The corporation absorbed volunteer programs formerly administered by ACTION and serves its mission through three major programs: (1) AmeriCorps engages volunteers to meet educational, public safety, human and environmental needs; a notable feature of AmeriCorps is the award of $4,725 per year for one or two years of service, which may be applied to college or vocational education or to repay student loans; other AmeriCorps programs include the National Civilian Community Corps, a residential service learning project concentrating on environmental needs, and Volunteers in Service to America (VISTA) which addresses poverty-related issues. (2) Learn and Serve America supports service learning from kindergarten through graduate school. (3) National Senior Service Corps includes the Retired and Senior Volunteers, the Foster Grandparents, and the Senior Companion Program. Many programs are administered by state or local governments and by private agencies through grants from the corporation. *See also* VOLUNTARISM, page 515.

Significance   The Corporation for National and Community Service resulted from strong initiatives by President Clinton to promote a culture of voluntarism, civic responsibility, and service among people of all ages and backgrounds. While voluntary community action in worthy causes is common in America, recent domestic experiences indicate a falling off of such activities and a lessening of civic spirit. The provision for educational funds under AmeriCorps has been controversial because of its potential costs; Congress has limited participation to 100,000 people. A substantial portion of the corporation's activities had been underway through ACTION.

Department of Education   A Cabinet-level department, established in 1979, consolidating under a Secretary of Education various educational functions formerly exercised by the Department of Health, Education, and Welfare (renamed the Department of Health and Human Services) and several other agencies of the national government. Its major units supervise federal programs in elementary, secondary, and postsecondary education; education research; vocational, adult, special, rehabilitative, bilingual, and overseas education programs; and civil rights. In the legislation creating the Department of Education, Congress specifically provides for the primacy of state and local governments over educational policies, programs, and personnel. *See also* FEDERAL AID TO EDUCATION, page 506.

Significance   The establishment of a separate Cabinet department for education represents the increasing role the national government has assumed in all levels and kinds of educational programs, as well as the close ties that education has to other governmental functions. The new department fulfilled a campaign pledge of President Jimmy Carter. His successor, President Ronald Reagan, pledged to reduce the agency's status on the grounds that its enhanced status would lead to greater federal control over education.

Congress, however, has resisted substantial cuts in federal support of education in the face of growing national concern over the need to upgrade American schools. Under Presidents Bush and Clinton, the department took a more activist stance.

Department of Health and Human Services (HHS)   A major department of the national government established in 1953 as the Department of Health, Education, and Welfare in order to unify administration of federal activities in the fields of health, education, and Social Security. In 1979, the educational function was transferred to a new Cabinet-level Department of Education. The Social Security Administration was given independent status in 1995. A secretary who is a member of the Cabinet heads HHS. Its major operating units include (1) the Administration on Aging, which administers a program of aid to the states under the Older Americans Act of 1965; (2) the Public Health Service, which carries out far-flung programs in health and hospital care and disease control and research; (3) Health Care Financing, which is concerned mainly with Medicare, Medicaid, and long-term care of the aged; (4) the Administration for Children and Families, which oversees child welfare services enforcement, foster care, adoption, and Head Start; and (5) the Substance Abuse and Mental Health Services Administration. *See also* CATEGORICAL ASSISTANCE, page 504; MEDICARE, page 509; PUBLIC HEALTH SERVICE, page 520; SOCIAL SECURITY ACT OF 1935, page 527.

Significance   The department reflects the commitment of the national government to protect the public health and welfare through vast programs of economic assistance, family support, and disease prevention. Most of these programs, once highly controversial, are now accepted by both major political parties and by the American people. Considerable differences of opinion do exist, however, over the desirable scope of welfare programs and the extent of national—as opposed to state and local—administration of these programs. Touching the lives of many Americans, HHS is often referred to as the "people's department."

Department of Housing and Urban Development (HUD)   A major department of Cabinet status, established in 1965, with responsibility for the housing, home finance, and community development functions of the national government. The department, headed by a secretary, has as its major functions programs related to the production and financing of housing, both public and private; community planning and development, with responsibility for urban renewal, home ownership for low-income persons, and homelessness programs; and civil rights in housing and in employment pertaining to housing and urban development. *See also* HOUSING ACT OF 1949, page 525; HOUSING AND COMMUNITY DEVELOPMENT ACT OF 1974, page 525.

Significance   Cabinet status for HUD climaxed years of effort to have the problems of metropolitan areas considered at the highest levels of government. It represents a national commitment to meet the growing crises in the areas of housing, urban renewal, and metropolitan planning. With more than 77 percent of the American people living in urban areas, HUD is an important center for governmental action programs. Many of its programs were restrained during the Reagan administration. Through its administration of the Federal Housing Administration (FHA), which insures mortgages on private homes, and the Government National Mortgage Association (GNMA, "Ginnie Mae"), which provides secondary mortgage market financing to FHA as well as veterans' home loans, HUD touches the lives of many American homeowners. A private counterpart authorized by Congress, the Federal National Mortgage Association (FNMA, "Fannie Mae"), provides general secondary mortgage market financing.

Department of Veterans Affairs (DVA)   A major department of Cabinet status responsible for programs affecting military veterans and their dependents. Originally established in 1930 as an independent agency (the Veterans Administration), the DVA achieved major departmental status in 1989 and is headed by a secretary appointed by the President with Senate consent. The DVA is essentially divided into two major units: Veterans Benefits Administration and Veterans Health Administration. Included within its responsibilities are such programs as compensation for service- or nonservice-connected disabilities or death, vocational rehabilitation, education, home mortgages, life insurance, hospitalization, care of disabled veterans, and burial of veterans. National Guard and reserve unit members are covered if called into active duty. *See also* COURT OF VETERANS APPEALS, page 259; VETERANS ORGANIZATIONS, page 514.

Significance   The Department of Veterans Affairs represents the aftercost of war. Even as the World War II generation decreases, about 26 million Americans still hold veterans' status. Including their families, who are actual or potential beneficiaries, nearly half of the American people are affected by the operations of DVA. It is larger than any other federal department except for the Defense Department. The DVA supervises the largest health care system in the nation, with more than 170 hospitals and 170 clinics and nursing homes. It also manages more than 100 cemeteries. Millions of veterans and, in some cases, their survivors receive disability payments, pensions, life insurance, home loans, education, and job training through DVA programs. The cost of such programs continues to skyrocket as veterans grow older. Provisions are made for veterans to appeal benefits decisions of the DVA to the agency's Board of Veterans Appeals and from there to the Court of Veterans Appeals. Congress and the President find it difficult to cut financing of veterans' programs.

Legal Services Corporation   A private, nonprofit agency established by Congress in 1974 to make grants and contracts with individuals, law firms, or private organizations to provide legal aid to the poor in noncriminal proceedings. Legal services may be provided for such issues as welfare rights, family problems, and personal finance. Lawsuits involving desegregation of schools, Selective Service problems, prisoners, illegal aliens, or nontherapeutic abortions are specifically prohibited. The Legal Services Corporation is governed by an eleven-member board appointed by the President and confirmed by the Senate. Advisory councils are established in each state.

Significance   The Legal Services Corporation was formerly a program within the Office of Economic Opportunity (OEO). Critics charged that

OEO legal services personnel had used their positions to further social activist causes through lawsuits. Consequently, in establishing the Legal Services Corporation as a separate entity, Congress placed curbs on partisan political activities of persons associated with the corporation, limited funding of independent legal research centers that might become involved in activist political goals, and placed bans on certain kinds of lawsuits. Most bar associations have had "legal aid" services to help poor persons with legal problems, and a number of interest groups provide *pro bono publico* (for the public good) legal services in the interest of social causes. These have not adequately served many persons who are either unaware of their rights or fearful of getting involved with legal processes. The Legal Services Corporation can fill an important need by making services available in poor communities. However, it has angered some public officials by bringing suits against them for alleged violations of the rights of the poor. Since its inception, the Legal Services Corporation has been an object of controversy at all levels of government. Conservatives have advocated abolishing it or turning the function over to states. Controversy has surrounded appointments to the governing board, with the Senate finally confirming a board in 1985 after a four-year hiatus. Though the agency has survived, its budget and authority have been continuously reduced.

National Foundation on the Arts and Humanities   An independent agency established in 1965 to encourage and support progress in education and performance in the arts and humanities. The foundation is best known for its two major components: the National Endowment for the Arts (NEA) and the National Endowment for the Humanities (NEH) Each has its own council composed of a chair and 26 members appointed by the President. A Federal Council on the Arts and Humanities with 20 members coordinates their activities. The foundation also supports an Institute of Museum Services. The NEA promotes involvement in the arts by individuals, private organizations, and state and local entities. The NEH has a broad definition of humanities that covers many subject areas in literature, language, history, philosophy, and social science.

Significance   Both the NEA and NEH seek to promote creative activity and to bring such activity to the broader community. They are frequently involved in controversy over specific grants, which may appear to some citizens and political leaders as contrary to decency or religious belief or acceptable political thought. Such episodes sometimes result in congressional action that reduces appropriations or tries to define proper standards. In most cases, these endowments have succeeded in developing and transmitting the diverse American heritage in art and the humanities.

National Science Foundation (NSF)   An independent agency that has primary responsibility for encouraging scientific inquiry and science education programs. Established by the National Science Foundation Act of 1950, the agency is headed by the National Science Board, consisting of 24 part-time members and the NSF director, *ex officio*. Board members are selected for six-year terms by the President with Senate consent to represent the scientific leadership of the nation and are known for their distinguished service in science, medicine, engineering, agriculture, education, public affairs, research management, and industry.

Significance   The National Science Foundation has done much to spur the growth of basic and applied research and to improve science education. Much of the research carried on in the nation's universities and colleges is partially or wholly subsidized by the NSF. International programs that encourage cooperative scientific research and exchange programs have also been strongly supported. Many students and teachers have received financial support for their science projects since 1950, including many in the social sciences.

Public Health Service   A major division within the Department of Health and Human Services charged with promoting and protecting the health of the American people. Its major components include the Food and Drug Administration, the Centers for Disease Control, the Health Resources and Services Administration, and the National Institutes of Health. It is actively involved in protecting people against mental and physical hazards to health, providing adequate health education and staffing, the delivery of community health services, and research into the causes of health disorders.

Significance   The Public Health Service was established in 1798 to provide hospital care for merchant seamen. Subsequent legislation has vastly broadened the scope of its activities from communicable disease control to comprehensive management of the nation's health delivery system. An expanding population, rising medical costs, and the growing prevalence of certain health problems, such as mental illness, heart disease, cancer, AIDS, and drug abuse, have led Congress to increase the duties of the Public Health Service. Notable examples include the National Mental Health Act of 1946, a nationwide program for the care and treatment of mental illness; the Partnership for Health Act (Comprehensive Health Planning and Public Health Service Act of 1966), which provides grants to the states for comprehensive health planning; and the National Health Planning and Resources Development Act of 1974, which created a network of Health System Agencies (HSA) to coordinate health care delivery. More recently, Congress has expanded the Public Health Service's responsibility to protect the public against hazardous and toxic substances in the environment.

Social Security Administration (SSA)   A major agency of the national government given independent status by Congress in 1994, effective March 1995. It was established in 1935 as a freestanding agency but was made part of the Department of Health and Human Services (HHS) in 1946. It is administered by a commissioner and a deputy commissioner appointed by the President with Senate consent to six-year terms. Three members of the seven-member advisory board are appointed by the President, and the Speaker of the House and President pro tempore of the Senate appoint two members each. The agency is responsible for the Old Age, Survivors, and Disability Insurance program and the Supplemental Security Income program. It is one of the largest agencies in government with numerous field offices. *See also* OLD AGE, SURVIVORS, AND DISABILITY INSURANCE, page 510; SUPPLEMENTAL SECURITY INCOME, page 513.

Significance   The Social Security Administration is of great significance to every American. It assigns Social Security numbers, monitors the earnings of all people, and eventually touches every family with whatever social insurance programs apply to its circumstances. The separation of SSA from HHS raises the stature of the agency and removes it from the controversies surrounding the welfare missions of HHS. Independence also removes SSA from the direct control of the President through the cabinet status of HHS. The vital importance and huge costs of social security will keep the SSA on center stage.

IMPORTANT CASES

Goldberg v. Kelly, 397 U.S. 254 (1970): Held that welfare benefits may not be terminated without due process. This requires a predetermination hearing with adequate notice, oral presentation, confrontation and cross-examination, right to retain an attorney, an impartial decision maker, and a decision based on rules and evidence adduced in the hearing. The hearing, said the Court, need not have the characteristics of a trial, but should have minimal procedural safeguards adapted to the educational and social characteristics of the welfare recipient. *See also* CATEGORICAL ASSISTANCE, page 504; ENTITLEMENTS, page 505; PRIVILEGE, page 330.

Significance The *Goldberg* ruling epitomizes a dramatic new direction in American law that recognizes economic and social benefits as rights rather than privileges. The concept of entitlement to an economic benefit that cannot be arbitrarily withdrawn is common in American law, such as subsidies to businesses and farms or grants of airline routes and television channels, but extension of similar benefits to the poor is a relatively new trend. In 1969, the Court declared that state residence requirements to qualify for welfare violated equal protection by imposing an unreasonable obstacle to the right of the poor to travel freely throughout the land (*Shapiro v. Thompson*, 394 U.S. 618). The Court also held that notice and hearing were essential prior to garnishment of wages (*Sniadach v. Family Finance Corp.*, 395 U.S. 337 [1969]) and prior to eviction from federally assisted housing (*Thorpe v. Housing Authority*, 393 U.S. 268 [1969]). Subsequent decisions have narrowed somewhat the scope of when a pretermination hearing is required. While some hearing is necessary before loss of a benefit, a pretermination hearing is necessary even for a temporary deprivation when it affects programs for people on the very margin of subsistence (*Mathews v. Eldridge*, 424 U.S. 319 [1976]).

Social Security Cases Two cases in which the Supreme Court upheld the Social Security Act of 1935. In *Steward Machine Co. v. Davis*, 301 U.S. 548 (1937), the Court upheld the unemployment insurance feature of the Act. The Court reasoned that the tax for relief of the unemployed was within the power of Congress to provide for the national welfare, and the states were not coerced to join the plan. In *Helvering v. Davis*, 301 U.S. 619 (1937), decided the same day, the Court upheld the Old Age, Survivors, and Disability Insurance provisions. The Court recognized the broad power of Congress to promote the general welfare and maintained that the scope of the general welfare was for Congress to determine. The Court denied that the tax on payrolls for Old Age, Survivors, and Disability Insurance benefited only a particular class of persons or invaded the powers of the state. *See also* SOCIAL SECURITY ACT OF 1935, page 527.

Significance   The Social Security cases involved major interpretations of the general welfare clause of the Constitution. The decisions gave Congress almost unlimited power to tax and spend for whatever purposes it deems necessary to promote the general welfare. These cases established the legal framework for the extensive system of social welfare measures carried on by the national government with the cooperation of state and local governments.

IMPORTANT STATUTES

Economic Opportunity Act of 1964   An act to help the poor become productive citizens through a "War on Poverty." The Act stresses education and training through such programs as the Job Corps, Neighborhood Youth Corps, and work-study programs. Community action programs are encouraged under the Act to stimulate local action to meet the needs of low-income people. Loan programs are made available to farmers and small-business operators. Programs are administered by the Department of Labor, the Department of Health and Human Services, and the Corporation for National and Community Service. *See also* COMMUNITY ACTION PROGRAM, page 505; JOB CORPS, page 508.

Significance   The Economic Opportunity Act is aimed at overcoming the causes of poverty by encouraging both community and individual programs of education and training for employment. While the Act provides for aid to older persons, it stresses programs for the young, including preschool children and college youth. Opponents of the War on Poverty have criticized it for not involving sufficient numbers of low-income people and for its potential control by political machines. More basic criticism is aimed at the underlying purposes of the program and the enlarged role of the national government in meeting social and economic problems.

Elementary and Secondary Education Act of 1965   The first general aid-to-education law enacted by Congress. It provides federal aid to most of the nation's school districts. The Act authorizes aid on the basis of the number of children from low-income families in each district. It applies to both public and nonpublic schools. Other major provisions authorize grants for textbooks and library materials for all schools, educational centers to provide programs that individual schools cannot afford, and grants for improvement of educational research and administration. In 1974, Congress also extended aid to programs of emerging importance such as reading, career education, and adult education. The 1974 law also provides for parent and student access to school records to protect the students' right to privacy. Congress declared the neighborhood school to be the proper basis for pupil assignment and sharply restricted the use of busing to achieve racial integration. A 1972 amendment to the Act outlaws sex discrimination in schools, and in 1975 Congress required that states provide appropriate education for handicapped persons ages 3 to 21. *See also* FEDERAL AID TO EDUCATION, page 506.

Significance   The Elementary and Secondary Education Act of 1965 is a landmark in relations between the nation and the states, representing a commitment on the part of both to nationwide equality of educational opportunity. Numerous past efforts to enact such legislation failed because of fear of federal control of education, racial segregation in schools, and controversy over aid to nonpublic, church-related schools. Many opponents of federal aid were defeated in the Democratic landslide of 1964, the school segregation issue was no longer legally relevant, and the church-state issue was overcome by basing the school aid formula on benefiting low-income children rather than the parochial schools directly. Extensive de facto racial segregation has given rise to persistent problems in the administration of the Act, as have complex questions growing out of rules promulgated by the Department of Education to enforce equality of treatment for the handicapped and both sexes. Whatever its merits, it is clear that federal aid to education has involved the national government in the education of the nation's children and remains controversial.

Family and Medical Leave Act of 1993   Legislation mandating up to 12 weeks of unpaid leave for workers in the event of personal illness; need to care for a spouse, child, or parent; or need to care for a child following birth, adoption, or foster placement. Coverage extends to employers of more than 50 employees and employees of at least a year's duration. Upon return, an employee must be placed in the same or an equivalent position.

Significance   The Family and Medical Leave Act was enacted after much effort by women's groups and in response to a major problem faced by two-income families. The 50-employee minimum for coverage excludes more than half the workforce, so pressure to extend coverage can be anticipated. A number of states have similar laws, which in some cases extends to grandparents, siblings, and unmarried domestic partners. Employers view the law as an additional regulatory burden, while labor sees it as a job protection measure. The Act is also a response to growing public concern with health care and family values.

Higher Education Act of 1965   An act to broaden higher education opportunities through federal aid. Major programs include scholarships, work-study programs, guaranteed low-interest loans, aid to developing colleges, aid to college and university community service programs with emphasis on urban problems, aid for library resources, a National Teachers Corps to work in slum areas, and aid for fellowships for present and future teachers. In addition, the Act increased aid under the Higher Education Facilities Act of 1963, which authorized grants and loans for construction of public and private academic facilities. Recent extensions of the Act have stressed student aid and career education. *See also* FEDERAL AID TO EDUCATION, page 506; STUDENT AID PROGRAMS, page 512.

Significance   The Higher Education Act of 1965 is a major extension of existing federal aid to higher education. A notable innovation provides scholarships, grants, and loans for general undergraduate education. The Act's major purpose is to overcome rising costs of higher education for low-

and middle-income families. Soaring and then declining enrollments in colleges and universities strained the resources of most institutions of higher learning, while the desire to secure a college education has become common throughout the population. The Higher Education Act, together with the Elementary and Secondary Education Act of 1965, commits the national government to extensive involvement in education from the preschool level through graduate education. The Supreme Court upheld construction grants to church-related colleges under the Higher Education Facilities Act but voided a provision that would authorize use of such buildings for religious purposes after twenty years (*Tilton v. Richardson,* 403 U.S. 672 [1971]).

Homeless Assistance Act of 1987   An Act to provide the nation's homeless with emergency housing, food, health care, training, and other community services. Numerous public and private agencies are involved in homeless assistance programs, especially the Department of Housing and Urban Development. The homeless are estimated to number up to 3 million people.

Significance   The Homeless Assistance Act opens a new avenue of welfare programs aimed at resolving a real but little-understood crisis in many cities. The growing number of homeless people is attributed partly to the release of persons from mental hospitals under new rules designed to confine only those receiving treatment and release those who are not a danger to themselves or others. Other factors include an acute shortage of inexpensive housing, high unemployment among blue-collar workers, and the apparent preference of some people to live on the streets, in that existing emergency shelters tend to be both dangerous and unsanitary. The Act, passed after advocates for the homeless staged sit-ins and demonstrations at the Capitol, may lay the foundation for a continuing commitment to end homelessness in America.

Housing Act of 1949   An act providing for federal assistance to local governments for low-rent public housing, slum clearance, and urban renewal. The Housing Act of 1949 continued a program, begun under the Housing Act of 1937, that had been interrupted by World War II. The 1949 Act called for the construction of 810,000 housing units over a period of six years, but Congress reduced this figure in subsequent legislation. In amendments to the Act since 1949, additional housing units have been authorized and increased emphasis given to urban renewal and new community development. Various specialized housing programs have been instituted, such as those for college dormitories, housing for the aged, and rent subsidies for the poor. Funds have also been made available for municipal public works, such as sewers and transportation. In 1974, Congress consolidated many of the programs and authorized block grants to local governments. The Department of Housing and Urban Development supervises administration of the Act. *See also* HOUSING AND COMMUNITY DEVELOPMENT ACT OF 1974, page 525; PUBLIC HOUSING, page 511; URBAN RENEWAL, page 514.

Significance   In the Housing Act of 1949, Congress declared its goal to be "a decent home and a suitable living environment for every American family." The national government is now committed to a "total" housing program that takes account of all aspects of community development. These programs result from an acute housing shortage for low-income families, slums and blight, and increasing urbanization, which multiplies the service needs of millions of city dwellers and suburbanites. Many object to the intrusion of the national government into these areas, but Congress has continued existing programs, encouraging the use of private capital when possible. Under the Reagan administration, public housing programs slackened considerably. The fate of housing legislation and of the Department of Housing and Urban Development remain controversial.

Housing and Community Development Act of 1974   A major revision and extension of urban development programs, which consolidates ten categorical programs into block grants for comprehensive community development and establishes an extensive rental subsidy program for low- and moderate-income families. The Act also continues public housing programs, mortgage credit, and expanded aid for rural housing development. Each eligible community is apportioned funds based on a formula that takes into account the ratio of poverty, population, and housing needs. Cities, in turn, must survey their needs more accurately than in the past and avoid undue concentrations of low-income housing and people in special neighborhoods. Additionally, the Act puts new emphasis on cash subsidies for rentals in nonpublic housing. Public participation in formulation of development plans is required. Block grants may be used, at the discretion of the community, for urban renewal, model cities, housing code enforcement, open spaces, neighborhood facilities, water and sewer facilities, planning, and aid to displaced families. *See also* HOUSING ACT OF 1949, page 525; PUBLIC HOUSING, page 511; URBAN RENEWAL, page 514.

Significance   The Housing and Community Development Act of 1974 was the first major housing bill passed in many years. It gives metropolitan areas, in particular, unprecedented freedom in deciding how to spend federal funds on urban redevelopment. The Act is designed to provide stability to a wide variety of programs that had been characterized by waste, politics, and confusion. Because the Act requires communities to develop comprehensive plans to receive the block grants and to take into consideration both physical and human factors involved in the rehabilitation of decaying communities, it charted a new course for national-local relations in community development. In extending the Act in 1981, Congress revised the block grant formula to ease federal controls even more. The Reagan administration, however, resisted new initiatives in housing and community development, and no new legislation on those issues was enacted until 1987.

Older Americans Act of 1965   An act to stimulate state and local programs to aid the elderly (60 or older), support community service jobs for older workers (age 65 or older), and support senior volunteer programs. Most of the aid programs, administered by the Administration on Aging in the Department of Health and Human Services, are concerned with transportation, home health, legal aid, and housing renovation. A major amendment to the Older Americans Act in 1975 bans "unreasonable" discrimination on the basis of age in federally funded programs beginning in 1979. Also, the Age Discrimination Act of 1967 prohibits discrimination in employment against persons 40 to 70 years of age, except where age is a bona fide occupational qualification. In 1986, Congress abolished mandatory retirement for most workers, with a 7-year delay in the application of this rule for some occupations, such as police, firefighters, and tenured college professors (now lifted).

Significance   The major goal of the Older Americans Act is to help the elderly remain self-sufficient by providing the essentials of life to the needy and useful activity for the able. The Act is a response to the aging of the American population. The termination of mandatory retirement may have a dramatic impact upon a variety of labor and social welfare laws. For example, a gradual increase in the normal retirement age of 65 to receive Social Security, to age 67 by the year 2025, has been established by Congress. In the early 1990s, more than 12 percent of the population was 65 or older, a growth of 12 percent in a decade, with the median age of the population up from 30 to 32. Political realities suggest that more legislation in support of the elderly will be forthcoming, and the impact of public policies on the elderly will receive continuing political attention.

Rehabilitation Act of 1973   An act to protect the rights of the disabled by extending to them rights accorded other minority groups with respect to equal employment opportunities and to require accessibility for the handicapped in buildings and transportation. The Act's most significant provision, known as Section 504, provides "no otherwise qualified handicapped individual...shall solely by reason of his handicap, be excluded from participation in, be denied benefits of, or be subjected to discrimination under any program or activity receiving federal financial assistance." The Act also provides for vocational training programs for handicapped persons. *See also* AMERICANS WITH DISABILITIES ACT OF 1990, page 375; CIVIL RIGHTS ACT OF 1991, page 379; VOCATIONAL REHABILITATION, page 515.

Significance   The Rehabilitation Act of 1973 received little attention until 1977, when the Department of Health, Education, and Welfare, acting under pressure from handicapped groups, issued regulations interpreting Section 504. The resultant costs, notably in the areas of transportation and education, have been staggering and led to intense debate over whether the disabled must be "mainstreamed" to participate fully in society or be provided separate facilities. The Supreme Court has ruled that federally funded colleges need not admit all handicapped applicants or make extensive facility modifications to accommodate every disabled student (*Southeastern Community College v. Davis*, 442 U.S. 397 [1979]). The Court has also held that a school need not provide all the aid necessary to assure that a handicapped child realizes his or her maximum potential (*Board of Education of the Hendrick Hudson Central School District v. Rowley*, 458 U.S. 176 [1982]), but a school must provide supportive health services to keep a handicapped child in school (*Irving Independent School District v. Tatro*, 468 U.S. 883 [1984]). The Act and its subsequent interpretations represent a major extension of civil rights to a large and heretofore neglected group of people. Congress has continued to demonstrate support for the handicapped by putting increased emphasis on aid for disabled preschool children and by banning discrimination against the handicapped in access to airlines and polling places. In 1990, a major reaffirmation and extension of the rights of the disabled was enacted—the Americans with Disabilities Act—which placed the rights of handicapped persons on the same level as the rights of other minorities.

Social Security Act of 1935   The basic social welfare legislation embodying social insurance, public assistance, and child health and welfare services. Social insurance programs include Old Age, Survivors, and Disability Insurance; Medicare; and unemployment insurance. Public assistance is provided under the categorical assistance and Supplemental Security Income programs to the needy aged, blind, or permanently and totally disabled and to dependent children. Child health and welfare services are provided under the Social Security Act for maternal care, crippled children, and general child welfare services. With the exception of the Old Age, Survivors, and Disability Insurance and Medicare programs, which are financed and administered exclusively by the national government, all others are administered in cooperation with the states. Responsibility for overall supervision rests mainly with the Social Security Administration and with the Department of Health and Human Services. In addition, the Social Security Act provides for widespread public health services through grants to the states. *See also* AID TO FAMILIES WITH DEPENDENT CHILDREN, page 504; CATEGORICAL ASSISTANCE, page 504; MATERNAL AND CHILD WELFARE PROGRAM, page 509; MEDICARE, page 509; OLD AGE, SURVIVORS, AND DISABILITY INSURANCE, page 510; SOCIAL SECURITY CASES, page 522; SUPPLEMENTAL SECURITY INCOME, page 513; UNEMPLOYMENT INSURANCE, page 458.

Significance   The Social Security Act is the most comprehensive social welfare legislation passed in the United States. The program grew out of the experience of the Great Depression and reflected a basic change in public attitudes toward the needy and the role of the government. The Act, at first highly controversial, is now generally accepted by the American people; both major political parties have expanded the scope of benefits available under the law. The partnership of the national and state governments in the administration of the Act provides a leading example of cooperative federalism in action to meet common national problems. The movement toward complete national assumption of welfare programs was reversed with the election of President Reagan in 1980, and a trend toward state assumption of responsibility has grown since that time. The sluggish economy and conservative political resurgence led to substantial reductions in many state programs during the 1990s.

Welfare Reform Act of 1996 (Personal Responsibility and Work Opportunity Reconciliation Act of 1996)   Landmark legislation that ended 61 years of federal entitlement to welfare benefits. Its most noteworthy provisions replace the Aid to Families with Dependent Children (AFDC) program with block grants to the states, which are given broad discretion to determine eligibility for financial assistance. Major provisions of the law (1) require the head of every family on welfare to work within 2 years or lose benefits; (2) limit lifetime welfare benefits to 5 years with some hardship exemptions; (3) permit aid to an unwed teen parent only if living with a parent and enrolled in school; (4) permit states to deny additional aid for children born to welfare recipients; (5) limit food stamps to three months for unemployed adults not raising children; (6) require reduction in aid to mothers who fail to establish paternity and strengthen collection of child support; and (7) deny aid for five years to future legal immigrants and end eligibility of current legal immigrants who do not become citizens to food stamps, supplementary security income, Medicaid, and various other social services. The act maintains existing Medicaid coverage for most people and folds major child care programs into block grants for the states. Prior to enactment of the reform, most states had already received federal waivers to experiment with work and welfare programs that may be continued until the waivers expire. *See also* AID TO FAMILIES WITH DEPENDENT CHILDREN (AFDC), page 504; FOOD STAMPS, page 507; SUPPLEMENTAL SECURITY INCOME (SSI), page 513.

Significance   The Welfare Reform Act responds in large measure to the concerns of many critics that welfare appeared to be a way of life for many people and that existing rules discouraged work and traditional family values, while encouraging immigration. It also reflected the growing conservatism of the American electorate and a decided change in the federal system to encourage return of state and local control over welfare. The act represents a major philosophical shift away from more than six decades of guaranteed assistance to the poor to a more limited program rooted in work requirements. About 14 million people are affected by the welfare programs and more than 25 million by changes in food stamp requirements. Opponents of the legislation predict dire consequences, doubtful that the states will be able to meet the job requirements, provide adequate child care, or compel a dramatic shift in behavior. Some fear that reduced federal grants and insufficient existing state resources will make it impossible to meet the basic needs of millions of poor children, especially in heavily populated states. As the new system unfolds, it will undoubtedly lead to continuing political and legal controversy.

13

Foreign Policy
and National Defense

Aggression The use of armed force by a state against the sovereignty, territorial integrity, or political independence of another state. Much of the literature of international law is concerned with the problem of identifying aggression and differentiating it from self-defense. The Cold War was characterized by nations arming and concluding alliances to protect themselves from aggression. The United Nations collective security system was established to protect states from aggression, or to deal with aggression collectively, should it occur. *See also* COLLECTIVE SECURITY, page 538; SANCTIONS, page 576.

Significance The community of nations has seldom been able to agree on a definition of what constitutes aggression. On occasion, however, international bodies have identified and fixed responsibility for aggression. For example, individuals were punished for the crimes of waging aggressive war and for committing acts against humanity in the post–World War II Nuremberg and Tokyo trials of Nazi and Japanese war leaders, respectively. The United Nations Charter does not define aggression; aggression has occurred when an authorized organ of the world organization makes such a determination through its voting procedure. Such was the case in 1950, when the Security Council branded North Korea an aggressor. The United Nations Special Committee on the Question of Defining Aggression in 1974 submitted its objective criteria to be used in deciding whether acts of aggression have been committed. Extensive Assembly debates have been carried on, but final agreement by the world community has not been reached, except for agreement that the Security Council has primary responsibility for making a determination of when aggression has been committed. In 1990, the Security Council unanimously voted to declare Iraq an aggressor following its invasion of Kuwait, and economic sanctions were levied against the aggressor. An American-led military buildup began that was designated Operation Desert Shield. Then, in 1991, the Security Council gave its full support to Operation Desert Storm, which involved a crushing military attack and defeat of Iraqi forces by the United States and more than twenty supporting nations. The question of aggression rose again in the 1990s, among the former regions of Yugoslavia that became Croatia, Bosnia-Herzegovina, and Serbia. Serb forces, with military equipment provided by the former Yugoslavian army, committed acts of aggression while engaging in "ethnic cleansing" in the form of mass murder and rape. United Nation peacekeepers sought to keep roads open, keep supplies flowing, and protect "safe areas" but met with failure much of the time. In 1995, NATO, with U.S. leadership, used its air power to stop Serbian aggression and bring the three parties to a conference table. They met at Wright-Patterson Air Force Base at Dayton, Ohio, to work out a peaceful solution to the problem of ethnonationalism in the Balkans. Following the signing of the peace agreement, NATO forces, including 20,000 U.S. troops, entered the area to oversee the carrying out of the provisions of the Dayton accord. In 1993, a special court, the International War Crimes Tribunal, was established by the United Nations at The Hague in the Netherlands, to bring alleged war criminals from the Balkans to trial and to provide legal punishment for their aggressive actions.

Alliance   A multilateral agreement by states to improve their power position by joining together in defense of their common interests. Most alliances are now characterized by agreement to regard "an attack upon any member of the alliance as an attack upon all." Hence, an alliance is a way of informing friend and foe that an attack against any individual nation will precipitate a general war. Balance of power systems tend to encourage the growth of alliances. *See also* BALANCE OF POWER, page 533; NORTH ATLANTIC TREATY ORGANIZATION, page 568.

Significance   Throughout most of American history, President George Washington's advice to "steer clear of permanent alliances" was carefully observed. With the advent of the Cold War, however, the United States, rejecting its time-honored policy of isolationism, assumed a position of leadership in the anti-communist world and became the world's leading advocate of security through defensive alliances. Alliances were concluded by the United States with more than 40 nations to forestall a communist attack or to meet it if it should occur. Mutual security alliances included the Rio Treaty, the North Atlantic Treaty (NATO), the Southeast Asia Treaty (SEATO), a trilateral treaty with Australia and New Zealand (ANZUS), and bilateral pacts with Japan, the Philippines, and South Korea. Today, NATO remains the key alliance system for the United States, with the rest largely discarded or ineffectual. With the ending of the Cold War and the dissolution of the Warsaw Pact, along with the unification of East and West Germany, NATO has moved in the direction of being predominantly political rather than military. However, in 1995, NATO, acting under United Nations guidelines, undertook military action against the Bosnian Serb forces in seeking to cope with their ethnoviolent actions. After the signing of the Dayton accord, NATO alliance forces were authorized to oversee the administration of the peace treaty.

Alliance for Progress   A program of foreign aid for Latin America developed by the Kennedy administration. Congress authorized $500 million in 1961 to initiate the program. Latin American countries—all except Cuba—participated in Alliance programs. Continued aid to these nations was offered if internal economic reforms were instituted and if social progress moved forward with economic development. The Inter-American Development Bank was created in 1961 to play a major role in implementing the program through development loans. Its efforts were supplemented by the

Development Loan Fund, the Export-Import Bank, and the Agency for International Development. *See also* ORGANIZATION OF AMERICAN STATES, page 570.

Significance The emphasis in the Alliance for Progress program was on securing economic and social progress in Latin America through close hemispheric cooperation. American help was intended to aid these countries in getting started on the road to self-sustaining growth. Closer economic ties leading to some measure of economic integration were encouraged by the program. Additional objectives included the strengthening of political relations through the Organization of American States (OAS) and the collective security system under the Rio Treaty. By the 1980s, much of the vitality and early enthusiasm for the Alliance program had disappeared. The vast amounts of private capital anticipated by the program have not been invested in the Latin American region, and a population explosion, internal strife, reduced American aid, heavy inflation, and soaring international debts have combined to frustrate development efforts in many Latin states. As a result of these failures, many of the countries of Latin America were beset with guerrilla warfare and bloody governmental reprisal actions. A prime example of this type of problem is the plight of Mexico, with political assassinations, drastic devaluation of the peso, and an armed rebellion in the poverty-stricken Indian state of Chiapas.

Ambassador The top-ranking diplomat sent by the government of a sovereign state as its official representative. Most ambassadors are accredited to foreign countries, but the President may also appoint ambassadors at large, ambassadors plenipotentiary, and ambassadors accredited to international organizations, such as the United Nations. An ambassador typically is the head of an embassy in the capital city of the foreign state. Official relations between governments are carried on mainly through an exchange of ambassadors. An American ambassador is the personal representative of the President in his role as chief of state. *See also* DIPLOMATIC PRIVILEGES AND IMMUNITIES, page 546; PERSONA NON GRATA, page 572.

Significance In the United States, ambassadors are appointed by the President and confirmed by the Senate. Personal and political considerations, such as campaign contributions and party service, may be important in making such appointments. The trend, however, is in the direction of appointing foreign service career diplomats. An ambassador, as the personal representative of the President, is charged with implementing the foreign policy of the administration in power in the United States. Consequently, some ambassadors, especially those assigned to the more important posts, are replaced after a new President takes office.

ANZUS Pact A tripartite security treaty concluded in 1951 among Australia, New Zealand, and the United States. The ANZUS treaty, which has no terminal date, declares that an attack upon any of the members would constitute a common danger, and each would act to meet it according to its constitutional processes. *See also* ALLIANCE, page 530.

Significance The ANZUS pact is an attempt to provide security against communist encroachment in a large area of the Pacific. The pact reflected a growing dependence upon the United States for leadership in providing security in that area. In 1954, the security system of the ANZUS Pact was expanded into the Southeast Asia Treaty Organization (SEATO) defense arrangement. Although SEATO has been disbanded, the Southeast Asia Collective Defense Treaty and the ANZUS Pact remain in force. In 1986, however, New Zealand barred nuclear-equipped American naval vessels from its ports, which led to a rupture in the ANZUS alliance when the United States retaliated by withdrawing its security guarantees from New Zealand.

Appeasement   A term used to describe concessions made to warlike potential foes in the hope that they will satiate their appetite for expansion and that peace will be secure. Prime Minister Neville Chamberlain's agreement at Munich in 1938 to accept Adolf Hitler's demand for the partition of Czechoslovakia in exchange for a vague guarantee of "peace in our time" is a classic example of appeasement that failed. *See also* DIPLOMACY, page 546.

Significance   The fear of appeasement makes diplomatic negotiations extremely difficult. Successful diplomacy requires concessions from both sides. Frequently, the cry of "appeasement" can sabotage a diplomat's position. Concessions are played up, while counterconcessions are overlooked. The problem of appeasement is particularly acute when diplomats are engaged in "open" or "public" negotiations. The League of Nations, in 1935, became a victim of appeasement when it failed to take collective action against Italian aggression in Ethiopia. Some United Nations critics have suggested that the failure of the UN to take collective action against the Bosnian Serb aggression in the early stages of conflict was an act of appeasement. In 1995, however, NATO forces, acting under UN guidelines, took military action that quelled the critics' charges of appeasement.

Arbitration   A method of settling a dispute between states by judges selected by the parties to the dispute. The judges, who have standing as international jurists, must render a decision or award based on international law, and the parties agree in advance to accept the decisions as binding. Arbitration dates back many centuries, but its modern use began with the famous *Alabama Claims* settlement between the United States and Great Britain growing out of Civil War controversies. In arbitration, disputing parties enter into a *compromis* or agreement that specifies the issues to be resolved and procedures to be followed. *See also* PACIFIC SETTLEMENT OF DISPUTES, page 571.

Significance   Many conflicts between states involving their secondary interests have been solved through arbitration. Generally, states are reluctant to submit disputes involving their *primary* national interests to an arbitration tribunal. Contrary to popular myth, states that have accepted arbitration have almost always abided by the decision of the tribunal. The main weakness of arbitration is the difficulty of getting states to accept it as a means of settling their dispute. To overcome this problem, many treaties include clauses in which the signatories agree to arbitrate any future disagreements over treaty provisions.

Attaché   A technical specialist who functions as an official with diplomatic rank and who is attached to an embassy or foreign mission. Attachés specialize in political, military, economic, agricultural, informational, labor, aviation, petroleum, and cultural fields. *See also* DIPLOMACY, page 546.

Significance   Attachés seek to establish good relations with similar officials in the country to which they are accredited. They also comprise the eyes and ears of the United States in gaining specialized information concerning the conditions that exist in that country.

Balance of Payments   The net balance between total income and expenditures of a nation in its business and trade relations with the rest of the world. A balance of payments includes all debit and credit monetary transactions, such as imports and exports of goods, tourist expenditures, investments, and income from investments. The balance of trade that includes all transactions involving tangible goods is often the key component of the balance of payments. *See also* ECONOMIC NATIONALISM, page 548.

Significance   Nations usually seek to maintain a "favorable" balance of payments. This means that they strive to increase income over expenditure, to the extent that balances of foreign currencies and gold can be built up. Nations with "unfavorable" or deficit balances are like individuals who spend beyond their income. In the short run, this situation may not be serious. If it persists, corrective action must be taken. This may take the form of higher tariffs, exchange controls, export subsidies, austerity programs, currency depreciation, or other kinds of state action. The United States has suffered from a deficit balance of payments for many years, resulting mainly from a huge deficit in its trade balances. The balance of payments can be used as an analytical tool for determining the relative economic positions of nations. In the 1980s, the deficits in the American balance of trade and in the nation's overall balance of payments each amounted to substantially over $100 billion annually, emphasizing the deteriorating economic position of the United States in the world economy. American trade deficits, for example, amounted to $156 billion in 1986 and $171 billion in 1987. The United States has changed from a creditor to a debtor nation, and by 1987, with a foreign debt of $368 billion, it was the world's largest debtor nation. The foreign debt of the United States has continued to grow and by the 1990s ranged into trillions of dollars.

Balance of Power   A system of power alignments in which peace and security may be maintained through an equilibrium of power between rival states or blocs of states. States participating in a balance of power system enter into alliances with friendly states to protect their power positions. *See also* ALLIANCE, page 530.

Significance   If a balance of power works well, peace may be maintained for a period of years. So long as a near-equilibrium is thought to exist, neither side will dare launch an attack upon the other. However, with the military buildup characteristic of a balance of power system, there is always the danger that war will result from border incidents, miscalculations, escalations, or other causes than planned attack. Historically, balance of power systems have kept the peace for short and long periods, but have often deteriorated into war. For 40 years a worldwide balance of power system existed between the communist and capitalist world camps, resulting in the greatest armaments race in history. By 1990, however, the Cold War had ended, numerous arms control and disarmament treaties were operational, communist governments were rapidly changing to democratic and capitalistic systems, the Warsaw Pact was dissolved, the two Germanys were united, and the Soviet threat essentially ended, with the Soviet Union broken up into its constituent parts and Russia emerging as the major state.

Balance of Trade   The nation's net surplus or deficit based on the value of its total imports and exports, usually measured over a monthly, quarterly, and one-year time period. The balance of trade involves only tangible articles of commerce and is only one of many components that comprise the nation's balance of payments. All foreign sales of American-produced merchandise, food, fiber, and energy take the form of credits, while all purchases of foreign goods that are imported into the United States are debits. If credits exceed debits, the nation has an international balance of trade surplus; if debits exceed credits, the nation has a trade deficit. *See also* COMPETITIVENESS, page 437; ECONOMIC NATIONALISM, page 548; GENERAL AGREEMENT ON TARIFFS AND TRADE (GATT), page 551; NORTH AMERICAN FREE TRADE ASSOCIATION (NAFTA), page 567; WORLD TRADE ORGANIZATION, page 592.

Significance   The United States has had a large international trade deficit for many years, typically over $100 billion annually. This has benefited countries such as Japan and Germany, whose consumer products have been attractive to Americans, as well as raw material–supplying countries (especially in Latin America and the Middle East), which sell huge quantities of oil, gas, foods, and fibers to American industries and consumers. The soaring price of oil that resulted from the 1990 Iraq-Kuwait crisis reversed an improving American trade deficit position. A global slowdown of national economies in the early 1990s contributed to a lessening demand for American goods abroad, thus adding to the nation's deficit. This trend, however, was offset somewhat by a weakened dollar exchange rate that made imports more expensive for Americans and exports of American goods less expensive, and thus more desirable, for foreign buyers.

Bipartisanship   Close cooperation between the two major American political parties in dealing with foreign problems. Bipartisanship usually takes the form of frequent consultations between the leaders of both parties in Congress and between these leaders and the President. During time of war or threat of war, when bipartisanship typically comes into vogue, the President may appoint members of the opposition party to key Cabinet posts. *See also* PRESIDENTIAL-CONGRESSIONAL BUDGET NEGOTIATION, page 198; WAR POWERS ACT, page 603.

Significance   Bipartisanship is a means by which a democracy can overcome its divisions and present a solid front to the world. "Partisanship ends at the water's edge" is a frequently repeated description of bipartisanship. Disadvantages resulting from such cooperation include the loss of the function of the "loyal opposition" within the government and the lack of critical discussion of vital issues. Flexibility is usually reduced, a solid wall of consensus may develop, freezing all options except those put forth by the administration, and criticism of government policy may be equated with disloyalty. Typically, bipartisanship has been invoked—or at least attempted—whenever the President has ordered American troops into action abroad and has tried to silence congressional critics. In 1990, for example, President George Bush was beset with angry partisan differences on budgetary and tax matters, though both parties initially backed him when he sent large numbers of troops to defend Saudi Arabia and to deal with Iraq's invasion of Kuwait. Soon, however, Bush was beset with numerous critics, especially congressional Democrats, who demanded that Congress participate in making military decisions in the Middle East and other foreign trouble areas. The success of Operations Desert Shield (1990) and Desert Storm (1991), though silencing the President's critics of his Middle East policy, was followed by widespread criticism that he spent too much time and effort on foreign policy problems while neglecting domestic issues, such as the economic recession.

Boland Amendments   A series of congressional policy statements concerning the U.S. aid to the contra rebels attempting to overthrow the Sandinista government of Nicaragua. The first version of the Boland Amendment, which covered the period from December 1982 to December 1983, forbade the CIA and the Defense Department from providing military aid to the contras. The second Boland Amendment, covering the period from December 1983 to September 1984, set a limit on the amount of military aid that could be given to the contras by the Defense Department, the CIA, or any other agency or entity involved in intelligence activities. The third version of the Boland Amendment, in effect from October 1984 to September 1985, prohibited the same group of agencies from "supporting, directly or indirectly, military or paramilitary operations in Nicaragua." Thereafter, a version of the Boland Amendment permitted only "humanitarian" aid and, subsequently, a fifth and final version authorized $100 million for contra aid in the 1986–1987 fiscal year, with no strings attached concerning the nature of that aid. *See also* CHIEF DIPLOMAT, page 186.

Significance   The various versions of the Boland Amendment were attempts by Congress to play a key role in dealing with a critical foreign policy issue rather than permitting the President and his administration to dominate the policy-making process through congressional inaction. As a result of disclosures of illegal military aid provided to the contras, with some of the aid money derived from secret sales of arms to Iran, the Congress in 1987 began a series of investigations and hearings into what became known as the Iran-contra affair. The main thrust of the inquiries dealt with questions concerning the role of the executive branch in providing aid to the contras in violation of the Boland Amendments. Although the President signed the Boland Amendments and claimed he adhered to its provisions, his ultimate defense in the Iran-contra inquiries was that Congress cannot limit his freedom of action in the foreign policy field. The Boland Amendment series demonstrates how a great power state can progressively use political, military, and economic power to cope with a foreign policy situation.

Camp David Accords   Agreements negotiated in 1978 at the President's retreat in the Catoctin Mountains in Maryland between Egyptian President Anwar Sadat and Israeli Prime Minister Menachem Begin. The Camp David

Accords led to the signing of a formal peace treaty between the two Middle Eastern nations in 1979, ending the state of war that had existed since the creation of Israel in 1948 and the start of the First Arab-Israeli War. President Jimmy Carter played a critical role in bringing the two parties into negotiations and in overcoming major diplomatic obstacles. *See also* DIPLOMACY, page 546; GOOD OFFICES, page 552; PACIFIC SETTLEMENT OF DISPUTES, page 571; SUMMIT DIPLOMACY, page 580.

Significance President Jimmy Carter achieved an outstanding breakthrough in orchestrating the Camp David Accords. They led to the first peace treaty ever concluded between Israel and an Arab state. The treaty has proved durable, although some critics charge that the billions of dollars in foreign aid provided annually to the two countries by the United States since the conclusion of the treaty constitute a form of bribery. The accords highlight the American president's role as chief diplomat and chief of foreign policy. They also emphasize the critical international role available to an American president who is inclined to provide leadership in solving foreign policy problems. Because of his role in making peace with Israel, Anwar Sadat was assassinated by Arab extremists in 1981. The success of this agreement has led to Israeli-Arab negotiations aimed at securing peace accords with other states throughout the region. In 1993, Yasir Arafat, as head of the Palestine Liberation Organization (PLO), signed an accord with Israel that would lead to self-rule in the Gaza Strip and the West Bank. In 1996, elections were held for president and members of the national council. Yasir Arafat was elected president with 85 percent of the vote. A peace treaty between Jordan and Israel was signed in 1995. Further agreements with Arafat have allowed Arabs control over education, tax collection, and social services. Syria keeps open the doors to peace, but insists on a pledge from Israel to withdraw from the Golan Heights. The lifting of economic boycotts by a number of Arab states gives evidence that the peace process is advancing. Not all actions in the peace process have been positive. Radical pro-Islamic groups, such as Hamas, have been responsible for many violent acts against Jews. This has been balanced by violence from radical Jewish groups, one member of which sought to stop the peace process by the assassination, in November 1995, of Yitzhak Rabin, Prime Minister of Israel and prime leader of the peace movement. American presidents, especially President Bill Clinton, have encouraged, supported, and assisted the Middle East peace process, with some of the agreements concluded at the White House. Israel's new prime minister, Benjamin Netanyahu, elected in June 1996, was opposed to the "land for peace" program nurtured by Yitzhak Rabin and his successor, Shimon Peres. Netanyahu favors a more rigid program of "peace with security." U.S. leaders are concerned by the change in policy because peace in the Middle East is a vital national interest.

Chargé d'Affaires The Foreign Service official temporarily placed in charge of an embassy or legation in the absence of the ambassador or minister. Technically, the official's full title is *chargé de'affaires ad interim*. *See also* DIPLOMACY, page 546.

Significance When the United States seeks to indicate displeasure with the actions of a foreign government but does not wish to take the serious step of severing diplomatic relations, it usually withdraws its ambassador. Under such conditions, the *chargé de affaires* assumes a position of grave importance. In this way, a "listening post" in the foreign country is kept open, as are diplomatic channels.

Chemical/Biological Weapons (CBW)   Toxic or poisonous agents and delivery systems that can be utilized as weapons of mass destruction. Chemical and biological (bacteriological) weapons (CBW) have been banned from use in warfare under international law by the Geneva Protocol of 1925, signed and ratified by almost every nation. However, the Geneva Protocol bans only the *use* of such weapons, not their production and stockpiling. Recent international initiatives by the United States have been aimed at securing a treaty that would completely outlaw such weapons, including their production, stockpiling, and use. The Reagan administration, claiming that development of new chemical weapons would encourage agreement on a treaty to ban them, began to develop new binary chemical weapons in 1987 with the approval of Congress. *Binary* weapons differ from the more common *unitary* weapons in that the latter carry a chemical agent in a deadly form that is ready to use, whereas binary weapons carry two separated stable chemicals that are combined just prior to their use into a powerful and deadly agent.

Significance   American policymakers believed for some time that the Soviets were far ahead of the United States in the production and storage of new chemical weapons. The 1987 initiative by the United States was aimed at overcoming this alleged lead and encouraging agreement on a total ban. Much of the stockpile of American chemical weapons has deteriorated dangerously over many years, posing very serious disposal problems. Biological or bacteriological weapons have been brought under a measure of international control by a 1972 Biological Weapons Convention that prohibits the possession or use of biological weapons and toxin weapons derived from natural poisons such as snake venom. Nearly 100 countries have accepted both the Geneva Protocol of 1925 and the Biological Weapons Convention of 1972, leaving more than 60 countries that have not agreed to them, especially not to the latter treaty. Although the United States and the Soviet Union avowedly have favored elimination of both chemical and biological weapons, serious disagreements over such matters as inspection, verification, and enforcement remain to be resolved. In 1990, Iraq seized its neighbor, Kuwait, and threatened to use its arsenal of chemical weapons to defend its action. This led to Iraq's defeat in the 1991 Desert Storm campaign, followed by a United Nations investigatory team's discovery that Iraq was in the process of developing weapons of mass destruction, including nuclear and chemical.

Civilian Control   The American constitutional principle of civilian supremacy over the military to safeguard republican institutions. Civilian control is maintained through constitutional provisions that make the President commander in chief of the armed forces and grant Congress power to raise and support armies, make military law, declare war, and appropriate money for military expenditures for no more than two-year periods. The Second and Third Amendments buttress the principle by forbidding the quartering of troops without consent and by granting the people the right to keep and bear arms. Statutory enactments, such as the legal requirement that the Secretary of Defense and the Secretaries of the Army, Navy, and Air Force departments must be civilians, also encourage civilian control. *See also Ex Parte Milligan,* page 599; MILITARY-INDUSTRIAL COMPLEX, page 562.

Significance   Civilian control is especially significant in a democratic nation that is threatened by potential enemies and has built up a great military power. Many developing countries appear to be democratic but are controlled by military cliques. Many people in the United States have become fearful of the rising power and influence of the military. Yet national defense considerations have increased the nation's dependence upon the military, while at the same time alerting the country to the dangers inherent in a military-industrial complex.

Collective Security   A worldwide security system by which all or most nations agree in advance to take collective action against any state or states that break the peace by committing aggression. Collective security is based on the assumption that, normally, no nation or group of nations would dare to challenge the power of the world community, but, if an attack should occur, nations would honor their commitments to take collective police action. The United Nations embodies the concept of collective security. Under Chapter VII of its Charter, the organization can take such action, including diplomatic, economic, or military, as may be necessary to preserve world peace. Primary responsibility was vested in the five great powers (the United States, the Soviet Union (now Russia), Britain, France, China), each having the veto power in the Security Council. Since 1950, the General Assembly also has been empowered under the Uniting for Peace Resolution to authorize collective security action if the Security Council is stymied with a veto. Collective security is occasionally, but inaccurately, used to describe mutual security alliances established under a balance of power system. *See also* SANCTIONS, page 576; UNITED NATIONS SECURITY COUNCIL, page 589.

Significance   The first universal collective security agreement, the League of Nations, broke down in the 1930s under the impact of aggressions by the Axis powers—Germany, Italy, and Japan. Collective security military sanctions were invoked by the United Nations in 1950 against North Korea for its attack upon South Korea. Although this police action left much to be resolved, the United Nations was successful in halting the aggression. In 1956, the world organization was faced simultaneously with an attack by the Soviet Union upon Hungary and an attack by Britain, France, and Israel against Egypt. Although the United Nations was able to cope with the latter successfully, in the Hungarian case only moral sanctions were employed because of a fear of general war. The organization refrained from undertaking any form of collective security action during the Vietnam War, and it preferred to handle Middle Eastern conflicts and the 1979 incursion of Soviet forces into Afghanistan as international disputes rather than as acts of aggression. There is a general belief that a collective security action undertaken against a nuclear power—the United States, Russia, China, France, or Britain—would not be a police action but rather could result in a major war. In 1990, the United Nations collective security system for the first time worked as the UN's founders had intended when the Security Council unanimously declared Iraq to be an aggressor and levied economic sanctions against it. Subsequently, the council approved collective military actions against Iraq in the Desert Storm campaign, which was conducted successfully in 1991 by over twenty nations led by the United States. In the 1990s, the United Nations faced its greatest challenge to the principle of collective security. Bosnian Serb forces engaged in aggression against the Bosnian government in the form of mass murder and rape of civilian populations. Lacking leadership, the collective security system failed in the early years of the Balkan wars. United Nation peacekeepers were sent in to protect the "safe areas" and to keep roads open and supplies flowing but most often met with failure. It was thought that diplomacy would bring peace to the area, however, diplomacy seemed to become synonymous with appeasement. Finally in 1995, NATO forces, under UN auspices, used its military air power to reduce the level of hostilities, arrange a cease-fire, and bring the combatants to the conference table. After the signing of the Dayton accord, collective security action took the form of a NATO force placed in Bosnia to oversee the carrying out of the peace treaty provisions.

Comparative Advantage   A theory, first advanced by David Ricardo in 1817, that explains why each country tends to specialize in the production of those commodities for which its costs are relatively lowest. The concept of *comparative* advantage or comparative cost modified Adam Smith's theory of an international specialization based on *absolute* national advantage. In rebutting Smith's doctrine, Ricardo noted that few countries have a clear cost superiority in the production of goods for the world market and that labor, capital, and enterprise are relatively immobile internationally and unlikely to move to those places where absolute advantage could be maintained. *See also* BALANCE OF TRADE, page 534; LAISSEZ-FAIRE, page 15.

Significance   The Ricardian comparative advantage doctrine has served as a theoretical base for positing an international division of labor to maximize trade. According to the theory, if each country specializes in the production of those articles of commerce that it can produce most efficiently and trades with other countries to obtain the things it needs, all will be likely to enjoy a higher standard of living. These ideas continue to serve as the basic American rationale for supporting freer international trade. Critics challenge comparative advantage on the grounds that it has produced huge deficits in the American balance of trade and has helped to change the United States from a creditor to a debtor nation during the 1980s and 1990s.

Consul   An official appointed by a government to reside in a foreign country in order to assist citizens of the appointing state and advance their commercial interests. American consuls are members of the Foreign Service. *See also* DIPLOMACY, page 546.

Significance   The United States maintains consulates in most of the important commercial cities of the world. Responsibilities of an American consul include jurisdiction over American vessels (the settling of shipboard disputes, sanitary inspections, sending mutinous and shipwrecked sailors home), granting visas to foreigners seeking entry into the United States, and opening up new business and trade opportunities.

Containment   A general policy adopted in 1947 by the Truman administration to build "situations of strength" around the periphery of the Soviet Union and Eastern Europe in order to contain communist power within its existing boundaries. Underlying the containment policy was a belief that, if Soviet expansion could be stopped, communism would collapse of its own internal weaknesses. The policy was developed by George Kennan and was first applied in the Truman Doctrine of 1947 in a program of military aid to Greece and Turkey. *See also* TRUMAN DOCTRINE, page 584.

Significance   Under general guidelines of containment policy, the Truman administration embarked on vast new programs that included (1) rearmament, (2) establishment of military bases around the world, (3) mutual security alliances with friendly powers, (4) an economic aid program to rebuild war-shattered economies in Western Europe (Marshall Plan), and (5) a program of technical and economic aid to underdeveloped countries. Through these and other programs, communist expansion was slowed down but not completely halted. American actions in Korea and South Vietnam were based on the policy of containing communist power. After a period of détente in the 1970s, American policy began again in the 1980s to place major emphasis on the containment of Soviet power. In 1969, President Richard Nixon recognized the limits of containment policy, as related to Korea and Vietnam, when he proclaimed the Nixon Doctrine, which provided that small countries threatened by internal or external aggression must play a major role in their own defense while helped by the United States with military and economic aid. Critics of containment policy charge that it encouraged a massive Soviet-American arms race, that it fostered the Cold War, and that it was built on the false assumption of Soviet military expansionism. Supporters of the containment doctrine claim that the liberalizations that occurred in the Soviet Union and Eastern Europe in the late 1980s and early 1990s were the product of a successful 40-year containment policy that produced the kinds of changes predicted by George Kennan in 1947.

Convergence Theory   The view that capitalist and communist systems were evolving in their economic functions and modes of operations in increasingly similar ways. Ultimately, the convergence theory held, the two systems would become almost indistinguishable in their basic forms and consequently would no longer constitute a threat to each other. Furthermore, both systems were being shaped by the same forces of science and technology, cybernetics and automation, and by the industrial and urban cultures of the space age. *See also* CAPITALISM, page 4; COMMUNISM, page 5; DÉTENTE, page 544.

Significance   The evidence on which the convergence theory was based included the growing role of the government in capitalist states in subsidizing, regulating, and promoting the "free" economy; the increasing collective control of private corporations and divorcing of management from ownership; and the growing need for government control of scarce energy sources and supplies. On the communist side, changes in the 1970s and 1980s included increasing decentralization of economic decision making, more emphasis on production of consumer goods, growing competition among producers, and cash incentives for increased productivity. Then, in the 1990s, movement toward the creation of a limited "market economy" governed by supply-demand forces occurred in most communist states. Critics of the convergence theory had held that the gulf that exists between the two systems was too large and fundamental to be overcome by a few surface similarities. Yet the policies of *glasnost* (openness) and *perestroika* (restructuring) developed by Soviet leader Mikhail Gorbachev in the 1980s and 1990s led to the actual convergence of the two systems in terms of military, political, and economic policies.

Counterinsurgency   Military force employed against a revolutionary group trying to overthrow an established regime. Counterinsurgency operations describe the efforts of American and indigenous military forces to prevent a Communist takeover through revolution, guerrilla warfare, subversion, and related techniques.

Significance   Counterinsurgency operations have developed as a response to the communist doctrine of promoting "wars of national liberation." In Vietnam, counterinsurgency operations were carried on by American, South Korean, Australian, New Zealand, and South Vietnamese units against Vietcong guerrillas and North Vietnamese forces. The development of counterinsurgency during the early 1960s helped contribute to confidence in a military solution that led to an expanding American involvement in Southeast Asia during the latter half of the 1960s. The ultimate failure of counterinsurgency operations in Indochina reopened the question of how the United States can react effectively to national liberation wars. Conversely, in Nicaragua and in several African states, the United States, in a policy known as the Reagan Doctrine, promoted insurgencies against socialist and communist regimes. With the ending of the Cold War, military leaders have pleaded for maintaining sizable and highly mobile forces that will be able to meet the challenges of insurgencies in Third World countries through vigorous counterinsurgency actions. They stress that the appeal of communism is not dead in the countries of Africa, Asia, and Latin America.

Coup d'État (pronounced "coo-day-taa")   A French phrase that describes a swift, decisive seizure of government power by a military or political group. A coup d'état, typically, is attempted from within an existing system. It differs from a revolution in that it is not based on a popular uprising and does not involve a drastic change in the political and social institutions of the society, although such changes may occur if the coup d'état succeeds. Organizers of a coup usually attempt to carry it out by capturing or killing top military and civilian leaders, by seizing control of key government buildings and public utilities, and by using the mass media to calm the masses and obtain their support for the new regime. Resembling a coup d'état, the German word *putsch* describes a revolt or uprising aimed at changing a political system and its leadership. It is an action typically carried out by a nation's military leaders, a disgruntled group of officers, or a paramilitary ethnic group. *See also* ABSOLUTISM, page 1.

Significance   Although the United States has never experienced a coup d'état, military officers denied their pay during the Washington administration threatened to oust Congress and take over the government, whereupon Congress voted to give them the five years' back pay owed to them. Also,

Abraham Lincoln's assassination was part of a coup attempt that never materialized. Throughout history, the coup d'état has been used frequently in many countries. In recent years, numerous coups have occurred in the developing countries of Africa, Asia, and Latin America, with most involving seizures of power by military cliques from constitutionally elected leaders. In 1991, a group from within the Communist party attempted a coup aimed at retaining communism within the Soviet Union, but its failure led to revolutionary changes by which democracy and capitalism replaced communism and socialism in that country.

Court-martial   A military tribunal that conducts trials of military personnel accused of violating military law. A *summary* court-martial consists of a single officer who tries enlisted persons for minor offenses. A *special* court-martial, which can be convened only by a high-ranking officer, usually consists of three officers, who may impose moderately severe penalties, such as six months at hard labor, bad conduct discharges, and reductions in rank. A *general* court-martial may be convened by the President, Secretary of Defense, or a commanding general or admiral. It consists of five or more members, one-third of whom may be enlisted persons (if they are requested by the accused). Severe penalties, such as the death penalty, life imprisonment, or dishonorable discharge, may be imposed. *See also* COURT OF APPEALS FOR THE ARMED FORCES, page 257; MILITARY LAW, page 563.

Significance   The court-martial has become an important part of the American system of justice because of the large numbers of Americans in the armed forces. During World War II, almost one-third of the nation's criminal cases were decided by courts-martial. Charges of unfair procedures and lack of justice led Congress to establish a new Uniform Code of Military Justice in 1950, to provide for enlisted persons to serve on *general* courts-martial, and to create a five-person civilian Court of Appeals for the Armed Forces, to which convicted military personnel can appeal decisions made by the Courts of Military Review of the Army, Navy, and Air Force. The Military Justice Act of 1968 created an independent military judiciary designed to parallel the civilian judiciary. In 1983, Congress authorized the Supreme Court to review cases on direct appeal from the Court of Appeals for the Armed Forces. Courts-martial came under closer public observation as a result of the trials of American soldiers accused of acts of mass murder of civilians during the Vietnam War. Enlisted persons may serve on either a special or a general court-martial if requested by an accused enlisted person. On the question of civil versus military jurisdiction, the Supreme Court held in 1969 that a serviceperson is entitled to trial by a civilian court for non-service-connected crimes committed off the post and out of uniform (*O'Callahan v. Parker*, 395 U.S. 258). This rule was tempered by the Court in 1971, when it held that an offense committed by a service person on a military post against a civilian is "service-connected" and subject to court-martial (*Relford v. U.S. Disciplinary Commandant*, 401 U.S. 355). In 1976, the Court held that a person undergoing a summary court-martial does not have a constitutional right to legal counsel because not all civilian rights apply to the military (*Middendorf v. Henry*, 425 U.S. 25). This trend of weakening the legal rights of military personnel continued in the 1980s. In 1987, for example, the Court reaffirmed governmental immunity from suit even when a serviceman was given LSD without his knowledge as part of an experiment that damaged his mind. (*United States v. Stanley,* 483 U.S. 660) and held that soldiers may be tried in military courts for crimes committed while in the service whether service-connected or not (*Solorio v. United States,* 483 U.S. 435). With the end of the military draft and the building of a professional military, fewer courts-martial need be utilized, especially with a great reduction in cases such as those dealing with AWOL (Absent Without Leave) and desertion. However, 175 officers were implicated in the Tailhook scandal, in which dozens of women were sexually assaulted at a 1991 convention of naval aviators. Efforts to bring criminal charges against the officers involved were thwarted by lack of evidence and conflicting evidence. Court-martial charges were dropped against a number of officers charged in the scandal. The Secretary of the Navy resigned and a number of admirals were reprimanded for failure to investigate the charges. In 1996, an American soldier assigned to serve in a United Nations monitoring mission in the Balkans refused to wear the UN insignia and was court-martialed, convicted of disobedience, and given a bad-conduct discharge.

Declaration of War   A formal announcement by a nation that a state of hostilities exists with another nation. Constitutionally, in the United States, only Congress can declare war (Art. I, sec. 8). Under the usual procedure, the President requests a declaration of war, the Congress adopts it by joint resolution, and the President signs it. In over 200 years of U.S. history, Congress has declared war only five times: the War of 1812, the Mexican War, the Spanish-American War, World War I, and World War II. According to the Department of Defense, American war dead total 1,153,541, which includes the Civil War, 497,000; World War II, 406,000; World War I, 116,000; Vietnam, 58,000; Korea, 54,000; Mexican War, 13,000; Revolutionary War, 4,000; Spanish-American War, 2,400; War of 1812, 2,000; Indian Wars, 1,000; and Persian Gulf, 141. In addition, several thousand Americans have been killed in various police actions around the globe. *See also* WAR POWERS ACT, page 603.

Significance   Under conditions of modern war, Congress has lost most of its discretionary power to determine when and if war should be declared. Congress may merely recognize that a state of hostilities already exists, as in its declaration of war against the Axis powers following the attack upon Pearl Harbor in 1941. Moreover, the President, as commander in chief, may commit American forces to action without congressional declaration of war, as when President Franklin Roosevelt ordered a naval convoy for merchant ships prior to America's actual entry into World War II. In the Korean War, American troops ordered into action by President Harry Truman fought from 1950 to 1953 under the United Nations banner without a formal declaration of war by Congress. In South Vietnam, Presidents Dwight Eisenhower, John Kennedy, Lyndon Johnson, and Richard Nixon committed large numbers of American troops to action, and Presidents Johnson and Nixon ordered massive bombing of North Vietnam, Laos, and Cambodia, all without a congressional declaration of war. Today, with missiles and hydrogen bombs poised for attack, the decision to launch or repel an attack may be made by the President or, conceivably in an emergency situation, by a military commander in the field, with Congress having little to do with the decision. Currently, the United States is the only nuclear weapons state in which one individual—the President acting as commander in chief of the armed forces—can act alone to order a nuclear attack anywhere in the world. However, the controversy over whether Congress has the constitutional power to participate in the making of military decisions, as provided in the War Powers Act of 1973, remains unresolved. President George Bush, in ordering over 500,000 American troops to the Middle East in 1990 to defend Saudi Arabia from an Iraqi military takeover and to free Kuwait from Iraqi aggression, informed Congress and received its support, though refusing to accept the War Powers Resolution as binding. Bush headed a United Nations force that, in Operation Desert Storm, won a major victory over Saddam Hussein's Iraqi army in a brief period of hostilities.

Defense Contract   An agreement between the Department of Defense (DOD) and a private business or industry by which the latter agrees to do research on new weapons systems or supply hardware, equipment, supplies, or services to the military. The three main types of defense contracts are (1) the *competitive bid* contract, which ordinarily would be awarded to that company offering to provide the hardware or service at the lowest cost; (2) the *negotiated* contract, in which Defense officials discuss and reach agreement with a private company concerning materials or services and their costs; and (3) the *cost-plus* contract, in which the DOD guarantees the private company repayment of all costs involved in producing the hardware or service, plus a stipulated amount or percentage of costs as profit. *See also* DEPARTMENT OF DEFENSE, page 594; MILITARY-INDUSTRIAL COMPLEX, page 562.

Significance   During peacetime, the Defense Department utilizes mainly competitive bid contracting, but, under the pressures of World War II and the Korean and Vietnam wars, negotiated and cost-plus contracts were used extensively. The latter types are used to expedite procurement of hardware and services, typically at much greater cost than under competitive bidding. Under cost-plus contracting, for example, the contracting company is encouraged to boost costs of production because the size of its profit may be determined by the magnitude of its costs in producing the military equipment. Congressional committee investigations into DOD procurement activities have uncovered many cases of defense profiteering resulting from excessively high prices paid to private contractors. Under current competitive bidding practices for developing major new weapons systems, private companies have often given low bids to win contracts and later requested the Defense Department and Congress to cover major cost overruns, amounting to billions of dollars. Nevertheless, the trend in defense contracting in recent years has been toward greater use of competitive bidding. In 1988, a major scandal involving the Defense Department and various private companies revealed that the competitive bidding process was often illegally manipulated in the procurement of weapons. With the ending of the Cold War and the substantial reductions in budget allotments for purchasing military items, defense contract competition has greatly increased, with many companies dependent on receiving such contracts to avoid bankruptcy and remain profitable.

Détente   A French diplomatic term that describes a condition of an easing of confrontations and reduced strain between two or more countries. A period of détente offers an improved environment that may contribute to the resolution of specific issues or reduce the tensions stemming from the political problems that created the hostile relationship. A détente may result from understandings reached between heads of state at a summit meeting, from concluding a major treaty, or from changes in basic strategies and tactics of the states involved. *See also* CONVERGENCE THEORY, page 540; STRATEGIC ARMS REDUCTION TALKS (START), page 579.

Significance   Achievement of a measure of détente between the United States and the Soviet Union, and between the United States and the People's Republic of China, constituted the major foreign policy achievements of the Nixon and Ford administrations during the first half of the 1970s. American-Soviet détente was initiated through personal summit diplomacy involving President Richard M. Nixon and Communist Party Secretary Leonid Brezhnev. American-Chinese détente began with conversations between President Nixon and Chinese Premier Chou En-lai and Communist Party Chairman Mao Tse-tung. The Soviet-American and Chinese-American détentes reflected the exploding costs and dangers of the nuclear arms race, the belief that improved relations and increased trade would benefit both sides, general acceptance of peaceful coexistence as a working diplomatic construct, and deteriorating relations between the Soviet Union and Communist China that encouraged both to seek improved relations with the United States. The period of Soviet-American détente involved a major shift in foreign policy away from the ideas of containment, the Truman Doctrine, and the Cold War. It resulted in American troop withdrawals from Indochina; in great-power consultation over Middle East issues; in scientific exchanges in such fields as cancer research, weather forecasting, and space probes; and in SALT negotiations and agreements to limit nuclear weapons systems. In the 1980s, détente between the United States and the Soviet Union ended and a new phase of the Cold War began as a result of Soviet intervention in Afghanistan and a massive military buildup carried out by the Reagan administration with the support of Congress. Chinese-American détente, however, remained firm and led to an expansion of trade relations, the granting of most-favored-nation status to China, and various cultural exchanges. In the 1980s, Soviet leader Mikhail Gorbachev initiated new policies aimed at achieving détente with the West. The internal policies of *glasnost* (openness) and *perestroika* (restructuring) have been supplemented by a new emphasis on human rights and a new effort to conclude disarmament agreements with the United States. With the dissolution of the Soviet Union into fifteen independent republics, Gorbachev lost political power to Boris Yeltsin, President of the Russian Republic and of the newly created Commonwealth of Independent States (CIS) that succeeded the USSR. Under Yeltsin, communism and socialism were replaced by democracy and capitalism, which, along with additional disarmament agreements, contributed to détente.

Deterrence   Retaliatory capability of a nation's military forces that discourages a potential enemy from launching an attack. The concept implies that a nation's military defenses are so large, diversified, and well protected that a first strike by an enemy would not cripple its ability to retaliate decisively. *See also* STRATEGY, page 579.

Significance   Nuclear weapons have made deterrence an effective and credible strategy. Even if most of a nuclear power's retaliatory capability were destroyed in an initial strike, the potential for mass destruction of enemy cities would remain. Deterrence implies that the people and industry of rival nuclear powers remain perpetual hostages to deter a planned attack by either. The U.S. deterrent power included MIRV (multiple independently targeted reentry vehicles), intercontinental missiles protected by underground silos, cruise and Pershing II missiles, nuclear-powered submarines with Poseidon multiple-warhead nuclear-tipped missiles, and the strategic nuclear bomber fleet, some of which is constantly airborne. Soviet retaliatory power and capabilities (and, hence, deterrence posture) during the Cold War era approximated those of the United States. The former Soviets under Boris Yeltsin's leadership, however, are reducing their military forces rapidly and returning them to Soviet soil from former Warsaw Pact bases in Eastern Europe; the United States has dismantled underground silos and reduced its stockpile of nuclear weapons. These actions, resulting from numerous agreements by leaders of the United States and Russia, reduced the importance of the deterrent systems that had been constructed during the Cold War.

Diplomacy   The total process by which states carry on political relations with each other. The machinery of diplomacy includes a policy-making foreign office (Department of State in the United States) and diplomatic missions abroad (Foreign Service). Diplomacy may be carried on through open or conference negotiations, or in secret. Occasionally, diplomacy is undertaken by heads of state, a process called "summit" diplomacy. *See also* APPEASEMENT, page 532; DIPLOMATIC PRIVILEGES AND IMMUNITIES, page 546; PACIFIC SETTLEMENT OF DISPUTES, page 571; SUMMIT DIPLOMACY, page 580.

Significance   Diplomacy is an art that can be mastered only by skilled negotiators. A good diplomat knows how, when, and what to compromise and how to achieve maximum benefit. In critical situations, war may result if diplomacy fails. Diplomacy contributes to an orderly system of international relations and is the key technique used in the peaceful settlement of international disputes. Appeasement occurs when diplomacy fails and deterrence lacks vigor. Prussian military analyst Karl von Clausewitz described war as diplomacy carried on by other means.

Diplomatic Privileges and Immunities   Under international law, ambassadors and other diplomatic officials enjoy special rights and are immune from the jurisdiction of the state to which they are accredited. The embassy grounds may not be trespassed by local officials unless permission is granted by the diplomat or by his or her government. The diplomat and the diplomat's family and official staff are immune from arrest and from civil jurisdiction unless his or her own government waives this immunity. *See also* PERSONA NON GRATA, page 572.

Significance   The purpose of diplomatic immunity is to ensure that diplomats will have the freedom to carry on effective relations between their states. Though not subject to the laws of the state to which they are accredited, diplomats nevertheless are expected to abide by them under normal conditions. Diplomats who misuse their immunity may be reported to their superiors for discipline or, in severe cases, their recall may be demanded by the government of the state to which they are accredited, and they may be declared *personae non gratae* (unacceptable).

Dollar Diplomacy   A concept used historically by Latin Americans to show their disapproval of the role the American government and giant American corporations have played in using economic, diplomatic, and military power to open up foreign markets and to exploit the people. The term was originally coined by President William Howard Taft, who claimed that U.S. operations in Latin America had changed from warlike and political to peaceful and economic. Under the Roosevelt Corollary of the Monroe Doctrine, American Marines were frequently sent into countries of Central America. Protectorates were established over Cuba, Haiti, Nicaragua, and Santo Domingo in the early part of the twentieth century. The term "dollar diplomacy" may also be used in the contemporary world to describe any use of a state's economic, political, or military power to further the economic interests of its citizens or large business enterprises in foreign lands. *See also* GOOD NEIGHBOR POLICY, page 552.

Significance   After years of dollar diplomacy, American relations with Latin America improved with the inauguration of the Good Neighbor policy in the 1930s and the establishment of the Alliance for Progress aid program in 1961. Mutual solving of problems through the Organization of American States has further improved the position of the United States with Latin America. Yet reservoirs of ill feeling remain and are exploited by political leaders unfriendly to the United States. New contemporary forms of economic imperialism, which use political and economic pressures rather than military interventions and are carried on by large powerful American corporations, have also tended to weaken relations and to recall earlier days of dollar diplomacy and Yankee Imperialism for Latin Americans. These political-economic-military actions, for many years despised by Latin Americans, have in recent years been replaced by a doctrine of noninterference in their domestic affairs and by mutually agreed-upon trade relations, including, for example, NAFTA and the construction of a free trade area for all the Americas.

Domino Theory   The doctrine that holds that if some key nation or geographical region falls into communist control, a string of other nations will subsequently topple "like a row of dominoes." The Domino Theory was applied by President Dwight D. Eisenhower and his top advisers in 1954 to describe the dangers of communist expansion in Asia if Indochina were to fall. *See also* CONTAINMENT, page 540.

Significance   The Domino Theory has been expounded periodically since 1954 by top American leaders who used it as justification for expanding military programs in Southeast Asia. Originally applied to all of Indochina, the doctrine was subsequently linked to South Vietnam as the key state in the region by the Johnson administration, which intervened in the latter half of the 1960s with over one-half million American troops to keep that "first domino" from falling. Supporters of the Domino Theory argued that a communist victory would mean that American alliance guarantees for other small nations would no longer be credible, and a series of Communist victories could be expected. Critics of the theory charged that the Indochinese wars were largely indigenous in nature, that no such monolithic force as "world communism" exists, and that the theory was used as a propaganda scare tactic to try to justify unwarranted intervention policies. In the 1980s, the Domino Theory was used to justify American interventions in Central America (Nicaragua, Panama, and El Salvador) and the Caribbean region (Grenada).

Economic Nationalism   An economic policy by which a nation seeks to attain economic prosperity or to correct a disequilibrium in its balance of payments by protecting the home market and/or opening up foreign markets through unilateral or bilateral government action. It is the opposite of a multilateral trading system with free flow of trade and free convertibility of currencies. It is characterized by extensive governmental control of trade and the subjection of economic matters to overriding considerations of political or military policy. Techniques employed by states pursuing policies of economic nationalism include (1) austerity programs, (2) barter arrangements, (3) currency depreciation, (4) exchange controls, (5) export subsidies, (6) licensing, (7) quota restrictions, and (8) tariffs. *See also* GENERAL AGREEMENT ON TARIFFS AND TRADE (GATT), page 551; TARIFF, page 581; WORLD TRADE ORGANIZATION (WTO), page 592.

Significance   A state cannot normally pursue policies of economic nationalism without inciting retaliatory action from other states that have suffered harm from such policies. The great danger is that, once started, the process tends to escalate, with action and counteraction building up to the point of stifling most trade. This is what happened in the 1930s, when the Smoot-Hawley Tariff Act raised tariff rates to the highest point in American history in a desperate effort to avoid a major depression by protecting the home market from foreign competition. The average duty paid on imports into the United States under that law was approximately 60 percent, as contrasted with the 4.2 percent on dutiable items in 1988. The Smoot-Hawley action touched off extensive retaliation, which precipitated a world trade crisis. Today, bloc trading systems, such as the European Community, Commonwealth Preferences, and NAFTA, tend to reduce restrictive trade practices among members, but outside nations regard the regional systems as discriminatory. The low tariff rates on imports in the 1980s and 1990s are largely the result of GATT (General Agreement on Tariffs and Trade) bargaining and the granting by the United States of most-favored-nation (MFN) status to more than 150 trading nations, including Russia in 1992.

Executive Agreement   An international agreement between the President and foreign heads of state that, unlike a treaty, does not require Senate consent. Most notably, trade agreements are concluded under powers granted to the President by Congress. Others are concluded by the President acting under his constitutional powers over foreign relations. The Constitution makes no explicit provision for executive agreements. *See also* EXECUTIVE AGREEMENT, page 190; GENERAL AGREEMENT ON TARIFFS AND TRADE (GATT), page 551; TREATY, page 583.

Significance   Legally, an executive agreement is similar to a treaty. In recent years, the trend has been toward more agreements and fewer treaties. For example, in 1930, 11 agreements and 25 treaties were concluded; in 1958, there were 182 agreements and 3 treaties; in 1968, more than 200 agreements and 16 treaties. Today, the United States is party to almost 1,000 treaties and to more than 4,000 executive agreements. Advantages of the executive agreement include avoidance of the power of the Senate to cripple or kill a treaty and the maintenance of secrecy when desirable, as in a wartime agreement. Disadvantages include the frequent need for further implementation of the agreement by *both* houses of Congress through statutes and appropriations. When secrecy is involved, congressional and public suspicions may be aroused. When substantial public support is needed, presidents usually fall back on the treaty procedure. Executive agreements concluded by presidents in recent years, without congressional consent, have committed the nation to military action in Indochina and provided for the sale of huge quantities of wheat to the Soviet Union. Reacting against secret agreements, Congress adopted the Case Amendment in 1972, which requires the President to inform Congress of every foreign commitment he makes. An example of the utility of the executive agreement is found in the role of GATT (General Agreement on Tariffs and Trade). When the Senate refused to consent to the ratification of the treaty to establish an International Trade Organization following the end of World War II, the President then helped to establish GATT as an alternative based on executive agreements not needing Senate approval, an approach that has worked well for more than 40 years. In 1994, the World Trade Organization (WTO) came into existence and the U.S. role in the WTO was approved in both the House and the Senate.

Extradition   Return by one nation to another of a person accused of a crime. The extradition process resembles that of interstate rendition, which occurs between states within the United States. In the international field, extradition usually depends upon treaty arrangements between the two nations concerned. *See also* INTERSTATE RENDITION, page 44; INTERNATIONAL TERRORISM, page 558.

Significance   Because there is no international criminal law, without extradition a criminal could escape punishment by simply crossing a border. In 1992, however, the Supreme Court held that a criminal suspect could be kidnapped by U.S. authorities in a foreign country and brought to the United States for trial in violation of the procedures set forth in the extradition treaty between the two countries. (*United States v. Alvarez Machain*, 504 U.S. 655). States usually extradite, but political offenses are not generally recognized as grounds for extradition. Major controversies sometimes arise between two nations over what constitutes a political offense. In the case of terrorism, such as the bombing of Pan American World Airways jetliner over Lockerbie, Scotland, in 1988, the nation seeking extradition regards the terrorists as murderers, whereas the other nation refuses to extradite on the basis that the individuals are "freedom fighters" who have committed political or military offenses. In the United States, the President is not legally empowered to extradite in the absence of treaty provisions. Libya has consistently failed to extradite two terrorist suspects in the bombing, bringing the

United Nations into the extradition controversy to levy sanctions against Libya.

Foreign Aid   The granting of economic or military assistance to foreign countries. American economic aid includes disposal of food surpluses, technical assistance, development loans, capital grants, and investment guarantees. The aid has been offered to over 100 countries bilaterally and to additional nations through United Nations and regional programs. Major programs in which the United States participates include the Alliance for Progress, the Peace Corps, the Colombo Plan, the Organization for Economic Cooperation and Development, the Asian and Inter-American Development Banks, the World Bank Group (IBRD, IDA, and IFC), the International Monetary Fund, and the United Nations Development Program. Military aid, taking the form of weapons, training, and defense support (paying civilian costs to make up for money the aid-receiving country has spent in its own defense), is given on a selective basis to strengthen resistance to external or internal aggression. Foreign economic aid programs are administered by the Defense Department. Other aid outlets include the World Bank, the International Development Association (IDA), the International Monetary Fund (IMF), and the Asian, African, and Inter-American Development Banks and Funds. *See also* AGENCY FOR INTERNATIONAL DEVELOPMENT, page 593; FOOD FOR PEACE, page 484; PEACE CORPS, page 597.

Significance   The United States has provided approximately $500 billion in aid to foreign countries in the period 1945–1990. Aid programs started with Lend-Lease assistance to the Allies in World War II and in postwar years included the Marshall Plan to aid European recovery, the Truman Doctrine of military and economic assistance to Greece and Turkey to "contain" communism, and the Mutual Security Program of military aid to bolster NATO defenses in Western Europe. Since the 1960s, most American aid has gone to developing countries to encourage their "self-help" efforts. Approaches have included encouragement of internal reforms by the Alliance for Progress, offering human resources through the Peace Corps, and disposing of surplus food to needy peoples through the Food for Peace (Public Law 480) program. Most American foreign aid has gone to a few key countries of great strategic importance or to those that policymakers believed to be most critical in the pursuit of American foreign policy objectives. India and several African countries have been the major beneficiaries of American food aid, and South Vietnam, South Korea, Israel, Egypt, and Taiwan have been major beneficiaries of military aid. Currently, Israel, Egypt, and Pakistan receive almost half of all U.S. economic and military assistance. Most foreign aid must be used to pay for purchases of American products and services, thus constituting a substantial subsidy for American industry and labor. Whereas recipient countries have preferred capital aid to help them industrialize, American programs have focused mainly on technical assistance, infrastructure development, military security, import subsidies, food, health, and educational forms of aid, with the assumption that private investors—such as multinational corporations—will provide the capital needed for industrialization. The annual foreign aid budget runs between $15 billion and $20 billion. President George Bush's annual foreign aid budgets totaled over $5 billion each year, with much emphasis on military aid. Although the need for aid in the

Third and Fourth Worlds has grown tremendously, American aid is limited by the budget crisis and the fact that the United States is, itself, the world's largest debtor nation. American actions in Grenada, El Salvador, Nicaragua, and Panama in recent years have created additional foreign aid demands. The Third World includes approximately 130 developing nations in Africa, Asia, Latin America, and the Pacific, all recipients of foreign aid. About 50 nations of this group—the poorest of the developing bloc—have been designated members of the Fourth World by the United Nations. Although their need is greatest, most receive very little foreign aid from major aid-giving nations because they lack strategic and/or political importance.

General Agreement on Tariffs and Trade (GATT)   An international organization that promotes trade among its members by serving as a center for harmonizing trade policies and reducing tariffs and other barriers. It first met at Geneva in 1947 as an ad hoc conference to start a multilateral attack on trade barriers, prior to the establishment of the proposed International Trade Organization (ITO) as a specialized agency of the United Nations. When the U.S. Senate refused to approve the ITO, GATT—which is based on executive agreements rather than on a treaty requiring Senate approval—was developed as the main instrument to encourage freer trade. Its membership has increased from its original 23 participants to 125 members. Its main functions are negotiating reciprocal reductions in tariffs and other trade barriers, developing new trade policies, adjusting trade disputes, and establishing rules to govern the trade policies of members. Because all GATT agreements to lower tariffs include the most-favored-nation clause, concessions apply equally to all members, whether or not they are parties to the agreement. *See also* MOST-FAVORED-NATION STATUS, page 564; TARIFF, page 581; URUGUAY ROUND, page 590; WORLD TRADE ORGANIZATION (WTO), page 592.

Significance   The members of GATT have successfully negotiated reductions in tariffs and other trade barriers over a period of almost five decades. Tariffs on industrial goods have been substantially lowered, especially between the United States, Western Europe, and Japan, but many national barriers to imports of primary commodities remain high, and nontariff barriers to trade, such as quotas, continue to impede the flow of commerce. Efforts to liberalize trade also have been weakened by the refusal of many developing countries to join what they refer to as "the rich man's club." However, many western industrialized states, as members of GATT, have adopted a General System of Preferences (GSP) to aid the economic development of these countries by giving preferential treatment to their exports. A new major series of trade negotiations by GATT known as the Uruguay Round began in 1986. The Trade Act of 1988 gave the President the authority to work out fairer trade rules in GATT. The Uruguay Round, the eighth round of talks in GATT's history, was aimed at removing taxes and trade restrictions on exports and imports by all member countries. The main obstacle to reaching agreement was that of freeing up agriculture, which is heavily protected in many member countries and in recent years has enjoyed bumper crop yields. The Uruguay Round finally concluded in December 1993 and was signed on April 15, 1994, at a ceremony in Marrakech, Morocco. It called for the reduction of agricultural export subsidies, a further lowering of tariffs around the globe, and the creation of an international body, the World Trade

Organization (WTO), to oversee the enforcement of the new trade accord and penalize nations that violate it. The Congress approved U.S. participation in late 1994. Dramatic changes in Eastern Europe during the late 1980s and early 1990s led most of these states, including those of the former Soviet Union, to seek membership in GATT and other Western-dominated political and economic organizations.

Good Neighbor Policy   American policy toward Latin America initiated in the early 1930s. President Franklin Roosevelt described the change in policy in his inaugural address in March 1933 as follows: "In the field of world policy, I would dedicate this nation to the policy of the good neighbor—the neighbor who resolutely respects himself and, because he does so, respects the rights of others." Although the policy was directed toward the world at large, it soon came into general usage as descriptive of the American policy of treating Latin American nations as friends and equals. *See also* ORGANIZATION OF AMERICAN STATES, page 570.

Significance   From the turn of the century until the adoption of the Good Neighbor policy, the United States played the role of "Big Brother" to Latin America. Unilateral actions, dollar diplomacy, and frequent military interventions characterized that policy. Terms such as "Yankee imperialists" and "Colossus of the North" came into common usage in Latin America to indicate displeasure with American policies. The Good Neighbor policy was an about-face, a repudiation of earlier actions. Since its inception, the policy has resulted in two military pacts of mutual assistance (the Act of Chapultepec of 1945 and the Rio Treaty of 1947), the creation of the Organization of American States (OAS), the creation of a trade agreement (the North American Free Trade Association, or NAFTA), and a general improvement in relations between the United States and Latin American countries. The policy occasionally has been strained over U.S. relations with dictatorial regimes and over unilateral actions by the United States, such as the military intervention in the Dominican Republic in 1965, covert interventions in Chile in the 1970s and in El Salvador and Nicaragua in the 1980s, and by the invasion of Grenada by American troops in 1983. In a 34-nation Summit of the Americas in 1994, an agreement was reached on creating a free trade area of the Americas by the year 2005. Stretching from the northernmost parts of Alaska and Canada to the southern tip of South America, this duty-free trading area will serve a potential market of 850 million.

Good Offices   A method of peaceful settlement by which a third nation seeks to bring two disputing nations into agreement. The state offering its good offices merely seeks to create favorable conditions under which the states in conflict can talk over their differences. Good offices does not include participation in the negotiations or offering a suggested solution, although the disputing states may request them. When they do, the good offices approach is converted into mediation. *See also* PACIFIC SETTLEMENT OF DISPUTES, page 571.

Significance   Good offices can be a useful device in breaking the ice between disputing states by getting them to talk things over. Neither disputant may be willing to initiate proposals for such talks for fear of demonstrating weakness in its position. The third state that offers its good offices is playing the role of peacemaker on behalf of the world community. In recent years, the United Nations has often taken over the role of offering good offices to disputing states, usually through the Security Council, the General Assembly, or the Secretary-General. The United States, through its Secretary of State, has also tendered its good offices to disputants in the Middle East and in the Balkans. In the latter case, the United States, in 1995, invited the three warring parties, the Bosnians, Croats, and Serbs, to meet at the Wright-Patterson Air Force Base at Dayton, Ohio, where they engaged in direct negotiations and reached a peace agreement, known as the Dayton Accord.

Ideological Warfare   A psychological tactic used by the communist and free-world blocs in the Cold War. Each side sought to achieve ideological conformity among its own people while trying to convert the large masses of humankind outside its borders to its basic values and "way of life." Ideology comprises the ideas and ideals of a political and economic system. The pre-Gorbachev struggle in the Soviet Union involved competition between Soviet-style communism with its one-party rule and Western-style capitalism and democracy, and between Soviet and Chinese communist systems. *See also* IDEOLOGY, page 13; PROPAGANDA, page 105.

Significance   The communism-socialism versus democracy-capitalism ideological war (1917–1990) developed an inclination toward good and bad classification of national and international actions as each side tried to convince millions of people of the soundness and rightness of its position and the imperialistic, warlike, aggressive nature of the other side. Various psychological techniques were used in disseminating propaganda. In the 1970s and early 1980s, however, a détente between the rival camps encouraged a reduction in propaganda, a lessening of tensions, and an expansion in communication and understanding. The basic ideological competition between rival belief systems, however, continued and increased as détente tended to give way to a return to the Cold War. However, with Mikhail Gorbachev's *glasnost* (openness) and *perestroika* (restructuring) reforms, Cold War attitudes began to give way to increased cooperation and successful disarmament agreements and cultural exchanges, beginning in 1986. In addition, ideological conformity in the Soviet system began to change as democratic and capitalistic ideas were adopted to moderate the Soviet system of socialism. In Russia, following the breakup of the Union of Soviet Socialist Republics (USSR), under the leadership of Boris Yeltsin, communism has been in retreat, and there has been a general rejection of communism in Eastern Europe with a growing emphasis on capitalistic and democratic ideals and practices. The newborn capitalism has not quickly provided the expected improved standard of living, however, and a return to communism through the democratic process is possible. President Boris Yeltsin won a critical reelection in July 1996 over the communist candidate, Gennady Zyuganov, insuring continuation of social, political, and economic reforms for the present.

Inherent Powers   Powers exercised by the national government in foreign affairs that are neither expressed nor implied in the Constitution. These are derived from the fact that the United States exists in a world of nations and, therefore, must possess powers to meet its international responsibilities. *See* *also* INHERENT POWERS, page 43; PRESIDENTIAL POWER: PREROGATIVE THEORY, page 202; *United States v. Curtiss-Wright Export Corp.,* page 600.

Significance   The inherent powers doctrine enables the national government to act in foreign affairs to protect the security and well-being of the American people. The extent to which such action would be permissible has not been specified, although the Supreme Court has stated (*United States v. Curtiss-Wright Export Corp.,* 299 U.S. 304 [1936]) that: "As a member of the family of nations, the right and power of the United States in that field are equal to the right and power of the other nations of the international family." Inherent powers are also known as "prerogative powers."

Intelligence   Gathering information about the capabilities and intentions of foreign governments. Most intelligence is secured by analyzing data found in governmental and private publications, but some requires the use of clandestine cloak-and-dagger methods. American agencies actively engaged in the gathering and/or analysis of intelligence include (1) the Central Intelligence Agency (CIA), which carries on undercover activities around the globe and serves as a central focus for the receipt and evaluation of intelligence; (2) the National Security Agency (NSA), which engages in coding and decoding operations and electronic surveillance; (3) Army Intelligence (G2), which secures data on ground forces and new weapons; (4) Air Force Intelligence (A2), which covers air and space affairs; (5) the Office of Naval Intelligence (ONI), which ferrets out information on foreign navies and fleet movements; (6) the Bureau of Intelligence and Research (I & R) in the State Department, which obtains economic, scientific, sociological, and political data and forecasts trends; (7) the Defense Intelligence Agency (DIA) of the Department of Defense, which evaluates the capabilities of allies and potential enemies; (8) the Department of Energy, which obtains and disseminates information about foreign energy supplies, production, intentions, and policies; (9) the Federal Bureau of Investigation (FBI), which obtains information on internal threats to security; (10) the Treasury Department, which collects foreign investment, monetary, and general economic intelligence; and (11) the Drug Enforcement Administration (DEA), which collects information on foreign and domestic production and traffic in narcotics. The United States Intelligence Board, headed by the Director of the CIA, meets regularly to sift information gathered by intelligence agencies and to give a "national intelligence estimate" to the President. *See also* CENTRAL INTELLIGENCE AGENCY, page 593.

Significance   Technological advances in warfare have increased the need for governments to obtain vital information related to the security of the state. Intelligence objectives relate mainly to the military field, but states also gather data on political, economic, and social factors. Not only potential enemies but also friendly and allied nations constitute the subjects of intelligence operations. Congressional investigations in the 1970s revealed that large numbers of American citizens were also under direct surveillance by various American intelligence agencies. Some critics charge that the multiplicity of American intelligence agencies leads to confusion and duplication. When intelligence failures permit a surprise attack—as at Pearl Harbor in 1941—or provide erroneous assessment of a foreign situation—as in the abortive Bay of Pigs invasion of Cuba in 1961—the results may endanger a nation's vital security interests. The Vietnam War provided numerous examples of the failures of military intelligence agencies to obtain reliable tactical and strategic information and to provide useful estimates about the enemy's intentions and capabilities.

International Bank for Reconstruction and Development (IBRD)   A specialized agency of the United Nations, known informally as the World Bank, that makes loans for economic development purposes. The bank was created by the Bretton Woods Agreement of 1944 to promote the economic growth of its members by making loans when private capital is not available. Its chief sources of funds are capital subscriptions from member nations and sales of its own bonds to private investors. One-fourth of the initial capital of the bank was subscribed by the United States. With the exception of a few communist states, such as Cuba and North Korea, most countries are members of the bank. To meet criticism of the bank's conservative lending policies, the International Finance Corporation (IFC) was created in 1956 to lend to private enterprises and, in 1960, the International Development Association (IDA) was created as a "soft loan" affiliate of the bank to offer long-term, no-interest loans. The Multilateral Investment Guarantee Agency (MIGA) was established in 1988 to encourage entrepreneurship by guaranteeing investments in private companies. The IBRD, the IFC, the IDA, and the MIGA are known collectively as the World Bank Group. *See also* FOREIGN AID, page 550.

Significance   By 1981, the World Bank Group had made 3,383 loans, amounting to a total of approximately $85 billion, with IBRD's share amounting to about $60 billion. In 1980, the bank made 144 loans at an average interest rate of 8.25 percent. Loans are made only after careful and detailed studies convince the bank's governing board of the soundness of the ventures. Recently, the World Bank Group in a single year lent more than $12 billion to developing member countries, with $4 billion lent on concessional terms to the poorest nations of the Fourth World. In 1979, the industrial nations agreed to a $40 billion capital increase for World Bank development lending, with $8.8 billion to be provided by the United States in the 1980s. Because loan decisions are made by the board using a system of voting weighted on the basis of contributions to the bank's capitalization, these decisions are controlled by a small group of Western countries, with the United States possessing about 20 percent of the total votes of the bank's members. Terms of loans have varied, with interest rates running close to those in private capital markets and with payment periods ranging from 10 to 35 years. Loans have been granted for such projects as irrigation, mining, agriculture, transport, communication, and general development. The bank has also undertaken a broad technical assistance program to help prepare the ground for useful loans and to help recipients make effective use of loans received. Efforts are also made in granting loans to finance those projects that are most likely to encourage an inflow of private investment capital. Although the bank has progressively increased the pace of its lending activities, its ability to help developing states meet their capital needs is limited. Increasingly, the World Bank Group has joined in consortium arrangements with a number of other international, national, and private banks to collectively finance major projects. In recent years, many loans have been aimed at increasing the capability of Third World countries to make payments on their massive loans that have precipitated a world debt crisis. The World Bank works closely with the International Monetary Fund (IMF) on these and other major international problems, including holding joint meetings every year. In the 1990s, the former communist countries of Eastern Europe and the republics of the former Soviet Union applied for membership in both the World Bank and the IMF. In 1995, the World Bank announced a new policy of making microloans as low as $100 to individuals in the developing countries, mainly women; such borrowers have excellent records of repaying. By 1996, there were 180 members in the World Bank and the IMF.

International Labor Organization (ILO)   A specialized agency of the United Nations that seeks through research and recommendation to improve working conditions throughout the world. Established in 1919, the ILO was the only major agency associated with the League of Nations in which the United States participated. The ILO is concerned with problems of full employment, labor standards, migration of workers, collective bargaining, Social Security, and workers' health. Its headquarters are in Geneva, and it functions through a General Conference comprised of delegates representing labor, employers, and government. Between annual conferences, an executive Governing Body supervises the operations of ILO committees and commissions and prepares the agenda for future conferences.

Significance   Although the ILO cannot make binding decisions, its recommendations have been adopted by many member countries, resulting in improved working and living conditions for millions of workers. Improvements in labor standards can best be accomplished when they are instituted simultaneously by many nations; otherwise, those nations acting alone would place themselves at a competitive disadvantage as far as labor costs are concerned. In recent years, much ILO activity has been directed toward the underdeveloped areas of the world. Hundreds of ILO experts have provided technical assistance to countries in Asia, Africa, Latin America, and the Middle East. As world economic conditions changed in the 1970s, the ILO became concerned with the problems of millions of immigrants who had entered the industrialized countries during the labor-shortage years. In 1977, the United States notified the ILO of its withdrawal from membership, an action that reflected its loss of a leadership role in the agency and its concern about ILO decisions. In 1980, however, the United States returned to the ILO as a result of a changing political atmosphere in the organization.

International Criminal Tribunal for the Former Yugoslavia   An independent body created in 1993 by the Security Council to investigate, prosecute, and penalize those involved in genocide, war crimes, and crimes against humanity. Based in The Hague, Netherlands, it is the first body to apply the 1948 international laws against genocide and the 1949 Geneva Convention that protects civilians during wartime. *See also* INTERNATIONAL LAW, page 557; INTERNATIONAL TERRORISM, page 558; UNITED NATIONS INTERNATIONAL COURT OF JUSTICE, page 587.

Significance   In 1996, the International Criminal Tribunal for the former Yugoslavia began the first war crimes hearings since similar cases were held in Nuremberg and Tokyo 50 years ago. The tribunal consists of eleven judges with no more than two from the same region of the world and numerous investigators and prosecutors. At the present, only a few of the 74 individuals indicted for war crimes are in custody. The tribunal operates under severe constraints. It has no power to arrest, cannot try persons in absentia, and cannot impose the death sentence. It has been charged that an estimated 8,000 Bosnian Muslims were massacred by the Bosnian Serbs under the direct supervision of their top military commanders. The tribunal is trying to accomplish in the courts what the United Nations peacekeepers were unable to do on the ground. If it fails to bring justice to the thousands of victims of atrocities in Bosnia, then the UN's status as defender of human rights may be undermined. One of the tribunal's chief justices recently commented that success should not be measured by the number of cases tried but by the very existence of an international tribunal to apply the Nuremberg principles that have been on the books for 50 years and not enforced.

International Law   A body of rules and principles that guides the relations among nations and between governments and foreign nationals. Sources of international law include treaties, authority (for example, decisions of international courts), reason, and custom. Treaties and other forms of international agreements are the most important source today, as custom was earlier, in the development of international law. The law has been classified into the following categories: peace, war, and neutrality, based on the nature of the law; and into public, private, and administrative, based on the different sources of the law. *See also* UNITED NATIONS INTERNATIONAL COURT OF JUSTICE, page 587.

Significance   Although international law evolved out of the European nation-state system, it has gained nearly universal acceptance by the world community of states. Some theorists reject the entire concept of international law, holding that law must be handed down by a sovereign authority, enforcement agencies must exist, and courts must provide sanctions against violators. Because none of these conditions exists in the state system, the existence of *law* is denied. Others refute this position by noting the universal acceptance of some elements of international law by the world community (such as diplomacy and commerce) and the general obedience of states to its rules. With the world caught up in revolutionary ferment, international law has unquestionably depreciated in importance. Efforts of the United Nations to foster its growth and adherence to its principles continue, however. The updating and modernization of international law received a major setback when President Ronald Reagan refused to sign the comprehensive Law of the Sea Treaty. This treaty was negotiated over a ten-year period by almost all nations of the world in an attempt to bring law and order into the exploitation of the resources of the world's oceans and seabeds. In 1993, an International Criminal Tribunal was established at The Hague in the Netherlands. This tribunal was the first of its kind since the Nuremberg and Tokyo war crimes trials after World War II. Questions remain concerning the arrest, trial, and punishment procedures of the court. Nevertheless, this court provides a beginning to cope with war criminals indicted for rape, genocide, and other crimes against humanity. The experience of this court demonstrates that if the world community is willing to punish war criminals who commit aggression on their neighbors, then international law may serve as the guide-post for a meaningful instrument for justice.

International Monetary Fund (IMF)   A specialized agency of the United Nations established by the Bretton Woods Monetary and Financial Conference of 1944 to promote international monetary cooperation. The major objectives of the fund include (1) promotion of exchange stability, (2) establishment of a worldwide multilateral payments system, and (3) provision of monetary reserves to help member nations overcome short-run disequilibria in their balances of payments. By the 1990s, 180 members had joined the fund and subscribed to quotas totaling over $25 billion. Voting power in the IMF is determined by the size of a member's contribution, with the United States casting about one-fifth of the total. The industrial nations function as a caucus (Group of 30) to reach decisions in the IMF to defend currency values and to promote international liquidity. *See also* DEVALUATION, page 395; GOLD STANDARD, page 403; WORLD DEBT CRISIS, page 591.

Significance   Creation of the International Monetary Fund was aimed at preventing a return to the anarchic financial conditions of the 1930s, with wildly fluctuating exchange rates and competitive devaluations. For many years, major exchange depreciations were generally avoided, but because of deteriorating world economic conditions in recent years, exchange stability has been greatly weakened. The main problems facing the fund have been the persistent deficits in the balance of payments of most developing countries. Other problems include the shortage of international reserves at a time when international trade has expanded rapidly and a dangerously high level of inflation in most countries. Balance of payments financing has involved annual loans of billions of dollars and other currencies to deficit states by the IMF in an effort to avoid a general default on international loans. The situation is critical because many countries must borrow the money from the IMF to make their annual payments to private and public banks and loan agencies on the principal and interest owed on outstanding loans. In the 1990s, Russia and other republics of the former Soviet Union, as well as former communist states of Eastern Europe, applied for membership in both the IMF and the World Bank.

International Terrorism   Actions undertaken by governments, individuals, or groups using violence or threats of violence for political purposes. International terrorism has included aircraft hijackings, political kidnappings, assassinations, bombing, arson, sabotage, and the holding of hostages. Most terrorism is practiced by groups representing extremist political parties or positions. Typically, terrorism of the Left is aimed at promoting revolution against the established order, and terrorism of the Right is used to preserve and protect a privileged group or class. *See also* ANTITERRORISM AND EFFECTIVE DEATH PENALTY ACT OF 1996, page 375; EXTRADITION, page 549; DOMESTIC TERRORISM, page 73.

Significance   Terrorism has been used increasingly in recent years by movements seeking to gain political and economic independence and to call attention to their cause. Terrorism has also been used to maintain positions of power, once secured. Citizens and officials of the United States, including diplomatic personnel, military officials, airline personnel, corporation executives, and tourists, have increasingly become the victims of terrorism. The United States government has been directly affected by terrorist actions. For example, American diplomatic and military hostages were seized by Iranian militants in 1979 and held for 444 days, with the connivance of the Iranian revolutionary government, before being released. Two bombings in Beirut in 1983 resulted in the deaths of more than 300 U.S. military and diplomatic personnel, and in 1995 and 1996, truck bombings of U.S. military facilities in Saudi Arabia killed 24 Americans. Terrorism is difficult to combat because innocent lives are often in jeopardy and the terrorists appear willing to sacrifice their own. Basically, the problem of dealing with terrorists comes down to the following question: Should counterviolence be used against terrorists, or should an effort be made to placate them through political compromises? Although most countries have agreed through the United Nations not to give sanctuary to terrorists and hijackers, the problem continues. The use of military force by national armies to achieve political objectives constitutes a form of terrorism used especially in the Middle East in recent years. In 1990, Iraq invaded Kuwait and seized thousands of hostages, whom they placed near strategic targets in an effort to deter an American attack from bases in Saudi Arabia. The United States and its allies were not deterred and won an easy military victory over Iraq in Operation Desert Storm in 1991. In 1992, the United Nations invoked economic sanctions against Libya because of that nation's refusal to extradite two alleged terrorists charged with planting a bomb on a civilian airliner. The bomb destroyed the plane over Lockerbie, Scotland; hundreds were killed. In 1996, President Bill Clinton signed a bill that would punish foreign businesses that invest in Iran and Libya, "two of the most dangerous supporters of terrorism in the world." There was a swift response from our European allies saying that this would "create a particularly dangerous precedent for the security and development of commerce."

Isolationism   The theory and practice of noninvolvement in affairs of other nations. Isolationism as a political ideology is nurtured by geographical, ideological, and cultural separateness. Isolationism is the opposite of a policy of internationalism, which is the theory and practice of national involvement in collective efforts to resolve security, political, economic, and social problems. *See also* COLLECTIVE SECURITY, page 538; SANCTIONS, page 576; UN SECURITY COUNCIL, page 589.

Significance   The United States pursued a policy of isolation during the nineteenth and part of the twentieth century. It was particularly operative in American intentions to remain aloof from the power struggles of Europe by remaining independent of Europe's system of entangling alliances. The doctrine was instrumental in conditioning the American public's belief that the United States should maintain neutrality during the early stages of World War I and World War II and not join the League of Nations. After World War II, American isolationism gave way to deep commitment to internationalism. Indications of a national trend back toward isolationism, however, began to appear during the 1980s. In 1990, some conservatives opposed President George Bush's action in sending major military forces to the Persian Gulf and, with the collapse of Soviet power, demanded that American troops overseas be returned to the United States. Public opinion in the 1980s and increasingly in the 1990s has been against committing American troops to action in trouble spots around the world. In the Balkans, this growing isolationism led to a situation in which horrible atrocities were committed and the United Nations, especially the NATO group, failed to intercede on behalf of the victims of aggression. After three years of watchful waiting, NATO forces finally launched air attacks that led to a cease-fire and brought the combatants to the conference table at Wright-Patterson Air Force Base near Dayton, Ohio, where a peace settlement was negotiated.

League of Nations   The first general international organization established to preserve peace and security and to promote cooperation among nations in economic and social fields. The League was created by the victorious powers of World War I in 1919 under the leadership of President Woodrow Wilson, but the United States did not join. The organization operated under a constitutional system established through its covenant, a section of the Versailles peace treaty. A council and assembly were the major organs (similar to the Security Council and General Assembly of the United Nations), and subsidiary committees and commissions were established to deal with special problems in areas such as mandates, military affairs, and disarmament. A Secretariat, headed by a secretary-general and staffed with international civil servants, provided continuity and expertise in record keeping and research. A world court (the Permanent Court of International Justice, forerunner of the present International Court of Justice) and the International Labor Organization were independent of the League but worked closely with it. Sixty-three nations joined the League, which had its headquarters at Geneva. *See also* UNITED NATIONS CHARTER, page 584.

Significance   In its first decade, the League resolved many postwar problems and settled numerous disputes that threatened the peace. The Great Depression that swept across the world in 1929–1930 rekindled aggressive nationalism and reduced the League's effectiveness. Failure of the League to deal resolutely with the Japanese conquest of Manchuria in 1931, the Italian conquest of Ethiopia in 1935, and the Nazi aggressions in the late 1930s brought about its collapse. Most observers believe that the League's breakdown resulted not only from internal constitutional weaknesses but also from the failure of key member states to support its principles and from the refusal of the United States to join. Despite its failure to maintain peace, the League did succeed in promoting extensive international cooperation in economic and social affairs and in developing new ideas and procedures for international organizations, which have proved useful to its successor, the United Nations. Although the United States never became a member of the League, it was more active and provided more funds for the League's activities than most members. The League voted itself out of existence in 1946 and transferred its assets to the United Nations. Because of the failure of the United Nations to take resolute actions against aggressors in Africa and in the Balkans in the 1990s, some observers fear that the UN might suffer the same fate as the League.

Limited War   Any war that is fought without all major weapons and for objectives other than the complete defeat of the enemy. Limited war involves the use of conventional military forces rather than of nuclear superweapons in the pursuit of specific political objectives. *See also* COLLECTIVE SECURITY, page 538; PACIFIC SETTLEMENT OF DISPUTES, page 571.

Significance   In the Korean conflict of the early 1950s, the Vietnam War of the 1960s and 1970s, and the Gulf War of the early 1990s, the United States and other nations fought limited wars with conventional military forces. Fear that limited wars may spread into a general worldwide conflagration makes decisive victories difficult to achieve. Many critics opposed American defense policies in the 1950s on the ground that too much emphasis was placed upon weapons of mass destruction at the expense of mobile tactical forces of the type needed to fight limited wars. The Kennedy and Johnson administrations sought to achieve a "balanced force" of conventional and nuclear weapons. The Nixon administration, reacting to the Vietnam War experience, enunciated the Nixon Doctrine, by which it sought to avoid direct limited war involvements by insisting that each ally assume primary responsibility for its own defense, rather than depending on intervention by American forces. The Reagan administration sought to strengthen American strategic and tactical forces, particularly conventional forces in NATO, whereas the Bush administration was active in reaching agreement with the Russians to substantially reduce both nuclear and conventional forces in Europe. These actions contributed to the end of the Cold War, the dissolution of the Soviet Union, and the breakup of the Eastern European alliance.

Marshall Plan   A proposal made by Secretary of State George C. Marshall in 1947 for a vast program of American economic aid to reconstruct the war-devastated economies of Western Europe. The U.S. Congress accepted the plan and, in 1948, established the European Recovery Program, under which sixteen nations of Western Europe (later joined by West Germany) received $15 billion in grants and loans from 1948 to 1952. Under the Marshall program, the participating European nations on American request joined together in the Organization for European Economic Cooperation (OEEC) for the purpose of drawing up a collective inventory of resources and requirements. The Soviet Union and other communist countries were invited to participate but rejected the offer. *See also* FOREIGN AID, page 550.

Significance   The Marshall Plan was successful in thwarting communist aims of exploiting the economic collapse and political turmoil of the post–World War II era in Western Europe. By 1951, all participating members had raised their production capacities beyond prewar levels. American attempts to promote the integration of European economies through the program were highly successful, especially on the Continent. The Marshall Plan, in the post–World War era, was the first of a series of economic and military programs through which the United States provided over $200 billion in grants and loans to over 100 countries. The Marshall Plan's OEEC was the forerunner of the contemporary Organization for Economic Cooperation and Development (OECD), which includes all of the industrialized capitalist countries as members.

Martial Law   Military government established over a civilian population during an emergency, in which military decrees supersede civilian laws and military tribunals replace civil courts. Martial law may be accompanied by the suspension of the writ of habeas corpus. Although the Constitution does not delegate specific power to declare martial law, it is implied from military and defense powers and can be invoked by the President when necessary for the security of the nation. In the states, the governor as commander in chief of the state militia may declare martial law during an emergency occasioned by internal disorders or a natural disaster. Vast discretion is vested in military officers in enforcing martial law. *See also Ex Parte Milligan,* page 599.

Significance Martial law is sometimes erroneously used to describe the use of troops to aid civil authorities and civil courts in maintaining order, which is far more common than the suspension of civil authority. Rare occasions on which federal martial law has been invoked by the President include Abraham Lincoln's placing the southern and border states under martial law, and Franklin Roosevelt's placing Hawaii under it following the attack upon Pearl Harbor. Mass violence has occasionally led governors to invoke martial law to restore order in local communities.

Military Government Temporary government established by conquering military forces over occupied enemy territory. Areas occupied by American forces are governed under statutes enacted by Congress, supplemented by orders issued by the President as commander in chief. The military governor of a territory under military government exercises supreme legislative, executive, and judicial authority. Civil government operates to the extent permitted by the military governor.

Significance Military government was used extensively by the United States and its allies during and following World War II in the occupation of enemy territory. Special army military government units were trained to perform occupation duties. Efforts were made to teach the enemy populace the principles and practices of democracy as defined and applied by the occupying forces. Sovereignty was later restored and military government units were withdrawn.

Military-Industrial Complex An informal alliance among key military, governmental, and corporate decision makers involved in the highly profitable weapons-procurement and military-support system. The phrase "military-industrial complex" was coined by President Dwight D. Eisenhower in his presidential farewell address, in which he warned the American people to guard against the growing and excessive militarization of society. The impact of the military-industrial complex can be determined through such indicators as the growth of the national defense budget, the increasingly militaristic posture of the nation in foreign policy, the magnitude of profits for those corporations engaged extensively in defense businesses, and the size of subsidies paid by the Pentagon to defense contractors. *See also* CIVILIAN CONTROL, page 537; DEFENSE CONTRACT, page 544.

Significance The military-industrial complex is a legacy of World War II, the Cold War, and the Korean and Vietnam Wars. It exists not only in the United States, where the phrase is commonly applied to the elites who wield economic, political, and social power as a result of the arms race, but in all societies caught up in the military technology race. Increasing militarism fostered by military-industrial complexes within many nations threatens the security of all. Within the United States, critics charge that the power of the military-industrial complex prohibits the nation from diverting funds from military expenditures to the many pressing problems that divide and weaken American society. In 1988, for example, the military-industrial complex became a focus for public criticism as a result of revelations of illegal activities in defense procurement involving billions of dollars in military equipment.

Military Law   Law, enacted by Congress, that governs the conduct of enlisted persons and officers of the armed forces of the United States. Military law also establishes the procedures for trial by court-martial for alleged infractions. Military law seeks to accord servicepersons accused of violations full due process of law. *See also* COURT-MARTIAL, page 542.

Significance   Prior to 1950, separate Articles of War applied to the Army, Navy, and Coast Guard. To secure uniformity and in response to criticism concerning the lack of military justice, Congress in 1950 enacted a single uniform code for all of the armed forces. This Uniform Code of Military Justice seeks to resolve the problem of balancing the need for discipline with justice. It also permits trial of servicepersons by civil courts for off-duty offenses committed in the United States. Military law, however, does not ordinarily apply to civilians who are abroad with the armed forces (*Reid v. Covert*, 354 U.S. 1 [1957]) or to discharged servicepersons for offenses committed while in the armed forces (*Toth v. Quarles*, 350 U.S. 11 [1955]). Critics of military law allege that military personnel enjoy less than first-class citizenship, in that full constitutional due process is not accorded to them. In an effort to correct that situation, Congress enacted the Military Justice Act of 1968, which established an independent military judiciary free from the control of local commanders and aimed at paralleling the civilian judiciary. The law also required judges and legal counsel in cases where they were not required in the past, and permitted defendants to be free when appealing a court-martial decision. In 1983, Congress revised and streamlined the Uniform Code of Military Justice and provided direct authority for the U.S. Supreme Court to review cases decided by military courts. These cases move from the Court of Appeals for the Armed Forces, the highest court in the military justice system, to the U.S. Supreme Court at the latter's discretion.

Mobilization   Preparing a nation to meet an attack or to fight a war. Mobilization involves placing the armed forces in readiness, calling up reserves to active duty, putting the nation's economy on a war footing, and establishing governmental controls over manpower, production, resources, and prices. Mobilization for modern war involves readying the totality of a nation's human and physical resources for military action. The Plans and Preparedness Office of the Federal Emergency Management Agency (FEMA) is responsible for plans and policies relating to peacetime and wartime emergencies and for planning the nation's nonmilitary defense effort, including managing its huge stockpile of strategic and critical materials. In addition, FEMA copes with natural disasters, such as floods, fires, earthquakes, hurricanes, and tornadoes, and with situations such as bombings and riots. *See also* EMERGENCY POWERS, page 189; FEDERAL EMERGENCY MANAGEMENT AGENCY, page 466; WAR POWERS, page 591.

Significance   Mobilization is directed by the President, whose constitutional authority as commander in chief is buttressed by vast delegations of emergency powers authorized by Congress for the duration of the war or crisis. Under the stress of war or threat of war, the courts have not generally interfered with the President's exercise of mobilization powers. Mobilization by a nation during peacetime may decrease the possibility of war by calling a potential aggressor's bluff; conversely, it may increase the likelihood of war if other nations consider it a threat to their security.

Monroe Doctrine   A unilateral declaration of American foreign policy made by President James Monroe in his annual message to Congress in 1823, opposing any European intervention in the affairs of the American continents. He also reaffirmed the American intention to refrain from interfering in European affairs. The doctrine was intended to stop the Holy Alliance from aiding Spain in a reconquest of the newly independent Latin American republics. *See also* DOLLAR DIPLOMACY, page 547; GOOD NEIGHBOR POLICY, page 552; ORGANIZATION OF AMERICAN STATES, page 570; RIO TREATY, page 575.

Significance   The Monroe Doctrine at the time of its enunciation was largely meaningless because only the British fleet stood between the Holy Alliance and the reconquest of Latin America. Over the years, however, it developed into one of the basic tenets of American policy through restatements, corollaries, and the growing ability of a powerful United States to intervene actively whenever the doctrine was challenged. Since the Declaration of Lima in 1942, and particularly the Rio Treaty of 1947, which provided for the multilateralization of the Doctrine, it has become a common principle by which the American republics have declared their determination to defend themselves against foreign intervention. In 1963, this definition of the Monroe Doctrine led to a failed American-sponsored invasion of Cuba by mercenary troops at the Bay of Pigs. An uneasy truce has existed since 1963, with the United States boycotting Cuba and treating the Castro government as a pariah nation. In 1995, President Bill Clinton modified the American policy with Cuba by concluding an immigration accord that allowed refugees to leave Guantanamo Bay for the United States, but all future refugees to be sent back to Cuba. Increased travel and the flow of remittances to Cuban families from Cuban-American citizens was also permitted. In 1996, a crisis erupted between the Fidel Castro regime and the United States over the shooting down of two civilian airplanes piloted by American citizens. The Helms-Burton law was passed, which tightens sanctions against Cuba and permits Americans to sue foreign companies using former American property in Cuba confiscated by Castro in 1959. The European Union has threatened retaliation even though Clinton has delayed this particular section of the bill, claiming that it offends and attacks trusted allies.

Most-Favored-Nation Status   Participation in a trading system in which all tariff concessions agreed upon by negotiating ("most-favored") states are extended to all other states. Inclusion of the most-favored-nation (MFN) clause in a trade agreement means that discrimination against third states is avoided by granting equal treatment to all. Although the term implies the granting of special treatment, it in fact ensures that all members of the trading system will receive the same advantages granted to the state "most favored." In the United States, Congress has delegated power to the President to withhold the application of MFN treatment from nations that discriminate against American exports. This power was used by presidents to withhold or withdraw MFN status from trade carried on with many communist states. *See also* GENERAL AGREEMENT ON TARIFFS AND TRADE, page 551; RECIPROCAL TRADE AGREEMENTS ACT, page 602.

Significance The most-favored-nation system can be used to turn an otherwise discriminatory series of bilateral trade agreements into an outward-looking program aimed at the general reduction of trade barriers. Under American leadership, for example, it has been used since 1934 to rebuild a liberal trading system out of the maze of discriminatory barriers established during the period of the Great Depression. Both the Reciprocal Trade Agreements Program and the General Agreement on Tariffs and Trade (GATT) have applied the MFN principle in all trade agreements. In the 1970s period of détente, the Soviet Union sought but did not receive MFN status from the United States. Tariff rates on imports coming from countries not granted MFN status date back to the Smoot-Hawley Tariff Act of 1930 and remain the highest in American history. Czechoslovakia in 1990 became the first former East bloc communist country in the post–Cold War era to conclude a comprehensive trade agreement with the United States, including the granting of MFN status to that nation. Most former communist countries of Eastern Europe, as well as Russia, have received MFN status. China was granted temporary MFN status by the Bush administration and has been extended with congressional approval for one-year periods by the Clinton administration. President Bill Clinton announced that, henceforth, MFN decisions would be based on economic rather than political factors.

National Guard The volunteer armed forces of the states, formerly called the militia. The Constitution provides for a cooperative system under which each state is responsible for appointing officers and Congress provides for organizing, arming, and disciplining the guard. Each governor is commander in chief of the state's national guard and may call it out for emergencies, such as floods, fires, and civil disorders. The guard may be called into federal service at any time, as occurred during World Wars I and II and during several Cold War emergencies, such as the Berlin Crisis in 1961, and the Gulf War in the 1990s.

Significance During much of American history, state volunteer militias constituted a relatively powerful and autonomous group of armed forces. Since 1916, the militias have been organized as the National Guard, an auxiliary of the regular army subject to substantial national control. Congress may authorize calling the guard into federal service at any time, but the President, as commander in chief, decides when units will be called, and all state jurisdiction ceases when the guard becomes part of the regular army. Racial and campus disorders during the 1960s and early 1970s led to the calling out of National Guard units in many states, sometimes with controversial results. The Reagan administration's military buildup in Central America during the 1980s included many National Guard units. In 1990, the Supreme Court held (*Perpich v. Department of Defense*, 496 U.S. 334) that Congress may authorize members of the National Guard to be ordered to active federal duty for purposes of training outside the United States (in this case, the Persian Gulf area) without the consent of the state governor or a declaration of national emergency. The pre-1916 definition of these units as militia has been reinvented and used by groups of radical right-wing elements. The members of the militia regard government as the enemy of the people. They believe that the federal government is out of control and that only an armed citizenry can keep it in check. They are organized into state groups and came into prominence as a result of the bombing of the Oklahoma City Federal Building in 1995. The alleged bombers are believed to have had ties with the militia movement.

National Interest   The concept of the security and well-being of the state, used in making foreign policy. A national interest approach to foreign policy demands "realistic" handling of international problems, based on the use of power divorced from moral principles and values. Conflicts of national interest in the state system are resolved through diplomacy, international law, international institutions, or, ultimately, war. Historically, national interest evolved as *raison d'état* (reason of state), a doctrine developed in the sixteenth century by Niccolò Machiavelli, which holds that security and national advantage are paramount considerations in state action.

Significance   The concept of national interest is hazy and subjective in its application. Exponents of a realistic approach argue that it reduces utopian expectations, recognizes the existence of power politics, produces a steady and sober involvement in world affairs, and limits a state to attainable objectives. Opponents argue that the strongest foreign policy is one built on a firm moral base and that reliance on unilateral policies of national interest fails to provide for reconciliation of international interests. The doctrine of national interest dictates that moral principles and commitments and agreements should be disregarded if they conflict with state policies or actions.

Nationalism   Social and psychological forces that spring from unique cultural and historical factors to provide unity and inspiration to a given people through a sense of belonging together and of sharing values. Nationalism binds together people who possess common cultural, linguistic, racial, historical, or geographical characteristics or experiences and who give their loyalty to the same political group. Modern nationalism began to make its appearance as a major political and ideological force in the early nineteenth century, particularly in Napoleonic France. Nationalism is strengthened in some states by *ethnocentrism* (the belief in the superiority of one's own group and culture) and by *xenophobia* (an exaggerated fear or distrust of foreigners and of the policies and objectives of other nations). *See also* NATION, page 20; SOVEREIGNTY, page 26.

Significance   The spirit of nationalism subjects people to the intangible forces of group psychology and collective behavior, especially when a crisis confronts them with a real or imaginary enemy. Nationalism tends to emphasize the separateness of and differences between groups, such as Germans versus French, Arabs versus Israelis, and Serbs versus Muslims in the former Yugoslavia. Most modern wars have been products of extreme nationalism in which mass emotional enthusiasm has been marshaled for one nation against another. It has played a significant role in the march to independence of numerous peoples. Nationalism is waning in Europe, its seedbed, and waxing strong in the new states of Asia and Africa. Nationalism is also a powerful internal force that helps produce unity, loyalty, and durable political, economic, and social institutions.

Neutrality   The legal status of a nation that does not participate in a war between other states. Under international law, such a state is free to defend its territory or neutral waters against attack by belligerents. Although public opinion and even the government of a neutral state may sympathize with one side or the other, to retain its neutral position a state may not engage in action that might favor one side in the war. Some states, such as Switzerland, Sweden, and Ireland, have espoused a doctrine of perpetual neutrality. *See also* INTERNATIONAL LAW, page 557.

Significance   The concept of neutrality has lost some of its meaning in modern times because of the increasingly ruthless nature of war, its expansion into global struggles, and the tendency of neutrals to show some favoritism based on ideological sympathies. In a future global war, neutrals may be placed in as great a position of danger as belligerents because of the possibilities of radioactive fallout, the spread of poisonous gases, and the employment of biological warfare by belligerents. Neutralism, a special form of neutrality that was espoused during the Cold War, provided a "third force" composed of states that followed policies of nonalignment toward the capitalist and communist blocs. In pursuit of a policy of neutralism, most nations of Asia, Africa, and the Middle East and a few states in Europe and Latin America refused to join military alliances propogated by either the United States or the Soviet Union.

North American Free Trade Agreement (NAFTA)   A major trade pact aimed at reducing or eliminating tariffs and other impediments to trade among the United States, Canada, and Mexico. It was approved by the Congress, signed by President Bill Clinton, and became effective January 1, 1994. The pact merges the economies of the United States, Canada, and Mexico over a fifteen-year period by phasing out most barriers to trade and investment. It calls for a trinational commission to mediate disputes. *See also* WORLD TRADE ORGANIZATION (WTO), page 592.

Significance   The North American Free Trade Agreement was designed to create the world's largest single marketplace. At the time of its creation, 370 million consumers and workers were producing $6.5 trillion worth of goods and services each year. It was an extension of the United States–Canada Free Trade Agreement, a trade pact between the United States and Canada that became effective January 1, 1989. This pact represented a victory for President Ronald Reagan's campaign to encourage free trade and open markets throughout the world. Shortly after NAFTA took effect, Mexico suffered an economic crisis and was forced to drastically devalue the peso. As a result, Mexican buying power was dramatically diminished, and United States exporters felt the crunch. The question is now being asked, Was NAFTA a mistake? Proponents say that it was the right decision, but it could take until the year 2000 for all expectations to be obtained. Chile stands next in line to join NAFTA, with formal talks already underway. Trade ministers of the Western Hemisphere met in 1995 to lay out the framework for a free trade zone encompassing the entire hemisphere by the year 2005—a goal set at the Summit of the Americas in Miami in December 1994. Trade experts believe that creating this large trade market has enhanced our ability to compete with Japan and with the European Community.

North Atlantic Treaty Organization (NATO) An organization established under the North Atlantic Treaty of 1949 to create a single unified defense force to safeguard the security of the North Atlantic area. Members agree under Article V of the Treaty to regard an attack on any of them as an attack on all, and, if an attack occurs, each will render such assistance as it deems necessary. The sixteen parties to the North Atlantic Treaty include the original twelve (Belgium, Britain, Canada, Denmark, France, Iceland, Italy, Luxembourg, the Netherlands, Norway, Portugal, and the United States), three states that joined NATO in the 1950s (Greece, Turkey, and West Germany), and its newest member, Spain, which joined NATO in 1982. Members seek, in addition to attainment of mutual security, "the further development of peaceful and friendly international relations . . . and to eliminate conflict in their international economic policies." *See also* ALLIANCE, page 530.

Significance NATO provides the basic framework of the political-military structure of the West. Important questions such as the rearmament of West Germany, the establishment of missile bases in Western Europe, the employment of nuclear weapons, and overall strategic and tactical plans were worked out through the political and military channels of cooperation established within the NATO framework. Its solidarity tended to wax and wane over the years as the Cold War grew more intense or cooled off. France, under de Gaulle, strained the alliance through independent actions that led ultimately to its withdrawal from NATO in 1966. In 1995, France ended its 29-year boycott and rejoined the military wing of the alliance. In 1974, Greece also ceased to participate for several years in the integrated military-political system of NATO, following a Turkish invasion of Cyprus using NATO weapons. Any NATO member may renounce the treaty by giving one year's notice, but none has invoked this provision. In 1984, NATO's unity was strained as a result of the controversy over the emplacement of American cruise and Pershing II missiles in NATO countries. In 1987, the United States and the Soviet Union, with the support of all NATO members, agreed in the INF Treaty to remove all short- and intermediate-range missiles and their nuclear warheads from Eastern and Western Europe. This action was followed in 1991 by the military, political, and economic dissolution of NATO's communist counterpart, the Warsaw Pact. The Berlin Wall no longer separated the two Germanys, which united into one nation that continued as a member of NATO. These events ushered in a post–Cold War era during the late 1980s and 1990s that left NATO's future in some doubt, as its members struggled to develop a new sense of mission. Another challenge to NATO suddenly developed in 1990 when Saddam Hussein's Iraq attacked and occupied Kuwait and threatened the stability of the entire Middle East. The success of Operation Desert Storm in defeating Iraq has led NATO to develop a small, flexible, highly mobile strike force to deal with future crises it faces. In response to requests for membership from former communist countries, in

1994 NATO adopted a historic plan, Partnership for Peace, which offered countries of the former Soviet bloc and republics of the former Soviet Union participation in certain military exercises, peacekeeping missions, and information exchanges but not full membership. Twenty-one nations, including Russia, are now members of the Partnership for Peace. In the early 1990s, NATO became involved in a crisis situation in the Balkans, where three rival ethnic groups—Croats, Muslims, and Serbs—fought each other, with the Serbs being the main perpetrators of aggression and atrocities, including rape and genocide. Lacking strong American and European leadership, NATO vacillated for a few years before becoming involved militarily by launching a series of air attacks on the Serbs in 1995. A highly mobile ground strike force, mainly of British and French troops, supported the air attacks. President Bill Clinton assumed a new leadership role. First, he secured a cease-fire and then brought the presidents of Bosnia, Croatia, and Serbia to a conference table in Dayton, Ohio, where he used his good offices and mediation roles to maneuver the leaders of the three groups to write and initial a peace treaty. More than 60,000 NATO troops, including 22,000 Americans, composed the NATO implementation force (IFOR), which was given the mission of maintaining a precarious peace. The Balkan situation has lent support to the idea that NATO's role in maintaining peace in the European region—working within the UN framework, with U.S. leadership and participation—is still viable.

Organization for Economic Cooperation and Development (OECD)   An international organization created in 1961 to achieve expanded cooperation and joint action among the United States, Western Europe, and Canada. It is an outgrowth of the Organization for European Economic Cooperation (OEEC), established in 1948 to decide how American aid granted under the Marshall Plan would be distributed. When OEEC was dissolved in 1960, its membership included 18 European nations, which, with the addition of the United States and 5 new members, comprised the membership of OECD. Sixteen of the 24 members of OECD are NATO allies—the United States, Canada, Belgium, Britain, Denmark, France, Greece, Iceland, Italy, Luxembourg, the Netherlands, Norway, Portugal, Spain, Turkey, and Germany. The other 8 are Australia, Austria, Finland, Ireland, Japan, New Zealand, Sweden, and Switzerland. Since the dissolution of the Warsaw Pact and the growing irrelevance of the communist world's COMECON, East European states have sought to participate in Western-oriented organizations like the OECD and GATT. In 1994, Mexico became the first Latin American country invited into membership in OECD, bringing the total membership to 25 countries. *See also* MARSHALL PLAN, page 561.

Significance   The objectives of OECD are (1) to encourage economic growth and financial stability for member nations, (2) to expand and improve Western aid to underdeveloped countries, (3) to expand trade among members and with the world through more liberal policies, and (4) to provide a forum in which members can consult on mutual economic problems. The United States was the main force behind the creation of OECD. American policymakers were particularly concerned with overcoming the balance of payments deficit, penetrating the Common Market trading bloc in Europe, and ensuring that all Western nations carried their fair share of the program for aiding underdeveloped countries. In the 1980s, OECD was used by the United States as a central negotiating forum for working out common policies for dealing with world inflation, the economic stability of the industrialized countries, and the problem of massive debt owed by Third World countries to private and public loan agencies in OECD countries.

Organization of American States (OAS)   A regional political organization comprised of the United States and 31 Latin American republics that was created at the Bogotá Conference in 1948. The original 21 members of the OAS were Argentina, Bolivia, Brazil, Chile, Colombia, Costa Rica, Cuba, Dominican Republic, Ecuador, El Salvador, Guatemala, Haiti, Honduras, Mexico, Nicaragua, Panama, Paraguay, Peru, United States, Uruguay, and Venezuela. Eleven new states have been admitted to membership: Antigua and Barbuda, the Bahamas, Barbados, Dominica, Grenada, Jamaica, Santa Lucia, Saint Kitts and Nevis, Saint Vincent and the Grenadines, Surinam, and Trinidad and Tobago. Only 22 OAS members have become parties to the Rio Treaty. The OAS now consists of (1) the General Assembly, which meets every 5 years to decide general policies; (2) the Council (with each member state represented by an ambassador), which oversees the implementation of general policies of OAS; (3) the Consultative Meetings of Ministers of Foreign Affairs, which occur whenever urgent problems confront the OAS; (4) the Pan-American Union, which operates through its headquarters in Washington, D.C., as a general secretariat of the OAS; (5) the Specialized Conferences, which are called periodically to enable the members to cooperate in dealing with technical problems; and (6) the Specialized Agencies, which are responsible for eliciting cooperation in economic, social, education, technical, and humanitarian problem areas. The OAS is a regional organization of the type encouraged by the United Nations Charter. Important provisions of the OAS Charter concern the peaceful settlement of disputes among members and procedures for mediation, arbitration, and adjudication. The OAS also implements the Rio Treaty's provision to safeguard the hemisphere from attack. *See also* ALLIANCE FOR PROGRESS, page 530; GOOD NEIGHBOR POLICY, page 552; MONROE DOCTRINE, page 564; RIO TREATY, page 575.

Significance   The OAS regional system has institutionalized the principles embodied in the Monroe Doctrine. All major hemispheric problems have been taken up since 1948 through the machinery of the OAS. Communist infiltration into Latin America has been the major problem facing OAS organs. In 1962, the Castro regime of Cuba was expelled for promoting communist subversion and revolution in Latin America. American unilateral military intervention in the Dominican Republic in 1965 created new strains in the OAS, even though the United States claimed that its role was to prevent a communist takeover, and an OAS peace force soon assumed control. The major challenge facing OAS in the future will be that of meeting increasing internal threats to the security of Latin American states as a result of population pressures, urbanization, and mass frustrations growing out of failures to make rapid progress in economic development and to alleviate poverty. United States foreign policy has aimed at replacing United Nations settlement efforts in the Western Hemisphere with those of the OAS, which more closely follow U.S. guidelines in their peaceful settlement efforts. The OAS efforts to find solutions to Central American problems, such as the revolution in El

Salvador and the American intervention in Nicaragua, have been supplemented by negotiations carried on by the Contadora Group of Mexico, Panama, Venezuela, and Colombia. In the Caribbean region, seven island states created the Organization of Eastern Caribbean States, which requested and supported a U.S. invasion of the island of Grenada in 1983 to replace its pro-Castro regime. In 1989, President George Bush sent combat troops into Panama to overthrow dictator Manuel Noriega and to protect Americans living there. Noriega surrendered on January 3, 1990, and was taken to the United States to face drug-trafficking charges. That year, a peaceful election was held in Nicaragua under international supervision in which the Sandinistas relinquished power to new President Violet Chamorro and her National Opposition Union party. The OAS is now working toward the creation of a hemispheric free trade zone.

Pacific Settlement of Disputes   The peaceful adjustment of international disputes by one or more of the following techniques: negotiation, inquiry, good offices, mediation, conciliation, arbitration, or adjudication. Sometimes several of these approaches may be used simultaneously, as in the conference of Balkan leaders at the Wright-Patterson Air Force Base, where the United States used good offices and also acted as mediator and conciliator. Pacific settlement may be employed through the traditional diplomatic channels, regional organizations or arrangements, or the organs or agencies of the United Nations. Chapter VI of the United Nations Charter details the political procedures available to the Security Council and the General Assembly, Chapter XV delegates peaceful settlement responsibilities to the Secretary-General, and Chapter XIV prescribes the legal processes by which the International Court of Justice may attempt to settle justiciable disputes. *See also* ARBITRATION, page 532; DIPLOMACY, page 546; GOOD OFFICES, page 552; UNITED NATIONS INTERNATIONAL COURT OF JUSTICE, page 587.

Significance   War occurs not only as a result of planned aggression but also from failure to keep international disputes within peaceful bounds. The United Nations system has bolstered traditional and regional settlement channels by establishing the principle of member responsibility to settle all disputes peacefully and by providing permanent machinery readily available to take up disputes. Although the United Nations has a good record of securing cease-fires, it has failed to settle major disputes, including those between India and Pakistan and between the Arab states and Israel. American mediation efforts conducted by President Jimmy Carter, however, led to the Camp David Accords in 1978 and a formal peace treaty between Israel and Egypt in 1979. Conflicts in Cyprus and the Congo and various Cold War transition problems have also proved to be difficult settlement problems for the United Nations. In the 1990s, treaties were concluded between Jordan and Israel, and between Yasir Arafat, leader of the Palestine Liberation Organization (PLO), and Israel.

Panama Canal Treaties   Two treaties concluded between the United States and Panama that provide for the operation and defense of the canal until the year 2000. The treaties, concluded in 1978, supersede all previous treaties relating to the Panama Canal. The first treaty includes provisions relating to the ownership, operation, and security of the canal. The second treaty, called the Treaty Concerning the Permanent Neutrality and Operation of the Panama Canal of 1978, lends support to the first treaty by providing for the canal's perpetual neutrality and for its defense, if aggression occurs, by the United States and/or Panama. Under the Panama Canal Treaty of 1978, the Canal Zone no longer exists, and the United States retains primary responsibility for the operation and security of the canal until the end of the twentieth century. During these years, the treaty provides for a progressive shifting of operational responsibilities to Panamanian citizens. Furthermore, the United States will continue to collect tolls but will turn over an increasing amount of such tolls to Panama to aid in its economic development. In the year 2000, Panama will assume full ownership of the canal, and the first treaty, which governs its operation and defense until that date, will expire, while the Neutrality and Operations Treaty will continue indefinitely. *See also* NEUTRALITY, page 567.

Significance   The two Panama Canal treaties were ratified by Panama following a national plebiscite, and by President Jimmy Carter after the U.S. Senate gave its consent (by a margin of one vote). The treaties were signed following fourteen years of negotiations and only after much rioting and many casualties along the Canal Zone border. The United Nations, the Organization of American States, and the Third World generated much pressure to get the United States to agree to the treaties. In 1989, President George Bush ordered a powerful United States military force to invade Panama, where it overthrew the dictatorship of General Manuel Noriega. He was captured and extradited to the United States to stand trial on drug-trafficking charges. In undertaking the invasion—dubbed "Operation Just Cause"—President Bush cited American obligations to defend the Panama Canal, as set forth in the 1978 treaties. This action was the thirteenth intervention in Panamanian affairs by the United States during the twentieth century. It was partly prompted by the DeConcini Reservation to the Neutrality Treaty, which provides that both Panama and the United States have the independent right to take military action in order to prevent the canal from being closed or its operations hampered.

Persona non Grata   An unacceptable person. *Persona non grata* relates particularly to the situation in which a nation declares that an ambassador or minister is no longer acceptable and requests that person's recall by the appointing government or expels him or her. All diplomatic officials are therefore regarded as *personae gratae* (acceptable) unless declared *personae non gratae* by the receiving state. *See also* DIPLOMATIC PRIVILEGES AND IMMUNITIES, page 546.

Significance   Each nation is free to accept or reject any person accredited to it as diplomatic agent. When a diplomat is declared *persona non grata,* the appointing government may consider it an affront, but the procedure is generally recognized and accepted. Numerous incidents involving the declaring of diplomatic agents *personae non gratae* occurred during the Cold War. In most such cases, retaliation followed, with a diplomat of equal status declared *persona non grata* following the first dismissal.

Police Action   A military action undertaken against a foreign foe without a congressional declaration of war. A police action initiated by the President has come to replace a state of war for several reasons: (1) under the United Nations Charter and earlier agreements, a declared war is of dubious legality under international law; (2) domestic public opinion may not support the nation's involvement in war; and (3) a President may fear that Congress would not vote for a requested declaration of war. *See also* COMMANDER IN CHIEF, page 188; DECLARATION OF WAR, page 543; WAR POWERS ACT OF 1973, page 603.

Significance   The advances of science and technology in the military weapons field have placed new emphasis on "police action" as a substitute for war. The time when the issue of whether the nation should go to war could be leisurely debated in the Congress is long past. Presidents have ordered troops into action in foreign lands without a declaration of war by Congress on more than 150 occasions in American history. The seriousness of the problem, however, has greatly increased because the Korean and Vietnam Wars, as examples of police actions, were major wars in terms of casualties, costs, domestic impact, and dangers involved. Congress, in the War Powers Act of 1973, sought to limit and regulate presidential powers involved in undertaking police actions, but all presidents since 1973 have considered the limitations and regulations of these powers to be unconstitutional and have refused to be bound by them.

Protectionism   An economic philosophy and a policy by which a government seeks to protect the nation's economy from foreign competition by regulating the volume or types of imports entering the state. Advocates of protectionism are philosophically challenged by supporters of laissez-faire, free trade doctrines, particularly those associated with the theory of comparative advantage. As a policy, protectionism is implemented through the use of various impediments to imports, such as tariffs, quotas, exchange control, licensing, and special taxes. Through such devices, imports can be reduced or eliminated, or their cost to the importer and hence the consumer can be substantially increased. The objective of protectionism is to help domestic industries compete with cheap imports from low-wage, low-cost countries or to ensure that certain domestic industries have a competitive edge in the home market. *See also* COMPARATIVE ADVANTAGE, page 539; GENERAL AGREEMENT ON TARIFFS AND TRADE (GATT), page 551; NORTH AMERICAN FREE TRADE AGREEMENT (NAFTA), page 567; TARIFF, page 581.

Significance   The amount of protectionism employed varies from nation to nation, but every country uses some protective measures. Throughout American history, the level of trade protection, especially through tariffs, has been an issue in almost every national election. Along with slavery, it was one of the leading issues involved in the Civil War, with the South demanding low tariffs or free trade and the North favoring a high protective tariff for its growing industries. Although average rates were boosted in the Smoot-Hawley Tariff Act of 1930 to the highest point in American history in a vain effort to forestall the Depression, this strategy failed because of trade retaliation. Since 1934, however, the United States has provided world leadership in a campaign to provide for freer trade. Whereas tariffs under the

Smoot-Hawley Tariff Act averaged 60 percent of the value of dutiable items, by 1987 that level of protectionism had been reduced through reciprocal trade agreements to only 4.2 percent. By the late 1980s, protectionism had once again become a major issue in American political and economic life, with Congress enacting trade laws to protect American industry and labor from foreign competition, and the Bush administration continuing to fight for freer trade. As an example of coping with protectionism, the North American Free Trade Agreement (NAFTA) was created in 1994, among Canada, the United States, and Mexico.

Quid pro Quo   A diplomatic bargaining concept meaning, literally, something for something. Negotiations are typically conducted on a basis of *quid pro quo* and depend on mutual compromises for success. *See also* DIPLOMACY, page 546; TRADE-OFF, page 115.

Significance   Any nation unable to demand a *quid pro quo* in exchange for its own concessions is in an inferior bargaining (and power) position. Reciprocal concessions are particularly useful in reducing tariffs and other trade barriers through *quid pro quo* bargaining.

Ratification   The formal action of the President in giving effect to a treaty that has been approved by the Senate. The President or his representative meets with representatives of the other signatory parties and exchanges ratifications with them. The treaty then is officially proclaimed and becomes legally enforceable. *See also* RATIFICATION, page 205; TREATY, page 583.

Significance   Contrary to popular belief, the Senate does not officially ratify a treaty when it gives its advice and consent. In giving its consent, the Senate may attach amendments or reservations that influence the decision of the President on ratification. The Senate's amendments or reservations, under which portions of a treaty will not be considered binding on the United States, leave the President with three choices: (1) renegotiation of the treaty; (2) ratification with reservations, if acceptable to other signatories; or (3) refusal to ratify. Of the nearly 1,600 treaties submitted to the Senate since 1789, about 70 percent have been approved. Many of those approved, however, failed to be ratified because amendments or reservations added by the Senate resulted in refusal of the President to put them in force, or they were rejected by other treaty parties. In addition, more than 60 treaties have been rejected outright by the Senate, thus eliminating the question of ratification. Many that failed to receive the Senate's consent for ratification have been among the most important treaties negotiated, including the League of Nations Covenant, the Statute of the first World Court, and the SALT II treaty. All amendments to a treaty adopted during the Senate process of giving its advice and consent must be renegotiated with other parties to the treaty, because no state can be bound by changes in a treaty that are made without its approval.

Recognition   The discretionary function exercised by the President of deciding whether the United States shall officially carry on relations with a new state or a new political regime in an existing state. *See also* RECOGNITION, page 206.

Significance Each state in the world must determine for itself if and when new states and governments are to be recognized. Premature recognition of a revolutionary regime may lead to a threat of war by the government fighting the insurgent group. Conversely, continued refusal to recognize an existing state or an established government may engender hostility toward the state that withholds it. American recognition policy has varied with different presidents but, since World War I, it has generally been one of withholding recognition from regimes distasteful to American citizens and of granting it to friendly governments. Worldwide ideological struggles have influenced presidential recognition policies in recent years. A major recognition controversy, linked also with the question of representation in the United Nations, involved the refusal of the United States for many years to accept East Germany and communist China in the family of nations. The United States continues to refuse to recognize North Korea and the Castro regime in Cuba. Recognition was given to Vietnam in 1995 by President Bill Clinton, with the result that American businesses have had new market opportunities and trade arrangements with Vietnam.

Reserves The Army, Navy, Air Force, Coast Guard, and National Guard units not regularly on active duty but available to supplement the regular military services during emergencies. Reservists are divided into "ready reserves," "standby reserves," and "retired reserves." The ready reserve may be called to active duty by the President or Congress. The standby reserve is a pool of trained military personnel who can be called up only in case of war or an emergency declared by Congress. A third category, the retired reserve, can be recalled to active duty by Congress during a major emergency. Congress, in 1976, gave the President authority for a limited reserve mobilization whenever the President deemed it necessary. *See also* NATIONAL GUARD, page 565.

Significance The reserves consist largely of men who have completed their active military duty, take weekly training, and attend summer training camps. The role of reserves in modern warfare depends on the nature of the military situation. In a major nuclear war, for example, decisive blows might be struck before reserves could be mustered. In a limited war, conversely, a reservoir of trained manpower would probably be essential. During the Berlin crisis in 1961, President John F. Kennedy called up some units of the ready reserves for one year of active duty to bolster the American military posture. In 1990, President George Bush called to active duty thousands of military reservists to serve in the Middle East. There they participated against Iraq in the 1991 collective military action known as Operation Desert Storm. President Bill Clinton, in 1995, called reservists to active duty for participation in the NATO force in Bosnia.

Rio Treaty The Inter-American Treaty of Reciprocal Assistance of 1947, by which 22 American republics agree "that an armed attack by any State against an American State shall be considered as an attack against all the American States." The Rio Treaty was the first mutual security pact entered into by the United States, and it became a model for all subsequent ones. The treaty establishes a hemispheric security zone stretching from the North Pole to the South Pole. If an attack occurs within the zone, members agree to consult about collective measures to be undertaken, while retaining freedom to act individually. The treaty also includes principles and means by which conflicts between American states can be settled peacefully. Decisions concerning implementation of the treaty are reached through organs of the Organization of American States. *See also* ALLIANCE, page 530; ORGANIZATION OF AMERICAN STATES, page 570.

Significance   The Rio Treaty gained new importance as a result of increasing economic and political pressures in Latin America that threatened the region's stability. The major challenge to the Rio Treaty was for many years that posed by the establishment of a communist regime in Cuba. The Organization of American States, under the leadership of the United States, has sought to forestall further undemocratic communist takeovers in the hemisphere by including military protection from internal threats of subversion and revolution within the mutual guarantees provided by the treaty. However, 10 members of the OAS refused to become signatories to the Rio Treaty. In addition, U.S. support of the contra rebels' campaign to overthrow the government of Nicaragua led to opposition and disarray within the alliance in the 1980s.

Sanctions   A collective punitive action involving diplomatic, economic, or military measures against a state. Under the United Nations Charter (Chapter VII), when the Security Council determines that a threat to the peace, breach of peace, or act of aggression exists, members may be called upon to invoke military or nonmilitary sanctions against the law-breaking state. Since the adoption of the Uniting for Peace Resolution in 1950, the General Assembly is also empowered to levy sanctions against an aggressor by a two-thirds vote. Sanctions may include such actions as breaking diplomatic relations, embargo or blockade, and the use of force. *See also* COLLECTIVE SECURITY, page 538.

Significance   An international law enforcement system, like a nation's, must provide enforcement action to be effective. The *threat* of collective sanctions may be more effective in preventing aggression than the enforcement system in dealing with actual aggressions. The League of Nations attempted only once to employ sanctions (an economic boycott was levied against Italy after its attack upon Ethiopia in 1935) but failed to deter the aggressor. The United Nations levied military and economic sanctions against North Korea in 1950 and applied trade and diplomatic sanctions against Rhodesia, South Africa, and Serbia. In the Balkans, in the 1990s, sanctions—including an embargo on military equipment—were imposed in a United Nations effort to cope with aggression and atrocities. Nations tend to be reluctant to undertake collective military action against aggressor nations when few or no national interest objectives are perceived. After vacillating for several years, NATO forces, with American participation, undertook military actions against the Serbs with a series of air attacks, as well as with ground forces. Regional organizations may also employ sanctions, such as the diplomatic and economic sanctions undertaken by the Organization of American States against the Castro regime. The Gulf War of 1991 involved major UN military as well as economic and political sanctions against Iraq for its invasion of Kuwait.

Secretary of State   The leading Cabinet officer, who heads the Department of State and is charged with responsibility for formulating policies and conducting relations with foreign states. The Secretary of State has been recognized by statute as first of the Cabinet officials in the line of succession to the presidency following the Vice President, Speaker, and President pro tempore. Responsibilities of the office include the direction and supervision of policymaking and administrative functions vested in the State Department in Washington, D.C., the diplomatic and consular services, and special missions and agencies abroad. *See also* DEPARTMENT OF STATE, page 595.

Significance   The decision-making role of the Secretary of State may be great or insignificant, depending on the President in office. Some presidents, like Woodrow Wilson and Franklin Roosevelt, largely ignored their secretaries of state and handled foreign policy matters directly and personally. Other presidents have delegated much responsibility to their secretaries of state in foreign affairs. Some have appointed personal assistants who have played a more important role in making foreign policy decisions than the Secretary of State. Still other presidents have depended mainly on personal friends or a "kitchen cabinet" to advise them on critical foreign issues. Regardless of where the President gets most of his advice, the Secretary of State typically becomes a political target for the opposition party and is often held responsible by the public for foreign policy failures.

Selective Service   The conscription system under which the national government has drafted men for service in the armed forces. Selective Service is based on the constitutional provisions that give Congress the powers necessary "to raise" armies and "to provide" a navy. *See also* CONSCIENTIOUS OBJECTOR, page 302; SELECTIVE DRAFT LAW CASES, page 600.

Significance   The national government has drafted manpower for military service during and since the Civil War for wartime or emergency service. During World Wars I and II, millions of Americans were conscripted for military service. Peacetime Selective Service systems were also instituted by Congress in 1940 and again in 1948. Selective Service activity increased in the 1960s because of larger draft quotas for the Vietnam War. This often resulted in anti–Selective Service demonstrations. Large numbers of young men refused induction and either served prison terms or evaded the draft, with thousands of the latter fleeing to havens in Canada and Sweden. The Supreme Court established a basic precedent in 1918 when it rejected the assertion that Selective Service violates the constitutional provision against "involuntary servitude" by holding that compulsory military service is, rather, an "involuntary duty" and that draft law violators may be punished (*Selective Draft Law Cases,* 245 U.S. 366 [1918]). The Nixon administration ended peacetime Selective Service, but in 1980, the Carter administration restored the requirement for young men to register, though it did not provide for inducting them into the military service. In 1981, the Supreme Court held in *Rostker v. Goldberg* (453 U.S. 57) that women can constitutionally be excluded from the draft.

Sovereignty   A legal concept that, in international affairs, means statehood, political independence, and freedom from external control. The concept of sovereignty is one of the most potent and persistent myths that has helped to shape the nature of the global state system. *See also* SOVEREIGNTY, page 26.

Significance The importance of sovereignty in the modern state system has come largely from the psychological effect it has had on the decision-making processes of states. It has been a difficult force to overcome in creating political, military, and economic international organizations with decision-making powers. Sovereignty remains one of the major legal and psychological obstacles to the effective operation of the United Nations system.

Status Quo A descriptive term used by international political analysts to describe the foreign policy of a state that aims at preserving the existing distribution of power in the world. The concept is derived from the diplomatic term *status quo ante bellum,* which is a clause typically inserted into peace treaties providing for the restoration of prewar conditions.

Significance The term "status quo" is used as an analytical tool in seeking to understand and describe the motivations and actions of states in the struggle for power that characterizes the state system. States pursuing policies of revision or expansion provide the challenge that forces the status quo grouping to develop defensive policies and alliances. Following World War II, for 45 years the United States pursued a policy of the status quo vis-à-vis the revisionistic policies of the Soviet bloc.

Stockpiling The accumulation of strategic raw materials for use during a national crisis. The United States has amassed a stockpile of about 80 essential raw materials and metals that must be obtained abroad or that might be needed quickly during an emergency. The Plans and Preparedness Office of the Federal Emergency Management Agency (FEMA) has responsibility for stockpiled materials, which range from steel and aluminum to natural rubber, industrial diamonds, and such rare items as selenium and tantalum. The storehouse of agricultural products acquired by the national government under its price support program buttresses the strategic materials stockpile. This reserve has dwindled, however, under the impact of the Food for Peace foreign aid program and the domestic school lunch and food stamp programs. *See also* MOBILIZATION, page 563.

Significance Stockpiling offers a country rich enough to indulge in the practice not only a hedge against future military demands but a powerful weapon for economic warfare as well. A stockpile has domestic as well as international implications. The Johnson administration, for example, released quantities of steel and aluminum for domestic consumption to ward off inflationary price increases. The American stockpiling program gave impetus to the export earnings of some of the developing countries while the materials were being acquired, but when the buying program cease, inflated productive capacities in these countries led to oversupply and a depressing of prices. The market value of the United States strategic materials stockpile has varied considerably because of widely fluctuating supply and demand conditions in the world market and heavy inflationary pressures on primary commodity price structures.

Strategic Arms Reduction Talks (START)   The primary bilateral negotiation forum for U.S.–Russian disarmament discussions, formerly known as the Strategic Arms Limitation Talks (SALT) until President Ronald Reagan renamed them START in 1982. His proposals, like those made by President Jimmy Carter, contained three steps: (1) the reduction of ground- and submarine-based ballistic missles to one-third of current level; (2) cutting down to half the total of ballistic missiles deployed on each side; and (3) placing an equal ceiling on other elements of U.S. and Russian strategic forces. *See also* DÉTENTE, page 544; UNITED STATES ARMS CONTROL AND DISARMAMENT AGENCY (USACDA), page 597.

Significance   The START talks were built on the framework of negotiations conducted under SALT I, which began in Helsinki in 1969, and SALT II, in 1972, which initiated a series of discussions to promote balanced and verifiable limitations on strategic nuclear weapons between the United States and the Soviet Union. Some agreement was reached. The Soviet Union invaded Afghanistan, and President Ronald Reagan, who felt we had been negotiating from a position of weakness and that the Soviets needed a greater incentive to disarm, began a great expansion of the arms race. In a 1988 meeting with General Secretary Mikhail Gorbachev, progress was made on a START treaty that greatly reduced strategic missiles on both sides. By 1992, Russian-American agreement had been reached by Presidents George Bush and Boris Yeltsin for achieving a major reduction in nuclear weapons and delivery systems, and destruction of nuclear weapons had begun. The U.S. Senate ratified this START II treaty in 1996. The end of the Cold War speeded up the implementation of all nuclear disarmament agreements. In 1994, President Bill Clinton reached an agreement with Russian President Boris Yeltsin, with each pledging that their nation's nuclear missiles would no longer be aimed at the other, but rather targeted on the oceans.

Strategy   A plan or preparations for the potential use of armed forces to achieve a specific goal or result. Strategy in the military field involves the science and art of planning and directing major military operations against a foe or potential foe. The President, aided by top-level military and civilian planning agencies, is responsible for developing the nation's basic defense strategies. Because events never transpire exactly as planned in basic strategies, contingency planning is an essential part of any successful strategy. *See also* TACTICS, page 581.

Significance   A broad, carefully developed strategy is indispensable in the achievement of most major goals, especially if they involve competitive situations. In the United States, current military strategic thinking provides for the execution, if necessary, of three simultaneous wars: nuclear, conventional, and brushfire. This strategic rationale has been used to justify recent military budgets. Included in current strategic thinking that guides the nation's policymakers are the assumptions that the East-West rapprochement will continue, that the United States will not be faced with the threat of military action from a collapsing communist world, and that the nation will be able to avoid a major land war in Asia, the Middle East, or Africa. By 1990, the major strategic considerations for the United States' policy makers involved the disintegration of the Warsaw Pact and domestic changes occurring in all East European countries and the former Soviet Union.

Summit Diplomacy   Discussions carried on between the leaders of countries who seek to gain an understanding of mutual problems and reach agreement on some of them. Most presidents, starting with Woodrow Wilson, have engaged in one form or another of summit diplomacy. President Ronald Reagan, for example, engaged in four summit conferences with his Soviet counterpart, Mikhail Gorbachev. Economic summits have also brought the leaders of the seven leading democratic states of the West together annually to discuss their mutual economic and political problems. In another summit approach, President Jimmy Carter brought Egypt's President Anwar Sadat and Israel's Prime Minister Menachem Begin to the conference table in 1978, leading to the signing of the Camp David Accords, followed in 1979 by a formal peace treaty. In 1994, President Clinton brought together two once-bitter enemies, Israeli Prime Minister Yitzhak Rabin and Yasir Arafat, chairman of the Palestine Liberation Organization (PLO), for a signing of an agreement for self-rule in Jericho and the Gaza Strip. Additional agreements followed. Both Anwar Sadat and Yitzhak Rabin were assassinated, the former by Muslim fundamentalists and the latter by a Jewish fundamentalist. *See also* CAMP DAVID ACCORDS, page 535; ECONOMIC SUMMIT, page 397.

Significance   Summit diplomacy is partly a public ceremony aimed at reducing international tension and partly an effort to achieve concrete results. It provides an opportunity for diverse personalities to meet and gain insights about each other. Although highly dramatic, summitry is unlikely to produce spectacular results, despite public expectations. Its main purpose may be to break deadlocks over specifics at lower diplomatic levels or reach agreement on principles at the highest level so that details can be worked out by subordinates. A summit conference is most successful and least controversial when details are worked out before the conference, and the leaders merely engage in formal acceptance. In the nuclear age, when major war would not only be catastrophic but suicidal, any summit movement in the direction of arms control or disarmament agreements has received overwhelming support from the American public. In the 1987 Washington Summit, President Reagan and First Secretary Gorbachev reached an unprecedented level of agreement to eliminate all short- and intermediate-range missiles in Europe, including their nuclear warheads, and this INF Treaty was ratified by the two leaders at the Moscow Summit. President George Bush, in his first two years in office, had three face-to-face meetings with President Gorbachev. Their third, in Helsinki in 1990, focused on the Middle East crisis and the problem of developing solidarity against Iraq's Saddam Hussein. In 1991, the two leaders met in Madrid where they sought to encourage Arab and Israeli delegations to work out a solution to basic Middle East problems. In 1992, with the Soviet Union dissolved and Boris Yeltsin the leader of Russia, President Bush continued his summit diplomacy with Yeltsin. President Clinton, in 1994, reached an agreement with President Boris Yeltsin of Russia; each nation would no longer aim their strategic nuclear missiles at each other but, rather, target them on the oceans.

Tactics   The art and science of making decisions concerning the deployment of troops, the weapons to be used, the timing of operations, and other decisions aimed at achieving a military success in a battle or limited engagement. Tactics, unlike strategy, involves short-term, relatively small-scale planning, usually carried out by commanders in the field or middle-level staffs. A decision to engage in terror bombing of enemy cities, for example, is a matter of strategy decided at the highest political and military levels, while the decision of a military commander to use bombing to support his troops in an offensive against enemy forces is a tactical decision. *See also* STRATEGY, page 579.

Significance   A successful military operation depends on effective overall strategic planning implemented by decisive tactical deployment and uses of military forces. Tactical errors may occasionally alter strategic plans, as in the abortive Bay of Pigs invasion of Cuba in 1961, which led to the American-Soviet missile crisis in 1962, and a pledge by the President that no further invasions would be attempted. In the field of nuclear weapons, many observers believe that, once employed in a tactical situation, it would be impossible to limit their use, and a massive strategic nuclear exchange would follow. To increase the nation's tactical capability, the Bush administration began in the 1990s to place increased emphasis on the development of a global Rapid Deployment Force (RDF), as a result of the Persian Gulf experience.

Tariff   A tax levied on imports to help protect a nation's industry, business, labor, and agriculture from foreign competition or to raise revenue. Tariffs are discriminatory if they apply unequally on similar products from different countries and are retaliatory if motivated by the creation of trade barriers by other countries. *See also* MOST-FAVORED-NATION STATUS, page 564; PROTECTIONISM, page 573; RECIPROCAL TRADE AGREEMENTS ACT, page 602; UNITED STATES INTERNATIONAL TRADE COMMISSION, page 599.

Significance   Tariffs have been used by the United States since 1789 as the principle means of protecting domestic producers from foreign competition. For many years prior to the adoption of an income tax, the tariff was also a primary source of revenue for the federal government. The United States encouraged mutual reductions in tariffs through the Reciprocal Trade Agreements Act of 1934, the General Agreement on Tariffs and Trade of 1947, the Trade Expansion Act of 1962, and the Trade Acts of 1974 and 1988. The process of lowering tariff rates among most trading countries continued in the Uruguay Round of the General Agreement on Tariffs and Trade (GATT). Most-favored-nation (MFN) status, accorded to more than 150 countries, has done much to moderate the impact of tariffs on trade. Tariffs were also lowered under a U.S.–Canada Free Trade Agreement that went into effect on January 1, 1989. This agreement was expanded under the Bush and Clinton administrations to include Mexico in the North American Free Trade Agreement (NAFTA). Critics argued that companies would move to low-wage sites in Mexico, with the resulting loss of American jobs. Supporters hold that free trade benefits all, tends to raise the standard of living, and, in the long haul, creates more jobs.

Third World   Those developing countries of Asia, Africa, and Latin America that constitute a majority of the international state system, that are—with the exception of the oil-exporting countries—relatively poor, "have-not," and underdeveloped in contrast with the capitalist (First) and former communist (Second) "worlds." The United Nations in its economic aid programs has recognized the existence within the Third World of about 50 countries that constitute a Fourth World group of nations. They are the poorest, with the lowest per capita incomes, few natural resources, and very limited financial reserves. Most Third World states have gained their freedom and independence from colonial rule and are now seeking to develop and modernize. The Third World as a powerful political force in international relations began to emerge in 1964 at the first meeting of the United Nations Conference on Trade and Development (UNCTAD), when a bloc of Asian, African, and Latin American nations began to meet as the "Caucus of the Seventy-Seven," or "Group of Seventy-Seven" (also known as G-77), to achieve political goals through voting solidarity. Membership (although there is no formal organization or membership roll) now exceeds 130 states. *See also* UNITED NATIONS GENERAL ASSEMBLY, page 586.

Significance   The Third World functions as an effective decision-making bloc in the United Nations General Assembly and at large international conferences. Third World nations split on some issues, such as those that grew out of the Cold War and those related to the law of the sea. On other issues, especially those dealing with economic development, ending colonialism, and human rights, they have a record of almost complete voting solidarity. On key issues, the Third World almost always raises a two-thirds majority vote in the General Assembly. As a result, the United States, Russia, and Western Europe are often on the losing side of issues, whereas China has increasingly voted with the Third World and is seeking to achieve a role of leadership in that bloc. Third World countries have also increasingly sought to secure capital for financing their development by joining together into cartel arrangements to control supply and fix world prices for such products as oil, copper, bauxite, sugar, and coffee. They have also obtained Generalized System of Preferences (GSP) concessions from Western nations, and some of their exports to these industrialized countries are free of import duties. Some Third World countries, for example, Cuba and North Korea, remain estranged from the capitalist countries of the world, especially the United States. A meeting of historic importance for the planet took place in 1992 in Rio de Janeiro, where 178 nations met to lay groundwork for solving global environmental problems. Participating Third World countries argued that environmental problems begin with economic inequality. They are truly faced with a dilemma: They criticize the industrial nations for excessive development of the environment, and, at the same time, call for help from these same nations to develop their own economies. As a result they, too, will become polluters of land, air and water. However, the Earth Summit concluded agreements on (1) protecting the ozone layer, (2) controlling global warming, (3) preserving world forests, (4) maintaining biodiversity of plant and animal species, (5) limiting greenhouse gas emissions, and (6) maintaining sustainable development. President George Bush refused to accept the agreement, but it was signed by President Bill Clinton.

Treaty   A formal agreement entered into between two or more countries. The treaty process includes negotiation, signing, ratification, exchange of ratifications, publishing and proclamation, and treaty execution. Treaties between only two signatory states are bilateral, whereas those with more than two parties are multilateral. Treaties may expire at the end of a specified time period, when certain conditions have been met, or by mutual agreement. Renunciation of a treaty by one of its parties may occur when a state of war exists or when conditions have been substantially altered (*rebus sic stantibus*). In the United States, all treaties are negotiated under the direction of the President, with some members of the Senate occasionally participating under the constitutional provision that treaties be made "by and with the advice and consent of the Senate." Treaties must be approved by a two-thirds vote in the Senate, followed by presidential ratification if the Senate's version is acceptable. *See also* EXECUTIVE AGREEMENT, page 190; *Missouri v. Holland,* page 600; RATIFICATION, page 574.

Significance   Multilateral treaties have become the major source of international law. In the United States, treaties are part of the supreme law of the land and take precedence over state constitutions and laws. The courts have never declared a treaty to be unconstitutional. The Supreme Court has held that a treaty may increase the powers of Congress beyond the powers prescribed in the Constitution (*Missouri v. Holland,* 252 U.S. 416 [1920]). Increasingly, American presidents have come to depend on executive agreements rather than treaties; the latter are used when strong congressional and public opinion support are essential. Very few treaties have been voted down by the Senate in the years since adoption of the Constitution, but many have been killed by Senate inaction. Treaties voted down, however, were often very important, such as those providing for U.S. membership in the League of Nations and the first World Court.

Trilateral Commission   An organization that meets annually to discuss and debate issues relevant to its three-region membership: North America, Japan, and Western Europe. Trilateral Commission members include several hundred nongovernmental representatives who reflect the interests of their respective regions. The organization was created in 1973 to provide a forum in which political, economic, and security issues affecting the three regions are discussed and debated. Because the Trilateral Commission represents three distinct regions of the world, its members have become obsessed with the number three, meeting each year for three days, rotating meetings among the three regions, and publishing task force *Triangle Papers* and a newsletter called the *Trialogue. See also,* PRESSURE GROUP, page 104.

Significance   The Trilateral Commission is a prestigious but controversial organization. Because it focuses mainly on economic problems and issues of the industrialized nations of the three regions, right-wing and left-wing groups have often charged it with playing a conspiratorial role in world affairs. The right views it as an agent of world socialism, whereas the left tends to regard it as a representative of monopoly capitalism. Its members include a number of well-known and highly respected former policy leaders from public as well as private sectors. This is why its recommendations are often taken seriously by American policy makers.

Truman Doctrine   The policy, adopted by President Harry Truman in 1947, that called for American support for all free peoples resisting armed subjugation by internal or outside forces. The policy was aimed expressly at halting communist expansion in southeastern Europe and was expounded in a speech to Congress in which President Truman asked for an appropriation of $400 million for military and economic aid to Greece and Turkey. The doctrine was linked with the policy of "containment" that called for the building of "situations of strength" around the periphery of communist power. *See also* CONTAINMENT, page 540; PRESIDENTIAL DOCTRINES, page 199.

Significance   The Truman Doctrine marked the official acceptance of the "containment" philosophy of building up free-world strength to halt communist expansionism. The Truman administration followed it up with the development of the Marshall Plan (1947), a technical assistance program (1949), the North Atlantic Treaty (1949), and a mutual security program (1951). The Truman Doctrine, as applied to Greece and Turkey, was successful in helping the loyalists win the Greek civil war and in building up Turkey as a bastion of free-world strength with a modern army. The policy of containment of communism embodied in the Truman Doctrine was continued by succeeding presidents, but more recent administrations sought to moderate the policy by fostering a détente between the United States and the two major communist states. In the late 1980s and early 1990s, the threat from the Soviets and East European communist states disintegrated as the Warsaw Pact collapsed, as East and West Germany became a single, unified state, and as the practice of communism began to change in many former communist states to democracy and capitalism. As a result, the Truman Doctrine became largely an anachronism. The ultimate success of the Truman Doctrine occurred when the Soviet Union was dissolved into fifteen independent and basically noncommunist states in the early 1990s.

Unification   The integration of the military services of the United States. Under the National Security Acts of 1947 and 1949, the Army, Navy, and Air Force were unified under a single Department of Defense. *See also* NATIONAL SECURITY ACTS, page 601.

Significance   Critics of separate military departments charged that the system promoted interservice rivalries, prevented integrated planning, increased military costs, encouraged recruiting competition, promoted budget battles, and resulted in duplication and inefficiency. Supporters of independent departments claimed that a single military chief would be too powerful, that it would lead to charges of favoritism against the single head, and that the separate service approach had proved itself in World Wars I and II. Unification has not, in fact, eliminated interservice rivalries. In addition, serious cleavages among the three branches, concerning such questions as basic strategy, budget allocation, and missile development responsibility, have continued.

United Nations Charter   A multilateral treaty that serves as the constitution for the United Nations Organization. The charter was drawn up and signed in San Francisco on June 26, 1945; it was ratified by 51 nations and put into effect on October 24, 1945, since designated United Nations Day. The document consists of a preamble and 111 articles that provide for the creation of 6 major organs and the powers to be exercised by each. The Charter has been amended 3 times, with 2 amendments increasing the size of the Economic and Social Council from 18 to 36 to 54. The third amendment increased the Security Council from 11 to 15 and changed the majority needed to make a decision from 7 to 9.

Significance   The charter represents an effort by the community of nations to establish norms of international conduct by outlawing war, providing for the peaceful settlement of international disputes, and encouraging cooperation among nations in dealing with economic and social problems. Like the U.S. Constitution, the charter has proved to be a flexible document, subject to broad interpretations. Without this feature of adaptability, the United Nations would probably have collapsed under the impact of the Cold War. For many years, the charter had to be adapted to deal with East-West Cold War problems and, more recently, to deal with North-South conflicts between Third World states and the industrialized states of the First (capitalist) World and the Second (former Communist) World. Since 1945, there has been more than a threefold increase in membership in the United Nations, with 185 nations of the world now subscribing to world community principles enunciated in the charter. The fiftieth anniversary of the ratification of the Charter and the creation of the United Nations was celebrated on October 24, 1995, with more than 100 world leaders, including President Fidel Castro of Cuba, in attendance at United Nations headquarters in New York.

United Nations Economic and Social Council (ECOSOC)   A major organ of the United Nations concerned with promoting higher standards of living and social justice throughout the world. The council originally consisted of 18 members but was enlarged by UN Charter amendment in 1965 to 27 and in 1973 to 54 members. All members are selected by the General Assembly of the United Nations for 3-year terms, with one-third elected each year. Responsibilities include (1) coordinating the activities of the Specialized Agencies, such as the World Health Organization (WHO) and the Food and Agriculture Organization (FAO); (2) administering United Nations functions in economic, social, educational, cultural, and related areas; (3) promoting worldwide observance of human rights and fundamental freedoms; and (4) recommending specific policies and programs for adoption by the General Assembly. *See also* THIRD WORLD, page 582.

Significance   The Economic and Social Council has successfully coordinated the operations of diverse agencies in seeking to solve pressing social and economic problems. It has established five economic commissions in the developing world: (1) the Economic Commission for Africa (ECA); (2) the Economic Commission for Europe (ECE); (3) the Economic Commission for Latin America and the Caribbean (ECLAC); (4) the Economic and Social Commission for Asia and the Pacific (ESCAP); and (5) the Economic and Social Commission for Western Asia (ESCWA). Each has the responsibility for making comprehensive studies and recommendations on how economic and social conditions can be improved in its region. It has also established various commissions to study international problems, including Fiscal, Human

Rights, Narcotic Drugs, Population, Social, Statistical, Status of Women, and Transport and Communications. The charter amendments enlarging ECOSOC were initiated by the Third World bloc of states, which demanded greater representation on the council.

United Nations General Assembly   The major organ of the United Nations in which all members are equally represented. The Assembly has evolved into the focus for the multifold activities of the United Nations. In one sense, it is a continuing international conference; in another, it is an international forum in which each member nation can discuss its international problems with all others. It is a "Town Meeting of the World," through which world public opinion can be aroused and brought to bear on a problem. Its functions directly or indirectly relate to almost all of the activities carried on by the world organization. Specific responsibilities include (1) election of some or all members of the other five major organs, (2) an annual review of the activities of all segments of the organization; (3) control over the budget; and (4) decision making and recommendations to members on all subjects within United Nations jurisdiction. Measures are adopted ordinarily by a simple majority vote, but "important questions," as defined by the charter or as determined by a majority of the Assembly, require a two-thirds vote of members present and voting. The most important power of the Assembly—to deal with acts of aggression and breaches of the peace when the Security Council is stalemated by a veto—was not vested in the Assembly by the charter but was assumed by it in 1950 through its adoption of the Uniting for Peace Resolution. *See also* UNITED NATIONS CHARTER, page 584.

Significance   Through an evolutionary process, the Assembly has become the central organ of the United Nations system. With the admittance of many new members, mostly African states, the prestige and responsibilities of the Assembly have grown accordingly. The Assembly in its 50-year history helped to settle many disputes, stopped several conflicts and adopted numerous resolutions setting forth norms for guiding international conduct. The Assembly has also helped in promotion of freer trade, the economic development of many nations, and the expansion of the scope of international law; further, it has aided colonial peoples in securing independence and statehood and has strengthened the concern for human rights in the world. Most of all, it has served as a conference center where representatives of almost every nation in the world can meet and discuss their mutual problems. Although the United States dominated the decision process in the General Assembly during its early years, influence and voting power have moved relentlessly toward the Third World majority, leading to a growing apprehension and, in some cases, open hostility toward the United Nations by the American public. However, the end of the Cold War resulted in a new effective role for the Security Council in meeting threats and acts of aggression, as demonstrated in the Persian Gulf situation that produced unanimous council votes declaring Iraq to be an aggressor. Thus, the role of the General Assembly in this important area has been substantially reduced, as the role of the Security Council has increased. The Security Council, working with the NATO command structure, demonstrated its capabilities in 1995 by launching air attacks on the Bosnian Serbs that were the key to bringing the leaders of Bosnia, Croatia, and Serbia to the conference table in Dayton, Ohio, where they successfully initialed a peace treaty.

United Nations International Court of Justice (ICJ)   An international tribunal, known as the World Court, established as one of the six major organs of the United Nations to adjudicate justiciable disputes among nations and to render advisory opinions to organs of the United Nations. The World Court was established in 1945 under an agreement that was annexed to the United Nations Charter and to which all United Nations member states are parties. Nonmembers of the United Nations may adhere to the agreement under conditions set by the General Assembly and the Security Council and may use The Court if they accept its jurisdiction. The Court, with its headquarters at the Hague, has fifteen judges elected by the General Assembly and the Security Council, no two of whom may be nationals of the same state. Decisions rendered by the Court are final and, if any party to a case refuses to heed the judgment of the Court, the other party has recourse to the Security Council, which may decide on a course of action. *See also* INTERNATIONAL CRIMINAL TRIBUNAL, page 556; INTERNATIONAL LAW, page 557.

Significance   The usefulness of the Court has been impaired because its jurisdiction (power to decide cases) extends only to cases in which the states concerned have accepted its jurisdiction. No national court system could function under such a limitation. Attempts to correct this weakness through compulsory jurisdiction under the "optional clause" (Article 36 of the Court's statute) have largely been unsuccessful because of self-serving reservations attached to the acceptance of compulsory jurisdiction by many nations, including the United States (Connally Amendment). Only about 40 cases had been decided and 17 advisory opinions rendered by the Court by 1982. Unless leading members of the United Nations resolve their major political differences, the Court may continue to play a limited role, having little impact on world affairs. The Court's weakness was demonstrated in 1980, when Iran ignored its order to release American hostages. The United States has generally supported the Court in the belief that world peace and security are unlikely to be achieved without world law and an effective court system. In 1984, the Sandinista government of Nicaragua brought a case to the Court claiming damages from the United States for its support of the contra rebels and for the mining of Nicaraguan harbors carried out by the CIA. Although the court in *Nicaragua v. United States* supported Nicaraguan claims, the United States did not participate in the case and refused to accept the jurisdiction of the Court or to honor its decision. The United States was criticized by many nations for its refusal to accept the Court's jurisdiction. In 1990, the Sandinistas were voted out of power, and the court cases became moot.

United Nations Secretariat   An organized body of officials and civil servants who have the responsibility of fulfilling administrative, secretarial, and housekeeping functions for an international organization. The United Nations Secretariat is one of the six major organs of the world organization. Its formal structure includes a secretary-general and eight assistant secretaries-general, each of the latter heading a major department (Security, Economic,

Social, Trusteeship, Legal, Information, General Services, and Administrative and Financial). *See also* UNITED NATIONS SECRETARY-GENERAL, page 588.

Significance   The success or failure of an international organization often depends on the efficiency of its secretariat and the capabilities and dedication of its staff. The United Nations has fostered the concept of an international civil service whose members serve the United Nations without regard for the views of their own countries. Every international organization utilizes some form of secretariat to perform the necessary routine functions of its day-to-day operations. Secretariat officials also pay an important role in the life of an international organization by taking the initiative in solving problems and by providing leadership, continuity, and professionalism.

United Nations Secretary-General   The chief administrative officer of the United Nations, who heads the Secretariat. The Secretary-General is chosen by the General Assembly, upon recommendation by the Security Council, for five-year terms. The United Nations Charter, in an attempt to strengthen the office of Secretary-General over that of its League of Nations predecessor, gave the Secretary-General authority to place security questions before the Security Council. *See also* UNITED NATIONS SECRETARIAT, page 587.

Significance   The role of the Secretary-General has greatly expanded with the assignment of various political responsibilities in addition to administrative duties. Although required to operate within the framework of Assembly or Security Council resolutions, the Secretary-General has considerable decision-making power in implementing these resolutions. Trygve Lie of Norway, the first Secretary-General of the United Nations, provided effective leadership until a Western-Soviet split over the Korean War reduced his ability to function in that role. Dag Hammarskjöld of Sweden, who replaced Lie in 1953, further expanded the executive role of the office and maintained the support of all United Nations members until the Congo crisis of 1960. At that time, the Soviet Union charged Hammarskjöld with partisanship in his handling of the Congo situation. Following the death of Hammarskjöld in 1961, U Thant of Burma was appointed Secretary-General. U Thant, who served for ten years, saw his role primarily as a conciliator. He was succeeded by Kurt Waldheim of Austria in 1972, who continued the U Thant conciliation approach, as did his successor Javier Pérez de Cuéllar, who assumed the office of Secretary-General in 1982 and was reelected for a second five-year term in 1987. In 1992, the African bloc finally succeeded in having one of its own—Egyptian diplomat Boutros Boutros-Ghali—placed at the helm of the world organization for a five-year term. In order to strengthen and revitalize the UN peacekeeping efforts, he developed the Agenda for Peace, which emphasized diplomacy and peacemaking. He recommended the creation of a rapid deployment force consisting of 1,000 troops from each member state, which would be ready within 24 hours to intercede in any country when conflict arose. The inability of the UN to halt the aggression of the Bosnian Serbs led to NATO air strikes in 1995, which were aided on the ground by a British-French rapid reaction force. These actions were successful in pushing back the Serbs, establishing a cease-fire, and bringing the three presidents of Bosnia, Croatia, and Serbia to the conference table in Dayton, Ohio. Boutros-Ghali's efforts to expand the UN peacekeeping endeavors as well as to assist developing countries—like efforts of his predecessors—suffered from financial problems stemming from member nations who failed to pay their dues. The United States was much criticized for its failure to do so; it owes more than any other nation. In 1996, the United States sought to block the re-election of Boutros-Ghali because of his failure to institute reforms.

United Nations Security Council   One of the six major organs of the United Nations, which was given primary responsibility for maintaining peace and security in the world. A charter amendment supported by the Third World bloc in 1965 increased the size of the Security Council from eleven to fifteen and provided for a vote of nine instead of seven for making decisions. There are five permanent members—Britain, China, France, Russia, and the United States—and ten nonpermanent members elected by the General Assembly for two-year periods, five chosen each year. Procedural and substantive decisions are made by an affirmative vote of nine members but, in the latter case, a negative vote cast by any permanent member constitutes a veto and stops all action. When considering peaceful settlement measures, a council member that is a party to the dispute must abstain from voting. Nations that are not members of the council may be invited to participate without a vote in council deliberations if they are involved in a dispute being considered. Chapter VII of the charter gives the Security Council the responsibility to "determine the existence of any threat to the peace, breach of the peace, or act of aggression." The council can make recommendations or take enforcement action to restore peace and security. *See also* COLLECTIVE SECURITY, page 538.

Significance   The Security Council was given the important responsibility by the charter on the assumption that the great powers would continue to cooperate in the postwar period to maintain peace and security. Instead, the major threats to world peace involved great-power rivalry, and more than 100 vetoes reduced the effectiveness of the council. A new role was thrust upon the General Assembly, which replaced the council as the central organ of the United Nations security system. Then, in 1990, when Iraq invaded Kuwait and threatened Saudi Arabia, the Security Council functioned as originally intended, levying sanctions against the aggressor with unanimous votes. These sanctions will continue until UN inspection teams are satisfied that all chemical, biological, and nuclear agents of war, and the means to deliver them, are destroyed. This newfound unity was a result of the end of the Cold War and a newly cooperative spirit on the part of China and some of the Third World nations. The importance of the council today includes its role of providing machinery for a continuous forum for great power negotiation. In the early 1990s, proposals were made to include Japan and Germany as permanent members, thus granting them the veto power, but no formal action has been taken. In its first major test since the end of the Cold War, the Security Council vacillated, thereby permitting aggressive actions, especially by the Bosnian Serb army. Under American leadership in 1995, this vacillation changed to a policy of involvement in diplomatic and military action. The Security Council working through NATO nations brought about a cease-fire, and a peace treaty was written and signed by the presidents of Bosnia, Croatia, and Serbia. This was followed by the creation of a NATO implementation force (IFOR) drawn from 25 member countries, with one-third of the 60,000 troops provided by the United States.

United Nations Trusteeship Council   One of the six major organs of the United Nations, established to help the General Assembly supervise the administration of the international trusteeship system. Members of the council included those nations that had administered trust territories, permanent members of the Security Council, and enough elected members to provide for parity between nontrust and trust-administering states on the council. Trust territories included (1) former mandates of the League of Nations, (2) Axis colonies, and (3) colonies voluntarily placed under trusteeship. No colonial power volunteered to place a colony under the system. Council powers included considering reports, accepting petitions, and making periodic visits to trust territories. Administration of "strategic" trust territories was supervised by the Security Council rather than by the Trusteeship Council, because of their military importance.

Significance   Through its supervisory role, the Trusteeship Council has helped all former trust territories achieve self-government. Libya and Tanganyika, for example, became independent states. Through an United Nations negotiated settlement, Namibia, after 75 years of South African rule, became the last African colony to achieve independence in March 1990. The United Nations Trust Territory of the Pacific Islands, which was administered by the United States under the jurisdiction of the United Nations, has been granted some measure of self-government and independence. The Northern Marianas Islands have been given Commonwealth status similar to Puerto Rico, and its peoples are citizens of the United States; the Republic of the Marshall Islands, the Federated States of Micronesia, and the Republic of Palau have entered into "compacts of free association" with the United States, in which they exercise authority in domestic affairs, but foreign relations and defense power remain with the United States. In total, the Trusteeship Council helped transform 11 trust territories into independent states and contributed to the march to independence of more than 70 nontrust colonies. Its mission has been completed, and the United Nations has begun debate on a replacement council, which many have suggested should be an environmental council.

Uruguay Round   A major series of multilateral trade negotiations aimed at keeping world markets open by combating protectionism. The Uruguay Round began in 1986 when officials from almost 100 member states of the General Agreement on Tariffs and Trade (GATT) met in Punta del Este to launch a new round of multilateral trade negotiations. Reductions in tariffs on both goods and services were considered in the negotiations. The Uruguay Round negotiations continued for several years at GATT's headquarters in Geneva and were concluded in 1993. *See also* GENERAL AGREEMENT ON TARIFFS AND TRADE, page 551; PROTECTIONISM, page 573; WORLD TRADE ORGANIZATION, page 592.

Significance   The Uruguay Round was an attempt to avoid a major catastrophe similar to the world Depression of the 1930s. It was the eighth major series of multilateral trade negotiations conducted by GATT since 1947, when the organization was created. The most important of these were the Kennedy Round (1964–1967), which opened up the European Community to trade from outside and lowered world tariffs by one-third, and the Tokyo Round (1973–1978), which sought to help Third World nations develop by opening Western markets to them and to encourage world trade by reducing quotas and other nontariff barriers. The Uruguay Round was a continuation of the half-century campaign to increase world trade. The Trade Act of 1988 increased the President's authority to negotiate in the Uruguay Round. In 1993, the Uruguay Round was concluded with the lowering of tariffs around the globe and the creation of the World Trade Organization (WTO), which the United States joined in 1994. The Uruguay Round for the first time attempted to set rules for international trade in services and intellectual property rights (patents, industrial designs, trademarks, and copyrights), as well as for trade-related investment measures.

War Powers   The authority expressly granted by the Constitution, implied from it, or inherent in the duty of protecting the nation from its enemies. War powers include those granted to Congress to tax and spend for the common defense, to declare war and make rules concerning captures, to raise and support armies and provide a navy, to enact military law, and to oversee the state militias. Moreover, the elastic clause permits Congress to do whatever is necessary and proper in executing these powers. The President, as commander in chief, has the inherent power to do whatever is necessary to protect the nation, subject to judicial scrutiny. In time of crisis, Congress delegates legislative powers to the President as "emergency powers." *See also* COMMANDER IN CHIEF, page 188; EMERGENCY POWERS, page 189; WAR POWERS ACT, page 603.

Significance   Although defense and war powers are subject to constitutional limitations in the same way as other powers, they have been stretched to their limits during serious crises. Presidents Abraham Lincoln, Franklin Roosevelt, and Harry Truman regarded the war powers as a special and undefined category of powers that can be exercised whenever the security of the nation is threatened. Congress, the public, and the courts have generally accepted the primacy of the President's role and his exercise of vast powers during time of war. Under conditions of modern warfare, the war powers include control over the domestic economic as well as the military phases of the conflict.

World Debt Crisis   The unstable international situation that results from the inability of many Third World and Eastern European states to make installment payments on their massive debts owed mainly to American and European banks and to governmental loan agencies. The world debt crisis involves overextended debt accumulation by receiving countries, overextended loans by many banks, and the threat of massive defaults that could lead to a severe weakening or collapse of the world economy. The rescheduling of debt payments for some of the debtor countries involves capital flows from thousands of separate banks. Most of the countries continue to borrow funds, which are then used to make payments on principal and interest owed. Many of the same banks that made the original loans are now involved in making additional loans to try to avoid default action by recipient governments. The International Monetary Fund (IMF) has taken the lead in the effort to meet the crisis and avoid fiscal disaster. In recognition of that threat, Congress passed the Monetary Control Act of 1980, which permits the Federal Reserve System to assume part of the international debt by issuing Federal Reserve notes as collateral. *See also* FEDERAL RESERVE SYSTEM, page 400; THIRD WORLD, page 582.

Significance   The world debt crisis has produced individual and collective actions by Western fiscal authorities who recognize that it could plunge much of the world into an unparalleled financial debacle. The IMF, the Bank for International Settlements (BIS), and the United States Federal Reserve System are working with lending agencies and with the debt-ridden countries in an effort to avoid additional defaults by renegotiating the debt and rescheduling payments. Economists and governmental experts from the Group of 30 (the 30 major industrialized nations) have tried to plan how to avoid a major collapse, or how to deal with it should it occur. The debt accumulation was largely a product of the oil crisis and the major inflation of the 1970s, plus the overwhelming desire of Third World countries to develop and modernize. The United States has taken the leadership in providing governmental funds to avoid major default action that could result in the bankruptcy of many American banks. Critics of such policies demand that the banks work out their own salvation and not depend on a government bailout. The United States, which in 1980 was still the world's largest creditor nation, by 1992 had become the world's largest debtor, but it was still not considered to be part of the world debt crisis.

World Trade Organization (WTO)   An international organization of more than 100 members created by the General Agreement on Tariffs and Trade (GATT) in 1994, at the conclusion of the Uruguay Round. The WTO consists of a council that functions as the political and governing arm of the organization, which is headed by a director-general, with seven top officers who oversee the implementation of the trade agreement. The WTO has authority to penalize nations that violate the principles set forth in the accord. *See also* GENERAL AGREEMENT ON TARIFFS AND TRADE, page 551; URUGUAY ROUND, page 590.

Significance   The World Trade Organization is in the process of developing a set of principles and practices to guide and govern the trade relationships among members. At the end of World War II, the economic game plan of the victorious allies was aimed at creating new international institutions to avoid the pitfalls that had restricted trade during the Great Depression of the 1930s. Three new organizations emerged to accomplish this: the International Monetary Fund, the World Bank, and the World Trade Organization. Whereas the first two were quickly accepted, numerous controversies developed over the nature and role of the third. As a result, GATT was created as a substitute, and trade arrangements were developed through the conclusion of trade agreements instead of trade treaties, thus keeping the U.S. Congress out of trade decision making. Now, 50 years later, the U.S. Congress has accepted the idea and signed the treaty for the new World Trade Organization. The members of the new WTO agreed to reduce tariffs, including those on agricultural products, which had been a major stumbling block for many years. Import quotas on certain items were also banned, as, for example, Japan's exclusion of rice imports from other nations. Protection for patents, trademarks, and copyrights was also provided. The first trade pact negotiated under the WTO, in 1995, made it easier for banks, insurance companies, and securities firms to do business around the world. The United States refused to participate, but its business groups will still benefit because all benefits are applicable to all members of WTO. In 1996, the United States was assessed a fine for "discriminatory pricing." The United States denied entrance to oil that contained more pollutants than is permitted by the Clean Air Act, but, in a suit filed with the WTO, Brazil and Venezuela asserted that the same quality of oil was in fact pumped, sold, and burned within the United States.

IMPORTANT AGENCIES

Agency for International Development (AID)   A semi-independent agency that functions as a component of the United States International Development Cooperation Agency (IDCA) in directing economic and technical assistance aid programs to foreign nations. Created by Congress in the Act for International Development of 1961, replacing the International Cooperation Administration (ICA), AID administers the foreign aid program through developmental loans and grants, investment surveys and guarantees, and developmental research. It is headed by an administrator who has a dual role as a chief of the operating agency and political adviser to the IDCA director and the President. *See also* FOREIGN AID, page 550; INTERNATIONAL DEVELOPMENT COOPERATION AGENCY, page 596.

Significance   The Agency for International Development was created particularly to implement President John F. Kennedy's Alliance for Progress program, but its operations became worldwide. It became increasingly important as the United States stepped up the pace of its competition with the Soviet Union and other communist states in helping less developed nations progress. Although military aid outweighed economic aid during the 1950s, the Kennedy, Johnson, Nixon, Ford, and Carter administrations all stressed economic aid programs during the 1960s and 1970s. The role of AID, however, was reduced in the 1980s as a result of substantial budget cuts made by the Reagan administration and Congress in economic aid and a major expansion in military aid. In the 1990s, job losses and poor economic conditions led to a growing opposition to foreign aid among American voters.

Central Intelligence Agency (CIA)   An agency, headed by a director appointed by the President with Senate approval, that functions under the National Security Council to coordinate intelligence activities in the interest of national security. The CIA evaluates raw intelligence data supplied by the Army, Navy, Air Force, State Department, and other intelligence-gathering civilian and military agencies. This information is disseminated among various units of the national government to aid in decision making. The CIA also engages in worldwide intelligence gathering and such clandestine activities as political assassinations, coups and revolutions, and extensive surveillance of American citizens. Congress has created a watchdog select committee to oversee CIA operations, but its findings are not subject to review by the entire Congress because of security requirements. The CIA's Cold War activities included the worldwide dissemination of propaganda and disinformation through the mass media. *See also* INTELLIGENCE, page 554.

Significance   The CIA's operations are supersecret in nature, and its financial status is also unknown because many of its appropriations are hidden in the general budget. In its operations, experts estimate that the major portion of intelligence information is secured through foreign publications and other materials of an open nature, with only a small amount of information obtained through clandestine "cloak-and-dagger" methods. In 1975, Congress and a special commission appointed by President Gerald R. Ford undertook investigations that revealed that the CIA had carried on extensive surveillance of American citizens in direct violation of the law under which it was established. An effort to challenge the budget secrecy under which the CIA operates was rejected by the Supreme Court (*United States v. Richardson,* 418 U.S. 166 [1974]). In the 1980s, the CIA was active in Central America, seeking to promote a civil war in Nicaragua and to defeat a revolution in El Salvador. With the end of the Cold War and the communist threat, questions began to arise concerning the future role of the CIA and the ten other U.S. government agencies engaged in intelligence-gathering activities. In 1994, the American public, as well as intelligence officials, were shocked at the disclosure that a high ranking CIA employee, Aldrich Ames, had revealed the identity of numerous Soviet and later Russian citizens working as CIA spies to the Soviet and later Russian intelligence, resulting in the execution of many. Ames was convicted and sentenced to life imprisonment. These disclosures led to Congressional investigations into the CIA's personnel and operations. Efforts to cut the agency's budget and calls for radical reforms followed. Critics have claimed that the CIA is a relic of the Cold War and cite the fact that, in the 1990s, it failed to detect a most important fact—that the Soviet Union was about to collapse as a political entity. Despite these failures, the agency continues to receive strong financial support, and the critics work for change.

Department of Defense (DOD)   A major department of the national government with responsibility to formulate military policies and to maintain the armed forces of the United States. Since 1961, it has assumed responsibility for civil defense functions. The secretary who heads the Department of Defense, a civilian appointed by the President with the Senate's approval, serves as a member of the Cabinet. The three major military departments of the Army, Navy, and Air Force are each headed by a civilian secretary responsible to the Secretary of Defense. The Chiefs of Staff of the Army and the Air Force and the Chief of Naval Operations are the top military officers in each service who advise the civilian secretaries. These three military leaders join with the Chief of Staff to the Secretary of Defense to form the Joint Chiefs of Staff. *See also* MILITARY-INDUSTRIAL COMPLEX, page 562.

Significance   The Defense Department has been the most important department in the national government in numbers of employees and amounts of money spent. At its peak, Defense had over one million civilian employees, almost one-half of all national civil servants. The Secretary of Defense ranks after the Secretaries of State and Treasury as Cabinet adviser to the President and in the line of succession to that office. Major expenditures of the department fall into four categories: procurement of military items, salaries and benefits to personnel, operations, and research and development. Military bases are maintained around the world, and coordinated programs are worked out with the more than 40 nations with which the United States is militarily allied. Increasing emphasis is being placed on research and development as the budget is severely cut in other areas. Unity of command has been achieved through the National Security Acts of 1947 and 1949 and the Defense Reorganization Act of 1958, but interservice rivalries have not completely given way to unity of purpose, especially during budget making. The "threat of peace" and what it would do to the Defense Department's future role became somewhat of a reality in the early 1990s with the end of the Cold War and the conclusion of a number of disarmament and arms control agreements. Iraq's seizure of Kuwait, however, changed the situation to a "threat of war," and in 1991 a punishing military action (Desert Storm) was successfully conducted against Iraq by the United States and its allies. The success of Desert Storm, combined with the ending of the communist threat in the world, has resulted in major reductions in military troop levels and budgets, as well as many base closings.

Department of State   The agency primarily responsible for making and executing American foreign policy. The Secretary of State, who heads the department, is appointed by the President with Senate approval and serves as the President's official adviser on foreign policy matters. The first responsibility of the department is to formulate programs and policies for the United States in its relations with other nations. Next in importance are its duties of administering laws relating to foreign affairs and conducting the day-to-day relations with foreign countries. The latter responsibility is carried out primarily by the Foreign Service, which is administratively tied to the Department of State. Specific duties of the Department include (1) negotiating treaties and agreements with foreign states; (2) carrying on extensive communications with foreign governments and American units abroad; (3) issuing passports and, through consular officials abroad, granting visas; (4) promoting cultural relations between foreign peoples and the American people; (5) carrying on propaganda and information programs overseas; and (6) planning and administering economic aid programs. The department and its secretary are responsible to the President. Important policy-making and primary contact with field operations and foreign missions are carried on through six regional bureaus (the African, Inter-American, European, East Asian and Pacific, Near Eastern, and South Asian Bureaus) and a Bureau of International Organization Affairs, each headed by an assistant secretary. The Agency for International Development is a semiautonomous agency within the State Department. See also SECRETARY OF STATE, page 577.

Significance   The State Department is the major agency for foreign policy decision making. The importance of its role, however, depends on the President. President Franklin Roosevelt, for example, relied heavily on his own abilities and those of close friends in making foreign policy decisions. The historic conflict over the role of the department has involved the question of whether it should confine itself to policy making or be charged additionally with administering foreign programs. This problem has never been resolved, although its primary responsibility remains that of developing policy. The State Department is one of the smallest of the departments represented in the President's Cabinet in personnel and budget, but its secretary is ranked first among Cabinet members. In the 1990s, secretaries of state have functioned as "roving ambassadors," regularly meeting with and seeking to reconcile conflicts and negotiate and mediate disputes in the Middle East, Europe, Asia, Africa, and Latin America. Warren Christopher was an outstanding Secretary of State during these years, with great skills in negotiating and bringing adversaries together. He sometimes visited trouble spots on two continents on the same day, bringing pressure on the disputants as only a representative of a great power state could do.

International Development Cooperation Agency (IDCA) An independent agency established in 1979 with responsibility for economic matters affecting relations of the United States with developing countries. The IDCA is headed by a Director who serves as the principal international development adviser to the President and to the Secretary of State. Differences between the Director and the Secretary of State are resolved by the President. The Agency for International Development (AID) is a component of IDCA and its Administrator reports to the IDCA Director. The Trade and Development Program (TDP) is an organizational unit within IDCA, and the Overseas Private Investment Corporation (OPIC) functions as a component of IDCA. *See also* AGENCY FOR INTERNATIONAL DEVELOPMENT, page 593; THIRD WORLD, page 582.

Significance The creation of IDCA was largely the result of pressures by the more than 130 developing countries of the Third World seeking greater assistance from the United States. The IDCA's mission includes (1) ensuring that development goals are fully considered by all U.S. agencies in making decisions on trade, finance, and monetary policy and (2) providing strong American leadership in helping the nations of the Third World through bilateral and multilateral aid programs. For many years, the administrative status of the AID remained a major problem. Should the agency be located in the State Department, or should it be independent? By creating the IDCA as an independent agency and providing that AID report to IDCA, but holding the IDCA director responsible to the Secretary of State, administrative experts believed they had finally found an effective answer to the problem of where to locate the AID. In its operations, the IDCA and Treasury Department work closely with the United Nations, the Organization of American States, the World Bank Group, the International Monetary Fund, and the regional development banks in pursuit of modernization goals.

National Security Council (NSC) A staff agency in the Executive Office of the President, established by the National Security Act of 1947, that advises the President on domestic and foreign matters involving national security. The council is composed of the President, the Vice President, and the Secretaries of State and Defense. The director of Central Intelligence and the chairman of the Joint Chiefs of Staff function as statutory advisers to the council, and other officials serve at the request of the President. The council's main role is to assess and appraise the objectives, commitments, and risks of the United States in the interests of national security and to make recommendations to the President on specific policies and decisions. *See also* BOLAND AMENDMENTS, page 535; CENTRAL INTELLIGENCE AGENCY, page 593.

Significance The National Security Council is the highest policy-recommending body in defense and foreign policy fields and has responsibility for integration of domestic, foreign, and military policies relating to national security. When a serious crisis erupts anywhere in the world, the President may summon the council into an immediate session. The President is free to reject the advice of the council, but this is unlikely because it is composed of the highest leaders of the administration in the defense and foreign policy fields. The continuing role and influence of the NSC have depended on the President, with some presidents using it regularly or expanding its membership and role, whereas others have rarely called it into session. Under President Ronald Reagan, the National Security Council staff was used to carry out secret operations involving the sale of arms to Iran and the diversion of funds from these sales to provide aid for the contra rebels in Nicaragua in violation of the Boland Amendment passed by Congress. As a result, Congress and an independent prosecutor in 1987 conducted extensive investigations of these actions, with four indictments resulting from the latter's investigations.

Peace Corps An agency that administers the foreign aid program under which American volunteers are sent to developing countries to teach skills and help improve living standards. More than 80,000 Peace Corps volunteers have served in over 62 countries of Asia, Africa, Eastern Europe, Russia, and Latin America. Established within the State Department in 1961, the Peace Corps was transferred to the ACTION Agency in 1971 and was made an independent agency in 1981. *See also* FOREIGN AID, page 550.

Significance The Peace Corps employs a new approach to foreign aid in using human resources to help developing societies help themselves through person-to-person contacts. Many other Western countries followed the American example by establishing similar volunteer programs. Most Third World countries have welcomed Peace Corps volunteers and praised their efforts, but several have been highly critical of the program and have ordered the Peace Corps removed from their territory for allegedly supporting rebel causes and providing information to the CIA. A 1977 amendment to the Peace Corps Act emphasized a commitment by the corps to meet the basic needs of people living in the poorest areas of the countries in which the Peace Corps operates. A domestic version of the Peace Corps was created by President Bill Clinton in 1993, called "AmeriCorps." It is a national service program that will give up to 100,000 youths college money, small cash stipends, and health insurance in exchange for community service.

United States Arms Control and Disarmament Agency (USACDA) An independent agency established in 1961 to conduct research and to develop disarmament policies. Also known as ACDA, USACDA is headed by a director, appointed by the President with Senate consent, who also serves as principal adviser to the President and the Secretary of State on arms control and disarmament matters. *See also* STRATEGIC ARMS REDUCTION TALKS (START), page 579.

Significance   Established in response to demands that greater efforts be expended to reach a disarmament agreement, USACDA has carried on "peace research" and participated in thermonuclear and conventional disarmament negotiations at Geneva and other locations. Many of its studies are carried on by private and public institutions on a contractual basis. Major objectives of negotiation and research include banning all nuclear testing, implementing the antiproliferation treaty to prevent the spread of nuclear weapons among additional states, solving technical and political problems concerned with the enforcement of a disarmament agreement, and developing new approaches to disarmament and arms control. The USACDA research studies contributed to the concluding of SALT strategic arms limitation agreements and to START (Strategic Arms Reduction Talks) negotiations between the United States and the Soviet Union (and later Russia). It has also engaged in supplying research and support studies on such issues as mutual force reductions in Central Europe, preventing the spread of nuclear weapons, controlling chemical and bacteriological weapons, and monitoring the world arms trade. The USACDA's efforts contributed to the signing and ratification of the Intermediate Range Nuclear Forces (INF) Treaty in 1988 at the Moscow Summit. Under this Treaty, all American and Russian short- and intermediate-range nuclear missiles will be removed from Western and Eastern Europe using on-site inspection to ensure compliance. Additional agreements were reached in the 1990s to reduce the numbers of long-range strategic nuclear missiles at Bush-Gorbachev and Bush-Yeltsin summit conferences. Agreement on tactical nuclear weapons was also achieved in the 1990s. Also in the 1990s, President Bill Clinton and President Boris Yeltsin agreed to aim all strategic nuclear missiles at the oceans instead of at each other's targeted areas. While great numbers of nuclear weapons are being disarmed and dismantled, many more remain active and capable of being launched within minutes.

United States Information Agency (USIA)   An independent agency that has responsibility for the administration of the foreign information and cultural programs of the United States. Although originally established in 1953 as the USIA, in 1978 it was designated as the International Communication Agency (ICA), and in 1982 it was redesignated as the United States Information Agency. The best-known USIA operations are the Voice of America, which broadcasts a variety of programs with candor and credibility, and the Fulbright scholarship exchange program, which has provided for the exchange of thousands of professors and students with 120 countries all over the world. *See also* IDEOLOGICAL WARFARE, page 553.

Significance   The USIA directs American governmental efforts in psychological warfare around the globe. One of its main stated objectives is to "bring about greater understanding between the people of the United States and the peoples of the world." Activities include round-the-clock radio broadcasts, television programs, distribution and showings of documentary, feature, and newsreel films, and distribution of leaflets, pamphlets, news bulletins, and related propaganda materials. The USIA operates many information centers and libraries abroad, some of which have been damaged or destroyed in anti-American demonstrations. The agency employs Americans and foreign nationals in more than 100 countries. The four functional elements of the agency are the International Bureau of Broadcasting (comprised of the Voice of America, which broadcasts in English and in 46 foreign languages over 2,000 affiliate stations worldwide; the WORLDNET Television Service; Radio and TV Marti, which broadcast to Cuba; Radio Free Europe, aimed at Eastern Europe, and Radio Liberty, directed at Russia); the Bureau of Educational and Cultural Affairs, which oversees the Fulbright Programs and other educational and cultural exchange programs; and the Bureaus of Information and Management. The future of these broadcasting operations remains questionable as the end of the Cold War and the demise of communism in Russia and Eastern Europe may have ended the utility of their role. In addition, budget-balancing problems have raised questions of the financial drain that results from the operation of these expensive propaganda efforts.

United States International Trade Commission An independent agency that gives information to Congress and the President on American and foreign tariff and trade matters. The six members of the commission, three from each of the two major parties, are appointed by the President, with the Senate's approval, for six-year terms. The Trade Commission's main responsibilities are to furnish studies, reports, and recommendations concerning international trade and tariffs to the President, Congress, and federal agencies. Under the Trade Act of 1974, the Trade Commission replaced the United States Tariff Commission, which had functioned since 1916. *See also* TARIFF, page 581; URUGUAY ROUND, page 590; WORLD TRADE ORGANIZATION, page 592.

Significance Congress has used the International Trade Commission as a means of keeping the President's tariff decisions within some degree of congressional supervision and control. If the President rejects the advice of the commission, Congress can override him by a two-thirds vote in both houses. The role of the Trade Commission was substantially increased by the Trade Reform Act of 1974, the Trade Agreements Act of 1979, and the Trade Act of 1988, all of which expanded American bargaining power. Negotiations through GATT in the Uruguay Round led to the creation of the World Trade Organization (WTO) in which more than 100 members agreed to reduce tariffs, ban import quotas, and protect patents, trademarks, and copyrights.

IMPORTANT CASES

Ex parte Milligan, 4 Wallace 2 (1866): Held in a famous Civil War case that the suspension of the right of writ of habeas corpus and the trial of a civilian by a military tribunal while the civilian courts are operating violate the Constitution. The Court held that neither the President nor Congress could legally deny the accused a civil trial by jury in an area outside an actual theater of war. *See also* CIVILIAN CONTROL, page 537; COURT-MARTIAL, page 542; MARTIAL LAW, page 561.

Significance The *Milligan* case reaffirmed the principles of civilian control over the military and the maintenance of due process of law free from military interference. There have been no further attempts to suspend the writ of habeas corpus in the continental United States. In 1941, following the attack upon Pearl Harbor, President Franklin Roosevelt placed the Hawaiian Islands under martial law, and all civil courts were replaced by military tribunals. In a case after the war (*Duncan v. Kahanamoku,* 327 U.S. 304 [1946]), the Court held this action invalid on the ground that the territorial governor of Hawaii, acting for the President, could not suspend constitutional guarantees through a declaration of martial law.

Missouri v. Holland,   252 U.S. 416 (1920): Upheld the validity of a federal statute based on a treaty for the protection of waterfowl migration between Canada and the United States. The basic legal question was whether the national government could acquire, through a treaty, power to legislate on domestic matters otherwise reserved to the states. A similar federal law had earlier been declared unconstitutional by the federal courts. *See also* TREATY, page 583.

Significance   The decision in *Missouri. v. Holland* means that the national government can actually add to its powers by concluding treaties with foreign states. Opponents of increasing federal powers have argued since 1920 that the case should be overturned because it obliterates the distinction between the national government's delegated powers and the state's reserved powers. This viewpoint crystallized in the 1950s in the Bricker Amendment proposal, which, if adopted, would have allowed treaties to become effective within the United States only through legislation valid in the absence of a treaty. Supporters of the decision point out that the alleged danger has not materialized and that to limit the treaty-making powers would constitute a greater danger to the country.

Selective Draft Law Cases,   245 U.S. 366 (1918): Upheld the constitutional authority of Congress to draft men into the military forces. The Supreme Court rejected the argument that conscription is "involuntary servitude" in violation of the Thirteenth Amendment, holding that such service by the citizen was "his supreme and noble duty." *See also* CONSCIENTIOUS OBJECTOR, page 302; SELECTIVE SERVICE, page 577.

Significance   Although the *Selective Draft Law Cases* dealt with a wartime conscription measure, the constitutionality of the peacetime draft is also based on this precedent. During war, and occasionally in peacetime, the military services have depended heavily upon the draft to supply needed manpower, but in the early 1970s the nation ended the peacetime draft in favor of a system based on voluntary enlistment.

United States v. Curtiss-Wright Export Corp.,   299 U.S. 304 (1936): Upheld the validity of a joint resolution of Congress that delegated broad powers to the President to prohibit arms shipments to foreign belligerents. In question was a presidential proclamation levying an embargo on shipment of war material to either side in the Gran Chaco war between Bolivia and Paraguay. In the *Curtiss-Wright* case, the Court distinguished between permissible delegations of congressional lawmaking power in domestic areas and those in foreign affairs. The Court noted: "As a member of the family of nations, the right and power of the United States . . . are equal to the right and power of the other nations of the international family. Otherwise the United States is not completely sovereign." *See also* INHERENT POWERS, page 553.

Significance   The Court recognized in the *Curtiss-Wright* case the full responsibility of the national government in foreign affairs and the importance of the President's role in this field. By authorizing congressional and presidential actions in foreign affairs that might not be valid in domestic matters, the Court recognized that, in addition to the enumerated and implied powers, a third category of powers, *inherent* in nature, may be exercised by the President in foreign affairs. The Court reaffirmed the primacy of the national government in foreign affairs in *United States v. Pink*, 315 U.S. 203 (1942), asserting that power over foreign relations "is not shared by the states; it is vested in the national government exclusively." Federalism, the Court noted, stops at the water's edge.

IMPORTANT STATUTES

Foreign Service Act of 1980   A major revision of the Foreign Service aimed at upgrading and modernizing it and improving its personnel system. Main provisions of the law (1) eliminated the "domestic" category for employees who served only in the United States, with all employees henceforth available for assignment anywhere in the world; (2) established a new Senior Foreign Service (SFS) with appointments made strictly on the basis of merit; (3) reaffirmed the "up or out" principle whereby officials not promoted within a stipulated time period must resign; (4) created an "employee bill of rights," authorized collective bargaining, and established a Foreign Service Labor Relations Board to hear grievances; and (5) applied personnel provisions of the law to the State Department, the International Development Cooperation Agency, the United States Information Agency, and those employees of the Departments of Commerce and Agriculture engaged in foreign policy programs. *See also* ROGERS (FOREIGN SERVICE) ACT OF 1924, page 602.

Significance   The Foreign Service Act of 1980 was the first comprehensive reorganization of the Foreign Service since 1946. Some of the provisions of the new law were aimed at attracting and holding highly qualified personnel, a major problem in recent years. The Act provides for incentive awards, strengthens career programs, and authorizes the President to establish a pay scale that meets the standards of the Federal Pay Comparability Act, which is aimed at keeping pay scales for Foreign Service personnel equal to those of civil service employees and private sector employees.

National Security Acts of 1947 and 1949   The Act of 1947 provided the nation's most comprehensive reorganization of its defense structure. It established a new National Security Organization and placed the three major military forces—Army, Navy, and Air Force—in a National Military Establishment under a single civilian Secretary of Defense. The National Security Council was established as a top-level advisory body. In the National Security Act of 1949, the National Military Establishment was replaced with a single executive department—the Department of Defense—and the National Security Council was transferred to the Executive Office as a staff agency to the President. *See also* DEPARTMENT OF DEFENSE, page 594.

Significance   The National Security Acts of 1947 and 1949 were aimed at unifying and coordinating the efforts of the nation's armed services. Although the 1947 Act stated that the services were not to be merged, it called for "their integration into an efficient team of land, naval, and air forces." The authority given to the Secretary of Defense in the Act of 1947 proved insufficient to unify three separate military services, each largely autonomous in its operations and protective of its traditional role. The Act of 1949 sought to reduce these interservice rivalries by strengthening the hand of the Secretary of Defense. The National Security Acts provide the most cogent example of a major functional consolidation in the national administration.

Reciprocal Trade Agreements Act of 1934   A broad tariff program under which the President negotiates trade agreements with foreign countries that provide for mutual reductions in tariff rates. It incorporates the "most-favored-nation" principle of nondiscrimination, under which concessions contained in agreements apply to all other nations with which we have most-favored-nation agreements. The original enactment in 1934 provided that tariff rates of the United States could be lowered or raised up to 50 percent of the existing rates, but renewals have given the President authority to seek additional cuts. Amendments to the Act include "peril-point" and "escape-clause" provisions. The peril-point amendment provides that the International Trade Commission inform the President and Congress at what level a tariff rate might allow imports to threaten or injure a domestic producer. Escape-clause procedures require that agreements lowering tariff rates be nullified if they injure domestic producers. Since 1974, a Special Representative for Trade Negotiations located in the Executive Office of the President is responsible for supervising the trade agreements program and directing American participation in trade negotiations. *See also* MOST-FAVORED-NATION STATUS, page 564; TARIFF, page 581; WORLD TRADE ORGANIZATION, page 592.

Significance   The Reciprocal Trade Agreements Act sought to increase the two-way flow of trade by transferring rate-setting powers from Congress, in which political considerations and logrolling tactics flourished, to the President, who was empowered to lower rates only on a *quid pro quo* basis. Reciprocal bargaining has been facilitated through multilateral negotiations carried on through the former General Agreement on Tariffs and Trade (GATT) system, now embodied in the new World Trade Organization (WTO), which became operational in 1994 with a membership of more than 100 of the world's trading nations. Protectionist sentiment has increased in Congress in recent years as a result of growing competition from imports.

Rogers (Foreign Service) Act of 1924   The basic law that established the organization and functions of the Foreign Service as it exists today. The Rogers Act unified the diplomatic and consular services into an integrated Foreign Service, created a career service based on merit, and established the Foreign Service Institute. Subsequent amendments added in the Foreign Service Acts of 1946 and 1949 have sought to professionalize the service. Additional changes based on the report of the Wriston Committee in 1954 sought to "democratize" the service and integrate its personnel with that of the State Department. *See also* DEPARTMENT OF STATE, page 595; FOREIGN SERVICE ACT OF 1980, page 601.

Significance   The Rogers Act initiated a series of reforms that have re-shaped the Foreign Service over the years and developed it into a first-rate organization. Appointment to the Foreign Service today is open to most Americans, yet it involves the most careful selection process developed by any government agency. The Foreign Service organization and the quality of its personnel have a direct bearing on making foreign policy and conducting foreign affairs. The Foreign Service of the United States operates embassies and consulate offices around the world, the former in capital cities and the latter in major cities and trading centers.

War Powers Act of 1973   A declaration of congressional authority to par-ticipate with the President in making national decisions to use American armed forces abroad. The War Powers Act provides that the President can commit American troops to action only (1) following a declaration of war by Congress, (2) by specific congressional authorization, and (3) when an attack upon the United States or its armed forces creates a national emergency. When such an attack occurs, the President must report immediately to Con-gress; if Congress does not thereupon declare war within 60 days, the Presi-dent must terminate his commitment of American troops. If, however, the President certifies to Congress that military conditions require it for the safety of American troops, an additional 30 days will be permitted under the War Powers Act. After 90 days, the Congress may, by concurrent resolu-tion not subject to a presidential veto, require the President to disengage all troops involved in the hostilities. *See also* COMMANDER IN CHIEF, page 188; DEC-LARATION OF WAR, page 543; WAR POWERS, page 591.

Significance   The War Powers Act was largely a reaction to the disas-trous involvement of American troops in Indochina as a result of decisions made by several presidents, with little in the way of congressional controls over their actions. Throughout American history, presidents have committed the nation's armed forces abroad without a declaration of war or other form of congressional consent. The supporters of the War Powers Act sought to close this constitutional loophole by providing for a sharing of the powers to decide when, where, and under what circumstances military interventions could occur in the future. The Act also reflected the effort by Congress to re-dress the balance of decision-making power that has moved relentlessly from the legislative to the executive branch as a result of the President's reacting to a series of domestic and foreign crises over a 50-year period. Critics have charged that the new congressional role undermines the nation's ability to act decisively during an international crisis. This, they assert, encourages po-tential enemies to take provocative actions and weakens our relations with our allies. Although the Act gives Congress the *legal* power to participate in all decisions involving the commitment of American troops abroad, the *po-litical* will to invoke it to restrain a president's actions in the field of national security remains problematical. In addition, no president since 1973 has ac-cepted the Act as a direct limitation of the constitutional powers of the Pres-ident to function as commander in chief of the armed forces. In 1990, Congress gave full support to President George Bush after he had made a de-cision calling for a large-scale involvement of American combat troops in the Persian Gulf. As the huge American troop buildup continued, congressional critics from both parties demanded a larger role by Congress in the decision processes involved in the Desert Shield (1990) and Desert Storm (1991) military actions. President Bush consulted with Congress but rejected the claim that the Congress had a statutory or constitutional right and power to participate in making decisions concerning the undertaking of hostilities abroad. This position was continued by President Bill Clinton in making the decision in 1995 to commit 20,000 American troops to join with 40,000 combat troops from 25 other nations to maintain the peace agreement reached by the presidents of Bosnia, Croatia, and Serbia.

14

State and Local Government

Alderman   A member of a city council. The term originated in England and was used in the American colonies to designate officials chosen by the common council of the city to exercise judicial power and to share in the governing of the city. In the nineteenth century, when bicameral legislatures were common in cities, one house was designated as the Board of Aldermen, the other, as the Common Council. *See also* WARD, page 630.

Significance   The term "alderman" is generally associated with cities in which ward systems of representation for the city council function under a mayor-council plan of government. The commission and council-manager plans of city government have been accompanied by the use of the terms "commissioner" or "councilman" to designate members of the city legislative body.

Annexation   The addition of territory to a unit of government. Annexation usually denotes the addition by a city of land adjacent to it as an aggressive policy of growth or to meet the problems of metropolitan expansion. Procedures for annexation are established by state law and generally require an affirmative vote of both the central city and of the area concerned. In a few states, such as Virginia and Texas, areas may be annexed by action of the city alone or through judicial procedures. *See also* CONSOLIDATION, page 610; METROPOLITAN AREA, page 621.

Significance   Annexation is viewed as one solution to the problems caused by the urbanization of fringe areas of a city. Through annexation a community seeks to eliminate conflicts of authority and duplication of services and to protect orderly city growth, which is hampered by the existence of numerous units of government. Fringe area dwellers often fear high city taxes and prefer to retain their identity as a community. Cities that annex residential fringe areas not having the broad tax base provided by business and industry, and with soaring needs for costly services, find the annexed areas to be costly for city taxpayers. Also, many annexed areas lack proper planning and zoning, posing special problems for the city administration. Prior to heavy suburban growth, annexation was used to spur city growth or to control development of uninhabited land. The more highly developed a suburban community gets, the less likely it is to consent to annexation.

Attorney General   The chief legal officer of the state. The office of attorney general is elective in 43 states (nominated and elected jointly with the governor in 24 of those states). The attorney general serves as legal adviser to the governor and to state agencies, represents the state in legal proceedings, and may have supervisory powers over local prosecuting attorneys. *See also* ATTORNEY GENERAL, page 250; CORPORATION COUNSEL, page 613; DISTRICT ATTORNEY, page 260.

Significance   Opinions of the attorney general have the force of law unless they are overturned by a court. Many students of state government argue that the office should be appointive so that the governor has full confidence in his or her chief legal adviser, similar to that placed by a client in his or her attorney. The state attorney general holds an office that frequently leads to the governorship or to a judicial appointment.

Board of Education   The state or local governing body for public education. State boards of education establish statewide educational and teacher certification standards, determine curricula, and control state educational funds. Most state boards are appointed by the governor; others are elected. Boards usually include the state superintendent of schools, who is often elected, although the trend is toward appointment by the board. Local school boards are chosen by popular vote in school districts in most states, with a few appointed by the city council. The local school board determines policy but leaves much responsibility in the hands of a school superintendent, whom they appoint. Local school boards determine teacher salaries, curricula, and building needs. *See also* SCHOOL DISTRICT, page 624; SUPERINTENDENT OF PUBLIC INSTRUCTION, page 627.

Significance   Boards of education administer the largest share of state and local expenditures. The independent status of most boards of education is in keeping with the tradition that schools be "kept out of politics." Schools, however, develop "politics" of their own, and no public agency spending huge sums of money is "out of politics." Typically, school boards are controlled by the same political group that dominates other government functions of a community and are subject to considerable community pressures to have the schools reflect the views of the community. Financial pressures and educational policy differences have put most school boards under continuous controversy.

Borough   A municipal corporation, generally smaller than a city. Boroughs are found mainly in Pennsylvania, Connecticut, and New Jersey and resemble the villages or towns of other states. "Borough" is also the name assigned to major local government divisions in Alaska, comparable to counties. The city of New York is divided into five boroughs: Manhattan, Brooklyn, Queens, Bronx, and Staten Island. *See also* COUNTY, page 614.

Significance   The term "borough" is a holdover from England and colonial America. In New York City, the boroughs represent an attempt to decentralize the operations of that huge metropolis. The use of the term in the constitution of Alaska represents a noteworthy departure from tradition. In order to avoid some of the pitfalls of county government and to adapt local government to their peculiar needs, the people of Alaska provided for the creation of boroughs that would embrace an area and population with common interests and that would have a high degree of home rule.

Charter The basic law of a local government unit that defines its powers, responsibilities, and organization. Charters are granted, under state constitutional or statutory provisions, to municipal corporations and, in some states, to counties or townships. Charters may be provided by (1) special act of the legislature applicable to one city; (2) general laws applicable to all cities within a certain classification; (3) optional charter laws, whereby a city may choose a charter from a group provided by law; or (4) home rule, whereby the people of a city draw up their own charter. *See also* GENERAL LAWS, page 617; HOME RULE, page 618; OPTIONAL CHARTER, page 622; SPECIAL ACT, page 625.

Significance In one sense, every unit of local government has a "charter" composed of the local government provisions of state constitutions, statutes, and the common law. Many cities or other municipal corporations, such as villages, do not have a charter in the form of a *document,* particularly when they operate under special acts or general laws. A charter document is generally found in cities operating under home rule and, sometimes, under optional charters. All local governments are subject to the state constitution and laws, and all actions taken under a charter must conform to these higher laws and to the charter as well.

City A municipal corporation, chartered by the state, that is usually larger and more densely populated than a village, town, borough, or other incorporated area. The term is a legal concept, and exactly what constitutes a city is defined by state law. It is generally based on population but may be based on assessed valuation. The International City Management Association identifies about 7,000 municipalities as "cities." The Census Bureau has identified 19,200 "municipal corporations" including villages, towns, and boroughs, as of 1990, comprising about 23 percent of 83,186 local governmental units. *See also* BOROUGH, page 606; INCORPORATED AND UNINCORPORATED AREAS, page 619; MUNICIPALITY, page 622; TOWN, page 628; VILLAGE, page 630.

Significance Cities are generally accorded more authority over fiscal matters and services than are other incorporated units. Cities, too, are organized differently, with the mayor-council plan, commission plan, and council-manager plan generally made available by state law. Most Americans live in cities and their suburbs, and city culture has replaced the traditions of a rural society. Cities have long fought for greater freedom from state control, and the trend is toward giving cities home rule.

City Council The policy-making and, in some instances, administrative board of a city. The structure and powers of city councils vary with the plan of city government. In the weak-mayor and commission plans, the council plays a large role in lawmaking and in the direction and control of administrative departments. In the strong-mayor and council-manager plans, the council's job is largely in the realm of lawmaking, with only general oversight of administration. In all cases, the most important job of the council is to pass ordinances that determine public policy including control over the purse strings. Other functions, which vary from city to city, may include serving as a board of review for tax assessments, issuing licenses, and making appointments. Members of city councils are elected, on a partisan or nonpartisan basis, from wards or districts, at large, or by a combination of both. *See also* COMMISSION PLAN, page 609; COUNCIL-MANAGER PLAN, page 613; MAYOR-COUNCIL PLAN, page 620.

Significance   City councils are typically unicameral bodies, most commonly of 5 or 7 members, but they range up to 50. The commission and council-manager forms of city government, which replaced the cumbersome and often corrupt bicameral city councils, have raised the prestige and quality of council members. Each state determines by law the structure and powers of city councils.

City-County Consolidation   The merger of county government with all other units within the county to form one unit of government. The plan is suggested as one solution to the problems of a metropolitan area, particularly when it coincides with the county boundary. *See also* METROPOLITAN AREA, page 621; URBAN COUNTY PLAN, page 630.

Significance   City-county consolidation simplifies the government of a metropolitan county by reducing fragmentation of services and allowing for areawide planning and administration of services. In many areas, city and county boundaries are actually or substantially the same. Where several units are involved, residents of smaller municipalities and rural parts of the county tend to resist consolidation. They fear increased costs and want to maintain their individual identity. As a solution to metropolitan problems, however, the city-county consolidation plan does not meet the problems of urbanized areas that overlap counties or extend though many counties or even states. Fewer than 25 city-county consolidations were achieved during the years 1947 to 1995 and only 7 remain: Milford, Connecticut; Jacksonville, Florida; Columbus, Georgia; Indianapolis, Indiana; Butte, Montana; Nashville, Tennessee; and, the only one since 1990, Athens, Georgia.

City-County Separation   Political separation of the city from the county. Cities are generally part of the county in which they lie, and the city residents pay county taxes and receive certain county services. More than 40 cities in Virginia, and the cities of St. Louis, Denver, Carson City, Baltimore, and San Francisco are separated from their counties and provide their residents with county services. *See also* METROPOLITAN AREA, page 621.

Significance   City-county separation is designed to increase the efficiency of the urban area and to eliminate overlapping government. The urban area, however, tends to continue to spread beyond the city limits. Moreover, the rural areas of the county and smaller municipalities are left without the financial help of the city, and the county must continue to provide services. These problems have been met in part in Virginia by permitting the judiciary to adjust boundary lines to meet urban growth. At one time city-county separation was considered a solution to metropolitan problems, but, except for the state of Virginia, it is rarely used today.

Classification of Cities   The grouping of cities by a state legislature according to population for the purpose of enacting laws or city charters. The practice of classification results from the requirement found in most state constitutions that the legislature must deal with local governments by general law rather than by special act applicable to one unit. Because general laws may result in putting all cities, large and small, into a uniform mold, legislatures have classified cities and passed general laws applicable to each class. *See also* GENERAL LAWS, page 617.

Significance   A classification must be reasonable and attainable by others not yet within the group. State legislatures have tried to evade the purposes of general law requirements by creating classes based on location or size in such a way as to have the effect of a special act applicable to only one community. Laws applicable to cities with populations exceeding 1 million, for example, may actually apply to only one city, but theoretically, other cities may reach the population figure. Classification schemes are used to determine forms of government as well as specific powers that a city may exercise. The courts determine whether a scheme of classification is reasonable.

Commission Plan   One of the forms of city government in the United States in which both legislative and executive powers are exercised by a commission of three to nine members. Variations in structure are found around the country, but the essential ingredients of the commission plan include (1) the concentration of legislative and executive powers in a small group elected at large on a nonpartisan ballot; (2) the collective responsibility of the commission to pass ordinances and control the purse strings; (3) the individual responsibility of each commissioner to head a city department, such as public works, finance, or public safety; and (4) the selection of the mayor from among the commissioners, with reduction of the office to that of ceremonial leadership. *See also* CITY COUNCIL, page 607.

Significance   The commission plan enjoyed great popularity from its inception in Galveston, Texas, in 1901 until about 1920. Its simplicity and its resemblance to business corporation organization appealed to reformers who sought an end to the long ballot and the extremes of partisan politics in municipal government. As its defects became apparent, however, its popularity declined. A major defect is the failure to separate legislative and executive authority, with the result that there is little check on spending, and administration is in the hands of amateurs. The lack of a chief executive makes it difficult for the voter to fix responsibility, and, in turn, the city suffers from the absence of political leadership. Furthermore, trying to fit the number of city agencies to the number of commissioners leads to rigidity in organization. To meet these defects, many cities followed the lead of Des Moines, Iowa, and added the initiative, referendum, and recall to the plan, as well as a merit system for selection of governmental employees. By 1994, only 154 cities, most under 25,000 in population, were using the commission plan.

Congressional Township   A 6-mile-square area established under laws of Congress for the purpose of surveying land. The system was started by the Confederation Congress in 1785 and was applied to the land in most states. Excluded are the original 13 states and Maine, Kentucky, Tennessee,

Vermont, West Virginia, and Texas. Under the law, land is divided into townships of 36 square miles, and each township is divided into 36 square-mile sections. Each section is further subdivided into quarter sections and less. By the assignment of numbered base lines, similar to the longitude and latitude patterns on maps, any parcel of land may be identified. *See also* TOWNSHIP, page 629.

Significance   The congressional township system of land surveying was instituted to replace the haphazard "metes and bounds" method of identifying tracts of land in which landmarks were used rather than precise, numerical points of reference. Accurate records, particularly for real estate transfers, are made possible by the congressional township plan. A congressional township is not a unit of government and, frequently, the township overlaps county and state boundaries. Many township units of government, however, do follow the congressional township line, accounting for the 36-square-mile civil township. Congress reserved one section of the township (section 16) for the support of public schools, and many states provide that the proceeds from this section constitute a permanent fund for school purposes.

Consolidation   The union of two or more units of government to form a single unit. Consolidation is often recommended as a solution to metropolitan area problems, but is also recommended in rural areas as a means of reducing the large number of local governments in existence. State constitutions or statutes designate consolidation procedures, generally requiring the separate consent of all units. *See also* ANNEXATION, page 605; METROPOLITAN AREA, page 621; SCHOOL DISTRICT, page 624.

Significance   Through consolidation, it is expected that services may be improved, costs cut, and much confusion eliminated. In the metropolitan areas, consolidation has the same benefits and meets the same opposition as do annexation proposals. It eliminates conflicting authority and duplication of services but meets opposition from suburban communities desiring to retain their identity. In rural areas, consolidation is viewed as a means of strengthening counties and townships that were established many years ago and no longer contain sizable populations or the means to carry on governmental functions efficiently. Nonetheless, legal intricacies, tradition, and the opposition of vested interests militate against consolidation. Many school districts, established prior to modern means of transportation, however, have consolidated in order to realize the benefits of larger enrollments and school plants, although this, too, meets strong opposition. The major change in the number of governmental units since the 1940s has been the reduction in the number of school districts through consolidation.

Constitution, State   The organic law of a state that defines and limits governmental power and guarantees the rights of the people. Each state has a constitution, and its provisions may not conflict with the U.S. Constitution. Because state governments have all powers not delegated to the national government, state constitutions, typically, are filled with restrictions on legislative and executive power rather than grants of authority. *See also* CONSTITUTION, page 34.

Significance   State constitutions tend to be unduly lengthy and filled with details better left to statutes. The authority of the legislature and executive is typically restricted in taxation, expenditures, and administration. Local governments and major state services, such as education and highways, tend to be frozen into a specific mold. These defects, among others, have led to considerable agitation for state constitutional reform because the people's representatives often have their hands tied by the constitution in their attempts to meet day-to-day problems. This has resulted in the frequent amendment of many state constitutions and the thorough revision of others. Proponents of reform seek a document more like the national Constitution, with emphasis on fundamentals rather than details. Opposition to change, however, comes from those whose interests are protected by specific provisions, as well as from many who tend to view a constitution as a sacred document.

Constitutional Amendments, State   Changes in a state constitution or additions to it. Amendment procedures are detailed in each state's constitution. Generally, two proposal methods are available: legislative, by an extraordinary majority, and initiative of the people. Ratification by the people is usually accomplished by simple majority vote, but a few states require an extraordinary majority. Under the initiative method, permitted in eighteen states, the voters draw up a petition with a specified number of signatures (8 or 10 percent of the voters in most cases, though the requirement ranges from 3 to 15 percent) requesting the desired change. If the petition is in order, the proposal goes on the ballot for ratification by the people. *See also* AMENDMENT PROCESS, page 29.

Significance   Most state constitutions have been amended numerous times to meet changing conditions or the desires of strong interest groups. The legislative proposal method has been used most often because it is simpler and less expensive than a constitutional convention. The requirement of extraordinary majorities, however, often makes it difficult to propose controversial measures. Unlike the national Constitution, however, state constitutions have required frequent amendment because of their inflexibility. The initiative method serves as an important weapon for the people when the legislature fails to respond to their particular interests. It tends, however, to be abused by pressure groups, and many such proposals are rejected. During 1992 and 1993, there were 36 initiative proposals on state ballots, many in California and Colorado. Many states with extremely difficult amending procedure suffer from outmoded organization and procedures in the daily workings of government. Often the average citizen fails to realize that the state constitution may be a stumbling block to effective government.

Constitutional Commission   A group of citizens selected by the legislature, the governor of a state, or both to study the constitution and to make recommendations for change.

Significance   Constitutional commissions have been used in a number of states when revision of the constitution has been under consideration. A notable instance took place in Georgia in 1945, where a commission, established by the legislature, had its proposed revision of the entire constitution ratified by the people as a single amendment to replace the old constitution. In other cases, a commission has served as an educational medium, prior to the calling of a constitutional convention. In still others, and with increasing frequency, the legislature submits to the people the specific proposals of a commission as amendments. Through the commission device, a group of leading citizens, making use of expert advice, can contribute to better understanding of constitutional problems. During the 1990s, constitutional commissions were operating in Arkansas, California, Florida, New York, and Utah.

Constitutional Convention   A body selected by the people to rewrite the constitution. Most state constitutions make provisions for the calling of a constitutional convention (usually called "Con-Con"), but, even if no provisions are made, the power to call a convention is considered to be inherent in the people in their sovereign capacity. Fourteen states provide for a mandatory, periodic submission to the people of the question of whether they wish to call a convention. The procedures for a constitutional convention generally involve (1) the placing of the question on the ballot by the legislature, usually by an extraordinary majority unless it is mandatory for that year; (2) the election of delegates, should the people approve the call; (3) the meeting of the convention, which has deliberations similar in method and procedure to legislative bodies; and (4) the submission of the new constitution to the people for ratification. *See also* CONSTITUTIONAL CONVENTION, page 35.

Significance   A constitutional convention is a historic event. About 230 have been held in the United States. About 16 states have held just 1 convention, but some states have held 10 or more. Twelve conventions were held during the 1970s, and 2 more during the 1980s, the most recent being Louisiana in 1986. In addition, the District of Columbia held a constitutional convention and submitted a document to Congress in 1982, seeking to become the fifty-first state, and the commonwealth territory of the Northern Marianas Islands held a convention in 1993. Constitutional conventions are expensive, and many people fear that vested interests or long-standing practices will be disturbed. Yet, conventions represent the highest voice of the people and have tended to attract able citizen talent. The voter is brought into the picture at several stages, and the entire process has an excellent educational effect. The provision for the mandatory call of a convention is based on the Jeffersonian assumption that each generation should have the opportunity to revise its basic law.

Constitutional Officer   A public official, usually in the executive branch, whose office is established and required by the constitution. Sate constitutions generally name numerous state and local officials and designate their terms of office and duties. For example, most state constitutions provide for the election of such statewide officers as secretary of state, attorney general, state treasurer, and state auditor. On the local level, the constitution may require election of such officers as sheriff, county clerk, township supervisor, and highway commissioner. *See also* SHORT BALLOT, page 111.

Significance   Constitutional officers present one of the troublesome aspects of state government today because they enjoy much immunity from legislative power and may resist direction from the chief executive, particularly when they belong to different political parties. Reform of state and local government is difficult because these offices cannot be abolished without constitutional change. Supporters of provisions for constitutional officers maintain that they reduce concentration of power in the chief executive and retain greater control in the hands of voters.

Corporation Counsel   The attorney for a municipal corporation. The term "corporation counsel" is used to distinguish the city, village, or township attorney from the district attorney or county prosecutor, who serves to enforce statewide and criminal law in the local communities. The corporation counsel is appointed by the mayor and/or council and serves mainly to advise on noncriminal matters. Most local governmental units do not have a regular attorney attached to the official staff but hire a law firm to serve as counsel as needed. *See also* ATTORNEY GENERAL, page 250; DISTRICT ATTORNEY, page 260.

Significance   Corporation counsel, like their counterparts at other levels of government, play a vital role in the communities they serve. Increasing reliance on legal advice by largely amateur and part-time public officials enhances their authority, particularly as local governments become more involved in state and national relations and various aspects of community development. Where no full-time corporation counsel or legal staff exists, the business for the lawyer or firm chosen to represent the municipal corporation can be lucrative.

Council-Manager Plan   A form of city government in which the city council appoints a professional administrator, a manager, to act as the chief executive. With variations from city to city, the essentials of this plan are (1) a small council or commission of five or seven members elected at large on a nonpartisan ballot, with power to make policy and to hire and fire the manager; (2) a professionally trained manager, with authority to hire and fire subordinates, who is responsible to the council for efficient administration of the city; and (3) a mayor chosen separately or from within the council, but with no executive functions. The council must refrain from bypassing the manager by interfering with his or her subordinates or in the details of administration, and the manager must follow the policies outlined by the council. A merit system for selection of employees is generally used under this plan. *See also* CITY COUNCIL, page 607; COUNTY-MANAGER PLAN, page 616; GENERAL MANAGEMENT MUNICIPALITY, page 618; MAYOR-ADMINISTRATOR PLAN, page 620.

Significance   The council-manager plan, first adopted in 1912 in Sumpter, South Carolina, is now well established in the United States and growing in popularity. Nearly 3,000 cities use the manager system. A small percentage of cities have abandoned the plan after trying it, usually because of lack of citizen understanding of its operations. More than 40 percent of cities with populations of 5,000 to 25,000 use the manager plan, as well as about half of those over 25,000, but only five cities with more than 500,000 people (Dallas, Phoenix, San Antonio, San Diego, and San Jose) have adopted it. Advantages of the plan include its simplicity, clarification of responsibility for both policy and administration, and use of experts to adopt and utilize modern techniques of budgeting, planning, and overall administration. The profession of city manager has gained in status, and many universities train managers. The manager may also be of invaluable aid to the council and the public in suggesting policy alternatives. Opponents of the plan criticize the lack of a strong political leader, particularly essential in large cities where strong mayors play this role. Some view the manager plan as undemocratic, but the council, responsible to the people, has full control over the manager.

Councils of Government   Voluntary regional organizations of counties and municipalities concerned with areawide problems. Nearly 700 regional councils were established, mainly since 1966, under incentives furnished by federal grants. Most surviving councils are located in metropolitan areas (for example, the South East Michigan Council of Governments [SEMCOG]) and, under authority granted by participating units, undertake such tasks as regional planning, community development, pollution control, developing and operating water systems, and airport construction. Congress has encouraged this development by requiring such councils to determine the regional effects of programs funded by federal grants. In some cases, the council becomes the "designated agency" through which federal departments, such as the Department of Housing and Urban Development, work in making grants to local communities. Some have hired professional managers similar to a city manager. *See also* METROPOLITAN AREA, page 621.

Significance   Councils of government are voluntary associations with only advisory power but actually possess coercive power because of their authority under federal law to review and clear regional programs. Their widespread development resulted from a combination of massive problems that transcend artificial geographic boundaries and the reluctance of communities to federate or consolidate into metropolitan governments. The councils also demonstrate the power inherent in the use of federal programs to promote goals that otherwise would not be met. Cutbacks in federal funding, however, can easily weaken their authority. Such was the case during the Reagan administration, resulting in the collapse of about 125 councils. Critics charge that the councils simply add another layer of government to the metropolitan confusion and that they tend to ignore local social and political problems. By 1994, only 139 councils of government remained.

County   The major unit of local government in the United States, except in Connecticut, Rhode Island, and Alaska. Louisiana has county units but calls them "parishes." Alaska has a new major division of local government called a "borough." In New England, counties are relatively unimportant for governmental purposes. Otherwise, county governments exist as principal agencies of the state for statewide purposes and as important units of local government. There are 3,041 counties in the United States, ranging from 3 in Delaware to 254 in Texas. Their powers and functions vary from state to state and within states as well. Generally, counties perform such functions as law enforcement and maintenance of courts, highways, schools, and welfare agencies. In urban areas, counties may perform a variety of services usually handled by cities. Counties are governed by a board that differs in composition from state to state. Most counties have a large number of elected officials, such as sheriff, clerk, coroner, attorney, auditor, register of deeds, surveyor, and treasurer. *See also* COUNTY BOARD, page 615; COUNTY-MANAGER PLAN, page 616; COUNTY SINGLE-EXECUTIVE PLAN, page 616.

Significance   Counties were originally established as administrative subdivisions of the state and for local governmental purposes. The number of counties and their organizational patterns have undergone almost no change through the years, and tradition militates against change. Many are densely populated and integral parts of metropolitan areas. Others have lost population and are thoroughly rural. The metropolitan counties are faced with the need to expand their services; the rural counties find it difficult to support their regular functions. Thus, in some cases, the county has achieved new importance; in others, means are sought to relieve it of its burdens. Most counties suffer from outmoded administrative organization, the lack of a chief executive, the long ballot, and the spoils system. About 5 percent use either the county-manager plan or an independently elected executive.

County Board   The governing body of the county. The official title of this body varies from state to state, with as many as 27 different titles used. "Board of commissioners," "board of supervisors," and "county court" are common, but "county board" is the most popular term. Most county boards are composed of three to five commissioners or supervisors who are elected by the voters of the county. In states with township government, the board may be composed of township supervisors and representatives of cities within the county, but these are undergoing change to comply with "one person, one vote" rulings of the Supreme Court that have been applied to county boards (*Avery v. Midland County, Texas,* 390 U.S. 474 [1968]). In several states, the board is composed of county judges. The board administers state law in the county, levies taxes, appoints numerous officials, and supervises the general affairs of the county. *See also* COUNTY, page 614.

Significance   County boards are important strongholds of political power. The growing importance of the county in urban areas has added to the power and influence of these boards. In some areas, they have not been adequate to meet new responsibilities, and many persons advocate the use of a county manager or elected executive because under the present system no individual has overall responsibility for the county. Boards are handicapped by the large number of elected county officials over whom they exercise little control.

County Clerk   A county official, who is popularly elected in more than half the states. The principal duties of the county clerk include acting as secretary to the county board, supervising elections, issuing various business certificates and licenses, and handling birth, marriage, and death records, collectively known as "vital statistics."

Significance   The county clerk's office tends to become a central clearinghouse for county affairs, and the clerk is often an important political figure. The nature of the office has led some observers to consider it the logical place to vest principal administrative and supervisory duties in the absence of a regular county executive.

County-Manager Plan   A plan patterned after the council-manager plan used in may cities. The county-manager plan envisages a small county board for policy determination and an appointed professional manager to serve as the executive officer of the county. About 125 of the more than 3,000 counties in the United States have adopted some form of the manager plan. *See also* COUNCIL-MANAGER PLAN, page 613; COUNTY SINGLE-EXECUTIVE PLAN, page 616; GENERAL MANAGEMENT MUNICIPALITY, page 618.

Significance   The county-manager plan is designed to overcome the defects common to most counties: the long ballot, the lack of an integrating executive officer, and the spoils system. General public apathy and a tradition-bound attitude toward county government have made for slow adoption of the plan since its introduction in 1930 in Durham County, North Carolina. State constitutional provisions also make it difficult for counties to reorganize. Such reforms as county home rule or optional charters will probably be necessary before the county-manager plan can spread. Supporters of the plan hold that, in both urban and rural counties, it can make the operation of county government more efficient and clearly fix responsibility. Critics argue that, because the county is principally an administrative arm of the state, the manager would obstruct state supervision of county activities.

County Single-executive Plan   A form of county government that provides for the election of a single executive in whom responsibility is placed to administer county functions. The first such elected county executives were chosen in 1938 in suburban counties around New York City (Westchester and Nassau counties). In 1990, New York State had 13 elected county executives. The International City Management Association lists more than 70 counties with a single elected executive, including Baltimore County, Maryland; Milwaukee County, Wisconsin; and Baton Rouge (Parish), Louisiana. *See also* COUNTY, page 614; COUNTY BOARD, page 615; COUNTY-MANAGER PLAN, page 616.

Significance   The single-executive plan gives the county a form of government more suited to highly urbanized areas than the typical county government characterized by large numbers of elected officials. Like the county-manager plan, which involves an appointed rather than elected executive, the elective plan is designed to integrate executive functions and reduce the impact of political patronage. Constitutional barriers in most states and the entrenched political power of county officials make change difficult. Nevertheless, a growing number of counties are being permitted to exercise needed authority to mold county government to meet contemporary needs. Elected county executives are a new force in local and national politics.

Dillon's Rule   A rule enunciated in 1872 by Judge John F. Dillon of Iowa, an authority on municipal corporations, to the effect that a municipal corporation can exercise only those powers expressly granted to it by state law, those necessarily implied from the granted powers, and those essential for the purposes of the organization. If any doubt exists, it is to be resolved against the local unit, in favor of the state. *See also* FEDERAL ANALOGY, page 617; HOME RULE, page 618; UNITARY STATE, page 53.

Significance The spread of home rule has weakened the force of Dillon's Rule, and some state constitutions overrule Dillon by providing that local governmental powers are to be liberally interpreted. Yet, Dillon's Rule underscores the subordinate relationship of local government to the state. The rule applies to all local units. Local government is a creature of the state and has only those powers permitted by state constitutions and laws.

Federal Analogy A concept, usually incorrectly applied, that assumes that the relationship of local governments to state governments is the same as that of the states to the national government. The relationship between the national and state governments is "federal"—a division of power defined by the Constitution; the relationship between a state government and its local subdivision is "unitary"—the local units are subordinate to the state and have only those powers authorized by state law. *See also* CHARTER, page 607; DILLON'S RULE, page 616; FEDERALISM, page 401; HOME RULE, page 618; *Reynolds v. Sims*, page 178; UNITARY STATE, page 53.

Significance The federal analogy is usually applied by those who seek to have counties or cities treated as independent entities similar to the states themselves. Thus, it is argued that a county or a city is to the state as the state is to the national government, or that the state senate is to the state legislature what the United States Senate is to Congress. The latter analogy was specifically rejected by the Supreme Court when it held the "one person, one vote" principle of legislative apportionment applicable to both houses of a state legislature (*Reynolds v. Sims*, 377 U.S. 533 [1964]). The Court declined to hold that one house of a state legislature could be treated like the U.S. Senate, where representation is based on the equality of states in the Union. Some modification of the unitary principle takes place when a state adopts home rule for local governments, but such authority may usually be withdrawn or circumscribed by state law.

Functional Consolidation The cooperation of two or more units of government in providing services to their constituents. Several counties may cooperate for common administration of health services, or two cities may agree to have a common water supply or sewerage system. *See also* COUNCILS OF GOVERNMENT, page 614; FUNCTIONAL CONSOLIDATION, page 226; METROPOLITAN AREA, page 621.

Significance Functional consolidation can help metropolitan areas, with their complex of overlapping governments, as well as rural areas, which lack financial resources. It provides a satisfactory alternative to complete consolidation of units, which often meets strong opposition. Another form of consolidation of functions takes place when a state takes over a service, such as highways or education, and relieves local units of these burdens. Functional consolidation has made headway in metropolitan areas because it solves technical problems while permitting units of government to retain their separate political identities.

General Laws Laws applicable to all local government units of a similar type. Most state constitutions now provide that the legislature may pass only laws of general application rather than special acts applicable only to one unit. To allow for variations, the legislatures often classify units according to population. *See also* CLASSIFICATION OF CITIES, page 609; SPECIAL ACT, page 625.

Significance   General law requirements free both the state legislature and the local unit of government from the pressure, favoritism, and political infighting that characterized the special act system that permitted the legislatures to make decisions for individual cities or other units. Often, however, the legislature's classifications are so specific as to apply, in fact, to only a single unit of government.

General Management Municipality   A form of local government in which an appointed official is responsible for administrative affairs. A general manager has authority similar to that of a traditional city manager under the council-manager plan and more than that typically held by the administrator under the mayor-administrator system. In 1969, the International City Managers' Association recognized the similar roles of professional managers, regardless of formal governmental systems, and changed its name to the International City Management Association (ICMA). By 1994, the ICMA recognized 1,007 cities, 199 counties, and 139 councils of government as general management municipalities, in addition to the cities and counties using the regular council or county-manager plans. *See also* COUNCIL-MANAGER PLAN, page 613; COUNCILS OF GOVERNMENT, page 614; COUNTY-MANAGER PLAN, page 616; MAYOR-ADMINISTRATOR PLAN, page 620.

Significance   The need for professional general management has increased as urbanization continues to spread and as new governmental structures, such as councils of government or urban county governments, take shape. Through the appointment of a general manager, difficult governmental structural reform may be avoided, and professional management to handle complex budgeting and personnel developments is provided.

Home Rule   The power vested in a local unit of government, usually a city, to draft or change its own charter and to manage its affairs. Home rule limits legislative interference in local affairs. Most states permit some degree of freedom for cities, and an increasing number are granting it to counties. Home rule may be required or permitted by the state constitution or be granted by the legislature without specific constitutional authorization. Under home rule, the voters choose a commission to draft a charter that may be approved or rejected by the voters. This is in contrast to the granting of charters by the legislature under special acts, general laws, or optional plans. The city under home rule has control over its local problems, provided it does not violate the state constitution or general laws of the state. *See also* CHARTER, page 607; DILLON'S RULE, page 616; FEDERAL ANALOGY, page 617; UNITARY STATE, page 53.

Significance   Home rule introduces a measure of federalism into state-local relations to modify the usual unitary relation. The legislature is relieved of the burden of handling a variety of local problems that are better handled by those most intimately affected by them. Moreover, it strengthens democracy and local self-government and increases citizen interest. The major problem of home rule is the determination of what constitutes a local problem. The attitude of the legislature and of the courts determines the effectiveness of home rule provisions. A classic and continuing home rule controversy is that involving the relationship between Washington, D.C., and Congress; since 1974, the District has its own home rule charter, but Congress retains and exercises considerable control over District affairs.

Incorporated and Unincorporated Areas   The legal status of a local unit of government. Incorporated units include cities and, in some states, villages, towns, and boroughs. Unincorporated units include counties, townships, New England towns, and school districts. Incorporated areas are also called "municipal corporations," and unincorporated places are known as "quasi-corporations."

Significance   Though variations are found in the laws of the states, incorporated units or municipal corporations have a distinct legal entity and are usually created at the request and for the benefit of the inhabitants of the area. Incorporated units have a charter granted under special, general, or optional laws or under home rule. As municipal corporations, they usually have a large measure of self-government and provide services needed by the residents. Unincorporated units or quasi-corporations are created by the state constitution or laws without regard to the wishes of the inhabitants of the area and are primarily designed to carry on state services. The distinction between incorporated and unincorporated areas is rapidly disappearing in many states, as unincorporated units are increasingly given powers formerly reserved for incorporated areas.

Lieutenant Governor   The elected official in 42 American states who succeeds to the governorship when that office is declared vacant. Typically, the lieutenant governor presides over the state senate and casts the deciding vote in case of a tie. The lieutenant governor is elected at the same time and for the same term as the governor. In some states he or she serves as an ex officio member of the governor's administrative council and several boards and commissions.

Significance   Like the Vice President in the national government, the lieutenant governor's most important function is being available to take over as chief executive. When the governor is temporarily absent from the state, the lieutenant governor usually takes over until the governor's return. In states without a lieutenant governor, the president pro tempore of the senate or the secretary of state succeeds to the office of governor.

Local Option   Authority vested in local units to approve, reject, or select specific or alternative forms of action. Local option often refers to the power of local units to determine by popular vote whether liquor can be served in the community. It may also be used to describe the action taken by communities to select a charter from those made available by state law.

Significance   Local option prevents state governments from imposing the same controls over all units of local government. This has proved to be popular in the case of liquor sales because each community may decide for itself whether it will be "wet" or "dry." Local option is in accord with traditional American theories of local self-government.

Mayor   The chief executive and/or the ceremonial leader of a city. The role of the mayor varies with the form of city government. Under the strong mayor-council plan, the mayor has extensive power, including control over appointments and removals of city officials, and the veto power. Under a weak mayor-council plan, the mayor has limited executive powers. The mayor in the commission and manager plans is largely a ceremonial figure. *See also* MAYOR-COUNCIL PLAN, page 620.

Significance   The power and prestige of the mayor vary not only with the structure of city government but also with the personal qualities and political influence of the individual. In most cities, the mayor is a part-time official, but in cities like New York and Chicago the mayor's responsibilities are greater than those of many governors. In all cities, people look to the mayor for leadership in municipal affairs. Though many mayors of large cities have achieved national prominence and significant influence in national politics, the position has not generally been a stepping-stone to national office.

Mayor-administrator Plan   A plan of city government in which an administrative officer is appointed to assist the mayor in managing the affairs of the city. The plan has been adopted in a number of large cities, such as Los Angeles and Washington, D.C., to free the mayor for broader policy-making duties while using expert aid to supervise the routine administration of city government. The administrator, called the chief administrative officer, is appointed by the mayor with or without council approval and may have extensive appointment and removal power over administrative officials. Duties of the office include budget supervision, coordination of city agencies, personnel direction, and technical advice for the mayor. *See also* COUNCIL-MANAGER PLAN, page 613; GENERAL MANAGEMENT MUNICIPALITY, page 618; STRONG-MAYOR PLAN, page 626.

Significance   The mayor-administrator plan is a recent development used in large cities under a strong-mayor plan of government. The plan makes use of some of the features of the city manager form while retaining the political leadership of a strong mayor. It differs from the council-manager plan in retaining the position of strong mayor and in making the administrator responsible to the mayor rather than to the council.

Mayor-council Plan   A plan of city government in which the mayor is elected to serve as the executive officer of the city and an elective council serves as the legislative body. Wide variations exist from city to city, but the plan usually takes the form of a weak or strong mayor-council plan, depending upon the power of the mayor in the system. *See also* CITY COUNCIL, page 607; STRONG-MAYOR PLAN, page 626; WEAK-MAYOR PLAN, page 631.

Significance   The mayor-council plan reflects the traditional separation of powers between the legislative and executive branches and is used in about half of the nation's 7,000 cities. While the role of the mayor is the key to the nature of any specific application of the plan in a city, the council, in all cases, plays a major role as the legislative body. In recent years, the mayor-council plan has lost ground to the council-manager plan, particularly in small and middle-sized cities. In large cities, however, the plan continues to be in use, with the strong-mayor plan favored over the weak-mayor plan.

Metropolitan Area   A large city and its surrounding suburbs, which are socially and economically integrated although composed of separate units of government. The term "metropolitan" is derived from the Greek terms "meter" ("mother") and "polis" ("city"). As of 1994 the Office of Management and Budget (OMB) identified 253 "metropolitan statistical areas" (MSA). These are determined through application of a complex definition set by OMB, which generally includes groups of densely populated cities, suburbs, and counties that are economically and socially integrated. In addition, 19 areas, typified by New York, Chicago, and Los Angeles, are designated as "consolidated metropolitan statistical areas" (CMSA) composed of several contiguous metropolitan areas called "primary metropolitan statistical areas" (PMSA), of which there are 76. *See also* ANNEXATION, page 605; CITY-COUNTY CONSOLIDATION, page 608; CITY-COUNTY SEPARATION, page 608; CONSOLIDATION, page 610; COUNCILS OF GOVERNMENT, page 614; FUNCTIONAL CONSOLIDATION, page 617; METROPOLITAN FEDERATION, page 621; SUBURBIA, page 627; URBAN COUNTY PLAN, page 630.

Significance   Nearly 80 percent of the American people live in metropolitan areas, although these occupy only about 10 percent of the land area of the United States. About 55 percent of the population lives in metropolitan areas of 1 million or more. This rapidly increasing phenomenon of the twentieth century has brought with it a host of political, social, and economic challenges. Metropolitan areas are characterized by numerous governmental units sharing such major problems as transportation, housing, sewage disposal, and water supply. In recent years, central cities have been losing population to the suburbs, creating severe governmental and fiscal problems for both areas. Proposed solutions to the metropolitan problem include annexation, consolidation, federation, and functional consolidation. None of these proposals has, as yet, proved satisfactory, due largely to the reluctance on the part of people to change established patterns. More than three-fourths of the national population growth during the period of 1960 to 1970 took place in metropolitan areas, and 90 percent of the growth during the 1980s occurred in metropolitan areas of 1 million or more. In metropolitan areas, central cities are declining in population while suburban areas are growing, resulting, in many large metropolitan areas, in racial minority concentration in central cities. Some areas, such as the 450 miles from Boston to Washington, D.C., are continuous chains of metropolitan areas.

Metropolitan Federation   A proposed solution to the problems of metropolitan areas that would create a central metropolitan government to handle problems of the entire metropolitan region, reserving to the local units control over local matters. The plan is based on the principle of federalism, which is in effect at the national-state level. The plan has been put into effect in Toronto, Ontario, and the metropolitan government of Dade County (Miami), Florida, resembles a federation. Under a federated plan, the metropolitan or central unit might handle such common problems as highways, air terminals, water supply, sewerage, and air pollution. The local units could continue to act in the areas of police, schools, and other matters that the people desire to retain as strictly local functions. *See also* METROPOLITAN AREA, page 621.

Significance   Federation is viewed as one of the more practical means of solving metropolitan problems because it does not destroy the identity of local units. At the same time, areawide services can be provided to units unable to finance them alone. The plan is flexible because functions can be arranged as need demonstrates, and new units can be added as they become part of the metropolitan area. It is difficult, however, to determine what constitutes an areawide or local problem. Further, the plan simply adds another unit of government to an already large number. Disagreement is apt to arise over proper representation of local units in the metropolitan government.

Municipality   A subordinate public entity authorized by a central government and vested with the legal rights of a corporation. The term (derived from "municipum," the local unit of Roman government) generally refers to urban communities such as cities, villages, towns, and boroughs. A municipal corporation establishes local self-government under a charter so that needed public services such as police and fire protection and water, sewer, health, and similar services may be provided. *See also* CHARTER, page 607; CITY, page 609; DILLON'S RULE, page 616; INCORPORATED AND UNINCORPORATED AREAS, page 619; VILLAGE, page 630.

Significance   Municipal corporations recognize the need for special governmental arrangements to meet local problems arising out of urbanization. Many issues that loom large in an urban community, such as refuse disposal, have little if any impact upon a rural community or may be treated largely as an individual matter. The precise concept and authority of a municipality varies from state to state and rests primarily on state law and judicial decisions. Municipalities are presumed to provide a measure of self-government and do more than carry out state functions, but such distinctions are disappearing as other local units, such as counties, take on urban functions.

Optional Charter   A plan in effect in about one-third of the states that permits a city to choose a charter from among several provided by state law. Typically, cities may choose various forms of the mayor-council plan, the commission plan, or the council-manager plan. *See also* CHARTER, page 607.

Significance   The optional charter plan represents a compromise between complete legislative domination of cities through special acts and local self-government under home rule. It permits cities to choose their own forms of government by public referendum. The plan is, however, unlike home rule in that the legislature may change the content of the options at any time. Under home rule, the city itself frames and changes its charter.

Ordinance   A legislative enactment of a local governing body. Ordinances have the force of law, but the term is to be distinguished from the statute-making power of national and state legislatures. Ordinances are issued under authority granted by the sovereign power and, in the case of local governments, must comply with state constitutions, charters, and general laws.

Significance   The subordinate position of local government in its relations to the state is underscored by the fact that the former has only ordinance-making rather than statutory power as that term is generally understood. An interesting example of the use of the term is that Congress under the Articles of Confederation had only ordinance-making power, demonstrating the sovereignty of the member states.

Planning   Preparation and execution of projects for the future economic, social, and physical development of a community. Planning may be nationwide or statewide in situations in which it encompasses all types of governmental problems, but it is more often associated with the physical development of municipal governments. This includes planning street layouts, parks, public utility routes, and the zoning of areas for residential and commercial purposes. In recent years, emphasis has turned from purely physical aspects of city planning and beautification to social and economic concerns such as urban redevelopment and housing. In metropolitan areas, stress is now being put on the need for countywide or regional planning to provide orderly development. Sound planning must take into consideration population and economic trends as well as future fiscal needs. Many cities and states have official planning agencies. *See also* COUNCILS OF GOVERNMENT, page 614; HOUSING AND COMMUNITY DEVELOPMENT ACT, page 525; ZONING, page 631.

Significance   The American people have been slow to accept the concept of planning, perhaps conceiving it to be similar to the planned economies associated with socialism. Lack of planning has, however, resulted in the waste of natural resources and the need for expensive corrective action. The failure of most communities to provide for suitable streets and parking facilities to meet the demands of the automotive age is a major example. Today, planning is generally accepted as a necessary aspect of governmental operations, although it is never a politically neutral exercise. A large number of cities now have master plans for future growth and require that new developments fit into the master plan. Planning is now considered to be a professional specialty, with many colleges and universities offering courses of training.

Register of Deeds   A county officer, sometimes called "recorder of deeds," who is elected in about half the states and whose major duty is to record and preserve legal documents relating mainly to real estate ownership and transfers. This function is designed to protect landowners and prospective purchasers of land against flaws in titles to property.

Significance   Few students of government support the idea of electing a register or recorder of deeds. The position is an important one but is not of a policy-making nature. Most counties have adopted modern techniques of recording legal papers through microfilm or other technical processes, but some continue to keep longhand records in bound volumes.

Resident   A person who lives in a political jurisdiction long enough to qualify for certain rights or privileges. Residency is generally determined by place of domicile, work, or school. Where one legally resides determines various matters such as voting rights, college tuition, use of courts as in a divorce suit, the right to public employment, or special licenses. *See also* RESIDENCE, page 110.

Significance   The free mobility of the American people, coupled with the existence of numerous units of government, exacerbates the issue of residency in American life. The courts have frowned upon efforts to limit essential or important rights or privileges to those with lengthy residence in a community. Thus the Supreme Court has voided lengthy residence requirements for voting (*Dunn v. Blumstein*, 405 U.S. 330 [1972]) or any residence requirement for welfare benefits (*Shapiro v. Thompson*, 394 U.S. 618 [1969]). It has sustained extended residence requirements in the case of state university tuition (*Vlaudis v. Kline*, 412 U.S. 441 [1973]) where the burden of support for the privilege is borne by bona fide residents and a distinction between residents and transients is reasonable. A problem shared by many communities involves the requirement that those working for a unit of government (such as city, county, or school district) must live in that unit. Contemporary metropolitan life, however, makes enforcement difficult and controversial.

School District   A governmental unit for the maintenance of schools. In about half the states, school districts are administratively and financially independent and do not follow township, city or county lines. The town or township plan is dominant in New England, whereas the county plan is dominant in the South. In Delaware and Hawaii, the entire state comprises one school district. Typically, school districts are governed by elective boards, which choose a superintendent to administer the system. In some areas, the school district is part of city government, and the board is selected by the mayor or council. Approximately 18 percent of all local units of government are school districts, and they account for 40 percent of all expenditures by local units of government. *See also* BOARD OF EDUCATION, page 606; CONSOLIDATION, page 610.

Significance   In 1942, school districts comprised more than two-thirds of all local governments. There has since been a dramatic consolidation of districts (from 108,000 to less than 15,000, or 18 percent of local government units), and this trend continues. The tradition of independent school districts is based on the belief that schools should not be part of the politics of regular governments or tied financially to other units. Some claim, however, that the independent school district develops a "politics" of its own and tends to detract from the financial needs of other units.

Secretary of State   A state official elected by popular vote in 36 states and appointed by the governor or legislature in 11 others. The lieutenant governor performs the function in Alaska, Hawaii, and Utah. Major duties of the office include the preservation of official documents, administration of elections, issuance of business licenses and certificates of incorporation, and registration and issuance of motor vehicle licenses. The secretary of state is also keeper of the state seal.

Significance   The office of secretary of state is not considered by political scientists to be one that justifies popular election. The office has few, if any, policy-making responsibilities, but its elective position reduces the governor's control over state administration. Appointment by the governor is generally recommended. In most states, the secretary of state enjoys political prominence because his or her name is affixed to numerous documents, such as driver's licenses. Many secretaries go on to higher office. Moreover, in states with widespread patronage or political appointments, this office controls numerous jobs that can be spread out to the party faithful.

Special Act   Legislation applicable to one unit of local government. The special act system prevailed from colonial times to the middle of the nineteenth century and is still in use in several states. Through special acts, state legislatures grant charters to municipalities, amend the charters, and pass legislation on a wide variety of purely local problems. *See also* CHARTER, page 607; GENERAL LAWS, page 617.

Significance   Special acts have the virtue of flexibility but are often abused. The net effect of much special legislation is to vest virtually complete authority over a local unit in the legislative representative from that area because other representatives rarely interfere with his or her desires. Often "ripper" acts are passed in such states; these abolish particular local offices, such as that of city manager, although such action may be contrary to local wishes. Special acts put a great burden on the legislature, and, in some states, more than half the legislation is special in nature. Most states now forbid special legislation by requiring general laws or by permitting home rule. In a few states, the people of an affected area may reject special acts by popular vote.

Special District   A unit of local government established to provide a single service. About half of the special districts in the United States are for fire protection, soil conservation, water, and drainage. Other common types of special districts provide cemetery, sewer, park, recreation, housing, and mosquito-abatement services. A school district may be classified as a special district, but the Census Bureau and political scientists classify it separately. Special districts are usually created to meet problems that transcend local government boundaries or to bypass taxation and debt restrictions imposed upon local units by state law. The number of special districts has nearly quadrupled since 1942 (8,000 to 31,500), and they now comprise 37 percent of all local units. The special district is created under state law, usually requires the consent of the people in the district, and is governed by a small board that has taxing and bonding authority, the power to levy user fees, and, in some cases, power of eminent domain.

Significance   The dramatic increase in the use of the special district device illustrates the inability of existing units of government to meet modern needs. Tax and debt restrictions can be evaded and high costs shared by several units without upsetting traditional government boundary lines. Paradoxically, while attempts are under way to decrease the number of local units of government, the special district is adding to the complexity of local government. The device, however, has strong appeal to interest groups that want to keep a function separate. Many people believe that a special district keeps a function "out of politics," when, in fact, it may exercise great power, spend large sums of money, and have an important impact upon community life. Most special districts and their governing officials have very low public visibility and may not be effectively accountable to the people.

State Aid   Funds provided to local governments by the state in the form of grants-in-aid or shared taxes. State grants go primarily to school districts for educational purposes and to counties for welfare and highway functions. Shared taxes are administered by the state, which gives a portion of sales or income taxes to local units, including cities. The amount provided to each unit is usually based on a formula keyed to population, use, and need. *See also* BLOCK GRANT, page 388.

Significance   Local units must rely heavily upon the general property tax for income. Since this source has proved insufficient, state aid has increased substantially in recent years and accounts for about one-third of local revenues. Grants-in-aid are usually accompanied by state supervision of the expenditure and a requirement that the local unit put up a matching amount or some percentage of the grant. Such grants have improved local government standards while retaining some measure of local control. Shared taxes are usually free of state controls but, because tax collections vary from year to year, local units cannot depend upon specific amounts.

State Auditor   A state official elected in seventeen states and appointed by the governor or legislature in others. In some states, the title "comptroller" is used. The state auditor's major duty is to act as a watchdog over expenditures of state agencies by postauditing accounts. In some states, however, the state auditor has preauditing and accounting duties as well. *See also* AUDITOR, page 387.

Significance   The position of auditor is essential for ensuring accountability of public expenditures. Political scientists, however, doubt the wisdom of electing or of having this official appointed by the governor. Selection by and responsibility to the legislature is considered the most desirable situation because the auditor's job is to ensure that expenditures have been made in accordance with the legislature's enactments.

State Treasurer   A state official popularly elected in 38 states and chosen by the governor or legislature in others. Major duties of the office are the safekeeping of state funds and the payment of bills on proper warrant. In some states, the treasurer has tax collection responsibilities as well.

Significance   The popular election of a treasurer is viewed as unnecessary by students of government. Financial matters, except for auditing, should be centralized in a finance office headed by an appointee of the governor. This would make the governor clearly responsible for the handling of state funds.

Strong-mayor Plan   A plan of city government in which the mayor is given complete executive authority. Its major features include (1) election of a mayor as chief executive; (2) concentration of administrative power in the hands of the mayor, including powers of appointment and removal; (3) a veto power over the city council; and (4) strong budgetary controls in the hands of the mayor. *See also* MAYOR-ADMINISTRATOR PLAN, page 620; MAYOR-COUNCIL PLAN, page 620; WEAK-MAYOR PLAN, page 631.

Significance   The strong-mayor plan is used in most large cities and is favored by political scientists over the weak-mayor plan. The main advantages of the plan are the centralization of authority and the clear fixing of executive responsibility. The plan permits the mayor to exercise strong political or policy-making leadership, a particularly desirable condition in large cities, with their variety of competing interests. In contrast to the weak-mayor plan, the strong-mayor plan encourages the use of modern administrative techniques and the appointment of able subordinates. Few people, however, combine top administrative and political talent. In several large cities, the mayor-administrator plan is in use to free the mayor from attention to administrative detail.

Suburbia   Areas adjacent to or near a city. Pulled by more space, larger homes, betters schools, and federally aided programs for highways and housing, a major shift of population to the suburbs occurred during the 1950s and 1960s. By 1970, the census showed that more than half the population of metropolitan areas lived in suburbia. Typically "bedroom" communities dependent upon the central city for jobs and cultural programs, suburbs rapidly became commercial and industrial in character and incorporated separately as cities. The result is hundreds of metropolitan areas composed of numerous separate units of government. In the case of the New York City metropolitan area, about 1,400 of these units exist. *See also* METROPOLITAN AREA, page 621.

Significance   Suburbia has had a major impact upon American politics. Congressional and state legislative representation has shifted in favor of suburbs. No longer dependent upon the central city, suburbs have become rivals to the cities as well as to other suburbs as centers of economic and cultural vitality. Indeed, suburbs increasingly look to central city populations as sources of labor. Racial and economic polarization also characterizes larger metropolitan areas, with minorities and the poor living in the central city and the white middle and upper classes in suburbs. Suburban communities enjoy and defend their political independence, but all are increasingly interdependent for solving problems of water supply, sanitation, air and water pollution, roads, and land use.

Superintendent of Public Instruction   A state official whose function is to supervise the public school system of the state. In some states, the official is known as "superintendent of schools" or "commissioner of education." The superintendent of public instruction is elected in 15 states, appointed by the governor in 11, and, in increasing numbers of states (23 in 1994), chosen by the state board of education. In most cases, the superintendent serves on the state board of education and acts as its chief administrative officer. Duties of the office generally include the establishment of standards for schools, curriculum development, teacher qualifications, and control of state-administered school funds. In some states, this authority extends to other educational institutions, such as state colleges and community colleges. *See also* BOARD OF EDUCATION, page 606.

Significance   The superintendent of public instruction holds a position of major responsibility because of the value placed on education in the United

States. Because of the high professional standards desirable for this office, many educators and political scientists favor the superintendent's appointment by an elected or appointed board of education or by the governor. Increasingly, superintendents of public instruction are embroiled in controversy over educational policy because of increased public demands for special programs in educational institutions at all levels and diminishing financial resources.

Supervisor   The chief elective officer of the township (called "trustee" in some states). The supervisor has overall responsibility for township government, presides over the township board, and may represent the township on the county board and serve as tax assessor. *See also* TOWNSHIP, page 629.

Significance   In states with township government, the supervisor is an important political figure who exercises considerable influence at the county and state levels. The growing urbanization of many townships and counties has forced new challenges upon township supervisors, whose functions were originally designed for a rural society.

Town   The major unit of local government in New England. The term is used in some states to designate a township or a small urban area but is generally used by political scientists to designate the New England town. With the exception of some incorporated cities, all six states of New England are divided into towns; this division includes both the rural and urban portions of each particular area. The town is responsible for most of those governmental services provided in other states by counties and cities. The town is governed by all the inhabitants through the town meeting and, between meetings, by a board of selectmen and other town officers. In many towns, however, representatives are chosen for town meetings, and some utilize a town manager. *See also* TOWN MEETING, page 628.

Significance   The New England town developed in the colonial period and is deeply rooted in tradition. Growing populations and urbanization of many towns have put a strain upon government arrangements suitable for a frontier rural society. Representative town meetings, special finance and budget committees, and town managers now characterize many towns.

Town Meeting   The governing authority of a town or township. All qualified voters may participate in the election of officers and in the passage of taxes or other legislation. Town meetings are used in New England towns and in many midwestern townships. *See also* TOWN, page 628.

Significance   The town meeting represents the ideal of direct democracy in action. It is a product of rural society, however, and has lost much of its vitality in recent years. Areas with large populations cannot hold meetings of all qualified voters; no building can accommodate them, and the meetings are unwieldy. Often people are apathetic, and power falls into the hands of the few who do attend or those who "pack" the meeting. Many midwestern townships have abolished the town meeting. In New England, representative town meetings are held; as is customary for most legislative bodies, these town meetings are comprised of delegates elected by the voters.

Township A unit of government, usually a subdivision of a county, found in twenty states, principally in the Midwest and in the Northeast. The term "midwestern township" is often used to distinguish it from the New England town. Townships vary in shape and size but tend to cover an area of 36 square miles as a result of the congressional township system of identifying land. Some townships have an annual town meeting, and all are governed by a township board, usually consisting of three members. Municipal areas are usually excluded from the township authority, but in some states, villages or towns remain part of the township. Township functions tend to be rural in nature, such as maintaining roads, cemeteries, and drains; minor law enforcement; and assessment of property. In urban areas, however, townships have taken on numerous urban services, such as police and fire protection and public works. In some states, the township is the unit for school administration. *See also* CONGRESSIONAL TOWNSHIP, page 609; TOWN, page 628.

Significance With some exceptions, township government has declined in importance. A product of frontier society and the New England town, it is too small for efficient administration. Modern communication makes it unnecessary as a subdivision of easily accessible county offices. Duplication of services in small areas results. Some states, such as Oklahoma and Iowa, have transferred most township functions to the county. Although there are nearly 16,700 township governments, comprising about 18 percent of local governmental units, a general lack of interest in them seems to characterize many areas. In some states, the township has gained strength by taking on municipal functions. Most political scientists favor abolition of the township as a unit of government and transfer of its functions to the county or, in some cases, to nearby city governments.

Uniform State Laws Laws proposed by the National Conference of Commissioners on Uniform State Laws, a few of which have been adopted by all or many states. Among those proposals that have had wide adoption are the Negotiable Instruments Act, the Warehouse Receipts Act, the Stock Transfer Act, others relating to sales, partnerships, bills of lading, and some traffic, criminal, and family matters. The National Conference has proposed more than 100 uniform laws since its inception in 1892, but it has met with only minor success. The conference consists of three commissioners from each state, usually lawyers, appointed by the governor. The Council of State Governments acts as secretariat for the conference. *See also* COUNCIL OF STATE GOVERNMENT, page 632; HORIZONTAL FEDERALISM, page 41.

Significance The wide diversity of state laws under the federal system has proved vexing to many people. Persons doing business in several states are often inconvenienced and confused. Confusion exists, too, in such matters as marriage and divorce and traffic laws. The increasing mobility of businesses and people in general has increased the need for more uniformity. The effort has been retarded by apathetic state legislatures and by the desires of many states to gain an advantage over others by having less stringent rules concerning business transactions or divorce, for example, in order to attract more business to the state.

Urban County Plan   A proposed solution to metropolitan area problems that involves the transfer to county governments of functions exercised by several units of government within the county. Several counties in California have taken over the functions of law enforcement, health services, tax assessments and collections, and prisons. Dade County, Florida, has been established as a metropolitan or urban county. Municipalities within that county, including Miami, have transferred to the county power over traffic problems, planning, sewerage, water supply, and other countywide problems. The urban county plan is to be distinguished from city-county consolidation, which contemplates the complete merger of county government with all other units within the county. *See also* CITY-COUNTY CONSOLIDATION, page 608; METROPOLITAN AREA, page 621.

Significance   Many metropolitan areas lie within a single county. This facilitates the transfer of functions because the county is an established unit of government. No new government need be created or any unit be abolished. Metropolitan areas are, however, rapidly spreading beyond county lines. Most county governments are poorly organized and have made little progress in the use of modern administrative techniques or of the merit system of personnel management. Most are ill equipped to handle urban services without considerable reform.

Village   A small urban area, called a town or borough in some states, that is a municipal corporation but one with less authority and simpler organization than a city. The term "village" is a legal concept, varying in meaning from state to state in which the designation is used. Village status may be based upon population, but many villages are larger than regular cities. Villages usually are governed by a small council and a village president or mayor. Limitations are placed by the state upon the taxing and borrowing powers of villages as well as upon the types of functions that they may perform.

Significance   Village government developed to accommodate the needs of trading centers in rural areas. Since the county or township could not provide needed services, such areas were permitted to incorporate as villages for limited purposes, such as street maintenance or water supply. Villages may attain city status by a vote of the people or by special act, but many people prefer the lesser designation and the informality of village organization. Increased population may, however, compel change to city status in order to get greater taxing and service authority.

Ward   The division of a city for purposes of electing members to the city council. The ward system is favored in the larger cities, but most cities use an at-large system of electing council members, particularly those using the commission or council-manager forms of government. A number of cities now use a combination of both methods, selecting some council members from wards and others at large. *See also* ALDERMAN, page 605.

Significance   The ward system has declined in recent years but still has many adherents. It provides a more representative council because voters can know their representatives more intimately and, in turn, the council member knows more about the ward. This system is particularly favored by

minority groups and labor interests, who seldom gain representation under
the at-large system. The main disadvantage of the ward system is the emphasis it tends to place on special interests of neighborhoods rather than on
the interest of the community as a whole. Further, it sometimes makes it
more difficult to get qualified candidates and leads inevitably to gerrymandering. These factors have led to the growth of the at-large system or a combination of both ward and at-large elections.

Weak-mayor Plan   A plan of city government in which the mayor must
share executive authority with other elected officials and the city council.
Most cities under the mayor-council plan use the weak-mayor form rather
than the strong-mayor plan. The major features of the weak-mayor plan include (1) a long ballot in which the people choose numerous department
heads, boards, and commissions, as well as the mayor, for administrative purposes; (2) a limited power of appointment and removal in the hands of the
mayor; (3) the appointment of numerous officials by the council alone; (4) a
weak veto power or a complete absence of it for the mayor; and (5) direct
participation by the council in administrative matters, including preparation
of the budget. *See also* MAYOR-COUNCIL PLAN, page 620; STRONG-MAYOR PLAN,
page 626.

Significance   In spite of its wide use, political scientists frown upon the
weak-mayor plan. The long ballot, the difficulty of fixing responsibility because of the lack of a responsible executive, the lack of coordination, and the
use of outmoded administrative and personnel techniques that characterize
the plan lead to a poor quality of municipal government. Yet the plan, which
is rooted in the traditions of Jacksonian Democracy, prevents the concentration of power and establishes an elaborate system of checks and balances.

Zoning   The division of a city or other unit of government into districts and
the regulation by law of the uses of the land. Zoning is concerned with the
nature of buildings (residential, industrial, or commercial), their height and
density, and the uses made of particular tracts of land. Zoning laws are enacted under the police power of communities to protect the health, safety,
and welfare of the people. The U.S. Supreme Court upheld zoning as a proper
exercise of police power in 1926 in *Euclid v. Amber Realty Co.,* 272 U.S. 365.
A zoning board of appeals is usually created to grant exceptions and vari-
ances to persons who might suffer undue hardships under a zoning regulation. *See also* EMINENT DOMAIN, page 308; TAKINGS CLAUSE, page 340; PLANNING,
page 623.

Significance   Comprehensive zoning has been in effect only since
the 1920s and still meets resistance in many areas in which the people object to legislative and administrative control of their property. Zoning,
however, protects property values in residential areas by forbidding industrial
or commercial uses of property. It also contributes to the environment
and appearance of a community. Zoning makes possible better planning and
administration of public services, such as fire protection and traffic supervision, and contributes to the health and well-being of a community by segre-
gating industrial plants from residential areas. Critics note that zoning is
often used by some communities to control the character and homogeneity

of population through requirements for land usage (lot size, placement of dwelling, construction) that result in costs beyond the capacity of all but the well-to-do. Zoning must be carried out with careful regard for constitutionally protected property rights. A zoning requirement may be challenged or compensation awarded if it lacks a public purpose or inappropriately denies an affected property owner of economic benefits.

IMPORTANT AGENCIES

Council of State Governments   An agency maintained by the state governments to serve as a secretariat, research agency, and clearinghouse for the improvement of state legislative, executive, and judicial administration. It has encouraged interstate cooperation and the general improvement of federal-state relations and state-local relations. The council's governing board includes the governor and two legislators from each state plus representatives of national organizations of elected state officials. The council serves as the secretariat for a variety of organizations representing state governmental officials and provides research, training, and support services to improve state government. It publishes a variety of materials including the biennial *Book of the States*. Its headquarters is in Lexington, Kentucky.

Significance   The Council of State Governments has sponsored conferences and research on problems of common state concern from crime control to fisheries. It has promoted better interstate relations and has influence in Washington and in the state capitals. Its publications carry informative and up-to-date information on state government developments and problems, and the *Book of the States* is a major reference work on state and local government. Similarly, but in less official roles, a number of voluntary associations, including the National League of Cities, the National Association of County Officials, the United States Conference of Mayors, and the International City Management Association, carry on important activities for local governments.

Constitution of the United States

PREAMBLE

We the People of the United States, in Order to form a more perfect Union, establish Justice, insure domestic Tranquility, provide for the common defence, promote the general Welfare, and secure the Blessings of Liberty to ourselves and our Posterity, do ordain and establish this Constitution for the United States of America.

ARTICLE I

Section 1. All legislative Powers herein granted shall be vested in a Congress of the United States, which shall consist of a Senate and House of Representatives.

Section 2. The House of Representatives shall be composed of Members chosen every second Year by the People of the several States, and the Electors in each State shall have the Qualifications requisite for Electors of the most numerous Branch of the State Legislature.

No Person shall be a Representative who shall not have attained to the Age of twenty five Years, and been seven Years a Citizen of the United States, and who shall not, when elected, be an Inhabitant of that State in which he shall be chosen.

Representatives and direct Taxes shall be apportioned among the several States which may be included within this Union, according to their respective Numbers, which shall be determined by adding to the whole Number of free Persons, including those bound to Service for a Term of Years, and excluding Indians not taxed, three fifths of all other Persons. The actual Enumeration shall be made within three Years after the first Meeting of Congress of the United States, and within every subsequent Term of ten Years, in such Manner as they shall by Law direct. The Number of Representatives shall not exceed one for every thirty Thousand, but each State shall have at Least one Representative; and until such enumeration shall be made, the State of New Hampshire shall be entitled to chuse three, Massachusetts eight, Rhode-Island and Providence Plantations one, Connecticut five, New York six, New Jersey four, Pennsylvania eight, Delaware one, Maryland six, Virginia ten, North Carolina five, South Carolina five, and Georgia three.

When vacancies happen in the Representation for any State, the Executive Authority thereof shall issue Writs of Election to fill such Vacancies.

The House of Representatives shall chuse their Speaker and other Officers; and shall have the sole Power of Impeachment.

Section 3.   The Senate of the United States shall be composed of two Senators from each State, chosen by the Legislature thereof, for six Years; and each Senator shall have one Vote.

Immediately after they shall be assembled in Consequence of the first Election, they shall be divided as equally as may be into three Classes. The Seats of the Senators of the first Class shall be vacated at the Expiration of the second Year, of the second Class at the Expiration of the Fourth Year, and of the third Class at the Expiration of the sixth Year, so that one third may be chosen every second Year; and if Vacancies happen by Resignation, or otherwise, during the Recess of the Legislature of any State, the Executive thereof may make temporary Appointments until the next Meeting of the Legislature, which shall then fill such Vacancies.

No Person shall be a Senator who shall not have attained to the Age of thirty Years, and been nine Years a Citizen of the United States, and who shall not, when elected, be an Inhabitant of that State for which he shall be chosen.

The Vice President of the United States shall be President of the Senate, but shall have no Vote, unless they be equally divided.

The Senate shall chuse their other Officers, and also a President pro tempore, in the absence of the Vice President, or when he shall exercise the Office of President of the United States.

The Senate shall have the sole Power to try all Impeachments. When sitting for that Purpose, they shall be on Oath or Affirmation. When the President of the United States is tried, the Chief Justice shall preside: And no Person shall be convicted without the Concurrence of two thirds of the Members present.

Judgment in Cases of Impeachment shall not extend further than to removal from Office, and disqualification to hold and enjoy any Office of honor, Trust or Profit under the United States: but the Party convicted shall nevertheless be liable and subject to Indictment, Trial, Judgment and Punishment, according to Law.

Section 4.   The Times, Places and Manner of holding Elections for Senators and Representatives, shall be prescribed in each State by the Legislature thereof; but the Congress may at any time by Law make or alter such Regulations, except as to the Places of Chusing Senators.

The Congress shall assemble at least once in every Year, and such Meeting shall be on the first Monday in December, unless they shall by Law appoint a different Day.

Section 5.   Each House shall be the Judge of the Elections, Returns and Qualifications of its own Members, and a Majority of each shall constitute a Quorum to do Business; but a smaller number may adjourn from day to day, and may be authorized to compel the Attendance of absent Members, in such Manner, and under such Penalties as each House may provide.

Each House may determine the Rules of its Proceedings, punish its Members for disorderly Behaviour, and, with the Concurrence of two thirds, expel a Member.

Each House shall keep a Journal of its Proceedings, and from time to time publish the same, excepting such Parts as may in their Judgment require Secrecy; and the Yeas and Nays of the Members of either House on any question shall, at the Desire of one fifth of those Present, be entered on the Journal.

Neither House, during the Session of Congress, shall, without the Consent of the other, adjourn for more than three days, nor to any other Place than that in which the two Houses shall be sitting.

Section 6.   The Senators and Representatives shall receive a Compensation for their Services, to be ascertained by Law, and paid out of the Treasury of the United States. They shall in all Cases, except Treason, Felony and Breach of the Peace, be privileged from Arrest during their Attendance at the Session of their respective Houses, and in going to and returning from the same; and for any Speech or Debate in either House, they shall not be questioned in any other Place.

No Senator or Representative shall, during the Time for which he was elected, be appointed to any civil Office under the Authority of the United States, which shall have been created, or the Emoluments whereof shall have been encreased during such time; and no Person holding any Office under the United States, shall be a Member of either House during his Continuance in Office.

Section 7.   All Bills for raising Revenue shall originate in the House of Representatives; but the Senate may propose or concur with Amendments as on other Bills.

Every Bill which shall have passed the House of Representatives and the Senate, shall, before it become a Law, be presented to the President of the United States; If he approve he shall sign it, but if not he shall return it, with his Objections to that House in which it shall have originated, who shall enter the Objections at large on their Journal, and proceed to reconsider it. If after such Reconsideration two thirds of that House shall agree to pass the Bill, it shall be sent, together with the Objections, to the other House, by which it shall likewise be reconsidered, and if approved by two thirds of that House, it shall become a Law. But in all such Cases the Votes of both Houses shall be determined by Yeas and Nays, and the Names of the Persons voting for and against the Bill shall be entered on the Journal of each House respectively. If any Bill shall not be returned by the President within ten Days (Sunday excepted) after it shall have been presented to him, the Same shall be a Law, in like Manner as if he had signed it, unless the Congress by their Adjournment prevent its Return, in which Case it shall not be a Law.

Every Order, Resolution, or Vote to which the Concurrence of the Senate and House of Representatives may be necessary (except on a question of Adjournment) shall be presented to the President of the United States; and before the Same shall take Effect, shall be approved by him, or being disapproved by him, shall be repassed by two thirds of the Senate and House of Representatives, according to the Rules and Limitations prescribed in the Case of a Bill.

Section 8.   The Congress shall have Power To lay and collect Taxes, Duties, Imposts and Excises, to pay the Debts and provide for the common

Defence and general Welfare of the United States; but all Duties, Imposts and Excises shall be uniform throughout the United States;

To borrow money on the credit of the United States;

To regulate Commerce with foreign Nations, and among the several States, and with the Indian Tribes;

To establish an uniform Rule of Naturalization, and uniform Laws on the subject of Bankruptcies throughout the United States;

To coin Money, regulate the Value thereof, and of foreign Coin, and fix the Standard of Weights and Measures;

To provide for the Punishment of counterfeiting the Securities and current Coin of the United States;

To establish Post Offices and post Roads;

To promote the Progress of Science and useful Arts, by securing for limited Times to Authors and Inventors the exclusive Right to their respective Writings and Discoveries;

To constitute Tribunals inferior to the supreme Court;

To define and punish Piracies and Felonies committed on the high Seas, and Offences against the Law of Nations;

To declare War, grant Letters of Marque and Reprisal, and make Rules concerning Captures on Land and Water;

To raise and support Armies, but not Appropriation of Money to that Use shall be for a longer Term than two Years;

To provide and maintain a Navy;

To make Rules for the Government and Regulation of the land and naval Forces;

To provide for calling forth the Militia to execute the Laws of the Union, suppress Insurrections and repel Invasions;

To provide for organizing, arming, and disciplining the Militia, and for governing such Part of them as may be employed in the Service of the United States, reserving to the States respectively, the Appointment of the Officers, and the Authority of training the Militia according to the discipline prescribed by Congress;

To exercise exclusive Legislation in all Cases whatsoever, over such District (not exceeding ten Miles square) as may, by Cession of Particular States, and the Acceptance of Congress, become the Seat of the Government of the United States, and to exercise like Authority over all Places purchased by the Consent of the Legislature of the State in which the Same shall be, for the Erection of Forts, Magazines, Arsenals, dock-Yards, and other needful Buildings;—And

To make all Laws which shall be necessary and proper for carrying into Execution the foregoing Powers, and all other Powers vested by this Constitution in the Government of the United States, or in any Department or Officer thereof.

Section 9.   The Migration or Importation of such Persons as any of the States now existing shall think proper to admit, shall not be prohibited by the Congress prior to the Year one thousand eight hundred and eight, but a tax or duty may be imposed on such Importation, not exceeding ten dollars for each Person.

The privilege of the Writ of Habeas Corpus shall not be suspended, unless when in Cases of Rebellion or Invasion the public Safety may require it.

No Bill of Attainder or ex post facto Law shall be passed.

No capitation, or other direct, Tax shall be laid, unless in Proportion to the Census of Enumeration herein before directed to be taken.

No Tax or Duty shall be laid on Articles exported from any State.

No Preference shall be given by any Regulation of Commerce or Revenue to the Ports of one State over those of another; nor shall Vessels bound to, or from, one State, be obliged to enter, clear, or pay Duties in another.

No Money shall be drawn from the Treasury, but in Consequence of Appropriations made by Law; and a regular Statement and Account of the Receipts and Expenditures of all public Money shall be published from time to time.

No Title of Nobility shall be granted by the United States: And no Person holding any Office of Profit or Trust under them, shall, without the Consent of the Congress, accept of any present, Emolument, Office, or Title, or any kind whatever, from any King, Prince, or foreign State.

Section 10.   No State shall enter into any Treaty, Alliance, or Confederation; grant Letters of Marque and Reprisal; coin Money; emit Bills of Credit; make any Thing but gold and silver Coin a Tender in Payment of Debts; pass any Bill of Attainder, ex post facto Law, or Law impairing the Obligation of Contracts, or grant any Title of Nobility.

No State shall, without the Consent of the Congress, lay any Imposts or Duties on Imports or Exports, except what may be absolutely necessary for executing its inspection Laws: and the net Produce of all Duties and Imposts, laid by any State on Imports or Exports, shall be for the Use of the Treasury of the United States; and all such Laws shall be subject to the Revision and Controul of the Congress.

No State shall, without the Consent of Congress, lay any Duty of Tonnage, keep Troops, or Ships of War in time of Peace, enter into any Agreement or Compact with another State, or with a foreign Power, or engage in War, unless actually invaded, or in such imminent Danger as will not admit of delay.

ARTICLE II

Section 1.   The executive Power shall be vested in a President of the United States of America. He shall hold his Office during the Term of four Years, and, together with the Vice-President, chosen for the same Term, be elected as follows.

Each State shall appoint, in such Manner as the Legislature thereof may direct, a Number of Electors, equal to the whole Number of Senators and Representatives to which the State may be entitled in the Congress: but no Senator or Representative, or Person holding an Office of Trust or Profit under the United States, shall be appointed an Elector.

The Electors shall meet in their respective States, and vote by Ballot for two persons, of whom one at least shall not be an Inhabitant of the same State with themselves. And they shall make a List of all the Persons voted for, and of the Number of Votes for each; which List they shall sign and certify, and transmit sealed to the Seat of the Government of the United States, directed to the President of the Senate. The President of the Senate shall, in the Presence of the Senate and House of Representatives, open all the Certificates, and the Votes shall then be counted. The Person having the greatest Number of Votes shall be the President, if such Number be a Majority of the whole Number of Electors appointed; and if there be more than one who have such Majority, and have an equal Number of Votes, then the House of Representatives shall immediately chuse by Ballot one of them for President; and if no Person have a Majority, then from the five highest on the List the said House shall in like Manner chuse the President. But in chusing the President, the Votes shall be taken by States, the Representation from each State having one Vote; a quorum for this Purpose shall consist of a Member or Members from two thirds of the States, and a Majority of all the States shall be necessary to a Choice. In every Case, after the Choice of the President, the Person having the greatest Number of Votes of the Electors shall be the Vice President. But if there should remain two or more who have equal Votes, the Senate shall chuse from them by Ballot the Vice-President.

The Congress may determine the Time of chusing the Electors, and the Day on which they shall give their Votes; which Day shall be the same throughout the United States.

No person except a natural born Citizen, or a Citizen of the United States, at the time of the Adoption of this Constitution, shall be eligible to the Office of President; neither shall any Person be eligible to that Office who shall not have attained to the Age of thirty five Years, and been fourteen Years a Resident within the United States.

In Case of the Removal of the President from Office, or of his Death, Resignation, or Inability to discharge the Powers and Duties of the said Office, the same shall devolve on the Vice President, and the Congress may be Law, provide for the Case of Removal, Death, Resignation or Inability, both of the President and Vice President, declaring what Officer shall then act as President, and such Officer shall act accordingly, until the Disability be removed, or a President shall be elected.

The President shall, at stated Times, receive for his Services, a Compensation, which shall neither be encreased nor diminished during the Period for which he shall have been elected, and he shall not receive within that Period any other Emolument from the United States, or any of them.

Before he enter on the Execution of his Office, he shall take the following Oath or Affirmation:—"I do solemnly swear (or affirm) that I will faithfully execute the Office of President of the United States, and will to the best of my Ability, preserve, protect and defend the Constitution of the United States."

Section 2.   The President shall be Commander in Chief of the Army and Navy of the United States, and of the Militia of the several States when called into the actual Service of the United States; he may require the Opinion in writing, of the principal Officer in each of the executive Departments, upon any subject relating to the Duties of their respective Offices, and he shall have Power to grant Reprieves and Pardons for Offences against the United States, except in Cases of Impeachment.

He shall have Power, by and with the Advice and Consent of the Senate, to make Treaties, provided two-thirds of the Senators present concur; and he shall nominate, and by and with the Advice and Consent of the Senate, shall appoint Ambassadors, other public Ministers and Consuls, Judges of the supreme Court, and all other Officers of the United States, whose Appointments are not herein otherwise provided for, and which shall be established by Law: but the Congress may by Law vest the Appointment of such inferior Officers, as they think proper, in the President alone, in the Courts of Law, or in the Heads of Departments.

The President shall have Power to fill up all Vacancies that may happen during the Recess of the Senate, by granting Commissions which shall expire at the End of their next Session.

Section 3.   He shall from time to time give to the Congress Information of the State of the Union, and recommend to their Consideration such Measures as he shall judge necessary and expedient; he may, on extraordinary Occasions, convene both Houses, or either of them, and in Case of Disagreement between them, with Respect to the Time of Adjournment, he may adjourn them to such Time as he shall think proper; he shall receive Ambassadors and other public Ministers; he shall take Care that the Laws be faithfully executed, and shall Commission all the Officers of the United States.

Section 4.   The President, Vice President and all Civil Officers of the United States, shall be removed from Office on Impeachment for, and Conviction of, Treason, Bribery, or other high Crimes and Misdemeanors.

ARTICLE III

Section 1.   The judicial Power of the United States, shall be vested in one supreme Court, and in such inferior Courts as the Congress may from time to time ordain and establish. The Judges, both of the supreme and inferior Courts, shall hold their Offices during good Behaviour, and shall, at stated Times, receive for their Services, a Compensation, which shall not be diminished during their Continuance in Office.

Section 2.   The judicial Power shall extend to all Cases, in Law and Equity, arising under this Constitution, the Laws of the United States, and Treaties made, or which shall be made, under their Authority;—to all Cases affecting Ambassadors, other public Ministers and Consuls;—to all Cases of admiralty and maritime Jurisdiction;—to Controversies to which the United States shall be a Party;—to Controversies between two or more States;—between a State and Citizens of another State;—between Citizens of different States;—between Citizens of the same State claiming Lands under Grants of different States, and between a State, or the Citizens thereof, and foreign States, Citizens or Subjects.

In all Cases affecting Ambassadors, other public Ministers and Consuls, and those in which a State shall be Party, the supreme Court shall have original Jurisdiction. In all the other Cases before mentioned, the supreme Court shall have appellate Jurisdiction, both as to Law and Fact, with such Exceptions, and under such Regulations as the Congress shall make.

The trial of all Crimes, except in Cases of Impeachment, shall be by Jury; and such Trial shall be held in the State where the said Crimes shall have been committed; but when not committed within any State, the Trial shall be at such Place or Places as the Congress may by Law have directed.

Section 3.   Treason against the United States, shall consist only in levying War against them, of in adhering to their Enemies, giving them Aid and Comfort. No person shall be convicted of Treason unless on the Testimony of two Witnesses to the same overt Act, or on Confession in open Court.

The Congress shall have Power to declare the Punishment of Treason, but no Attainder of Treason shall work Corruption of Blood, or Forfeiture except during the Life of the Person attainted.

ARTICLE IV

Section 1.   Full Faith and Credit shall be given in each State to the public Acts, Records, and judicial Proceedings of every other State. And the Congress may by general Laws prescribe the Manner in which such Acts, Records and Proceedings shall be proved, and the Effect thereof.

Section 2.   The Citizens of each State shall be entitled to all Privileges and Immunities of Citizens in the several States.

A Person charged in any State with Treason, Felony, or other Crime, who shall flee from Justice, and be found in another State, shall on demand of the executive Authority of the State from which he fled, be delivered up, to be removed to the State having Jurisdiction of the Crime.

No Person held to Service or Labour in one State, under the Laws thereof, escaping into another, shall, in Consequence of any Law or Regulation therein, be discharged from such Service or Labour, but shall be delivered up on Claim of the Party to whom such Service or Labour may be due.

Section 3.   New States may be admitted by the Congress into this Union; but no new State shall be formed or erected within the Jurisdiction of any other State; nor any State be formed by the Junction of two or more States, or parts of States, without the Consent of the Legislatures of the States concerned as well as of the Congress.

The Congress shall have Power to dispose of and make all needful Rules and Regulations respecting the Territory or other Property belonging to the United States; and nothing in this Constitution shall be so construed as to Prejudice any Claims of the United States, or any particular State.

Section 4.   The United States shall guarantee to every State in this Union a Republican Form of Government, and shall protect each of them against Invasion; and on Application of the Legislature, or of the Executive (when the Legislature cannot be convened) against domestic Violence.

ARTICLE V

The Congress, whenever two thirds of both Houses shall deem it necessary, shall propose Amendments to this Constitution, or, on the Application of the Legislatures of two thirds of the several States, shall call a Convention for proposing Amendments, which, in either Case, shall be valid to all Intents and Purposes, as Part of this Constitution, when ratified by the Legislatures of three fourths of the several States, or by Conventions in three fourths thereof, as the one or the other Mode of Ratification may be proposed by the Congress: Provided that no Amendment which may be made prior to the Year One thousand eight hundred and eight shall in any Manner affect the first and fourth Clauses in the Ninth Section of the first Article; and that no State, without its Consent, shall be deprived of its equal Suffrage in the Senate.

ARTICLE VI

All Debts contracted and Engagements entered into, before the Adoption of this Constitution, shall be as valid against the United States under this Constitution, as under the Confederation.

This Constitution, and the Laws of the United States which shall be made in Pursuance thereof; and all Treaties made, or which shall be made, under the Authority of the United States, shall be the supreme Law of the Land; and the Judges in every State shall be bound thereby, any Thing in the Constitution or Laws of any State to the Contrary notwithstanding.

The Senators and Representatives before mentioned, and the Members of the several State Legislatures, and all executive and judicial Officers, both of the United States and of the several States, shall be bound by Oath or Affirmation, to support this Constitution; but no religious Test shall ever be required as a Qualification to any Office or public Trust under the United States.

ARTICLE VII

The Ratification of the Conventions of nine States shall be sufficient for the Establishment of this Constitution between the States so ratifying the Same.

AMENDMENTS

(First ten amendments ratified Dec. 15, 1791)

Amendment I   Congress shall make no law respecting an establishment of religion, or prohibiting the free exercise thereof; or abridging the freedom of speech, or of the press; or the right of the people peaceably to assemble, and to petition the Government for a redress of grievances.

Amendment II   A well regulated Militia, being necessary to the security of a free State, the right of the people to keep and bear Arms, shall not be infringed.

Amendment III   No Soldier shall, in time of peace be quartered in any house, without the consent of the Owner, nor in time of war, but in a manner to be prescribed by law.

Amendment IV   The right of the people to be secure in their persons, houses, papers, and effects, against unreasonable searches and seizures, shall not be violated, and no Warrants shall issue, but upon ·probable cause, supported by Oath or affirmation, and particularly describing the place to be searched, and the persons or things to be seized.

Amendment V   No person shall be held to answer for a capital, or otherwise infamous crime, unless on a presentment or indictment of a Grand Jury, except in cases arising in the land or naval forces, or in the Militia, when in actual service in time of War or public danger; nor shall any person be subject for the same offence to be twice put in jeopardy of life or limb; nor shall be compelled in any criminal case to be a witness against himself, nor be deprived of life, liberty, or property, without due process of law; nor shall private property be taken for public use, without just compensation.

Amendment VI   In all criminal prosecutions, the accused shall enjoy the right to a speedy and public trial, by an impartial jury of the State and district wherein the crime shall have been committed, which district shall have been previously ascertained by law, and to be informed of the nature and cause of the accusation; to be confronted with the witnesses against him; to have compulsory process for obtaining witnesses in his favor, and to have the Assistance of Counsel for his defence.

Amendment VII   In suits at common law, where the value in controversy shall exceed twenty dollars, the right of trial by jury shall be preserved, and no fact tried by a jury, shall be otherwise re-examined in any Court of the United States, than according to the rules of the common law.

Amendment VIII   Excessive bail shall not be required, nor excessive fines imposed, nor cruel and unusual punishments inflicted.

Amendment IX   The enumeration in the Constitution, of certain rights, shall not be construed to deny or disparage others retained by the people.

Amendment X   The powers not delegated to the United States by the Constitution, nor prohibited by it to the States, are reserved to the States respectively, or to the people.

Amendment XI   *(Ratified Feb. 7, 1795)*   The Judicial power of the United States shall not be construed to extend to any suit in law or equity, commenced or prosecuted against one of the United States by Citizens of another State, or by Citizens or Subjects of any Foreign State.

Amendment XII   *(Ratified June 15, 1804)*   The Electors shall meet in their respective states and vote by ballot for President and Vice-President, one of whom, at least, shall not be an inhabitant of the same state with themselves; they shall name in their ballots the person voted for as President, and in distinct ballots the person voted for as Vice-President, and they shall make distinct lists of all persons voted for as President, and of all person voted for as Vice-President, and of the number of votes for each, which lists they shall sign and certify, and transmit sealed to the seat of the government of the United States, directed to the President of the Senate;—The President of the Senate shall, in the presence of the Senate and House of Representatives, open all the certificates and the votes shall then be counted;—The person having the greatest number of votes for President, shall be the President, if such number be a majority of the whole number of Electors appointed; and if no person have such majority, then from the persons having the highest numbers not exceeding three on the list of those voted for as President, the House of Representatives shall choose immediately, by ballot, the President. But in choosing the President, the votes shall be taken by states, the representation from each state having one vote; a quorum for this purpose shall consist of a member or members from two-thirds of the states, and a majority of all the states shall be necessary to a choice. And if the House of Representatives shall not choose a President whenever the right of choice shall devolve upon them, before the fourth day of March next following, then the Vice-President shall act as President, as in the case of the death or other constitutional disability of the President.—The person having the greatest number of votes as Vice-President, shall be the Vice-President, if such number be a majority of the whole number of Electors appointed, and if no person have a majority, then from the two highest numbers on the lists, the Senate shall choose the Vice-President; a quorum for the purpose shall consist of two-thirds of the whole number of Senators, and a majority of the whole number shall be necessary to a choice. But no person constitutionally ineligible to the office of President shall be eligible to that of Vice-President of the United States.

Amendment XIII   *(Ratified Dec 6, 1865)*

Section 1.   Neither slavery nor involuntary servitude, except as a punishment for crime whereof the party shall have been duly convicted, shall exist within the United States, or any place subject to their jurisdiction.

Section 2.   Congress shall have power to enforce this article by appropriate legislation.

Amendment XIV   *(Ratified July 9, 1868)*

Section 1.   All persons born or naturalized in the United States, and subject to the jurisdiction thereof, are citizens of the United States and of the State wherein they reside. No State shall make or enforce any law which shall abridge the privileges or immunities of citizens of the United States; nor shall any State deprive any person of life, liberty, or property, without due process of law; nor deny to any person within its jurisdiction the equal protection of the laws.

Section 2.   Representatives shall be apportioned among the several States according to their respective numbers, counting the whole number of persons in each State, excluding Indians not taxed. But when the right to vote at any election for the choice of electors for President and Vice-President of the United States, Representatives in Congress, the Executive and Judicial officers of a State, or the members of the Legislature thereof, is denied to any of the male inhabitants of such State, being twenty-one years of age, and citizens of the United States, or in any way abridged, except for participation in rebellion, or other crime, the basis of representation therein shall be reduced in the proportion which the number of such male citizens shall bear to the whole number of male citizens twenty-one years of age in such State.

Section 3.   No person shall be a Senator or Representative in Congress, or elector of President and Vice President, or hold any office, civil or military, under the United States, or under any State, who having previously taken an oath, as a member of Congress, or as an officer of the United States, or as a member of any State legislature, or as an executive or judicial officer of any State, to support the Constitution of the United States, shall have engaged in insurrection or rebellion against the same, or given aid or comfort to the enemies thereof. But Congress may by a vote of two-thirds of each House, remove such disability.

Section 4.   The validity of the public debt of the United States, authorized by law, including debts incurred for payment of pensions and bounties for services in suppressing insurrection or rebellion, shall not be questioned. But neither the United States nor any State shall assume or pay any debt or obligation incurred in aid of insurrection or rebellion against the United States, or any claim for the loss or emancipation of any slave; but all such debts, obligations and claims shall be held illegal and void.

Section 5.   The Congress shall have power to enforce, by appropriate legislation, the provisions of this article.

Amendment XV   (Ratified Feb. 3, 1870)

Section 1.   The right of citizens of the United States to vote shall not be denied or abridged by the United States or by any State on account of race, color, or previous condition of servitude.

Section 2.   The Congress shall have power to enforce this article by appropriate legislation.

Amendment XVI   (Ratified Feb. 3, 1913)   The Congress shall have power to lay and collect taxes on incomes, from whatever source derived, without apportionment among the several States, and without regard to any census or enumeration.

Amendment XVII   (Ratified April 8, 1913)   The Senate of the United States shall be composed of two Senators from each State, elected by the people thereof, for six years; and each Senator shall have one vote. The electors in each State shall have the qualifications requisite for electors of the most numerous branch of the State legislatures.

When vacancies happen in the representation of any State in the Senate, the executive authority of such State shall issue writs of election to fill such vacancies: Provided, That the legislature of any State may empower the executive thereof to make temporary appointments until the people fill the vacancies by election as the legislature may direct.

This amendment shall not be so construed as to affect the election or term of any Senator chosen before it becomes valid as part of the Constitution.

Amendment XVIII   *(Ratified Jan. 16, 1919)*

Section 1.   After one year from the ratification of this article the manufacture, sale, or transportation of intoxicating liquors within, the importation thereof into, or the exportation thereof from the United States and all territory subject to the jurisdiction thereof for beverage purposes is hereby prohibited.

Section 2.   The Congress and the several States shall have concurrent power to enforce this article by appropriate legislation.

Section 3.   This article shall be inoperative unless it shall have been ratified as an amendment to the Constitution by the legislatures of the several States, as provided in the Constitution, within seven years from the date of the submission hereof to the States by the Congress.

Amendment XIX   *(Ratified Aug. 18, 1920)*   The right of citizens of the United States to vote shall not be denied or abridged by the United States or by any State on account of sex.

Congress shall have power to enforce this article by appropriate legislation.

Amendment XX   *(Ratified Jan. 23, 1933)*

Section 1.   The terms of the President and Vice President shall end at noon on the 20th day of January, and the terms of Senators and Representatives at noon on the 3d day of January, of the years in which such terms would have ended if this article had not been ratified; and the terms of their successors shall then begin.

Section 2.   The Congress shall assemble at least once in every year, and such meeting shall begin at noon on the 3d day of January, unless they shall by law appoint a different day.

Section 3.   If, at the time fixed for the beginning of the term of the President, the President elect shall have died, the Vice President elect shall become President. If a President shall not have been chosen before the time fixed for the beginning of his term, or if the President elect shall have failed to qualify, then the Vice President elect shall act as President until a President shall have qualified; and the Congress may by law provide for the case wherein neither a President elect nor a Vice President elect shall have qualified, declaring who shall then act as President, or the manner in which one who is to act shall be selected, and such person shall act accordingly until a President or Vice President shall have qualified.

Section 4.   The Congress may by law provide for the case of the death of any of the persons from whom the House of Representatives may choose a President whenever the right of choice shall have devolved upon them, and for the case of the death of any of the persons from whom the Senate may choose a Vice President whenever the right of choice shall have devolved upon them.

Section 5.   Sections 1 and 2 shall take effect on the 15th day of October following the ratification of this article.

Section 6.   This article shall be inoperative unless it shall have been ratified as an amendment to the Constitution by the legislatures of three-fourths of the several States within seven years from the date of its submission.

Amendment XXI   *(Ratified Dec. 5, 1933)*

Section 1.   The eighteenth article of amendment to the Constitution of the United States is hereby repealed.

Section 2.   The transportation or importation into any State, Territory or possession of the United States for delivery or use therein of intoxicating liquors, in violation of the laws thereof, is hereby prohibited.

Section 3.   This article shall be inoperative unless it shall have been ratified as an amendment to the Constitution by conventions in the several States, as provided in the Constitution, within seven years from the date of the submission hereof to the States by the Congress.

Amendment XXII   *(Ratified Feb. 27, 1951)*

Section 1.   No person shall be elected to the office of the President more than twice, and no person who has held the office of President, or acted as President, for more than two years of a term to which some other person was elected President shall be elected to the office of the President more than once. But this Article shall not apply to any person holding the office of President when this Article was proposed by the Congress, and shall not prevent any person who may be holding the office of President, or acting as President, during the term within which this Article becomes operative from holding the office of President or acting as President during the remainder of such term.

Section 2.   This Article shall be inoperative unless it shall have been ratified as an amendment to the Constitution by the legislatures of three-fourths of the several States within seven years from the date of its submission to the States by the Congress.

Amendment XXIII   *(Ratified Mar. 29, 1961)*

Section 1.   The District constituting the seat of Government of the United States shall appoint in such manner as the Congress may direct:
    A number of electors of President and Vice President equal to the whole number of Senators and Representatives in Congress to which the District would be entitled if it were a State, but in no event more than the least populous State; they shall be in addition to those appointed by the States, but they shall be considered, for the purposes of the election of President and Vice President, to be electors appointed by a State; and they shall meet in the District and perform such duties as provided by the twelfth article of amendment.

Section 2.   The Congress shall have power to enforce this article by appropriate legislation.

Amendment XXIV   *(Ratified Jan. 23, 1964)*

Section 1.   The right of citizens of the United States to vote in any primary or other election for President or Vice President, for electors for President or Vice President, or for Senators or Representatives in Congress, shall not be denied or abridged by the United States or any State by reason of failure to pay any poll tax or other tax.

Section 2.   The Congress shall have power to enforce this article by appropriate legislation.

Amendment XXV   *(Ratified Feb. 10, 1967)*

Section 1.   In case of the removal of the President from office or of his death or resignation, the Vice President shall become President.

Section 2.   Whenever there is a vacancy in the office of the Vice President, the President shall nominate a Vice President who shall take office upon confirmation by a majority vote of both Houses of Congress.

Section 3.   Whenever the President transmits to the President pro tempore of the Senate and the Speaker of the House of Representatives his written declaration that he is unable to discharge the powers and duties of his office, and until he transmits to them a written declaration to the contrary, such power and duties shall be discharged by the Vice President as Acting President.

Section 4.   Whenever the Vice President and a majority of either the principal officers of the executive departments or of such other body as Congress may by law provide, transmit to the President pro tempore of the Senate and the Speaker of the House of Representatives their written declaration that the President is unable to discharge the powers and duties of his office, the Vice President shall immediately assume the powers and duties of the office as Acting President.

Thereafter, when the President transmits to the President pro tempore of the Senate and the Speaker of the House of Representatives his written declaration that no inability exists, he shall resume the powers and duties of his office unless the Vice President and a majority of either the principal officers of the executive department or of such other body as Congress may by law provide, transmit within four days to the President pro tempore of the Senate and the Speaker of the House of Representatives their written declaration that the President is unable to discharge the powers and duties of his office. Thereupon Congress shall decide the issue, assembling within forty-eight hours for that purpose if not in session. If the Congress, within twenty-one days after receipt of the latter written declaration, or, if Congress is not in session, within twenty-one days after Congress is required to assemble, determines by two-thirds vote of both Houses that the President is unable to discharge the powers and duties of his office, the Vice President shall continue to discharge the same as Acting President; otherwise, the President shall resume the powers and duties of his office.

Amendment XXVI *(Ratified July 1, 1971)*

Section 1. The right of citizens of the United States, who are eighteen years of age or older, to vote shall not be denied or abridged by the United States or by any State on account of age.

Section 2. The Congress shall have power to enforce this article by appropriate legislation.

Amendment XXVII *(Ratified May 18, 1992)*

Section 1. No law, varying the compensation for the services of the Senators and Representatives, shall take effect until an election of Representatives shall have intervened.

Index

Page references in **bold** type indicate main entry in dictionary.

B

C

D

E

G

I

J

N

O

P

Q

R

S

V

W

X